INTRODUCTION TO COMPUTER THEORY

Daniel I. A. Cohen

Hunter College
City University of New York

John Wiley & Sons, Inc.
New York   Chichester   Brisbane   Toronto   Singapore

Copyright © 1986, by John Wiley & Sons, Inc.

All rights reserved. Published simultaneously in Canada.

Reproduction or translation of any part of
this work beyond that permitted by Sections
107 and 108 of the 1976 United States Copyright
Act without the permission of the copyright
owner is unlawful. Requests for permission
or further information should be addressed to
the Permissions Department, John Wiley & Sons.

Library of Congress Cataloging-in-Publication Data:

Cohen, Daniel I. A., 1946–
  Introduction to computer theory.

  Includes Index
    1. Electronic digital computers.   I. Title.
QA76.5.C558   1986   001.64   85-12077
ISBN 0-471-80271-9

Printed in the United States of America

10 9 8 7 6 5 4 3 2

Au Professeur M.-P. Schützenberger
comme un témoignage de profonde
et affectueuse reconnaissance

PREFACE

It has become clear that some abstract Computer Theory should be included in the education of undergraduate Computer Science majors.

Leaving aside the obvious worth of knowledge for its own sake, the terminology, notations, and techniques of Computer Theory are necessary in the teaching of courses on computer design, Artificial Intelligence, the analysis of algorithms, and so forth. Of all the programming skills undergraduate students learn, two of the most important are the abilities to recognize and manipulate context-free grammars and to understand the power of the recursive interaction of parts of a procedure. Very little can be accomplished if each advanced course has to begin at the level of defining rules of production and derivations. Every interesting career a student of Computer Science might pursue will make significant use of some aspects of the subject matter of this book.

Yet we find today, that the subjects of Automata Theory, Formal Languages, and Turing machines are almost exclusively relegated to the very advanced student. Only textbooks demanding intense mathematical sophistication discuss these topics. Undergraduate Computer Science majors are unlikely to develop the familiarity with set theory, logic, and the facility with abstract manipulation early enough in their college careers to digest the material in the existing excellent but difficult texts.

Bringing the level of sophistication to the exact point where it meets the expected preparation of the intended student population is the responsibility of every carefully prepared textbook. Of all the branches of Mathematics, Computer Science is one of the newest and most independent. Rigorous mathematical proof of the most profound theorems in this subject can be constructed without the aid of Calculus, Number Theory, Algebra, or Topology. Some degree of understanding of the notion of proof is, of course, required, but the techniques employed are so idiosyncratic to this subject that it is preferable to introduce them to the student from first principles. Characteristic methods, such as making accurate conclusions from diagrams, analyzing graphs, or searching trees, are not tools with which a typical mathematics major is familiar. Hardly any students come prepared for the convoluted surprise of the Halting Problem. These then are the goals of this textbook: (1) to introduce a student of Computer Science to the need for and the working of mathematical proof; (2) to develop facility with the concepts, notations, and techniques of the theories of Automata, Formal Languages, and Turing machines; and (3) to provide historical perspective on the creation of the computer with a profound understanding of some of its capabilities and limitations.

Basically, this book is written for students with no presumed background of any kind. Every mathematical concept used is introduced from scratch. Extensive examples and illustrations spell out everything in detail to avoid any possibility of confusion. The bright student is encouraged to read at whatever pace or depth seems appropriate.

For their excellent care with this project I thank the staff at John Wiley & Sons: Richard J. Bonacci, acquisitions editor, and Lorraine F. Mellon, Eugene Patti, Elaine Rauschal, and Ruth Greif of the editorial and production staffs. Of the technical people who reviewed the manuscript I thank Martin Kaliski, Adrian Tang, Martin Davis, and especially H. P. Edmundson, whose comments were invaluable and Martin J. Smith whose splendid special support was dispositive. Rarely has an author had an assistant as enthusiastic, dedicated, knowledgeable and meticulous as I was so fortunate to find in Mara Chibnik. Every aspect of this project from the classnotes to the page proofs benefited immeasurably from her scrutiny. Very little that is within these covers—except for the few mistakes inserted by mischievous Martians—does not bare the mark of her relentless precision and impeccable taste. Every large project is the result of the toil of the craftsmen and the sacrifice and forebearance of those they were forced to neglect. Rubies are beneath their worth.

Daniel I. A. Cohen

CONTENTS

CONTENTS

PART I

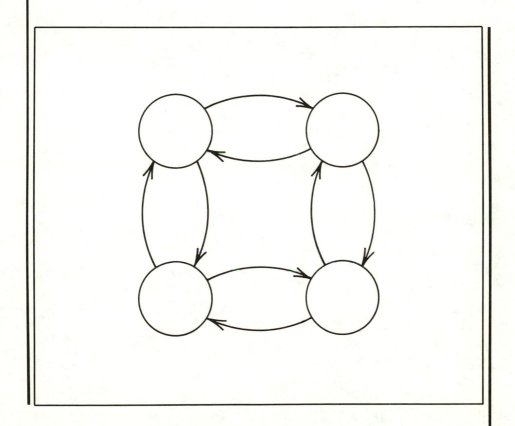

AUTOMATA
THEORY

CHAPTER 1

BACKGROUND

The twentieth century has been filled with the most incredible shocks and surprises: the theory of relativity, Communist revolutions, psychoanalysis, nuclear war, television, moon walks, genetic engineering, and so on. As astounding as any of these is the advent of the computer and its development from a mere calculating device into what seems like a "thinking machine."

The birth of the computer was not wholly independent of the other events of this century. The history of the computer is a fascinating story; however, it is not the subject of this course. We are concerned with the **Theory of Computers,** which means that we form several abstract mathematical models that will describe with varying degrees of accuracy parts of computers and types of computers and similar machines. Our models will not be used to discuss the practical engineering details of the hardware of computers, but the more abstract questions of the frontiers of capability of these mechanical devices.

There are separate courses that deal with circuits and switching theory (computer logic) and with instruction sets and register arrangements (computer architecture) and with data structures and algorithms and operating systems and compiler design and artificial intelligence and so forth. All of these courses have a theoretical component, but they differ from our study in two basic ways. First, they deal only with computers that already exist; our models, on

3

the other hand, will encompass all computers that do exist, will exist, and that can ever be dreamed of. Second, they are interested in how best to do things; we shall not be interested in optimality at all, but rather we shall be concerned with the question of possibility—what can and what cannot be done. We shall look at this from the perspective of what language structures the machines we describe can and cannot accept as input, and what possible meaning their output may have. This description of our intent is extremely general and perhaps a little misleading, but the mathematically precise definition of our study can be understood only by those who already know the concepts introduced in this course. This is often a characteristic of scholarship—after years of study one can just begin to define the subject. We are now embarking on a typical example of such a journey. In our last chapter (Chapter 31) we shall finally be able to define a computer.

The history of Computer Theory is also interesting. It was formed by fortunate coincidences, involving several seemingly unrelated branches of intellectual endeavor. A small series of contemporaneous discoveries, by very dissimilar people, separately motivated, flowed together to become our subject. Until we have established more of a foundation, we can only describe in general terms the different schools of thought that have melded into this field.

The most obvious component of Computer Theory is the theory of mathematical logic. As the twentieth century started, mathematics was facing a dilemma. Georg Cantor (1845–1918) had recently invented the Theory of Sets (unions, intersections, inclusion, cardinality, etc.). But at the same time he had discovered some very uncomfortable paradoxes—he created things that looked like contradictions in what seemed to be rigorously proven mathematical theorems. Some of his unusual findings could be tolerated (such as that infinity comes in different sizes), but some could not (such as that some set is bigger than the universal set). This left a cloud over mathematics that needed to be resolved.

David Hilbert (1862–1943) wanted all of mathematics put on the same sound footing as Euclidean Geometry, which is characterized by precise definitions, explicit axioms, and rigorous proofs. The format of a Euclidean proof is precisely specified. Every line is either an axiom, a previously proven theorem, or follows from the lines above it by one of a few simple rules of inference. The mathematics that developed in the centuries since Euclid did not follow this standard of precision. Hilbert believed that if mathematics were put back on the Euclidean standard the Cantor paradoxes would go away. He was actually concerned with two ambitious projects: first, to demonstrate that the new system was free of paradoxes; second, to find methods that would guarantee to enable humans to construct proofs of all the true statements in mathematics.

Hilbert wanted something formulaic—a precise routine for producing results, like the directions in a cookbook. First draw all these lines, then write all these equations, then solve for all these points, and so on and so on and the proof is done—some approach that is certain and sure-fire without any reliance on unpredictable and undependable brilliant mathematical insight. We simply follow the rules and the answer must come.

This type of complete, guaranteed, easy-to-follow set of instructions is called an **algorithm.** He hoped that algorithms or procedures could be developed to solve whole classes of mathematical problems. The collection of techniques called linear algebra provides just such an algorithm for solving all systems of linear equations. Hilbert wanted to develop algorithms for solving other mathematical problems, perhaps even an algorithm that could solve all mathematical problems of any kind in some finite number of steps. Before starting to look for such an algorithm, an exact notion of what is and what is not a mathematical statement had to be developed. After that, there was the problem of defining exactly what can and what cannot be a step in an algorithm. The words we have used: "procedure," "formula," "cookbook method," "complete instructions," are not part of mathematics and are no more meaningful than the word "algorithm" itself.

Mathematical logicians, while trying to follow the suggestions of Hilbert and straighten out the predicament left by Cantor, found that they were able to prove mathematically that some of the desired algorithms *cannot exist*—not only at this time, but they can never exist in the future, either. Their main result was even more fantastic than that.

Kurt Gödel (1906–1978) not only showed that there was no algorithm that could guarantee to provide proofs for all the true statements in mathematics, but he proved that not all the true statements even have a proof to be found. Gödel's **Incompleteness Theorem** implies that in a specific mathematical system either there are some true statements without any possible proof or else there are some false statements that can be "proven." This earth-shaking result made the mess in the philosophy of mathematics even worse, but very exciting.

If not every true statement has a proof, can we at least fulfill Hilbert's program by finding a proof-generating algorithm to provide proofs whenever they do exist? Logicians began to ask the question: Of what fundamental parts are all algorithms composed? The first general definition of an algorithm was proposed by Alonzo Church. Using his definition he and Stephen Cole Kleene and, independently, Emil Post were able to prove that there were problems that no algorithm could solve. While also solving this problem independently, Alan Mathison Turing (1912–1954) developed the concept of a theoretical "universal-algorithm machine." Studying what was possible and what was not possible for such a machine to do, he discovered that some tasks that we might have expected this abstract omnipotent machine to be able to perform are impossible, even for it. Turing's model for a universal-algorithm machine is directly connected to the invention of the computer. In fact, for completely different reasons (wartime code-breaking) Turing himself had an important part in the construction of the first computer, which he based on his work in abstract logic.

On a wildly different front, two researchers in neurophysiology, Warren

Sturgis McCulloch and Walter Pitts (1923–1969), constructed a mathematical model for the way in which sensory receptor organs in animals behave. The model they constructed for a "neural net" was a theoretical machine of the same nature as the one Turing invented, but with certain limitations. Mathematical models of real and abstract machines took on more and more importance. Along with mathematical models for biological processes, models were introduced to study psychological, economic, and social situations.

Again, entirely independent of these considerations, the invention of the vacuum tube and the subsequent developments in electronics enabled engineers to build fully automatic electronic calculators. These developments fulfilled the age-old dream of Blaise Pascal (1623–1662), Gottfried Wilhelm von Leibniz (1646–1716), and Charles Babbage (1792–1871), all of whom built mechanical calculating devices as powerful as their respective technologies would allow. In the 1940s, gifted engineers began building the first generation of computers: the computer Colossus at Bletchley, England (Turing's decoder), the ABC machine built by John Atanosoff in Iowa, the Harvard Mark I built by Howard Aiken, and ENIAC built by John Presper Eckert, Jr. and John William Mauchly (1907–1980) at the University of Pennsylvania.

Shortly after the invention of the vacuum tube, the incredible mathematician John von Neumann (1903–1957) developed the idea of a stored-program computer. The idea of storing the program inside the computer and allowing the computer to operate on (and modify) the program as well as the data was a tremendous advance. It may have been conceived decades earlier by Babbage and his co-worker Ada Augusta, Countess of Lovelace (1815–1853), but their technology was not adequate to explore this possibility. The ramifications of this idea, as pursued by von Neumann and Turing were quite profound.

The early calculators could perform only one predetermined set of tasks at a time. To make changes in their procedures, the calculators had to be physically rebuilt either by rewiring, resetting, or reconnecting various parts. Von Neumann permanently wired certain operations into the machine and then designed a central control section that, after reading input data, could select which operation to perform based on a program or algorithm encoded in the input and stored in the computer along with the raw data to be processed. In this way, the inputs determined which operations were to be performed on themselves. Interestingly, current technology has progressed to the point where the ability to manufacture dedicated chips cheaply and easily has made the prospect of rebuilding a computer for each program feasible again. However, by the last chapters of this book we will appreciate the significance of the difference between these two approaches.

Von Neumann's goal was to convert the electronic calculator into a real-life model of one of the logicians' ideal universal-algorithm machines, such as those Turing had described. Thus we have an unusual situation where the advanced theoretical work on the potential of the machine preceded the demonstration that the machine could really exist. The people who first discussed these machines only dreamed they might ever be built. Many were very surprised to find them actually working in their own lifetimes.

Along with the concept of programming a computer came the question: What is the "best" language in which to write programs? Many languages were invented, owing their distinction to the differences in the specific machines they were to be used on and to the differences in the types of problems for which they were designed. However, as more languages emerged, it became clear that they had many elements in common. They seemed to share the same possibilities and limitations. This observation was at first only intuitive, although Turing had already worked on much the same problem but from a different angle.

At the time that a general theory of computer languages was being developed, another surprise occurred. Modern linguists, some influenced by the prevalent trends in mathematical logic and some by the emerging theories of developmental psychology, had been investigating a very similar subject: What is language in general? How could primitive humans have developed language? How do people understand it? How do they learn it as children? What ideas can be expressed, and in what ways? How do people construct sentences from the ideas in their minds?

Noam Chomsky created the subject of mathematical models for the description of languages to answer these questions. His theory grew to the point where it began to shed light on the study of computer languages. The languages humans invented to communicate with one another and the languages necessary for humans to communicate with machines shared many basic properties. Although we do not know exactly how humans understand language, we do know how machines digest what they are told. Thus, the formulations of mathematical logic became useful to linguistics, a previously nonmathematical subject. Metaphorically, we could say that the computer then took on linguistic abilities. It became a word processor, a translator, and an interpreter of simple grammar, as well as a compiler of computer languages. The software invented to interpret programming languages was applied to human languages as well. One point that will be made clear in our studies is why computer languages are easy for a computer to understand whereas human languages are very difficult.

Because of the many influences on its development the subject of this book goes by various names. It includes three major fundamental areas: the **Theory of Automata**, the **Theory of Formal Languages**, and the **Theory of Turing Machines**. This book is divided into three parts corresponding to these topics.

Our subject is sometimes called **Computation Theory** rather than Computer Theory, since the items that are central to it are the types of tasks (algorithms or programs) that can be performed, not the mechanical nature of the physical computer itself. However, the name "computation" is also misleading, since it popularly connotes arithmetical operations that are only a fraction of what computers can do. The term "computation" is inaccurate when describing word

processing, sorting and searching and awkward in discussions of program verification. Just as the term "Number Theory" is not limited to a description of
calligraphic displays of number systems but focuses on the question of which
equations can be solved in integers, and the term "Graph Theory" does not
include bar graphs, pie charts, and histograms, so too "Computer Theory" need
not be limited to a description of physical machines but can focus on the
question of which tasks are possible for which machines.

We shall study different types of theoretical machines that are mathematical
models for actual physical processes. By considering the possible inputs on
which these machines can work, we can analyze their various strengths and
weaknesses. We then arrive at what we may believe to be the most powerful
machine possible. When we do, we shall be surprised to find tasks that even
it cannot perform. This will be our ultimate result, that no matter what machine
we build, there will always be questions that are simple to state that it cannot
answer. Along the way, we shall begin to understand the concept of **computability**, which is the foundation of further research in this field. This is
our goal. Computer Theory extends further to such topics as complexity and
verification, but these are beyond our intended scope. Even for the topics we
do cover—Automata, Languages, Turing Machines—much more is known than
we present here. As intriguing and engaging as the field has proven so far,
with any luck the most fascinating theorems are yet to be discovered.

CHAPTER 2

LANGUAGES

In English we distinguish the three different entities: letters, words, and sentences. There is a certain parallelism between the fact that groups of letters make up words and the fact that groups of words make up sentences. Not all collections of letters form a valid word, and not all collections of words form a valid sentence. The analogy can be continued. Certain groups of sentences make up coherent paragraphs, certain groups of paragraphs make up coherent stories, and so on.

This situation also exists with computer languages. Certain character strings are recognizable words (GOTO, END . . .). Certain strings of words are recognizable commands. Certain sets of commands become a program (with or without data).

To construct a general theory that unifies all these examples, it is necessary for us to adopt a definition of a "most universal language structure," that is, a structure in which the decision of whether a given string of units constitutes a valid larger unit is not a matter of guesswork but is based on explicitly stated rules.

It is very hard to state all the rules for the language "spoken English," since many seemingly incoherent strings of words are actually understandable utterances. This is due to slang, idiom, dialect, and our ability to interpret poetic metaphor and to correct unintentional grammatical errors in the sentences we hear. However, as a first step to defining a general theory of abstract languages, it is right for us to insist on precise rules, especially since computers are not quite as forgiving about imperfect input commands as listeners are about informal speech.

When we call our study the **Theory of Formal Languages,** the word "formal" refers to the fact that all the rules for the language are explicitly stated in terms of what strings of symbols can occur. No liberties are tolerated, and no reference to any "deeper understanding" is required. Language will be considered solely as symbols on paper and not as expressions of ideas in the minds of humans. In this basic model, language is not communication among intellects, but a game of symbols with formal rules. The term "formal" used here emphasizes that it is the *form* of the string of symbols we are interested in, not the *meaning*.

We begin with only one finite set of fundamental units out of which we build structures. We shall call this the **alphabet.** A certain specified set of strings of characters from the alphabet will be called the **language.** Those strings that are permissible in the language we call **words.** The symbols in the alphabet do not have to be Latin letters, and the sole universal requirement for a possible string is that it have only finitely many symbols in it. The question of what it means to "specify" a set of strings is one we discuss presently.

We shall wish to allow a string to have no letters. This we call the **empty string** or **null string,** and we shall denote it by the symbol Λ. No matter what language we are considering, the null string is always Λ. Two words are considered the same if all their letters are the same and in the same order so there is only one possible word of no letters. For clarity, we do not allow the symbol Λ to be part of the alphabet for any language.

The most familiar example of a language for us is English. The alphabet is the usual set of letters plus the apostrophe and hyphen. Let us denote the whole alphabet by the Greek letter capital sigma.

$$\Sigma = \{ a \quad b \quad c \quad d \quad e \quad \ldots \quad z \quad ' \quad - \}$$

Sometimes we shall list a set of elements separated by spaces and sometimes by commas. If we wished to be supermeticulous, we would also include in Σ the uppercase letters and the seldom used *diac*ritical marks.

We can now specify which strings of these letters are valid words in our language by listing them all, as is done in a dictionary. It is a long list, but a finite list, and it makes a perfectly good definition of the language. If we call this language ENGLISH-WORDS we may write

ENGLISH-WORDS = {all the words (main entries) in a standard dictionary}

In the line above, we have intentionally mixed mathematical notation (the equal sign, the braces denoting sets) and a prose phrase. This results in perfectly understandable communication; we take this liberty throughout. All of our investigations will be agglomerates of informal discussion and precise symbolism.

Of course, the language ENGLISH-WORDS, as we have specified it, does not have any grammar. If we wish to make a formal definition of the language of the sentences in English, we must begin by saying that this time our basic *alphabet* is the entries in the dictionary. Let us call this alphabet Γ, the capital gamma.

Γ = { the entries in a standard dictionary, plus a blank space, plus the usual punctuation marks }

In order to specify which strings of elements from Γ produce valid words in the language ENGLISH-SENTENCES, we must rely on the grammatical rules of English. This is because we could never produce a complete list of all possible words in this language; that would have to be a list of all valid English sentences. Theoretically, there are infinitely many different words in the language ENGLISH-SENTENCES. For example:

I ate one apple.

I ate two apples.

I ate three apples.

. . . .

The trick of defining the language ENGLISH-SENTENCES by listing all the rules of English grammar allows us to give a finite description of an infinite language.

If we go by the rules of grammar only, many strings of alphabet letters seem to be valid words, for example, "I ate three Tuesdays." In a *formal* language we must allow this string. It is *grammatically* correct; only its *meaning* reveals that it is ridiculous. Meaning is something we do not refer to in formal languages. As we make clear in Part II of this book, we are primarily interested in syntax alone, not semantics or diction. We shall be like the bad teacher who is interested only in the correct spelling, not the ideas in a homework composition.

In general, the abstract languages we treat will be defined in one of two ways. Either they will be presented as an alphabet and the exhaustive list of all valid words, or else they will be presented as an alphabet and a set of rules defining the acceptable words.

Earlier we mentioned that we could define a language by presenting the alphabet and then *specifying* which strings are words. The word "specify" is trickier than we may at first suppose. Consider this example of the language called MY-PET. The alphabet for this language is

$$\{a \quad c \quad d \quad g \quad o \quad t\}$$

There is only one word in this language, and for our own perverse reasons we wish to *specify* it by this sentence:
If the Earth and the Moon ever collide, then

$$\text{MY-PET} = \{\ cat\ \}$$

but, if the Earth and the Moon never collide, then

$$\text{MY-PET} = \{\ dog\ \}$$

One or the other of these two events will occur, but at this point in the history of the universe it is impossible to be certain whether the word *dog* is or is not in the language MY-PET.

This sentence is not an adequate specification of the language MY-PET because it is not useful. To be an acceptable specification of a language, a set of rules must enable us to decide, in a finite amount of time, whether a given string of alphabet letters is or is not a word in the language.

The set of rules can be of two kinds. They can either tell us how to test a string of alphabet letters that we might be presented with, to see if it is a valid word; or they can tell us how to construct all the words in the language by some clear procedures. We investigate this distinction further in the next chapter.

Let us consider some simple examples of languages. If we start with an alphabet having only one letter, the letter x,

$$\Sigma = \{\ x\ \}$$

we can define a language by saying that any nonempty string of alphabet characters is a word.

$$L_1 = \{\ x \quad xx \quad xxx \quad xxxx \dots \}$$

or to write this in an alternate form:

$$L_1 = \{\ x^n \quad \text{for } n = 1 \quad 2 \quad 3 \quad \dots \}$$

Because of the way we have defined it, this language does not include the null string. We could have defined it so as to include Λ, but we didn't.

In this language, as in any other, we can define the operation of **concatenation,** in which two strings are written down side by side to form a new longer string. In this example, when we concatenate the word xxx with the word xx, we obtain the word $xxxxx$. The words in this language are clearly analogous to the positive integers, and the operation of concatenation is analogous to addition:

$$x^n \text{ concatenated with } x^m \text{ is the word } x^{n+m}$$

It will often be convenient for us to designate the words in a given language by new symbols, that is, other than the ones in the alphabet. For example, we could say that the word *xxx* is called *a* and that the word *xx* is *b*. Then to denote the word formed by concatenating *a* and *b* we write the letters side by side:

$$ab = xxxxx$$

It is not always true that when two words are concatenated they produce another word in the language. For example if the language is

$$
\begin{aligned}
L_2 &= \{\, x \quad xxx \quad xxxxx \quad xxxxxxx \ldots \,\} \\
&= \{\, x^{odd} \,\} \\
&= \{\, x^{2n+1} \quad \text{for } n = 0 \quad 1 \quad 2 \quad 3 \quad \ldots \,\}
\end{aligned}
$$

then $a = xxx$ and $b = xxxxx$ are both words in L_2, but their concatenation $ab = xxxxxxxx$ is not in L_2. Notice that the alphabet for L_2 is the same as the alphabet for L_1. Notice also the liberty we took with the middle definition.

In these simple examples, when we concatenate *a* with *b* we get the same word as when we concatenate *b* with *a*. We can depict this by writing:

$$ab = ba$$

But this relationship does not hold for all languages. In English when we concatenate "house" and "boat" we get "houseboat," which is indeed a word but distinct from "boathouse," which is a different thing—not because they have different meanings but because they are different words. "Merry-go-round" and "carousel" mean the same thing, but they are different words.

EXAMPLE

Consider another language. Let us begin with the alphabet:

$$\Sigma = \{\, 0 \quad 1 \quad 2 \quad 3 \quad 4 \quad 5 \quad 6 \quad 7 \quad 8 \quad 9 \,\}$$

and define the set of words:

$L_3 = \{\,$ any finite string of alphabet letters that does not start with the letter zero $\}$

This language L_3 then looks like the set of all positive integers written in base 10.

$$L_3 = \{ 1 \quad 2 \quad 3 \quad 4 \quad 5 \quad 6 \quad 7 \quad 8 \quad 9 \quad 10 \quad 11 \quad 12 \ldots \}$$

We say "looks like" instead of "is" because L_3 is only a formal collection of strings of symbols. The integers have other mathematical properties. If we wanted to define the language L_3 so that it includes the string (word) 0, we could say:

L_3 = {any finite string of alphabet letters that, if it starts with a 0, has no more letters after the first} ■

The box, ■, which ends the line above is an **end marker.** When we present an example of a point in the text, we shall introduce it with the heading:

EXAMPLE

and finish it with an end marker ■. This will allow us to keep the general discussion separate from the specific examples. We shall use the same end marker to denote the end of a definition or a proof.

DEFINITION

_____
_____
_____ ■

PROOF

_____
_____
_____ ■

The old-fashioned end marker denoting that a proof is finished is Q.E.D. This box serves the same purpose.

DEFINITION

We define the function "**length** of a string" to be the number of letters in the string. We write this function using the word "length." For example, if $a = xxxx$ in the language L_1 above, then

$$\text{length}(a) = 4$$

If $c = 428$ in the language L_3, then

$$\text{length}(c) = 3$$

Or we could write directly that in L_1

$$\text{length}(xxxx) = 4$$

and in L_3

$$\text{length}(428) = 3$$

In any language that includes the empty string Λ we have:

$$\text{length}(\Lambda) = 0$$

For any word w in any language, if $\text{length}(w) = 0$ then $w = \Lambda$. ■

We can now present yet another definition of L_3.

L_3 = {any finite string of alphabet letters that, if it has length more than one, does not start with a zero}

This is not necessarily a better definition of L_3, but it does illustrate that there are often different ways of specifying the same language.

There is some inherent ambiguity in the phrase "any finite string," since it is not clear whether we intend to include the null string (Λ, the string of no letters). To avoid this ambiguity, we shall always be more careful. The language L_3 above does not include Λ, since we intended that that language should look like the integers, and there is no such thing as an integer with no digits. On the other hand, we may wish to define a language like L_1 but that does contain Λ.

$$L_4 = \{ \Lambda \quad x \quad xx \quad xxx \quad xxxx \ldots \}$$
$$= \{ x^n \quad \text{for } n = 0 \quad 1 \quad 2 \quad 3 \ldots \}$$

Here we have said that $x^0 = \Lambda$, not $x^0 = 1$ as in algebra. In this way x^n is always the string of n x's. This may seem like belaboring a trivial point, but the significance of being careful about this distinction will emerge over and over again.

In L_3 it is very important not to confuse 0, which is a string of length 1, with Λ. Remember, even when Λ is a word in the language, it is not a letter in the alphabet.

DEFINITION

Let us introduce the function **reverse.** If a is a word in some language L, then reverse(a) is the same string of letters spelled backward, called the reverse of a, even if this backward string is not a word in L.   ■

EXAMPLE

$$\text{reverse}(xxx) = xxx$$
$$\text{reverse}(xxxxx) = xxxxx$$
$$\text{reverse}(145) = 541$$

But let us also note that in L_3

$$\text{reverse}(140) = 041$$

which is not a word in L_3.   ■

DEFINITION

Let us define a new language called **PALINDROME** over the alphabet

$$\Sigma = \{a, b\}$$

PALINDROME = { Λ, and all strings x such that reverse(x) = x }   ■

If we begin listing the elements in PALINDROME we find

PALINDROME = { Λ, a, b, aa, bb, aaa, aba,
            bab, bbb, $aaaa$, $abba$ . . . }

The language PALINDROME has interesting properties that we shall examine later.

Sometimes when we concatenate two words in PALINDROME we obtain another word in PALINDROME such as when $abba$ is concatenated with $abbaabba$. More often, the concatenation is not itself a word in PALINDROME, as when aa is concatenated with aba. Discovering when this does happen is left as a problem at the end of this chapter.

DEFINITION

Given an alphabet Σ, we wish to define a language in which any string of letters from Σ is a word, even the null string. This language we shall call the **closure** of the alphabet. It is denoted by writing a star (an asterisk) after the name of the alphabet as a superscript

$$\Sigma*$$

This notation is sometimes known as the **Kleene star** after the logician who was one of the founders of this subject. ∎

EXAMPLE

If $\Sigma = \{ x \}$, then

$$\Sigma* = L_4 = \{ \Lambda \quad x \quad xx \quad xxx. . . \}$$

∎

EXAMPLE

If $\Sigma = \{ 0,1 \}$, then

$$\Sigma* = \{ \Lambda \quad 0 \quad 1 \quad 00 \quad 01 \quad 10 \quad 11 \quad 000 \quad 001. . . \}$$

∎

EXAMPLE

If $\Sigma = \{ a,b,c \}$, then

$$\Sigma* = \{ \Lambda \quad a \quad b \quad c \quad aa \quad ab \quad ac \quad ba \quad bb \quad bc \quad ca \quad cb \quad cc \quad aaa. . . \}$$ ∎

We can think of the Kleene star as an **operation** that makes an infinite language of strings of letters out of an alphabet. When we say "infinite language" we mean infinitely many words each of finite length.

Notice that when we wrote out the first several words in the language we put them in size order (words of shortest length first) and then listed all the words of the same length alphabetically. We shall usually follow this method of sequencing a language.

We shall now generalize the use of the star operator to sets of words, not just sets of alphabet letters.

DEFINITION

If S is a set of words, then by $S*$ we mean the set of all finite strings formed by concatenating words from S, where any word may be used as often as we like, and where the null string is also included.   ■

EXAMPLE

If $S = \{\ aa,b\ \}$, then

$S* = \{\ \Lambda$ plus any word composed of factors of aa and $b\ \}$

$\quad = \{\ \Lambda$ plus all strings of a's and b's in which the a's occur in even clumps $\}$

$\quad = \{\ \Lambda\quad b\quad aa\quad bb\quad aab\quad baa\quad bbb\quad aaaa\quad aabb\quad baab\quad bbaa\quad bbbb$
$\qquad aaaab\quad aabaa\quad aabbb\quad baaaa\quad baabb\quad bbaab\quad bbbaa\quad bbbbb \ldots \}$

The string $aabaaab$ is not in $S*$ since it has a clump of a's of length 3. The phrase "clump of a's" has not been precisely defined, but we know what it means anyway.   ■

EXAMPLE

Let $S = \{\ a,\ ab\ \}$. Then

$\quad S* = \{\Lambda$ plus any word composed of factors of a and $ab\}$

$\qquad = \{\Lambda$ plus all strings of a's and b's except those that start with b and those that contain a double $b\}$

$\qquad = \{\ \Lambda\quad a\quad aa\quad ab\quad aaa\quad aab\quad aaaa\quad aaab\quad aaba\quad abaa\quad abab$
$\qquad\quad aaaaa\quad aaaab\quad aaaba\quad aabaa\quad aabab\quad abaaa\quad abaab\quad ababa. \ldots \}$

By the phrase "double b" we mean the substring bb. For each word in $S*$ every b must have an a immediately to its left. The substring bb is impossible, as is starting with a b. Any string without the substring bb that begins with an a can be factored into terms of (ab) and (a).   ■

To prove that a certain word is in the closure language $S*$, we must show how it can be written as a concatenate of words from the base set S.

In the last example, to show that *abaab* is in $S*$ we can factor it as follows:

$$(ab)(a)(ab)$$

These three factors are all in the set S; therefore their concatenation is in $S*$. This is the only way to factor this string into factors of (a) and (ab). When this happens, we say that the factoring is **unique.**

Sometimes the factoring is not unique. For example, consider $S = \{xx, xxx\}$. Then:

$$S* = \{ \Lambda \text{ and all strings of more than one x } \}$$
$$= \{ x^n \text{ for } n = 0, \quad 2, \quad 3, \quad 4, \quad 5 \ldots \}$$
$$= \{ \Lambda \quad xx \quad xxx \quad xxxx \quad xxxxx \quad xxxxxx \ldots \}$$

Notice that the word x is not in the language $S*$. The string *xxxxxx* is in this closure for any of these three reasons. It is:

$$(xx)\ (xx)\ (xxx) \qquad \text{or} \qquad (xx)\ (xxx)\ (xx) \qquad \text{or} \qquad (xxx)\ (xx)\ (xx)$$

Also, x^6 is either $x^2x^2x^2$ or else x^3x^3.

It is important to note here that the parentheses, ( ), are not letters in the alphabet but are used for the sole purpose of demarcating the ends of factors. So we can write $xxxxx = (xx)(xxx)$. In cases where parentheses *are* letters of the alphabet,

$$\Sigma = \{ x\ (\ )\ \}$$
$$\text{length}(xxxxx) = 5$$
$$\text{but length}(\ (xx)(xxx)\ ) = 9$$

Let us suppose that we wanted to prove mathematically that this set $S*$ contains all x^n for $n \neq 1$. Suppose that somebody did not believe this and needed convincing. We could proceed as follows.

First, we consider the possibility that there were some powers of x that we could not produce by concatenating factors of (xx) and (xxx).

Obviously, since we can produce x^4, x^5, x^6, the examples of strings that we cannot produce must be large. Let us ask the question, "What is the smallest power of x (larger than 1) that we cannot form out of factors of *xx* and *xxx*?" Let us suppose that we start making a list of how to construct the various powers of x. On this list we write down how to form x^2, x^3, x^4, x^5, and so on. Let us say that we work our way successfully up to x^{373}, but then we cannot figure out how to form x^{374}. We become stuck, so a friend comes over to us and says, "Let me see your list. How did you form the word x^{372}?

Why don't you just concatenate another factor of xx in front of this and then you will have the word x^{374} that you wanted." Our friend is right, and this story shows that while writing this list out we can never really become stuck. This discussion can easily be generalized into a mathematical proof of the fact that $S*$ contains all powers of x greater than 1.

We have just established a mathematical fact by a method of proof that we have rarely seen in other courses. It is a proof based on showing that something exists (the factoring) because we can describe how to create it (by adding xx to a previous case). What we have described can be formalized into an algorithm for producing all the powers of x from the factors xx and xxx. The method is to begin with xx and xxx and, when we want to produce x^n, we take the sequence of concatenations that we have already found will produce x^{n-2}, and we concatenate xx on to that.

The method of proving that something exists by showing how to create it is called **proof by constructive algorithm.** This is the most important tool in our whole study. Most of the theorems in this book will be proven by the method of constructive algorithm. It is in general a very satisfying and useful method of proof, that is, providing that anybody is interested in the objects we are constructing. We may have a difficult time selling powers of x broken into factors of xx and xxx.

Let us observe that if the alphabet has no letters, then its closure is the language with the null string as its only word Symbolically, we write:

$$\text{If } \Sigma = \emptyset \quad \text{(the empty set)},$$
$$\text{then } \Sigma* = \{\Lambda\}$$

This is not the same as

$$\text{If } S = \{\Lambda\},$$
$$\text{then } S* = \{\Lambda\}$$

An alphabet may look like a set of one-letter words.

If for some reason we wish to modify the concept of closure to refer to only the concatenation of some (not zero) strings from a set S, we use the notation $^+$ instead of $*$. For example,

$$\text{If } \Sigma = \{x\}, \quad \text{then } \Sigma^+ = \{\, x \quad xx \quad xxx \dots \}$$

which is the language L_1 that we discussed before.

If $S = \{xx, xxx\}$ then S^+ is the same as $S*$ except for the word Λ, which is not in S^+. This is not to say that S^+ cannot in general contain the word Λ. It can, but only on condition that S contains the word Λ. In this case, Λ is in S^+, since it is the concatenation of some (actually one) word from

S (Λ itself). Anyone who does not think that the null string is confusing has missed something. It is already a problem, and it gets worse later.

If S is the set of three words

$$S = \{\, w_1 \quad w_2 \quad w_3 \,\}$$

then,

$$S^+ = \{\, w_1 \quad w_2 \quad w_3 \quad w_1w_1 \quad w_1w_2 \quad w_1w_3 \quad w_2w_1 \quad w_2w_2 \quad w_2w_3$$
$$w_3w_1 \quad w_3w_2 \quad w_3w_3 \quad w_1w_1w_1 \quad w_1w_1w_2 \ldots \}$$

no matter what the words w_1, w_2, and w_3 are.

If $w_1 = aa$, $w_2 = bbb$, $w_3 = \Lambda$, then
$S^+ = \{\, aa \quad bbb \quad \Lambda \quad aaaa \quad aabbb\ldots \}$

The words in the set S are listed above in the order corresponding to their w-sequencing, not in the usual size-alphabetical order.

What happens if we apply the closure operator twice? We start with a set of words S and look at its closure S^*. Now suppose we start with the set S^* and try to form *its* closure, which we denote as

$$(S^*)^* \quad \text{or} \quad S^{**}$$

If S is not the trivial empty set, then S^* is infinite, so we are taking the closure of an infinite set. This should present no problem since every string in the closure of a set is a combination of only finitely many words from the set. Even if the set S has infinitely many words, we use only finitely many at a time. This is the same as with ordinary arithmetic expressions, which can be made up of only finitely many numbers at a time even though there are infinitely many numbers to choose from.

From now on we shall let the closure operator apply to infinite sets as well as to finite sets.

THEOREM 1

For any set S of strings we have $S^* = S^{**}$.

CONVINCING REMARKS

First let us illustrate what this theorem means. Say for example that $S = \{a,b\}$. Then S^* is clearly all strings of the two letters a and b of any finite length whatsoever. Now what would it mean to take strings from S^* and concatenate

them? Let us say we concatenated (*aaba*) and (*baaa*) and (*aaba*). The end
result (*aababaaaaaba*) is no more than a concatenation of the letters *a* and
b, just as with all elements of *S**.

$$aababaaaaaba$$
$$= (aaba)(baaa)(aaba)$$
$$= [(a)(a)(b)(a)] \ [(b)(a)(a)(a)] \ [(a)(a)(b)(a)]$$
$$= (a)(a)(b)(a)(b)(a)(a)(a)(a)(a)(b)(a)$$

Let us consider one more illustration. If $S = \{aa, bbb\}$, then $S*$ is the set
of all strings where the *a*'s occur in even clumps and the *b*'s in groups of
3, 6, 9. . . Some words in $S*$ are

$$aabbbaaaa \quad bbb \quad bbbaa$$

If we concatenate these three elements of $S*$, we get one big word in $S**$,
which is again in $S*$.

$$aabbbaaaabbbbbbaa$$
$$= [(aa)(bbb)(aa)(aa)] \ [(bbb)] \ [(bbb)(aa)]$$

This theorem expresses a trivial but subtle point. It is analogous to saying
that if people are made up of molecules and molecules are made up of atoms,
then people are made up of atoms.

PROOF

Every word in $S**$ is made up of factors from $S*$. Every factor from $S*$ is
made up of factors from S. Therefore, every word in $S**$ is made up of
factors from S. Therefore, every word in $S**$ is also a word in $S*$. We can
write this as

$$S** \subset S*$$

using the symbol "⊂" from Set Theory, which means "is contained in or equal
to."

Now in general it is true that for any set A we know that $A \subset A*$, since
in $A*$ we can chose as a word any one factor from A. So if we consider A
to be our set $S*$, we have

$$S* \subset S**$$

Together, these two inclusions prove that

$$S* = S**$$

■

PROBLEMS

1. Consider the language $S*$, where $S = \{a, b\}$.
    How many words does this language have of length 2? of length 3? of length n?

2. Consider the language $S*$, where $S = \{aa, b\}$.
    How many words does this language have of length 4? of length 5? of length 6? What can be said in general?

3. Consider the language $S*$, where $S = \{ab, ba\}$. Write out all the words in $S*$ that have seven or fewer letters. Can any word in this language contain the substrings aaa or bbb?

4. Consider the language $S*$, where $S = \{a\ ab\ ba\}$. Is the string $(abbba)$ a word in this language? Write out all the words in this language with seven or fewer letters. What is another way in which to describe the words in this language? Be careful, this is not simply the language of all words without bbb.

5. Consider the language $S*$, where $S = \{aa\ aba\ baa\}$. Show that the words $aabaa$, $baaabaaa$, and $baaaaababaaaa$ are all in this language. Can any word in this language be interpreted as a string of elements from S in two different ways? Can any word in this language have an odd total number of a's?

6. Consider the language $S*$ where $S = \{xx\ xxx\}$. In how many ways can x^{19} be written as the product of words in S? This means: How many different factorizations are there of x^{19} into xx and xxx?

7. (i)   Prove that if x is in PALINDROME then so is x^n for any n.
    (ii) Prove that if y^3 is in PALINDROME then so is y.
    (iii) Prove that if z^n is in PALINDROME for some n (greater than 0) then z itself is also.
    (iv) Prove that PALINDROME has as many words of length 4 as it does of length 3.
    (v)   Prove that PALINDROME has as many words of length $2n$ as it has of length $2n-1$.

8. Show that if the concatenation of two words (neither Λ) in PALIN-DROME is also a word in PALINDROME then both words are powers of some other word; that is, if x and y and xy are all in PALINDROME then there is a word z such that $x = z^n$ and $y = z^m$ for some integers n and m (maybe n or $m = 1$).

9. Let $S = \{ab, bb\}$ and let $T = \{ab, bb, bbbb\}$. Show that $S^* = T^*$. What principle does this illustrate?

10. Let $S = \{ab, bb\}$ and let $T = \{ab, bb, bbb\}$.
    (i)   Show that $S^* \neq T^*$, but that $S^* \subset T^*$.
    (ii) Prove in general that if $S \subset T$ then $S^* \subset T^*$.
          Find examples of S and T for which:
    (iii) $S \subset T$ but $S \neq T$ and yet $S^* = T^*$.
    (iv) $S^* = T^*$ but $S \not\subset T$ and $T \not\subset S$. The symbol "$\not\subset$" means "is not contained in or equal to."

11. How does the situation in Problem 10 change if we replace the operator $*$ with the operator $^+$ as defined in this chapter? Note the language S^+ means the same as S^* but does not allow the "concatenation of no words" of S.

12. Prove that for all sets S,
    (i) $(S^+)^* = (S^*)^*$
    (ii) $(S^+)^+ = S^+$
    (iii) Is $(S^*)^+ = (S^+)^*$ for all sets S?

13. Suppose that for some language L we can always concatenate two words in L and get another word in L if and only if the words are *not* the same. That is, for any words w_1 and w_2 in L where $w_1 \neq w_2$, the word $w_1 w_2$ is in L but the word $w_1 w_1$ is not in L. Prove that this cannot happen.

14. By definition

$$(S^{**})^* = S^{***}$$

    is this set bigger than S^*? Is it bigger than S?

15. Give an example of two sets of strings, S and T, such that the closure of S added to (union with) the closure of T is different from the closure of the set S union T. (In this book we will use the $+$ sign for union of sets instead of the usual $\cup$.) What we want here are two sets, S and T, such that

$$S^* + T^* \neq (S + T)^*$$

    What can we say in general about sets S and T that satisfy $(S + T)^* = S^* + T^*$?

16. Give an example of a set S such that the language $S*$ has more six letter words than seven letter words. Give an example of an $S*$ that has more six letter words than eight letter words. Does there exist an $S*$ such that it has more six letter words than twelve letter words?

17. Let $S = \{a, bb, bab, abaab\}$. Is *abbabaabab* in $S*$? Is *abaabbabbaabb*? Does any word in $S*$ have an odd total number of b's?

18. (i) Consider the language $S*$ where $S = \{aa, ab, ba, bb\}$. Give another description of this language.

    (ii) Give an example of a set S such that $S*$ contains all possible strings of a's and b's that have length divisible by three.

19. One student suggested the following algorithm to test a string of a's and b's to see if it is a word in $S*$ where $S = \{aa, ba, aba, abaab\}$. Step 1, cross off the longest set of characters from the front of the string that is a word in S. Step 2, repeat step 1 until it is no longer possible. If what remains is the string Λ, the original string was a word in $S*$. If what remains is not Λ (this means some letters are left but we cannot find a word in S at the beginning), the original string was not a word in $S*$. Find a string that disproves this algorithm.

20. The reason * is called the "closure operator" is because the set $S*$ is *closed under concatenation*. This means that if we take any two words in $S*$ and concatenate them, we get another word in $S*$. If $S = \{ab, bbb\}$, then S is not closed under concatenation since *abab* is not in S, but $S*$ is closed under concatenation.

    (i) Let T be any set that contains all of S, and suppose T is closed under concatenation. Show that T contains $S*$.

    (ii) Explain why we may say "$S*$ is the smallest set that is closed under concatenation that contains S."

    (iii) What is the smallest set, closed under concatenation, that contains both the sets of words P and Q?

CHAPTER 3

RECURSIVE DEFINITIONS

One of the mathematical tools that we shall find extremely useful in our study, but which is largely unfamiliar in other branches of mathematics, is a method of defining sets called **recursive definition.** A recursive definition is characteristically a three-step process. First, we specify some basic objects in the set. Second, we give rules for constructing more objects in the set from the ones we already know. Third, we declare that no objects except those constructed in this way are allowed in the set.

Let us take an example. Suppose that we are trying to define the set of positive even integers for someone who knows about arithmetic but has never heard of the even numbers. One standard way of defining this set is:

EVEN is the set of all positive whole numbers divisible by 2.

Another way we might try is this:

EVEN is the set of all $2n$ where $n = 1$ 2 3 4 . . .

The third method we present is sneaky, by recursive definition:

The set EVEN is defined by these three rules:

Rule 1   2 is in EVEN.

Rule 2   If x is in EVEN then so is $x + 2$.

Rule 3   The *only* elements in the set EVEN are those that can be produced from the two rules above.

There is a reason that the third definition is less popular than the others: It is much harder to use in most practical applications.

For example, suppose that we wanted to prove that 14 is in the set EVEN. To show this using the first definition we divide 14 by 2 and find that there is no remainder. Therefore, it is in EVEN. To prove that 14 is in EVEN by the second definition we have to somehow come up with the number 7 and then, since $14 = (2)(7)$, we know that it is in EVEN. To prove that 14 is even using the recursive definition is a lengthier process. We could proceed as below:

By Rule 1, we know that 2 is in EVEN.

Then by Rule 2 we know that $2 + 2 = 4$ is also in EVEN.

Again by Rule 2 we know that since 4 has just been shown to be in EVEN, $4 + 2 = 6$ is also in EVEN.

The fact that 6 is in EVEN means that when we apply Rule 2 we deduce that $6 + 2 = 8$ is in EVEN, too.

Now applying Rule 2 to 8 we derive that $8 + 2 = 10$ is another member of EVEN.

Once more applying Rule 2, this time to 10, we infer that $10 + 2 = 12$ is in EVEN.

And, at last, by applying Rule 2 once more, to the number 12, we conclude that $12 + 2 = 14$ is, indeed, in EVEN.

Pretty horrible. This, however, is not the only recursive definition of the set EVEN. We might use:

The set EVEN is defined by these three rules.

Rule 1   2 is in even.

Rule 2   If x and y are both in EVEN then so is

$$x + y$$

Rule 3   No number is in EVEN unless it can be produced by Rules 1 and 2.

It should be understood that we mean we can apply Rule 2 also to the case where x and y stand for the same number.

We can now prove that 14 is in EVEN in fewer steps:

By Rule 1   2 is in EVEN

By Rule 2 $x = 2, y = 2 \rightarrow 4$ is in EVEN

By Rule 2 $x = 2, y = 4 \rightarrow 6$ is in EVEN

By Rule 2 $x = 4, y = 4 \rightarrow 8$ is in EVEN

By Rule 2 $x = 6, y = 8 \rightarrow 14$ is in EVEN

This is a better recursive definition of the set EVEN, because it produces shorter proofs that elements are in EVEN. The set EVEN, as we have seen, has some very fine definitions that are not recursive. In later chapters we shall be interested in certain sets that have no better definition than the recursive one.

Before leaving this example, let us note that although the second recursive definition is still harder to use (in proving that given numbers are even) than the two nonrecursive definitions, it does have some advantages. For instance, suppose we want to prove that the sum of two numbers in EVEN is also a number in EVEN. This is a trivial conclusion from the second recursive definition, but to prove this from the first definition is decidedly harder. Whether or not we want a recursive definition depends on two things: one, how easy the other possible definitions are to understand; and two, what types of theorems we may wish to prove about the set.

Let us consider the way polynomials are usually defined:

A polynomial is a finite sum of terms each of which is of the form a real number times a power of x (that may be $x^0 = 1$).

Now let us consider a recursive definition that is designed for people who know algebraic notation but do not know what a polynomial is.

The set POLYNOMIAL is defined by these four rules:

Rule 1   Any number is in POLYNOMIAL.

Rule 2   The variable x is in POLYNOMIAL.

Rule 3   If p and q are in POLYNOMIAL, then so are $p + q$ and (p) and pq.

Rule 4   POLYNOMIAL contains only those things which can be created by the three rules above.

The symbol pq, which looks like a concatenation of alphabet letters, in algebraic notation refers to multiplication.

These rules are very crude in that they make us write subtraction as $p + (-1)q$ and they do not show us how to simplify this to $p - q$. We could include rules for making the notation prettier, but the rules above do allow us to produce all polynomials in some form or another, and the rules themselves are simple.

Some sequence of applications of these rules can show that $3x^2 + 7x - 9$ is in POLYNOMIAL.

By Rule 1   3 is in POLYNOMIAL

By Rule 2 x is in POLYNOMIAL

By Rule 3 $(3)(x)$ is in POLYNOMIAL, call it $3x$

By Rule 3 $(3x)(x)$ is in POLYNOMIAL, call it $3x^2$

By Rule 1   7 is in POLYNOMIAL

By Rule 3 $(7)(x)$ is in POLYNOMIAL

By Rule 3 $3x^2 + 7x$ is in POLYNOMIAL

By Rule 1 -9 is in POLYNOMIAL

By Rule 3 $3x^2 + 7x + (-9) = 3x^2 + 7x - 9$ is in POLYNOMIAL.

In fact, there are several other sequences that could also produce this result.

There are some advantages to this definition as well as the evident disadvantages. On the plus side, it is immediately obvious that the sum and product of polynomials are both themselves polynomials. This is a little more complicated to see if we had to provide a proof based on the classical definition.

Suppose for a moment that we were studying calculus and we had just proven that the derivative of the sum of two functions is the sum of the derivatives and that the derivative of the product fg is $f'g + fg'$. As soon as we prove that the derivative of a number is 0 and that the derivative of x is 1 we have automatically shown that we can differentiate all polynomials. This becomes a theorem that can be proven directly from the recursive definition. It is true that we do not then *know* that the derivative of x^n is nx^{n-1}, but we do know that it can be calculated for every n.

In this way we can have proven that we can differentiate all polynomials without giving the best algorithm to do it. Since the topic of this book is Computer Theory, we are very interested in proving that certain tasks are possible for a computer to do even if we do not know the best algorithms by which to do them. What is even more astounding is that we shall be able to prove that certain tasks are theoretically impossible for *any computer* (remember: this includes all the models we have today and all the models that may be built in the future). It is for these reasons that recursive definitions are important to us.

Before proceeding to more serious matters, let us note that recursive definitions are not completely alien to us in the real world. What is the best definition of the set of people who are descended from Henry VIII? Is it not:

Rule 1   The children of Henry VIII are all elements of DESCENDANTS.

Rule 2   If x is an element of DESCENDANTS, then so are x's children.

Also in mathematics we often see the following definition of factorial:

Rule 1 $0! = 1$

Rule 2 $(n + 1)! = (n + 1)(n!)$

The reason that these definitions are called "recursive" is that one of the rules used to define the set mentions the set itself. We define EVEN in terms of previously known elements of EVEN, POLYNOMIAL in terms of previously known elements of POLYNOMIAL. We define $(n + 1)!$ in terms of the value of $n!$. In computer languages, when we allow a procedure to call itself we refer to the program as recursive. These definitions have the same self-referential sense.

EXAMPLE

Observe how natural the following definitions are:

Rule 1 x is in L_1

Rule 2   If Q is any word in L_1, then xQ is also in L_1.

$$L_1 = x^+ = \{ x \quad xx \quad xxx. \ . \ . \}$$

or

Rule 1 Λ is in L_4

Rule 2   If Q is any word in L_4, then xQ is also in L_4

$$L_4 = x^* = \{ \Lambda \quad x \quad xx \quad xxx \ . \ . \ . \}$$

or

Rule 1 x is in L_2

Rule 2   If Q is any word in L_2, then xxQ is also in L_2.

$$L_2 = \{x^{odd}\} = \{ x \quad xxx \quad xxxxx \ . \ . \ . \}$$

or

Rule 1   *1 2 3 4 5 6 7 8 9 are in L₃*

Rule 2   If Q is any word in L_3, then $Q0$, $Q1$, $Q2$, $Q3$, $Q4$, $Q5$, $Q6$, $Q7$, $Q8$, $Q9$ are also words in L_3.

$$L_3 = \{ 1 \quad 2 \quad 3 \quad 4 \quad \ldots \}$$

■

Suppose we ask ourselves what constitutes a valid arithmetic expression that can be typed on one line, in a form digestible by computers. The alphabet for this language is

$$\Sigma = \{ 0 \quad 1 \quad 2 \quad 3 \quad 4 \quad 5 \quad 6 \quad 7 \quad 8 \quad 9 + - * / ( ) \}$$

Obviously, the following strings are not good:

$$(3 + 5) + 6) \qquad 2(/ 8 + 9) \qquad (3 + (4 -)8) \qquad 2) - (4$$

The first contains unbalanced parentheses; the second contains the forbidden substring (/; the third contains the forbidden substring −); the fourth has a close parenthesis before the corresponding open parenthesis. Are there more rules? The subsequences // and */ are also forbidden. Are there still more? The most natural way of defining a valid arithmetic expression, AE, is by using a recursive definition rather than a long list of forbidden substrings. The definition can be written as:

Rule 1   Any number (positive, negative, or zero) is in AE.

Rule 2   If x is in AE, then so are (x) and $-(x)$.

Rule 3   If x and y are in AE, then so are
(i) $x + y$ (if the first symbol in y is not $-$)
(ii) $x - y$ (if the first symbol in y is not $-$)
(iii)) $x * y$
(iv) x / y
(v) $x**y$ (our notation for exponentiation)

We have called this the "most natural" definition because, even though we may never have articulated this point, it truly is the method we use for recognizing arithmetic expressions in real life. If we are presented with

$$(2 + 4) * (7 * (9 - 3) / 4) / 4 * (2 + 8) - 1$$

and asked to determine if it is a valid arithmetic expression, we do not really scan over the string looking for forbidden substrings or count the parentheses.

We imagine it in our mind broken down into its components. $(2 + 4)$ that's OK, $(9 - 3)$ that's OK, $7 * (9 - 3) / 4$ that's OK, and so on. We may never have seen a definition of "arithmetic expressions" before, but this is what we have always intuitively meant by the phrase.

This definition gives us the possibility of writing $2 + 3 + 4$, which is not ambiguous. But it also gives us $8/4/2$, which is. It could mean $8/(4/2) = 4$ or $(8/4)/2 = 1$. Also, $3 + 4 * 5$ is ambiguous. So we usually adopt conventions of operator hierarchy and left to right execution. By applying Rule 2 we could always put in enough parentheses to avoid any confusion if we so desired. We return to this point in Part II, but for now this definition adequately defines the language of all valid strings of symbols for arithmetic expressions. Remember, the ambiguity in the string $8/4/2$ is a problem of *meaning*. There is no doubt that the string is a word in AE, only doubt about what it means.

This definition determines the set AE in a manner useful for proving many theorems about arithmetic expressions.

THEOREM 2

An arithmetic expression cannot contain the character $.

PROOF

This character is not part of any number, so it cannot be introduced into an AE by Rule 1. If the character string x does not contain the character $, then neither do the strings (x) and $-(x)$, so it cannot be introduced into an AE by Rule 2. If neither x nor y contains the character $, then neither do any of the expressions defined by Rule 3. Therefore, the character $ can never get into an AE. ∎

THEOREM 3

No AE can begin or end with the symbol /.

PROOF

No number begins or ends with this symbol, so it cannot occur by Rule 1. Any AE formed by Rule 2 must begin and end with parentheses or begin with a minus sign, so the / cannot be introduced by Rule 2. If x does not begin with a / and y does not end with a /, then any AE formed by any clause in Rule 3 will not begin or end with a /. Therefore, these rules will never produce an expression beginning or ending with a /. ∎

These proofs are like the story of the three chefs making a stew. One can add only meat to the pot. One can add only carrots to the pot. One can add only potatoes to the pot. Even without knowing exactly in what order the chefs visit the pot or how often, we still can conclude that the pot cannot end up with an alarm clock in it. If no rule contributes a $, then one never gets in, even though if x had a $ then $x + y$ would also.

The symbol "/" has many names. In computer science it is usually called a "slash," other names are "oblique stroke," "solidus," and "virgule." It also has another theorem.

THEOREM 4

No AE can contain the substring //.

PROOF

For variation, we shall prove this result by contradiction, even though a direct argument similar to those above could easily be given.

Let us suppose that there were some AE's that contained the substring //. Let the shortest of these be a string called w. This means that w is a valid AE that contains the substring //, but there is no shorter word in AE that contains this substring. There may be more strings of the same length as w that contain //, but it does not matter which of these we begin with and choose to call w.

Now we know that w, like all words in AE, is formed by some sequence of applications of the Rules 1, 2, and 3. Our first question is: Which was the last rule used in the production of w? This is easy to answer. We shall show that it must have been Rule 3(iv). If it were Rule 3(iii), for instance, then the // must either be found in the x part or the y part. But x and y are presumed to be in AE so this would mean that there is some shorter word in AE than w that contains the substring //, which contradicts the assumption that w is the shortest. Similarly we can eliminate all the other possibilities. Therefore, the last rule used to produce w must have been 3(iv).

Now, since the // cannot have been contributed to w from the x part alone or from the y part alone (or else x or y are shorter words in AE with a double slash), it must have been included by finding an x part that ended in / or a y part that began with a /. But since both x and y are AE's, our previous theorem says that neither case can happen. Therefore, even Rule 3(iv) cannot introduce the substring //.

Therefore, there is no possibility left for the last rule from which w can be constructed. Therefore, w cannot be in the set AE. Therefore, there is no shortest AE that contains the substring //. Therefore, nothing in the set AE can have the substring //. ∎

This method of argument should sound familiar. It is similar to the proof that $\{xx, xxx\}^*$ contains all x^n, for $n \neq 1$.

The long-winded but careful proof of the last theorem is given to illustrate that recursive definitions can be conveniently employed in rigorous mathematical proofs. Admittedly, this was a trival example of the application of this method. Most people would be just as convinced by the following "proof."

How could an arithmetic expression contain the substring //? What would it mean? Huh? What are you, crazy or something?

We should bear in mind that we are only on the threshold of investigating a very complex and profound subject and that in this early chapter we wish to introduce a feel for the techniques and viewpoints that will be relied on heavily later, under far less obvious circumstances. We will use our learner's permit to spend a few hours driving around an empty parking lot before venturing onto the highway.

Another common use for recursive definitions is to determine what expressions are valid in Symbolic Logic. We shall be interested in one particular branch of Symbolic Logic called the Sentential Calculus or the Propositional Calculus. The version we shall define here uses only negation $\neg$ and implication $\rightarrow$ along with the phrase variables, although conjunction and disjunction could easily be added to the system. The valid expressions in this language are traditionally called WFF's for **well-formed formulas.**

As with AE, parentheses are letters in the alphabet

$$\Sigma = \{ \neg \rightarrow ( ) \quad a \quad b \quad c \quad d \quad \dots \}$$

There are other symbols sometimes used for negation, such as $\ulcorner$, $-$, and $\sim$. The rules for forming WFF's are:

Rule 1   Any single Latin letter is a WFF,
$\qquad a \quad b \quad c \quad d \quad \dots$

Rule 2   If p is a WFF, then so are
$\qquad (p)$ and $\neg p$.

Rule 3   If p and q are WFF's, then so is
$\qquad p \rightarrow q$.

Some sequences of applications of these rules enable us to show that;

$$p \rightarrow ((p \rightarrow p) \rightarrow q)$$

is a WFF. Without too much difficulty we can also show that

$$p \rightarrow \qquad \rightarrow p \qquad (p \rightarrow \quad p) \qquad p) \rightarrow p($$

are all not WFF's.

As a final note in this section, we should be wary that we have sometimes used recursive definitions to define *membership in a set*, as in the phrase "*x* is in POLYNOMIAL" or "*x* is in EVEN" and sometimes to define a *property*, such as in the phrase "*x* is a WFF" or "*x* is even." This should not present any problem.

PROBLEMS

1. Write another recursive definition for the language L_1 of Chapter 2.
2. Using the second recursive definition of the set EVEN, how many different ways can we prove that 14 is in EVEN?
3. Using the second recursive definition of EVEN, what is the smallest number of steps required to prove that 100 is EVEN? Describe a good method for showing that $2n$ is in EVEN.
4. Show that the following is another recursive definition of the set EVEN.

Rule 1   2 and 4 are in EVEN.

Rule 2   If *x* is in EVEN, then so is $x + 4$.

5. Show that there are infinitely many different recursive definitions for the set EVEN.
6. Using any recursive definition of the set EVEN, show that all the numbers in it end in the digits 0, 2, 4, 6, or 8.
7. The set POLYNOMIAL defined in this chapter contains only the polynomials in the one variable *x*. Write a recursive definition for the set of all polynomials in the two variables *x* and *y*.
8. Define the set of valid algebraic expressions ALEX as follows:

Rule 1   All polynomials are in ALEX.

Rule 2   If $f(x)$ and $g(x)$ are in ALEX then so are

      (i) $(f(x))$
     (ii) $-(f(x))$
    (iii) $f(x) + g(x)$
    (iv) $f(x) - g(x)$
     (v) $f(x)g(x)$
    (vi) $f(x) / g(x)$

(vii) $f(x)^{g(x)}$

(viii) $f(g(x))$

(a) Show that $(x + 2)^{3x}$ is in ALEX.

(b) Show that elementary calculus contains enough rules to prove the theorem that all algebraic expressions can be differentiated.

(c) Is Rule (viii) really necessary?

9. Using the fact that $3x^2 + 7x - 9 = (((((3)x) + 7)x) - 9)$, show how to produce this polynomial from the rules for POLYNOMIAL using multiplication only twice. What is the smallest number of steps needed for producing $x^8 + x^4$? What is the smallest number of steps needed for producing $7x^7 + 5x^5 + 3x^3 + x$?

10. Show that if n is less than 29, then x^n can be shown to be in POLYNOMIAL in fewer than eight steps.

11. In this chapter we mentioned several substrings of length 2 that cannot occur in arithmetic expressions, such as (/, +), // and */. What is the complete list of substrings of length 2 that cannot occur?

12. Are there any substrings of length 3 that cannot occur that do not contain forbidden substrings of length 2? (This means that /// is already known to be illegal because it contains the forbidden substring //.) What is the longest forbidden substring that does not contain a shorter forbidden substring?

13. The rules given above for the set AE, allow for the peculiar expressions

$$((((9))))) \quad \text{and} \quad -(-(-(-(9))))$$

It is not really harmful to allow these in AE, but is there some modified definition of AE that eliminates this problem?

14. Write out the full recursive definition for the propositional calculus that contains the symbols $\vee$ and $\wedge$ as well as $\neg$ and $\rightarrow$. What are all the forbidden substrings of length 2 in this language?

15. (i) When asked to give a recursive definition for the language PALINDROME over the alphabet $\Sigma = \{a, b\}$, a student wrote:

Rule 1 a and b are in PALINDROME

Rule 2   If x is in PALINDROME, then so are axa and bxb

Unfortunately all of the words in the language defined above have an odd length and so it is not all of PALINDROME. Fix this problem.

(ii) Give a recursive definition for the language EVENPALINDROME of all palindromes of even length.

16. (i)   Give a recursive definition for the set ODD = {1,3,5,7 . . . }.
    (ii) Give a recursive definition for the set of strings of digits 0, 1, 2, 3, . . . 9 that cannot start with the digit 0.
17. (i)   Give a recursive definition for the language $S*$ where $S = \{aa,b\}$.
    (ii) Give a recursive definition for the language $T*$ where

$$T = \{w_1,\ w_2,\ w_3,\ w_4\},$$

where these w's are some particular words.

18. Give two recursive definitions for the set

$$\text{POWERS-OF-TWO} = \{1\ 2\ 4\ 8\ 16\ \ldots\}$$

Use one of them to prove that the product of two powers of two is also a power of two.

19. Give recursive definitions for the following languages over the alphabet $\{a,b\}$:
    (i)   The language EVENSTRING of all words of even length.
    (ii) The language ODDSTRING of all words of odd length.
    (iii) The language AA of all words containing the substring aa.
    (iv) The language NOTAA of all words not containing the substring aa.

20. (i)   Consider the following recursive definition of 3-PERMUTATION
    (a) 123 is a 3-PERMUTATION
    (b) if xyz is a 3-PERMUTATION then so are

$$zyx \quad \text{and} \quad yzx$$

Show that there are six different 3-PERMUTATION's.
    (ii) Consider the following recursive definition of 4-PERMUTATION
    (a) 1234 is a 4-PERMUTATION
    (b) if $xyzw$ is a 4-PERMUTATION then so are

$$wzyx \text{ and } yzwx$$

How many 4-PERMUTATION's are there (by this definition)?

CHAPTER 4

REGULAR EXPRESSIONS

We wish now to be very careful about the phrases we use to define languages. We defined L_1 in Chapter 2 by the symbols:

$$L_1 = \{x^n \quad \text{for } n = 1 \quad 2 \quad 3 \quad \dots\}$$

and we presumed that we all understood exactly which values n could take. We might even have defined the language L_2 by the symbols

$$L_2 = \{x^n \quad \text{for } n = 1 \quad 3 \quad 5 \quad 7 \quad \dots\}$$

and again we could presume that we all agree on what words are in this language.

We might define a language by the symbols:

$$L_5 = \{x^n \quad \text{for } n = 1 \quad 4 \quad 9 \quad 16 \quad \dots\}$$

but now the symbols are becoming more of an IQ test than a clear definition.

38

What words are in the language

$$L_6 = \{x^n \quad \text{for } n = 3 \quad 4 \quad 8 \quad 22 \quad \ldots\} \; ?$$

Perhaps these are the ages of the sisters of Louis XIV when he assumed the throne of France. More precision and less guesswork is required, especially where computers are concerned. In this chapter we shall develop some new language-defining symbolism that will be much more precise than the ellipsis (which is what the three dots . . . are called).

The language-defining symbols we are about to create are called **regular expressions.** We will define the term regular expression itself recursively. The languages that are associated with these regular expressions are called **regular languages** and are also said to be defined by **finite representation.**

These terms will make more sense when they are associated with concepts. Let us reconsider the language L_4 of Chapter 2.

$$L_4 = \{ \Lambda \quad x \quad xx \quad xxx \quad xxxx \ldots \}$$

In that chapter we presented one method for indicating this set as the closure of a smaller set.

$$\text{Let } S = \{x\}. \text{ Then } L_4 = S*$$

As shorthand for this we could have written:

$$L_4 = \{x\}*$$

We now introduce the use of the Kleene star applied not to a set but directly to the letter x and written as a superscript as if it were an exponent.

$$\mathbf{x}*$$

The simple expression $\mathbf{x}*$ will be used to indicate some sequence of x's (maybe none at all).

$$\mathbf{x}* = \Lambda \quad \text{or} \quad x \quad \text{or} \quad x^2 \quad \text{or} \quad x^3 \quad \text{or} \quad x^4 \ldots$$
$$= x^n \quad \text{for some } n = 0 \quad 1 \quad 2 \quad 3 \quad 4 \ldots$$

We can think of the star as an unknown power or undetermined power. That is $\mathbf{x}*$ stands for a string of x's, but we do not specify how many. It stands for any string of x's in the language L_4.

The star operator applied to a letter is analogous to the star operator applied to a set. It represents an arbituary concatenation of copies of that letter (maybe none at all). This notation can be used to help us define languages by writing

$$L_4 = \text{language } (\mathbf{x}*)$$

Since $\mathbf{x}^*$ is any string of x's, L_4 is then the set of all possible strings of x's of any length (including Λ).

We should not confuse $\mathbf{x}^*$, which is a language-defining symbol, with L_4, which is the name we have given to a certain language. This is why we use the word "language" in the equation. We shall soon give a name to the world in which this symbol $\mathbf{x}^*$ lives but not quite yet. Suppose that we wished to describe the language L over the alphabet $\Sigma = \{a,b\}$ where

$$L = \{\, a \quad ab \quad abb \quad abbb \quad abbbb \quad \ldots \,\}$$

We could summarize this language by the English phrase "all words of the form one a followed by some number of b's (maybe no b's at all.)"

Using our star notation, we may write:

$$L = \text{language } (\mathbf{a} \ \mathbf{b}^*)$$

or without the space,

$$L = \text{language } (\mathbf{ab}^*)$$

The meaning is clear: This is a language in which the words are the concatenation of an initial a with some or no b's (that is $\mathbf{b}^*$). Whether we put a space inside $\mathbf{ab}^*$ or not is only for the clarity of reading; it does not change the set of strings this represents. No string can contain a blank unless a blank is a character in the alphabet Σ. If we want blanks to be in the alphabet, we normally introduce some special symbol to stand for them, as blanks themselves are invisible to the naked eye. The reason for putting a blank between $\mathbf{a}$ and $\mathbf{b}^*$ in the product above is to emphasize the point that the star operator is applied to the b only. We have now used a boldface letter without a star as well as with a star.

We can apply the Kleene star to the string ab if we want, as follows:

$$(\mathbf{ab})^* = \Lambda \quad \text{or} \quad ab \quad \text{or} \quad abab \quad \text{or} \quad ababab \ldots$$

Parentheses are not letters in the alphabet of this language, so they can be used to indicate factoring without accidently changing the words. Since the star represents some kind of exponentiation, we use it as powers are used in algebra, where by universal understanding the expression xy^2 means $x(y^2)$, not $(xy)^2$.

If we want to define the language L_1 this way, we may write

$$L_1 = \text{language } (\mathbf{xx}^*)$$

This means that we start each word of L_1 by writing down an x and then we follow it with some string of x's (which may be no more x's at all). Or we may use the $^+$ notation from Chapter 2 and write

$$L_1 = \text{language } (\mathbf{x}^+)$$

meaning all words of the form x to some positive power (that is, not $x^0 = \Lambda$). The $^+$ notation is a convenience but is not essential since we can say the same thing with *'s alone.

EXAMPLE

The language L_1 can be defined by any of the expressions below:

$$\mathbf{xx^*} \quad \mathbf{x^+} \quad \mathbf{xx^*x^*} \quad \mathbf{x^*xx^*} \quad \mathbf{x^+x^*} \quad \mathbf{x^*x^+} \quad \mathbf{x^*x^*x^*xx^*}$$

Remember $\mathbf{x}^*$ can always be Λ. ■

EXAMPLE

The language defined by the expression

$$\mathbf{ab^*a}$$

is the set of all strings of a's and b's that have at least two letters, that begin and end with a's, and that have nothing but b's inside (if anything at all).

language $(\mathbf{ab^*a}) = \{aa \quad aba \quad abba \quad abbba \quad abbbba \quad \ldots\}$

It would be a subtle mistake to say only that this language is the set of all words that begin and end with an a and have only b's in between, because this description may also apply to the word "a," depending on how it is interpreted. Our symbolism eliminates this ambiguity. ■

EXAMPLE

The language of the expression

$$\mathbf{a^*b^*}$$

contains all the strings of a's and b's in which all the a's (if any) come before all the b's (if any).

language $(\mathbf{a^*b^*}) = \{\Lambda \quad a \quad b \quad aa \quad ab \quad bb \quad aaa \quad aab \quad abb \quad bbb \quad aaaa \ldots\}$

Notice that *ba* and *aba* are not in this language. Notice also that there need not be the same number of *a*'s and *b*'s. ∎

Here we should again be very careful to observe that

$$\mathbf{a*b*} \neq \mathbf{(ab)*}$$

since the language defined by the expression on the right contains the word *abab*, which the language defined by the expression on the left does not. This cautions us against thinking of the * as a normal algebraic exponent.

The language defined by the expression **a*b*a*** contains the word *baa* since it starts with zero *a*'s followed by one *b* followed by two *a*'s.

EXAMPLE

The following expressions both define the language $L_2 = \{x^{odd}\}$

$$\mathbf{x(xx)*} \quad or \quad \mathbf{(xx)*x}$$

but the expression

$$\mathbf{x*xx*}$$

does not since it includes the word $(xx) \, x \, (x)$. ∎

We now introduce another use for the plus sign. By the expression $\mathbf{x + y}$ where x and y are strings of characters from an alphabet, we mean "either x or y". This means that $\mathbf{x + y}$ offers a choice, much the same way that $\mathbf{x*}$ does. Care should be taken so as not to confuse this with $^+$ as an exponent.

EXAMPLE

Consider the language T defined over the alphabet $\Sigma = \{a, b, c\}$

$$T = \{a \quad c \quad ab \quad cb \quad abb \quad cbb \quad abbb \quad cbbb \quad abbbb \quad cbbbb \quad \ldots \}$$

All the words in T begin with an a or a c and then are followed by some number of *b*'s. Symbolically, we may write this as

$$T = \text{language } ((\mathbf{a + c})\mathbf{b*})$$
$$= \text{language (either } a \text{ or } c \text{ then some } b\text{'s)}$$

We should, of course, have said "some or no b's". We often drop the zero-option because it is tiresome. We let the word "some" always mean "some or no," and when we mean "some positive number of" we say that.

We say that the expression $(\mathbf{a} + \mathbf{c})\mathbf{b}*$ defines a language in the following sense. Every $^+$ and $*$ ask us to make a choice. For each $*$ or $^+$ used as a superscript we must select some number of factors for which it stands. For each other $+$ we must decide whether to choose the right-side expression or the left-side expression. For every set of choices we have generated a particular string. The set of all strings produceable by this method is the language of the expression. In the example

$$(\mathbf{a} + \mathbf{c})\mathbf{b}*$$

we must choose either the a or the c for the first letter and then we choose how many b's the $\mathbf{b}*$ stands for. Each set of choices is a word. If from $(\mathbf{a} + \mathbf{c})$ we choose c and we choose $\mathbf{b}*$ to mean bbb, we have the word $cbbb$. ∎

EXAMPLE

Now let us consider a finite language L that contains all the strings of a's and b's of length exactly three.

$$L = \{aaa \quad aab \quad aba \quad abb \quad baa \quad bab \quad bba \quad bbb\}$$

The first letter of each word in L is either an a or a b. The second letter of each word in L is either an a or a b. The third letter of each word in L is either an a or a b. So we may write

$$L = \text{language } ((\mathbf{a} + \mathbf{b})(\mathbf{a} + \mathbf{b})(\mathbf{a} + \mathbf{b}))$$

or for short,

$$L = \text{language } ((\mathbf{a} + \mathbf{b})^3) \qquad ∎$$

If we want to define the set of all seven letter strings of a's and b's, we could write $(\mathbf{a} + \mathbf{b})^7$. In general, if we want to refer to the set of all possible strings of a's and b's of any length whatsoever we could write,

$$(\mathbf{a} + \mathbf{b})*$$

This is the set of all possible strings of letters from the alphabet $\Sigma = \{a, b\}$

including the null string. This is a very important regular expression and we use it often.

Again this expression represents a language. If we decide that * stands for 5, then

$$(\mathbf{a} + \mathbf{b})*$$

gives

$$(\mathbf{a} + \mathbf{b})^5 = (\mathbf{a}+\mathbf{b})(\mathbf{a}+\mathbf{b})(\mathbf{a}+\mathbf{b})(\mathbf{a}+\mathbf{b})(\mathbf{a}+\mathbf{b})$$

We now have to make five more choices: either a or b for the first letter, either a or b for the second letter, ...

This is a very powerful notation. We can describe all words that begin with the letter a simply as:

$$\mathbf{a}(\mathbf{a} + \mathbf{b})*$$

that is, first an a, then anything (as many choices as we want of either letter a or b).

All words that begin with an a and end with a b can be defined by the expression

$$\mathbf{a}(\mathbf{a} + \mathbf{b})*\mathbf{b} = a \text{ (arbitrary string) } b$$

EXAMPLE

Let us consider the language defined by the expression

$$(\mathbf{a} + \mathbf{b})*\mathbf{a}(\mathbf{a} + \mathbf{b})*$$

At the beginning we have $(\mathbf{a} + \mathbf{b})*$, which stands for anything, that is any string of a's and b's, then comes an a, then another anything. All told, the language is the set of all words over the alphabet $\Sigma = \{a, b\}$ that have an a in them somewhere. The only words left out are those that have only b's and the word Λ.

For example, the word *abbaab* can be considered to be of this form in three ways:

$$(\Lambda) \ a \ (bbaab) \quad \text{or} \quad (abb) \ a \ (ab) \quad \text{or} \quad (abba) \ a \ (b)$$

■

EXAMPLE

The language of all words that have at least two a's can be described by the expression

$$(a + b)*a(a + b)*a(a + b)*$$

= (some beginning)(the first important a)(some middle)(the second
  important a)(some end)

where the arbitrary parts can have as many a's (or b's) as they want.   ■

    In the last three examples we have used the notation $(a + b)*$ as a factor to mean "any possible substring," just as we have seen it stand for the language of all words. In this sense, the expression $(a + b)*$ is a wild card.

EXAMPLE

Another expression that denotes all the words with at least two a's is:

$$b*ab*a(a + b)*$$

We scan through some jungle of b's (or no b's) until we find the first a, then more b's (or no b's), then the second a, then we finish up with anything. In this set are *abbbabb* and *aaaaa*.
    We can write:

$$(a + b)*a(a + b)*a(a + b)* = b*ab*a(a + b)*$$

where by the equal sign we do not mean that these expressions are equal algebraically in the same way as

$$x + x = 2x$$

but that they are equal because they describe the same item, as with

$$16\text{th President} = \text{Abraham Lincoln}$$

  We could write

      language $((a + b)*a(a + b)*a(a + b)*)$
= language $(b*ab*a (a + b)*)$
= all words with at least two a's.

To be careful about this point, we say that two regular expressions are **equivalent** if they describe the same language.

The expressions below also describe the language of words with at least two a's.

$$(a + b) * ab * ab *$$

↑　　↑

next to　　last a

last a

and

$$b*a(a + b)*ab*$$

↑　　　　↑

first a　　last a　　　　　　　　　　　■

EXAMPLE

If we wanted all the words with *exactly* two a's, we could use the expression

$$b*ab*ab*$$

which describes such words as *aab, baba,* and *bbbabbbab*. To make the word *aab*, we let the first and second **b*** become Λ and the last becomes b. ■

EXAMPLE

The language of all words that have at least one a and at least one b is somewhat trickier. If we write

$$(a + b)*a(a + b)* \ b(a + b)*$$
$$= (\text{arbitrary}) \ a(\text{arbitrary}) \ b(\text{arbitrary})$$

we are then requiring that an a precede a b in the word. Such words as *ba* and *bbaaaa* are not included in this set. Since, however, we know that either the a comes before the b or the b comes before the a, we could define this set by the expression:

$$(a+b)*a(a+b)*b(a+b)* \ + \ (a+b)*b(a+b)*a(a+b)*$$

Here we are still using the plus sign in the general sense of disjunction (or). We are taking the union of two sets, but it is more correct to think of this + as offering alternatives in forming words.

There is a simpler expression that defines the same language. If we are confident that the only words that are omitted by the first term

$$(a + b)*a(a + b)*b(a + b)*$$

are the words of the form some b's followed by some a's, then it would be sufficient to add these specific exceptions into the set. These exceptions are all defined by the regular expression:

$$bb*aa*$$

The language of all words over the alphabet $\Sigma = \{a, b\}$ that contain both an a and a b is therefore also defined by the expression:

$$(a+b)*a(a+b)*b(a+b)* \ + \ bb*aa*$$

Notice that it is necessary to write **bb*aa*** because **b*a*** will admit words we do not want, such as *aaa*. ∎

These language-defining expressions cannot be treated like algebraic symbols. We have shown that

$$(a+b)*a(a+b)*b(a+b)*+(a+b)*b(a+b)*a(a+b)*=(a+b)*a(a+b)*b(a+b)*+bb*aa*$$

The first terms on both sides of this equation are the same, but if we cancel them we get

$$(a+b)*b(a+b)*a(a+b)* \ = \ bb*aa*$$

which is false, since the left side includes the word *aba,* which the expression on the right side does not.

The only words that do not contain both an a and a b in them somewhere are the words of all a's, all b's, or Λ. When these are added into the language, we get everything. Therefore, the regular expression:

$$(a+b)*a(a+b)*b(a+b)* \ + \ bb*aa* \ + \ a* \ + \ b*$$

defines all possible strings of a's and b's. The word Λ is included in both **a*** and **b***.

We can then write:

$$(a + b)* \ = \ (a+b)*a(a+b)*b(a+b)* \ + \ bb*aa* \ + \ a* \ + \ b*$$

which is not a very obvious equivalence at all.

EXAMPLE

All temptation to treat these language-defining expressions as if they were algebraic polynomials should be dispelled by these equivalences:

$$(\mathbf{a+b})* = (\mathbf{a+b})* + (\mathbf{a+b})*$$
$$(\mathbf{a+b})* = (\mathbf{a+b})* \ (\mathbf{a+b})*$$
$$(\mathbf{a+b})* = \mathbf{a(a+b)}* + \mathbf{b(a+b)}* + \Lambda$$
$$(\mathbf{a+b})* = (\mathbf{a+b})* \ \mathbf{ab(a+b)}* + \mathbf{b*a*}$$

The last of these equivalences requires some explanation. It means that all the words that do not contain the substring *ab* (which are accounted for in the first term) are all *a*'s, all *b*'s, Λ, or some *b*'s followed by some *a*'s. All four missing types are covered by **b*a***. ∎

Usually when we employ the star operator, we are defining an infinite language. We can represent a finite language by using the plus (union sign) alone. If the language L over the alphabet $\Sigma = \{a, \ b\}$ contains only the finite list of words given below,

$$L = \{abba \quad baaa \quad bbbb\}$$

then we can represent L by the symbolic expression

$$L = \text{language } (\mathbf{abba + baaa + bbbb})$$

Every word in L is some choice of options of this expression.

If L is a finite language that includes the null word Λ, then the expression that defines L must also employ the symbol Λ.

For example, if

$$L = \{\Lambda \quad a \quad aa \quad bbb\}$$

then the symbolic expression for L must be

$$L = \text{language } (\Lambda + \mathbf{a} + \mathbf{aa} + \mathbf{bbb})$$

The symbol Λ is a very useful addition to our system of language-defining symbolic expressions.

EXAMPLE

Let V be the language of all strings of *a*'s and *b*'s in which the strings are either all *b*'s or else there is an *a* followed by some *b*'s. Let V also contain the word Λ.

$$V = \{\Lambda \ a \ b \ ab \ bb \ abb \ bbb \ abbb \ bbbb \ \ldots \}$$

We can define V by the expression

$$\mathbf{b^* + ab^*}$$

where the word Λ is included in the term $\mathbf{b^*}$. Alternatively, we could define V by the expression:

$$\mathbf{(\Lambda + a)b^*}$$

This would mean that in front of the string of some b's we have the option of either adding an a or nothing. Since we could always write $\mathbf{b^* = \Lambda b^*}$, we have what appears to be some sort of distributive law at work.

$$\mathbf{\Lambda b^* + ab^* = (\Lambda + a)b^*}$$

We have factored out the $\mathbf{b^*}$ just as in algebra. It is because of this analogy to algebra that we have denoted our disjunction by the plus sign instead of the union sign $\cup$ or the symbolic logic sign $\vee$.

∎

We have a hybrid system: the $*$ is somewhat like an exponent and the $+$ is somewhat like addition. But the analogies to algebra should be approached very suspiciously, since addition in algebra never means choice and algebraic multiplication has properties different from concatenation (even though we sometimes conventionally refer to it as product):

$$ab = ba \qquad \text{in algebra}$$
$$ab \neq ba \qquad \text{in formal languages}$$

Let us reconsider the language

$$T = \{a \ c \ ab \ cb \ abb \ cbb \ \ldots \}.$$

T can be defined as above by

$$\mathbf{(a + c)b^*}$$

but it can also be defined by

$$\mathbf{ab^* + cb^*}$$

This is another example of the distributive law.

It is now time for us to provide a rigorous definition for the expressions we have been playing with.

We have all the parts we need in order to define regular expressions recursively. The symbols that appear in regular expressions are: the letters of the alphabet Σ, the symbol for the null string Λ, parentheses, the star operator, and the plus sign.

DEFINITION

The set of regular expressions is defined by the following rules:

Rule 1   Every letter of Σ can be made into a regular expression by writing it in boldface; Λ is a regular expression.

Rule 2   If $\mathbf{r}_1$ and $\mathbf{r}_2$ are regular expressions, then so are

$$(\mathbf{r}_1) \quad \mathbf{r}_1\mathbf{r}_2 \quad \mathbf{r}_1 + \mathbf{r}_2 \quad \mathbf{r}_1{}^*$$

Rule 3   Nothing else is a regular expression.   ■

We could have included the plus sign as a superscript $\mathbf{r}_1{}^+$ as part of the definition, but since we know that $\mathbf{r}_1{}^+ = \mathbf{r}_1\mathbf{r}_1{}^*$, this would add nothing valuable.

This is a language of language definers. It is analogous to a book that lists all the books in print. Every word in this book is a book-definer. The same confusion occurs in everyday speech. The string "French" is both a word (an adjective) and a language-defining name (a noun). However difficult Computer Theory may seem, English is much harder.

Because of Rule 1 we may have trouble in distinguishing when we write an a whether we mean a the letter in Σ, a the word in Σ^*, $\{a\}$ the one word language, or $\mathbf{a}$ the regular expression for that language. Context and typography will guide us.

As with the recursive definition of arithmetic expressions, we have included the use of parentheses as an option, not a requirement. Let us emphasize again the implicit parentheses in $\mathbf{r}_1{}^*$. If $\mathbf{r}_1 = \mathbf{aa} + \mathbf{b}$ then the expression $\mathbf{r}_1{}^*$ technically refers to the expression

$$\mathbf{r}_1{}^* = \mathbf{aa} + \mathbf{b}^*$$

which is the formal concatenation of the symbols for $\mathbf{r}_1$ with the symbol $*$, but what we generally mean when we write $\mathbf{r}_1{}^*$ is actually $(\mathbf{r}_1)^*$

$$(\mathbf{r}_1)^* = (\mathbf{aa} + \mathbf{b})^*$$

which is different. Both are regular expressions and both can be generated from the rules. Care should always be taken to produce the expression we actually want, but this much care is too much to ask of mortals, and when we write r_1^* in the rest of the book we really mean $(r_1)^*$.

Another example of excessive care is the worry about the language that contains no words at all. The set of words in this language is the null set, not the null word. The null word is a word, so the language that contains no words cannot contain it. The language of no words cannot technically be defined by a regular expression since Rule 1 starts by putting something into the language. We finesse this point by saying that the language of no words is defined by the regular expression of no symbols.

To make the identification between the regular expressions and their associated languages more explicit, we need to define the operation of multiplication of sets of words.

DEFINITION

If S and T are sets of strings of letters (whether they are finite or infinite sets), we define the product set of strings of letters to be

$$ST = \{\text{all combinations of a string from } S \text{ concatenated with a string from } T \}$$
∎

EXAMPLE

If

$$S = \{a \quad aa \quad aaa\} \qquad T = \{bb \quad bbb\}$$

then

$$ST = \{abb \quad abbb \quad aabb \quad aabbb \quad aaabb \quad aaabbb\}$$

Note that these words are not in proper order.
∎

EXAMPLE

If

$$S = \{a \quad bb \quad bab\} \qquad T = \{a \quad ab\}$$

then

$$ST = \{aa \quad aab \quad bba \quad bbab \quad baba \quad babab\}$$
∎

EXAMPLE

If

$$P = \{a \quad bb \quad bab\} \qquad Q = \{\Lambda \qquad bbbb\}$$

then

$$PQ = \{a \quad bb \quad bab \quad abbbb \quad bbbbb \quad babbbbb\}$$

∎

EXAMPLE

If

$$M = \{\Lambda \quad x \quad xx\} \qquad N = \{\Lambda \quad y \quad yy \quad yyy \quad yyyy \ldots\}$$

then

$$MN = \quad \{\Lambda \quad y \quad yy \quad yyy \quad yyyy \ldots$$
$$\quad x \quad xy \quad xyy \quad xyyy \quad xyyyy \ldots$$
$$\quad xx \quad xxy \quad xxyy \quad xxyyy \quad xxyyyy \ldots\}$$

∎

Using regular expressions, these four examples can be written as:

$$(a + aa + aaa)(bb + bbb) = abb + abbb + aabb + aabbb + aaabb + aaabbb$$
$$(a + bb + bab)(a + ab) = aa + aab + bba + bbab + baba + babab$$
$$(a + bb + bab)(\Lambda + bbbb) = a + bb + bab + ab^4 + b^6 + bab^5$$
$$(\Lambda + x + xx)(y*) = y* + xy* + xxy*$$

EXAMPLE

If FRENCH and GERMAN are their usual languages, then the product
FRENCHGERMAN is the language of all strings that start with a FRENCH word and
finish with a GERMAN word. Some words in this language are ennuiverboten and
souffléGesundheit.

∎

It might not be clear why we can not just leave the rules for associating
a language with a regular expression on the informal level, with the expression

"make choices for **+** and __*__." The reason is that the informal phrase "make choices" is much harder to explain precisely than the formal mathematical presentation below.

We are now ready to give the rules for associating a language with every regular expression. As we might suspect, the method for doing this is given recursively.

DEFINITION

The following rules define the **language associated** with any regular expression.

Rule 1   The language associated with the regular expression that is just a single letter is that one-letter word alone and the language associated with Λ is just $\{\Lambda\}$, a one-word language.

Rule 2   If r_1 is a regular expression associated with the language L_1 and r_2 is a regular expression associated with the language L_2 then,

(i)   The regular expression (r_1) (r_2) is associated with the language L_1 times L_2.

$$\text{language } (r_1 \ r_2) = L_1 L_2$$

(ii)   The regular expression $r_1 + r_2$ is associated with the language formed by the union of the sets L_1 and L_2.

$$\text{language } (r_1 + r_2) = L_1 + L_2$$

(iii)   The language associated with the regular expression (r_1)* is L_1*, the Kleene closure of the set L_1 as a set of words.

$$\text{language } (r_1\text{*}) = L_1\text{*}$$ ∎

Once again this collection of rules proves recursively that there is some language associated with every regular expression. As we build up a regular expression from the rules, we simultaneously are building up the corresponding language.

The rules seem to show us how we can interpret the regular expression as a language, but they do not really tell us how to *understand* the language. By this we mean that if we apply the rules above to the regular expression

$$(a + b)\text{*}a(a + b)\text{*}b(a + b)\text{*} + bb\text{*}aa\text{*}$$

we can develop a description of some language, but can we understand that this is the language of all strings that have an *a* and a *b* in them? This is a question of meaning.

This correspondence between regular expressions and languages leaves open two other questions. We have already seen examples where completely different regular expressions end up describing the same language. Is there some way of telling when this happens? By "way" we mean, of course, an algorithm. We present an algorithmic procedure in Chapter 12 to determine whether or not two regular expressions define the same language.

Another fundamental question is this: We have seen that every regular expression is associated with some language; is it also true that every language can be described by a regular expression? In our next theorem we show that every finite language can be defined by a regular expression. The situation for languages with infinitely many words is different. We prove in Chapter 11 that there are some languages that cannot be defined by any regular expression.

As to the first and perhaps most important question, the question of understanding regular expressions, we haven't a clue. Before we can construct an algorithm for obtaining understanding we must have some good definition of what it means to understand. We may be centuries away from being able to do that, if it can be done at all.

THEOREM 5

If L is a finite language (a language with only finitely many words), then L can be defined by a regular expression.

PROOF

To make one regular expression that defines the language L, turn all the words in L into boldface type and stick pluses between them. Voilà.

For example, the regular expression that defines the language

$$L = \{baa \quad abbba \quad bababa\}$$

is

baa + abbba + bababa

If

$$L = \{aa \quad ab \quad ba \quad bb\}$$

the algorithm described above gives the regular expression

aa + ab + ba + bb

Another regular expression that defines this language is

$$(a + b)(a + b)$$

so the regular expression need not be unique.

The reason this trick only works for finite languages is that an infinite language would become a regular expression that is infinitely long, which is forbidden. ∎

EXAMPLE

Let

$$L = \{\, \Lambda \quad x \quad xx \quad xxx \quad xxxx \quad xxxxx \,\}$$

The regular expression we get from the theorem is

$$\Lambda + x + xx + xxx + \quad xxxx + xxxxx$$

A more elegant regular expression for this language is

$$(\Lambda + x)^5$$

Of course the 5 is, strictly speaking, not a legal symbol for a regular expression although we all understand it means

$$(\Lambda + x)(\Lambda + x)(\Lambda + x)(\Lambda + x)(\Lambda + x)$$

∎

Let us examine some regular expressions and see if we are lucky enough to understand something about the languages they represent.

EXAMPLE

Consider the expression:

$$(a + b)*(aa + bb)(a + b)*$$

This is the set of strings of a's and b's that at some point contain a double letter. We can think of it as

(arbitrary)(double letter)(arbitrary)

Let us now ask, "What strings do not contain a double letter?" Some ex-

amples are: Λ a b ab ba aba bab $abab$ $baba$ .... The expression **(ab)***
covers all of these except those that begin with b or end in a. Adding these
choices gives us the regular expression

$$(\Lambda + b) \; (ab)^* \; (\Lambda + a)$$

■

EXAMPLE

Consider the regular expression below:

$$E = (a + b)^*a (a + b)^* (a + \Lambda) \qquad (a + b)^*a(a + b)^*$$
$$= (\text{arbitrary}) \; a \; (\text{arbitrary}) \; [a \text{ or nothing}] \; (\text{arbitrary}) \; a \; (\text{arbitrary}).$$

One obvious fact is that all the words in the language of E must have at least
two a's in them. Let us break up the middle plus sign into its two cases:
either the middle factor contributes an a or else it contributes a Λ. Therefore,

$$E = (a+b)^*a(a+b)^*a(a+b)^*a(a+b)^*$$
$$+ (a+b)^*a(a+b)^* \; \Lambda \; (a+b)^*a(a+b)^*$$

This is a more detailed use of the distributive law. The first term above clearly
represents all words that have at least three a's in them. Before we analyze
the second term let us make the observation that

$$(a + b)^* \; \Lambda \; (a + b)^*$$

which occurs in the middle of the second term is only another way of saying
"any string whatsoever" and could be replaced with the more direct expression

$$(a + b)^*$$

This would reduce the second term of the expression to

$$(a + b)^*a(a + b)^*a(a + b)^*$$

which we have already seen is a regular expression representing all words that
have at least two a's in them.

Therefore, the language associated with E is the union of all strings that
have three or more a's with all strings that have two or more a's. But since
all strings with three or more a's are themselves already strings with two or
more a's, this whole language is just the second set alone.

The language associated with E is no different from the language associated with

$$(a + b)*a(a + b)*a(a + b)*$$

which we have examined before with three of its avatars.   ∎

It is possible by repeated application of the rules for forming regular expressions to produce an expression in which the star operator is applied to a subexpression that already has a star in it.
Some examples are:

$$(a + b*)*   (aa + ab*)*   ((a + bbba*) + ba*b)*$$

In the first of these expressions, the internal * adds nothing to the language

$$(a + b*)* = (a + b)*$$

since all possible strings of a's and b's are described by both expressions.
Also, in accordance with Theorem 1,

$$(a*)* = a*$$

However,

$$(aa + ab*)* \neq (aa + ab)*$$

since the language for the expression on the left includes the word *abbabb*, which the language on the right does not. (The language defined by the regular expression on the right cannot contain any word with a double b.)

EXAMPLE

Consider the regular expression:

$$(a*b*)*$$

The language defined by this expression is all strings that can be made up of factors of the form $a*b*$, but since both the single letter a and the single letter b are words of the form $a*b*$, this language contains all strings of a's and b's. It cannot contain more than everything, so

$$(a*b*)* = (a + b)*$$ ∎

EXAMPLE

One very interesting example, which we consider now in great detail and carry with us through the book is

$$E = [\mathbf{aa} + \mathbf{bb} + (\mathbf{ab} + \mathbf{ba})(\mathbf{aa} + \mathbf{bb})^*(\mathbf{ab} + \mathbf{ba})]^*$$

This regular expression represents the collection of all words that are made up of "syllables" of three types:

$$\text{type}_1 = \mathbf{aa}$$
$$\text{type}_2 = \mathbf{bb}$$
$$\text{type}_3 = (\mathbf{ab} + \mathbf{ba})(\mathbf{aa} + \mathbf{bb})^*(\mathbf{ab} + ba)$$
$$E = [\text{type}_1 + \text{type}_2 + \text{type}_3]^*$$

Suppose that we are scanning along a word in the language of E from left to right reading the letters two at a time. First we come to a double a (type$_1$), then to a double b (type$_2$), then to another double a (type$_1$ again). Then perhaps we come upon a pair of letters that are not the same. Say, for instance, that the next two letters are ba. This must begin a substring of type$_3$. It starts with an undoubled pair (either ab or ba), then it has a section of doubled letters (many repetitions of either aa or bb), and then it finally ends with another undoubled pair (either ab or ba again). One property of this section of the word is that it has an even number of a's and an even number of b's. If the section started with a ba, it could end with an ab still giving two a's and two b's on the ends with only doubled letters in between. If it started with a ba and ended with an ab, again, it would give an even number of a's and an even number of b's. After this section of type$_3$ we could proceed with more sections of type$_1$ or type$_2$ until we encountered another undoubled pair, starting another type$_3$ section. We know that another undoubled pair will be coming up to balance off the initial one. The total effect is that every word of the language of E contains an even number of a's and an even number of b's.

If this were all we wanted to conclude, we could have done so more quickly. All words in the language of E are made up of these three types of substrings and, since each of these three has an even number of a's and an even number of b's, the whole word must, too. However, a stronger statement is also true. *All* words with an even number of a's and an even number of b's belong to the language of E. The proof of this parallels our argument above.

Consider a word w with even a's and even b's. If the first two letters are the same, we have a type$_1$ or type$_2$ syllable. Scan over the doubled letter pairs until we come to an unmatched pair such as ab or ba. Continue scanning by skipping over the double a's and double b's that get in the way until we find the *balancing unmatched* pair (ab or ba) to even off the count of a's and b's. If the word ends before we find such a pair, the a's and b's are not even. Once we have found the balancing unmatched pair, we have completed a syllable of type₃. By "balancing" we do not mean it has to be the same unmatched pair: *ab* can be balanced by either *ab* or *ba*. Consider them book-ends or open and close parentheses; whenever we see one we must later find another. Therefore, *E* represents the language of all strings with even *a*'s and even *b*'s.

Let us consider this as a computer algorithm. We are about to feed in a long string of *a*'s and *b*'s, and we want to determine if this string has the property that the number of *a*'s is even and the number of *b*'s is even. One method is to keep two binary flags, the *a*-flag and the *b*-flag. Every time an *a* is read, the *a*-flag is reversed (0 to 1, or 1 to 0); every time a *b* is read, the *b*-flag is reversed. We start both flags at 0 and check to be sure they are both 0 at the end. This method will work.

But there is another method that also works that uses only one flag—the method that corresponds to the discussion above. Let us have only one flag called the type₃-flag. We read the letters in two at a time. If they are the same, then we do not touch the type₃-flag, since we have a factor of type₁ or type₂. If, however, the two letters read do not match, we throw the type₃-flag. If the flag starts at 0, then whenever it is 1 we are in the middle of a type₃-factor; whenever it is 0 we are not. If it is 0 at the end, then the input string contains an even number of *a*'s and an even number of *b*'s.

For example, if the input is

$$(aa)(ab)(bb)(ba)(ab)(bb)(bb)(bb)(ab)(ab)(bb)(ba)(aa)$$

the flag is reversed six times and ends at 0.

We will refer to this language again later, so we give it the name EVEN-EVEN.

$$\text{EVEN-EVEN} = \{\Lambda \quad aa \quad bb \quad aabb \quad abab \quad abba$$
$$baab \quad baba \quad bbaa \quad aaaabb \quad aaabab \quad \ldots\}$$

Notice that there do not have to be the same number of *a*'s and *b*'s, just an even quantity of each. ∎

EXAMPLE

Consider the language defined by the regular expression:

$$\mathbf{b^*(abb^*)^*(\Lambda + a)}$$

This is the language of all words without a double *a*. The typical word here starts with some *b*'s. Then come repeated factors of the form **abb*** (an *a* followed by at least one *b*). Then we finish up with a final *a* or we leave the last *b*'s as they are. This is another starred expression with a star inside. ∎

PROBLEMS

1. Let r_1, r_2, and r_3 be three regular expressions. Show that the language associated with $(r_1 + r_2)r_3$ is the same as the language associated with $r_1r_3 + r_2r_3$. Show that $r_1(r_2 + r_3)$ is equivalent to $r_1r_2 + r_1r_3$. This will be the same as "proving a distributive law" for regular expressions.

    Construct a regular expression defining each of the following languages over the alphabet $\Sigma = \{a, b\}$.

2. All words in which a appears tripled, if at all. This means that every clump of a's contains 3 or 6 or 9 or 12 . . . a's.

3. All words that contain at least one of the strings s_1 s_2 s_3 or s_4.

4. All words that contain exactly three b's in total.

5. All words that contain exactly two b's or exactly three b's, not more.

6. (i)   All strings that end in a double letter.

    (ii) All strings that have exactly one double letter in them.

7. All strings in which the letter b is *never* tripled. This means that no word contains the substring bbb.

8. All words in which a is tripled or b is tripled, but not both. This means each word contains the substring aaa or the substring bbb but not both.

9. (i)   All strings that do not have the substring ab.

    (ii) All strings that do not have both the substrings bba and abb.

10. All strings in which the *total* number of a's is divisible by three, such as $aabaabbaba$.

11. (i)   All strings in which any b's that occur are found in clumps of an odd number at a time, such as $abaabbbbab$.

    (ii) All strings that have an even number of a's and an odd number of b's.

    (iii) All strings that have an odd number of a's and an odd number of b's.

12. Let us reconsider the regular expression

$$(a + b)*a(a + b)*b(a + b)*$$

(i) Show that this is equivalent to

$$(a + b)*ab(a + b)*$$

in the sense that they define the same language.

(ii) Show that

$$(a + b)*ab(a + b)* + b*a* = (a + b)*$$

(iii) Show that

$$(a + b)* ab[(a + b)*ab(a + b)* + b*a*] + b*a* = (a + b)*$$

(iv) Is (iii) the last variation of this theme or are there more beasts left in this cave?

13. We have defined the product of two sets of strings in general. If we apply this to the case where both factors are the same set, $S = T$, we obtain squares, S^2. Similarly we can define S^3, S^4, ... Show that

(i) $S* = \Lambda + S + S^1 + S^2 + S^3 + S^4 + \ldots$
(ii) $S^+ = S + S^1 + S^2 + S^3 + S^4 + \ldots$

Show that the following pairs of regular expressions define the same language over the alphabet $\Sigma = \{a, b\}$.

14. (i) **(ab)*a**   and   **a(ba)***
     (ii) **(a* + b)***   and   **(a + b)***
     (iii) **(a* + b*)***   and   **(a + b)***

15. (i) **Λ***   and   **Λ**
     (ii) **(a*b)*a***   and   **a*(ba*)***
     (iii) **(a*bbb)*a***   and   **a*(bbba*)***

16. (i) **((a + bb)*aa)***   and   **Λ + (a + bb)*aa**
     (ii) **(aa)*(Λ + a)**   and   **a***
     (iii) **a(aa)*(Λ + a)b + b**   and   **a*b**

17.   (i) **a(ba + a)*b**   and   **aa*b(aa*b)***
    (ii) **Λ + a(a + b)* + (a + b)* aa(a + b)***   and   **((b*a)*ab*)***

Describe (in English phrases) the languages associated with the following regular expressions.

18.   (i)   **(a + b)* a(Λ + bbbb)**
    (ii) **(a(a + bb)*)***
    (iii) **(a(aa)*b(bb)*)***
    (iv) **(b(bb)*)*(a(aa)*b(bb)*)***
    (v) **(b(bb)*)*(a(aa)*b(bb)*)*(a(aa)*)***
    (vi) **((a + b)a)***

19.   (D.N. Arden) Let R, S, and T be three languages and assume that Λ is not in S. Prove the following statements.
    (i) From the premise that $R = SR + T$, we can conclude that $R = S*T$.
    (ii) From the premise that $R = S*T$, we can conclude that $R = SR + T$.

20.   Explain why we can take any pair of equivalent regular expressions and replace the letter a in both with any regular expression **R** and the letter b with any regular expression **S** and the resulting regular expressions will have the same language. For example, 15.(ii)

$$(a*b)*a* = a*(ba*)*$$

becomes the identity

$$(R*S)*R* = R*(SR*)*$$

which is true for all regular expressions **R** and **S**. In particular **R = a + bb**, **S = ba*** results in the complicated identity

$$((a + bb)*(ba*))*(a + bb)* = (a + bb)* ((ba*)(a + bb)*)*$$

What is the deeper meaning of this transformation?
What identity would result from using

$$R = (ba*)* \qquad S = (\Lambda + b)$$

CHAPTER 5

FINITE AUTOMATA

Several games that children play fit the following description. Pieces are set up on a playing board. Dice are thrown (or a wheel is spun), and a number is generated at random. Depending on the number, the pieces on the board must be rearranged in a fashion completely specified by the rules. The child has no options about changing the board. Everything is determined by the dice. Usually it is then some other child's turn to throw the dice and make his or her move, but this hardly matters, since no skill or choice is involved. We could eliminate the opponent and have the one child move first the white pieces and then the black. Whether or not the white pieces win the game is dependent entirely on what sequence of numbers is generated by the dice, not on who moves them.

Let us look at all possible positions of the pieces on the board and call them **states.** The game changes from one state to another in a fashion determined by the input of a certain number. For each possible number there is one and only one resulting state. We should allow for the possibility that after a number is entered the game is still in the same state as it was before. (For example, if a player who is in "jail" needs to roll doubles in order to get out, any other roll leaves the board in the same state.) After a certain number of rolls, the board arrives at a state that means a victory for one of the players and the game is over. We call this a **final state.** There might be many possible final states. In Computer Theory these are also called **halting states** or **terminal states** or **accepting states.**

Beginning with the initial state (which we presume to be unique) some input sequences of numbers lead to victory for the first child and some do not.

Let us put this game back on the shelf and take another example. A child has a simple computer (input device, processing unit, memory, output device) and wishes to calculate the sum of 3 plus 4. The child writes a program, which is a sequence of instructions that are fed into the machine one at a time. Each instruction is executed as soon as it is read, and then the next instruction is read. If all goes well, the machine outputs the number 7 and terminates execution. We can consider this process to be similar to the board-game. Here the board is the computer and the different arrangements of pieces on the board correspond to the different arrangements of 0's and 1's in the cells of memory. Two machines are in the same state if their output pages look the same and their memories look the same cell by cell.

The computer is also **deterministic,** by which we mean that, on reading one particular input instruction, the machine converts itself from one given state to some particular other state (or remains in the same state if given a NO-OP) where the resultant state is completely determined by the prior state and the input instruction. Nothing else. No choice is involved. No knowledge is required of the state the machine was in six instructions ago. Some sequences of input instructions may lead to success (printing the 7) and some may not. Success is entirely determined by the sequence of inputs. Either the program will work or it won't.

As in the case of the board-game, in this model we have one initial state and the possibility of several successful final states. Printing the 7 is what is important; what is left in memory does not matter.

One small difference between these two situations is that in the child's game the number of pieces of input is determined by whether either player has yet reached a final state whereas with the computer the number of pieces of input is a matter of choice made before run time. Still, the input string is the sole determinant as to whether the game child or the computer child wins his or her victory.

In the first example, we can consider the set of all dice rolls to be the letters of an alphabet. We can then define a certain language as the set of strings of those letters that lead to success; that is, lead to a final state. Similarly, in the second example we can consider the set of all computer instructions as the letters of an alphabet. We can then define a language to be the set of all words over this alphabet that lead to success. This is the language with *words* that are all *programs* that print a 7.

The most general model, of which both of these examples are instances, is called a **finite automaton**—"finite" because the number of possible states and number of letters in the alphabet are both finite, and "automaton" because the change of states is totally governed by the input. It is automatic (involuntary and mechanical) not willful, just as the motion of the hands of a clock is automatic while the motion of the hands of a human is presumably the result of desire and thought. We present the precise definition below. "Automaton" comes to us from the Greek, so its correct plural is "automata."

DEFINITION

A **finite automaton** is a collection of three things:

1. A finite set of states, one of which is designated as the initial state, called the **start state,** and some (maybe none) of which are designated as **final states.**
2. An alphabet Σ of possible input letters, from which are formed strings, that are to be read one letter at a time.
3. A finite set of **transitions** that tell for each state and for each letter of the input alphabet which state to go to next.   ∎

The definition above is incomplete in the sense that it describes what a finite automation is but not how it works. It works by being presented with an input string of letters that it reads letter by letter starting at the leftmost letter. Beginning at the start state the letters determine a sequence of states. The sequence ends when the last input letter has been read.

Instead of writing out the whole phrase "finite automaton" it is customary to refer to one by its initials, FA. Computer theory is rife with acronyms, so we have many in this book. The term FA is read by naming its letters, so we say "an FA" even though it stands for "a finite automaton" and we say "two FA's" even though it stands for "two finite automata".

Some people prefer to call the object we have just defined a **finite acceptor** because its sole job is to **accept** certain input strings and run on them. It does not do anything like print output or play music. Even so, we shall stick to the terminology "finite automaton." When we build some in Chapter 9 that do do something, we give them special names, such as "finite automaton with output."

Let us begin by considering in detail one particular example.

Suppose that the input alphabet has only the two letters a and b. Throughout this chapter we use only this alphabet (except for a couple of problems at the end). Let us also assume that there are only three states, x, y, and z. Let the following be the rules of transition:

1. From state x and input a go to state y.
2. From state x and input b go to state z.
3. From state y and input a go to state x.

4. From state y and input b go to state z.

5. From state z and any input stay at state z.

Let us also designate state x as the starting state and state z as the only final state.

We now have a perfectly defined finite automaton, since it fulfills all three requirements demanded above: states, alphabet, transitions.

Let us examine what happens to various input strings when presented to this FA. Let us start with the string aaa. We begin, as always, in state x. The first letter of the string is an a, and it tells us to go to state y (by Rule 1). The next input (instruction) is also an a, and this tells us by Rule 3 to go back to state x. The third input is another a, and by Rule 1 again we go to state y. There are no more input letters in the input string, so our trip has ended. We did not finish up in the final state (state z), so we have an unsuccessful termination of our run.

The string aaa is not in the language of all strings that leave this FA in state z. The set of all strings that do leave us in a final state is called **the language defined by the finite automaton.** The input string aaa is not in the language defined by this FA. Using other terminology, we may say that the string aaa is **not accepted** by this finite automaton because it does not lead to a final state. We use this expression often. We may also say "aaa is **rejected** by this FA." The set of all strings accepted is the **language associated** with the FA. We say, this FA **accepts** the language L, or L is the **language accepted** by this FA. When we wish to be anthropomorphic, we say that L is the **language of** the FA. If language L_1 is contained in language L_2 and a certain FA accepts L_2 (all the words in L_2 are accepted and all the inputs accepted are words in L_2), then this FA also must accept all the words in language L_1 (since they are also words in L_2). However, we do not say "L_1 is accepted by this FA" since that would mean that all the words the FA accepts are in L_1. This is solely a matter of standard usage.

At the moment, the only job an FA does is define the language it accepts which is a fine reason for calling it an acceptor, or better still a **language recognizer.** This last term is good because the FA merely recognizes whether the input string is in its language much the same way we might recognize when we hear someone speak Russian without necessarily understanding what it means.

Let us examine a different input string for this same FA. Let the input be $abba$. As always, we start in state x. Rule 1 tells us that the first input letter, a, takes us to state y. Once we are in state y we read the second input letter, which is a b. Rule 4 now tells us to move to state z. The third input letter is a b, and since we are in state z, Rule 5 tells us to stay there. The fourth input letter is an a, and again Rule 5 says stay put. Therefore, after we have followed the instruction of each input letter we end up in state z. State z is designated a final state, so we have won this game. The input string $abba$

has taken us successfully to the final state. The string *abba* is therefore a word in the language associated with this FA. The word *abba* is accepted by this FA.

It is not hard for us to predict which strings will be accepted by this FA. If an input string is made up of only the letter *a* repeated some number of times, then the action of the FA will be to jump back and forth between state *x* and state *y*. No such word can ever be accepted. To get into state *z*, it is necessary for the string to have the letter *b* in it. As soon as a *b* is encountered in the input string, the FA jumps immediately to state *z* no matter what state it was in before. Once in state *z*, it is impossible to leave. When the input string runs out, the FA will still be in state *z*, leading to acceptance of the string.

The FA above will accept all strings that have the letter *b* in them and no other strings. Therefore, the language associated with (or accepted by) this FA is the one defined by the regular expression

$$(a + b)*b(a + b)*$$

The list of transition rules can grow very long. It is much simpler to summarize them in a table format. Each row of the table is the name of one of the states in the FA, and each column of the table is a letter of the input alphabet. The entries inside the table are the new states that the FA moves into—the transition states. The **transition table** for the FA we have described is:

		a	b
start	x	y	z
	y	x	z
final	z	z	z

We have also indicated along the left side which states are start and final states. This table has all the information necessary to define an FA.

Even though it is no more than a table of symbols, we consider an FA to be a **machine,** that is, we understand that this FA has dynamic capabilities. It moves. It processes input. Something *goes* from state to state as the input is read in and executed. We may imagine that the state we are in at any given time is lit up and the others are dark. An FA running on an input string then looks like a pinball machine.

From the table format it is hard to see the moving parts. There is a pictorial representation of an FA that gives us more of a feel for the motion. We begin by representing each state by a small circle drawn on a sheet of paper. From each state we draw arrows showing to which other states the different letters of the input alphabet will lead us. We **label** these arrows with the corresponding alphabet letters.

If a certain letter makes a state go back to itself, we indicate this by an arrow that returns to the same circle—this arrow is called a **loop.** We can indicate the start state by labeling it with the word "start" or by a minus sign, and the final states by labeling them with the word "final" or plus signs. The machine we have already defined by the transition list and the transition table can be depicted by the **transition diagram:**

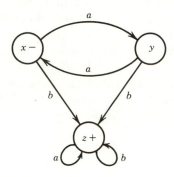

Sometimes a start state is indicated by an arrow and a final state by drawing a box or another circle around its circle. The minus and plus signs, when employed, are drawn inside or outside the state circles. This machine can also be depicted as:

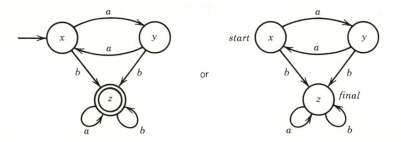

Every input string can be interpreted as traversing a path beginning at the start state and moving among the states (perhaps visiting the same state many times) and finally settling in some particular rest state. If it is a final state, then the path has ended in success. The letters of the input string dictate the directions of travel. They are the map and the fuel needed for motion. When we are out of letters we must stop.

Let us look at this machine again and at the paths generated by the input strings *aaaabba* and *bbaabbbb*.

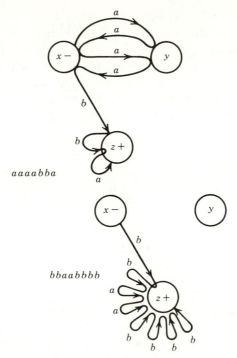

When we depict an FA as circles and arrows, we say that we have drawn a **directed graph.** Graph Theory is an exciting subject in its own right, but for our purposes there is no real need to understand directed graphs in any deeper sense than as a collection of circles and arrows. We borrow from Graph Theory the name **directed edge** or simply **edge** for the arrow between states. An edge comes from one state and leads to another (or the same, if it is a loop). Every state has as many **outgoing edges** as there are letters in the alphabet. It is possible for a state to have no **incoming edges.**

There are machines for which it is not necessary to give the states specific names. For example, the FA we have been dealing with so far can be represented simply as:

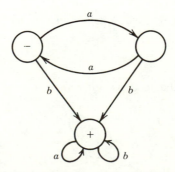

Notice that some states are neither − nor +.

Even though we do not have names for the states, we can still determine whether a particular input string is accepted by this *mach*ine. We start at the minus sign and proceed along the indicated edges until we are out of input letters. If we are then at a plus sign, we accept the word; if not, we reject it as not being part of the language of the machine.

Let us consider some more simple examples of FA's.

EXAMPLE

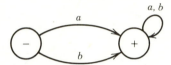

In the picture above we have drawn one edge from the state on the right back into itself and given this loop the two labels *a* and *b*, separated by a comma meaning that this is the path traveled if either letter is read. (We save ourselves from drawing a second loop edge.) At first glance it looks as if this machine accepts everything. The first letter of the input takes us to the right-hand state and, once there, we are trapped forever. When the input string runs out, there we are in the correct final state. This description, however, omits the possibility that the input is the null string Λ. If the input string is the null string, we are left back at the left-hand state, and we never get to the final state. There is a small problem about understanding how it is possible for Λ ever to be an input string to an FA, since a string, by definition, is executed (run) by reading its letters one at a time. By convention we shall say that Λ starts in the start state and then ends right there on all FA's.

The language accepted by this machine is the set of all strings except Λ. This has the regular expression definitions

$$(\mathbf{a} + \mathbf{b})(\mathbf{a} + \mathbf{b})^* = (\mathbf{a} + \mathbf{b})^+ \qquad\qquad \blacksquare$$

EXAMPLE

One of the many FA's that accepts all words is:

Here the sign ± means that the same state is both a start and a final state.

Since there is only one state and no matter what happens we must stay there, the language for this machine is:

$$(\mathbf{a} + \mathbf{b})^*$$ ■

Similarly, there are FA's that accept no language. These are of two types: FA's that have no final states, such as

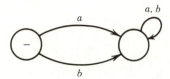

and FA's in which the circles that represent the final states cannot be reached from the start state. This may be either because the picture is in two separate components as with

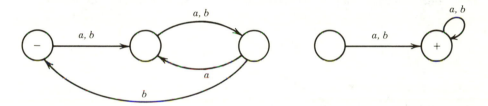

(in this case we say that the graph is **disconnected**) or for a reason such as that shown below.

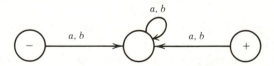

We consider these examples again in Chapter 12.

EXAMPLE

Suppose we want to build a finite automaton that accepts all the words in the language

$$\mathbf{a}(\mathbf{a} + \mathbf{b})^*$$

that is, all the strings that begin with the letter a. We start at state x and, if the first letter read is a b, we go to a dead-end state y. (A "dead-end state" is an informal way of describing a state that no string can leave once it has entered.) If the first letter is an a we go to the dead-end state z, where z is a final state. The machine looks like this:

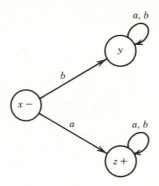

The same language may be accepted by a four-state machine, as below:

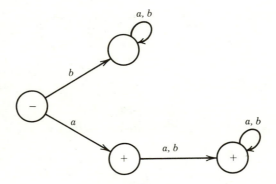

Only the word a ends in the first $+$ state. All other words starting with an a reach and finish in the second $+$ state where they are accepted.

This idea can be carried further to a five-state FA as below:

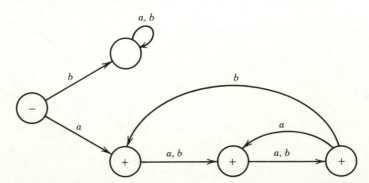

The examples above are FA's that have more than one final state. From them we can see that there is not a unique machine for a given language. We may then ask the question, "Is there always at least one FA that accepts each possible language? More precisely, if L is some language, is there necessarily a machine of this type that accepts exactly the inputs in L, while rejecting all others?" We shall see shortly that this question is related to the question, "Can all languages be represented by regular expressions?" We prove, in Chapter 7, that every language that can be accepted by an FA can be defined by a regular expression and, conversely, every language that can be defined by a regular expression can be accepted by some FA. However, we shall see that there are languages that are neither definable by a regular expression nor accepted by an FA. Remember, for a language to be *the* language accepted by an FA means not only that all the words in the language run to final states but also that *no strings not in the language do*.

Let us consider some more examples of FA's.

EXAMPLE

Consider the FA pictured below:

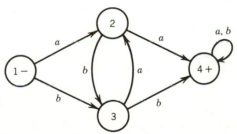

Before we begin to examine what language this machine accepts, let us trace the paths associated with some specific input strings. Let us input the string *ababa*. We begin at the start state 1. The first letter is an *a*, so it takes us to state 2. From there the next letter, *b*, takes us to state 3. The next letter, *a*, then takes us back to state 2. The fourth letter is a *b* and that takes us to state 3 again. The last letter is an *a* that returns us to state 2 where we end. State 2 is not a final state (no +), so this word is not accepted.

Let us trace the word *babbb*. As always, we start in state 1. The first letter *b* takes us to state 3. An *a* then takes us to state 2. The third letter *b* takes us back to state 3. Now another *b* takes us to state 4. Once in state 4, we cannot get out no matter what the rest of the string is. Once in state 4 we must stay in state 4, and since that is the final state the string is accepted.

There are two ways to get to state 4 in this FA. One is from state 2, and the other is from state 3. The only way to get to state 2 is by reading the input letter *a* (either while in state 1 or in state 3). So when we are in state 2 we know we have just read an *a*. If we read another *a* immediately, we go straight to state 4. Similarly with state 3. To get to state 3 we need to read a *b*. Once in state 3, if we read another *b* immediately, we go to state 4; otherwise, we go to state 2.

Whenever we encounter the substring *aa* in an input string the first *a* must take us to state 4 or state 2. Either way, the next *a* takes us to state 4. The situation with *bb* is analogous.

In summary, the words accepted by this machine are exactly those strings that have a double letter in them. This language, as we have seen, can also be defined by the regular expression

$$(\mathbf{a} + \mathbf{b})^*(\mathbf{aa} + \mathbf{bb})(\mathbf{a} + \mathbf{b})^* \qquad\qquad \blacksquare$$

EXAMPLE

Let us consider the FA pictured below:

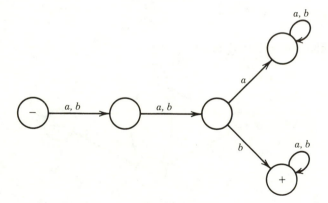

This machine will accept all words with *b* as the third letter and reject all other words. The first couple of states are only waiting states eating up the first two letters of input. Then comes the decision state. A word that has fewer than three letters cannot qualify, and its path ends in one of the three left-hand states, none of which is designated +.

Some regular expressions that define this set are

$$(\mathbf{aab} + \mathbf{abb} + \mathbf{bab} + \mathbf{bbb})(\mathbf{a} + \mathbf{b})^*$$

and

$$(\mathbf{a} + \mathbf{b})(\mathbf{a} + \mathbf{b})(\mathbf{b})(\mathbf{a} + \mathbf{b})^*$$

$$= (\mathbf{a} + \mathbf{b})^2\mathbf{b} \ (\mathbf{a} + \mathbf{b})^*$$

Notice that this last formula is not strictly speaking a regular expression, since it uses the symbol "2," which is not included in the kit.   ■

EXAMPLE

Let us consider a very specialized FA, one that accepts only the word *baa*.

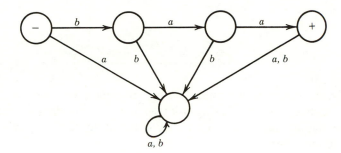

Starting at the start state, anything but the sequence *baa* will drop down into the collecting bucket at the bottom, never to be seen again. Even the word *baabb* will fail. It will reach the final state marked with a + but then the next letter will suicide over the edge.

The language accepted by this FA is

$$L = \{baa\}$$ ■

EXAMPLE

The FA below accepts exactly the two strings *baa* and *ab*.   ■

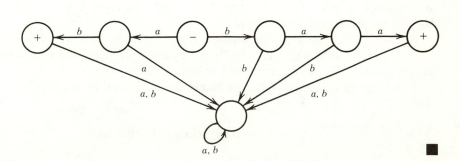

■

EXAMPLE

Let us take a trickier example. Consider the FA shown below:

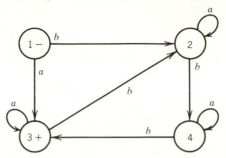

What is the language accepted by this machine? We start at state 1, and if we are reading a word starting with an *a* we go straight to the final state 3. We can stay at state 3 as long as we continue to read only *a*'s. Therefore, all words of the form

aa*

are accepted by this machine. What if we began with some *a*'s that take us to state 3 but then we read a *b*? This then transports us to state 2. To get back to the final state, we must proceed to state 4 and then to state 3. These trips require two more *b*'s to be read as input. Notice that in states 2, 3, and 4 all *a*'s that are read are ignored. Only *b*'s cause a change of state.

Recapitulating what we know: If an input string begins with an *a* and then has some *b*'s, it must have three *b*'s to return us to state 3, or six *b*'s to make the trip (state 2, state 4, state 3) twice, or 9 *b*'s or 12 *b*'s . . . . In other words, an input string starting with an *a* and having a total number of *b*'s divisible by 3 will be accepted. If it starts with an *a* and has a total number of *b*'s not divisible by 3, then the input is rejected because its path through the machine ends at state 2 or state 4.

What happens to an input string that begins with a *b*? It finds itself in state 2 and needs two more *b*'s to get to state 3 (these *b*'s can be separated by any number of *a*'s). Once in state 3, it needs no more *b*'s, or three more *b*'s, or six more *b*'s, and so on.

All and all, an input string, whether beginning with an *a* or a *b* must have a total number of *b*'s divisible by 3 to be accepted. It is also clear that any string meeting this requirement will reach the final state.

The language accepted by this machine can be defined by the regular expression

a*(a*ba*ba*ba*)*(a + a*ba*ba*ba*)

The only purpose for the last factor is to guarantee that Λ is not a possibility since it is not accepted by the machine. If we did not mind Λ being included in the language, we could have used this simpler FA.

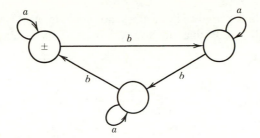

The regular expression

$$(a + ba*ba*b)^+$$

also defines the original (non-Λ) language. ■

EXAMPLE

The following FA accepts only the word Λ

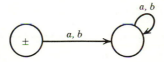

   Notice that the left state is both a start and a final state. All words other than Λ go to the right state and stay there. ■

EXAMPLE

Consider the following FA:

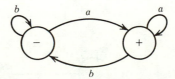

   No matter which state we are in, when we read an *a* we go to the right-hand state and when are read a *b* we go to the left-hand state. Any input string that ends in the + state must end in the letter *a*, and any string ending in *a* must end in +. Therefore, the language accepted by this machine is

$$(a + b)*a$$ ■

EXAMPLE

The language in the example above does not include Λ. If we add Λ we get
the language of all words that do not end in *b*. This is accepted by the FA
below.

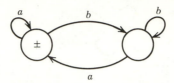

■

EXAMPLE

Consider the following FA:

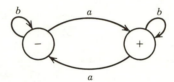

The only letter that causes motion between the states is *a*, *b*'s leave the
machine in the same state. We start at −. If we read a first *a*, we go to
+. A second *a* takes us back. A third *a* takes us to + again. We end at
+ after the first, third, fifth, seventh, . . . *a*. The language accepted by this
machine is all words with an odd number of *a*'s.

$$\mathbf{b*a(b*ab*ab*)*}$$

■

EXAMPLE

Consider the following FA:

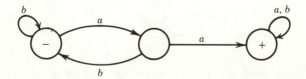

This machine will accept the language of all words with a double *a* in
them somewhere. We stay in the start state until we read our first *a*. This
moves us to the middle state. If the very next letter is another *a*, we move

to the + state where we must stay and be accepted. If the next letter is a
b, however, we go back to − to wait for the next *a*. An *a* followed by a
b will take us from − to middle to −, while an *a* followed by an *a* will
take us from − to middle to +.

The language accepted by this machine can also be defined by the regular
expression

$$\textbf{(a + b)*aa(a + b)*}$$

EXAMPLE

The following FA accepts all words that have different first and last letters.
If the word begins with an *a*, to be accepted it must end with a *b* and vice
versa.

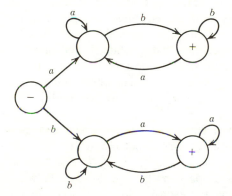

If we start with an *a*, we take the high road and jump back and forth
between the two top states ending on the right (at +) only if the last letter
read is a *b*. If the first letter read is a *b*, we get to the + on the bottom
only when we read *a* as the last letter.

This can be better understood by examining the path through the FA of
the input string *aabbaabb*, as shown below:

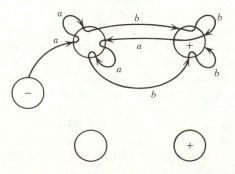

EXAMPLE

As the last example of an FA in this chapter, let us consider the picture below:

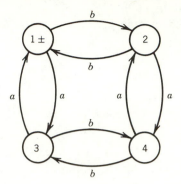

To process a string of letters, we start at state 1, which is in the upper left of the picture. Every time we encounter a letter *a* in the input string we take an *a* train. There are four edges labeled *a*. All the edges marked *a* go either from one of the upper two states (state 1 and state 2) to one of the lower two states (state 3 and state 4) or else from one of the lower two states to one of the upper two states. If we are north and we read an *a*, we go south. If we are south and we read an *a*, we go north. The letter *a* reverses our up/down status.

What happens to a word that gets accepted and ends up back in state 1? Without knowing anything else about the string, we can say that it must have had an even number of *a*'s in it. Every *a* that took us south was balanced by some *a* that took us back north. We crossed the Mason-Dixon line an even number of times, one for each *a*. So every word in the language of this FA has an even number of *a*'s in it. Also, we can say that every input string with an even number of *a*'s will finish its path in the north (state 1 or state 2).

There is more that we can say about the words that are accepted by this machine. There are four edges labeled *b*. Every edge labeled *b* either takes us from one of the two states on the left of the picture (state 1 and state 3) to one of the two states on the right (state 2 and state 4) or else it takes us from one of the two states on the right to one of the two states on the left. Every *b* we encounter in the input is an east/west reverser. If the word starts out in state 1, which is on the left, and ends up back in state 1 (on the left), it must have crossed the Mississippi an even number of times. Therefore, all the words in the language accepted by this FA have an even number of *b*'s as well as an even number of *a*'s. We can also say that every input string with an even number of *b*'s will leave us in the west (state 1 or state 3).

These are the only two conditions on the language. All words with an even number of *a*'s and an even number of *b*'s must return to state 1. All words that return to state 1 are in EVEN-EVEN. All words that end in state 2 have crossed the Mason-Dixon line an even number of times but have crossed the Mississippi an odd number of times; therefore they have an even number of a's and an odd number of b's. All the words that end in state 3 have an even number of b's but an odd number of a's. All words that end in state 4 have an odd number of a's and an odd number of b's. So again we see that all the EVEN-EVEN words must end in state 1 and be accepted.

One regular expression for the language EVEN-EVEN was discussed in detail in the previous chapter.

Notice how much easier it is to understand the FA than the regular expression. Both methods of defining languages have advantages, depending on the desired application. But we are still a little way from considering applications. ■

PROBLEMS

1. Write out the transition table for the FA's on pages 68, 70 (both), 73, 74 and 80 that were defined by pictures. If the states in the pictures were not labeled, assign them names so that we can build the table.

2. Build an FA that accepts only the language of all words with b as the second letter. Show both the picture and the transition table for this machine and find a regular expression for the language.

3. Build an FA that accepts only the words *baa, ab,* and *abb* and no other strings longer or shorter.

4. (i) Build a new FA that accepts only the word Λ.
   (ii) Build an FA with three states that accept all words.

5. Build an FA that accepts only those words that have an even number of letters total.

6. Build an FA that accepts only those words that do not end with *ba*.

7. Build an FA that accepts only those words that begin or end with a double letter.

8. (i) Build an FA that accepts only those words that have more than four letters.
   (ii) Build an FA that accepts only those words that have fewer than four letters.

9. Problems 2 through 12 of Chapter 4 include 14 languages that could be represented by regular expressions. For each of these find an FA that accepts exactly it.

10. So far we have been dealing with Fa's over the alphabet. {a, b}.
    Let us consider for the moment the alphabet $\Sigma = \{a, b, c\}$.

    (i)   If we had an FA over this alphabet with five states, how many entries would there be in the transition table?

    (ii) In the picture of this five-state machine, how many edges would need to be drawn in total (counting an edge with two labels double and an edge with three labels triple)?

    (iii) Build an FA that accepts all the words in this alphabet that have an a in them somewhere that is followed later in the word by some b that is followed later in the word by some c (the three being not necessarily in a row but in that order, as in abaac).

    (iv) Write a regular expression for the language accepted by this machine.

11. Recall from Chapter 4 the language of all words over the alphabet {a, b} that have both the letter a and the letter b in them, but not necessarily in that order. Build an FA that accepts this language.

12. Build an FA that accepts the language of all words with only a's or only b's in them. Give a regular expression for this language.

13. Draw pictures for all the FA's over the alphabet {a, b} that have exactly two states. Be careful to put the +'s in in all possible ways. (*Hint:* There are 48 different machines.)

14. (i)   Write out the transition tables for all the FA's in Problem 13.

    (ii) Write out regular expressions to represent all the languages defined by the machines in Problem 13.

15. Let us call two FA's *different* if their pictures are not the same but *equivalent* if they accept the language. How many different languages are represented by the 48 machines of Problem 13.

16. Show that there are exactly

$$3^6(8) = 5832$$

different finite automata with three states x, y, z over the alphabet $\{a,b\}$ where x is always the start state.

17. Find two FA's that satisfy these conditions: Between them they accept all words in (**a** + **b**)*, but there is no word accepted by both machines.

18. Describe the languages accepted by the following FA's.

(i)

(ii)

(iii)

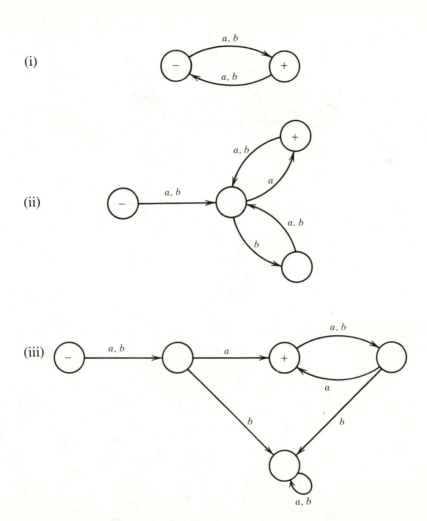

(iv) Write regular expressions for the languages accepted by these three machines.

19.   The following is an FA over the alphabet $\Sigma = \{a, b, c\}$. Prove that it accepts all strings that have an odd number of occurrences of the substring abc.

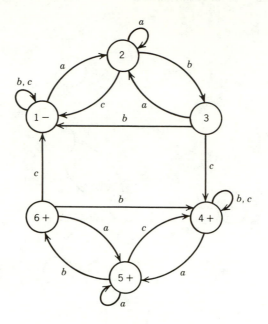

20.   Consider the following FA:

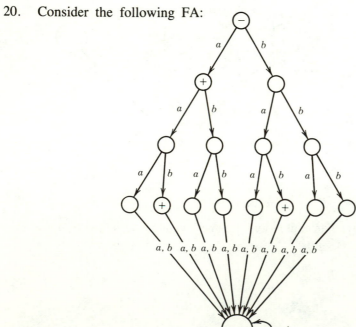

(i)   Show that any input string with more than three letters is not accepted by this FA.

(ii)   Show that the only words accepted are *a*, *aab*, and *bab*.

(iii)   Show that by changing the + signs alone we can make this FA accept the language {*bb, aba, bba*}

(iv)   Show that any language in which the words have fewer than four letters can be accepted by a machine that looks like this one with the + signs in different places.

(v)   Prove that if *L* is a finite language, then there is some FA that accepts *L*.

CHAPTER 6

TRANSITION GRAPHS

We saw in the last chapter that we could build an FA that accepts only the word *baa*. The example we gave required five states primarily because an FA can read only one letter from the input string at a time. Suppose we designed a more powerful machine that could read either one or two letters of the input string at a time and could change its state based on this information. We might design a machine like the one below:

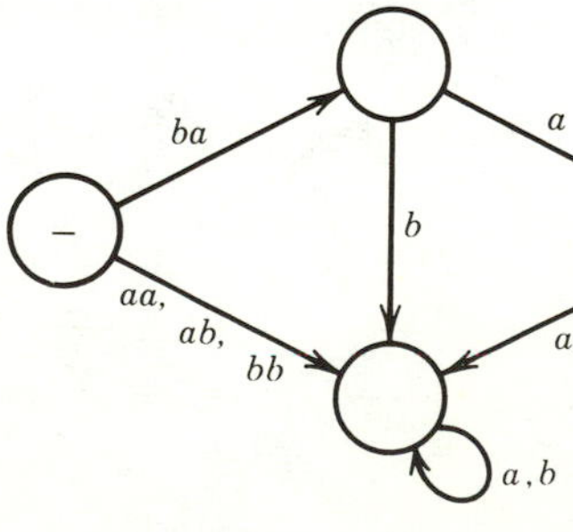

Since when we say "build a machine" all we have to do is scribble on paper—we do not have to solder, weld and screw—we could easily change the rules of what constitutes a machine and allow such pictures as the one above. The objects we deal with in this book are **mathematical models,** which we shall discover are abstractions and simplifications of how certain actual machines do work. This new rule for making models will also turn out to be practical. It will make it easier for us to design machines that accept certain different languages. The machine above can read from the input string either one letter or two letters at a time, depending on which state it is in. Notice that in this machine an edge may have several labels separated by commas just as in FA's, indicating that the edge can be traveled on if the input letters are any of the indicated combinations.

If we are interested in a machine that accepts only the word *baa,* why stop at assuming that the machine can read just two letters at a time? A machine that accepts this word and that can read up to three letters at a time from the input string could be built with even fewer states.

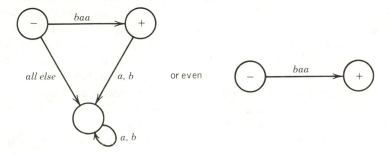

If we hypothesize that a machine can read one or two letters at a time, then one can be built using only two states that can recognize all words that contain a doubled letter.

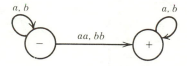

If we are going to bend the rules to allow for a machine like the last one, we must realize that we have changed something more fundamental than just the way the edges are labeled or the number of letters read at a time. This last machine makes us exercise some choice in its running. We must decide how many letters to read from the input string each time we go back for more. This decision is quite important.

Let us say, for example, that the input string is *baa.* It is easy to see how this string can be accepted by this machine. We first read in the letter *b,* which leaves us back at the start state by taking the loop on the left. Then we decide to read in both letters *aa* at once, which allows us to take the highway to the final state where we end. However, if after reading in the single character *b* we then decided to read in the single character *a,* we would loop back and be stuck at the start state again. When the third letter is read in, we would still be at the starting post. We could not then accept this string. There are two different paths that the input *baa* can take through the machine. This is totally different from the situation we had before, especially since one path leads to acceptance and one to rejection.

Another bad thing that might have happened is that we could have started processing the string *baa* by reading the first two letters at once. Since *ba* is not a double, we could not move to the final state. In fact, when we read in *ba,* no edge tells us where to go, since *ba* is not the label of any edge leaving the start state. The processing of this string breaks down at this point.

When there is no edge leaving a state corresponding to the group of input letters that have been read while in that state, we say that the input **crashes.** It also means that the input string is not accepted, but for a different reason than simply ending its path peacefully in a state that is not a final state.

The result of these considerations is that if we are going to change the definition of our abstract machine to allow for more than one letter to be read in at a time, we must also change the definition of acceptance. We have to say that a string is accepted by a machine if there is *some* way it could be processed so as to arrive at a final state. There may also be ways in which this string does not get to a final state, but we ignore all failures.

We are about to create machines in which any edge in the picture can be labeled by any string of alphabet letters, but first we must consider the consequences. We could now encounter the following additional problem:

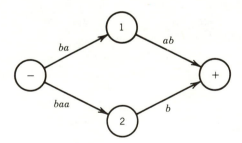

On this machine we can accept the word *baab* in two different ways. First, we could take *ba* from the start state to state 1 and then *ab* would take us to the final state. Or else we could read in the three letters *baa* and go to state 2 from which the final letter, *b,* would take us to the final state.

Previously, when we were dealing only with FA's, we had a unique path through the machine for every input string. Now some strings have no paths at all while some have several. What is this machine going to do with the input string *aaa?* There is no way to process this string (reading any grouping of letters at a time) that will allow us to get to the final state. Therefore, this string cannot be accepted by this machine. We use the word "rejected" to describe what must happen to this string. This rejection is different from the situation for the string *baa,* which, though it doesn't reach the final state, can at least be fully processed to arrive at some state. However, we are not yet interested in the different reasons for failure and we use the word "rejection" for both cases.

We now have observed many of the difficulties inherent in expanding our definition of "machine" to allow word-labeled edges (or, equivalently, to reading more than one letter of input at a time). We shall leave the definition of finite automation alone and call these new machines **transition graphs** because they are more easily understood as graphs than as tables.

DEFINITION

A **transition graph,** abbreviated **TG,** is a collection of three things:

1. A finite set of states at least one of which is designated as the start state (−) and some (maybe none) of which are designated as final states (+).
2. An alphabet Σ of possible input letters from which input strings are formed.
3. A finite set of transitions that show how to go from one state to another based on reading specified substrings of input letters (possibly even the null string Λ). ∎

When we give a pictorial representation of a transition graph, clause 3 in the definition means that every edge is labeled by some string of letters not necessarily to only one letter. We are also not requiring that there be any specific number of edges emanating from every state. Some states may have no edge coming out of them at all, and some may have thousands (for example, edges labeled *a, aa, aaa, aaaa, . . .*).

Transition graphs were invented by John Myhill in 1957 to simplify the proof of Theorem 6 which we shall meet in the next chapter.

A **successful path** through a transition graph is a series of edges forming a path beginning at some start state (there may be several) and ending at a final state. If we concatenate in order the strings of letters that label each edge in the path, we produce a word that is accepted by this machine.

For example, consider the following TG:

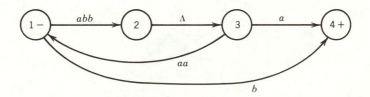

The path from state 1 to state 2 to state 3 back to state 1 then to state 4 corresponds to the string $(abb)(\Lambda)(aa)(b)$. This is one way of factoring the word *abbaab*, which, we now see, is accepted by this machine. Some other words accepted are *abba*, *abbaaabba*, and *b*.

When an edge is labeled with the string Λ, it means that we can take the ride it offers free (without consuming any letters from the input string). Remember that we do not *have* to follow that edge, but we can if we want to.

If we are presented with a particular string of *a*'s and *b*'s to run on a given TG, we must decide how to break the word into substrings that might correspond to the labels of edges in a path. If we consider the input string *abbab* for the machine above, we see that from state 1, where we must start, we can proceed along the outgoing edge labeled *abb* or the one labeled *b*. This word then moves along the edge from state 1 to state 2. The input letters *abb* are read and consumed. What is left of the input string is *ab*, and we are now in state 2. From state 2 we must move to state 3 along the Λ-edge. At state 3 we cannot read *aa*, so we must read only *a* and go to state 4. Here we have a *b* left in the input string but no edge to follow, so we must crash and reject the input string *abbab*.

Because we have allowed some edges to be traversed for free, we have also allowed for the possibility of more than one start state. The reason we say that these two points are related is that we could always introduce more start states if we wanted to, simply by connecting them to the original start state by edges labeled Λ. This point is illustrated by the following example. There is no difference between the TG

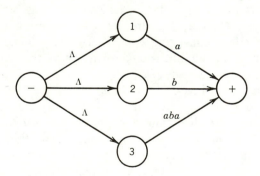

and the TG

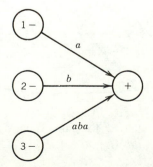

in the sense that all the strings accepted by the first are accepted by the second and vice versa. There are differences between the two machines such as the number of total states they have, but as *language acceptors* they are equivalent.

It is extremely important for us to understand that every FA is also a TG. This means that any picture that represents an FA can be interpreted as a picture of a TG. Of course, not every TG satisfies the definition of an FA.

Let us consider some more examples of TG's.

The picture above represents a TG that accepts nothing, not even the null string Λ. To be able to accept anything, it must have a final state.

The machine

accepts only the string Λ. Any other string cannot have a successful path to the final state through labels of edges since there are no edges (and hence no labels).

Any TG in which some start state is also a final state will always accept the string Λ; this is also true of FA's. There are some other TG's that accept the word Λ, for example:

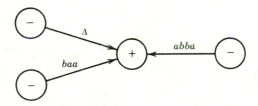

This machine accepts only the words Λ, *baa*, and *abba*. Anything read while in the + state will cause a crash, since the + state has no outgoing edges.

EXAMPLE

Consider the following TG:

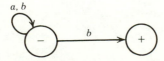

We can read all the input letters one at a time and stay in the left-side state. When we read a *b* in the − state there are two possible edges we can follow. If the very last letter is a *b*, we can use it to go to the + state. It must be the very last letter, since once in the right-side state if we try to read another letter we crash.

Notice that it is also possible to start with a word that does end with a *b* but to follow an unsuccessful path that does not lead to acceptance. We could either make the mistake of following the non-loop *b*-edge too soon (on a non-final *b*) in which case we crash on the next letter; or else we might make the mistake of looping back to − when we read the last *b*, in which case we reject without crashing. But still, all words that end in *b* *can* be accepted by some path, and that is all that is required.

The language accepted by this TG is all words ending in *b*. One regular expression for this language is **(a + b)*b** and an *FA* that accepts the same language is:

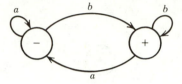

EXAMPLE

The following TG:

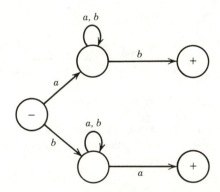

accepts the language of all words that begin and end with different letters.

EXAMPLE

The following TG:

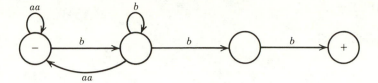

accepts the language of all words in which the *a*'s occur only in even clumps and that end in three or more *b*'s. ∎

EXAMPLE

Consider the following TG:

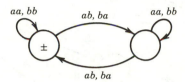

In this TG every edge is labeled with a pair of letters. This means that for the string to be accepted it must have an even number of letters that are read in and processed in groups of two's. Let us call the left state the balanced state and the right state the unbalanced state. If the first pair of letters that we read from the input string is a double (*aa* or *bb*), then the machine stays in the balanced state. In the balanced state the machine has read an even number of *a*'s and an even number of *b*'s. However, when a pair of unmatched letters is read (either *ab* or *ba*), the machine flips over to the unbalanced state which signifies that it has read an odd number of *a*'s and an odd number of *b*'s. We do not return to the balanced state until another "corresponding" unmatched pair is read (not necessarily the same unmatched pair, any unequal pair). The discovery of two unequal pairs makes the total number of *a*'s and the total number of *b*'s read from the input string even again. This TG is an example of a machine that accepts exactly the old and very familiar language EVEN-EVEN of all words with an even number of *a*'s and an even number of *b*'s.

Of the three examples of definitions or descriptions of this language we have had (the regular expression, the FA, and the TG); this last is the most understandable. ∎

There is a practical problem with TG's. There are occasionally so many possible ways of grouping the letters of the input string that we must examine many possibilities before we know whether a given string is accepted or rejected.

EXAMPLE

Consider this TG:

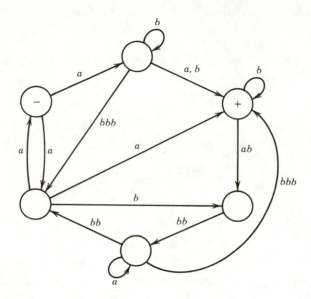

Is the word *abbbabbbabba* accepted by this machine? (Yes, in two ways.) ■

    When we allow Λ-edges we may have an infinite number of ways of grouping the letters of an input string. For example, the input string *ab* may be factored as:

                 (*a*) (*b*)
                 (*a*) (Λ) (*b*)
                 (*a*) (Λ) (Λ) (*b*)
                 (*a*) (Λ) (Λ) (Λ) (*b*)

                 . . . .

    Instead of presenting a definite algorithm right now for determining whether a particular string is accepted by a particular TG, we shall wait until Chapter 12 when the task will be easier. There are, of course, difficult algorithms for performing this task that are within our abilities at this moment. One such is outlined in Problem 20 below.

PROBLEMS

1. For the four FA's pictured in Problems 5-18, 5-19 and 5-20 determine whether a TG could be built that can accept the same language but requires fewer states.

2. The notion of transition table can be extended to TG's. The rows of the table would be the states of the machine and the columns of the table would be all those strings of alphabet characters that are ever used as the label for any edge in the TG. However, the mere fact that a certain string is the label for an edge coming from state 1 does not mean that it is also the label of an edge coming out of state 2. Therefore, in the transition table some entries are likely to be blank (that is, no new state is reached from the prior state given this input sequence). The TG

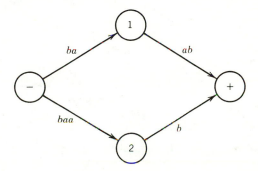

discussed in this section has the following transition table:

	b	ab	ba	baa
$-$			1	2
1		$+$		
2	$+$			
$+$				

Calculate the transition table for the TG's defined by pictures on pages 86, 87, 89 (bottom), 90, 91 (third), 93 (second), and 94.

One advantage of defining a TG by such a table is that in complicated cases it may be easier to read the table than a cluttered picture having many edges with long string labels. (Remember that in cases where not all the states have names it is necessary to give them names to build the table.)

3. Draw a four-state TG that accepts *all* the input strings from {a, b}* that are *not* in EVEN-EVEN. Is there a two-state TG that accepts this language?

4.   Here are six TG's. For each of the next 10 words decide which of these machines accepts the given word.

TG_1

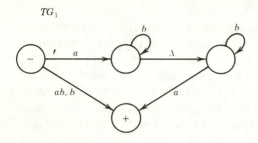

TG_4

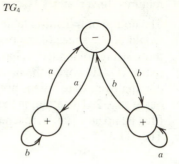

TG_2

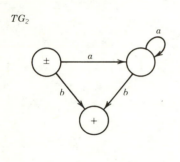

TG_5

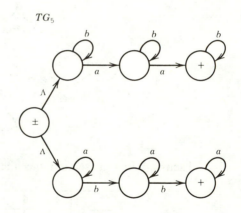

TG_3

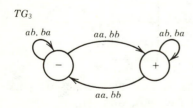

TG_6

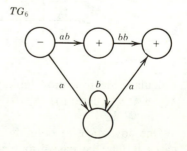

         (i) Λ (vi)   *aba*

       (ii)   *a*   (vii)   *abba*

     (iii)   *b*   (viii)   *bab*

     (iv)   *aa*   (ix)   *baab*

      (v)   *ab*   (x)   *abbb*

5. Find regular expressions defining the language accepted by each of the six TG's above.

6. Show that any language that can be accepted by a TG can be accepted by a TG with an even number of states.

7. How many different TG's are there over the alphabet $\{a, b\}$ that have two states?

8. Show that for every finite language L there is a TG that accepts exactly the words in L and no others. Contrast this with Theorem 5.

9. Prove that for every TG there is another TG that accepts the same language but has only one + state.

10. Build a TG that accepts the language L_1 of all words that begin and end with the same doubled letter, either of the form $aa \ldots aa$ or $bb \ldots bb$. Note: aaa and bbb are not words in this language.

11. Build a TG that accepts the language of all strings that end in a word from L_1 of Problem 10 above.

12. If OURSPONSOR is a language that is accepted by a TG called Henry, prove that there is a TG that accepts the language of all strings of a's and b's that end in a word from OURSPONSOR.

13. Given a TG for some arbitrary language L, what language would it accept if every + state were to be connected back to every − state by Λ-edges? For example, by this method:

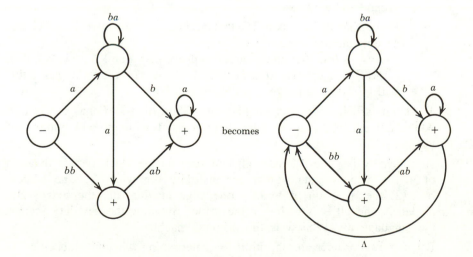

Hint: Why is the answer not always $L*$?

14. Let the language L be accepted by the finite automaton F and let L not contain the word Λ. Show how to build a new finite automaton that accepts exactly all the words in L and the word Λ.

15. Let the language L be accepted by the transition graph T and let L not contain the word Λ. Show how to build a new TG that accepts exactly all the words in L and the word Λ.

16. Let the language L be accepted by the transition graph T and let L not contain the word ba. We want to build a new TG that accepts exactly L and the word ba.

(i)   One suggestion is to draw an edge from $-$ to $+$ and label it ba. Show that this does not always work.

(ii)   Another suggestion is to draw a new $+$ state and draw an edge from a $-$ state to it labeled ba. Show that this does not always work.

(iii) What does work?

17. Let L be any language. Let us define the **transpose** of L to be the language of exactly those words that are the words in L spelled backward. For example, if

$$L = \{a \quad abb \quad bbaab \quad bbbaa\}$$

then

$$\text{transpose } (L) = \{a \quad bba \quad baabb \quad aabbb\}$$

(i)   Prove that if there is a FA that accepts L, then there is a TG that accepts the transpose of L.

(ii)   Prove that if there is a TG that accepts L, then there is a TG that accepts the transpose of L.
       Note: It is true, but much harder to prove that if an FA accepts L then some FA accepts the transpose of L. However, after Chapter 7 this will be trivial to prove.

18. Transition graph T accepts language L. Show that if L has a word of odd length, then T has an edge with a label with an odd number of letters.

19. A student walks into a classroom and sees on the blackboard a diagram of a TG with two states that accepts only the word Λ. The student reverses the direction of exactly one edge leaving all other edges and all labels and all $+$'s and $-$'s the same. But now the new TG accepts the language $\mathbf{a}^*$. What was the original machine?

20. Let us now consider an algorithm for determining whether a specific TG that has no Λ-edges accepts a given word.
     Step 1   Number each edge in the TG in any order with the integers 1, 2, 3 . . . x, where x is the number of edges in the TG.

Step 2   Observe that if the word has y letters and is accepted at all by this machine, it can be accepted by tracing a path of not more than y edges.

Step 3   List all strings of y or fewer integers each of which $\leq x$. This is a finite list.

Step 4   Check each string on the list in Step 3 by concatenating the labels of the edges involved to see if they make a path from a $-$ to a $+$ corresponding to the given word.

Step 5   If there is a string in Step 4 that works, the word is accepted. If none work, the word is not in the language of the machine.

(i) Prove this algorithm does the job.

(ii) Why is it necessary to assume that the TG has no Λ-edges?

CHAPTER 7

KLEENE'S THEOREM

In the last three chapters we introduced three separate ways of defining a language: by regular expression, by finite automaton, and by transition graph. (Remember that the language defined by a machine is the set of all words it accepts.) In this chapter we will present a theorem proved by Kleene in 1956, which (in our version) says that if a language can be defined by any one of these three ways, then it can also be defined by the other two. One way of stating this is to say that all three of these methods of defining languages are *equivalent*.

THEOREM 6

Any language that can be defined by

　　　　1. regular expression

or　　　2. finite automaton

or　　　3. transition graph

can be defined by all three methods.

This theorem is the most important and fundamental result in the Theory of Finite Automata. We are going to take extreme care with its proof. In the

100

process we shall introduce four algorithms that have the practical value of enabling us actually to construct the corresponding machines and expressions. More than that, the importance of this chapter lies in its value as an illustration of thorough theoretical thinking in this field.

The logic of this proof is a bit involved. If we were trying to prove the mathematical theorem that the set of all ZAPS (whatever they are) is the same as the set of all ZEPS, we could break the proof into two parts. In Part 1, we would show that all ZAPS are also ZEPS. In Part 2 we would show that all ZEPS are also ZAPS. Together, this would demonstrate the equivalence of the two sets.

Here we have a more ambitious theorem. We wish to show that the set of ZAPS, the set of ZEPS, and the set of ZIPS are all the same. To do this, we need three parts. In Part 1 we shall show that all ZAPS are ZEPS. In Part 2 we shall show that all ZEPS are ZIPS. Finally, in Part 3 we shall show that all ZIPS are ZAPS. Taken together, these three parts will establish the equivalence of the three sets.

$$(\text{ZAPS} \subset \text{ZEPS} \subset \text{ZIPS} \subset \text{ZAPS}) \equiv (\text{ZAPS} = \text{ZEPS} = \text{ZIPS})$$

PROOF

The three sections of our proof will be:

Part 1   Every language that can be defined by a finite automaton can also be defined by a transition graph.

Part 2   Every language that can be defined by a transition graph can also be defined by a regular expression.

Part 3   Every language that can be defined by a regular expression can also be defined by a finite automaton.

When we have proven these three parts, we have finished our theorem.

The Proof of Part 1

This is the easiest part. Every finite automaton *is* itself a transition graph. Therefore, any language that has been defined by a finite automaton has already been defined by a transition graph. Done.

The Proof of Part 2

The proof of this part will be by constructive algorithm. This means that we present a procedure that starts out with a transition graph and ends up with a regular expression that defines the same language. To be acceptable as a method of proof, any algorithm must satisfy two criteria. It must work for every conceivable TG, and it must guarantee to finish its job in a finite time (a finite number of steps). For the purposes of theorem-proving alone, it does not have to be a good algorithm (quick, least storage used, etc.). It just has to work in every case.

Let us start by considering an abstract transition graph T. T may have many start states. We first want to simplify T so that it has only one start state. We do this by introducing a new state that we label with a minus sign and that we connect to all the previous start states by edges labeled with the string Λ. Then we drop the minus signs from the previous start states. Now all words must begin at the new unique start state. From there, they can proceed free of charge to any of the old start states. If the word w used to be accepted by starting at previous start state 3 and proceeding through the machine to a final state, it can now be accepted by starting at the new unique start state and progressing to the old start state 3 along the edge labeled Λ. This trip does not use up any of the input letters. The word then picks up its old path and becomes accepted. This process is illustrated below on a TG that has three start states: 1, 3, and 5.

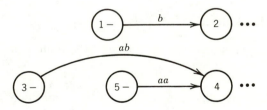

becomes

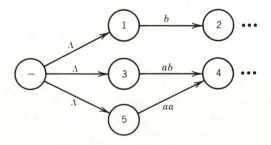

The ellipses in the pictures above indicate other, but irrelevant, sections of the TG.

Another simplification we can make in T is that it can be modified to have a unique final state without changing the language it accepts. (If T had no final states to begin with, then it accepts no strings at all and has no language and we need produce no regular expression.) If T has several final states, let us introduce a new unique final state labeled with a plus sign. We draw new edges from all the old final states to the new one, drop the old plus signs, and label each new edge with the null string Λ. We have a free ride from each old final state to the new unique final state. This process is depicted below.

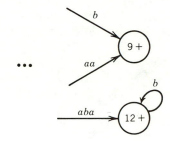

becomes

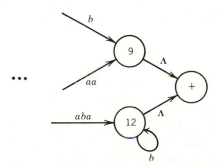

We shall require that the unique final state be a different state from the unique start state.

It should be clear that the addition of these two new states does not affect the language that T accepts. Any word accepted by the old T is also accepted by the new T, and any word rejected by the old T is also rejected by the new T.

We are now going to build the regular expression that defines the same language as T piece by piece. To do so we extend our notion of transition graph. We previously allowed the edges to be labeled only with strings of alphabet letters. For the purposes of this algorithm, we allow the edges to be labeled with regular expressions. This will mean that we can travel along an edge if we read from the input string any substring that is a word in the language defined by the regular expression labeling that edge. For example, if an edge is labeled $(\mathbf{a} + \mathbf{baa})$ as below,

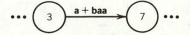

we can cross from state 3 to state 7 by reading from the input string either the letter *a* alone or else the sequence *baa*. The ellipses on each side of the picture in this example indicate that there is more transition graph on each side of the edge, but we are focusing close up on this edge alone.

Labeling an edge with the regular expression (**ab**)* means that we can cross the edge by reading any of the input sequences

$$\Lambda, \ ab, \ abab, \ ababab \ \ldots$$

Let us suppose that T has some state (called state x) inside it (not the $-$ or $+$ state) that has more than one loop circling back to itself,

where $\mathbf{r}_1$, $\mathbf{r}_2$, and $\mathbf{r}_3$ are all regular expressions or simple strings. In this case, we can replace the three loops by one loop labeled with a regular expression.

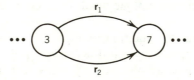

The meaning here is that from state x we can read any string from the input that fits the regular expression $\mathbf{r}_1 + \mathbf{r}_2 + \mathbf{r}_3$ and return to the same state.

Similarly, suppose two states are connected by more than one edge going in the same direction:

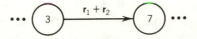

where the labels $\mathbf{r}_1$ and $\mathbf{r}_2$ are each regular expressions or simple strings. We can replace this with a single edge that is labeled with a regular expression.

We can now define the **bypass operation.** In some cases, if we have three states in a row connected by edges labeled with regular expressions (or simple strings), we can eliminate the middleman and go directly from one outer state to the other by a new edge labeled with a regular expression that is the concatenation of the two previous labels.

For example, if we have:

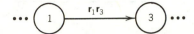

we can replace this with:

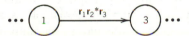

We say "replace," because we no longer need to keep the old edges from state 1 to state 2 and state 2 to state 3 unless they are used in paths other than the ones from state 1 to state 3. The elimination of edges is our goal.

We can do this trick only as long as state 2 does not have a loop going back to itself. If state 2 does have a loop, we must use this model:

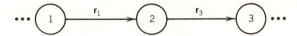

becomes

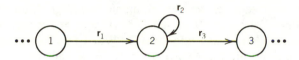

We have had to introduce the * because once we are at state 2 we can loop the loop edge as many times as we want, or no times at all, before proceeding to state 3. Any string that fits the description $r_1 r_2^* r_3$ corresponds to a path from state 1 to state 3 in either picture. The Kleene star and the option of looping indefinitely correspond perfectly.

If state 1 is connected to state 2 and state 2 is connected to more than one other state (say to states 3, 4, and 5), then when we eliminate the edge from state 1 to state 2 we have to add edges that show how to go from state 1 to states 3, 4, and 5. We do this as in the pictures below.

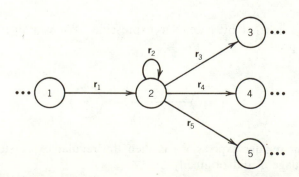

becomes

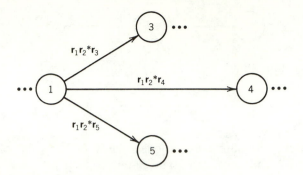

We see that in this way we can eliminate the edge from state 1 to state 2, bypassing state 2 altogether.

In fact, every state that leads into state 2 can be made to bypass state 2. If state 9 leads into state 2, we can eliminate the edge from state 9 to state 2 by adding edges from state 9 to states 3, 4, and 5 directly. We can repeat this process until nothing leads into state 2. When this happens, we can eliminate state 2 entirely, since it then cannot be in a path that accepts a word. We drop it, and the edges leading from it, from the picture for T.

What have we done to transition graph T? Without changing the set of words that it accepts, we have eliminated one of its states.

We can repeat this process again and again until we have eliminated all the states from T except for the unique start state and the unique final state. (We shall illustrate this presently.)

What we come down to is a picture that looks like this:

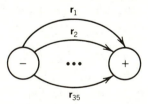

with each edge labeled by a regular expression. We can then combine this once more to produce:

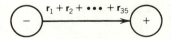

The resultant regular expression, is then the regular expression that defines the same language T did originally.

For example, if we have:

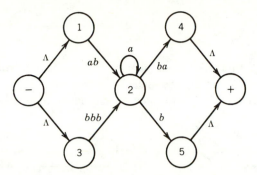

we can bypass state 2 by including a path from state 1 to state 4 labeled **aba*ba,** a path from state 1 to state 5 labeled **aba*b,** a path from state 3 to state 4 labeled **bbba*ba,** and a path from state 3 to state 5 labeled **bbba*b.** We can then erase the edges from state 1 to state 2 and from state 3 to state 2. Without these edges, state 2 becomes unreachable. The edges from state 2 to states 4 and 5 are then useless because they cannot be part of any path from − to +. Dropping this state and these edges will not affect whether any word is accepted by this TG.

The machine that results from this operation is:

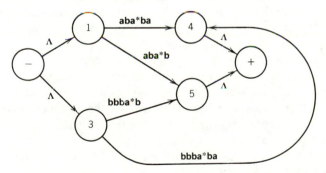

Before we claim to have finished describing this algorithm, there are some special cases that we must examine more carefully. In this picture

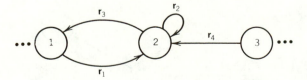

we might want to eliminate the edge from state 1 to state 2. Since state 2 goes nowhere except into state 1, we might think that we can rewrite this part of T as:

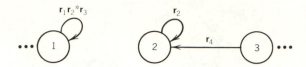

but this is wrong. In the original picture, we could go from state 3 to state 1, while in the modified picture that is impossible. Therefore, we must introduce an edge from state 3 to state 1 and label it as below.

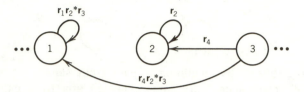

Whenever we remove an edge or a state we must be sure that we have not destroyed any paths through T that may previously have existed. Destroying paths could change the language of words accepted, which we do not want to do. Since there are only finitely many paths in the whole TG (not counting looping and repeating circuits), we can check this possibility in a finite number of steps.

This example is symptomatic of the only problem that arises with this algorithm, so we now have a well-described method of producing regular expressions equivalent to given transition graphs. All words accepted by T are paths through the picture of T. If we change the picture but preserve all paths and their labels, we must keep the language unchanged.

This algorithm terminates in a finite number of steps, since T has only finitely many states to begin with, and one state is eliminated with each iteration. The other important observation is that the method works on all transition graphs. Therefore, this algorithm provides a satisfactory proof that there is a regular expression for each transition graph.

Before proceeding to the proof of Part 3, let us illustrate the algorithm above on a particular example.

The TG we shall consider is the one below, which accepts all words that begin and end with double letters (having at least four different letters). This is by no means the only TG that accepts this language.

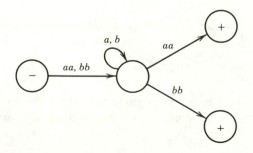

As it stands, this machine has only one start state, but it has two final states, so we must introduce a new unique final state following the method prescribed by the algorithm.

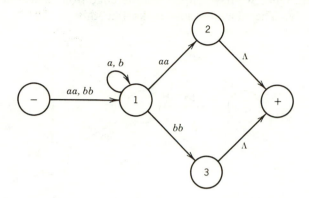

The next modification we perform is to note that the edge from the start state to state 1 is a double edge—we can travel over it by an *aa* or a *bb*. We replace this by the regular expression **aa + bb**. We also note that there is a double loop at state 1. We can loop back to state 1 on a single *a* or on a single *b*. The algorithm says we are supposed to replace this double loop by a single loop labeled with the regular expression **a + b**. The picture of the machine has now become:

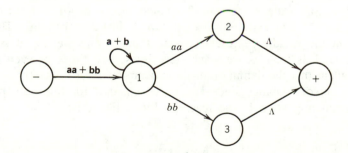

Let us choose for our next modification the path from state 1 to state 2 to state +. The algorithm does not actually tell us which section of the TG we must attack next. The order is left up to our own discretion. The algorithm tells us that it really does not matter. As long as we continue to eliminate edges and states, we shall be simplifying the machine down to a single regular expression representation.

The path we are considering now is:

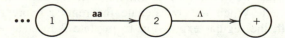

The algorithm says we can replace this with one edge from state 1 to state + that bears the label that is the concatenation of the regular expressions on the two parts of the path. In this case, *aa* is concatenated with Λ, which is only *aa* again. Once we have eliminated the edge from state 1 we can eliminate state 2 entirely. The machine now looks like this.

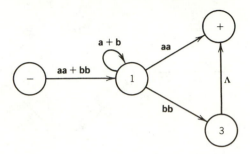

It seems reasonable now for us to do the same thing with the path that goes from state 1 to state 3 to state +. But the algorithm does not require us to be reasonable, and since this is an illustrative example and we have already seen something like this path, we shall choose a different section of *T* to modify.

Let us try to bypass state 1. Only one edge comes into state 1 and that is from state −. There is a loop at state 1 with the label (**a** + **b**). State 1 has edges coming out of it that lead to state 3 and state +.

The algorithm explains that we can eliminate state 1 and replace these edges with an edge from state − to state 3 labeled (**aa** + **bb**)(**a** + **b**)*(**bb**) and an edge from state − to state + labeled (**aa** + **bb**)(**a** + **b**)*(**aa**). The starred expression in the middle represents the fact that while we are at state 1 we can loop around as long as we want—ten times, two times or even no times. It is no accident that the definition of the closure operator * exactly corresponds to the situation of looping, since Kleene invented it for this very purpose.

After eliminating state 1, the machine looks like this:

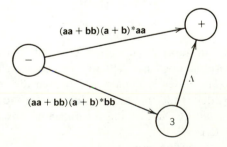

It is obvious that we must now eliminate state 3, since that is the only bypassable state left. When we concatenate the regular expression from state − to state 3 with the regular expression from state 3 to state +, we are left with the machine:

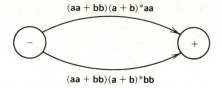

(aa + bb)(a + b)*aa

(aa + bb)(a + b)*bb

Now by the last rule of the algorithm, this machine defines the same language as the regular expression

$$(aa + bb)(a + b)*(aa) + (aa + bb)(a + b)*(bb)$$

If we had to make up a regular expression for the language of all strings that begin and end with double letters, we would probably write:

$$(aa + bb)(a + b)*(aa + bb)$$

which is equivalent to the regular expression that the algorithm produced because the algebraic distributive law applies to regular expressions.

Without going through lengthy descriptions, let us watch the algorithm work on one more example. Let us start with the TG that accepts strings with an even number of a's and an even number of b's, the language EVEN-EVEN. (We keep harping on these strings not because they are so terribly important, but because it is the hardest example we thoroughly understand, and rather than introduce new hard examples we keep it as an old conquest.)

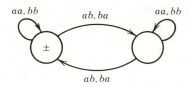

becomes first

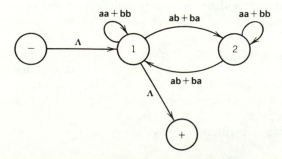

When we eliminate state 2, the path from 1 to 2 to 1 becomes a loop at state 1:

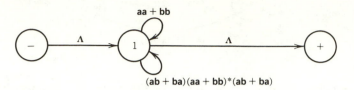

which becomes:

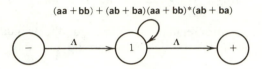

which becomes:

which reduces to the regular expression:

$$[(aa + bb) + (ab + ba)(aa + bb)*(ab + ba)]*$$

which is exactly the regular expression we used to define this language before. Anyone who was wondering how we could have thought up that complicated regular expression we presented in Chapter 4 can see now that it came from the obvious TG for this language by way of our algorithm.

We still have one part of Kleene's theorem yet to prove. We must show that for each regular expression we can build a finite automaton that accepts the same language.

The Proof of Part 3

The proof of this part will be by recursive definition and constructive algorithm at the same time. This is the hardest part of our whole theorem, so we shall go very slowly.

We know that every regular expression can be built up from the letters of the alphabet and Λ by repeated application of certain rules: addition, concatenation, and closure. We shall see that as we are building up a regular expression, we could at the same time be building up an FA that accepts the same language.

We present our algorithm recursively.

Rule 1 There is an FA that accepts any particular letter of the alphabet. There is an FA that accepts only the word Λ.

For example: If x is in Σ, then the FA

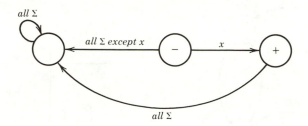

accepts only the word x.

One FA that accepts only Λ is

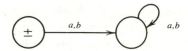

Rule 2 If there is an FA called FA_1 that accepts the language defined by the regular expression $\mathbf{r}_1$ and there is an FA called FA_2 that accepts the language defined by the regular expressions $\mathbf{r}_2$, then there is an FA called FA_3 that accepts the language defined by the regular expression $(\mathbf{r}_1 + \mathbf{r}_2)$.

We are going to prove this by showing how to construct the new machine in the most reasonable way.

Before we state the general principles, let us demonstrate them in a specific example. Suppose we have the machine FA_1, which accepts the language of all words over the alphabet

$$\Sigma = \{a, b\}$$

that have a double a somewhere in them,

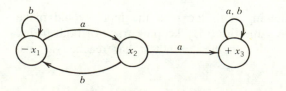

	a	b
$-\ x_1$	x_2	x_1
x_2	x_3	x_1
$+\ x_3$	x_3	x_3

and the familiar machine FA_2, which accepts all words that have both an even number of total a's and an even number of total b's (this is the language EVEN-EVEN).

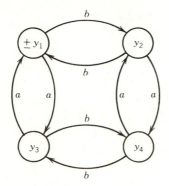

	a	b
$\pm\ y_1$	y_3	y_2
y_2	y_4	y_1
y_3	y_1	y_4
y_4	y_2	y_3

We shall show how to design a machine that accepts both sets. That is, we will build a machine that accepts all words that either have an *aa* or are in EVEN-EVEN and rejects all strings with neither characteristic.

The language the new machine accepts will be the *union* of these two languages. We shall call the states in this new machine z_1, z_2, z_3, and so on, for as many as we need. We shall define this machine by its transition table.

Our guiding principle is this: The new machine will simultaneously keep track of where the input would be if it were running on FA_1 and where the input would be if it were running on FA_2.

First of all, we need a start state. This state must combine x_1, the start state for FA_1, and y_1, the start state for FA_2. We call it z_1. If the string were running on FA_1, it would start in x_1, on FA_2 in y_1.

What new states can occur if the input letter a is read in? If the string were being run on the first machine, it would put the machine into state x_2. If the string were running on the second machine, it would put the machine into state y_3. Therefore, on our new machine an a puts us into state z_2, which means either x_2 or y_3, in the same way that z_1 means either x_1 or y_1. Since y_1 is a final state, for FA_2, z_1 is also a final state in the sense that any word whose path ends there on the z-machine would be accepted by FA_2.

$$z_1 = x_1 \text{ or } y_1$$

$$z_2 = x_2 \text{ or } y_3$$

On the machine FA_3 we are following both the path the input would make on FA_1 and the path on FA_2 at the same time. By keeping track of both paths, we know when the input string ends whether or not it has reached a final state on either machine.

If we are in state z_1 and we read the letter b, we then go to state z_3, which represents either x_1 or y_2. The x_1 comes from being in x_1 on FA_1 and reading a b, whereas the y_2 comes from being in y_1 on FA_2 and reading a b.

$$z_3 = x_1 \text{ or } y_2$$

The beginning of our transition table for FA_3 is:

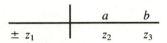

	a	b
$\pm\ z_1$	z_2	z_3

Suppose that somehow we have gotten into state z_2 and then we read an a. If we were in FA_1, we would now go to state x_3, which is a final state. If we were in FA_2, we would now go back to y_1, which is also a final state. We will call this condition z_4, meaning either x_3 or y_1. Since this string could now be accepted on one of these two machines, z_4 is a final state for FA_3. As it turns out, in this example the word is accepted by both machines at once, but this is not necessary. Acceptance by either machine FA_1 or FA_2 is enough for acceptance by FA_3.

If we are in state z_2 and we happen to read a b, then in FA_1 we are back to x_1 whereas in FA_2 we are in y_4. Call this new condition $z_5 = $ state x_1 or y_4.

$$+\ z_4 = x_3 \text{ or } y_1$$

$$z_5 = x_1 \text{ or } y_4$$

At this point our transition table looks like this:

	a	b
$\pm\ z_1$	z_2	z_3
z_2	z_4	z_5

What happens if we start from state z_3 and read an a? If we were in FA_1, we are now in x_2, if in FA_2, we are now in y_4. This is a new state; call it state z_6.

$$z_6 = x_2 \text{ or } y_4$$

What if we are in z_3 and we read a b? In FA_1 we stay in x_1, whereas in FA_2 we return to y_1. This means that if we are in z_3 and we read a b we return to state z_1.

Our transition table now looks like this:

	a	b
$+ \; z_1$	z_2	z_3
z_2	z_4	z_5
z_3	z_6	z_1

What if we are in z_4 and we read an a? FA_1 remains in x_3, whereas FA_2 goes to y_3. This is a new state; call it z_7. If we are in z_4 and we read a b, the FA_1 part stays at x_3 whereas the FA_2 part goes to y_2. This is also a new state; call it z_8.

$$+ \; z_7 = x_3 \text{ or } y_3$$

$$+ \; z_8 = x_3 \text{ or } y_2$$

Both of these are final states because a string ending here on the z-machine will be accepted by FA_1, since x_3 is a final state for FA_1.

If we are in z_5 and we read an a, we go to x_2 or y_2, which we shall call z_9.
If we are in z_5 and we read a b, we go to x_1 or y_3, which we shall call z_{10}.

$$z_9 = x_2 \text{ or } y_2$$

$$z_{10} = x_1 \text{ or } y_3$$

If we are in z_6 and we read an a, we go to x_3 or y_2, which is our old z_8.
If we are in z_6 and we read a b, we go to x_1 or y_3, which is z_{10} again.
If we are in z_7 and we read an a we go to x_3 or y_1, which is z_4 again.
If we are in z_7 and we read a b, we go to x_3 or y_4, which is a new state, z_{11}.

$$+ \; z_{11} = x_3 \text{ or } y_4$$

If we are in z_8 and we read an a, we go to x_3 or $y_4 = z_{11}$. If in z_8 we read a b, we go to x_3 or $y_1 = z_4$.
If we are in z_9 and we read an a, we go to x_3 or $y_4 = z_{11}$. If in z_9 we read a b, we go to x_1 or $y_1 = z_1$.
If we are in z_{10} and we read an a, we go to x_2 or y_1, which is our last new state, z_{12}.

$$+ \; z_{12} = x_2 \text{ or } y_1$$

If we are in z_{10} and we read a b, we go to $(x_1$ or $y_4) = z_5$.

If we are in z_{11} and we read an a, we go to $(x_3$ or $y_2) = z_8$.

If we are in z_{11} and we read a b, we go to $(x_3$ or $y_3) = z_7$.

If we are in z_{12} and we read an a, we go to $(x_3$ or $y_3) = z_7$.

If we are in z_{12} and we read a b, we go to $(x_1$ or $y_2) = z_3$.

Our machine is now complete. The full transition table is:

	a	b
$\pm\ z_1$	z_2	z_3
z_2	z_4	z_5
z_3	z_6	z_1
$+\ z_4$	z_7	z_8
z_5	z_9	z_{10}
z_6	z_8	z_{10}
$+\ z_7$	z_4	z_{11}
$+\ z_8$	z_{11}	z_4
z_9	z_{11}	z_1
z_{10}	z_{12}	z_5
$+\ z_{11}$	z_8	z_7
$+\ z_{12}$	z_7	z_3

If a string traces through this machine and ends up at a final state, it means that it would also end at a final state either on machine FA_1 or on machine FA_2. Also, any string accepted by either FA_1 or FA_2 will be accepted by this FA_3.

The general description of the algorithm we employed above is as follows. Starting with two machines, FA_1 with states x_1, x_2, x_3, . . . and FA_2 with states y_1, y_2, y_3, . . ., build a new machine FA_3 with states z_1, z_2, z_3, . . . where each z is of the form "$x_{\text{something}}$ or $y_{\text{something}}$". If either the x part or the y part is a final state, then the corresponding z is a final state. To go from one z to another by reading a letter from the input string, we see what happens to the x part and to the y part and go to the new z accordingly. We could write this as a formula:

$$z_{\text{new}} \text{ after letter } p = [x_{\text{new}} \text{ after letter } p] \text{ or } [y_{\text{new}} \text{ after letter } p]$$

Since there are only finitely many x's and y's, there can be only finitely many possible z's. Not all of them will necessarily be used in FA_3. In this way, we can build a machine that can accept the sum of two regular expressions if there are already machines to accept each of the component regular expressions separately.

Let us go through this very quickly once more on the two machines:

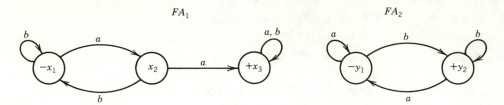

FA_1 accepts all words with a double a in them, and FA_2 accepts all words ending in b.

The machine that accepts the union of the two languages for these two machines begins:

$$- \quad z_1 = x_1 \quad \text{or} \quad y_1$$

In z_1 if we read an a, we go to $(x_2 \text{ or } y_1) = z_2$.

In z_1, if we read a b, we go to $(x_1 \text{ or } y_2) = z_3$, which is a final state since y_2 is.

The partial picture of this machine is now:

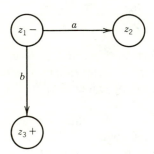

In z_2 if we read an a, we go to $(x_3 \text{ or } y_1) = z_4$, which is a final state because x_3 is. In z_2 if we read a b, we go to $(x_1 \text{ or } y_2) = z_3$.

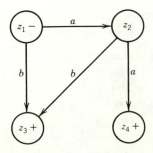

In z_3 if we read an a, we go to $(x_2$ or $y_1) = z_2$.

In z_3 if we read a b, we go to $(x_1$ or $y_2) = z_3$.

In z_4 if we read an a, we go to $(x_3$ or $y_1) = z_4$.

In z_4 if we read a b, we go to $(x_3$ or $y_2) = z_5$, which is a final state.

In z_5 if we read an a, we go to $(x_3$ or $y_1) = z_4$.

In z_5 if we read a b, we go to x_3 or $y_2 = z_5$.

The whole machine looks like this:

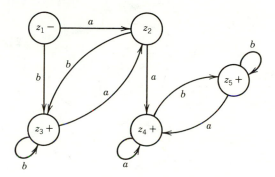

This machine accepts all words that have a double a *or* that end in b.

The seemingly logical possibility

$$z_6 = (x_2 \quad \text{or} \quad y_2)$$

does not arise. This is because to be in x_2 on FA_1 means the last letter read is an a. But to be in y_2 on FA_2 means the last letter read is a b. These cannot both be true at the same time, so no input string ever has the possibility of being in state z_6.

This algorithm establishes the existence of the machine FA_3 that accepts the union of the languages for FA_1 and FA_2.

EXAMPLE (Inside of the proof of Theorem 6)

Let FA_1 be the machine below that accepts all words that end in a:

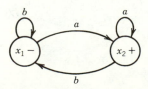

and let FA_2 be the machine below that accepts all words with an odd number of letters (odd length):

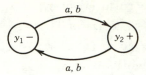

Using the algorithm produces the machine below that accepts all words that either have an odd number of letters or that end in a:

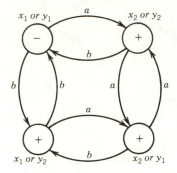

The only state that is not a $+$ state is the $-$ state. To get back to the start state, a word must have an even number of letters *and* end in b.   ∎

EXAMPLE (Inside of the proof of Theorem 6)

Let FA_1 be:

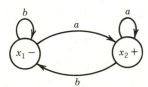

which accepts all words ending in a, and let FA_2 be:

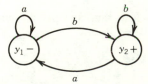

which accepts all words ending in b.

Using the algorithm, we produce:

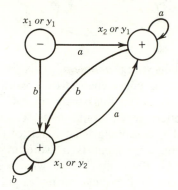

which accepts all words ending in a or b, that is, all words except Λ. Notice that the state x_2 or y_2 cannot be reached since x_2 means "we have just read an a" and y_2 means "we have just read a b." ■

We still have two rules to go.

Rule 3   If there is an FA_1 that accepts the language defined by the regular expression $\mathbf{r}_1$ and an FA_2 that accepts the language defined by the regular expression $\mathbf{r}_2$ then there is an FA_3 that accepts the language defined by the concatenation $\mathbf{r}_1\mathbf{r}_2$, the product language.

Again, we shall verify this rule by constructive algorithm.

Let L_1 be the language of all words with b as the second letter. One machine that accepts L_1 is FA_1 below:

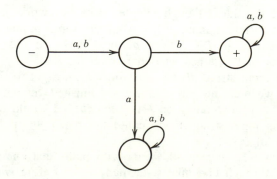

Let L_2 be the language of all words that have an odd number of a's. One machine for L_2 is FA_2 on the next page.

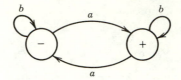

Now consider the input string *ababbaa*. This is a word in the product language L_1L_2, since it is the concatenation of a word in L_1 (*ab*) with a word in L_2 (*abbaa*). If we begin to run this string on FA_1, we would reach the + state after the second letter. If we could now somehow automatically jump over into FA_2, we could begin running what is left of the input, *abbaa*, starting in the − state. This remaining input is a word in L_2, so it will finish its path in the + state of FA_2. Basically, this is what we want to build—an FA_3 that processes the first part of the input string as if it were FA_1; then when it reaches the FA_1 + state, it turns into the − state on FA_2. From there it continues processing the string until it reaches the + state on FA_2, and we can then accept the input.

Tentatively, let us say FA_3 looks something like this:

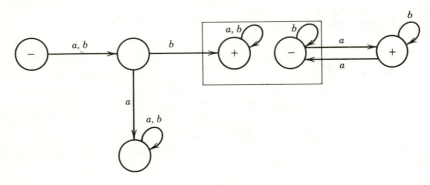

Unfortunately, this idea, though simple, does not work. We can see this by considering a different input string from the same product language. The word *ababbab* is also in L_1L_2, since *abab* is in L_1 (it has *b* as its second letter) and *bab* is in L_2 (it has an odd number of *a*'s).

If we run the input string *ababba* first on FA_1, we get to the + state after two letters, but we must not say that we are finished yet with the L_1 part of the input. If we stopped running on FA_1 after *ab*, we would reach + in FA_1, but the remaining input string *abbab* could not reach + on FA_2 since it has an even number of *a*'s.

Remember that FA_1 accepts all words with paths that *end* at a final state. They could pass through that final state many times before *ending* there. This is the case with the input *abab*. It reaches + after two letters. However, we must continue to run the string on FA_1 for two more letters. We loop back to + twice. Then we can jump to FA_2 and run the remaining string *bab* on

FA_2. The input bab will start on FA_2 in the $-$ state and finish in the $+$ state.

Our problem is this: "How do we know when to jump from FA_1 to FA_2?" With the input $ababbaa$ we should jump when we first reach the $+$ in FA_1. With the input $ababbab$ (which differs only in the last letter), we have to stay in FA_1 until we have looped back to the $+$ state some number of times before jumping to FA_2. How can a finite automaton, which must make a mandatory transition on each input letter without looking ahead to see what the rest of the string will be, know when to jump from FA_1 to FA_2?

This is a subtle point, and it involves some new ideas.

We have to build a machine that has the characteristic of starting out like FA_1 and following along it until it enters a final state at which time an option is reached. Either we continue along FA_1 waiting to reach another $+$ or else we switch over to the start state of FA_2 and begin circulating there. This is tricky, since the r_1 part of the input string can generate an arbitrarily long word if it has a star in it, and we cannot be quite sure of when to jump out of FA_1 and into FA_2.

As before, we first illustrate how to build such an FA_3 for a specific example. The two machines we shall use are

$$FA_1 = \text{the machine that accepts only strings with a double } a \text{ in them}$$
$$\text{and}$$
$$FA_2 = \text{the machine that accepts all words that end in the letter } b.$$

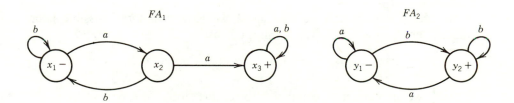

We shall start with the state z_1, which is exactly like x_1. It is a start state, and it means that the input string is being run on FA_1. From z_1 if we read a b, we must return to the same state x_1, which is z_1 again. From z_1 if we read an a, we must go to state x_2 because we are interested in seeing that the first section of the input string is a word accepted by FA_1. Therefore, z_2 is the same as x_2. From the state z_2 if we read a b, we must go back to z_1. Therefore, we have the relationships

$$z_1 = x_1$$
$$z_2 = x_2$$

The picture of FA_3 starts out just like the picture of FA_1.

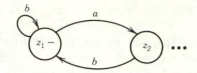

Now if we are in z_2 and we read an a, we must go to a new state z_3, which in some ways corresponds to the state x_3 in FA_1. However, x_3 has a dual identity. Either it means that we have reached a final state for the first half of the input as a word in the language. for FA_1 and it is where we cross over and run the rest of the input string on FA_2, or else it is merely another state that the string must pass through to get eventually to its last state in FA_1. Many strings, some of which are accepted and some of which are rejected, pass through several + states on their way through any given machine.

If we are now in z_3 in its capacity as the final state of FA_1 for the first part of this input string, we must begin running the rest of the input string as if it were input of FA_2 beginning at state y_1. Therefore, the full meaning of being in z_3 is:

$$z_3 = \begin{cases} x_3, \text{ and we are still running on } FA_1 \\ \qquad\qquad \text{or} \\ y_1, \text{ and we have begun to run on } FA_2 \end{cases}$$

Notice the similarity between this disjunctive (either/or) definition of z_3 and the disjunctive definitions for the z states produced by the algorithm given for the addition of two FA's.

If we are in state z_3 and we read an a, we have now three possible interpretations for the state into which this puts us:

$$\begin{cases} \text{we are back in } x_3 \text{ continuing to run the string on } FA_1 \\ \qquad\qquad \text{or} \\ \text{we have just finished on } FA_1 \text{ and we are now in } y_1 \\ \text{beginning to run on } FA_2 \\ \qquad\qquad \text{or} \\ \text{we have looped from } y_1 \text{ back to } y_1 \text{ while already running on} \\ FA_2 \end{cases}$$

$$= x_3 \text{ or } y_1$$

(since being in y_1 is the same whether we are

there for the first time or not)

$$= z_3$$

Therefore, if we are in z_3 and we read an a, we loop back to z_3.

If we are in state z_3 and we read a b, we go to state z_4, which has the following meaning:

$$+ z_4 = \begin{cases} \text{we are still in } x_3 \text{ continuing to run on } FA_1 \\ \qquad\qquad\qquad \text{or} \\ \text{we have just finished running on } FA_1 \text{ and are now in } y_1 \text{ on } FA_2 \\ \qquad\qquad\qquad \text{or} \\ \text{we are now in } y_2 \text{ on } FA_2 \text{ having reached there via } y_1 \end{cases}$$

$$= \quad x_3 \text{ or } y_1 \text{ or } y_2$$

If an input string ends its path in this state z_4, that means that it could have been broken into two sections, the first going from x_1 to x_3 and the second from y_1 to y_2; therefore, it must be accepted, so z_4 is a final state.

So far our machine looks like this:

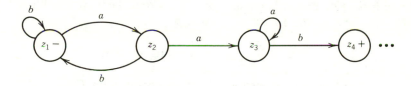

If we are in z_4 and we read an a, our choices are:

$$\begin{cases} \text{remaining in } x_3 \text{ and continuing to run on } FA_1 \\ \qquad\qquad \text{or} \\ \text{having just finished } FA_1 \text{ and beginning at } y_1 \\ \qquad\qquad \text{or} \\ \text{having moved from } y_2 \text{ back to } y_1 \text{ in } FA_2 \end{cases}$$

$$= x_3 \text{ or } y_1$$

However, this is exactly the definition of z_3 again. So, in summary, if we are in z_4 and read an a, we go back to z_3.

If we are in z_4 and read a b, our choices are:

$$\begin{cases} \text{remaining in } x_3 \text{ and continuing to run on } FA_1 \\ \qquad\qquad\qquad \text{or} \\ \text{having just finished } FA_1 \text{ and beginning at } y_1 \\ \qquad\qquad\qquad \text{or} \\ \text{having looped back from } y_2 \text{ to } y_2 \text{ running on } FA_2 \end{cases}$$

$$= x_3 \text{ or } y_1 \text{ or } y_2$$

$$= z_4$$

Accordingly, if we are in z_4 and read a b, we loop back to z_4. The whole machine then looks like this:

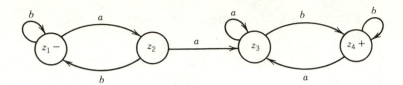

Thus we have produced a machine that accepts exactly those strings that have a front section with a double a followed by a back section that ends in b. This we can see because without a double a we never get to z_3 and we end in z_4 only if the whole word ends in b.

In general, we can describe the algorithm for forming the machine FA_3 as follows. First we make a z state for every nonfinal x state in FA_1. For each final state in FA_1 we establish a z state that expresses the options that we are continuing on FA_1 or are beginning on FA_2. From there we establish z states for all situations of the form

are in $x_{\text{something}}$ continuing on FA_1

or

have just started y_1 about to continue on FA_2

or

are in $y_{\text{something}}$ continuing on FA_2

There are clearly only finitely many possibilities for such z states, so FA_3 is a finite machine. The transition from one z state to another for each letter of the alphabet is determined uniquely by the transition rules in FA_1 and FA_2. So FA_3 is a well-defined finite automaton that clearly does what we want, that is, it accepts only strings that first reach a final state on FA_1 and then reach a final state on FA_2.

EXAMPLE (Inside the proof of Theorem 6)

Let FA_1 be:

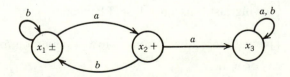

which accepts the language L_1 of all words that do *not* contain the substring *aa*.

Let FA_2 be:

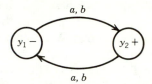

which accepts the language L_2 of all words with an odd number of letters.

Using the algorithm above, we produce the following machine to accept the product language L_1L_2.

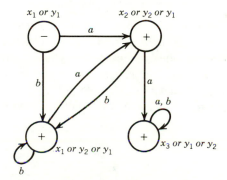

All states except the $-$ state are final states. The $-$ state is left the instant an input letter is read, and it can never be reentered. Therefore, the language this machine accepts is all words but Λ. This actually *is* the product language L_1L_2, since if a word w has an odd number of letters, we can factor it as $(\Lambda)(w)$, where Λ is in L_1 and w is in L_2. If w has an even (not 0) number of letters, we can factor it as

$$w = (\text{first letter})(\text{the rest})$$

where (first letter) must be in L_1 and (the rest) is in L_2. Only the word Λ cannot be factored into a part in L_1 and a part in L_2. ∎

We are now ready for our last rule.

Rule 4   If **r** is a regular expression and FA_1 is a finite automaton that accepts exactly the language defined by **r**, then there is an FA called FA_2 that will accept exactly the language defined by **r***.

The language defined by **r*** must always contain the null word. To accept the null string Λ we must indicate that the start state is also a final state. This could be an important change in the machine FA_1, since strings that return to x_1 might not have been accepted before. They may not be in the language of the expression **r**. The building of our new machine must be done carefully.

We shall, as in the other cases, first illustrate the algorithm for manufacturing this machine on a simple example. We cannot use most of the examples we have seen recently because their closure is not different from themselves (except for the possibility of the word Λ). This is just a curious accident of these examples and not usual for regular expressions. The concatenation of several strings of words ending in b is itself a word ending in b. The concatenation of several strings containing aa is itself a string containing aa. The concatenation of EVEN-EVEN strings is itself an EVEN-EVEN string.

Let us consider the regular expression

$$\mathbf{r} = \mathbf{a}* + \mathbf{aa}*\mathbf{b}$$

The language defined by **r** is all strings of only a's and the strings of some (not zero) a's ending in a single b. The closure of this language is defined by $(\mathbf{a}* + \mathbf{aa}*\mathbf{b})*$, which includes all words in which each b has an a on its left. Here **r*** is clearly not equal to **r**, since such words as aba and $ababaa$ are in **r*** but not in the language of **r**.

The machine we use to accept **r** is FA_1 pictured below.

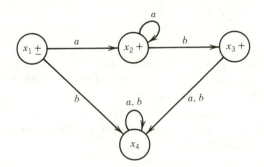

Notice that x_4 is a reject state. Any string that enters it stays there and is eventually rejected. A word that goes to x_2 and stops there is a word of all a's and it is accepted. To get to x_3 and stop there, we need exactly one b after the a's. It is true that x_1 is also a final state, but the only word that ends there is Λ.

The machine we shall build, FA_2, to accept the language defined by **r*** begins as follows.

$$\pm \; z_1 = x_1$$

If we are in z_1 and read a b, we go to the reject state x_4, which we call z_2.

$$z_2 = x_4$$

If we are in z_1 and read an a, we go to z_3, which means a little more than x_2 alone.

$$+z_3 = \begin{cases} x_2 \text{ and we continue processing the middle of a longer factor} \\ \text{of type } \mathbf{r} \text{ that itself may be only one of many substrings of} \\ \text{type } \mathbf{r} \text{ that the input word is composed of} \\ \qquad\qquad\qquad\qquad \text{or} \\ \text{we have just accepted a section of the input string as being} \\ \text{in the proper form for } \mathbf{r} \text{ and now we are back in } x_1 \text{ starting} \\ \text{again on the next section of the input string} \end{cases}$$

What we are trying to say here is that while we are scanning the input string we may have arrived at a break between one factor of type $\mathbf{r}$ and another factor of type $\mathbf{r}$, in which case the first ends correctly at a $+$ and the second should begin at the $-$. However, a factor of type $\mathbf{r}$ does not have to stop at the first $+$ that it comes to. It may terminate at the fourth $+$, and the new type $\mathbf{r}$ factor may then pick up at the $-$.

As we saw with the product of two machines when we hit a $+$ on the first machine we can continue on that machine or jump to the $-$ on the second. Here when we hit a $+$, we can also jump back to the $-$ (on the same machine) or we can ignore the $+$ status of the state and continue processing or (a new option) we can end.

This situation is like a bus with passengers. At each stop (final state) there is the possibility that some people get off while others stay on the bus waiting for their correct stops. Those that get off may jump back to start and get on another bus immediately. We are trying to trace where all these people could be at any given time. Where they are must be some collection of bus stops (states), and they are either finished, still inside the bus riding, or back at start.

If we ever get to z_2, the total input is to be rejected, so we stay at z_2. We know this mechanically (which means here that we know it without any intelligent insight, which is important since we should never need anything that the algorithm does not automatically provide) because x_4 loops back to x_4 by a and by b and therefore z_2 must do the same.

If we are in z_3 and we read a b, we go different places depending on which clause in the definition of z_3 was meant in a particular case. If z_3 meant x_2, we now go to x_3, but if z_3 meant that we are back in x_1, then we now go to x_4. Therefore, we have a new state. However, even when we are in x_3 we could be there in two ways. We could be continuing to run a string on FA_1 and proceed as normal or else we could have just accepted a part of the string and we are starting to process the next section from scratch at x_1. Therefore, z_4 has a triple meaning:

$$+ z_4 = x_1 \quad \text{or} \quad x_3 \quad \text{or} \quad x_4$$

Since x_3 is an accept state, z_4 can also accept a string that ends its path there.

Where do we go if we are in z_3 and we read an a? If we were in x_2 we stay there, whereas if we were back in x_1 we would go to x_2. Therefore, we return to z_3. Remember again that every $+$ state is also automatically a possible restart state jumping back to x_1.

If we are in z_4 and we read a b, whether we are in x_1, x_3, or x_4, we definitely go to x_4, which is z_2.

If we are in z_4 and we read an a, we go (if we were in x_1) to x_2 or (if we were in x_3) to x_4 or (if we were in x_4) to x_4. Therefore, we are in a new state

$$+ z_5 = x_1 \quad \text{or} \quad x_2 \quad \text{or} \quad x_4$$

which must be a final state since x_2 is.

From z_5 an a gets us to (x_1 or x_2 or x_4), which is z_5, whereas a b gets us to (x_1 or x_3 or x_4), which is z_4 again.

This finishes the description of the whole machine. It is pictured below.

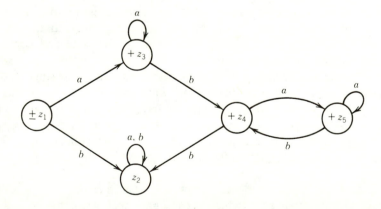

This is not actually a bad machine for the language defined by

$$(a^* + aa^*b)^*$$

The general rule for this algorithm is that each z state corresponds to some collection of x states. We must remember each time we reach a final state it is possible that we have to start over again at x_1. There are only finitely many possible collections of x states, so the machine produced by this algorithm has only finitely many states. The transitions from one collection of x states to another based on reading certain input letters is determined completely by the transition rules for FA_1. Therefore, this algorithm will always produce an FA, and the FA it produces satisfies our requirements.

Let us do another example. Consider the regular expression:

$$r = aa*bb*$$

This defines the language of all words where all the a's (of which there is at least one) come before all the b's (of which there is at least one). One FA that accepts this language is:

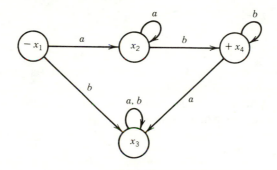

Now let us consider the language defined by $r*$.

$$r* = (aa*bb*)*$$

This is a collection of a's then b's then a's then b's and so on. Most words fit this pattern. In fact, the only strings not in this language are those that start with a b and those that end with an a. All other strings are words defined by $r*$. This $r*$ is almost equivalent to

$$a(a + b)*b$$

For example, *aababbb* is in $r*$ since (*aab*) is in r and (*abbb*) is in r. (Every string in $r*$ can be uniquely factored into its substrings of type r, but this is a side issue.) The string *abba* is definitely not in $r*$ since it ends in a.

Now let us build an FA for $r*$.
We begin with the start state:

$$- z_1 = x_1$$

Reading an a takes us to

$$z_2 = x_2$$

Reading a b in state z_1 takes us to

$$z_3 = x_3$$

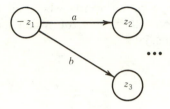

Like its counterpart x_3, z_3 is a point of no return (abandon all hope, ye that enter).

From z_2 if we read an a, we return to z_2, just as with x_2. From z_2 if we read a b, we proceed to a new state called z_4.

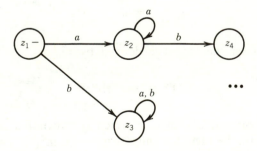

However, z_4 is not just x_4. Why? Because when we are processing the string $abab b$ and we get to z_4, we may have just accepted the first factor (ab) as being of the form **r** and be about to process the second factor starting again in the state x_1. On the other hand, if we are processing the string $abbab$ and we have only read the first two letters, even though we are in z_4 we have not completed reading the whole first factor of type **r**. Therefore,

$$+ \; z_4 = x_1 \text{ or } x_4$$

Because it is possible to end here and accept a string, this must be a final state, but we must have the option of continuing to read another factor (substring) of type **r** or to finish reading a factor we are in the middle of. If we are in z_4 and we read an a, we go to x_3 (if we were in x_4) or x_2 (if we were in x_1). Therefore, we could say that we are going to a new state:

$$z_5 = x_2 \text{ or } x_3$$

However, the option of being in x_3 is totally worthless. If we ever go there, we cannot accept the string. Remember x_3 is Davy Jones's locker. No string that gets there ever leaves or is ever accepted. So if we are interested in the paths by which strings can be accepted, we need only consider that when in z_4 if we read an a it is because we were in the x_1 part of z_4, not the x_4 part. This a, then, takes us back to z_2. (This is a touch of extra insight not actually provided by the algorithm. The algorithm requires us blindly to form a new state, z_6. We shall build both machines, the smart one and the algorithm one.)

If we are in z_2 and we read a b, we go to x_4 (if we were in x_4) or x_3 (if we were in x_1). Again, we need not consider the option of going to x_3 (the suicide option), since a path going there could accept no words. So instead of inventing a new state:

$$z_6 = x_1 \text{ or } x_3 \text{ or } x_4$$

which the algorithm above tells us to construct, we can simply assume that from z_4 a b always takes us to x_4. This is, of course, really the combination $(x_4 \text{ or } x_1)$ because we could now continue the processing of the next letter as if it were in the state x_1 having just accepted a factor of type **r**. This is the case with the word *abbab*.

These options, x_1 or x_4, are already the definition of state z_4, so we have finished our machine.

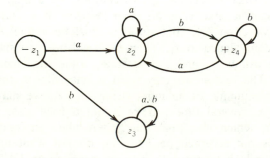

If we had mechanically followed the algorithm in the proof, we would have constructed

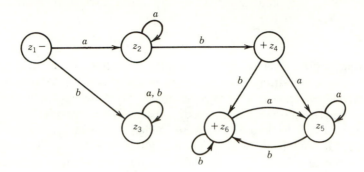

For some applications it may be important to construct the entire machine mechanically as above because accepting an input string in z_4 may somehow be different from accepting it in z_6 (the cost could be different, or the storage space, etc.). For our simple purposes, there is no difference between these two machines.

In both of these diagrams it is clear that in order to be accepted the only conditions a string must satisfy are that it begin with an a and end with a b. Therefore, because we understand the language $\mathbf{r}^*$ and we understand these two machines, we know that they truly represent the language $\mathbf{r}^*$ as desired.

Before we feel completely satisfied with ourselves we should realize that neither of the machines we have built accepts the word Λ, which must be in the closure of any language. What went wrong was at the very beginning when we said that z_1 was the equivalent of x_1. This is true only when x_1 is also a final state, since otherwise z_1, which must be a final state, cannot be its true twin. z_1 can act like x_1 in all other respects as a starting state for the acceptance of a word on FA_1, but since z_1 must be a final state, we cannot simply posit its equivalence to x_1. What we need are two states that are like x_1. One of them will be x_1 and a final state, while the other will be x_1 and a nonfinal state. The reason we may need a state like x_1 that is not a final state is that in the running of an input string on FA_1 we may be required to reenter the state x_1 several times. If x_1 is not a final state in FA_1, but we convert it into z_1, which is a final state, then when an input string ends in x_1 on FA_1 and is not accepted on FA_1, we do not want mistakenly to say that it ends in z_1, which then causes it to be accepted on FA_2. In the machine we have at present, this is no problem since the state x_1 on FA_1 can never be reentered (no edges go into x_1). Therefore, we can say that the z_1 we have is sufficient to represent x_1 in all its uses. An accurate machine for the language defined by **(aa*bb*)*** is this:

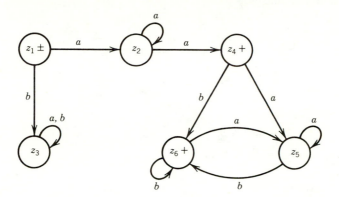

To illustrate the possible need for two different states representing x_1, we have to start with a machine that does not accept Λ but that does allow the state x_1 to be reentered in the path for some input words. One such FA is the one below, which accepts the language of all words with an odd number of b's.

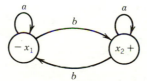

Let us practice our algorithm on this machine.

The first state we want is z_1, which must be like x_1 except that it is also a final state. If we are in z_1 and we read an a, we come back to x_1, but this time in its capacity as a nonfinal state. We have to give a different name to this state; let us call it z_2.

$$z_1 = x_1 \text{ and a final state}$$
$$z_2 = x_1 \text{ and a nonfinal state}$$

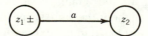

If we are in z_1 and we read a b, we must go to a state like x_2. Now since x_2 is a final state, we must also include the possibility that once we enter x_2

we immediately proceed as if we were back in x_1. Therefore, the state z_3 that we go to is simply x_1 or x_2 and a final state because of x_2.

At this point the machine looks like this:

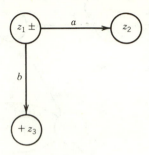

If we are in z_2 and we read an a, we stay in z_2. If we are in z_2 and we read a b, we go to z_3. If we are in z_3 and we read an a, it will take us back to z_3, since if we were in x_1 we would stay in x_1 and if we were in x_2 we would stay in x_2. If we are in z_3 and we read a b, then we also return to z_3, since if we were in x_1, then we would go to x_2, and if we were in x_2 we would go to x_1. The whole machine is this:

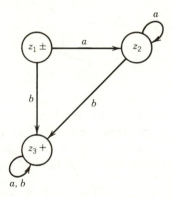

The only words not accepted by this machine are words of solid a's. All other words are clearly the concatenation of substrings with one b each and are therefore in the closure of the language of FA_1.

This is another example of how the null string may have no letters yet still be a royal pain in the neck. One regular expression defining the language of all words with an odd number of b's is

$$r = a*b(a*ba*b)*a*$$

therefore the regular expression

$$r* = [a*b(a*ba*b)*a*]*$$

defines the language of all words that are not of the form **aa***. Another regular expression for this language is

$$\Lambda + (a + b)*b(a + b)*$$

Therefore,

$$\Lambda + (a + b)*b(a + b)* = [a*b(a*ba*b)*a*]*$$

It is hard to imagine an algebraic proof of this equation. The problem of determining when two regular expressions define the same language will be discussed in Chapter 12.

We have now developed algorithms that, when taken together, finish the proof of part three of Kleene's theorem. (We have been in the middle of this project for so long it is possible to lose our perspective.)

Because of Rule 1, Rule 2, Rule 3, and Rule 4, we know that all regular expressions have corresponding finite automata that give the same language. This is because while we are building the regular expression from the recursive definition we can simultaneously be building the corresponding FA from the four algorithms shown above. This is a powerful example of the strength of recursive definitions.

As an example, suppose we want to find an FA to accept the language for the regular expression **(ab)*a(ab + a*)***. Since this is a regular expression, it can be built up by repeated applications of the rules: any letter, sum, product, star.

The lengthy process of expression and machine-building can proceed as follows: a is a letter in the alphabet, so there is an FA that accepts it called FA_1. Now b is a letter in the alphabet, so there is a machine that accepts it, FA_2. Then **ab** is the language of the product of the two machines FA_1 and FA_2, so there is a machine to accept it, FA_3. Then **(ab)*** is the language of the closure of the machine FA_3, so there is a machine to accept it, call it FA_4.

Now **a*** is the language of the closure of the machine FA_1, so there is an FA to accept it called FA_5. Now **ab + a*** is the language of the sum of FA_3 and FA_5, so there is a machine to accept it, FA_6. Now **(ab + a*)*** is the language of the closure of FA_6; therefore, there is a machine to accept it, FA_7. Now **a(ab + a*)*** is the product of FA_1 and FA_7, so there is a machine to accept it, FA_8. Now **(ab)*a(ab + a*)*** is the product of machines FA_4 and FA_8, call it FA_9. Done.

All regular expressions can be handled the same way. We have shown that every language accepted by an FA can be accepted by a TG, every language accepted by a TG can be defined by a regular expression, and every language defined by a regular expression can be accepted by an FA. This concludes the proof of all of Kleene's theorem.   ■

The proof has been **constructive,** which means that we have not only shown that there is a correspondence between regular expressions, FA's and TG's, but we have also shown exactly how to find examples of the things that correspond. Given any one we can build the other two using the techniques outlined in the proof above.

Because TG's seem more understandable, we often work with them instead of struggling with the rigors of FA's (especially having to specify what happens in every state to every letter).

The biggest surprise of this theorem may be that TG's are not any more powerful than FA's in the sense that there are no extra languages that TG's can accept that FA's could not handle already. This is too bad because we shall soon show that there are some languages that FA's cannot accept, and we shall need a more powerful type of machine than a TG to deal with them.

Even though with a TG we had the right to exercise some degree of judgment—we made some decisions about sectioning the reading of the input string—we could do no better than a purely automatic robot like an FA. The human input factor was worth essentially nothing.

PROBLEMS

For the following transition graphs use the algorithm of this chapter to find an equivalent regular expression. Then simplify the expression if possible.

1.

2.

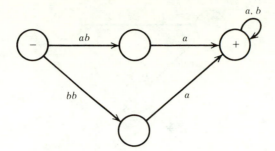

3.

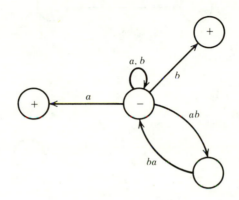

4.

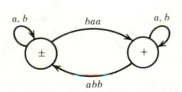

5.

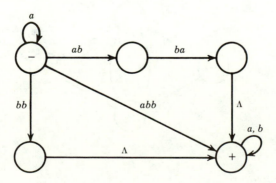

6.

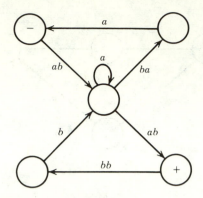

7. Consider the following finite automata:

FA_1 FA_2

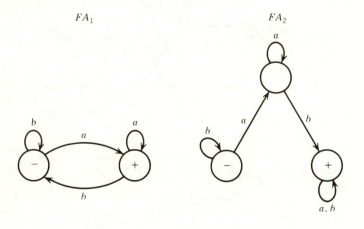

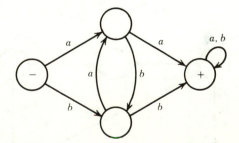

Find regular expressions r_1, r_2, r_3 for these, respectively, and simplify the expressions if possible. Describe these languages in English.

Using the algorithms in this chapter and the three FA's from Problem 7 find FA's for the following:

8. $r_1 + r_2$

9. $r_1 + r_3$

10. $r_2 + r_3$

11. r_1r_2

12. r_1r_3

13. r_2r_3

14. r_2r_1

15. r_1r_1

16. $(r_1)^*$

17. $(r_2)^*$

18. $(r_3)^*$

19. Based on the regular expressions in Problems 8 through 18, answer these questions: Is the machine for r_1r_2 the same as the machine for r_2r_1? Why? Is the machine for $r_1 + r_2$ the same as the machine for $r_2 + r_1$? Why? Is the machine for r_1r_1 the same as the machine for $(r_1)^*$? Why? Would the machine for r_2r_2 be the same as the machine for $(r_2)^*$? Why?

20. If some automaton, FA_1, has n_1 states and some other automaton, FA_2, has n_2 states, what is the maximum number of states possible in the machines the algorithms in this chapter produce for the automata corresponding to

    (i) $FA_1 + FA_2$

    (ii) FA_1FA_2

    (iii) $(FA_1)^*$

CHAPTER 8

NONDETERMINISM

In our discussion of transition graphs in Chapter 6, there was one point that we glossed over that is actually a subtlety of great depth. We said that we would label every edge of the graph with any string of alphabet letters (perhaps even the null string Λ). We even allowed two edges coming out of the same state to have exactly the same label:

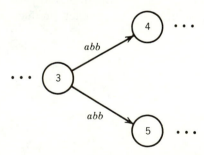

If we tried to forbid people from writing this directly, they could sneak it into TG's in other ways:

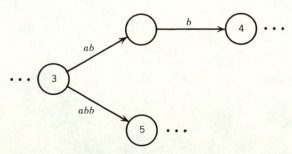

Even if we restrict labels to strings of only one letter or Λ, we may indirectly permit these two equivalent situations:

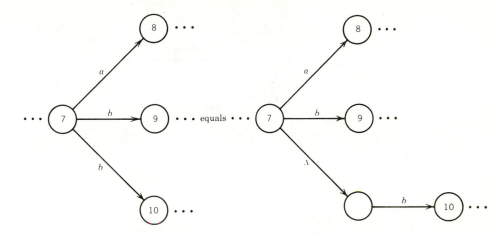

We have already seen that in a TG a particular string of input letters may trace through the machine on different paths, depending on our choice of grouping. For instance, *abb* can go from state 3 to 4 or 5 in the middle example above depending on whether we read the letters two and one or all three at once. The ultimate path through the machine is not determined by the input alone. Therefore, we say this machine is **nondeterministic.** Human choice becomes a factor in selecting the path; the machine does not make all its own determinations. Remember that a string is accepted by the machine if *at least one* sequence of choices leads to a path that ends at a final state.

In 1959, Michael Oser Rabin and Dana Scott introduced the notion of nondeterminism for language-recognizing finite automata.

DEFINITION

A **nondeterministic finite automaton** (NFA) is a collection of three things:

1. A finite set of states with one start state $(-)$ and some final states $(+)$.
2. An alphabet Σ of possible input letters.
3. A finite set of transitions that describe how to proceed from each state to other states along edges labeled with letters of the alphabet (but not Λ), where we allow the possibility of more than one edge with the same label from any state and some states for which certain input letters have no edge. ∎

Some authors argue that an NFA is not a special case of a TG since they insist in their definition that a TG is not allowed more than one edge from one state with the same label. (We did not insist on this in our definition.)

Let us observe that we can replace all same-labeled edges using this trick:

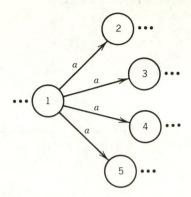

is equivalent to

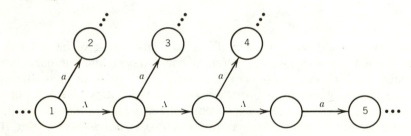

or this trick:

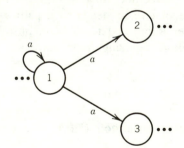

is equivalent to

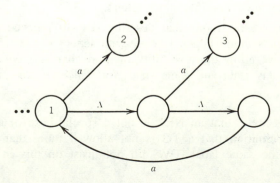

Therefore, we can convert any NFA into a TG with no repeated labels from any single state.

Let us also observe that every deterministic finite automaton can be considered as an example of an NFA where we did not make use of the extra possible features. Nowhere in the definition of NFA did we *insist* that an NFA have nondeterministic branching. Any FA will satisfy the definition of an NFA. So we have:

1. Every FA is an NFA.
2. Every NFA has an equivalent TG.
3. By Kleene's theorem, every TG has an equivalent FA.

Therefore:

$$\text{languages of FA's} \subset \text{languages of NFA's} \subset \text{languages of TG's} = \text{languages of FA's}$$

THEOREM 7

$$FA = NFA$$

by which we mean that any language definable by a nondeterministic finite automaton is also definable by a deterministic (ordinary) finite automaton and vice versa. We say then that they are of **equal power**. ■

Let us not mistake the equation FA = NFA as meaning that every NFA *is itself* an FA. This is not true. Only that for every NFA there is *some* FA that is equivalent to it as a language acceptor.

NFA's may sometimes be easier or more intuitive to use than FA's to define a given language. One example of this is a machine to combine two FA's, one that accepts the language of the regular expression r_1 and the other for the language of the regular expression r_2. If the start states in these two machines have no edges coming into them, we can produce an NFA_3 that accepts exactly the language of $r_1 + r_2$ by amalgamating the two start states. This is illustrated below.

Let FA_1 be

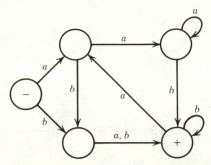

And let FA_2 be

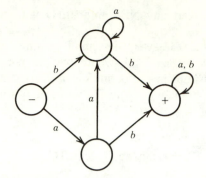

Then $NFA_3 = FA_1 + FA_2$ is

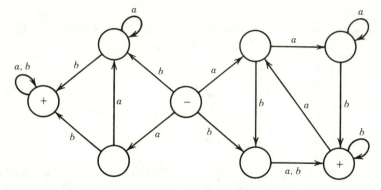

Nondeterminism does not increase the power of an FA, but we shall see that it does increase the power of the more powerful machines introduced later.

EXAMPLE

It is sometimes easier to understand what a language is from the picture of an NFA that accepts it than from the picture of an FA. Let us take, for example, the language of all words that contain either a triple a (the substring aaa) or a triple b (the substring bbb) or both. The NFA below does an obvious job of accepting this language.

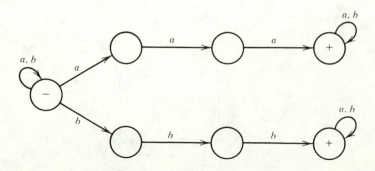

If a word contains *aaa* somewhere inside of it, it can be accepted by a path along the high road. If it contains *bbb*, it can be accepted along the low road. If a word has both, it can use either route. Clearly, anything that gets to + has one of these substrings.

Let us now build an FA that accepts this language. It must have a start state. From the start state, it must have a path of three edges to accept the word *aaa*. It needs three edges because otherwise a shorter string of *a*'s could be accepted. Therefore, we begin our machine with

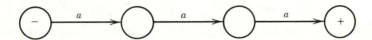

For similar reasons, we can deduce that there must be a path for *bbb* that has no loop and uses entirely different states. If it shared any of the same states, we could begin with *a*'s and pick up with *b*'s. So we must have at least two more states since we could share the last state of the three-edge path with one of the *a* states already drawn.

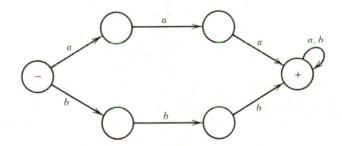

If we are along the *a* path and read a *b* before the third *a*, we jump to the beginning of the *b* path and vice versa. The whole FA then looks like this:

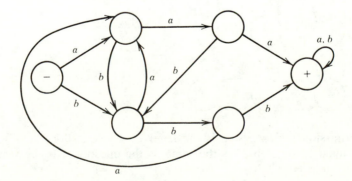

We can understand this FA because we have seen it built, but the NFA is still much easier to interpret. ∎

Nondeterminism can have important practical applications, in particular in the subject of artificial intelligence (AI). We shall demonstrate this on one simple example.

Suppose the problem we want to solve is the maze below:

−	░		░
	░		░
	░		+

The rules are that we start at − and can proceed from square to adjacent square. We can walk only in empty squares, the dark squares are walls. When we get to the + we stop. This is not a very hard maze to figure out, but we are only taking an illustrative example.

Let us number the open squares as follows:

−	1	2	3
4	░	5	░
6	░	7	░
8	░	9	+

Let us build the following nondeterministic finite automaton in which every state represents a square in the maze and one state can be reached from the other in the NFA only if the same move is possible in the maze.

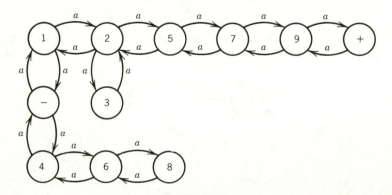

The permission for each step is the letter a. The question, "Does this maze have a solution in six steps?" is the same as the question, "Is the word $aaaaaa$ accepted by this NFA?"

If the language for the NFA of some other maze was {aaa, $aaaaa$}, that would mean that there was a solution path of three steps and one of five steps.

An algorithm that found all the words accepted by an NFA would automatically tell us all the lengths of the solution paths to all mazes. We already have such an algorithm. If we consider this NFA as a TG and apply the TG into regular expression conversion algorithm of Chapter 7, we discover, after simplification, that the language accepted by this machine is defined by **aaaaaa(aa)***, which means that there are solutions of six steps, eight steps, ten steps, and so on.

COMPARISON TABLE FOR AUTOMATA (Version 1)

	FA	**TG**	**NFA**
Start states	One	One or more	One
Final states	Some or none	Some or none	Some or none
Edge labels	Letters from Σ	Words from Σ^*	Letters from Σ
Number of edges from each state	One for each letter in Σ	Arbitrary	Arbitrary
Deterministic (Every input string has one path)	Yes	Not necessarily	Not necessarily
Every path represents one word	Yes	Yes	Yes

PROBLEMS

1. In the example for NFA_3 above, why was it necessary to stipulate that no edges come into the two different start states? What can be done to add two machines when this condition fails?

2. Suppose NFA_1 is a machine for the regular expression r_1 and NFA_2 for the regular expression r_2. Further suppose that NFA_1 has only one $+$ state and that this state has no edges leading out of it (even back to itself). Show how to make a simple NFA for the language r_1r_2.

3. Can anything be done, similar to Problem 2, for $(\mathbf{r}_1)^*$?

4. (i)   How many NFA's are there with exactly two states where there can be 0, 1, or 2 final states and where the states may even be disconnected?

    (ii) How many are there if the states cannot be disconnected?

    (iii) How many different connected NFA's are there with two states that accept at least one word? (Be careful: We are counting machines not languages.)

Let us now introduce a machine called "a nondeterministic finite automaton with null string labels," abbreviated NFA-Λ. This machine follows the same rules as an NFA except that we are allowed to have edges labeled with the null string Λ, as in the example below:

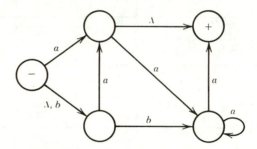

5. What words are accepted by the machine pictured above?

6. Prove that NFA-Λ's have the same power as FA's, that is, show that any language accepted by a machine of one type can also be accepted by a machine of the other.

7. Show that NFA-Λ's can be added, concatenated, and starred quite easily (without the extra conditions required for NFA's).

Convert the following NFA-Λ's into FA's.

8.   9.

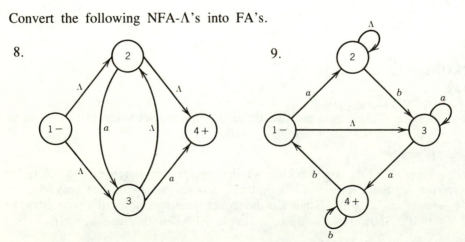

What is the language for each of the NFA's pictured below? Write regular expressions for each.

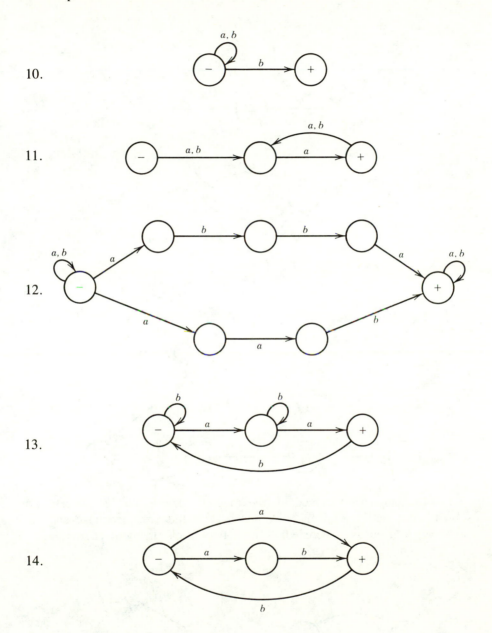

10.

11.

12.

13.

14.

15.   Build FA's for the languages in Problems 10 through 14.

For each of the following FA's, find NFA's that have fewer states and accept the same language.

16.

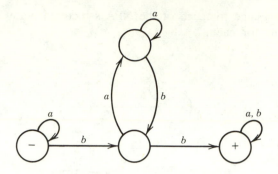

17.

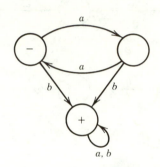

18.

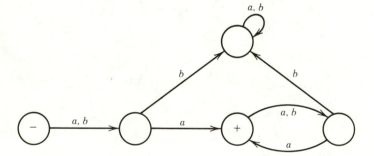

19. For the language accepted by the machine below, find a different FA with four states. Find an NFA that accepts the same language and has only seven edges (where edges with two labels are counted twice).

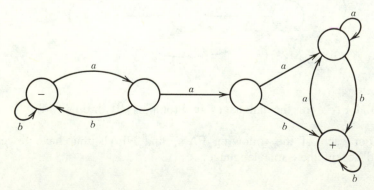

20. A one-person game can be converted into an NFA as follows. Let every possible board situation be a state. If any move (there may be several types of moves but we are not interested in distinguishing among them) can change some state x into some state y, then draw an edge from x to y and label it m. Label the initial position $-$ and the winning positions $+$. "This game can be won in five moves" is the same as saying "m^5 is accepted by this NFA." Once we have the NFA we use the algorithm of Chapter 7 to convert it into a regular expression. The language it represents tells us how many moves are in each winning sequence.

Let us do this with the following example. The game of Flips is played with three coins. Initially they are all heads. A move consists of flipping two coins simultaneously from whatever they were to the opposite side. For example, flipping the end coins changes THH into HHT. We win when all three coins are tails. There are eight possible states: HHH, HHT,. . . . TTT. The only $-$ is HHH; the only $+$ is TTT. Draw this NFA, labeling any edge that can flip between states with the letter m.

Convert this NFA into a regular expression. Is m^3 or m^5 in the language of this machine? The shortest word in this language is the shortest solution of this puzzle. What is it?

CHAPTER 9

FINITE AUTOMATA WITH OUTPUT

In our discussion of finite automata in Chapter 5, our motivation was in part to design a mathematical model for a computer. We said that the input string represents the program and input data. Reading the letters from the string is analogous to executing instructions in that it changes the state of the machine, that is, it changes the contents of memory, changes the control section of the computer, and so on. Part of this "and so on," that was not made explicit before is the question of output. We mentioned that we could consider the output as part of the total state of the machine. This could mean two different things: one, that to enter a specific computer state means change memory a certain way and print a specific character, or two, that a state includes both the present condition of memory plus the total output thus far. In other words, the state could reflect what we are now printing or what we have printed in total. One natural question to ask is, "If we have these two different models, do these machines have equal power or are there some tasks that one can do that the other cannot?"

154

If we assume that all the printing of output is to be done at the end of the program run, at which time we have an instruction that dumps a buffer, then we have a maximum on the number of characters that the program can print, namely the size of the buffer. However, theoretically we should be able to have outputs of any finite length. For example, we might simply want to print out a copy of the input string, which could be arbitrarily long.

These are questions that have to be faced if we are to claim that our mathematical models of FA's and TG's represent actual physical machines. So far we have used finite automata only as acceptors or recognizers of languages; in this chapter we shall investigate two different models for FA's with output capabilities. These were created by G. H. Mealy (1955) and, independently, by E. F. Moore (1956). The original purpose of the inventors was to design a mathematical model for sequential circuits, which are only one component of a whole computer. It is an important component, and as we shall see, acts as a machine all by itself. We shall present these two models, prove that they are equivalent, and give some examples of how they arise in sequential circuits.

DEFINITION

A **Moore machine** is a collection of five things:

1. A finite set of states q_0, q_1, q_2 . . . where q_0 is designated as the start state.

2. An alphabet of letters for forming the input string
$$\Sigma = \{ a, b, c, \ldots \}.$$

3. An alphabet of possible output characters
$$\Gamma = \{ x, y, z, \ldots \}.$$

4. A transition table that shows for *each* state and *each* input letter what state is reached next.

5. An output table that shows what character from Γ is printed by each state that is entered. ∎

Notice that we did not assume that the input alphabet Σ is the same as the output alphabet Γ. When dealing with twentieth-century machines, both input and output are usually encoded strings of 0's and 1's. However, we may interpret the input bit strings as instructions in a programming language. We may also wish to group the strings of output bits into codes for typewriter characters. We discuss whether it is necessary to have more than two letters in an alphabet in Chapter 29.

To keep the output alphabet separate from the input alphabet, we give it a different name, Γ instead of Σ, and for its letters we use symbols from the other end of the Latin alphabet: $\{x, y, z \ldots\}$ or numbers $\{0, 1 \ldots\}$ instead of $\{a, b, c \ldots\}$. Moreover, we refer to the input symbols (as we always have) as **letters,** while we call the output symbols **characters.**

As we shall see from our circuitry examples, the knowledge of which state is the start state is not always important in applications. If the machine is run several times, it may continue from where it left off rather than restart. Because of this, we can define the Moore machine in two ways: Either the first symbol printed is the character always specified in the start state or else it is the character specified in the next state, which is the first state *chosen.* We shall adopt the policy that a Moore machine always begins by printing the character dictated by the mandatory start state. This difference is not significant (see Problem 13 below). If the input string has 7 letters, then the output string will have 8 characters because it includes eight states in its path.

Because the word "outputted" is so ugly, we shall say "printed" instead, even though we realize that the output device does not technically have to be a printer.

A Moore machine does not define a language of accepted words, since every input string creates an output string and there is no such thing as a final state. The processing is terminated when the last input letter is read and the last output character is printed. Nevertheless, there are subtle ways to turn Moore machines into language definers (see Problem 12 below).

Moore machines have pictorial representations very similar to their cousins the FA's. We start with little circles depicting the states and directed edges between them labeled with input letters. The difference is that instead of having only the name of the state inside the little circle, we also specify the output character printed by that state. The two symbols inside the circle are separated by a slash "/". On the left side is the name of the state and on the right is the output from that state.

EXAMPLE

Let us consider an example defined first by a table:

Input alphabet: $\Sigma = \{a, b\}$
Output alphabet: $\Gamma = \{0, 1\}$
Names of states: q_0, q_1, q_2, q_3, ($q_0 = $ start state)

	Transition Table		Output Table
	New State		(The Character Printed in the
Old State	After Input a	After Input b	Old State)
$- \ q_0$	q_1	q_3	1
q_1	q_3	q_1	0
q_2	q_0	q_3	0
q_3	q_3	q_2	1

The pictorial representation of this Moore machine is

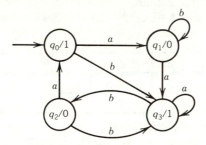

In Moore machines, so much information is written inside the state circles that there is no room for the minus sign indicating the start state. We usually indicate the start state by an outside arrow as shown above. As mentioned before there is no need for any plus signs either, since any input string will generate an output string and can end in any state having done an acceptable job.

Let us trace the operation of this machine on the input string *abab*. We always start this machine off in start q_0, which automatically prints out the character 1. We then read the first letter of the input string, which is an *a* and which sends us to state q_1. This state tells us to print a 0. The next input letter is a *b*, and the loop shows that we return to state q_1. Being in q_1 again, we print another 0. Then we read an *a*, go to q_3, and print a 1. Next we read a *b*, go to q_2, and print a 0. This is the end of the run. The output sequence has been 10010. ∎

EXAMPLE

Suppose we were interested in knowing exactly how many times the substring *aab* occurs in a long input string. The following Moore machine will "count" this for us:

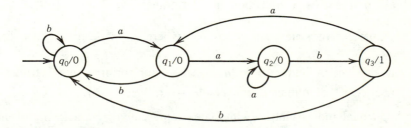

Every state of this machine prints out the character 0 except for state q_3, which prints a 1. To get to state q_3, we must have come from state q_2 and have just read a *b*. To get to state q_2, we must have just read at least two *a*'s in a row, having started in any state. After finding the substring *aab* and tallying a 1 for it, we begin to look for the next *aab*. If we read a *b*, we start the search in q_0; if we read an *a*, we start in q_1. The number of substrings *aab* in the input string will be exactly the number of 1's in the output string.

Input	String		a	a	a	b	a	b	b	a	a	b	b
	State	q_0	q_1	q_2	q_2	q_3	q_1	q_0	q_0	q_1	q_2	q_3	q_0
	Output	0	0	0	0	1	0	0	0	0	0	1	0

To count up how many 1's are in the output string we could use bit collection methods from assembly-language programming, depending on the application we have in mind. ∎

The example above is part of a whole class of useful Moore machines. Given a language *L* and an FA that accepts it, if we add the printing instruction 0 to any nonfinal state and 1 to each final state, the 1's in any output sequence mark the end position of all substrings of the input string starting from the first letter that are words in *L*. The machine above with $q_0 = -$, $q_3 = +$ accepts all words that end in *aab*.

Our next subject is another variation of the FA called the **Mealy machine.** A Mealy machine is like a Moore machine except that now we do our printing while we are traveling along the edges, not in the states themselves. If we are in state q_4 and we are proceeding to q_7, we do not simply print what q_7 tells us. What we print depends on the edge we take. If there are two different edges from q_4 to q_7, one an *a*-edge and one a *b*-edge, it is possible that they will have different printing instructions for us. We take no printing instructions from the state itself.

DEFINITION

A **Mealy machine** is a collection of four things:

1. A finite set of states q_0, q_1, q_2 . . . where q_0 is designated as the start state.

2. An alphabet of letters $\Sigma = \{a, b, \ldots\}$ for forming input strings.

3. An alphabet of output characters $\Gamma = \{x, y, z \ldots\}$.

4. A pictorial representation with states represented by small circles and directed edges indicating transitions between states. Each edge is labeled with a compound symbol of the form *i/o* where *i* is an input letter and *o* is an output character. *Every* state must have exactly one outgoing edge for *each* possible input letter The edge we travel is determined by the input letter *i*; while traveling on the edge we must print the output character *o*. ∎

We have for the sake of variation defined a Mealy machine by its pictorial representation. Another reason is that the table definition is not as simple as that for a Moore machine (see the problem section below).

EXAMPLE

The following picture represents a Mealy machine:

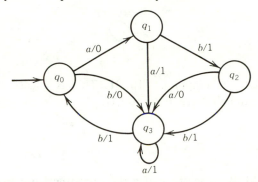

Notice that when we arrive in state q_3 we may have just printed a 1 or a 0. If we came from state q_0 by the b-road, we printed a 0. If we got there from q_1 by the a-road, we printed a 1. If we got there from q_2, it depends on whether we took the a-road and printed a 0 or the b-road and printed a 1. If we were in q_3 before and looped back on the input a, we then printed a 1. Every time we enter q_1 we have just printed a 0, but it is not always possible to tell this information from the destination state alone.

Let us trace the running of this machine on the input sequence $aaabb$. We start in state q_0. In distinction to the Moore machine, here we do not have to print the same character each time we start up, even before getting a look at the input. The first input letter is an a, which takes us to q_1 and prints a 0. The second letter is an a, which takes to q_3 and prints a 1. The third letter is an a, which loops us back to q_3 and prints a 1. The fourth letter is a b, which takes us back to q_0 and prints a 1. The fifth letter is a b, which takes us to q_3 and prints a 0. The output string for this input is 01110. ■

Notice that in a Mealy machine the output string has the same number of characters as the input string has letters. As with the Moore machine, the Mealy machine does not define a language, so it has no final states. However, we will see shortly that there is a sense in which it can recognize a language.

If there are two edges going in the same direction between the same pair of states, we can draw only one arrow and represent the choice of label by the usual comma.

EXAMPLE

The simplest example of a useful Mealy machine is one that prints out the
1's complement of an input bit string. This means that we want to produce
a bit string that has a 1 wherever the input string has a 0 and a 0 wherever
the input has a 1. For example, the input 101 should become the output 010.
One machine that does this is:

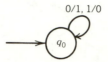

If the input is 001010 the output is 110101. This is a case where the input
alphabet and output alphabet are both {0, 1}.   ∎

EXAMPLE

We now consider a Mealy machine called the **increment machine** that assumes
that its input is a binary number and prints out the binary number that is one
larger. We assume that the input bit string is a binary number fed in backwards,
that is, units digit first (then 2's digit, 4's digit . . .). The output string will
be the binary representation of the number one greater and will also be generated units bit first (backwards).

   The machine will have three states: start, owe-carry, no-carry. The owe-
carry state represents the overflow when two bits equal to 1 are added—we
print a 0 and we carry a 1.

   From the start state we read the first bit. If we read in a 0, we print a
1 and we do not owe a carry bit. If we read a 1, we print a 0 and we do
owe a carry bit. If at any point in the process we are in no-carry (which
means that we do not owe a carry), we print the next bit just as we read it
and remain in no-carry. However, if at some point in the process we are in
owe-carry, the situation is different. If we read a 0, we print a 1 and go to
the no-carry state. If we are in owe-carry and we read a 1, we print a 0 and
we loop back to owe-carry. The complete picture for this machine is:

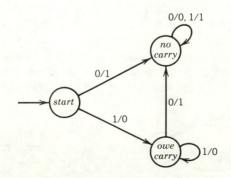

Let us watch this machine in action on the binary representation for the number eleven, 1011. The string is fed into the machine as 1101 (backwards). The first 1 causes a 0 to be printed and sends us to owe-carry. The next 1 causes a 0 to be printed and loops back to owe-carry. The next input letter is a 0 and causes a 1 to be printed on our way to no-carry. The next bit, 1, is printed out, as it is fed in, on the no-carry loop. The total output string is 0011, which when reversed is 1100, and is, as desired, the binary representation for the number twelve.

As simple as this machine is, it can be simplified even further (see Problem 18).

This machine has the typical Mealy machine property that the output string is exactly as long as the input string. This means that if we ran this incrementation machine on the input 1111 we would get 0000. We must interpret the owe-carry state as an overflow situation if a string ever ends there. ■

There is a connection between Mealy machines and sequential circuits (which we touch on at the end of this chapter) that makes them a very valuable component of Computer Theory. The two examples we have just presented are also valuable to computing. Once we have an incrementer, we can build a machine that can perform the addition of binary numbers, and then we can use the 1's complementing machine to build a subtracting machine based on the following principle:

If a and b are strings of bits, then the subtraction a − b can be performed by (1) adding the 1's complement of b to a ignoring any overflow digit and (2) incrementing the results by 1.

For example,

$$
\begin{aligned}
14 - 5 \text{ (decimal)} &= 1110 - 0101 \text{ (binary)} \\
&\rightarrow 1110 + 1\text{'s complement of } 0101 + 1 \text{ (binary)} \\
&= 1110 + 1010 + 1 \text{ (binary)} \\
&= [1]1001 \text{ binary} \rightarrow \text{(dropping the [1])} = 9 \text{ (decimal)}
\end{aligned}
$$

$$
\begin{aligned}
18 - 7 &= 10010 - 00111 \rightarrow 10010 + 11000 + 1 \\
&= [1]01011 \rightarrow 01011 = 11 \text{ (decimal)}
\end{aligned}
$$

The same trick works in decimal notation if we use 9's complements, that is, replace each digit d in the second number by the digit $(9 - d)$. For example, $46 - 17 \rightarrow 46 + 82 + 1 = [1]29 \rightarrow 29$.

EXAMPLE

Even though a Mealy machine does not accept or reject an input string, it can recognize a language by making its output string answer some questions about the input. We have discussed before the language of all words that have a double letter in them. The Mealy machine below will take a string of *a*'s and *b*'s and print out a string of 0's and 1's such that if the *n*th output character is a 1 it means that the *n*th input letter is the second in a pair of double letters. For example *ababbaab* becomes 00001010 with 1's in the position of the second of each pair of repeated letters.

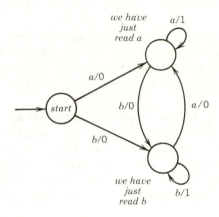

This is similar to the Moore machine that recognized the number of occurrences of the substring *aab*. This machine recognizes the occurrences of *aa* or *bb*. Notice that the triple letter word *aaa* produces the output 011 since the second and third letters are both the back end of a pair of double *a*'s. ∎

So far, our definition of the equivalence of two machines has been that they accept the same language. In this sense we cannot compare a Mealy machine and a Moore machine. However, we may say that two output automata are equivalent if they always give the same output string when presented with the same input string. In this way, two Mealy machines may be equivalent and two Moore machines may be equivalent, but a Moore machine can never be equivalent to a Mealy machine because the length of the output string from a Moore machine is one longer than that from a Mealy machine given the same input. The problem is that a Moore machine always begins with one automatic start symbol.

To get around this difficulty, we define a Mealy machine to be equivalent to a Moore machine whenever they always result in the same output if the automatic start symbol for the Moore machine is deleted from the front of the output.

DEFINITION

Given the Mealy machine *Me* and the Moore machine *Mo*, which prints the automatic start-state character *x*, we will say that these two machines are **equivalent** if for every input string the output string from *Mo* is exactly *x* concatenated with the output from *Me*. ∎

Rather than debate the merits of the two types of machine, we prove that for every Moore machine there is an equivalent Mealy machine and for every Mealy machine there is an equivalent Moore machine. We can then say that the two types of machine are completely equivalent.

THEOREM 8

If *Mo* is a Moore machine, then there is a Mealy machine *Me* that is equivalent to it.

PROOF

The proof will be by constructive algorithm. Consider any particular state in *Mo*—call it q_4. It gives instructions to print a certain character—call it *t*. Let us consider all the edges that enter this state. Each of them is labeled with an input letter. Let us change this. Let us relabel all the edges coming into q_4. If they were previously labeled *a* or *b* or *c* . . . , let them now be labeled *a/t* or *b/t* or *c/t* . . . and let us erase the *t* from inside the state q_4. This means that we shall be printing a *t* on the incoming edges before they enter q_4.

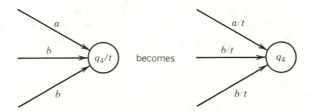

We leave the outgoing edges from q_4 alone. They will be relabeled to print the character associated with the state to which they lead.

If we repeat this procedure for every state q_0, q_1, . . . , we turn *Mo* into a Mealy machine *Me*. As we move from state to state, the things that get printed are exactly what *Mo* would have printed itself.

The symbol that used to be printed automatically when the machine started in state q_0 is no longer the first output character, but this does not stop the rest of the output string from being the same.

Therefore, every *Mo* is equivalent to some *Me*. ∎

EXAMPLE

Below, a Moore machine is converted into a Mealy machine by the algorithm of the proof above. ∎

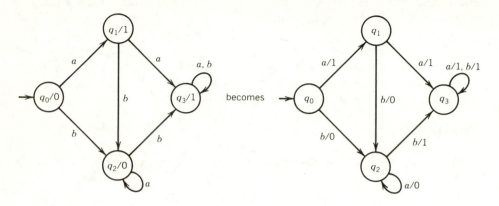

THEOREM 9

For every Mealy machine *Me* there is a Moore machine *Mo* that is equivalent to it.

PROOF

Again the proof will be by constructive algorithm.

We cannot just do the reverse of the previous procedure. If we were to try to push the printing instruction from the edge as it is in *Me* to the inside of the state as it should be for a Moore machine, we might end up with a conflict. Two edges might come into the same state but have different printing instructions, as in this example.

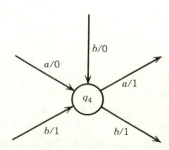

What we need then are twin copies of the same state. The edge $a/0$ will go into $q_4{}^1$ (q_4 copy 1) and the edge $b/1$ will go into $q_4{}^2$ (q_4 copy 2). The edge labeled $b/0$ will also go into q_4^1. Inside these states, we include the printing instuctions $q_4^1/0$ and $q_4^2/1$. The arrows coming out of each of these copies of what used to be q_4 must be the same as the edges coming out of q_4 originally. We get two sets of the output edges each equal to the original out-edges but the one set of original in-edges is divided between the two copies. The example above becomes:

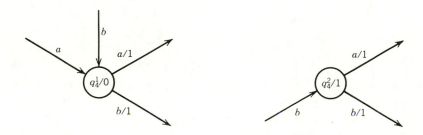

The instruction to print a 0 or a 1 is now found inside the state, not along the edge.

State by state we repeat this procedure. If all the edges coming into the object state have the same printing instruction, then we can simply move that printing instruction into the state. This does not effect the edges coming out of the state.

If there is more than one possibility for printing as we enter the state, then we need a copy of the state for each character we might have to print. (We may need as many copies as there are characters in Γ.) All the edges that entered a certain state that used to be labeled

something / t

now lead into the copy of that state that instructs us to print the character t. Each of the copies of the orginal state retains a complete set of the original outgoing edges. The labels on the incoming edges lose their printing instructions. The letters on the outgoing edges retain them if they have not lost them already. This algorithm slowly turns a Mealy into a Moore state by state.

One interesting consequence of this algorithm is that an edge that was a loop in *Me* may become one edge that is not a loop and one that is a loop in *Mo*. For example,

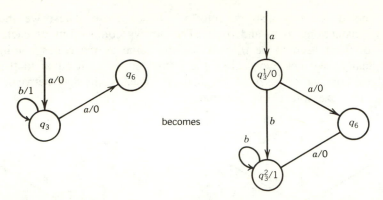

What happens in the example above is that the edge labeled $a/0$ has to enter a version of q_3 that prints a 0. We call this $q_3{}^1/0$. The loop labeled $b/1$ at q_3 has to enter a version of q_3 that prints a 1. We call this $q_3{}^2/1$. When we enter q_3 from the edge $a/0$, we enter $q_3{}^1/0$, but we must also be able to loop with b's while staying in a q_3-like state. Therefore, an edge labeled b must connect $q_3{}^1/0$ to $q_3{}^2/1$. Since we must be allowed to repeat as many b's as we want there must be a b loop at the state $q_3{}^2/1$. Each b loop we go around prints another 1 when it reenters $q_3{}^2$. As with all such twin descendants, they must both be connected to q_6 by $a/0$.

If there is ever a state that has no edges entering it, we can assign it any printing instruction we want, even if this state is the start state.

Let us repeat this process for each state of *Me*, q_0, q_1, ... This will produce *Mo*. If we have to make copies of the start state in *Me*, we can let any one of them be the start state in *Mo* since they all give the identical directions for proceeding to other states. Having a choice of start states means that the conversion of *Me* into *Mo* is not unique. We should expect this since any *Me* is equivalent to more than one *Mo*. It is equivalent to the *Mo* with automatic start symbol 0, or to the *Mo* with automatic start symbol 1, ...

As we run a string on the *Mo* that we have produced, we move from state to state very much as in the *Me*. It may not be the exact same state that we enter but one of the clones of the original. But this copy sends us along the same direction that the original did. We end up printing the same sequence of output characters.

The only difference is that when we start up the machine initially we print some unpredictable character, specified by the start state, that does not correspond to any output from *Me*, because *Me* never prints before reading an input letter. But we allowed for this discrepancy in the definition of equivalence, so there is no problem. ∎

Together, **Theorems** 8 and 9 allow us to say

$$Me = Mo.$$

When we went from *Mo* to *Me*, we kept the same number of states and same number of edges. When we go from *Me* to *Mo*, these can both increase drastically.

EXAMPLE

Let us start with the following Mealy machine:

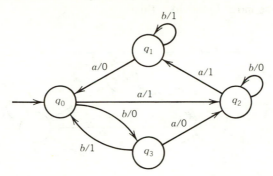

We can begin the conversion process anywhere because the algorithm does not specify the order of replacing states; so let us first consider the state q_0. Two edges come into this state, one labeled $a/0$ and one labeled $b/1$. Therefore, we need two copies of this state: one that prints a 0 (called q_0^1) and one that will print a 1 (called q_0^2). Both of these states must be connected to q_2 through an edge labeled $a/1$ and to q_3 through an edge labeled $b/0$. There is no loop at q_0, so these two states are not connected to each other. The machine becomes:

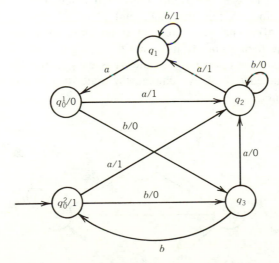

We must select the start state for the new machine, so let us arbitrarily select q_0^2. Notice that we now have two edges that cross. This sometimes happens, but aside from making a messier picture, there is no real problem in understanding which edge goes where. Notice that the edge from q_1 to q_0, which used to be labeled $a/0$, is now only labeled a because the instruction to print the 0 is found in the state $q_0^1/0$. The same is true for the edge from q_3, which also loses its printing instruction.

State q_1 has only two edges coming into it: one from q_2 labeled $a/1$ and a loop labeled $b/1$. So whenever we enter q_1 we are always printing a 1. We have no trouble here transferring the print instructions from the edges into the state. The machine now looks like this:

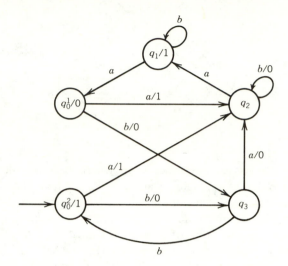

What we have now is a partially converted machine or a hybrid. We could run an input string on this machine, and it would give us the same output as the original *Me*. The rules are that if an edge says print, then print; if a state says print, then print. If not, don't.

Let us continue the conversion. State q_3 is easy to handle. Two edges come into it, both labeled $b/0$, so we change the state to $q_3/0$ and simplify the edge labels to b alone.

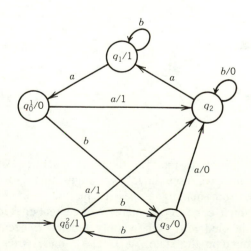

The only job left is to convert state q_2. It has some 0-printing edges entering it and some 1-printing edges (actually two of each, counting the loop). Therefore, we must split it into two copies, q_2^1 and q_2^2. Let the first print a 0 and the second print a 1. The two copies will be connected by a b edge going from q_2^2 to q_2^1 (to print a 0). There will also be a b loop at q_2^1. The final machine is this:

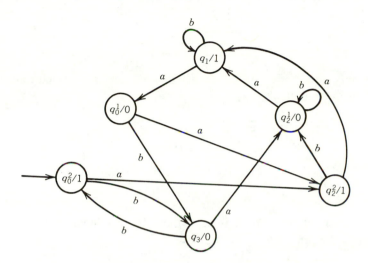

The student of Computer Science may already have met these machines in courses on Computer Logic or Architecture. They are commonly used to describe the action of sequential circuits that involve flip-flops and other feedback electronic devices for which the output of the circuit is not only a function of the specific instantaneous inputs but also a function of the previous state of the system. The total amount of history of the input string that can be "remembered" in a finite automaton is bounded by the number of states the automaton has. A machine can recognize a language of arbitrarily long words, but it cannot remember a particular word that has more letters than the machine has states. A 6-state machine cannot remember the last 7 input letters but it can remember a specific five-letter word like *aabaa*. Chapter 11 will deal with this subject in more depth. Automata with input and output are sometimes called **transducers** because of their connection with electronics.

EXAMPLE

Let us consider an example of a simple sequential circuit. The box labeled NAND means "not and." Its output wire carries the complement of the Boolean AND of its input wires. The output of the box labeled DELAY is the same as its previous input. It delays transmission of the signal along the wire by one step (clock pulse). The DELAY is sometimes called a **D flip-flop.** The AND and OR are as usual. Current in a wire is denoted by the value 1, no current by 0.

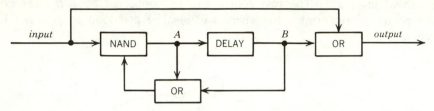

We identify four states based on whether or not there is current at points A and B in the circuit.

$$q_0 \text{ is } A = 0 \quad B = 0$$
$$q_1 \text{ is } A = 0 \quad B = 1$$
$$q_2 \text{ is } A = 1 \quad B = 0$$
$$q_3 \text{ is } A = 1 \quad B = 1$$

The operation of this circuit is such that after an input of 0 or 1 the state changes according to the following rules:

$$\text{new } B = \text{old } A$$
$$\text{new } A = (\text{input}) \text{ NAND (old } A \text{ OR old } B)$$
$$\text{output} = (\text{input}) \text{ OR (old } B)$$

At various discrete pulses of a time clock input is received, the state changes, and output is generated.

Suppose we are in state q_0 and we recive the input 0:

$$\text{new } B = \text{old } A = 0$$
$$\text{new } A = (\text{input}) \text{ NAND (old } A \text{ OR old } B)$$
$$= (0) \qquad \text{NAND (0} \qquad \text{OR} \qquad 0)$$
$$= 0 \text{ NAND } 0$$
$$= 1$$
$$\text{output} = 0 \text{ OR } 0 = 0$$

The new state is q_2 (since new $A = 1$, new $B = 0$).

If we are in state q_0 and we receive the input 1:

$$\text{new } B = \text{old } A = 0$$
$$\text{new } A = 1 \text{ NAND (0 OR 0)} = 1$$

$$\text{output} = 1 \text{ OR } 0 = 1$$

The new state is q_2 (since the new $A = 1$ and the new $B = 0$).

If we are in q_1 and we receive the input 0:

$$\text{new } B = \text{old } A = 0$$
$$\text{new } A = 0 \text{ NAND } (0 \text{ OR } 1) = 1$$
$$\text{output} = 0 \text{ OR } 1 = 1$$

The new state is q_2.

If we are in q_1 and we receive the input 1:

$$\text{new } B = \text{old } A = 0$$
$$\text{new } A = 1 \text{ NAND } (0 \text{ OR } 1) = 0$$
$$\text{output} = 1 \text{ OR } 1 = 1$$

The new state is q_0.

If we are in state q_2 and we receive the input 0:

$$\text{new } B = \text{old } A = 1$$
$$\text{new } A = 0 \text{ NAND } (1 \text{ OR } 0) = 1$$
$$\text{output} = 0 \text{ OR } 0 = 0$$

The new state is q_3 (since new $A = 1$, new $B = 1$).

If we are in q_2 and we receive the input 1:

$$\text{new } B = \text{old } A = 1$$
$$\text{new } A = 1 \text{ NAND } (1 \text{ OR } 0) = 0$$
$$\text{output} = 1 \text{ OR } 0 = 1$$

The new state is q_1.

If we are in q_3 and we receive the input 0:

$$\text{new } B = \text{old } A = 1$$
$$\text{new } A = 0 \text{ NAND } (1 \text{ OR } 1) = 1$$
$$\text{output} = 0 \text{ OR } 1 = 1$$

The new state is q_3.

If we are in q_3 and we receive the input 1:

$$\text{new } B = \text{old } A = 1$$
$$\text{new } A = 1 \text{ NAND } (1 \text{ OR } 1) = 0$$
$$\text{output} = 1 \text{ OR } 1 = 1$$

The new state is q_1.

Old state	After input 0		After input 1	
	New state	Output	New state	Output
q_0	q_2	0	q_2	1
q_1	q_2	1	q_0	1
q_2	q_3	0	q_1	1
q_3	q_3	1	q_1	1

The action of this sequential feedback circuit is equivalent to the following Mealy machine.

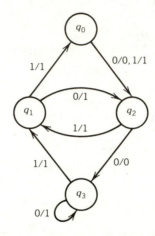

If we input two 0's no matter which state we started from, we will get to state q_3. From there the input string 011011 will cause the output sequence 111011.

COMPARISON TABLE FOR AUTOMATA (version 2)

	FA	**TG**	**NFA**	**NFA-Λ**	**MOORE**	**MEALY**
Start states	One	One or more	One	One	One	One
Final states	Some or none	Some or none	Some or none	Some or none	None	None
Edge labels	Letters from Σ	Words from Σ^*	Letters from Σ	Letters from Σ and Λ	Letters from Σ	i/o i from Σ o from Γ
Number of edges from each state	One for each letter in Σ	Arbitrary	Arbitrary	Arbitrary	One for each letter in Σ	One for each letter in Σ
Deterministic	Yes	No	No	No	Yes	Yes
Output	No	No	No	No	Yes	Yes
Page defined	65	89	143	150	155	158

PROBLEMS

Each of the following is a Moore machine with input alphabet $\Sigma = \{a,b\}$ and output alphabet $\Gamma = \{0,1\}$. In Problems 1 through 5, draw the machines given the transition and output tables. In Problems 6 through 10, construct the transition and output tables given the pictorial representations of the machines.

1.

	a	b	Output
q_0	q_1	q_2	1
q_1	q_1	q_1	0
q_2	q_1	q_0	1

2.

	a	b	Output
q_0	q_0	q_2	0
q_1	q_1	q_0	1
q_2	q_2	q_1	1

3.

	a	b	Output
q_0	q_0	q_1	1
q_1	q_0	q_2	0
q_2	q_2	q_2	1
q_3	q_1	q_1	0

4.

	a	b	Output
q_0	q_3	q_2	0
q_1	q_1	q_0	0
q_2	q_2	q_3	1
q_3	q_0	q_1	0

5.

	a	b	Output
q_0	q_1	q_2	0
q_1	q_2	q_3	0
q_2	q_3	q_4	1
q_3	q_4	q_4	0
q_4	q_0	q_0	0

6.

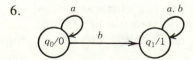

7.

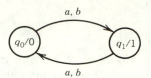

8.

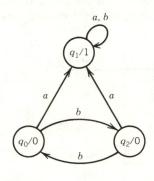

9.

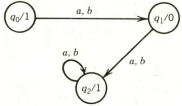

10.

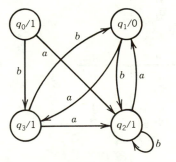

11.   On each of the Moore machines in Problems 1 through 10, run the input sequence *aabab*. What are the respective outputs?

12.   Even though a Moore machine does not define a language of the strings that it accepts as input, we can still use it to recogonize a language in the following sense. We can arrange that the last character printed out by the machine is an *A* for accept or an *R* for reject. For example, the following Moore machine will recognize the language of all words of

the form **(a + b)*aa(a + b)*** in the sense that these words and only these words will cause the last character printed by the machine to be *A*.

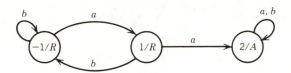

Show that all languages defined by regular expressions can be recognized by Moore machines in this fashion.

13. Suppose we define a Less machine to be a Moore machine that does not automatically print the character of the start state. The first character it prints is the character of the second state it enters. From then on, for every state it enters it prints a character, even when it reenters the start state. In this way the input string gets to have some say in what the first character printed is going to be. Show that these Less machines are equivalent to Mealy machines in the direct sense, that is, for every Less machine there is a Mealy machine that has the same output for every input string.

Mealy machines can also be defined by transition tables. The rows and the columns are both labeled with the names of the states. The entry in the table is the label of the edge (or edges) going from the row state to the column state (if there is no such edge, this entry is blank).

Construct the transition table for each of the four Mealy machines shown below.

14.

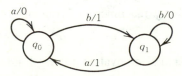

15.

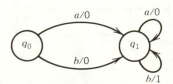

16.

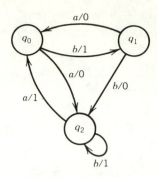

17.

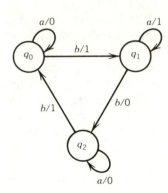

18. The example of the increment machine on page 160 used three states to perform its job. Show that two states are all that are needed.

19. (i) Convert the Moore machines in Problems 1 through 10 into Mealy machines.
    (ii) Convert the Mealy machines in Problems 14 through 17 into Moore machines.

20. Draw a Mealy machine equivalent to the following sequential circuit.

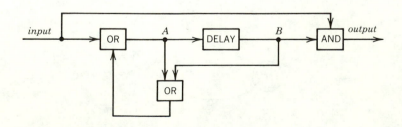

CHAPTER 10

REGULAR LANGUAGES

A language that can be defined by a regular expression is called a **regular language.** In the next chapter we address the important question, "Are all languages regular?" The answer is no. But before beginning to prove this, we discuss some of the properties of the class of all languages that are regular.

The information we already have about regular languages is summarized in the following theorem.

THEOREM 10

If L_1 and L_2 are regular languages, then $L_1 + L_2$, L_1L_2 and L_1* are also regular languages.

Remark

$L_1 + L_2$ means the language of all words in either L_1 or L_2. L_1L_2 means the language of all words formed by concatentating a word from L_1 with a word from L_2. L_1* means strings that are the concatenation of arbitrarily many factors from L_1. The result stated in this theorem is often expressed by saying: The

177

set of regular languages is *closed* under union, concatenation, and the Kleene star operator.

PROOF 1 (by Regular Expressions)

If L_1 and L_2 are regular languages, there are regular expressions $\mathbf{r}_1$ and $\mathbf{r}_2$ that define these languages. Then $(\mathbf{r}_1 + \mathbf{r}_2)$ is a regular expression that defines the language $L_1 + L_2$. The language L_1L_2 can be defined by the regular expression $\mathbf{r}_1\mathbf{r}_2$. The language $L_1{}^*$ can be defined by the regular expression $(\mathbf{r}_1)^*$. Therefore, all three of these sets of words are definable by regular expressions and so are themselves regular languages. ∎

The proof of Theorem 10 above uses the fact that L_1 and L_2 must be definable by regular expressions if they are regular languages. Regular languages can also be defined in terms of machines, and as it so happens machines can also be used to prove this theorem.

PROOF 2 (by Machines)

Since L_1 and L_2 are regular languages, there must be TG's that accept them. Let TG_1 accept L_1 and TG_2 accept L_2. Let us further assume that TG_1 and TG_2 each have a unique start state and a unique separate final state. If this is not the case originally, we can modify the TG's so that it becomes true as in Theorem 6, Part 2.

The TG described below accepts the language $L_1 + L_2$:

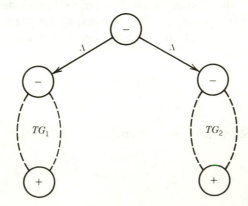

Starting at the $-$ of TG_1, our only option is to follow a path on TG_1. Starting at the $-$ of TG_2, we can only follow a path on TG_2. Starting at the new − state, we must choose to go to one machine or the other; once there, we stay there. This machine proves that $L_1 + L_2$ is regular.

The TG described below accepts the language L_1L_2:

where 1 is the former + of TG_1 and 2 is the former − of TG_2.

The TG described below accepts the language L_1*:

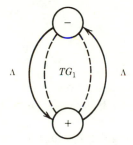

Here we begin at the − of TG_1 and trace a path to the + of TG_1. At this point, we could stop and accept the string or jump back, at no cost, to the − of TG_1 and run another segment of the input string back down to +. We can repeat this process as often as we want. The edge that goes directly from − to + allows us to accept the word Λ, but otherwise it has no effect on the language accepted.   ■

EXAMPLE

Let the alphabet be $\Sigma = \{a,b\}$.
Let

$L_1 =$ all words of two or more letters
that begin and end with the same letter

and

$L_2 =$ all words that contain the substring *aba*

For these languages we will use the following TG's and regular expressions:

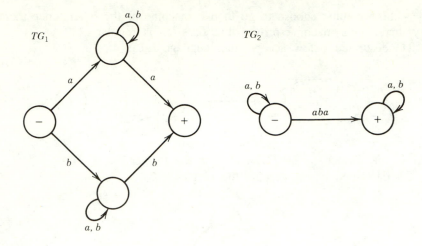

$$\mathbf{r_1}$$
$$\mathbf{a(a + b)*a + b(a + b)*b}$$

$$\mathbf{r_2}$$
$$\mathbf{(a + b)* \ aba \ (a + b)*}$$

The language $L_1 + L_2$ is regular because it can be defined by the regular expression:

$$[\mathbf{a(a+b)*a + b(a+b)*b}] + [\mathbf{(a+b)* \ aba \ (a+b)*}]$$

(for the purpose of clarity we have employed brackets instead of nested parentheses) and is accepted by the TG:

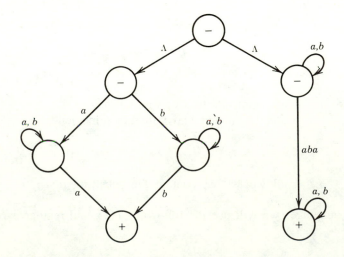

The language L_1L_2 is regular because it can be defined by the regular expression:

$$[a(a+b)*a \; + \; b(a+b)*b] \; [(a+b)* \; aba \; (a+b)*]$$

and is accepted by the TG:

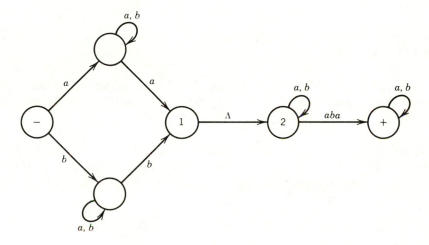

The language L_1* is regular because it can be defined by the regular expression:

$$[a(a+b)*a \; + \; b(a+b)*b]*$$

and is accepted by the TG:

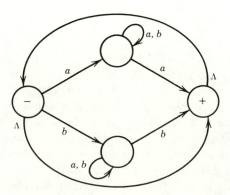

DEFINITION

If L is a language over the alphabet, Σ, we define its **complement,** L', to be the language of all strings of letters from Σ that are not words in L. ∎

Many authors use the bar notation $\overline{L}$ to denote the complement of the language L, but, as with most writing for computers, we will use the more typable form.

EXAMPLE

If L is the language over the alphabet $\Sigma = \{a,b\}$ of all words that have a double a in them, then L' is the language of all words that do not have a double a. ∎

It is important to specify the alphabet Σ or else the complement of L might contain "cat", "dog", "frog". . . , since these are definitely not strings in L.

Notice that the complement of the language L' is the language L. We could write this as

$$(L')' = L.$$

This is a theorem from Set Theory that is not restricted only to languages.

THEOREM 11

If L is a regular language, then L' is also a regular language. In other words, the set of regular languages is closed under complementation.

PROOF

If L is a regular language, we know from Kleene's Theorem that there is some FA that accepts the language L. Some of the states of this FA are final states and, most likely, some are not. Let us reverse the final status of each state, that is, if it was a final state, make it a nonfinal state, and if it was a nonfinal state, make it a final state. If an input string formerly ended in a nonfinal state, it now ends in a final state and vice versa. This new machine we have built accepts all input strings that were not accepted by the original FA (all the words in L') and rejects all the input strings that the FA used to accept (the words in L). Therefore, this machine accepts exactly the language L'. So by Kleene's Theorem, L' is regular. ∎

EXAMPLE

An FA that accepts only the strings *aba* and *abb* is shown below:

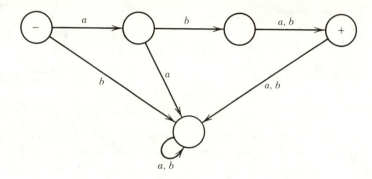

An FA that accepts all strings other than *aba* and *abb* is

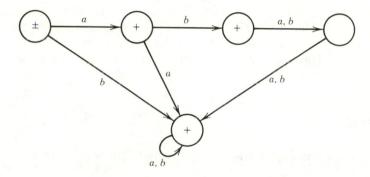

Notice that we have to reverse the final/nonfinal status of the start state as well.   ∎

THEOREM 12

If L_1 and L_2 are regular languages, then $L_1 \cap L_2$ is also a regular language. In other words, the set of regular languages is closed under intersection.

PROOF

By DeMorgan's Law for sets of any kind (regular languages or not):

$$L_1 \cap L_2 = (L_1' + L_2')'$$

This is illustrated by the Venn diagrams below.

$(L_1' + L_2') =$ 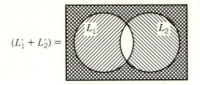 　　　 $(L_1' + L_2')' =$ 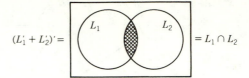 $= L_1 \cap L_2$

This means that the language $L_1 \cap L_2$ consists of all words that are not in either L_1' or L_2'. Since L_1 and L_2 are regular, then so are L_1' and L_2'. Since L_1' and L_2' are regular, so is $L_1' + L_2'$. And since $L_1' + L_2'$ is regular, then so is $(L_1' + L_2')'$, which means $L_1 \cap L_2$ is regular. ■

This is a case of "the proof is quicker than the eye." When we start with two languages L_1 and L_2, which are known to be regular because they are defined by FA's, finding the FA for $L_1 \cap L_2$ is not as easy as the proof makes it seem. If L_1 and L_2 are defined by regular expressions finding $L_1 \cap L_2$ can be even harder. However, all the algorithms that we need for these constructions have already been developed.

EXAMPLE

Let us work out one example in complete detail. We begin with two languages over $\Sigma = \{a,b\}$.

$$L_1 = \text{all strings with a double } a$$
$$L_2 = \text{all strings with an even number of } a\text{'s.}$$

These languages are not the same, since aaa is in L_1 but not in L_2 and aba is in L_2 but not in L_1.

They are both regular languages because they are defined by the following regular expressions (among others).

$$\mathbf{r_1 = (a + b)^*aa(a + b)^*}$$
$$\mathbf{r_2 = b^*(ab^*ab^*)^*}$$

The regular expression $\mathbf{r_2}$ is somewhat new to us. A word in the language L_2 can have some b's in the front, but then whenever there is an a it is balanced (after some b's) by another a. This gives us factors of the form (**ab*ab***). The word can have as many factors of this form as it wants. It can end in an *a* or a *b*.

Since these two languages are regular, Kleene's Theorem says that they can also be defined by FA's. The two smallest of these are:

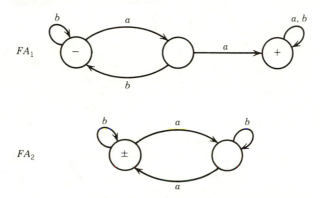

In the first machine we stay in the start state until we read our first *a*, then we move to the middle state. This is our opportunity to find a double *a*. If we read another *a* from the input string while in the middle state, we move to the final state where we remain. If we miss our chance and read a *b*, we go back to −. If we never get past the middle state, the word has no double *a* and is rejected.

The second machine switches from left state to right state or from right state to left state every time it reads an *a*. It ignores all *b*'s. If the string begins on the left and ends on the left, it must have made an even number of left/right switches. Therefore, the strings this machine accepts are exactly those in L_2.

Now the first step in building the machine (and regular expression) for $L_1 \cap L_2$ is to find the machines that accept the complementary languages L_1' and L_2'. Although it is not necessary for the successful execution of the algorithm, the English description of these languages is:

$$L_1' = \text{all strings that do not contain the substring } aa$$

$$L_2' = \text{all strings having an odd number of } a\text{'s}$$

In the proof of the theorem that the complement of a regular language is regular we gave the algorithm for building the machines that accept these languages. All that we have to do is reverse what is a final state and what is not a final state. The machines for these languages are then

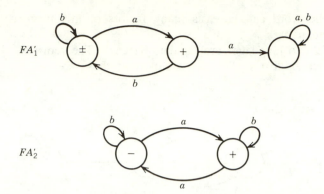

Even if we are going to want both the regular expression and the FA for the intersection language, we do not need to find the regular expressions that go with these two component machines. However, it is good exercise and the algorithm for doing this was presented as part of the proof of Kleene's Theorem. Recall that we go through stages of transition graphs with edges labeled by regular expressions. FA_1' becomes:

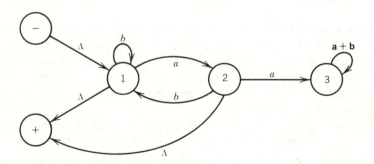

State 3 is part of no path from $-$ to $+$, so it can be dropped. When we eliminate the edge from state 2 to state 1, we are destroying a loop of ab at state 1, a loop of **bb*a** at state 2, and the path: state 2, state 1, $+$, which adds a **bb***-edge from 2 to $+$.

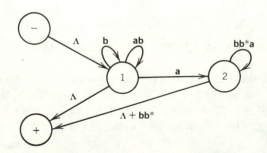

The possible paths from $-$ to $+$ are now from $-$ to state 1 to $+$, which is labeled $(\mathbf{b} + \mathbf{ab})^*$, and from $-$ to state 1 to state 2 to $+$ labeled

$$(\mathbf{b} + \mathbf{ab})^*\mathbf{a}(\mathbf{bb}^*\mathbf{a})^*(\Lambda + \mathbf{bb}^*)$$

The regular expression we have produced for L_1' is then:

$$(\mathbf{b} + \mathbf{ab})^* + (\mathbf{b} + \mathbf{ab})^*\mathbf{a}(\mathbf{bb}^*\mathbf{a})^*(\Lambda + \mathbf{b}^*)$$

There are many regular expressions for this set. Rather than use this complicated formula, let us note that the term $(\mathbf{b} + \mathbf{ab})^*$ alone covers all words that have no double a and end in b. Therefore, we can produce the same set by adding the factor (nothing or a) to the end of this expression:

$$\mathbf{r}_1' = (\mathbf{b} + \mathbf{ab})^*(\Lambda + \mathbf{a})$$

This is the regular expression we use for L_1'.

Let us now do the same thing for the language L_2'. FA_2' becomes:

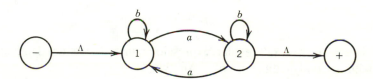

Let us start the simplification of this picture by eliminating the edge from state 1 to state 2. We must ask what paths this destroys that we must replace. One path it destroys is a loop back to state 1. We replace this with a loop at state 1 labeled $\mathbf{ab}^*\mathbf{a}$, which is what the old loop through state 2 amounted to. The other path this elimination destroys is the path from state 1 to state 2 to $+$. We must include an edge for this path labeled $\mathbf{ab}^*$. This picture is now:

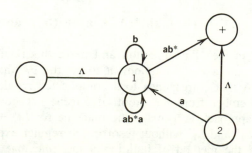

We can now see that there is no way to get to state 2, so it cannot be part of any path from $-$ to $+$. Therefore, we can eliminate it and its two edges. (Strictly speaking, to work entirely according to the algorithm, we should eliminate its edges first and then notice that it can be dropped. We have taken the liberty of taking an insightful shortcut.) The two loops at state 1 can be combined to give:

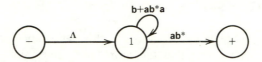

We can now eliminate state 1 and we have

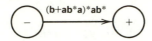

which gives us the regular expression

$$r_2' = (b + ab^*a)^*ab^*$$

This is one of several regular expressions that define the language of all words with an odd number of a's. Another is

$$b^*ab^*(ab^*ab^*)^*$$

which we get by adding the factor **b*a** in front of the regular expression for L_1. This works because words with an odd number of a's can be interpreted as **b*a** in front of words with an even number of a's. The fact that these two different regular expressions define the same language is not obvious. The question, "How can we tell when two regular expressions are equal?", will be answered in Chapter 12.

We now have regular expressions for L_1' and L_2', so we can write the regular expression for $L_1' + L_2'$. This will be

$$r_1' + r_2' = (b + ab)^*(\Lambda + a) + (b + ab^*a)^*ab^*$$

We must now go in the other direction and make this regular expression into an FA so that we can take its complement to get the FA that defines $L_1 \cap L_2$.

To build the FA that corresponds to a complicated regular expression is no picnic, as we remember from the proof of Kleene's Theorem.

An alternative approach is to make the machine for $L_1' + L_2'$ directly from the machines for L_1' and L_2' without resorting to regular expressions. We have already developed the method of building a machine that is the sum of two FA's also in the proof of Kleene's Theorem.

Let us label the states in the two machines for FA_1' and FA_2' as shown:

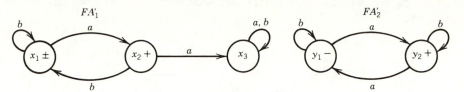

where the start states are x_1 and y_1 and the final states are x_1, x_2, and y_2. The six possible combination states are:

$z_1 = x_1$ or y_1 start, final (words ending here are accepted in FA_1')

$z_2 = x_1$ or y_2 final (words ending here are accepted on FA_1' and FA_2')

$z_3 = x_2$ or y_1 final (words ending here are accepted on FA_1')

$z_4 = x_2$ or y_2 final (words ending here are accepted on FA_1' and FA_2')

$z_5 = x_3$ or y_1 not final

$z_6 = x_3$ or y_2 final (words ending here are accepted on FA_2')

The transition table for this machine is:

	a	b
$+z_1$	z_4	z_1
$+z_2$	z_3	z_2
$+z_3$	z_6	z_1
$+z_4$	z_5	z_2
z_5	z_6	z_5
$+z_6$	z_5	z_6

And so the machine can be pictured like this:

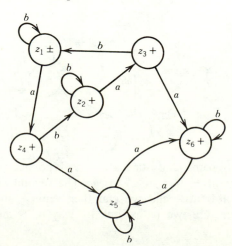

This is an FA that accepts the language $L_1' + L_2'$. If we reverse the status of each state from final to nonfinal and vice versa, we produce an FA for the language $L_1 \cap L_2$. This is it:

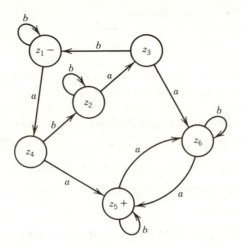

This can be made into a regular expression as follows. First we observe that there is only one $-$ and one $+$, so we do not have to add extra terminal states. Let us begin by removing the edge from z_2 to z_3. The whole path from z_4 to z_2 to z_3 can be replaced with an edge labeled **bb*a**. Let us also eliminate the edge from z_3 to z_6 and let z_3 go directly into $+$ on an edge labeled **ab*a**. There is no need to include in the z_3 path the possible looping back and forth between z_6 and $+$ that can be done once z_3 leads into $+$. Once we get to $+$, we can hop out and back again. We can then replace z_6 with a loop at $+$ labeled **ab*a**.

The picture is now

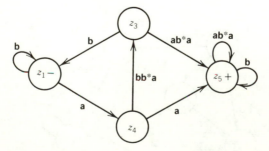

There are now two paths that start at $-$ and go back to $-$, the simple loop at $-$ and the circuit $-$ to z_4 to z_3 to $-$. The second path can be reduced to the loop labeled (**abb*ab**), and we can then remove the edge from z_3 to $-$. From z_4 to $+$ there are two paths: one by way of z_3 and the other direct.

We can remove the edge z_4 to z_3 (and then the whole state z_3) by labeling the direct edge z_4 to $+$ with both alternatives as shown below:

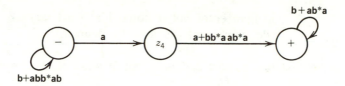

This whole machine reduces to the regular expression:

$$\textbf{(b + abb*ab)*a(a + bb*aab*a)(b + ab*a)*}$$

Even though we know this expression must be our answer because we know how it was derived, let us try to analyze it anyway to see if we can understand what this language means in some more intuitive sense.

As it stands, there are four factors (the second is just an **a** and the first and fourth are starred). Every time we use one of the options from the two end factors we incorporate an even number of a's into the word (either none or two). The second factor gives us an odd number of a's (exactly one). The third factor gives us the option of taking either one or three a's. In total, the number of a's must be even. So all the words in this language are in L_2.

The second factor gives us an a, and then we must immediately concatenate this with one of the choices from the third factor. If we choose the a, then we have formed a double a. If we choose the other expression, **bb*aab*a,** then we have formed a double a in a different way. By either choice the words in this language all have a double a and are therefore in L_1.

This means that all the words in the language of this regular expression are contained in the language $L_1 \cap L_2$. But are *all* the words in $L_1 \cap L_2$ included in the language of this expression?

The answer to this is yes. Let us look at any word that is in $L_1 \cap L_2$. It has an even number of a's and a double a somewhere in it. There are two possibilities to consider separately:

1. Before the first double a there are an even number of a's.
2. Before the first double a there are an odd number of a's.

Words of type 1 come from the expression below.

(even number of a's but not doubled) (first aa)
(even number of a's may be doubled)
= **(b + abb*ab)* (aa)(b + ab*a)***
= type 1.

Notice that the third factor defines the language L_1 and is a shorter expression than the $\mathbf{r}_1$ we used above.

Words of type 2 come from the expression:

(odd number of not doubled a's) (first aa)
(odd number of a's may be doubled)

Notice that the first factor must end in b, since none of its a's is part of a double a.

$$= [(\mathbf{b} + \mathbf{abb^*ab})^*\mathbf{abb^*}] \ \mathbf{aa} \ [\mathbf{b^*a}(\mathbf{b} + \mathbf{ab^*a})^*]$$
$$= (\mathbf{b} + \mathbf{abb^*ab})^*(\mathbf{a})(\mathbf{bb^*} \ \mathbf{aab^*a})(\mathbf{b} + \mathbf{ab^*a})^*$$
$$= \text{type } 2$$

Adding type 1 and type 2 together (and factoring out like terms using the distributive law), we obtain the same expression we got from the algorithm. We now have two proofs that this is indeed a regular expression for the language $L_1 \cap L_2$. ∎

This completes the calculation that was started on page 184.

The proofs of the last three theorems are a tour de force of technique. The first was proved by regular expressions and TG's, the second by FA's, and the third by a Venn diagram.

We must confess now that the proof of the theorem that the intersection of two regular languages is again a regular language was an evil pedagogical trick. The theorem is not really as difficult as we made it seem. We chose the hard way to do things because it was a good example of mathematical thinking: *Reduce the problem to elements that have already been solved.*

This procedure is reminiscent of a famous story about a theoretical mathematician. Professor X is surprised one day to find his desk on fire. He runs to the extinguisher and douses the flames. The next day he looks up from his book to see that his wastepaper basket is on fire. Quickly he takes the basket and empties it onto his desk which begins to burn. Having thus reduced the problem to one he has already solved, he goes back to his reading. (The students who find this funny are probably the ones who have been setting the fires in his office.)

The following is a more direct proof that the intersection of two regular languages is regular.

GOOD PROOF OF THEOREM 12

Let us recall the method we introduced as part of the proof of Kleene's Theorem to show that for any FA_1 and FA_2 there is an FA_3 that accepts the language that is the union of these two languages, that is, FA_3 accepts any string accepted by either FA_1 or FA_2.

To prove this we showed how to build a machine with states $z_1, z_2, \ldots$ of the form $x_{\text{something}}$ if the input is running on FA_1 or $y_{\text{something}}$ if the input is running on FA_2. If either the x state or the y state was a final state, we made the z state a final state.

Let us now build the exact same machine FA_3 but let us change the designation of final states. Let the z state be a final state only if *both* the corresponding x state *and* the corresponding y state are final states. Now FA_3 accepts only strings that reach final states simultaneously on both machines.

The words in the language for FA_3 are words in both the languages for FA_1 and FA_2. This is therefore a machine for the intersection language. ∎

Not only is the proof shorter but also the construction of the machine has fewer steps.

EXAMPLE

In the proof of Kleene's Theorem, we took the sum of the machine that accepts words with a double a

	a	b
$-x_1$	x_2	x_1
x_2	x_3	x_1
$+x_3$	x_3	x_3

and the machine that accepts all words in EVEN-EVEN

	a	b
$\pm y_1$	y_3	y_2
y_2	y_4	y_1
y_3	y_1	y_4
y_4	y_2	y_3

The resultant union-machine was

	a	b	Old States
$\pm z_1$	z_2	z_3	x_1 or y_1
z_2	z_4	z_5	x_2 or y_3
z_3	z_6	z_1	x_1 or y_2
$+z_4$	z_7	z_8	x_3 or y_1
z_5	z_9	z_{10}	x_1 or y_4
z_6	z_8	z_{10}	x_2 or y_4
$+z_7$	z_4	z_{11}	x_3 or y_3
$+z_8$	z_{11}	z_4	x_3 or y_2
z_9	z_{11}	z_1	x_2 or y_2
z_{10}	z_{12}	z_5	x_1 or y_3
$+z_{11}$	z_8	z_7	x_3 or y_4
$+z_{12}$	z_7	z_3	x_2 or y_1

The intersection machine is identical to this except that it has only one final state. In order for the z state to be a final state, both the x and y states must be final states. If FA_1 and FA_2 have only one final state, then FA_3 can have only one final state (if it can be reached at all). The only final state in our FA_3 is z_4, which is (x_3 or y_1).

This complicated machine is pictured below:

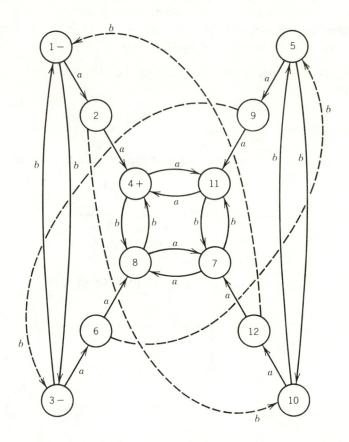

The dashed lines are perfectly good edges, but they have to cross other edges. With a little imagination, we can see how this machine accepts all EVEN-EVEN with a double a. All north-south changes are caused by b's, all east-west by a's. To get into the inner four states takes a double a.   ■

EXAMPLE

Let us rework the example in the first proof once again, this time by the quick method. This is like the citizens of the fabled city of Chelm who on learning that they did not have to carry all of their logs down from the top of the mountain were so overjoyed that they carried them all back up again so that they could use the clever work-saving method of rolling them down.

$L_1 =$ all strings with a double a

FA_1

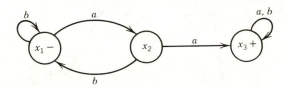

$L_2 =$ all strings with an even number of a's

FA_2

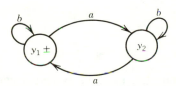

The machine that simulates the same input running on both machines at once is:

	a	b	Old States
$-z_1$	z_4	z_1	x_1 or y_1
z_2	z_3	z_2	x_1 or y_2
z_3	z_6	z_1	x_2 or y_1
z_4	z_5	z_2	x_2 or y_2
z_5	z_6	z_5	x_3 or y_1
z_6	z_5	z_6	x_3 or y_2

To be accepted by FA_1 an input string must have its path end in x_3. To be accepted by FA_2, an input string must have its path end in y_1. To be accepted by both machines at once, an input string on the z-machine, starting its processing in z_1, must end its path in state z_5 and only z_5. ■

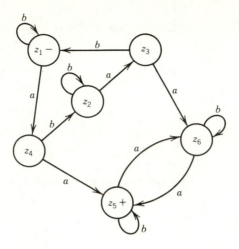

EXAMPLE

Let us work through one last example of intersection. Our two languages will be

$$L_1 = \text{all words that begin with an } a$$
$$L_2 = \text{all words that end with an } a$$
$$\mathbf{r_1} = \mathbf{a\,(a + b)*}$$
$$\mathbf{r_2} = \mathbf{(a + b)*\,a}$$

The intersection language will be

$$L_1 \cap L_2 = \text{all words that begin and end with the letter } a$$

The language is obviously regular since it can be defined by the regular expression

$$\mathbf{a(a + b)*a + a}$$

Note that the first term requires that the first and last a's be different, which is why we need the second choice "$+ \mathbf{a}$."

In this example we were lucky enough to "understand" the languages, so we could concoct a regular expression that we "understand" represents the intersection. In general, this does not happen, so we follow the algorithm presented in the proof, which we can execute even without the benefit of understanding.

For this we must begin with FA's that define these languages:

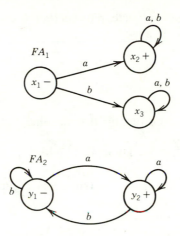

As it turns out, even though the two regular expressions are very similar, the machines are very different. There is a three-state version of FA_2 but no two-state version of FA_1.

We now build the transition table of the machine that runs its input strings on FA_1 and FA_2 simultaneously.

State	Read a	Read b	New names
x_1 or y_1	x_2 or y_2	x_3 or y_1	$-z_1$
x_2 or y_2	x_2 or y_2	x_2 or y_1	z_2
x_3 or y_1	x_3 or y_2	x_3 or y_1	z_3
x_2 or y_1	x_2 or y_2	x_2 or y_1	z_4
x_3 or y_2	x_3 or y_2	x_3 or y_1	z_5

The machine looks like this:

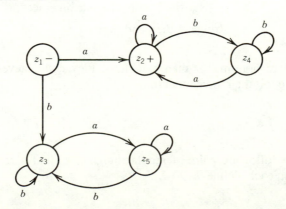

If were building the machine for

$$L_1 + L_2 = \text{all words in either } L_1 \text{ or } L_2 \text{ or in both}$$

We would put $+$'s at any state representing acceptance by L_1 or L_2, that is, any state with an x_2 or a y_2:

$$z_2 \, +$$
$$z_4 \, +$$
$$z_5 \, +$$

Since we are instead constructing the machine for

$$L_1 \cap L_2 = \text{all words in both } L_1 \text{ and } L_2$$

we put a $+$ only after the state that represents acceptance by both machines at once:

$$z_2 \, + \; = x_2 \text{ or } y_2$$

Strings ending here are accepted by FA_1 if being run on FA_1 (by ending in x_2) *and* by FA_2 if being run on FA_2 (by ending in y_2).   ■

Do not be fooled by this slight confusion

$$z_2 = x_2 \; \underline{\text{or}} \; y_2 = \text{accepted by } FA_1 \; \underline{\text{and}} \; \text{by } FA_2$$

The poor plus sign is perilously overworked.

$2 + 2$	(sometimes read "2 $\underline{\text{and}}$ 2 are 4")
$(\mathbf{a} + \mathbf{b})^*$	(a $\underline{\text{or}}$ b repeated as often as we choose)
$\mathbf{a}^+$	(a string of at least one a)
$L_1 + L_2$	(all words in L_1 $\underline{\text{or}}$ in L_2)
$+z_2, z_2 \, +$	(z_2 is a final state, the machine accepts input strings if they end here)

If humans were not smarter than machines, they could never cope with the mess they make of their own notation.

PROBLEMS

For each of the following pairs of regular languages, find a regular expression and an FA that each define $L_1 \cap L_2$.

L_1	L_2
1. (a + b)*a	b(a + b)*
2. (a + b)*a	(a + b)*aa(a + b)*
3. (a + b)*a	(a + b)*b
4. (a + b)b(a + b)*	b(a + b)*
5. (a + b)b(a + b)*	(a + b)*aa(a + b)*
6. (a + b)b(a + b)*	(a + b)*b
7. (b + ab)*(a + Λ)	(a + b)*aa(a + b)*
8. (b + ab)*(a + Λ)	(b + ab*a)*ab*
9. (b + ab)*(a + Λ)	(a + ba)*a
10. (ab*)*	b(a + b)*
11. (ab*)*	a(a + b)*
12. (ab*)*	(a + b)*aa(a + b)*
13. all strings of even length = (aa + ab + ba + bb)*	b(a + b)*
14. even length strings	(a + b)*aa(a + b)*
15. even length strings	(b + ab)*(a + Λ)
16. odd length strings	a(a + b)*
17. even length strings	EVEN-EVEN
18. (i) even length strings	strings with an even number of *a*'s
(ii) even length strings	strings with an odd number of *a*'s
19. (i) even length strings	strings with an odd number of *a*'s and an odd number of *b*'s
(ii) even length strings	strings with an odd number of *a*'s and an even number of *b*'s

20. We have seen that since the regular languages are closed under union and complement, they must be closed under intersection. Find a collection of languages that is closed under union and intersection but *not* under complement.

CHAPTER 11

NONREGULAR LANGUAGES

By using FA's and regular expressions, we have been able to define many languages. Although these languages have had many different structures, they took only a few basic forms: languages with required substrings, languages that forbid some substrings, languages that begin or end with certain strings, languages with certain even/odd properties, and so on. We will now turn our attention to some new forms, such as the language PALINDROME of Chapter 3 or the language PRIME of all words a^p where p is a prime number. In this chapter we shall see that neither of these is a regular language. We can describe them in English, but they cannot be defined by an FA. More powerful machines are needed to define them, machines that we build in later chapters.

DEFINITION

A language that cannot be defined by a regular expression is called a **nonregular** language. ∎

By Kleene's theorem, a nonregular language can also not be accepted by any FA or TG. All languages are either regular or nonregular, none are both. Let us first consider a simple case. Let us define the language L.

$$L = \{ \Lambda \quad ab \quad aabb \quad aaabbb \quad aaaabbbb \quad aaaaabbbbb \ldots \}$$

We could also define this language by the formula

$$L = \{a^n b^n \quad \text{for } n = 0 \ 1 \ 2 \ 3 \ 4 \ 5 \ldots\}$$

or for short

$$L = \{a^n b^n\}$$

When the range of the abstract exponent n is unspecified we mean to imply that it is $0,1,2,3, \ldots$

We shall now show that this language is nonregular. Let us note, though, that it is a subset of many regular languages, such as **a*b***, which, however, also includes such strings as aab and bb that $\{a^n b^n\}$ does not.

Let us be very careful to note that $\{a^n b^n\}$ is not a regular expression. It involves the symbols $\{\ \}$ and n that are not in the alphabet of regular expressions. This is a language-defining expression that is not regular. Just because this is not a regular expression does not mean that none exists; this we shall now prove.

Suppose on the contrary that this language were regular. Then there would have to exist some FA that accepts it. Let us picture one of these FA's (there might be several) in our mind. This FA might have many states. Let us say that it has 95 states, just for the sake of argument. Yet we know it accepts the word $a^{96} b^{96}$. The first 96 letters of this input string are all a's and they trace a path through this machine. The path cannot visit a new state with each input letter read because there are only 95 states. Therefore, at some point the path returns to a state that it has already visited. The first time it was in that state it left by the a-road. The second time it is in that state it leaves by the a-road again. Even if it only returns once we say that the path contains a circuit in it. (A **circuit** is a loop that can be made of several edges.) First the path wanders up to the circuit and then it starts to loop around the circuit, maybe many times. It cannot leave the circuit until a b is read in. Then the path can take a different turn. In this hypothetical example the path could make 30 loops around a three-state circuit before the first b is read.

After the first b is read, the path goes off and does some other stuff following b edges and eventually winds up at a final state where the word $a^{96} b^{96}$ is accepted.

Let us, for the sake of argument again, say that the circuit that the a-edge path loops 'around has seven states in it. The path enters the circuit, loops around it madly and then goes off on the b-line to a final state. What would happen to the input string $a^{96+7}b^{96}$? Just as in the case of the input string $a^{96}b^{96}$, this string would produce a path through the machine that would walk up to the same circuit (reading in only a's) and begin to loop around it in exactly the same way. However, the path for $a^{96+7}b^{96}$ loops around this circuit one more time than the path for $a^{96}b^{96}$—precisely one extra time. Both paths, at exactly the same state in the circuit, begin to branch off on the b-road. Once on the b-road, they both go the same 96 b-steps and arrive at the same final state. But this would mean that the input string $a^{103}b^{96}$ is accepted by this machine. But that string is not in the language $L = \{a^nb^n\}$.

This is a contradiction. We assumed that we were talking about an FA that accepts exactly the words in L and then we were able to prove that the same machine accepts some word that is not in L. This contradiction means that the machine that accepts exactly the words in L does not exist. In other words, L is nonregular.

Let us review what happened. We chose a word in L that was so large (had so many letters) that its path through the FA had to contain a circuit. Once we found that some path with a circuit could reach a final state, we asked ourselves what happens to a path that is just like the first one, but that loops around the circuit one extra time and then proceeds identically through the machine. The new path also leads to the same final state, but it is generated by a different input string—an input string not in the language L.

Perhaps the picture below can be of some help in understanding the idea behind this discussion. Let the path for a^9b^9 be:

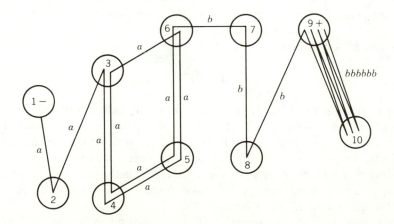

We have not indicated all the edges in this FA, only those used in the path of the word a^9b^9. State 6 is the only state for which we see both an a-exit edge and a b-exit edge.

In the path this input string takes to acceptance we find two circuits. The a-circuit 3-4-5-6 and the b-circuit 9-10. Let us concentrate on the a-circuit. What would be the path through this FA of the input string $a^{13}b^9$? The path for $a^{13}b^9$ would begin with the same nine steps as the path for a^9b^9 ending after nine steps in state 6. The input string a^9b^9 now gives us a b to read, which makes us go to state 7. However, the path for $a^{13}b^9$ still has four more a-steps to take, which is one more time around the circuit, and then it follows the nine b-steps.

The path for $a^{13}b^9$ is shown below:

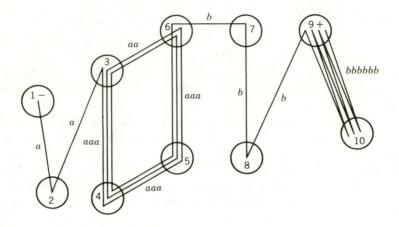

Let us return to our first consideration.

With the assumptions we made above (that there were 95 states and that the circuit was 7 states long), we could also say that $a^{110}b^{96}$, $a^{117}b^{96}$, $a^{124}b^{96}$, . . . are also accepted by this machine.

They can all be written in this form

$$a^{96}(a^7)^m b^{96}$$

where m is any integer $0,1,2,3, \ldots$. If m is 0, the path through this machine is the path for the word $a^{96}b^{96}$. If m is 1, the path looks the same, but it loops the circuit one more time. If $m = 2$, the path loops the circuit two more times. In general, $a^{96}(a^7)^m b^{96}$ loops the circuit exactly m more times. After doing this looping it gets off the circuit at exactly the same place $a^{96}b^{96}$ does and proceeds along exactly the same route to the final state. All these words, though not in L, must be accepted.

Suppose that we had considered a different machine to accept the language L, perhaps a machine that has 732 states. When we input the word $a^{733}b^{733}$, the path that the a's take must contain a circuit. We choose the word $a^{733}b^{733}$ to be efficient. The word $a^{9999}b^{9999}$ also must loop around a circuit in its a-part of the path. Suppose the circuit that the a-part follows has 101 states. Then $a^{733+101}b^{733}$ would also have to be accepted by this machine, because its path is the same in every detail except that it loops the circuit one more time. This second machine must also accept some strings, that are not in L:

$$a^{834}b^{733} \qquad a^{935}b^{733} \qquad a^{1036}b^{733} \ldots$$
$$= a^{733}(a^{101})^m b^{733} \quad \text{for } m = 1 \quad 2 \quad 3 \ldots$$

For each different machine we suggest to define L there is a different counter-example proving that it accepts more than just the language L.

There are machines that include L in the language they accept, but for each of them there are infinitely many extra words they must also accept.

All in all, we can definitely conclude that there is no FA that accepts all the strings in L and only the strings in L. Therefore L is nonregular.

The reason why we cannot find an FA that accepts L is not because we are stupid, but because none can exist.

The principle we have been using to discuss the language L above can be generalized so that it applies to consideration of other languages. It is a tool that enables us to prove that certain other languages are also nonregular. We shall now present the generalization of this idea, called the **Pumping Lemma** for regular languages, which was discovered by Yehoshua Bar-Hillel, Micha A. Perles, and Eliahu Shamir in 1961.

The name of this theorem is interesting. It is called "pumping" because we pump more stuff into the middle of the word, swelling it up without changing the front and the back part of the string. It is called a "lemma" because, although it is a theorem, its main importance is as a tool in proving other results of more direct interest, namely, it will help us prove that certain languages are nonregular.

THEOREM 13

Let L be any regular language that has infinitely many words. Then there exist some three strings x, y, and z (where y is not the null string) such that all the strings of the form

$$xy^n z \quad \text{for } n = 1 \quad 2 \quad 3 \quad \ldots$$

are words in L.

PROOF

If L is a regular language, then there is an FA that accepts exactly the words in L. Let us focus on one such machine. Like all FA's, this machine has only finitely many states. But L has infinitely many words in it. This means that there are arbitrarily long words in L. (If there were some maximum on the length of all the words in L, then L could have only finitely many words in total.)

Let w be some word in L that has more letters in it than there are states in the machine we are considering. When this word generates a path through the machine, the path cannot visit a new state for each letter because there are more letters than states. Therefore, it must at some point revisit a state that it has been to before. Let us break the word w up into three parts.

Part 1   All the letters of w starting at the beginning that lead up to the first state that is revisited. Call this part x. Notice that x may be the null string if the path for w revisits the start state as its first revisit.

Part 2   Starting at the letter after the substring x, let y denote the substring of w that travels around the circuit coming back to the same state the circuit began with. Since there must be a circuit, y cannot be the null string. y contains the letters of w for exactly one loop around this circuit.

Part 3   Let z be the rest of w starting with the letter after the substring y and going to the end of the string w. This z could be null. The path for z could also possibly loop around the y circuit or any other. What z does is arbitrary.

Clearly from the definition of these three substrings

$$w = xyz$$

and w is accepted by this machine.

What is the path through this machine of the input string

$$xyyz \ ?$$

It follows the path for w in the first part x and leads up to the beginning of the place where w looped around a circuit. Then like w it inputs the string y, which causes the machine to loop back to this same state again. Then, again like w, it inputs a string y, which causes the machine to loop back to this same state yet another time. Then, just like w, it proceeds along the path dictated by the input string z and so ends on the same final state that w did. This means that $xyyz$ is accepted by this machine, and therefore it must be in the language L.

If we traced the paths for $xyyz$, $xyyyz$, and $xyyyyyyyyyyyyz$, they would all be the same. Proceed up to the circuit. Loop around the circuit some number of times. Then proceed to the final state. All these must be accepted by the machine and therefore are all in the language L. In fact, L must contain all strings of the form:

$$xy^n z \quad \text{for } n = 1 \quad 2 \quad 3 \quad . . .$$

as the theorem claims.

Perhaps these pictures can be helpful in understanding the argument above.

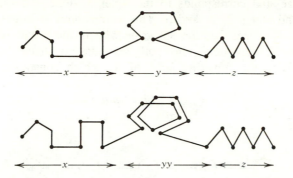

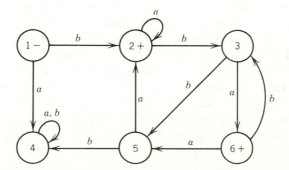

Notice that in this theorem it does not matter whether there is another circuit traced in the z part or not. All we need to do is find one circuit, and then we keep pumping it for all it is worth. Notice also that we did not assume that the x, y, or z parts were repetitions of the same letter as was the case in our discussion of $\{a^n b^n\}$. They could have been any arbitrary strings. ∎

EXAMPLE

Let us illustrate the action of the Pumping Lemma on a concrete example of a regular language. The machine below accepts an infinite language and has only six states.

Any word with six or more letters must correspond to a path that includes a circuit. Some words with fewer than six letters correspond to paths with circuits, such as *baaa*. The word we will consider in detail is

$$w = bbbababa$$

which has more than six letters and therefore includes a circuit. The path that this word generates through the FA can be decomposed into three stages:

The first part, the x-part, goes from the $-$ state up to the first circuit. This is only one edge and corresponds to the letter b alone. The second stage is the circuit around states 2, 3, and 5. This corresponds to edges labeled b, b, and a. We therefore say that the substring bba is the y-part of the word w. After going around the circuit, the path procedes to states 3, 6, 3, and 6. This corresponds to the substring $baba$ of w, which constitutes the z-part.

$$w = b \quad bba \quad baba$$
$$x \quad y \quad z$$

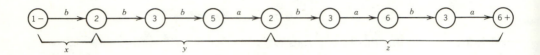

Now let us ask what would happen to the input string $xyyz$.

$$x \ y \ y \ z = b \quad bba \quad bba \quad baba$$

Clearly, the x-part (the letter b) would take this path from $-$ to the beginning of the circuit in the path of w. Then the y-part would circle the circuit in the same way that the path for w does when it begins xy.

At this point, we are back at the beginning of the circuit. We mark off the circuit starting at the first repeated state, which in this case is state 2 and consider it to be made up of exactly as many edges as it takes to get back there (in this case 3 edges). Even though in the original path for w we proceed again from state 2 to state 3 as in the circuit, this is not part of the first simple looping and so not part of y. Therefore, we can string two y-parts together since the second y begins in the state in which the first leaves us. The second y-part circles the circuit again and leaves us in the correct state to resume the path of the word w. We can continue after xyy with the z path exactly as we continued w with the z path after its y-part. This means again that the z path will take us to a $+$ state for $xyyz$ just as it did for $w = xyz$. In other words, we will accept the word $xyyz$ just as we accepted w.

Path for xyz

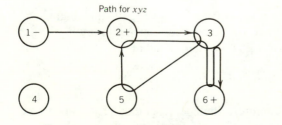

Path for $xyyz$

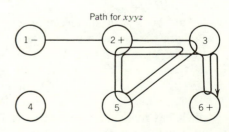

The same thing happens with $xyyyz$, $xyyyyz$, and in general for xy^nz. This is all that the Pumping Lemma says. ∎

Suppose for a moment that we did not already have a discussion of the language

$$L = \{a^nb^n \quad \text{for} \quad n = 0 \quad 1 \quad 2 \quad 3 \quad \ldots\}$$

Let us see how we could apply the Pumping Lemma directly to this case.

The Pumping Lemma says that there must be strings x, y, and z such that all words of the form xy^nz are in L. Is this possible? A typical word of L looks like

$$aaa \ldots aaaabbbb \ldots bbb$$

How do we break this into three pieces conformable to the roles x, y, and z? If the middle section y is going to be made entirely of a's, then when we pump it to $xyyz$ the word will have more a's than b's, which is not allowed in L. Similarly, if the middle part, y, is composed of only b's, then the word $xyyz$ will have more b's than a's. The solution is that the y part must have some positive number of a's and some positive number of b's. This would mean that y contains the substring ab. Then $xyyz$ would have two copies of the substring ab. But every word in L contains the substring ab exactly once. Therefore, $xyyz$ cannot be a word in L. This proves that the Pumping Lemma cannot apply to L and therefore L is not regular.

EXAMPLE

Once we have shown that the language $\{a^nb^n\}$ is nonregular, we can show that the language EQUAL, of all words with the same total number of a's and b's, is also nonregular. (Note the number of a's and b's do not have to be even, they just have to be the same.)

$$\text{EQUAL} = \{\Lambda \quad ab \quad ba \quad aabb \quad abab \quad abba \quad baab \quad baba \quad bbaa \quad aaabbb \ldots\}$$

The language $\{a^nb^n\}$ is the intersection of all words defined by the regular expression $\mathbf{a^*b^*}$ and the language EQUAL.

$$\{a^nb^n\} = \mathbf{a^*b^*} \cap \text{EQUAL}$$

Now if EQUAL were a regular language, then $\{a^nb^n\}$ would be the intersection of two regular languages and by Theorem 12 it would have to be regular itself. Since $\{a^nb^n\}$ is not regular, EQUAL cannot be. ∎

For the example $\{a^n b^n\}$, and in most common instances, we do not need the full force of the Pumping Lemma as stated. It is often just as decisive to say that w can be decomposed into xyz where $xyyz$ is also in the language. The fact that $xy^n z$ is in the language for all $n > 2$ is also interesting and will be quite useful when we discuss whether certain languages are finite or infinite, but often $n = 2$ is adequate to show that a given language is nonregular.

The proof that we gave of the Pumping Lemma actually proved more than was explicitly stated in the lemma. By the method of proof that we used we showed additionally that the string x and the string y together do not have any more letters than the machine in question has states. This is because as we proceed through x and y we visit our first repeated state at the end of y; before that, all the states were entered only once each.

The same argument that proved Theorem 13 proves the stronger theorem below.

THEOREM 14

Let L be an infinite language accepted by a finite automaton with N states. Then for all words w in L that have more than N letters there are strings x, y, and z

where y is not null

and where length(x) + length(y) does not exceed N
such that

$$w = xyz$$

and all strings of the form

$$xy^n z \quad (\text{for } n = 1 \quad 2 \quad 3 \quad \ldots)$$

are in L. ■

We put the end of proof symbol ■ right after the statement of the theorem to indicate that we have already provided a proof of this result.

The purpose of stressing the question of length is illustrated by our next example.

EXAMPLE

We shall show that the language PALINDROME is nonregular. We cannot use the first version of the Pumping Lemma to do this because the strings

$$x = a \qquad y = b \qquad z = a$$

satisfy the lemma and do not contradict the language. All words of the form

$$xy^n z = ab^n a$$

are in PALINDROME.

However, let us consider one of the FA's that might accept this language. Let us say that the machine we have in mind has 77 states. Now the palindrome

$$w = a^{80} b a^{80}$$

must be accepted by this machine and it has more letters than the machine has states. This means that we can break w into the three parts, x, y, and z. But since the length of x and y must be in total 77 or less, they must both be made of solid a's, since the first 77 letters of w are all a's. That means when we form the word $xyyz$ we are adding more a's on to the front of w. But we are not adding more a's on to the back of w since all the rear a's are in the z part, which stays fixed at 80 a's. This means that the string $xyyz$ is not a palindrome since it will be of the form

$$a^{\text{more than } 80} \, b \, a^{80}$$

But the second version of the Pumping Lemma said that PALINDROME has to include this string. Therefore, the second version does not apply to the language PALINDROME, which means that PALINDROME is nonregular.

This demonstration did not really rely on the number of states in the hypothetical machine being 77. Some people think that this argument would be more mathematically sound if we called the number of states m. This is silly. ∎

EXAMPLE

Let us consider the language

$$\text{PRIME} = \{a^p \text{ where } p \text{ is a prime}\}$$
$$= \{aa, \quad aaa, \quad aaaaa, \quad aaaaaaa, \dots\}$$

Is PRIME a regular language? If it is, then there is some some FA that accepts exactly these words. Let us keep one such automaton in mind. Let us suppose, for the sake of argument, that it has 345 states. Let us choose a prime number bigger than 345, for example 347. Then a^{347} can be broken into parts x, y, and z such that $xy^n z$ is in PRIME for any value of n. The parts x, y, and z are all just strings of a's. Let us take the value of $n = 348$.

By the Pumping Lemma, the word $xy^{348}z$ must be in PRIME. Now

$$x \ y^{348} \ z = x \ y \ z \ y^{347}$$

We can write this because the factors x, y, and z are all solid clumps of a's, and it does not matter in what order we concatenate them. All that matters is how many a's we end up with.

Let us write

$$xyz \ y^{347} = a^{347} \ y^{347}$$

This is because x, y, and z came originally from breaking up a^{347} into three parts. We also know that y is some (nonempty) string of a's. Let us say that $y = a^m$ for some integer m that we do not know.

$$
\begin{aligned}
a^{347} \ y^{347} &= a^{347}(a^m)^{347} \\
&= a^{347 + 347m} \\
&= a^{347(m + 1)}
\end{aligned}
$$

These operations are all standard algebraic manipulations.

What we have arrived at is that there is an element in PRIME that is of the form a to the power $347(m + 1)$. Now since $m \neq 0$, we know that $347(m + 1)$ is not a prime number. But this is a contradiction, since all the strings in PRIME are of the form a^p where the exponent is a prime number. This contradiction arose from the assumption that PRIME was a regular language. Therefore PRIME is nonregular. ∎

PROBLEMS

Prove that each of the following languages is nonregular

1.   SQUARE $= \{a^n$ where n is a square$\}$
          $= \{a, \quad aaaa, \quad aaaaaaaaa, \quad \ldots\}$

This language could also be written as $\{a^{n^2}\}$

2. DOUBLE = {the set of all repeated strings, that is, all words of the form
   ss where s is any string of a's and b's}
   = {*aa, bb, aaaa, abab, baba, bbbb, aaaaaa, aabaab,*
   abaaba, abbabb, . . .}

3. TRAILING-COUNT = { any string s followed by a number of a's equal
   to length(s)}
   = {*aa, ba, aaaa, abaa, baaa, bbaa, aaaaaa,*
   aabaaa, abaaaa, abbaaa, . . .}

4. $\{a^n b^{n+1}\}$ = {*abb, aabbb, aaabbbb,* . . .}

5. $\{a^n b^n a^n\}$ = {*aba, aabbaa, aaabbbaaa, aaaabbbbaaaa,* . . .}

6. (i) $\{a^n b^{2n}\}$ = {*abb aabbbb aaabbbbbb* . . .}
   (ii) $\{a^n b a^n\}$ = {*aba, aabaa, aaabaaa,* . . .}

7. $\{a^n b^n a^m$ where $n = 0,1,2, \ldots$ and $m = 0,1,2, \ldots\}$
   = $\{\Lambda$ a aa ab aaa aba . . .}

8. EVENPALINDROME = {all words of the form $s(\text{reverse}(s))$ where s is
   any string}.
   = {all words in PALINDROME that have even length}
   = {*aa, bb, aaaa, abba, baab, bbbb,* . . .}

9. ODDPALINDROME = {all words in PALINDROME that have odd length}

10. DOUBLEPRIME   = $\{a^p b^p$ where p is any prime}

11. DOUBLESQUARE   = $\{a^{n^2} b^{n^2}$ where $n = 1, 2, 3, \ldots\}$

12. PRIME-PRIME   = {all words of a's and b's such that the total number
    of a's is a prime and the total number of b's is a
    prime, but not necessarily the same prime}

13. SQUAREA = {all words of a's and b's such that the number of a's is
    a square and the b's are arbitrary}

14. (i) FACTORIAL = $\{a^{n!}, \quad n = 1, \quad 2, \quad 3, \quad \ldots\}$
    (ii) DOUBLEFACTORIAL = $\{a^{n!} b^{n!}, \quad n = 1, \quad 2, \quad 3. \quad \ldots\}$

15. Just for this problem let the alphabet be $\Sigma = \{a,b,c\}$. Show that the language of all words of the form $a^n b^n c^n$, for $n = 1, 2, 3, \ldots$

$$= \{abc, \ aabbcc, \ aaabbbccc \ldots\}$$

is nonregular.

16. (i) Give an example of a regular language R and a nonregular language N such that $R + N$ is regular.
    (ii) Give an example of a regular language R and a nonregular language N such that $R + N$ is nonregular.

17. Consider the following language:

$$\text{PRIME}' = \{a^n \text{ where } n \text{ is not a prime}\}$$
$$= \{\Lambda \ a \ aaaa \ aaaaaa \ aaaaaaaa \ldots\}$$

(i) Prove that PRIME$'$ is nonregular.
(ii) Prove, however, that PRIME$'$ *does* satisfy the Pumping Lemma.

18. (i) Show that if we add a finite set of words to a regular language the result is a regular language.
    (ii) Show that if we subtract a finite set of words from a regular language the result is a regular language.

19. (i) Show that if we add a finite set of words to a nonregular language the result is a nonregular language.
    (ii) Show that if we subtract a finite set of words from a nonregular language the result is a nonregular language.

20. Consider what happens when an FA is built for an infinite language over the one-letter alphabet $\Sigma = \{a\}$. When the input is a string of a's that is longer than the number of states, the path it traces must take the form of some initial sequence of edges followed by a circuit. Since all the

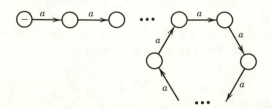

words in the language accepted by the machine are strings of a's, all the long words accepted by this FA follow the same path up to the circuit and then around and around as in the picture below:

Some of the states leading up to the circuit may be final states and some of the states in the circuit may be final states. This means that by placing $+$ signs judiciously along the path to the circuit we can make the machine accept any finite set of words S_1. While going around the circuit the first time the FA can accept another finite set of words S_2. If the length of the circuit is n all words of the form a^n times a word in S_2 will also be accepted on the second go-round of the circuit.

(i) Prove that if L is a regular language over the alphabet $\Sigma = \{a\}$ then there are two finite sets of words S_1 and S_2 and an integer n such that

$$L = S_1 + S_2(a^n)^*$$

(ii) Consider the language L defined as:

$\qquad L = \{a^n$ where n is any integer with an even number of digits in base 10$\}$

$\qquad\quad = \{\Lambda\ a^{10}\ a^{11}\ a^{12} \ldots\}$

Prove that L is nonregular.

CHAPTER 12

DECIDABILITY

In this part of the book we have laid the foundations of the Theory of Finite Automata. The pictures and tables that we have called "machines" can actually be built out of electronic components and operate exactly as we have described. Certain parts of a computer and certain aspects of a computer obey the rules we have made up for FA's. We have not yet arrived, though, at the mathematical model for a whole computer. That we shall present in Part III. But before we leave this topic, we have some unfinished business to clear up. Along the way we asked some very basic questions that we deferred considering. We now face three of these issues.

1. How can we tell if two regular expressions define the same language?
2. How can we tell if two FA's are equivalent?
3. How can we tell if the language defined by an FA has finitely many or infinitely many words in it?

In mathematical logic we say that a problem is **effectively solvable** if there is an algorithm that provides the answer in a finite number of steps, no matter what the particular inputs are. The maximum number of steps the algorithm will take must be predictable before we begin to execute the procedure. For example, if the problem was, "What is the solution to a quadratic equation?"

then the quadratic formula provides an algorithm for calculating the answer in a predetermined number of arithmetic operations: four multiplications, two subtractions, one square root, and one division. The number of steps in the algorithm is never greater than this no matter what the particular coefficients of the polynomial are. Other suggestions for solving a quadratic equation (such as "keep guessing until you find a number that satisfies the equation") that do not guarantee to work in a fixed number of steps are not considered effective solutions.

DEFINITION

An effective solution to a problem that has a yes or no answer is called a **decision procedure.** A problem that has a decision procedure is called **decidable.** ■

We want to decide whether two regular expressions determine the exact same language. We might, very simply, use the two expressions to generate many words from each language until we find one that obviously is not in the language of the other. To be even more organized, we may generate the words in size order, smallest first. In practice, this method works fairly well but there is no mathematical guarantee that we find such an obvious benchmark word at any time in the next six years. Suppose we begin with the two expressions:

$$\textbf{a(a + b)*} \qquad \text{and} \qquad \textbf{(b + }\Lambda\textbf{)(baa + ba*)*}.$$

It is obvious that all the words in the language represented by the first expression begin with the letter a and all the words in the language represented by the second expression begin with the letter b. These expressions have no word in common; and this fact is very clear. However, consider these two expressions:

$$\textbf{(aa + ab + ba + bb)*} \qquad \text{and} \qquad \textbf{((ba + ab)*(aa + bb)*)*}$$

They both define the language of all strings over $\Sigma = \{a, b\}$ with an even number of letters. If we did not recognize this, how could we decide the question of whether they are equivalent? We could generate many examples of words from the languages each represents, but we would not find a difference. Could we then conclude that they are equivalent? It is logically possible that the smallest example of a word that is in one language but not in the other has 96 letters. Maybe the smallest example has 2 million letters. This is not an effective procedure, and it does not decide the problem.

The following two expressions are even less clear:

$$\textbf{((b*a)*ab*)*} \qquad \text{and} \qquad \Lambda \textbf{ +a(a + b)* + (a + b)*aa(a + b)*}$$

They both define the language of all words that either start with an *a* or else have a double *a* in them somewhere or else are null.. The suggestion that we should "interpret what the regular expressions mean and see if they are the same," is, of course hopeless.

Before we answer the first major question of this chapter, let us note that it is virtually the same as the second question. If we had a decision procedure to determine whether two regular expressions were equivalent, we could use it to determine whether two FA's were equivalent. First, we would convert the FA's into regular expressions and then decide about the regular expressions. The process of converting FA's into regular expressions is an effective procedure that we developed in the proof of Kleene's Theorem in Chapter 7. The number of steps required can be predicted in advance based on the size of the machine to be converted. Since the conversion process eliminates at least one state with each step, a machine with 15 states will take at most 16 steps to convert into a regular expression (counting the step that creates a unique $-$ and a unique $+$).

Similarly, if we had an effective procedure to determine whether two FA's were equivalent, we could use it to decide the problem for regular expressions by converting them into FA's.

Fortunately we have already developed all the algorithms necessary to decide the "equivalency problem" for FA's and regular expressions. We need only recognize how to apply them.

Given two languages L_1 and L_2 defined either by regular expressions or by FA's, we have developed (in Chapter 10) the procedures necessary to produce finite automata for the languages L_1', L_2', $L_1 \cap L_2'$, and $L_2 \cap L_1'$. Therefore, we can produce an FA that accepts the language

$$(L_1 \cap L_2') + (L_2 \cap L_1')$$

This machine accepts the language of all words that are in L_1 but not L_2 or else in L_2 but not L_1. If L_1 and L_2 are the same language, this machine cannot accept any words. If this machine accepts even one word, then L_1 is not equal to L_2; even if the one word is the null word. If L_1 is equal to L_2, then the machine for the language above accepts nothing at all.

To make this discussion into an effective decision procedure, we must show that we can tell by some algorithm when an FA accepts no words at all. This is not a very hard task, and there are several good ways to do it. We make a big fuss about this since it is so simple that it might seem unimportant, which is wrong. It is a basic question in its own right—not just as part of the decidability of the equivalence of regular languages.

How to determine whether an FA accepts any words:

Method 1   Convert the FA into a regular expression. Every regular expression defines some words. We can prove this by an algorithm. First delete all stars. Then for each + we throw away the right half of the sum and the $+$ sign itself. When we have no more *'s or $+$'s, we remove the parentheses and we have a concatenation of a's, b's, and Λ's. These taken together form a word. For example:

$$(a + \Lambda)(ab^* + ba^*)^*(\Lambda + b^*)^*$$

becomes (after removing *'s)

$$(a + \Lambda)(ab + ba)\ (\Lambda + b)$$

which becomes (throwing away right halves)

$$(a)(ab)(\Lambda)$$

which becomes (eliminating parentheses)

$$a\ ab\ \Lambda$$

which is the word

$$aab$$

This word must be in the language of the regular expression since the operations of choosing * = power 1, and $+$ = left half, are both legal choices for forming words. If every regular expression defines at least one word, it *seems* at first glance that this means that every FA must accept at least one word. How then could we ever show that two languages are equal? If we first build an FA for the language

$$(L_1 \cap L_2') + (L_2 \cap L_1')$$

and then when we convert this machine into a regular expression, is it not true that by the argument above we must find some word in the language of the regular expression and therefore $L_1 \neq L_2$ no matter what they are? No. The hole in this reasoning is that the process of converting this FA into a regular expression breaks down. We come down to the last step where we usually have several edges running from $-$ to $+$ that we add together to form the regular expression.

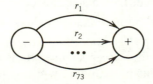

However, when we get to this last step we suddenly realize that there are no paths from − to + at all.

This could happen theoretically in three different ways: the machine has no final states, such as this one:

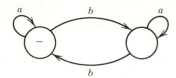

or the final state is disconnected from the start state, as with this one:

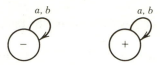

or the final state is unreachable from the start state, as with this one:

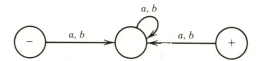

We shall see later in this chapter which of these situations does arise if the languages are actually equal.

Method 2   Examine the FA to see if there is any path from − to +. If there is any path, then the machine must accept some words—for one, the word that is the concatenation of the labels of the edges in the path from − to + just discovered. In a large FA with thousands of states and millions of directed edges, it may be impossible to decide if there is a path from − to + without the aid of an effective procedure. One such procedure is this:

Step 1   Paint the start state blue.

Step 2   From every blue state follow each edge that leads out of it and paint the connecting state blue, then delete this edge from the machine.

Step 3   Repeat Step 2 until no new state is painted blue, then stop.

Step 4   When the procedure has stopped, if any of the final states are painted blue, then the machine accepts some words and, if not, it does not.

Let us look at this procedure at work on the machine

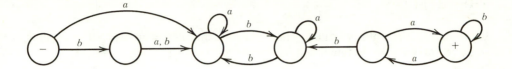

after Step 1:

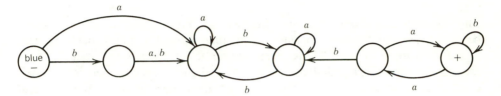

after Step 2:

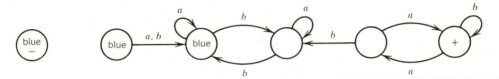

after Step 2 again:

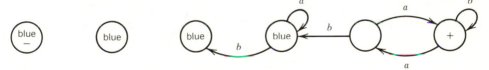

after Step 2 again:

No new states were painted blue this time, so the procedure stops and we examine the + state. The + state is not blue, so the machine accepts no words.

While we were examining the second method we might have noticed that Step 2 cannot be repeated more times than there are total states in the machine. If the machine has N states, after N iterations of Step 2 either they are all colored blue or we have already stopped. We can summarize this as a theorem.

THEOREM 15

Let F be an FA with N states. Then if F accepts any words at all it accepts some word with N or fewer letters.

PROOF

The shortest path from $-$ to $+$ (if there is any) cannot contain a circuit because if we go from $-$ to state 7 and then around a circuit back to state 7 and then to $+$ it would have been shorter to go from $-$ to state 7 to $+$ directly. If there is a path from $-$ to $+$ without a circuit, then it can visit each state at most one time. The path can then have at most N edges and the word that generates it can have at most N letters. ■

The proof actually shows that the shortest word must have at most $N - 1$ letters, since if the start state is a final state, then the word Λ is accepted and with $N - 1$ letters we can visit the other $N - 1$ states. The FA below has four states, but it accepts no word with fewer than three letters, so we see that the bound $N - 1$ is the best possible.

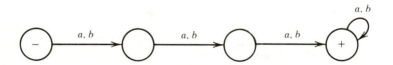

This gives us a third method for determining whether an FA accepts any words.

Method 3 Test all words with fewer than N letters by running them on the FA. If the FA accepts none of them, then it accepts no words at all. There are a predictable number of words to test, and each word takes a finite predictable time to run, so this is an effective decision procedure.

These methods are all effective; the question of which is more efficient is a whole other issue, one that we do not (often) raise in this book. As soon as we know that there is at least one way to accomplish a certain task we lose interest because our ultimate concern is the question, "What can be done and what cannot?" The only motivation we have for investigating alternative methods is that maybe they can be generalized to apply to new problems that our original approach could not be extended to cover.

EXAMPLE

Let us illustrate the effective decision procedure described above that determines whether two regular expressions are equivalent. We shall laboriously execute the entire process on a very simple example. Let the two regular expressions be:

$$r_1 = a^* \quad \text{and} \quad r_2 = \Lambda + aa^*$$

Luckily in this case we can understand that these two define the same language. Let us see how the decision procedure proves this. Some machines for FA_1, FA_1', FA_2, and FA_2' are shown below:

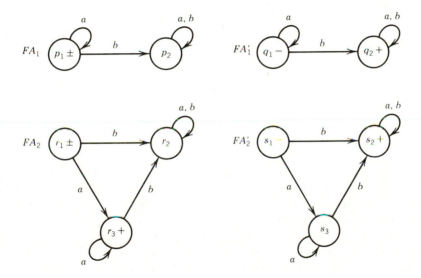

If we did not know how to produce these, algorithms in previous chapters would show us how. We have labeled the states with the letters p, q, r, and s for clarity. Instead of using the logical formula:

$$(L_1 \cap L_2') + (L_2 \cap L_1')$$

we build our machine based on the equivalent Set Theory formula

$$(L_1' + L_2)' + (L_2' + L_1)'$$

The machine for the first half of this formula is $(FA_1' + FA_2)'$

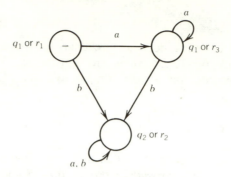

The machine for the second half is $(FA_2' + FA_1)'$

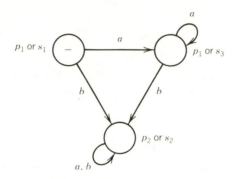

It was not an oversight that we failed to mark any of the states in these two machines with a $+$. Neither machine has any final states. For $(FA_1' + FA_2)'$ to have a final state, the machine $(FA_1' + FA_2)$ must have a nonfinal state. The start state for this machine is (q_1 or r_1). From there, if we read an a we go to (q_1 or r_3), and if we read instead a b we go to (q_2 or r_2). If we ever get to (q_2 or r_2) we must stay there. From (q_1 or r_3) an input b takes us to (q_2 or r_2) and an input a leaves us at (q_1 or r_3). All in all, from $-$ we cannot get to any other combination of states, such as the potential (q_2 or r_1) or (q_1 or r_2). Now since q_2 is a $+$ and r_1 and r_3 are both $+$, all three states (q_1 or r_1), (q_1 or r_3), and (q_2 or r_2) are all $+$, which means that the complement has no final states.

The exact same thing is true for the machine for the second half of the formula. Clearly, if we added these two machines together we would get a machine with nine states and no final state. Since it has no final state, it accepts no words and the two languages L_1 and L_2 are equivalent. This ends the decision procedure. There are no words in one language that are not in the other, so the two regular expressions define the same language and are equivalent. ∎

This example is a paradigm for the general situation. The machine for $(L_1' + L_2)'$ accepts only those words in L_1 but not in L_2. If the languages are in fact equal, this machine will have no final states. The same will be true for the machine for $(L_2' + L_1)'$. It will never be necessary to combine these two machines, since if either accepts a word, then $L_1 \neq L_2$.

When we listed three ways that a machine could accept no words the first way was that there be no final states and the second and third ways were that the final states not be reachable from the start state. We counted these situations separately. When we form a machine by adding two machines to-gether, we do not usually bother describing the states that are not reachable from the start state. The algorithm that we described in Chapter 7 never gets to consider combinations of states of the component machines that are never referred to. However, if we used a different algorithm, based on writing down the whole table of possible combinations and then drawing edges between the resultant states as indicated, we would, in this example, produce a picture with a final state but it would be unreachable from the start state. In the example above, the full machine for $(FA_1' + FA_2)'$ is this:

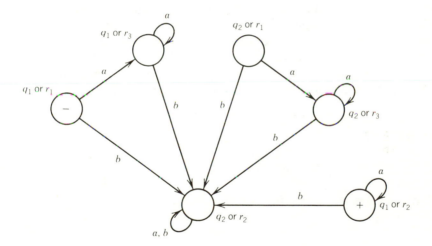

The only final state, $(q_1 \text{ or } r_2)$, cannot be reached from anywhere (in par-ticular not from the start state $(q_1 \text{ or } r_1)$. So the machine accepts no words.

We can summarize what we have learned so far in the following theorem.

THEOREM 16

(i)   There is an effective procedure to decide whether a given FA accepts any words.

(ii)   There is an effective procedure to decide whether two FA's are equivalent.

(iii) There is an effective procedure to decide whether two regular expressions are equivalent.   ■

Let us now answer our last question of decidability. How can we tell whether an FA, or regular expression, accepts a finite language or an infinite language?

With regular expressions this is easy. The closure of any nonempty set, whether finite or infinite, is itself infinite. Even the closure of one letter is infinite. Therefore, if when building the regular expression from the recursive definition we have ever had to use the closure operator, the resulting language is infinite. This can be determined by scanning the expression itself to see whether it contains the symbol *. If the regular expression does contain a *, then the language is infinite. The one exception to this rule is Λ*, which is just Λ. This one exception can however be very tricky. Of the two regular expressions:

$$(\Lambda + a\ \Lambda^*)\ (\Lambda^* + \Lambda)^* \quad \text{and} \quad (\Lambda + a\ \Lambda)^*\ (\Lambda^* + \Lambda)^*$$

only the second defines an infinite language.

If the regular expression does not contain a *, then the language is necessarily finite. This is because the other rules of building regular expressions (any letter, sum, and product) cannot produce an infinite set from finite ones. Therefore, as we could prove recursively, the result must be finite.

If we want to decide this question for an FA, we could first convert it to a regular expression. On the other hand, there are ways to determine whether an FA accepts an infinite language without having to perform the conversion.

THEOREM 17

Let F be an FA with N states. Then

(i)   If F accepts an input string w such that

$$N \leq \text{length } (w) < 2N$$

then F accepts an infinite language.

(ii)   If F accepts infinitely many words, than F accepts some word w such that

$$N \leq \text{length } (w) < 2N$$

PROOF

(i)   If there is some word w with N or more letters, then by the second version of the Pumping Lemma, we can break it into three parts:

$$w = x\ y\ z$$

The infinitely many different words $x \, y^n \, z$ for $n = 1, 2, 3 \ldots$ are all accepted by F.

(ii) Now we are supposing that F does accept infinitely many words. Then it must accept a word so large that its path must contain a circuit, maybe several circuits. Each circuit can contain at most N states because F has only N states in total. Let us change the path of this long word by keeping the first circuit we come to and bypassing all the others. To bypass a circuit means to come up to it, go no more than part way around it, and leave at the first occurrence of the state from which the path previously exited.

This one-circuit path corresponds to some word accepted by F. The word can have at most $2N$ letters, since at most N states are on the one circuit and at most N states are encountered off that circuit. If the length of this word is more than N, then we have found a word whose length is in the range that the theorem specifies. If, on the other hand, the length of this word is less than N, we can increase it by looping around the one circuit until the length is greater than N. The first time the length of the word (and path) becomes greater than N, it is still less than $2N$, since we have increased the word only by the length of the circuit, which is less than N. Eventually, we come to an accepted word with a length in the proper range. ∎

EXAMPLE

Consider this example:

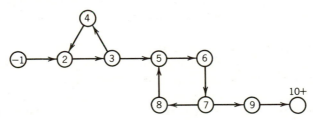

The first circuit is 2-3-4. It stays. The second circuit is 5-6-7-8. It is bypassed to become 5-6-7-9.

The path that used to be

$$1\text{-}2\text{-}3\text{-}4\text{-}2\text{-}3\text{-}5\text{-}6\text{-}7\text{-}8\text{-}5\text{-}6\text{-}7\text{-}8\text{-}5\text{-}6\text{-}7\text{-}9\text{-}10$$

becomes

$$1\text{-}2\text{-}3\text{-}4\text{-}2\text{-}3\text{-}5\text{-}6\text{-}7\text{-}9\text{-}10$$

This demonstrates the existence of a simple one-circuit path in any FA that accepts infinitely many words. ∎

This theorem provides us with an effective procedure for determining whether F accepts a finite language or an infinite language. We simply test the finitely many strings with lengths between N and $2N$ by running them on the machine and seeing if any reach a final state. If none does, the language is finite. Otherwise it is infinite.

THEOREM 18

There is an effective procedure to decide whether a given FA accepts a finite or an infinite language.

PROOF

If the machine has N states and the alphabet has m letters, then in total there are

$$m^N + m^{N+1} + m^{N+2} + \ldots + m^{2N-1}$$

different input strings in the range

$$N \leqslant \text{length of string} < 2N.$$

We can test them all by running them on the machine. If any are accepted, the language is infinite. If none are accepted, the language is finite. ■

It may often be more efficient to convert the FA to a regular expression. However, suppose the FA is an actual physical machine that is sitting in front of us. We may not know its exact structure inside or it may be extremely complicated. Even though we have an effective procedure for converting it into a regular expression, we may not have the capacity (storage or time or inclination) to do so. Yet there might be an automatic way of feeding in all combinations of letters in the interesting range. Even if this situation never arises, the theorem we have covered is a prototype for decidability of more complex questions.

In the case where the machine has 3 states and the alphabet has 2 letters, the number of strings we have to test is

$$2^3 + 2^4 + 2^5 = 8 + 16 + 32 = 56$$

which is not too bad. However, an FA with 3 states can be converted into a regular expression in very few steps.

PROBLEMS

Show by the method described in this chapter that the following pairs of FA's are equivalent.

1.

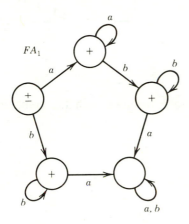 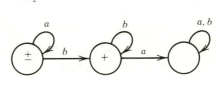

2.

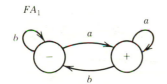 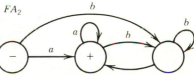

3.

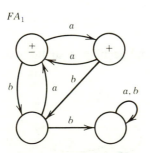 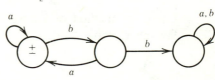

4.

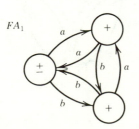

5. FA_1

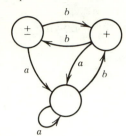

       FA_2

6.   Using the method of intersecting each machine with the complement of the other show that:

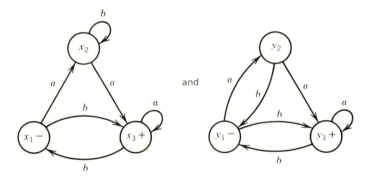

     do not accept the same language.

7.   Using the method of intersecting each machine with the complement of the other, show that:

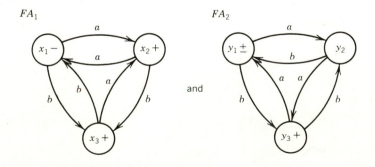

     do not accept the same language.

8.   List the 56 strings that will suffice to test whether a 3-state FA over $\Sigma = \{a, b\}$ has a finite language.

By using blue paint, determine which of the following FA's accept any words.

9.

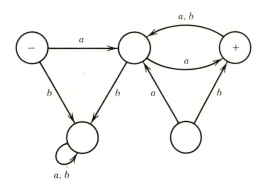

10.

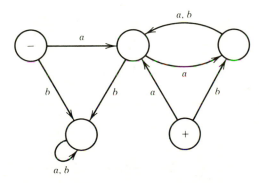

11.

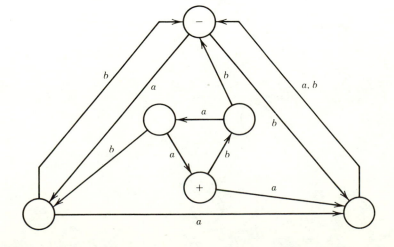

12.

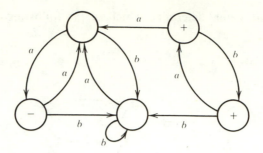

Which of the following FA's accepts a finite language and which an infinite one?

13.   (i)

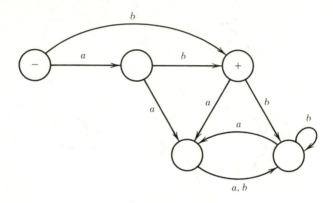

(ii)

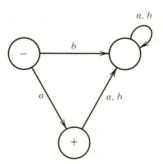

(iii)

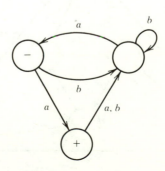

(iv)

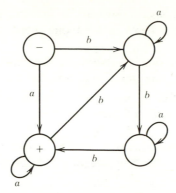

14. Without converting it into a regular expression or an FA, give an algorithm that decides whether a TG accepts any words.

15. Without converting it into a regular expression or an FA, give an algorithm that decides whether the language of an NFA is empty, finite, or infinite.

16. Do the same as Problem 15 for NFA-Λ's (see Chapter 8, Problem 9). Be careful. The machine

has an infinite language, whereas the machine

has a one-word language.

17. Consider the following simplified algorithm to decide if an FA with exactly N states has an empty language.

Step 1 Take the edges coming out of each final state and turn them into loops going back to the state they started from.

Step 2 Relabel all edges with the letter x. (We now have an NFA.)

Step 3 The original FA has a nonempty language if and only if this new NFA accepts the word x^N.

Illustrate this algorithm and prove it always works.
Is this an effective procedure?

18. By moving the start state, construct a decision procedure to determine whether a given FA accepts at least one word that starts with an a.

19. (i)   Construct a decision procedure to determine whether a given FA accepts at least one word that contains the letter b.

     (ii) Construct a decision procedure to determine whether a given FA accepts some words of even length.

20. Given two regular expressions r_1 and r_2, construct a decision procedure to determine whether the language of r_1 is contained in the language of r_2.

PART II

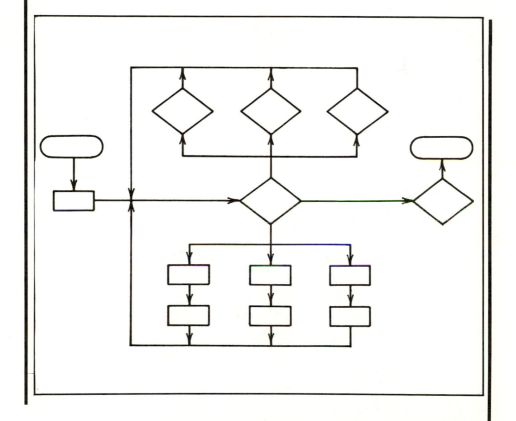

PUSHDOWN
AUTOMATA
THEORY

CHAPTER 13

CONTEXT-FREE GRAMMARS

Our overall goal is the study of computers: What are they? Of what are they composed? What can they and what can't they do? What will they be able to do in ten thousand years? The machines of Part I could not do much. This is because they did not have enough components. We shall soon rectify this shortcoming. In Part II we shall connect the topics of Part I directly to some of the problems in Computer Science with which we are already familiar.

The earliest computers, just like the programmable hand calculators of the 1970s, accepted no instructions except those in their own machine language or (almost equivalently) in their own assembly language. Every procedure, no matter how complicated, had to be spelled out in the crudest set of instructions: LOAD this, STORE that, ADD the contents of these two registers, and so forth. It could take dozens of these primitive instructions to do anything useful. In particular, it could take quite a few to evaluate one complicated arithmetic expression.

For example, in statistics, we often want to calculate something like

$$S = \sqrt{\frac{(7-9)^2 + (9-9)^2 + (11-9)^2}{2}}$$

Unfortunately, we cannot just throw this expression into the machine. One of the first hurdles the inventors of computers had to overcome was the problem of formula display. A human sees the picture of this formula drawn on five different levels. A 2 is on the bottom. Above it is a division line. Above that are the three subtractions. Above them and to the right are exponents indicating that these subtractions are to be squared. Above all of that and to the left is the square root sign. We must check the tail on the left of the square root sign to be sure that the bottom 2 is included in the root taking.

This converts to numerous assembly language instructions, especially since square roots are not standard hard-wired instructions on most computers.

The problem of making computers attractive to a wide variety of potential users (a problem important to those people who wanted to sell computers) clearly required that some "higher-level" language be invented—a language in which one mathematical step, such as evaluating the formula above, could be converted into one single computer instruction.

Because of the nature of early computer input devices, such as keypunches, paper tape, magnetic tape, and typewriters, it was necessary to develop a way of writing this expression in one line of standard typewriter symbols. Some few new symbols could be invented if necessary, but the whole expression had to be encoded in a way that did not require a five-level display or depend on the perception of spatial arrangement. Formulas had to be converted into linear strings of characters.

Several of the adjustments that had to be made were already in use in the scientific literature for various other reasons. For example, the use of the slash as a divide sign was already accepted by the mathematical public. Most publishers have special symbols for the popular fractions such as $\frac{1}{2}$ and $\frac{1}{4}$, but eight-elevenths was customarily written as 8/11.

Still, before the days of the computer no one would ever have dreamed of writing a complicated compound fraction such as

$$\frac{\dfrac{1}{2} + 9}{4 + \dfrac{8}{21} + \dfrac{5}{3 + \dfrac{1}{2}}}$$

in the parentheses-laden one-line notation

$$((1/2) + 9)/(4 + (8/21) + (5/(3 + (1/2))))$$

The most important reason for not using the one-line version unless necessary is that in the picture version we can easily see that the number we are looking at is a little more than 9 divided by a little more than 5, so it obviously has a value between 1 and 2. Looking at the parentheses notation, it is not even obvious which of the slash marks separates the numerator from the denominator of the major division.

The main advantage of the one-level version is that we can feed it into a computer. At some time in the future a computer might be able to digest the multilevel expression and the one-line nightmare can be forgotten forever.

How can a computer scan over this one-line string of typewriter characters and figure out what is going on? That is, how can a computer convert this string into its personal language of LOAD this, STORE that, and so on?

The conversion from a high-level language into assembler language code is done by a program called the **compiler.** This is a superprogram. Its data are other people's programs. It processes them and prints out an equivalent program written in assembler language. To do this it must figure out in what order to perform the complicated set of arithmetic operations that it finds written out in the one-line formula. It must do this in a mechanical, algorithmic way. It cannot just look at the expression and understand it. Rules must be given by which this string can be processed—rules, perhaps, like those the machines we discussed in Part I could follow.

Consider the language of valid input strings over the alphabet

$$0\ 1\ 2\ 3\ 4\ 5\ 6\ 7\ 8\ 9\ +\ -\ /\ *\ )\ ($$

Could some FA, directed from state to state by the input of a one-line formula, print out the equivalent assembly-language program? This would have to be an output FA like the Mealy or Moore machines for which the output alphabet would be assembler language statements.

The solution is not quite as easy as that, but it is within our reach.

We also want our machine to be able to reject strings of symbols that make no sense as arithmetic expressions, such as "((9)+". This input string should not take us to a final state in the machine. However, we cannot know that this is a bad input string until we have reached the last letter. If the + were changed to a), the formula would be valid. An FA that translated expressions into instructions as it scanned left to right would already be turning out code before it realized that the whole expression is nonsense.

Before we try to build a compiling machine, let us return to the discussion of what is and what is not a valid arithmetic expression as defined in Chapter 3 by recursive definition.

All valid arithmetic expressions can be built up from the following rules. Anything not produceable from these rules is not a valid arithmetic expression:

Rule 1   Any number is in the set AE.

Rule 2   If x and y are in AE then so are:

$$(x) \qquad -(x) \qquad (x + y) \qquad (x - y) \qquad (x*y) \qquad (x/y) \qquad (x**y)$$

This time we have included parentheses around every component factor. This avoids the ambiguity of expressions like 3 + 4 * 5 and 8/4/2 by making them illegal. We shall present a better definition of this set later.

First we must design a machine that can figure out how a given input string was built up from these basic rules. Then we should be able to translate this sequence of rules into an assembler language program, since all of these rules are pure assembler language instructions (with the exception of exponentiation, which presents a totally different problem; but since this is not a course in compiler design, we ignore this embarrassing fact).

For example, if we present the input string

$$((3 + 4) * (6 + 7))$$

and the machine discovers that the way this can be produced from the rules is by the sequence

3 is in *AE*

4 is in *AE*

(3 + 4) is in *AE*

6 is in *AE*

7 is in *AE*

(6 + 7) is in *AE*

((3 + 4) * (6 + 7)) is in *AE*

we can automatically convert this into

LOAD 3 in Register 1

LOAD 4 in Register 2

ADD the contents of Register 2 into Register 1

LOAD 6 in Register 3

LOAD 7 in Register 4

ADD the contents of Register 3 into Register 4

MULTIPLY Register 1 by Register 4

or some such sequence of instructions depending on the architecture of the particular machine (not all computers have so many arithmetic registers) and the requirements of the particular assembler language (multiplication is not always available).

The hard part of the problem is to figure out by mechanical means how the input string can be produced from the rules. The second part—given the sequence of rules that create the expression to write a computer program to duplicate this process—is easy.

The designers of the first high-level languages realized that this problem is analogous to the problem humans have to face hundreds of times every day when they must decipher the sentences that they hear or read in English. Here we have again the ever-present parallelism: Recognizing what a computer language instruction is saying is analogous to recognizing what a sentence in a human language means.

Elementary School used to be called Grammar School because one of the most important subjects taught was English Grammar. A grammar is the set of rules by which the valid sentences in a language are constructed. Our ability to understand what a sentence means is based on our ability to understand how it could be formed from the rules of grammar. Determining how a sentence can be formed from the rules of grammar is called *parsing the sentence*.

When we hear or read a sentence in our native language, we do not go through a conscious act of parsing. Exactly why this is the case is a question for other sciences. Perhaps it is because we learned to speak as infants by a trial and error method that was not as mathematical and rigorous as the way in which we learn foreign languages later in life. When we were born we spoke no language in which the grammar of our native tongue could be described to us. However, when we learn a second language the rules of grammar for that language can be explained to us in English. How we can possibly learn our first language is a problem discussed by linguists, psychologists, philosophers, and worried parents. It does not concern us here because when we come to teach a computer how to understand the languages it must recognize, a few printed circuits will do the trick.

Even though human languages have rules of grammar that can be stated explicitly, it is still true that many invalid sentences, those that are not strictly speaking grammatical, can be understood. Perhaps this is because there are tacit alternative rules of grammar that, although not taught in school, nevertheless are rules people live by. But this will not concern us either. No computer yet can forgive the mess, "Let x equal two times the radius times that funny looking Greek letter with the squiggly top that sounds like a pastry, you know what I mean?" The rules of computer language grammar are prescriptive—no ungrammatical strings are accepted.

Since the English word "grammar" can mean the study of grammar as well as the set of rules themselves, we sometimes refer to the set of rules as forming a "generative grammar." This emphasizes the point that from them and a dictionary (the alphabet) we can generate all the sentences (words) in the language.

Let us look at the rule in English grammar that allows us to form a sentence by juxtaposing a noun and a verb (assuming that the verb is in the correct person and number). We might produce

Birds sing.

However, using the same rule might also produce

Wednesday sings.   or   *Coal mines sing.*

If these are not meant to be poetical or metaphoric, they are just bad sentences. They violate a different kind of rule of grammar, one that takes into account the meaning of words as well as their person, number, gender, and case.

Rules that involve the meaning of words we call **semantics** and rules that do not involve the meaning of words we call **syntax.** In English the meaning of words can be relevant but in arithmetic the meaning of numbers is rarely cataclysmic. In the high-level computer languages, one number is as good as another. If

$$X = B + 9$$

is a valid formulation then so are

$$X = B + 8 \qquad X = B + 473 \qquad X = B + 9999$$

So long as the constants do not become so large that they are out of range, and we do not try to divide by 0, and we do not try to take the square root of a negative number, and we do not mix fixed-point numbers with floating-point numbers in bad ways, one number is as good as another. It could be argued that such rules as "thou shalt not divide by zero" as well as the other restrictions mentioned are actually semantic laws, but this is another interesting point that we shall not discuss.

In general, the rules of computer language grammar are all syntactic and not semantic.

There is another way in which the parsing of arithmetic expressions is easier than the parsing of English sentences. To parse the English sentence, "Birds sing." it is necessary to look up in a dictionary whether "birds" is a noun or a verb. To parse the arithmetic expression "(3 + 5)*6" it is not necessary to know any other characteristics of the numbers 3, 5, and 6. We shall see more differences between simple languages and hard languages as we progress through Part II.

Let us go back to the analogy between computer languages and English. Some of the rules of English grammar are these:

1.   A _sentence_ can be a _subject_ followed by a _predicate_.

2.   A _subject_ can be a _noun-phrase_.

3.   A _noun-phrase_ can be an _adjective_ followed by a _noun-phrase_.

4.   A _noun-phrase_ can be an _article_ followed by a _noun-phrase_.

5.   A _noun-phrase_ can be a _noun_.

6.   A _predicate_ can be a _verb_ followed by a _noun-phrase_.

7.   A _noun_ can be:

$$apple \qquad bear \qquad cat \qquad dog$$

8. A *verb* can be:

eats   *follows*   *gets*   *hugs*

9. An *adjective* can be:

itchy   *jumpy*

10. An *article* can be:

a   *an*   *the*

Let us, for the moment, restrict the possibility of forming sentences to the laws stated above. Within this small model of English there are hundreds of sentences we can form. For example:

The itchy bear hugs the jumpy dog.

The method by which this sentence can be generated is outlined below:

1.	*sentence* ⇒ *subject predicate*	Rule 1
2.	⇒ *noun-phrase predicate*	Rule 2
3.	⇒ *noun-phrase verb noun-phrase*	Rule 6
4.	⇒ *article noun-phrase verb noun-phrase*	Rule 4
5.	⇒ *article adjective noun-phrase verb noun-phrase*	Rule 3
6.	⇒ *article adjective noun verb noun-phrase*	Rule 5
7.	⇒ *article adjective noun verb article noun-phrase*	Rule 4
8.	⇒ *article adjective noun verb article adjective noun-phrase*	Rule 3
9.	⇒ *article adjective noun verb article adjective noun*	Rule 5
10.	⇒ *the adjective noun verb article adjective noun*	Rule 10
11.	⇒ *the itchy noun verb article adjective noun*	Rule 9
12.	⇒ *the itchy bear verb article adjective noun*	Rule 7
13.	⇒ *the itchy bear hugs article adjective noun*	Rule 8
14.	⇒ *the itchy bear hugs the adjective noun*	Rule 10
15.	⇒ *the itchy bear hugs the jumpy noun*	Rule 9
16.	⇒ *the itchy bear hugs the jumpy dog*	Rule 7

The arrow indicates that a substitution was made according to the rules of grammar stated above.

A law of grammar is in reality a suggestion for possible substitutions. What happened above is that we started out with the initial symbol *Sentence*. We then applied the rules for producing sentences listed in the generative grammar. In most cases we had some choice in selecting which rule we wanted to apply.

There is a qualitative distinction between the word "_noun_" and the word "_bear_." To show this we have underlined the words that stand for parts of speech and are not to be considered themselves as words for the finished sentences. Of course, in the complete set of rules for English the words "verb," "adjective," and so on are all perfectly good words and would be included in our final set of rules as usable words. They are all nouns. But in this model the term _verb_ is a transitory place holder. It means, "stick a verb here." It must eventually be replaced to form a finished sentence.

Once we have put in the word "bear" we are stuck with it. No rule of grammar says that a bear can be replaced by anything else. The words that cannot be replaced by anything are called **terminals.** Words that must be replaced by other things we call **nonterminals.** We will give a more general definition of this shortly.

Midway through the production procedure we developed the sentence into as many nonterminals as it was going to become.

9. _article_ _adjective_ _noun_ _verb_ _article_ _adjective_ _noun_

From this point on the procedure was only one of selecting which terminals were to be inserted in place of the nonterminals. This middle stage in which all the terminals are identified by their nonterminal names is the "grammatical parse" of the sentence. We can tell what noun each adjective modifies because we know how it got into the sentence in the first place. We know which noun-phrase produced it. "Itchy" modifies "bear" because they were both introduced in Step 5 by application of Rule 3.

There is an element of recursive definition lurking in these rules. We have allowed a noun-phrase to be an adjective followed by a noun-phrase. This could lead to:

$$_noun\text{-}phrase_ \Rightarrow \text{_adjective_ _noun\text{-}phrase_}$$

$$\Rightarrow \text{_adjective_ _adjective_ _noun\text{-}phrase_}$$

$$\Rightarrow \text{_adjective_ _adjective_ _adjective_ _noun\text{-}phrase_}$$

$$\Rightarrow \text{_adjective_ _adjective_ _adjective_ _noun_}$$

$$\Rightarrow \text{_itchy_ _adjective_ _adjective_ _noun_}$$

$$\Rightarrow \text{_itchy_ _itchy_ _adjective_ _noun_}$$

$$\Rightarrow \text{_itchy_ _itchy_ _itchy_ _noun_}$$

$$\Rightarrow \text{_itchy_ _itchy_ _itchy_ bear}$$

If we so desired, we could produce fifty itchy's. Using the Kleene closure operator we could write

$$_noun\text{-}phrase_ \Rightarrow \text{_adjective_* _noun_}$$

But now we are getting ahead of ourselves.

The rules we have given above for this simplified version of English allow for many dumb sentences such as:

Itchy the apple eats a jumpy jumpy jumpy bear.

Because we are not considering the limitations of semantics, diction, or good sense, we must consider this string of terminals as a good sentence. This is what we mean by the phrase "formal language," which we used in Part I. It is a funny phrase because it sounds as if we mean the stuffy language used in diplomatic circles. In reality it means that any string of symbols satisfying the rules of grammar (syntax alone) is as good as any other. The word "formal" here means "strictly formed by the rules," not "highly proper." The Queen of England is unlikely to have made the remark above about Itchy the apple.

We can follow the same model for defining arithmetic expressions. We can write the whole system of rules of formation as the list of possible substitutions shown below:

$$Start \rightarrow (AE)$$
$$AE \rightarrow (AE + AE)$$
$$AE \rightarrow (AE - AE)$$
$$AE \rightarrow (AE * AE)$$
$$AE \rightarrow (AE / AE)$$
$$AE \rightarrow (AE ** AE)$$
$$AE \rightarrow (AE)$$
$$AE \rightarrow -(AE)$$
$$AE \rightarrow ANY\text{-}NUMBER$$

Here we have used the word "Start" to begin the process, as we used the word "Sentence" in the example of English. Aside from Start, the only other nonterminal is AE. The terminals are the phrase "any number" and the symbols

$$+ \ - \ * \ / \ ** \ (\ )$$

Either we could be satisfied that we know what is meant by the words "any number" or else we could define this phrase by a set of rules, thus converting it from a terminal into a nonterminal.

Rule 1 ANY-NUMBER → FIRST-DIGIT
Rule 2 FIRST-DIGIT → FIRST-DIGIT OTHER-DIGIT

Rule 3   FIRST-DIGIT → 1 2 3 4 5 6 7 8 9
Rule 4   OTHER-DIGIT → 0 1 2 3 4 5 6 7 8 9

Rules 3 and 4 offer choices of terminals. We put spaces between them to indicate "choose one," but we soon shall introduce another disjunctive symbol. We can produce the number 1066 as follows:

Rule 1 ANY-NUMBER ⇒ FIRST-DIGIT

Rule 2   ⇒ FIRST-DIGIT OTHER-DIGIT

Rule 2   ⇒ FIRST-DIGIT OTHER-DIGIT
                    OTHER-DIGIT

Rule 2   ⇒ FIRST-DIGIT OTHER-DIGIT
                    OTHER-DIGIT OTHER-DIGIT

Rules 3 and 4   ⇒ 1066

Here we have made all our substitutions of terminals for nonterminals in one swoop, but without any possible confusion. One thing we should note about the definition of AE is that some of the grammatical rules involve both terminals and nonterminals together. In English, the rules were either of the form

one Nonterminal → string of Nonterminals

or

one Nonterminal → choice of terminals

In our present study, we shall see that the form of the grammar has great significance.

The sequence of applications of the rules that produces the finished string of terminals from the starting symbol is called a **derivation.** The grammatical rules are often called **productions.** They all indicate possible substitutions. The derivation may or may not be unique, by which we mean that by applying productions to the start symbol in two different ways we may still produce the same finished product. (See Problem 6 below.)

We are now ready to define the general concept of which all these examples have been special cases. We call this new structure a **context-free grammar** or **CFG.** The full meaning of the term "context-free" will be made clear later. The concept of CFG's was invented by the linguist Noam Chomsky in 1956.

Chomsky gave several mathematical models for languages, and we shall see more of his work later.

DEFINITION

A **context-free grammar,** called a **CFG,** is a collection of three things:

1   An alphabet Σ of letters called **terminals** from which we are going to make strings that will be the words of a language.
2   A set of symbols called **nonterminals,** one of which is the symbol S, standing for "start here."
3   A finite set of **productions** of the form

    one nonterminal $\rightarrow$ finite string of terminals and/or nonterminals

where the strings of terminals and nonterminals can consist of only terminals or of only nonterminals, or any mixture of terminals and nonterminals or even the empty string. We require that at least one production has the nonterminal S as its left side.   ∎

So as not to confuse terminals and nonterminals, we always insist that nonterminals be designated by capital letters while terminals are usually designated by lowercase letters and special symbols.

DEFINITION

The **language generated** by a CFG is the set of all strings of terminals that can be produced from the start symbol S using the productions as substitutions. A language generated by a CFG is called a **context-free language,** abbreviated **CFL.**   ∎

There is no great uniformity of opinion among experts about the terminology to be used here. The language generated by a CFG is sometimes called the **language defined** by the CFG, or the **language derived** from the CFG, or the **language produced** by the CFG. This is similar to the problem with regular expressions. We should say "the language defined by the regular expression" although the phrase "the language of the regular expression" has a clear meaning. We usually call the sequence of productions that form a word a **derivation** or a **generation** of the word.

EXAMPLE

Let the only terminal be a.
Let the productions be:

$$\text{Prod 1}\quad S \rightarrow aS$$
$$\text{Prod 2}\quad S \rightarrow \Lambda$$

If we apply Production 1 six times and then apply Production 2, we generate the following:

$$S \Rightarrow aS$$
$$\Rightarrow aaS$$
$$\Rightarrow aaaS$$
$$\Rightarrow aaaaS$$
$$\Rightarrow aaaaaS$$
$$\Rightarrow aaaaaaS$$
$$\Rightarrow aaaaaa\Lambda$$
$$= aaaaaa$$

This is a derivation of a^6 in this CFG. The string a^n comes from n applications of Production 1 followed by one application of Production 2. If we apply Production 2 without Production 1, we find that the null string is itself in the language of this CFG. Since the only terminal is a it is clear that no words outside of **a*** can possibly be generated. The language generated by this CFG is exactly **a***. ■

In the examples above, we used two different arrow symbols. The symbol "$\rightarrow$" we employ in the statement of the productions. It means "can be replaced by", as in $S \rightarrow aS$. The other arrow symbol "$\Rightarrow$" we employ between the unfinished stages in the generation of our word. It means "can develop into" as in $aaS \Rightarrow aaaS$. These "unfinished stages" are strings of terminals and nonterminals that we shall call **working strings.**

Notice that in this last example we have both $S \rightarrow aS$ as a production in the abstract and $S \Rightarrow aS$ as the first step in a particular derivation.

EXAMPLE

Let the only terminal be a.
Let the productions be:

$$\text{Prod 1}\quad S \rightarrow SS$$
$$\text{Prod 2}\quad S \rightarrow a$$
$$\text{Prod 3}\quad S \rightarrow \Lambda$$

In this language we can have the following derivation.

$$S \Rightarrow SS$$
$$\Rightarrow SSS$$
$$\Rightarrow SaS$$
$$\Rightarrow SaSS$$
$$\Rightarrow \Lambda\, a\, S\, S$$
$$\Rightarrow \Lambda\, a\, a\, S$$
$$\Rightarrow \Lambda\, a\, a\, \Lambda$$
$$= aa$$

The language generated by this set of productions is also just the language **a***, but in this case the string *aa* can be obtained in many (actually infinitely many) ways. In the first example there was a unique way to produce every word in the language. This also illustrates that the same language can have more than one CFG generating it. Notice above that there are two ways to go from *SS* to *SSS*—either of the two *S*'s can be doubled. ■

In the previous example the only terminal is *a* and the only nonterminal is *S*. What then is Λ? It is not a nonterminal since there is no production of the form

$$\Lambda \rightarrow \text{something}$$

Yet it is not a terminal since it vanishes from the finished string $\Lambda aa\Lambda = aa$. As always, Λ is a very special symbol and has its own status. In the definition of a CFG we said a nonterminal could be replaced by any string of terminals and/or nonterminals even the empty string. To replace a nonterminal by Λ is to delete it without leaving any tangible remains. For the nonterminal *N* the production

$$N \rightarrow \Lambda$$

means that whenever we want, *N* can simply be deleted from any place in a working string.

EXAMPLE

Let the terminals be *a* and *b*, let the only nonterminal be *S*, and let the productions be

> PROD 1 $S \rightarrow aS$
> PROD 2 $S \rightarrow bS$
> PROD 3 $S \rightarrow a$
> PROD 4 $S \rightarrow b$

We can produce the word *baab* as follows:

$$S \Rightarrow bS \qquad \text{(by PROD 2)}$$
$$\Rightarrow baS \qquad \text{(by PROD 1)}$$
$$\Rightarrow baaS \qquad \text{(by PROD 1)}$$
$$\Rightarrow baab \qquad \text{(by PROD 4)}$$

The language generated by this CFG is the set of all possible strings of the letters *a* and *b* except for the null string, which we cannot generate.

We can generate any word by the following algorithm:

At the beginning the working string is the start symbol *S*. Select a word to be generated. Read the letters of the desired word from left to right one at a time. If an *a* is read that is not the last letter of the word, apply PROD 1 to the working string. If a *b* is read that is not the last letter of the word, apply PROD 2 to the working string. If the last letter is read and it is an *a*, apply PROD 3 to the working string. If the last letter is read and it is a *b*, apply PROD 4 to the working string.

At every stage in the derivation before the last, the working string has the form

$$\text{(string of terminals) } S$$

At every stage in the derivation, to apply a production means to replace the final nonterminal *S*. Productions 3 and 4 can be used only once and only one of them can be used. For example, to generate *babb* we apply in order Prods 2, 1, 2, 4, as below:

$$S \Rightarrow bS \Rightarrow baS \Rightarrow babS \Rightarrow babb \qquad \blacksquare$$

EXAMPLE

Let the terminals be *a* and *b*. Let the nonterminals be *S*, *X*, and *Y*. Let the productions be:

$$S \rightarrow X$$
$$S \rightarrow Y$$
$$X \rightarrow \Lambda$$
$$Y \rightarrow aY$$
$$Y \rightarrow bY$$
$$Y \rightarrow a$$
$$Y \rightarrow b$$

All the words in this language are either of type X, if the first production in their derivation is

$$S \rightarrow X$$

or of type Y, if the first production in their derivation is

$$S \rightarrow Y$$

The only possible continuation for words of type X is the production

$$X \rightarrow \Lambda$$

Therefore Λ is the only word of type X.

The productions whose left side is Y form a collection identical to the productions in the previous example except that the start symbol S has been replaced by the symbol Y. We can carry on from Y the same way we carried on from S before. This does not change the language generated, which contains only strings of terminals. Therefore, the words of type Y are exactly the same as the words in the previous example. That means, any string of a's and b's except the null string can be produced from Y as these strings were produced before from S.

Putting the type X and the type Y words together, we see that the total language generated by this CFG is all strings of a's and b's, null or otherwise. The language generated is $(a + b)^*$. ■

EXAMPLE

Let the terminals be a and b. Let the only nonterminal be S.
Let the productions be

$$S \rightarrow aS$$
$$S \rightarrow bS$$
$$S \rightarrow a$$
$$S \rightarrow b$$
$$S \rightarrow \Lambda$$

The word ab can be generated by the derivation

$$S \Rightarrow aS$$
$$\Rightarrow abS$$
$$\Rightarrow ab\Lambda$$
$$= ab$$

or by the derivation

$$S \Rightarrow aS$$
$$\Rightarrow ab$$

The language of this CFG is also $(\mathbf{a} + \mathbf{b})^*$, but the sequence of productions that is used to generate a specific word is not unique.

If we deleted the third and fourth productions, the language generated would be the same. ∎

EXAMPLE

Let the terminals be a and b, let the nonterminals be S and X, and let the productions be

$$S \rightarrow XaaX$$
$$X \rightarrow aX$$
$$X \rightarrow bX$$
$$X \rightarrow \Lambda$$

We already know from the previous example that the last three productions will allow us to generate any word we want from the nonterminal X. If the nonterminal X appears in any working string we can apply productions to turn it into any word we want. Therefore, the words generated from S have the form

anything *aa* anything

or

$$(\mathbf{a} + \mathbf{b})^*\mathbf{aa}(\mathbf{a} + \mathbf{b})^*$$

which is the language of all words with a double a in them somewhere.

For example, to generate *baabaab* we can proceed as follows:

$$S \Rightarrow XaaX \Rightarrow bXaaX \Rightarrow baXaaX \Rightarrow baaXaaX \Rightarrow baabXaaX$$
$$\Rightarrow baab\Lambda aaX = baabaaX \Rightarrow baabaabX \Rightarrow baabaab\Lambda = baabaab$$

There are other sequences that also derive the word *baabaab*. ∎

EXAMPLE

Let the terminals be a and b, let the nonterminals be S, X, and Y and let the productions be

$$S \rightarrow XY$$
$$X \rightarrow aX$$
$$X \rightarrow bX$$
$$X \rightarrow a$$
$$Y \rightarrow Ya$$
$$Y \rightarrow Yb$$
$$Y \rightarrow a$$

What can be derived from X? Let us look at the X productions alone.

$$X \rightarrow aX$$
$$X \rightarrow bX$$
$$X \rightarrow a$$

Beginning with the nonterminal X and starting a derivation using the first two productions we always keep a nonterminal X on the right end. To get rid of the X for good we must eventually replace it with an a by the third production. We can see that any string of terminals that comes from X must end in an a and any words ending in an a can be derived from X. For example, to derive the word $babba$ from X we can proceed as follows:

$$X \Rightarrow bX \Rightarrow baX \Rightarrow babX \Rightarrow babbX \Rightarrow babba$$

Similarly, the words that can be derived from Y are exactly those that begin with an a. To derive $abbab$, for example, we can proceed:

$$Y \Rightarrow Yb \Rightarrow Yab \Rightarrow Ybab \Rightarrow Ybbab \Rightarrow abbab$$

A Y always stays on the left end until it is replaced by an a. When an X part is concatenated with a Y part, a double a is formed.

We can conclude that starting from S we can derive only words with a double a in them, and all of these words can be derived.

For example, to derive $babaabb$ we know that the X part must end at the first a of the double a and that the Y part must begin with the second a.

$$S \Rightarrow XY \Rightarrow bXY \Rightarrow baXY \Rightarrow babXY \Rightarrow babaY$$
$$\Rightarrow babaYb \Rightarrow babaYbb \Rightarrow babaabb$$ ∎

EXAMPLE

Let the terminals be *a* and *b*. Let the three nonterminals be S, BALANCED, and UNBALANCED. We treat these nonterminals as if they were each a single symbol and nothing more confusing. Let the productions be

$$S \rightarrow SS$$
$$S \rightarrow \text{BALANCED } S$$
$$S \rightarrow S \text{ BALANCED}$$
$$S \rightarrow \Lambda$$
$$S \rightarrow \text{UNBALANCED } S \text{ UNBALANCED}$$
$$\text{BALANCED} \rightarrow aa$$
$$\text{BALANCED} \rightarrow bb$$
$$\text{UNBALANCED} \rightarrow ab$$
$$\text{UNBALANCED} \rightarrow ba$$

We shall show that the language generated from these productions is the set of all words with an even number of *a*'s and an even number of *b*'s. This is our old friend, the language EVEN-EVEN.

To prove this we must show two things: that all the words in EVEN-EVEN can be generated from these productions and that every word generated from these productions is in fact in the language EVEN-EVEN.

First we show that every word in EVEN-EVEN can be generated by these productions. From our earlier discussion of the language EVEN-EVEN we know that every word in this language can be written as a collection of substrings of

type **aa** or type **bb**
or type **(ab + ba) (aa + bb)* (ab + ba)**.

All three types can be generated from the nonterminal S from productions above. The various substrings can be put together by repeated application of the production

$$S \rightarrow SS$$

This production is very useful. If we apply it four times we can turn one S into five S's. Each of these S's can be a syllable of any of the three types. For example, the EVEN-EVEN word *aababbab* can be produced as follows:

$$S \Rightarrow \text{BALANCED } S$$
$$\Rightarrow aaS$$
$$\Rightarrow aa \text{ UNBALANCED } S \text{ UNBALANCED}$$

$\Rightarrow aa\ ba\ S$ UNBALANCED
$\Rightarrow aa\ ba\ S\ ab$
$\Rightarrow aa\ ba$ BALANCED $S\ ab$
$\Rightarrow aa\ ba\ bb\ S\ ab$
$\Rightarrow aa\ ba\ bb\ \Lambda\ ab$
$= aababbab$

To see that all the words that are generated by these productions are in the language EVEN-EVEN we need only to observe that words derived from S can be decomposed into two-letter syllables and the unbalanced syllables, ab and ba, come into the working string in pairs, which add two a's and two b's. Also, the balanced syllables add two of one letter and zero of the other letter. The sum total of a's and b's will be the sum of even numbers of a's and even numbers of b's. Both the a's and the b's in total will be even.

Therefore, the language generated by this CFG is exactly EVEN-EVEN. ■

EXAMPLE

Let the terminals be a and b. Let the nonterminals be S, A, and B. Let the productions be

$$S \rightarrow aB$$
$$S \rightarrow bA$$
$$A \rightarrow a$$
$$A \rightarrow aS$$
$$A \rightarrow bAA$$
$$B \rightarrow b$$
$$B \rightarrow bS$$
$$B \rightarrow aBB$$

The language that this CFG generates is the language EQUAL of all strings that have an equal number of a and b's in them. This language begins

EQUAL = {$ab\ ba\ aabb\ abab\ abba\ baab\ baba\ bbaa\ aaabbb$ . . . }

(Notice that previously we included Λ in this language, but for now it has been dropped.)

To prove that this is the language that is generated by these productions we need to demonstrate two things: first, that every word in EQUAL can be derived from S by these productions and, second, that every word generated by these productions is in EQUAL.

To do this we should note that the nonterminal A stands for any word that is a-heavy, that is, a word that has one more a than it has b's (for example, 7 a's and 6 b's). The nonterminal B stands for any word that is b-heavy, that is, that has one more b than it has a's, (for example 4 b's and 3 a's).

We are really making three claims at once.

Claim 1   All words in EQUAL can be generated by some sequence of productions beginning with the start symbol S.

Claim 2   All words that have one more a than b's can be generated from these productions by starting with the symbol A.

Claim 3   All words that have one more b than a's can be generated from these productions by starting with the symbol B.

If one of these three claims is false, then there is a smallest word of one of these three types that cannot be generated as we claim it can. We are looking for the smallest counterexample to any of these three claims. Let w be the smallest counterexample. For all words shorter than w the three claims must be true.

Which of these three claims does w disprove?

Let us first challenge Claim 1, by assuming that the word w is in the language EQUAL, but it cannot be produced from these productions starting with the symbol S. The word w either begins with an a or a b. Let us say that it begins with an a. It then is of the form a(rest). Since w is in the language EQUAL, the string (rest) must have exactly one more b in it than a's. By our claim (which holds for all words with fewer letters than w has), we know that (rest) can then be generated from these productions, starting with the symbol B. But then w can be generated from these productions starting with the symbol S, since the production

$$S \Rightarrow aB$$

then leads to

$$\Rightarrow a(\text{rest}) = w$$

A similar contradiction arises if we assume that w started with the letter b.

In this case the letters of w after the b form an A-heavy string that can be generated from A. $S{\rightarrow}bA$ then generates w. Therefore the smallest counterexample to these claims cannot be a word in EQUAL. That means that w does not disprove Claim 1.

Let us now entertain the possibility that w disproves Claim 2. That means that there is a word w that has one more a than b's but that cannot be produced from these productions starting with the symbol A, and further that all words smaller than w satisfy all three claims.

There are two cases we need to consider. The first is that the word w begins with the letter a and the second is that the word w begins with the letter b.

In the first case w must be of the form a(rest). Since w has one more a than b's, the substring (rest) has the same number of a's and b's. This means that it can be generated from these rules starting with the letter S, because (rest) has fewer letters than w does, and so Claim 1 applies to it.

However, if (rest) can be produced from S, then w can be produced from A starting with the production

$$A \Rightarrow aS$$

which leads to

$$\Rightarrow a(\text{rest}) = w$$

This contradicts the premise of our counterexample. Therefore, w cannot start with an a.

Now let us treat the second case. Suppose w begins with the letter b. The word w is still of the form b(rest), but now (rest) does not have the same number of a's and b's. The string (rest) has two more a's than it has b's. Let us scan down the string (rest) from left to right until we find a substring that has exactly one more a than it has b's. Call this the first half. What is left must also have exactly one more a than it has b's. Call it the second half. Now we know that the word w is of the form

$$b(\text{first half})(\text{second half})$$

Both halves are of type A and can be generated from the symbol A since they both have fewer letters than w has and Claim 2 must apply to them.

This time we can generate w starting with the production

$$A \Rightarrow bAA$$

leading eventually to

$$\Rightarrow b(\text{first half})(\text{second half})$$

Again, this contradicts the assumption that w is a counterexample to our second claim.

The case where the smallest counterexample is of type B is practically identical to the case where w is of type A. If we reverse the letters a and b and the letters A and B in the argument above we have the proof of this case.

We have now covered all possibilities, and we can conclude that there can be no smallest counterexample to any of our claims. Therefore, all three claims are true. In particular, Claim 1 is true: All the words in EQUAL can be generated from the symbol S.

Even though we have worked hard we are only half done. We still need to show that all the words that can be generated from S are in the language EQUAL.

Again we make three claims:

Claim 4   All words generated from S are in EQUAL.

Claim 5   All words generated from A have one more a than b's.

Claim 6   All words generated from B have one more b than a's.

Let us say that w is the smallest counterexample to any of these three claims. Let us first consider whether w can violate Claim 4. Let us say that w is produced from S but has unequal a's and b's. We are assuming that these three claims are true when applied to all words with fewer letters than w.

If w is produced from S, it either comes from $S \rightarrow aB$ or from $S \rightarrow bA$. Since these cases are symmetric, let us say that w comes from $S \rightarrow aB$. Now since this B generates a word with one fewer letter than w, we know that the three claims apply to the production that proceeds from this B. This means in particular that what is generated from B satisfies Claim 6 above and that it therefore generates a word with one more b than a. Therefore, w will have exactly the same number of b's and a's. The word w, then, satisfies Claim 4 and is not a counterexample.

Now let us treat the case where the smallest counterexample, is a word called w that disproves Claim 6; that is, it is generated from the symbol B but does not have exactly one more b than a's. It could not have come from $B \rightarrow b$ since then it would have one more b than a (one b, no a's). It could not come from the production $B \rightarrow bS$, since whatever is produced from the S part is a string of length less than w, which must then satisfy Claim 4 and have equal a's and b's leaving w in proper form. Lastly, it could not come from $B \rightarrow aBB$, since each of the B's is known by Claim 6 to produce words with one more b than a as long as the words are shorter than w. Taken together, they have two more b's than a's and with an a in front they have exactly one more b than a. But then w is not a counterexample to Claim 6.

All together, this contradicts the existence of any counterexample to Claim 6.

The case where the counterexample may be a word that disproves Claim 5 similarly leads to a contradiction. Therefore, there is no smallest counterexample, and the three claims are true, and in particular Claim 4, which is the one we needed. This concludes the proof that the language generated by these productions is the language EQUAL. ∎

It is common for the same nonterminal to be the left side of more than one production. We now introduce the symbol, |, a vertical line, to mean disjunction (or). Using it we can combine all the productions that have the same left side. For example,

$$S \rightarrow aS$$
$$S \rightarrow \Lambda$$

can be written simply as:

$$S \rightarrow aS \mid \Lambda$$

The CFG

$$S \rightarrow X$$
$$S \rightarrow Y$$
$$X \rightarrow \Lambda$$
$$Y \rightarrow aY$$
$$Y \rightarrow bY$$
$$Y \rightarrow a$$
$$Y \rightarrow b$$

can be written as:

$$S \rightarrow X \mid Y$$
$$X \rightarrow \Lambda$$
$$Y \rightarrow aY \mid bY \mid a \mid b$$

We have committed a small sloppiness here. We have called a set of productions a CFG when we know that by definition a CFG has three other parts. This error is common and forgivable since the sets of terminals and nonterminals can be deduced by examining the productions.

The notation we are using for CFG's is practically universal with the following minor changes:

Some authors use the symbol

$$\text{``::=''} \text{ instead of ``}\rightarrow\text{''}.$$

Some authors call nonterminals **variables.**

Some authors use a small epsilon, ε, or small lambda, λ, instead of Λ to denote the null string.

Some authors indicate nonterminals by writing them in angle brackets:

$$\langle S \rangle \rightarrow \langle X \rangle \mid \langle Y \rangle$$
$$\langle X \rangle \rightarrow \Lambda$$
$$\langle Y \rangle \rightarrow a\langle Y \rangle \mid b\langle Y \rangle \mid a \mid b$$

We shall be careful to use capital letters for nonterminals and small letters for terminals. Even if we did not do this, it would not be hard to determine when a symbol is a terminal. All symbols that do not appear as the left parts of productions are terminals with the exception of Λ.

Aside from these minor variations, we call this format—arrows, vertical bars, terminals, and nonterminals—for presenting a CFG, **BNF** standing for **Backus Normal Form** or **Backus-Naur Form.** It was invented by John W. Backus for describing the high-level language ALGOL. Peter Naur was the editor of the report in which it appeared, and that is why BNF has two possible meanings.

A FORTRAN identifier (variable or storage location name) can, by definition, be up to six alphanumeric characters long but must start with a letter. We can generate the language of all FORTRAN identifiers by a CFG.

$$S \rightarrow \underline{\text{LETTER}} \ X \ X \ X \ X \ X$$
$$X \rightarrow \underline{\text{LETTER}} \mid \underline{\text{DIGIT}} \mid \Lambda$$
$$\underline{\text{LETTER}} \rightarrow A \mid B \mid C \mid \ldots \mid Z$$
$$\underline{\text{DIGIT}} \rightarrow 0 \mid 1 \mid 2 \mid \ldots \mid 9$$

Not just the language of identifiers but the language of all proper FORTRAN instructions can be defined by a CFG. This is also true of all the statements in the languages PASCAL, BASIC, PL/I, and so on. This is not an accident. As we shall see in Chapter 22, if we are given a word generated by a specified CFG we can determine how the word was produced. This in turn enables us to understand the meaning of the word just as identifying the parts of speech helps us to understand the meaning of an English sentence. A computer must determine the grammatical structure of a computer language statement before it can execute the instruction.

Regular languages were easy to understand in the sense that we were able to determine how a given word could be accepted by an FA. But the class of languages they define is too restrictive for us. By this we mean that regular languages cannot express all of the deep ideas we may wish to communicate. Context free languages can handle more of these—enough for computer programming. And even this is not the ultimate language class, as we see in Chapter 20. We shall return to such philosophical issues in Part III.

PROBLEMS

1. Consider the CFG:

$$S \rightarrow aS \mid bb$$

Prove that this generates the language defined by the regular expression

a*bb

2. Consider the CFG:

$$S \rightarrow XYX$$
$$X \rightarrow aX \mid bX \mid \Lambda$$
$$Y \rightarrow bbb$$

Prove that this generates the language of all strings with a triple b in them, which is the language defined by

(a + b)*bbb(a + b)*

3. Consider the CFG:

$$S \rightarrow aX$$
$$X \rightarrow aX \mid bX \mid \Lambda$$

What is the language this CFG generates?

4. Consider the CFG:

$$S \rightarrow XaXaX$$
$$X \rightarrow aX \mid bX \mid \Lambda$$

What is the language this CFG generates?

5. Consider the CFG:

$$S \rightarrow SS \mid XaXaX \mid \Lambda$$
$$X \rightarrow bX \mid \Lambda$$

(i) Prove that X can generate any **b***.

(ii)   Prove that *XaXaX* can generate any **b*ab*ab***.

(iii)   Prove that *S* can generate (**b*ab*ab***)*.

(iv)   Prove that the language of this CFG is the set of all words in (**a** + **b**)* with an even number of *a*'s with the following exception: We consider the word Λ to have an even number of *a*'s, as do all words with no *a*'s, but of the words with no *a*'s only Λ can be generated.

(v)   Show how the difficulty in part (iv) can be alleviated by adding the production

$$S \rightarrow XS$$

6. (i)   For each of the CFG's in Problems 1 through 5 determine whether there is a word in the language that can be generated in two substantially different ways. By "substantially," we mean that if two steps are interchangeable and it does not matter which comes first, then the different derivations they give are considered "substantially the same" otherwise they are "substantially different."

    (ii)   For those CFG's that do have two ways of generating the same word, show how the productions can be changed so that the language generated stays the same but all words are now generated by substantially only one possible derivation.

7. Consider the CFG:

$$S \rightarrow XbaaX \mid aX$$
$$X \rightarrow Xa \mid Xb \mid \Lambda$$

What is the language this generates? Find a word in this language that can be generated in two substantially different ways.

8. (i)   Consider the CFG for "some English" given in this chapter. Show how these productions can generate the sentence:

    Itchy the bear hugs jumpy the dog.

    (ii)   Change the productions so that an article cannot come between an adjective and its noun.

9. (i)   Show how in the CFG for "some English" we can generate the sentence:

    The the the cat follows cat.

    (ii)   Change the productions so that the same noun cannot have more than one article. Do this for the modification in Problem 8 also.

10. Show that in the CFG for *AE* given in this chapter we can eliminate the nonterminal *AE*. In which other CFG's in this chapter can we eliminate a nonterminal?

Find a CFG for each of the languages defined by the following regular expressions.

11. **ab***

12. **a*b***

13. **(baa + abb)***

Find CFG's for the following languages over the alphabet $\Sigma = \{a,b\}$.

14. (i) All words in which the letter *b* is never tripled.
    (ii) All words that have exactly two or three *b*'s.

15. (i) All words that do not have the substring *ab*.
    (ii) All words that do not have the substring *baa*.

16. All words that have different first and last letters:

$$\{ab \ ba \ aab \ abb \ baa \ bba \ . \ . \ . \}$$

17. Consider the CFG:

$$S \rightarrow AA$$
$$A \rightarrow AAA$$
$$A \rightarrow bA \mid Ab \mid a$$

Prove that the language generated by these productions is the set of all words with an even number of *a*'s, but not no *a*'s. Contrast this grammar with the CFG in Problem 5.

18. Describe the language generated by the following CFG:

$$S \rightarrow SS$$
$$S \rightarrow XXX$$
$$X \rightarrow aX \mid Xa \mid b$$

19. Write a CFG to generate the language of all strings that have more a's than b's (not necessarily only one more, as with the nonterminal A for the language EQUAL, but any number more a's than b's).

$$\{a \ aa \ aab \ aba \ baa \ aaaa \ aaab \ \dots\}$$

20. Let L be any language. Define the transpose of L to be the language of all the words in L spelled backward (see Chapter 6, Problem 17). For example, if

$$L = \{a \ baa \ bbaab \ bbbaa\}$$

then

$$\text{transpose } (L) = \{a \ aab \ baabb \ aabbb\}$$

Show that if L is a context-free language then the transpose of L is context-free also.

CHAPTER 14

TREES

In old-fashioned English grammar courses students were often asked to diagram a sentence. This meant that they were to draw a **parse tree,** which is a picture with the base line divided into subject and predicate. All words or phrases modifying these were drawn as appendages on connecting lines. For example,

> *The quick brown fox jumps over the lazy dog.*

becomes:

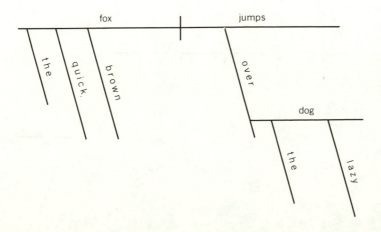

If the fox is dappled grey, then the parse tree would be:

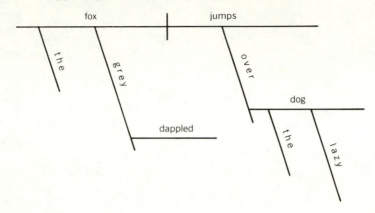

since dappled modifies grey and therefore is drawn as a branch off the grey line.

The sentence, "I shot the man with the gun." can be diagrammed in two ways:

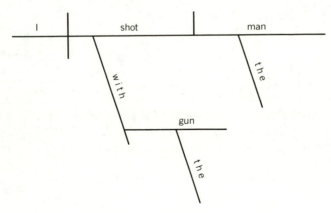

or

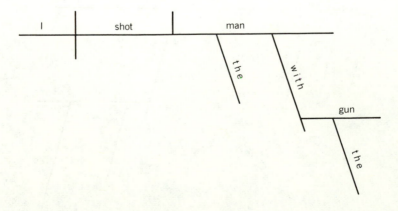

In the first diagram "with the gun" explains how I shot. In the second diagram "with the gun" explains who I shot.

These diagrams help us straighten out ambiguity. They turn a string of words into an interpretable idea by identifying who does what to whom.

A famous case of ambiguity is the sentence, "Time flies like an arrow." We humans have no difficulty identifying this as a poetic statement, technically a simile, meaning, "Time passes all too quickly, just as a speeding arrow darts across the endless skies"—or some such euphuism.

This is diagrammed by the following parse tree:

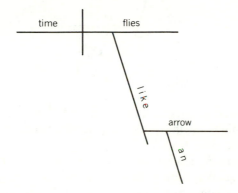

Notice how the picture grows like a tree when "an" branches from "arrow." A Graph Theory tree, unlike an arboreal tree, can grow sideways or upside down.

A nonnative speaker of English with no poetry in her soul (a computer, for example) who has just yesterday read the sentence, "Horse flies like a banana." might think the sentence should be diagrammed as

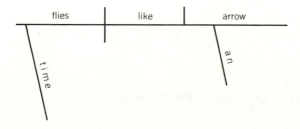

where she thinks "time flies" may have even shorter lives than drosophilae.

Looking in our dictionary, we see that "time" is also a verb, and if so in this case, the sentence could be in the imperative mood with the understood subject "you," in the same way that "you" is the understood subject of the sentence "Close the door." A race track tout may ask a jockey to do a favor and "Time horses like a trainer" for him. The computer might think this sentence should be diagrammed:

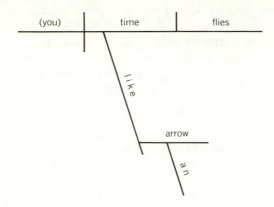

Someone is being asked to take a stopwatch and "time" some racing "flies" just as "an arrow" might do the same job, although one is unlikely to meet a straight arrow at the race track.

The idea of diagramming a sentence to show how it should be parsed carries over easily to CFG's. We start with the symbol S. Every time we use a production to replace a nonterminal by a string, we draw downward lines from the nonterminal to each character in the string.

Let us illustrate this on the CFG

$$S \rightarrow AA$$
$$A \rightarrow AAA \mid bA \mid Ab \mid a$$

We begin with S and apply the production $S \rightarrow AA$.

To the left-hand A let us apply the production $A \rightarrow bA$. To the right-hand A let us apply $A \rightarrow AAA$.

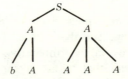

The *b* that we have on the bottom line is a terminal, so it does not descend further. In the terminology of trees it is called a **terminal node.** Let the four *A*'s, left to right, undergo the productions $A \rightarrow bA$, $A \rightarrow a$, $A \rightarrow a$, $A \rightarrow Ab$ respectively. We now have

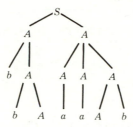

Let us finish off the generation of a word with the productions $A \rightarrow a$ and $A \rightarrow a$:

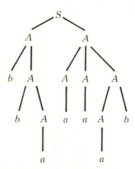

Reading from left to right, the word we have produced is *bbaaaab*.

As was the case with diagramming a sentence, we understand more about the finished word if we see the whole tree. The third and fourth letters are both *a*'s, but they are produced by completely different branches of the tree.

These tree diagrams are called **syntax trees** or **parse trees** or **generation trees** or **production trees** or **derivation trees.** The variety of names comes from the multiplicity of applications to linguistics, compiler design, and mathematical logic.

The only rule for formation of such a tree is that every nonterminal sprouts branches leading to every character in the right side of the production that replaces it. If the nonterminal *N* can be replaced by the string *abcde:*

$$N \rightarrow abcde$$

then in the tree we draw:

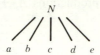

There is no need to put arrow heads on the edges because the direction of production is always downward.

EXAMPLE

One CFG for a subsystem of Propositional Calculus is:

$$S \rightarrow (S) \mid S{\supset}S \mid {\sim}S \mid p \mid q$$

The only nonterminal is S. The terminals are $p \; q \sim \supset (\;)$ where "$\supset$" is the symbol for implication.

In this grammar consider the diagram:

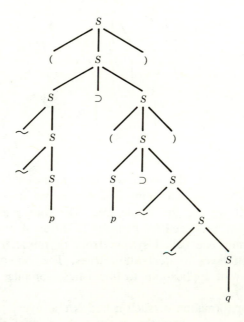

This is a derivation tree for the 13-letter word

$$(\sim\sim p \supset (p \supset \sim\sim q))$$

We often say that to know the derivation tree for a given word in a given grammar is to understand the meaning of that word.

The concept of "meaning" is one that we shall not deal with mathematically in this book. We never presumed that the languages generated by our CFG's have any significance beyond being formal strings of symbols. However, in some languages the meaning of a string of symbols is important to us for reasons of computation. We shall soon see that knowing the tree helps us determine how to evaluate and compute.

EXAMPLE

Let us concentrate for a moment on an example of a CFG for a simplified version of arithmetic expressions:

$$S \rightarrow S + S \mid S * S \mid \underline{number}$$

Let us presume that we know precisely what is meant by "$\underline{number}$."
We are all familiar with the ambiguity inherent in the expression

$$3 + 4 * 5$$

Does it mean $(3 + 4) * 5$, which is 35, or does it mean $3 + (4 * 5)$, which is 23?

In the language defined by this particular CFG we do not have the option of putting in parentheses for clarification. Parentheses are not generated by any of the productions and are therefore not letters in the derived language. There is no question that $3 + 4 * 5$ is a word in the language of this CFG. The only queston is what does this word mean in terms of calculation?

It is true that if we insisted on parentheses by using the grammar:

$$S \rightarrow (S + S) \mid (S * S) \mid \underline{number}$$

we could not produce the string $3 + 4 * 5$ at all. We could only produce

$$S \Rightarrow (S + S) \Rightarrow (S + (S * S)) \Rightarrow \ldots \Rightarrow (3 + (4 * 5))$$
or
$$S \Rightarrow (S * S) \Rightarrow ((S + S) * S) \Rightarrow \ldots \Rightarrow ((3 + 4) * 5)$$

neither of which is an ambiguous expression.

In the practical world we do not need to use all these cluttering parentheses because we have adopted the convention of "hierarchy of operators," which says that * is to be executed before +. This, unfortunately, is not reflected in either grammar. Later, in Chapter 20, we present a grammar that generates unambiguous arithmetic expressions that will mean exactly what we want them to mean without the need for burdensome parentheses. For now, we can only distinguish between these two possible meanings for the expression 3 + 4 * 5 by looking at the two possible derivation trees that might have produced it.

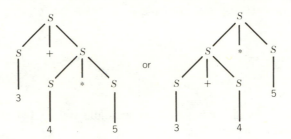

We can evaluate an expression in parse-tree form from the tree picture itself by starting at the bottom and working our way up to the top, replacing each nonterminal as we come to it by the result of the calculation that it produces. This can be done as follows:

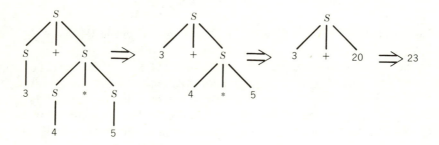

These examples show how the derivation tree can explain what the word means in much the same way that the parse trees in English grammar explain the meaning of sentences.

In the special case of *this particular grammar* (not for CFG's in general), we can draw meaningful trees of terminals alone using the start symbol *S* only once. This will enable us to introduce a new notation for arithmetic expressions—one that has direct applications to Computer Science.

The method for drawing the new trees is based on the fact that + and * are binary operations that combine expressions already in the proper form. The expression 3 + (4 * 5) is a sum. A sum of what? A sum of a number and a product. What product? The product of two numbers. Similarly (3 + 4) * 5 is a product of a sum and a number, where the sum is a sum of numbers. Notice the similarity to the original recursive definition of arithmetic expressions. These two situations are depicted in the following trees.

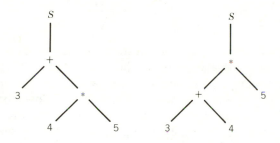

These are like derivation trees for the CFG:

$$S \rightarrow S + S \mid S * S \mid \underline{\text{number}}$$

except that we have eliminated most of the *S*'s. We have connected the branches directly to the operators instead.

The symbols * and + are no longer terminals, since they must be replaced by numbers. These are actually standard derivation trees taken from a new CFG in which *S*, * and + are nonterminals and <u>number</u> is the only terminal. The productions are:

$$S \rightarrow * \mid + \mid \underline{\text{number}}$$
$$+ \rightarrow + + \mid + * \mid + \underline{\text{number}} \mid * + \mid * * \mid * \underline{\text{number}} \mid \underline{\text{number}} + \mid$$
$$\underline{\text{number}} * \mid \underline{\text{number}} \ \underline{\text{number}}$$
$$* \rightarrow + + \mid + * \mid + \underline{\text{number}} \mid * + \mid * * \mid * \underline{\text{number}} \mid \underline{\text{number}} + \mid$$
$$\underline{\text{number}} * \mid \underline{\text{number}} \ \underline{\text{number}}$$

As usual <u>number</u> has been underlined because it is only one symbol. The only words in this language are strings of <u>number</u>. But we are interested in the derivation trees themselves, not in these dull words.

From these trees we can construct a new notation for arithmetic expressions. To do this, we walk around the tree and write down the symbols, once each, as we encounter them. We begin our trip on the left side of the start symbol *S* heading south. As we walk around the tree, we keep our left hand always on the tree.

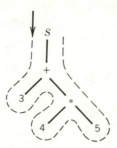

The first symbol we encounter on the first tree is +. This we write down as the first symbol of the expression in the new notation. Continuing to walk around the tree, keeping it on our left, we first meet 3 then + again. We write down the 3, but this time we do not write + down because we have already included it in the string we are producing. Walking some more we meet *, which we write down. Then we meet 4, then * again, then 5. So we write down 4, then 5. There are no symbols we have not met, so our trip is done. The string we have produced is:

$$+ \; 3 \; * \; 4 \; 5.$$

The second derivation tree when converted into the new notation becomes:

$$* \; + \; 3 \; 4 \; 5.$$

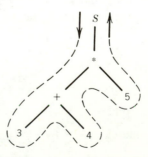

This tree-walking method produces a string of the symbols +, *, and number, which summarizes the picture of the tree and thus contains the information necessary to understand the meaning of the expression. This is information that is lacking in our usual representation of arithmetic expressions, unless parentheses are required. We shall show that these strings are unambiguous in that each determines a unique calculation without the need for establishing the convention of times before plus. These representations are said to be in **operator prefix notation** because the operator is written in front of the operands it combines.

Since $S \rightarrow S + S$ has changed from

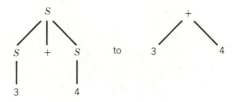

the left-hand tracing changes $3 + 4$ into $+\ 3\ 4$.

To evaluate a string of characters in this new notation, we proceed as follows. We read the string from left to right. When we find the first substring of the form

       operator-operand-operand   (call this o-o-o for short)

we replace these three symbols with the one result of the indicated arithmetic calculation. We then rescan the string from the left. We continue this process until there is only one number left, which is the value of the entire original expression.

In the case of the expression $+\ 3\ *\ 4\ 5$, the first substring we encounter of the form operator-operand-operand is $*\ 4\ 5$, so we replace this with the result of the indicated multiplication, that is, the number 20. The string is now $+\ 3\ 20$. This itself is in the form o-o-o, and we evaluate it by performing the addition. When we replace this with the number 23 we see that the process of evaluation is complete.

In the case of the expression $*\ +\ 3\ 4\ 5$ we find that the o-o-o substring is $+\ 3\ 4$. This we replace with the number 7. The string is then $*\ 7\ 5$, which itself is in the o-o-o form. When we replace this with 35, the evaluation process is complete.

Let us see how this process works on a harder example. Let us start with the arithmetic expression

$$((1 + 2) * (3 + 4) + 5) * 6.$$

This is shown in normal notation, which is called **operator infix notation** because the operators are placed in between the operands. With infix notation we often need to use parentheses to avoid ambiguity, as is the case with the expression above. To convert this to operator prefix notation, we begin by drawing its derivation tree:

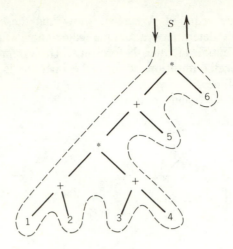

Reading around this tree gives the equivalant prefix notation expression

$$* + * + 1\ 2 + 3\ 4\ 5\ 6$$

Notice that the operands are in the same order in prefix notation as they were in infix notation, only the operators are scrambled and all parentheses are deleted.

To evaluate this string we see that the first substring of the form operator-operand-operand is $+\ 1\ 2$, which we replaced with the number 3. The evaluation continues as follows:

String	First o-o-o substring
$* + * 3 + 3\ 4\ 5\ 6$	$+\ 3\ 4$
$\Downarrow$	
$* + * 3\ 7\ 5\ 6$	$* 3\ 7$
$\Downarrow$	
$* + 21\ 5\ 6$	$+\ 21\ 5$
$\Downarrow$	
$* 26\ 6$	$* 26\ 6$
$\Downarrow$	
156	

which is the correct value for the expression we started with.

Since the derivation tree is unambiguous, the prefix notation is also unambiguous and does not rely on the tacit understanding of operator hierarchy or on the use of parentheses.

This clever parenthesis-free notational scheme was invented by the Polish logician Jan Łukasiewicz (1878–1956) and is often called Polish notation. There is a similar operator postfix notation, which is also called Polish notation, in which the operation symbols $(+, *, \ldots)$ come after the operands. This can be derived by tracing around the tree from the other side, keeping our right hand on the tree and then reversing the resultant string. Both of these methods of notation are useful for computer science, and we consider them again in Chapter 22. ∎

Let us return to the more general case of languages other than arithmetic expressions. These may also suffer from the problem of ambiguity. Substantive ambiguity is a difficult concept to define.

EXAMPLE

Let us consider the language generated by the following CFG:

$$\text{PROD 1} \quad S \rightarrow AB$$
$$\text{PROD 2} \quad A \rightarrow a$$
$$\text{PROD 3} \quad B \rightarrow b$$

There are two different sequences of applications of the productions that generate the word ab. One is PROD 1, PROD 2, PROD 3. The other is PROD 1, PROD 3, PROD 2.

$$S \Rightarrow AB \Rightarrow aB \Rightarrow ab \qquad \text{or} \qquad S \Rightarrow AB \Rightarrow Ab \Rightarrow ab$$

However, when we draw the corresponding syntax trees we see that the two derivations are essentially the same:

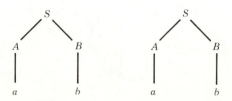

This example, then, presents no substantive difficulty because there is no ambiguity of interpretation. This is related to the situation in Chapter 13 in which we first built up the grammatical structure of an English sentence out of *noun, verb,* and so on, and then substituted in the specific words of each category either one at a time or all at once. When all the possible derivation trees are the same for a given word then the word is unambiguous. ∎

DEFINITION

A CFG is called **ambiguous** if for at least one word in the language that it generates there are two possible derivations of the word that correspond to different syntax trees.   ■

EXAMPLE

Let us reconsider the language PALINDROME, which we can now define by the CFG below:

$$S \to aSa \mid bSb \mid a \mid b \mid \Lambda$$

At every stage in the generation of a word by this grammar the working string contains only the one nonterminal S smack dab in the middle. The word grows like a tree from the center out. For example.:

$$\dots baSab \Rightarrow babSbab \Rightarrow babbSbbab \Rightarrow babbaSabbab \dots$$

When we finally replace S by a center letter (or Λ if the word has no center letter) we have completed the production of a palindrome. The word *aabaa* has only one possible generation:

$$S \Rightarrow aSa$$
$$\Rightarrow aaSaa$$
$$\Rightarrow aabaa$$

If any other production were applied at any stage in the derivation, a different word would be produced.

We see then that this CFG is **unambiguous.** Proving this rigorously is left to Problem 13 below.   ■

EXAMPLE

The language of all nonnull strings of a's can be defined by a CFG as follows:

$$S \rightarrow aS \mid Sa \mid a$$

In this case the word a^3 can be generated by four different trees:

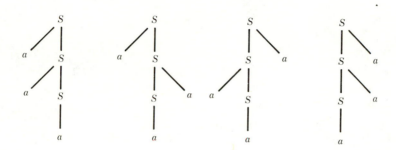

This CFG is therefore ambiguous.

However the same language can also be defined by the CFG:

$$S \rightarrow aS \mid a$$

for which the word a^3 has only one production:

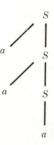

(See Problem 14 below). This CFG is not ambiguous.   ■

From this last example we see that we must be careful to say that it is
the CFG that is ambiguous, not that the language itself is ambiguous.

So far in this chapter we have seen that derivation trees carry with them
an additional amount of information that helps resolve ambiguity in cases where
meaning is important. Trees can be useful in the study of formal grammars
in other ways.

For example, it is possible to depict the generation of all the words in the
language of a CFG simultaneously in one big (possibly infinite) tree.

DEFINITION

For a given CFG we define a tree with the start symbol S as its root and whose nodes are working strings of terminals and nonterminals. The descendants of each node are all the possible results of applying every production to the working string, one at a time. A string of all terminals is a terminal node in the tree. The resultant tree is called the **total language tree** of the CFG. ∎

EXAMPLE

For the CFG

$$S \rightarrow aa \mid bX \mid aXX$$
$$X \rightarrow ab \mid b$$

the total language tree is:

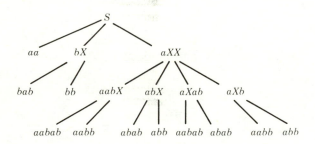

This total language has only seven different words. Four of its words (*abb, aabb, abab, aabab*) have two different possible derivations because they appear as terminal nodes in this total language tree in two different places. However, the words are not generated by two different derivation trees and the grammar is unambiguous. For example:

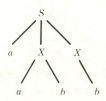

EXAMPLE

Consider the CFG:

$$S \rightarrow aSb \mid bS \mid a$$

We have the terminal letters a and b and three possible choices of substitutions for S at any stage. The total tree of this language begins:

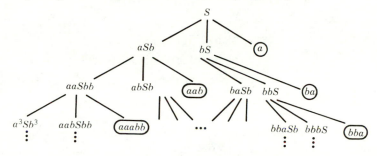

Here we have circled the terminal nodes because they are the words in the language generated by this CFG. We say "begins" because since the language is infinite the total language tree is too.

We have already generated all the words in this language with one, two, or three letters.

$$L = \{ a \quad ba \quad aab \quad bba \ldots \}$$

These trees may get arbitrarily wide as well as infinitely long. ∎

EXAMPLE

$$S \rightarrow SAS \mid b$$
$$A \rightarrow ba \mid b$$

Every string with some S's and some A's has many possible productions that apply to it, two for each S and two for each A.

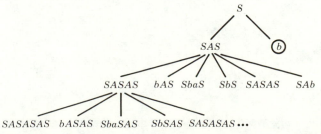

The essence of recursive definition comes into play in an obvious way when some nonterminal has a production with a right-side string containing its own name, as in this case:

$$X \rightarrow (\text{blah}) \ X \ (\text{blah})$$

The total tree for such a language then must be infinite since it contains the branch:

$$X \Rightarrow (\text{blah}) \ X \ (\text{blah})$$
$$\Rightarrow (\text{blah}) \ (\text{blah}) \ X \ (\text{blah}) \ (\text{blah})$$
$$\Rightarrow (\text{blah})^3 \ X \ (\text{blah})^3$$
$$\cdots$$

This has a deep significance which will be important to us shortly.

Surprisingly, even when the whole language tree is infinite, the language may have only finitely many words.

EXAMPLE

Consider this CFG:

$$S \rightarrow X \mid b$$
$$X \rightarrow aX$$

The total language tree begins:

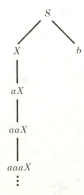

Clearly the only word in this language is the single letter b. X is a bad mistake; it leads to no words. It is a *useless* symbol in this CFG. We shall be interested in matters like this again in Chapter 23.   ■

PROBLEMS

1. Chomsky finds three different interpretations for "I had a book stolen." Explain them.

Below is a set of words and a set of CFG's. For each word, determine if the word is in the language of each CFG and, if it is, draw a syntax tree to prove it.

Words	CFG's
2. *ab*	CFG 1. $S \to aSb \mid ab$
3. *aaaa*	
	CFG 2. $S \to aS \mid bS \mid a$
4. *aabb*	
5. *abaa*	CFG 3. $S \to aS \mid aSb \mid X$ $X \to aXa \mid a$
6. *abba*	
7. *baaa*	CFG 4. $S \to aAS \mid a$ $A \to SbA \mid SS \mid ba$
8. *abab*	
9. *bbaa*	CFG 5. $S \to aB \mid bA$ $A \to a \mid aS \mid bAA$ $B \to b \mid bS \mid aBB$
10. *baab*	

11. Find an example of an infinite language that does not have any production of the form

$$X \to \text{(blah)} \ X \ \text{(blah)}$$

for any nonterminal X

12. Show that the following CFG's are ambiguous by finding a word with two distinct syntax trees.
    (i) $S \to SaSaS \mid b$
    (ii) $S \to aSb \mid Sb \mid Sa \mid a$
    (iii) $S \to aaS \mid aaaS \mid a$
    (iv) $S \to aS \mid aSb \mid X$
            $X \to Xa \mid a$

(v) $S \rightarrow AA$
      $A \rightarrow AAA \mid a \mid bA \mid Ab$

13.   Prove that the CFG

$$S \rightarrow aSa \mid bSb \mid a \mid b \mid \Lambda$$

does generate exactly the language PALINDROME as claimed in the chapter and is unambiguous.

14.   Prove that the CFG

$$S \rightarrow aS \mid a$$

is unambiguous.

15.   Show that the following CFG's that use Λ are ambiguous
      (i) $S \rightarrow XaX$
             $X \rightarrow aX \mid bX \mid \Lambda$
      (ii) $S \rightarrow aSX \mid \Lambda$
             $X \rightarrow aX \mid a$
      (iii) $S \rightarrow aS \mid bS \mid aaS \mid \Lambda$

16.   (i)   Find unambiguous CFG's that generate the three languages in Problem 15.
      (ii)   For each of the three languages generated in Problem 15, find an unambiguous grammar that generates exactly the same language except for the word Λ. Do this by not employing the symbol Λ in the CFG's at all.

17.   Begin to draw the total language trees for the following CFG's until we can be sure we have found all the words in these languages with one, two, three, or four letters. Which of these CFG's are ambiguous?
      (i) $S \rightarrow aS \mid bS \mid a$
      (ii) $S \rightarrow aSaS \mid b$
      (iii) $S \rightarrow aSa \mid bSb \mid a$
      (iv) $S \rightarrow aSb \mid bX$
             $X \rightarrow bX \mid b$
      (v) $S \rightarrow bA \mid aB$
             $A \rightarrow bAA \mid aS \mid a$
             $B \rightarrow aBB \mid bS \mid b$

18. Convert the following infix expressions into Polish notation.
    (i)   1 * 2 * 3
    (ii)   1 * 2 + 3
    (iii) 1 * (2 + 3)
    (iv)   1 * (2 + 3) * 4
    (v)   ((1 + 2) * 3) + 4
    (vi)   1 + (2 * (3 + 4))
    (vii) 1 + (2 * 3) + 4

19. Suppose that, while tracing around a derivation tree for an arithmetic expression to convert it into operator prefix notation, we make the following change: When we encounter a number we write it down, but we do not write down an operator until the *second* time we encounter it. Show that the resulting string is correct operator postfix notation for the diagrammed arithmetic expression.

20. Invent a form of prefix notation for the system of Propositional Calculus used in this chapter that enables us to write all well-formed formulas without the need for parentheses (and without ambiguity).

CHAPTER 15

REGULAR GRAMMARS

Some of the examples of languages we have generated by CFG's have been regular languages, that is, they are definable by regular expressions. However, we have also seen some nonregular languages that can be generated by CFG's (PALINDROME and EQUAL).

EXAMPLE

The CFG:

$$S \rightarrow ab \mid aSb$$

generates the language

$$\{a^n b^n\}$$

Repeated applications of the second production results in the derivation

$$S \Rightarrow aSb \Rightarrow aaSbb \Rightarrow aaaSbbb \Rightarrow aaaaSbbbb \ldots$$

Finally the first production will be applied to form a word having the same number of a's and b's, with all the a's first. This language as we demonstrated in Chapter 11, is nonregular. ∎

EXAMPLE

The CFG:

$$S \rightarrow aSa \mid bSa \mid \Lambda$$

generates the language TRAILING-COUNT of all words of the form:

$$s \; a^{\text{length}(s)} \qquad \text{for all strings } s \text{ in } (\mathbf{a} + \mathbf{b})^*$$

that is, any string concatenated with a string of as many a's as the string has letters. This language is also nonregular (See Chapter 11, Problem 10). ∎

What then is the relationship between regular languages and context-free grammars?

Several possibilities come to mind:

1. All languages can be generated by CFG's.
2. All regular languages can be generated by CFG's, and so can some non-regular languages but not all possible languages.
3. Some regular languages can be generated by CFG's and some regular languages cannot be generated by CFG's. Some nonregular languages can be generated by CFG's and some nonregular languages cannot.

Of these three possibilities, number 2 is correct. In this chapter we shall indeed show that all regular languages can be generated by CFG's. We leave the construction of a language that cannot be generated by any CFG for Chapter 20.

We now present a method for turning an FA into a CFG so that all the words accepted by the FA can be generated by the CFG and only the words accepted by the FA are generated by the CFG. The process of conversion is easier than we might suspect. It is, of course, stated as a constructive algorithm that we first illustrate on a simple example.

EXAMPLE

Let us consider the FA below, which accepts the language of all words with a double a:

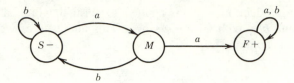

We have named the start state S, the middle state M, and the final state F.

The word *abbaab* is accepted by this machine. Rather than trace through the machine watching how its input letters are read, as usual, let us see how its path grows. The path has the following step-by-step development where a path is denoted by the labels of its edges concatenated with the symbol for the state in which it now sits:

S	(We begin in *S*)
aM	(We take an *a*-edge to *M*)
abS	(We take an *a*-edge then a *b*-edge and we are in *S*)
abbS	(An *a*-edge, a *b*-edge, and a *b*-loop back to *S*)
abbaM	(Another *a*-edge and we are in *M*)
abbaaF	(Another *a*-edge and we are in *F*)
abbaabF	(A *b*-loop back to *F*)
abbaab	(The finished path: an *a*-edge a *b*-edge . . .)

This *path development* looks very much like a derivation of a word in a CFG. What would the rules of production be?

(From *S* an *a*-edge takes us to *M*)	$S \rightarrow aM$
(From *S* a *b*-edge takes us to *S*)	$S \rightarrow bS$
(From *M* an *a*-edge takes us to *F*)	$M \rightarrow aF$
(From *M* a *b*-edge takes us to *S*)	$M \rightarrow bS$
(From *F* an *a*-edge takes us to *F*)	$F \rightarrow aF$
(From *F* a *b*-edge takes us to *F*)	$F \rightarrow bF$
(When at the final state *F*, we can	$F \rightarrow \Lambda$
stop if we want to).	

We shall prove in a moment that the CFG we have just described generates all paths from S to F and therefore generates all words accepted by the FA.

Let us consider another path from S to F, that of the word *babbaaba*. The path development sequence is

(Start here)	*S*
(A *b*-loop back to *S*)	*bS*
(An *a*-edge to *M*)	*baM*

(A *b*-edge back to *S*)	*babS*
(A *b*-loop back to *S*)	*babbS*
(An *a*-edge to *M*)	*babbaM*
(Another *a*-edge to *F*)	*babbaaF*
(A *b*-loop back to *F*)	*babbaabF*
(An *a*-loop back to *F*)	*babbaabaF*
(Finish up in *F*)	*babbaaba*

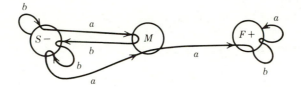

This is not only a path development but also a derivation of the word *babbaaba* from the CFG above.

The logic of this argument is roughly as follows. Every word accepted by this FA corresponds to a path from *S* to *F*. Every path has a step-by-step development sequence as above. Every development sequence is a derivation in the CFG proposed. Therefore, every word accepted by the FA can be generated by the CFG.

The converse must also be true. We must show that any word generated by this CFG is a word accepted by the FA. Let us take some derivation such as

Production Used	Derivation
$S \rightarrow aM$	$S \Rightarrow aM$
$M \rightarrow bS$	$\Rightarrow abS$
$S \rightarrow aM$	$\Rightarrow abaM$
$M \rightarrow aF$	$\Rightarrow abaaF$
$F \rightarrow bF$	$\Rightarrow abaabF$
$F \rightarrow \Lambda$	$\Rightarrow abaab$

This can be interpreted as a path development:

Production Used	Path Developed
$S \rightarrow aM$	Starting at *S* we take an *a*-edge to *M*
$M \rightarrow bS$	Then a *b*-edge to *S*
$S \rightarrow aM$	Then an *a*-edge to *M*
$M \rightarrow aF$	Then an *a*-edge to *F*
$F \rightarrow bF$	Then a *b*-edge to *F*
$F \rightarrow \Lambda$	Now we stop

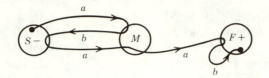

The path, of course, corresponds to the word *abaab*, which must be in the language accepted by the FA since its corresponding path ends at a final state.   ∎

The general rules for the algorithm above are:

$$\text{CFG derivation} \rightarrow \text{path development} \rightarrow \text{path} \rightarrow \text{word accepted}$$

and

$$\text{word accepted} \rightarrow \text{path} \rightarrow \text{path development} \rightarrow \text{CFG derivation}$$

For this correspondence to work, all that is necessary is that:

1. Every edge between states be a production:

and

2. Every production correspond to an edge between states:

or to the possible termination at a final state:

$$X \rightarrow \Lambda$$

only when X is a final state.

If a certain state Y is not a final state, we do *not* include a production of the form

$$Y \rightarrow \Lambda$$

for it.

At every stage in the derivation the working string has this form:

(string of terminals) (one Nonterminal)

until, while in a final state, we apply a production replacing the single non-terminal with Λ. It is important to take careful note of the fact that a path that is not in a final state will be associated with a string that is not all terminals, (i.e. not a word). These correspond to the working strings in the middle of derivations, not to words in the language.

DEFINITION

For a given CFG a **semiword** is a string of terminals (maybe none) concatenated with exactly one nonterminal (on the right), for example,

(terminal) (terminal) . . . (terminal) (Nonterminal)

■

Contrast this with **word,** which is a string of all terminals, and **working string,** which is a string of any number of terminals and nonterminals in any order.

Let us examine next a case of an FA that has two final states.
One easy example of this is the FA for the language of all words without double a's. This, the complement of the language of the last example, is also regular and is accepted by the machine FA'.

FA'

Let us retain for the moment the names of the nonterminals we had before: S for start, M for middle, and F for what used to be the final state, but is not anymore.
The productions that describe the labels of the edges of the paths are still

$$S \rightarrow aM \mid bS$$
$$M \rightarrow bS \mid aF$$
$$F \rightarrow aF \mid bF$$

as before.

However, now we have a different set of final states. We can accept a string with its path ending in S or M, so we include the productions:

$$S \rightarrow \Lambda$$

and

$$M \rightarrow \Lambda$$

but not

$$F \rightarrow \Lambda$$

The following paragraph is the explanation for why this algorithm works:

Any path through the machine FA' that starts at $-$ corresponds to a string of edge labels and simultaneously to a sequence of productions generating a semiword whose terminal section is the edge label string and whose right-end nonterminal is the name of the state the path ends in. If the path ends in a final state, then we can accept the input string as a word in the language of the machine, and simultaneously finish the generation of this word from the CFG by employing the production:

(Nonterminal corresponding to final state) $\rightarrow \Lambda$

Because our definition of CFG's requires that we always start a derivation with the particular start symbol S, it is always necessary to label the unique start state in an FA with the nonterminal name S. The rest of the choice of names of states is arbitrary.

This discussion was general and complete enough to be considered a proof of the following theorem:

THEOREM 19

All regular languages can be generated by CFG's.
This can also be stated as: All regular languages are CFL's. ∎

EXAMPLE

The language of all words with an even number of a's (with at least some a's) is regular since it can be accepted by this FA:

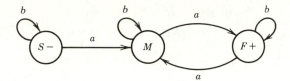

Calling the states S, M, and F as before, we have the following corresponding set of productions:

$$S \rightarrow bS \mid aM$$
$$M \rightarrow bM \mid aF$$
$$F \rightarrow bF \mid aM \mid \Lambda$$

We have already seen two CFG's for this language, but this CFG is substantially different. (Here we may ask a fundamental question: How can we tell whether two CFG's generate the same language? But fundamental questions do not always have satisfactory answers.) ■

Theorem 19 was discovered (or perhaps invented) by Noam Chomsky and George A. Miller in 1958. They also proved the result below, which seems to be the flip side of the coin.

THEOREM 20

If all the productions in a given CFG fit one of the two forms:

Nonterminal → semiword

or

Nonterminal → word

(where the word may be Λ) then the language generated by this CFG is regular.

PROOF

We shall prove that the language generated by such a CFG is regular by showing that there is a TG that accepts the same language. We shall build this TG by constructive algorithm.

Let us consider a general CFG in this form:

$$N_1 \rightarrow w_1 N_2 \qquad N_7 \rightarrow w_{10}$$
$$N_1 \rightarrow w_2 N_3 \qquad N_{41} \rightarrow w_{23}$$
$$N_2 \rightarrow w_3 N_4 \qquad \ldots$$
$$\ldots$$

where the N's are the nonterminals, the w's are strings of terminals, and the parts $w_y N_z$ are the semiwords used in productions. One of these N's must be S. Let $N_1 = S$.

Draw a small circle for each N and one extra circle labeled $+$. The circle for S we label $-$.

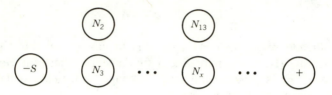

For every production rule of the form:

$$N_x \rightarrow w_y N_z$$

draw a directed edge from state N_x to N_z and label it with the word w_y.

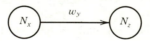

If the two nonterminals above are the same the path is a loop.
For every production rule of the form:

$$N_p \rightarrow w_q$$

draw a directed edge from N_p to $+$ and label it with the word w_q.

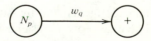

We have now constructed a transition graph. Any path in this TG from $-$ to $+$ corresponds to a word in the language of the TG (by concatenating labels) and simultaneously corresponds to a sequence of productions in the CFG generating the same word. Conversely, every production of a word in this CFG:

$$S \Rightarrow wN \Rightarrow wwN \Rightarrow wwwN \quad \ldots \quad \Rightarrow wwwww$$

corresponds to a path in this TG from $-$ to $+$.

Therefore, the language of this TG is exactly the same as the language of the CFG. Therefore, the language of the CFG is regular. ∎

We should note that the fact that the productions in some CFG are all in the required format does not guarantee that the grammar generates any words. If the grammar is totally discombobulated, the TG that we form from it will be crazy too and accept no words. However, if the grammar generates a language of some words then the TG produced above for it will accept that language.

DEFINITION

A CFG is called a **regular grammar** if each of its productions is of one of the two forms

$$\text{Nonterminal} \rightarrow \text{semiword}$$

or

$$\text{Nonterminal} \rightarrow \text{word} \qquad\qquad ∎$$

The two previous proofs imply that all regular languages can be generated by regular grammars and all regular grammars generate regular languages.

We must be very careful not to be carried away by the symmetry of these theorems. Despite both theorems it is still possible that a CFG that is not in the form of a regular grammar can generate a regular language. In fact we have seen examples of this very phenomenon in Chapters 13 and 14.

EXAMPLE

Consider the CFG:

$$S \rightarrow aaS \mid bbS \mid \Lambda$$

This is a regular grammar and so we may apply the algorithm to it. There is only one nonterminal, S, so there will be only two states in the TG, $-$ and the mandated $+$. The only production of the form

$$N_p \rightarrow w_q$$

is

$$S \rightarrow \Lambda$$

so there is only one edge into $+$ and that is labeled Λ. The productions $S \rightarrow aaS$ and $S \rightarrow bbS$ are of the form $N_1 \rightarrow wN_2$ where the N's are both S. Since these are supposed to be made into paths from N_1 to N_2 they become loops from S back to S. These two productions will become two loops at $-$ one labeled aa and one labeled bb. The whole TG is shown below:

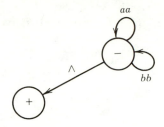

By Kleene's theorem, any language accepted by a TG is regular, therefore the language generated by this CFG (which is the same) is regular.

It corresponds to the regular expression

$$(\mathbf{aa} + \mathbf{bb})^*$$

■

EXAMPLE

Consider the CFG:

$$S \rightarrow aaS \mid bbS \mid abX \mid baX \mid \Lambda$$
$$X \rightarrow aaX \mid bbX \mid abS \mid baS$$

The algorithm tells us that there will be three states: $-, X, +$. Since there is only one production of the form

$$N_p \rightarrow w_q$$

there is only one edge into $+$. The TG is:

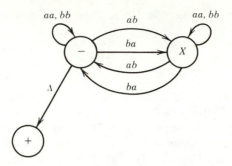

which we immediately see accepts our old friend the language EVEN-EVEN. (Do not be fooled by the Λ edge to the $+$ state. It is the same as relabeling the $-$ state $\pm$.) ∎

EXAMPLE

Consider the CFG:

$$S \rightarrow aA \mid bB$$
$$A \rightarrow aS \mid a$$
$$B \rightarrow bS \mid b$$

The corresponding TG constructed by the algorithm in Theorem 20 is:

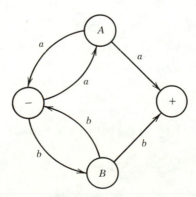

The language of this CFG is exactly the same as the language of the CFG two examples ago except that it does not include the word Λ. This language can be defined by the regular expression $(\mathbf{aa} + \mathbf{bb})^{+}$. ∎

We should also notice that the CFG above does not have any productions of the form

$$N_x \rightarrow \Lambda$$

For a CFG to accept the word Λ, it must have at least one production of this form, called a Λ-production.

A theorem in the next chapter states that any CFL that does not include the word Λ can be defined by a CFG that includes no Λ-productions. Notice that a Λ-production need not imply that Λ is in the language, as with

$$S \rightarrow aX$$
$$X \rightarrow \Lambda$$

The language here is just the word a.

The CFG's that are constructed by the algorithm in Theorem 19 always have Λ-productions, but they do not always generate the word Λ. We know this because not all regular languages contain the word Λ, but the algorithm suggested in the theorem shows that they can all be converted into CFG's with Λ-productions.

PROBLEMS

Find CFG's that generate these regular languages over the alphabet $\Sigma = \{a, b\}$:

1.   The language defined by **(aaa + b)***

2.   The language defined by **(a + b)* (bbb + aaa) (a + b)***

3.   All strings without the substring aaa.

4.   All strings that end in b and have an even number of b's in total.

5.   The set of all strings of odd length.

6.   All strings with exactly one a or exactly one b.

7.   All strings with an odd number of a's or an even number of b's.

For the following CFG's find regular expressions that define the same language and describe the language.

8. $S \rightarrow aX \mid bS \mid a \mid b$
         $X \rightarrow aX \mid a$

9. $S \rightarrow bS \mid aX \mid b$
         $X \rightarrow bX \mid aS \mid a$

10. $S \rightarrow aaS \mid abS \mid baS \mid bbS \mid \Lambda$

11. $S \rightarrow aB \mid bA \mid \Lambda$
         $A \rightarrow aS$
         $B \rightarrow bS$

12. $S \rightarrow aB \mid bA$
         $A \rightarrow aB \mid a$
         $B \rightarrow bA \mid b$

13. $S \rightarrow aS \mid bX \mid a$
         $X \rightarrow aX \mid bY \mid a$
         $Y \rightarrow aY \mid a$

14. $S \rightarrow aS \mid bX \mid a$
         $X \rightarrow aX \mid bY \mid bZ \mid a$
         $Y \rightarrow aY \mid a$
         $Z \rightarrow aZ \mid bW$
         $W \rightarrow aW \mid a$

15. $S \rightarrow bS \mid aX$
         $X \rightarrow bS \mid aY$
         $Y \rightarrow aY \mid bY \mid a \mid b$

16.   (i)   Starting with the alphabet

$$\Sigma = \{\mathbf{a} \ \mathbf{b} \ (\ ) + *\}$$

           find a CFG that generates all regular expressions.

       (ii)   Is this language regular?

17.   Despite the fact that a CFG is not in *regular form* it still might generate a regular language. If so, this means that there is another CFG that defines the same language and *is* in regular form. For each of the examples below, find a regular form version of the CFG.

(i) $S \rightarrow XYZ$
$X \rightarrow aX \mid bX \mid \Lambda$
$Y \rightarrow aY \mid bY \mid \Lambda$
$Z \rightarrow aZ \mid \Lambda$

(ii) $S \rightarrow XXX$
$X \rightarrow aX \mid a$
$Y \rightarrow bY \mid b$

(iii) $S \rightarrow XY$
$X \rightarrow aX \mid Xa \mid a$
$Y \rightarrow aY \mid Ya \mid a$

18. Each of the following CFG's has a production using the symbol Λ and yet Λ is not a word in its language. Show that there are other CFG's for these languages that do not use Λ.

(i) $S \rightarrow aX \mid bX$
$X \rightarrow a \mid b \mid \Lambda$

(ii) $S \rightarrow aX \mid bS \mid a \mid b$
$X \rightarrow aX \mid a \mid \Lambda$

(iii) $S \rightarrow aS \mid bX$
$X \rightarrow aX \mid \Lambda$

19. Show how to convert a TG into a regular grammar without first converting it to an FA.

20. Let us, for the purposes of this problem only, allow a production of the form
$$N_1 \rightarrow \mathbf{r} \, N_2$$
where N_1 and N_2 are nonterminals and $\mathbf{r}$ is a regular expression. The meaning of this formula is that in any working string we may substitute for N_1 any string wN_2 where w is a word in the language defined by $\mathbf{r}$. This can be considered a short-hand way of writing an infinite family of productions, one for each word in the language of $\mathbf{r}$.
Let a grammar be called *bad* if all of its productions are of the two forms
$$N_1 \rightarrow \mathbf{r} \, N_2$$
$$N_3 \rightarrow \Lambda$$
Bad grammars generate languages the same way CFG's do.
Prove that even a bad grammar cannot generate a nonregular language, by showing how to construct one regular expression that defines the same language as the whole bad grammar.

CHAPTER 16

CHOMSKY NORMAL FORM

Context-free grammars come in a wide variety of forms. By definition, any finite string of terminals and nonterminals is a legal right-hand side of a production, for example,

$$X \rightarrow YaaYbaYXZabYb$$

This wide range of possibilities gives us considerable freedom, but it also adds to the difficulty of analyzing the languages these possibilities represent. We have seen in the previous chapter that it may be important to know the form of the grammar. In this chapter, we shall show that all context-free languages can be defined by CFG's that fit a more restrictive format, one more amenable to theoretical investigation.

The first problem we tackle is Λ. The null string is a perennial weed in our garden. It gave us trouble with FA's and TG's, and it will give us trouble now.

We have not yet committed ourselves to a definite stand on the social acceptability of **Λ-productions**, that is, productions of the form:

$$N \to \Lambda$$

where N is any nonterminal. We have employed them but we do not pay them equal wages. These Λ-productions will make our lives very difficult in the discussions to come, so we must ask ourselves, do we need them at all?

Any context-free language in which Λ is a word must have some Λ-productions in its grammar since otherwise we could never derive the word Λ from S. This statement is obvious, but it should be given some justification. Λ-productions are the only productions that shorten the working string. If we begin with the string S and apply only non-Λ-productions, we never develop a word of length 0.

However, there are some grammars that generate languages that do not include the word Λ but that contain some Λ-productions anyway. One such CFG that we have already encountered is

$$S \to aX$$
$$X \to \Lambda$$

for the single word a. There are other CFG's that generate this same language that do not include any Λ-productions.

The following theorem, which is the work of Bar-Hillel, Perles, and Shamir, shows that Λ-productions are not necessary in a grammar for a context-free language that does not contain the word Λ. It proves an even stronger result.

THEOREM 21

If L is a context-free language generated by a CFG that includes Λ-productions, then there is a different context-free grammar that has no Λ-productions that generates either the whole language L (if L does not include the word Λ) or else generates the language of all the words in L that are not Λ.

PROOF

We prove this by providing a constructive algorithm that will convert a CFG that contains Λ-productions into a CFG that does not contain Λ-productions that generates the same language with the possible exception of the word Λ.

Consider the purpose of the production

$$N \to \Lambda$$

If we apply this production to some working string, say *abAbNaB*, we get *abAbaB*. In other words, the net result is to delete *N* from the working string. If *N* was just destined to be deleted, why did we let it get there in the first place? Its mere presence in the working string cannot have affected the non-terminals around it since productions are applied to one symbol at a time no matter what its neighbors are. This is why we call these grammars *context free*. A nonterminal in a working string in a derivation is not a catalyst; it is not there to make other changes possible. It is only there so that eventually it will be replaced by one of several possibilities. It represents a decision we have yet to make, a fork in the road, a branching node in a tree.

If *N* is simply destined to be removed we need a means of avoiding putting that *N* into the string at all. This is not quite so simple as it sounds.

Consider the following CFG for EVENPALINDROME (the language of all palindromes with an even number of letters):

$$S \rightarrow aSa \mid bSb \mid \Lambda$$

In this grammar we have the following possible derivation:

$$\begin{aligned} S &\Rightarrow aSa \\ &\Rightarrow aaSaa \\ &\Rightarrow aabSbaa \\ &\Rightarrow aabbaa \end{aligned}$$

We obviously need the nonterminal *S* in the production process even though we delete it from the derivation when it has served its purpose.

The following rule seems to take care of using and deleting the nonterminals involved in Λ-productions.

Proposed Replacement Rule

If, in a certain CFG, there is a production of the form

$$N \rightarrow \Lambda$$

among the set of productions, where *N* is any nonterminal (even *S*), then we can modify the grammar by deleting this production and adding the following list of productions in its place.

For all productions of the form:

$$X \rightarrow \text{(blah 1)}\ N\ \text{(blah 2)}$$

where *X* is any nonterminal (even *S* or *N*) and where (blah 1) and (blah 2) are anything at all (even involving *N*), *add* the production

$$X \rightarrow \text{(blah 1)}\ \text{(blah 2)}$$

Notice, we do not delete the production $X \rightarrow$ (blah 1) N (blah 2), only the production $N \rightarrow \Lambda$.

For all productions that involve more than one N on the right side add new productions that have the other characters the same but that have all possible subsets of N's deleted.

For example, the production

$$X \rightarrow aNbNa$$

makes us add

$$X \rightarrow abNa \qquad \text{(deleting only the first } N\text{)}$$
$$X \rightarrow aNba \qquad \text{(deleting only the second } N\text{)}$$

and

$$X \rightarrow aba \qquad \text{(deleting both } N\text{'s)}$$

Also,

$$X \rightarrow NN$$

makes us add

$$X \rightarrow N \qquad \text{(deleting one } N\text{)}$$

and

$$X \rightarrow \Lambda \qquad \text{(deleting both } N\text{'s)}$$

Instead of using a production with an N and then dropping the N later we simply use the correct form of the production with the N already dropped. There is then no need to remove N later and so no need for the lambda production. This modification of the CFG will produce a new CFG that generates exactly the same words as the first grammar with the possible exception of the word Λ. This is the end of the Proposed Replacement Rule.   ∎

Let us see what happens when we apply this replacement rule to the following CFG.

$$S \rightarrow aSa \mid bSb \mid \Lambda$$

We remove the production $S \rightarrow \Lambda$ and replace it with $S \rightarrow aa$ and $S \rightarrow bb$, which are the first two productions with the right-side S deleted.

The CFG is now:

$$S \rightarrow aSa \mid bSb \mid aa \mid bb$$

which also generates EVENPALINDROME, except for the word Λ, which can no longer be derived.

The reason this rule works is that if the N was put into the working string by the production

$$X \rightarrow (\text{blah } 1) \; N \; (\text{blah } 2)$$

and later deleted by

$$N \rightarrow \Lambda$$

both steps could have been done at once by using the replacement production

$$X \rightarrow (\text{blah } 1) \; (\text{blah } 2)$$

in the first place. We have seen that, in general, a change in the order in which we apply the productions may change the word generated. However, in this case, no matter how far apart the productions

$$X \rightarrow (\text{blah } 1) \; N \; (\text{blah } 2)$$

and

$$N \rightarrow \Lambda$$

may be in the sequence of the derivation, if the N removed from the working string by the second production is the same N introduced by the first then these two can be combined into the single production

$$X \rightarrow (\text{blah } 1) \; (\text{blah } 2)$$

We must be careful not to remove N before it has served its full purpose. For example, the following EVENPALINDROME derivation is generated in the old CFG:

Derivation	Production Used
$S \Rightarrow aSa$	$S \rightarrow aSa$
$\Rightarrow aaSaa$	$S \rightarrow aSa$
$\Rightarrow aabSbaa$	$S \rightarrow bSb$
$\Rightarrow aabbaa$	$S \rightarrow \Lambda$

In the new CFG we can combine the last two steps into one:

Derivation	Production Used
$S \Rightarrow aSa$	$S \rightarrow aSa$
$\Rightarrow aaSaa$	$S \rightarrow aSa$
$\Rightarrow aabbaa$	$S \rightarrow bb$

It is only the last two steps for which we use the replacement production:

$$\left.\begin{array}{l} S \rightarrow bSb \\ \\ S \rightarrow \Lambda \end{array}\right\} \quad \text{becomes } S \rightarrow bb$$

We do not eliminate the entire possibility of using S to form words.

We can now use this proposed replacement rule to describe an algorithm for eliminating all Λ-productions from a given grammar.

If a particular CFG has several nonterminals with Λ-productions, then we replace these Λ-productions one by one following the steps of the proposed replacement rule. As we saw, we will get more productions (new right sides by deleting some N's) but shorter derivations (by combining the steps that formerly employed Λ-productions). We end up with a CFG that generates the exact same language as the original CFG (with the possible exception of the word Λ) but that has no Λ-productions.

A little discussion is in order here to establish that the new CFG actually does generate all the non-Λ words the old CFG does *and* that it generates no new words that the old CFG did not.

In the general case we might have something like this. In a long derivation in a grammar that includes the productions $B \rightarrow aN$ and $N \rightarrow \Lambda$ among other stuff we might find:

$$\begin{array}{ll} S \Rightarrow \ldots & \\ \Rightarrow a\,A\,N\,b\,B\,a & \\ \Rightarrow a\,A\,N\,b\,a\,N\,a & \text{from } B \rightarrow aN \\ \quad \ldots & \\ \Rightarrow a\,b\,b\,X\,y\,b\,a\,N\,a & \\ \Rightarrow a\,b\,b\,X\,y\,b\,a\,a & \text{from } N \rightarrow \Lambda \\ \quad \ldots & \end{array}$$

Notice that not all the N's have to turn into Λ's. The first N in the working string did not, but the second does. We trace back to the step at which this second N was originally incorporated into the working string. In this sketchy example, it came from the production $B \rightarrow aN$. In the new CFG we would have a corresponding production $B \rightarrow a$. If we had applied this production instead of $B \to aN$, there would be no need later to apply $N \to \Lambda$ to this particular N. Those never born need never die. (First statistician: "With all the troubles in this world, it would be better if we were never born in the first place." Second statistician: "Yes, but how many are so lucky? Maybe one in ten thousand.") So we see that we can produce all the old non-Λ words with the new CFG even without Λ-productions.

To show that the new CFG with its new productions does not generate any new words that the old CFG could not, we merely observe that each of the new added productions is just a combination of old productions and any new derivation corresponds to some old derivation that used the Λ-production.

Before we claim that this constructive algorithm provides the whole proof, we must ask if it is *finite*. It seems that if we start with some nonterminals N_1, N_2, N_3, which have Λ-productions and we eliminate these Λ-productions one by one until there are none left, nothing can go wrong. Can it?

What can go wrong is that the proposed replacement rule may create new Λ-productions that can not themselves be removed without again creating more. For example, in this grammar

$$S \to a \mid Xb \mid aYa$$
$$X \to Y \mid \Lambda$$
$$Y \to b \mid X$$

we have the Λ-production

$$X \to \Lambda$$

so by the replacement rule we can eliminate this production and put in its place the additional productions:

$$S \to b \qquad \text{(from } S \to Xb\text{)}$$

and

$$Y \to \Lambda \qquad \text{(from } Y \to X\text{)}.$$

But now we have created a new Λ-production which was not there before. So we still have the same number of Λ-productions we started with. If we now use the proposed replacement rule to get rid of $Y \to \Lambda$, we get

$$S \to aa \qquad \text{(from } S \to aYa\text{)}$$

and

$$X \to \Lambda \qquad \text{(from } X \to Y\text{)}$$

But we have now re-created the production $X \rightarrow \Lambda$. So we are back with our old Λ-production. In this particular case the proposed replacement rule will never eliminate all Λ-productions even in hundreds of applications.

Therefore, unfortunately, we do not yet have a proof of this theorem. However, we can take some consolation in having created a wonderful illustration of the need for careful proofs. Never again will we think that the phrase "and so we see that the algorithm is finite" is a silly waste of words.

Despite the apparent calamity, all is not lost. We can perform an ancient mathematical trick and patch up the proof. The trick is to eliminate all the Λ-productions at once.

DEFINITION (inside the proof of Theorem 21)

In a given CFG, we call a nonterminal N **nullable** if

  1. There is a production $N \rightarrow \Lambda$
or
  2. There is a derivation that starts at N and leads to Λ.
   $$N \Rightarrow \ldots \Rightarrow \Lambda$$

(end of definition, not proof) ∎

As we have seen, all nullable nonterminals are dangerous. We now state the careful formulation of the algorithm.

Modified Replacement Rule

  1. Delete all Λ-productions.
  2. Add the following productions: For every production

$$X \rightarrow \text{old string}$$

add enough new productions of the form $X \rightarrow \ldots$, that the right side will account for any modification of the old string that can be formed by deleting all possible subsets of nullable nonterminals, except that we do not allow $X \rightarrow \Lambda$ to be formed even if all the characters in this old right-side string are nullable.

For example, in the CFG

$$S \rightarrow a \mid Xb \mid aYa$$
$$X \rightarrow Y \mid \Lambda$$
$$Y \rightarrow b \mid X$$

we find that X and Y are nullable. So when we delete $X \rightarrow \Lambda$ we have to check all productions that include X or Y to see what new productions to add:

Old Productions with Nullables	Productions Newly Formed by the Rule
$X \rightarrow Y$	Nothing
$X \rightarrow \Lambda$	Nothing
$Y \rightarrow X$	Nothing
$S \rightarrow Xb$	$S \rightarrow b$
$S \rightarrow aYa$	$S \rightarrow aa$

The new CFG is

$$S \rightarrow a \mid Xb \mid aYa \mid b \mid aa$$
$$X \rightarrow Y$$
$$Y \rightarrow b \mid X$$

It has no Λ-productions but generates the same language.

This modified replacement rule works the way we thought the first replacement rule would work, that is, by looking ahead at which nonterminals in the working string will be eliminated by Λ-productions and offering alternate substitutions in which they have already been eliminated.

Before we conclude this proof, we should ask ourselves whether the modified replacement rule is really workable, that is, is it an effective procedure in the sense of our use of that term in Chapter 12? To apply the modified replacement rule we must be able to identify all the nullable nonterminals at once. How can we do this if the grammar is complicated? For example, in the CFG

$$S \rightarrow Xay \mid YY \mid aX \mid ZYX$$
$$X \rightarrow Za \mid bZ \mid ZZ \mid Yb$$
$$Y \rightarrow Ya \mid XY \mid \Lambda$$
$$Z \rightarrow aX \mid YYY$$

all the nonterminals are nullable, as we can see from

$$S \Rightarrow ZYX \Rightarrow YYYYX \Rightarrow YYYYZZ \Rightarrow YYYYYYYZ \Rightarrow YYYYYYYYY$$
$$\Rightarrow \ldots \Rightarrow \Lambda\Lambda\Lambda\Lambda\Lambda\Lambda\Lambda\Lambda\Lambda = \Lambda$$

The solution to this problem is blue paint (the same shade used in Chapter 12). Let us start by painting all the nonterminals with Λ-productions blue. We paint every occurrence of them, throughout the entire CFG, blue. Now for

Step 2 we paint blue all nonterminals that produce solid blue strings. For example, if

$$S \rightarrow ZYX$$

and Z, Y, and X are all blue, then we paint S blue. Paint all other occurrences of S throughout the CFG blue too. As with the FA's, we repeat Step 2 until nothing new is painted. At this point all nullable nonterminals will be blue.

This is an effective decision procedure to determine all nullables, and therefore the modified replacement rule is also effective.

This then successfully concludes the proof of this Theorem. ∎

EXAMPLE

Let us consider the following CFG for the language defined by **(a + b)*a**

$$S \rightarrow Xa$$
$$X \rightarrow aX \mid bX \mid \Lambda$$

The only nullable nonterminal here is X, and the productions that have right sides including X are:

Productions with Nullables	New Productions Formed by the Rule
$S \rightarrow Xa$	$S \rightarrow a$
$X \rightarrow aX$	$X \rightarrow a$
$X \rightarrow bX$	$X \rightarrow b$

The full new CFG is:

$$S \rightarrow Xa \mid a$$
$$X \rightarrow aX \mid bX \mid a \mid b$$

To produce the word *baa* we formerly used the derivation:

Derivation	Production Used
$S \Rightarrow Xa$	$S \rightarrow Xa$
$\Rightarrow bXa$	$X \rightarrow bX$
$\Rightarrow baXa$	$X \rightarrow aX$
$\Rightarrow baa$	$X \rightarrow \Lambda$

Now we combine the last two steps, and the new derivation in the new CFG is:

$$S \Rightarrow Xa \qquad\qquad S \rightarrow Xa$$
$$\quad \Rightarrow bXa \qquad\qquad X \rightarrow bX$$
$$\quad \Rightarrow baa \qquad\qquad X \rightarrow a$$

Since Λ was not a word generated by the old CFG, the new CFG generates exactly the same language. ∎

EXAMPLE

Consider this inefficient CFG for the language defined by

$$(a + b)^*bb(a + b)^*$$
$$S \rightarrow XY$$
$$X \rightarrow Zb$$
$$Y \rightarrow bW$$
$$Z \rightarrow AB$$
$$W \rightarrow Z$$
$$A \rightarrow aA \mid bA \mid \Lambda$$
$$B \rightarrow Ba \mid Bb \mid \Lambda$$

From X we can derive any word ending in b; from Y we can derive any word starting with b. Therefore, from S we can derive any word with a double b.

Obviously, A and B are nullable. Based on that, $Z \rightarrow AB$ makes Z also nullable. After that, we see that W is also nullable. X, Y, and S remain nonnullable. Alternately, of course, we could have arrived at this by azure artistry.

The modified replacement algorithm tells us to generate new productions to replace the Λ-productions as follows:

Old	Additional New Productions Derived from Old
$X \rightarrow Zb$	$X \rightarrow b$
$Y \rightarrow bW$	$Y \rightarrow b$
$Z \rightarrow AB$	$Z \rightarrow A$ and $Z \rightarrow B$
$W \rightarrow Z$	Nothing
$A \rightarrow aA$	$A \rightarrow a$
$A \rightarrow bA$	$A \rightarrow b$
$B \rightarrow Ba$	$B \rightarrow a$
$B \rightarrow Bb$	$B \rightarrow b$

Remember we do not eliminate all of the old productions, only the old Λ-productions.

The fully modified new CFG is:

$$S \rightarrow XY$$
$$X \rightarrow Zb \mid b$$
$$Y \rightarrow bW \mid b$$
$$Z \rightarrow AB \mid A \mid B$$
$$W \rightarrow Z$$
$$A \rightarrow aA \mid bA \mid a \mid b$$
$$B \rightarrow Ba \mid Bb \mid a \mid b$$

Since Λ was not a word generated by the old CFG, the new CFG generates exactly the same language. ∎

We now eliminate another needless oddity that plagues some CFG's.

DEFINITION

A production of the form

one Nonterminal → one Nonterminal

is called a **unit production.** ∎

Bar-Hillel, Perles, and Shamir tell us how to get rid of these too.

THEOREM 22

If there is a CFG for the language L that has no Λ-productions, then there is also a CFG for L with no Λ-productions and no unit productions.

PROOF

This will be another proof by constructive algorithm.

First we ask ourselves what is the purpose of a production of the form

$$A \rightarrow B$$

where A and B are nonterminals.

We can use it only to change some working string of the form

$$(\text{blah}) \; A \; (\text{blah})$$

into the working string

$$(\text{blah}) \; B \; (\text{blah})$$

why would we want to do that? We do it because later we want to apply a production to the nonterminal B that is different from any that we could produce from A. For example,

$$B \rightarrow (\text{string})$$

so

$$(\text{blah}) \; A \; (\text{blah}) \Rightarrow (\text{blah}) \; B \; (\text{blah}) \Rightarrow (\text{blah}) \; (\text{string}) \; (\text{blah})$$

which is a change we could not make without using $A \rightarrow B$, since we had no production $A \rightarrow (\text{string})$.

It seems simple then to say that instead of unit productions all we need are more choices for replacements for A. We now formulate a replacement rule for eliminating unit productions.

Proposed Elimination Rule

If $A \rightarrow B$ is a unit production and all the productions starting with B are

$$B \rightarrow s_1 \mid s_2 \mid \ldots$$

where $s_1, s_2, \ldots$ are strings, then we can drop the production $A \rightarrow B$ and instead include these new productions:

$$A \rightarrow s_1 \mid s_2 \mid \ldots$$

Again we ask ourselves, will repeated applications of this proposed elimination rule result in a grammar that does not include unit productions but defines exactly the same language?

The answer is that we still have to be careful. A problem analogous to the one that arose before can strike again.

The set of new productions we create may give us new unit productions. For example, if we start with the grammar:

$$S \rightarrow A \mid bb$$
$$A \rightarrow B \mid b$$

$$B \rightarrow S \mid a$$

and we try to eliminate the unit production $A \rightarrow B$, we get instead

$$A \rightarrow S \mid a$$

to go along with the old productions we are retaining. The CFG is now:

$$S \rightarrow A \mid bb$$
$$A \rightarrow b$$
$$B \rightarrow S \mid a$$

We still have three unit productions:

$$S \rightarrow A \quad A \rightarrow S \quad B \rightarrow S$$

If we now try to eliminate the unit production $B \rightarrow S$, we create the new unit production $B \rightarrow A$. If we then use the proposed elimination rule on $B \rightarrow A$, we will get back $B \rightarrow S$.

As was the case with Λ-productions, we must get rid of all unit productions in one fell swoop to avoid infinite circularity.

Modified Elimination Rule

For every pair of nonterminals A and B, *if* the CFG has a unit production $A \rightarrow B$ *or if* there is a chain of unit productions leading from A to B, such as

$$A \Rightarrow X_1 \Rightarrow X_2 \Rightarrow \ldots \Rightarrow B$$

where X_1, X_2 are some nonterminals, we *then* introduce new productions according to the following rule: If the nonunit productions from B are

$$B \rightarrow s_1 \mid s_2 \mid s_3 \mid \ldots$$

where s_1 s_2 and s_3 are strings, create the productions:

$$A \rightarrow s_1 \mid s_2 \mid s_3 \mid \ldots$$

We do the same for all such pairs of A's and B's simultaneously. We can then eliminate all unit productions.

This is what we meant to do originally. If in the derivation for some word w the nonterminal A is in the working string and it gets replaced by a unit production $A \rightarrow B$, *or* by a sequence of unit productions leading to B, and further if B is replaced by the production $B \rightarrow s_4$, we can accomplish the same thing and derive the same word w by employing the production $A \rightarrow s_4$ directly in the first place.

This modified elimination rule avoids circularity by removing all unit productions at once. If the grammar contains no Λ-productions, it is not a hard task to find all sequences of unit productions $A \rightarrow S_1 \rightarrow S_2 \rightarrow \ldots \rightarrow B$, since there are only finitely many unit productions and they chain up in only obvious ways. In a grammar with Λ-productions, and nullable nonterminals X and Y, the production $S \rightarrow ZYX$ is essentially a unit production. There are no Λ-productions allowed by the hypothesis of the theorem so no such difficulty is possible.

The modified method described in the proof is an effective procedure and it proves the theorem. ∎

EXAMPLE

Let us reconsider the troubling example mentioned in the proof above

$$S \rightarrow A \mid bb$$
$$A \rightarrow B \mid b$$
$$B \rightarrow S \mid a$$

Let us separate the units from the nonunits:

Unit Productions	Decent Folks
$S \rightarrow A$	$S \rightarrow bb$
$A \rightarrow B$	$A \rightarrow b$
$B \rightarrow S$	$B \rightarrow a$

We list all unit productions and sequences of unit productions, one nonterminal at a time, tracing each nonterminal through each sequence it heads. Then we create the new productions that allow the first nonterminal to be replaced by any of the strings that could replace the last nonterminal in the sequence.

$S \rightarrow A$	gives	$S \rightarrow b$
$S \rightarrow A \rightarrow B$	gives	$S \rightarrow a$
$A \rightarrow B$	gives	$A \rightarrow a$
$A \rightarrow B \rightarrow S$	gives	$A \rightarrow bb$
$B \rightarrow S$	gives	$B \rightarrow bb$
$B \rightarrow S \rightarrow A$	gives	$B \rightarrow b$

The new CFG for this language is:

$$S \rightarrow bb \mid b \mid a$$
$$A \rightarrow b \mid a \mid bb$$
$$B \rightarrow a \mid bb \mid b$$

which has no unit productions.

Parenthetically, we may remark that this particular CFG generates a finite language since there are no nonterminals in any string produced from S. ■

In our next result we will separate the terminals from the nonterminals in CFG productions.

THEOREM 23

If L is a language generated by some CFG, then there is another CFG that generates all the non-Λ words of L, all of whose productions are of one of two basic forms:

$$\text{Nonterminal} \rightarrow \text{string of only Nonterminals}$$

or

$$\text{Nonterminal} \rightarrow \text{one terminal}$$

PROOF

The proof will be by constructive algorithm. Suppose that in the given CFG the nonterminals are S, X_1, X_2, ...

(If these are not actually the names of the nonterminals in the CFG as given, we can rename them without changing the final language. Let Y be called X_1, let N be called X_2. . . .)

Let us also assume that the terminals are a and b.

We now add two new nonterminals A and B and the productions

$$A \rightarrow a$$
$$B \rightarrow b$$

Now for every previous production involving terminals we replace each a with the nonterminal A and each b with the nonterminal B. For example,

$$X_3 \rightarrow X_4 a X_1 S b b X_7 a$$

becomes

$$X_3 \rightarrow X_4 A X_1 S B B X_7 A$$

which is a string of solid nonterminals.

Even if we start with a string of solid terminals

$$X_6 \rightarrow aaba$$

we convert it into a string of solid nonterminals

$$X_6 \rightarrow AABA$$

All our old productions are now of the form

$$\text{Nonterminal} \rightarrow \text{string of Nonterminals}$$

and the two new productions are of the form

$$\text{Nonterminal} \rightarrow \text{one terminal}$$

Any derivation that formerly started with S and proceeded down to the word

$$aaabba$$

will now follow the same sequence of productions to derive the string

$$AAABBA$$

from the start symbol S. From here we apply $A \rightarrow a$ and $B \rightarrow b$ a number of times to generate the word $aaabba$. This convinces us that any word that could be generated by the original CFG can also be generated by the new CFG.

We must also show that any word generated by the new CFG could also be generated by the old CFG. Any derivation in the new CFG is a sequence of applications of those productions which are modified old productions and the two totally new productions from A and B. Because these two new productions are the replacement of one nonterminal by one terminal nothing they introduce into the working string is replaceable. They do not interact with the other productions. If all applications of these two productions are deleted from a derivation in the new CFG what will result from the productions left is a working string of A's and B's. This reduced derivation completely corresponds to a derivation of a word from the old CFG. It is the same word the new

CFG had generated before we monkeyed with the derivation. This long-winded discussion makes more precise the idea that there are no extraneous words introduced into the new CFG. Therefore, this the new CFG proves the theorem. ∎

EXAMPLE

Let us start with the CFG:

$$S \rightarrow X_1 \mid X_2aX_2 \mid aSb \mid b$$
$$X_1 \rightarrow X_2X_2 \mid b$$
$$X_2 \rightarrow aX_2 \mid aaX_1$$

After the conversion we have:

$$\begin{array}{ll} S \rightarrow X_1 & X_1 \rightarrow X_2X_2 \\ S \rightarrow X_2AX_2 & X_1 \rightarrow B \\ S \rightarrow ASB & X_2 \rightarrow AX_2 \\ S \rightarrow B & X_2 \rightarrow AAX_1 \\ & A \rightarrow a \\ & B \rightarrow b \end{array}$$

We have not employed the disjunction slash | but instead have written out all the productions separately so that we may observe eight of the form:

$$\text{Nonterminal} \rightarrow \text{string of Nonterminals}$$

and two of the form:

$$\text{Nonterminal} \rightarrow \text{one terminal}$$ ∎

In all cases where the algorithm of the theorem is applied the new CFG has the same number of terminals as the old CFG and more nonterminals (one new one for each terminal).

As with all our proofs by constructive algorithm, we have not said that this new CFG is the best example of a CFG that fits the desired format. We say only that it is one of those that satisfy the requirements.

One problem is that we may create unit productions where none existed before. For example, if we follow the algorithm to the letter of the law,

$$X \rightarrow a$$

will become

$$X \rightarrow A$$
$$A \rightarrow a$$

To avoid this problem, we should add a clause to our algorithm saying that any productions that we find that are already in one of the desired forms, should be left alone: "If it ain't broke, don't fix it." Then we do not run the risk of creating unit productions (or Λ-productions for that matter).

EXAMPLE

One student thought that it was a waste of effort to introduce a new nonterminal to stand for a if the CFG already contained a production of the form Nonterminal $\rightarrow a$. Why not simply replace all a's in long strings by this Nonterminal? For instance, why cannot

$$S \rightarrow Na$$

$$N \rightarrow a \mid b$$

become

$$S \rightarrow NN$$

$$N \rightarrow a \mid b$$

The answer is that bb is not generated by the first grammar but it is by the second. The correct modified form is

$$S \rightarrow NA$$

$$N \rightarrow a \mid b$$

$$A \rightarrow a$$

EXAMPLE

The CFG

$$S \rightarrow XY$$
$$X \rightarrow XX$$
$$Y \rightarrow YY$$
$$X \rightarrow a$$
$$Y \rightarrow b$$

(which generates **aa*bb***) and which is already in the desired format would, if we mindlessly attacked it with our algorithm, become:

$$S \rightarrow XY$$
$$X \rightarrow XX$$
$$Y \rightarrow YY$$
$$X \rightarrow A$$
$$Y \rightarrow B$$
$$A \rightarrow a$$
$$B \rightarrow b$$

which is also in the desired format but has unit productions. When we get rid of the unit productions using the algorithm of Theorem 22 we return to the original CFG.

To the true theoretician this meaningless waste of energy costs nothing. The goal was to *prove* the existence of an equivalent grammar in the specified format. The virtue here is to find the shortest, most understandable and most elegant proof, not an algorithm with dozens of messy clauses and exceptions. The problem of finding the best such grammar is also a question theoreticians are interested in, but it is not the question presented in Theorem 23. ■

The purpose of Theorem 23 was to prepare the way for the following theorem developed by Chomsky.

THEOREM 24

For any context-free language L the non-Λ words of L can be generated by a grammar in which all productions are of one of two forms:

> Nonterminal → string of exactly two Nonterminals
> Nonterminal → one terminal

PROOF

The proof will be by constructive algorithm.

From Theorems 21 and 22 we know that there is a CFG for L (or for all L except Λ) that has no Λ-productions and no unit productions.

Let us suppose further that we start with a CFG for L that we have made to fit the form specified in Theorem 23. Let us suppose its productions are:

$$S \rightarrow X_1 X_2 X_3 X_8 \qquad\qquad X_1 \rightarrow X_3 X_4 X_{10} X_4$$
$$S \rightarrow X_3 X_5 \qquad\qquad\qquad X_1 \rightarrow a$$
$$S \rightarrow b \qquad\qquad\qquad\quad X_3 \rightarrow X_4 X_9$$
$$\cdots$$

The productions of the form

$$\text{Nonterminal} \rightarrow \text{one terminal}$$

we leave alone. We must now make the productions with right sides having many nonterminals into productions with right sides that have only two non-terminals.

For each production of the form

$$\text{Nonterminal} \rightarrow \text{string of Nonterminals}$$

we propose the following expansion that involves the introduction of the new nonterminals R_1, R_2, ... The production

$$S \rightarrow X_1 X_2 X_3 X_8$$

should be replaced by

$$S \rightarrow X_1 R_1$$

where $\quad R_1 \rightarrow X_2 R_3$

and where $\quad R_3 \rightarrow X_3 X_8$

We use these new nonterminals nowhere else in the grammar; they are used solely to split this one production into small pieces. If we need to expand more productions we introduce new R's with different subscripts.

Let us think of this as:

$$S \rightarrow X_1(\text{rest}_1) \qquad (\text{where } \text{rest}_1 = X_2 X_3 X_8)$$
$$(\text{rest}_1) \rightarrow X_2(\text{rest}_2) \qquad (\text{where } \text{rest}_2 = X_3 X_8)$$
$$(\text{rest}_2) \rightarrow X_3 X_8$$

This trick works just as well if we start with an odd number of nonterminals on the right-hand side of the production:

$$X_8 \rightarrow X_2 X_1 X_1 X_3 X_9$$

should be replaced by

$$X_8 \rightarrow X_2 R_4 \qquad (\text{where } R_4 = X_1 X_1 X_3 X_9)$$
$$R_4 \rightarrow X_1 R_5 \qquad (\text{where } R_5 = X_1 X_3 X_9)$$
$$R_5 \rightarrow X_1 R_6 \qquad (\text{where } R_6 = X_3 X_9)$$
$$R_6 \rightarrow X_3 X_9$$

In this way we can convert productions with long strings of nonterminals into sequences of productions with exactly two nonterminals on the right side. As with the previous theorem, we are not finished until we have convinced ourselves that this conversion has not altered the language the CFG generates.

Any word formerly generated is still generatable by virtually the same steps, if we understand that some productions have been expanded into several productions that must be executed in sequence.

For example, in a derivation where we previously employed the production

$$X_8 \rightarrow X_2X_1X_1X_3X_9$$

we must now employ the sequence of productions:

$$X_8 \rightarrow X_2R_4$$
$$R_4 \rightarrow X_1R_5$$
$$R_5 \rightarrow X_1R_6$$
$$R_6 \rightarrow X_3X_9$$

in exactly this order.

This should give confidence that we can still generate all the words we could before that change. The real problem is to show that with all these new nonterminals and productions that we have not allowed any additional words to be generated. Let us observe that since the nonterminal R_5 occurs in only the two productions

$$R_4 \rightarrow X_1R_5$$

and

$$R_5 \rightarrow X_1R_6$$

any sequence of productions that generates a word using R_5 must have used

$$R_4 \rightarrow X_1R_5$$

to get R_5 into the working string, and

$$R_5 \rightarrow X_1R_6$$

to remove it from the final string.

This combination has the net effect of a production like:

$$R_4 \rightarrow X_1X_1R_6$$

Again R_4 could have been introduced into the working string only by one specific production. Also R_6 can be removed only by one specific production. In fact, the net effect of these R's must be the same as the replacment of X_8 by $X_2X_1X_1X_3X_9$. Because we use different R's in the expansion of each production the new nonterminals (R's) cannot interact to give us new words. Each is on the right side of only one production and on the left side of only one production. The net effect must be like that of the original production.

The new grammar generates the same language as the old grammar and is in the desired form. ∎

DEFINITION

If a CFG has only productions of the form

$$\text{Nonterminal} \rightarrow \text{string of two Nonterminals}$$

or of the form

$$\text{Nonterminal} \rightarrow \text{one terminal}$$

it is said to be in **Chomsky Normal Form, CNF.** ∎

Let us be careful to realize that any context-free language that does not contain Λ as a word has a CFG in CNF that generates exactly it. However, if a CFL contains Λ, then when its CFG is converted by the algorithms above into CNF the word Λ drops out of the language while all other words stay the same.

EXAMPLE

Let us convert

$$S \rightarrow aSa \mid bSb \mid a \mid b \mid aa \mid bb$$

(which generates the language PALINDROME except for Λ) into CNF. This language is called NONNULLPALINDROME.

First we separate the terminals from the nonterminal as in Theorem 23:

$$S \rightarrow ASA$$
$$S \rightarrow BSB$$
$$S \rightarrow AA$$
$$S \rightarrow BB$$
$$S \rightarrow a$$
$$S \rightarrow b$$
$$A \rightarrow a$$
$$B \rightarrow b$$

Notice that we are careful not to introduce the needless unit productions $S \rightarrow A$ and $S \rightarrow B$.

Now we introduce the R's:

$$S \rightarrow AR_1 \qquad\qquad S \rightarrow AA$$
$$R_1 \rightarrow SA \qquad\qquad S \rightarrow BB$$
$$S \rightarrow BR_2 \qquad\qquad S \rightarrow a$$
$$R_2 \rightarrow SB \qquad\qquad S \rightarrow b$$
$$A \rightarrow a$$
$$B \rightarrow b$$

This is in CNF, but it is quite a mess. Had we not seen how it was constructed we would have some difficulty recognizing this grammar as a CFG for NONNULLPALINDROME.

If we include with this list of productions the additional production $S \rightarrow \Lambda$, we have a CFG for the entire language PALINDROME. ∎

EXAMPLE

Let us convert the CFG

$$S \rightarrow bA \mid aB$$
$$A \rightarrow bAA \mid aS \mid a$$
$$B \rightarrow aBB \mid bS \mid b$$

into CNF. Since we use the symbols A and B in this grammar already, let us call the new nonterminals we need to incorporate to achieve the form of Theorem 23, X (for a) and Y (for b).

The grammar becomes:

$$S \rightarrow YA \qquad\qquad B \rightarrow XBB$$
$$S \rightarrow XB \qquad\qquad B \rightarrow YS$$
$$A \rightarrow YAA \qquad\qquad B \rightarrow b$$
$$A \rightarrow XS \qquad\qquad X \rightarrow a$$
$$A \rightarrow a \qquad\qquad Y \rightarrow b$$

Notice that we have left well enough alone in two instances:

$$A \rightarrow a \qquad \text{and} \qquad B \rightarrow b$$

We need to simplify only two productions:

$$A \rightarrow YAA \qquad \text{becomes} \qquad \begin{cases} A \rightarrow YR_1 \\ R_1 \rightarrow AA \end{cases}$$

and

$$B \rightarrow XBB \qquad \text{becomes} \qquad \begin{cases} B \rightarrow XR_2 \\ R_2 \rightarrow BB \end{cases}$$

The CFG has now become:

$$
\begin{aligned}
S &\rightarrow YA \mid XB \\
A &\rightarrow YR_1 \mid XS \mid a \\
B &\rightarrow XR_2 \mid YS \mid b \\
X &\rightarrow a \\
Y &\rightarrow b \\
R_1 &\rightarrow AA \\
R_2 &\rightarrow BB
\end{aligned}
$$

which is in CNF. This is one of the more obscure grammars for the language EQUAL. ∎

EXAMPLE

Consider the CFG

$$S \rightarrow aaaaS \mid aaaa$$

which generates the language a^{4n} for $n = 1\ 2\ 3. \ldots$

$$= \{a^4,\ a^8,\ a^{12}. \ldots\}$$

We convert this to CNF as follows: First into the form of Theorem 23:

$$
\begin{aligned}
S &\rightarrow AAAAS \\
S &\rightarrow AAAA \\
A &\rightarrow a
\end{aligned}
$$

which in turn becomes

$$S \rightarrow AR_1$$
$$R_1 \rightarrow AR_2$$
$$R_2 \rightarrow AR_3$$
$$R_3 \rightarrow AS$$
$$S \rightarrow AR_4$$
$$R_4 \rightarrow AR_5$$
$$R_5 \rightarrow AA$$
$$A \rightarrow a$$

∎

As the last topic in this chapter we show that not only can we standardize the form of the grammar but we can also standardize the form of the derivations.

DEFINITION

The **leftmost nonterminal** in a working string is the first nonterminal that we encounter when we scan the string from left to right. ∎

EXAMPLE

In the string $abNbaXYa$, the leftmost nonterminal is N. ∎

DEFINITION

If a word w is generated by a CFG by a certain derivation and at each step in the derivation a rule of production is applied to the leftmost nonterminal in the working string, then this derivation is called a **leftmost derivation**.

∎

EXAMPLE

Consider the CFG:

$$S \rightarrow aSX \mid b$$

$$X \rightarrow Xb \mid a$$

The following is a leftmost derivation:

$$S \Rightarrow aSX$$

$$\Rightarrow aaSXX$$

$$\Rightarrow aabXX$$

$$\Rightarrow aabXbX$$

$$\Rightarrow aababX$$

$$\Rightarrow aababa$$

At every stage in the derivation the nonterminal replaced is the leftmost one. ∎

EXAMPLE

Consider the CFG:

$$S \rightarrow XY$$
$$X \rightarrow XX \mid a$$
$$Y \rightarrow YY \mid b$$

We can generate the word *aaabb* through several different derivations, each of which follows one of these two possible derivation trees:

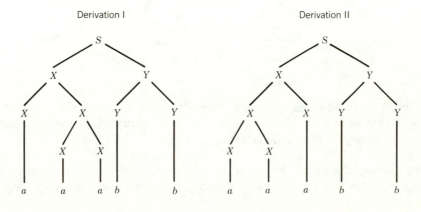

Derivation I   Derivation II

Each of these trees becomes a leftmost derivation when we specify in what order the steps are to be taken. If we draw a dotted line similar to the one that traces the Polish notation for us, we see that it indicates the order of productions in the leftmost derivation. We number the nonterminals in the order in which we first meet them on the dotted line. This is the order in which they must be replaced in a leftmost derivation.

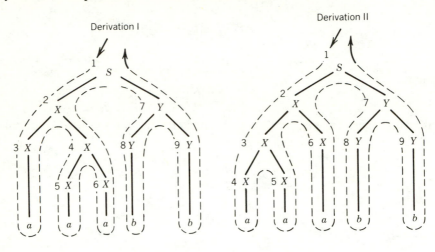

Derivation I	**Derivation II**
1. $S \Rightarrow \dot{X}Y$	1. $S \Rightarrow \dot{X}Y$
2. $\Rightarrow \dot{X}XY$	2. $\Rightarrow \dot{X}XY$
3. $\Rightarrow a\dot{X}Y$	3. $\Rightarrow \dot{X}XXY$
4. $\Rightarrow a\dot{X}XY$	4. $\Rightarrow a\dot{X}XY$
5. $\Rightarrow aa\dot{X}Y$	5. $\Rightarrow aa\dot{X}Y$
6. $\Rightarrow aaa\dot{Y}$	6. $\Rightarrow aaa\dot{Y}$
7. $\Rightarrow aaa\dot{Y}Y$	7. $\Rightarrow aaa\dot{Y}Y$
8. $\Rightarrow aaab\dot{Y}$	8. $\Rightarrow aaab\dot{Y}$
9. $\Rightarrow aaabb$	9. $\Rightarrow aaabb$

In each of these derivations we have drawn a dot over the head of the leftmost nonterminal. It is the one that must be replaced in the next step if we are to have a leftmost derivation. ∎

The method illustrated above can be applied to any derivation in any CFG. It therefore provides a proof by constructive algorithm the following theorem.

THEOREM 25

Any word that can be generated by a given CFG by some derivation also has a leftmost derivation. ∎

EXAMPLE

Consider the CFG:

$$S \rightarrow S \supset S \mid {\sim}S \mid (S) \mid p \mid q$$

To generate the symbolic logic formula

$$(p \supset ({\sim}p \supset q))$$

we use the following tree:

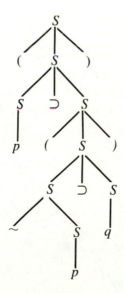

Remember that the terminal symbols are

$$(\quad) \supset \sim p \quad q$$

and the only nonterminal is S. We must always replace the left-most S.

$$S \Rightarrow (\dot{S})$$
$$\Rightarrow (\dot{S} \supset S)$$
$$\Rightarrow (p \supset \dot{S})$$
$$\Rightarrow (p \supset (\dot{S}))$$
$$\Rightarrow (p \supset (\dot{S} \supset S))$$
$$\Rightarrow (p \supset (\sim \dot{S} \supset S))$$
$$\Rightarrow (p \supset (\sim p \supset \dot{S}))$$
$$\Rightarrow (p \supset (\sim p \supset q)) \qquad \blacksquare$$

PROBLEMS

Each of the following CFG's has a production using the symbol Λ and yet Λ is not a word in its language. Using the algorithm in this chapter, show that there are other CFG's for these languages that do not use Λ-productions.

1. $S \rightarrow aX \mid bX$
    $X \rightarrow a \mid b \mid \Lambda$

2. $S \rightarrow aX \mid bS \mid a \mid b$
    $X \rightarrow aX \mid a \mid \Lambda$

3. $S \rightarrow aS \mid bX$
    $X \rightarrow aX \mid \Lambda$

4. $S \rightarrow XaX \mid bX$
    $X \rightarrow XaX \mid XbX \mid \Lambda$

5. Show that if a CFG does not have Λ-productions then there is another CFG that does have Λ-productions and that generates the same language.

Each of the following CFG's has unit productions. Using the algorithm presented in this chapter, find CFG's for these same languages that do not have unit productions.

6. $S \rightarrow aX \mid Yb$
   $X \rightarrow S$
   $Y \rightarrow bY \mid b$

7. $S \rightarrow AA$
   $A \rightarrow B \mid BB$
   $B \rightarrow abB \mid b \mid bb$

8. $S \rightarrow AB$
   $A \rightarrow B$
   $B \rightarrow aB \mid Bb \mid \Lambda$

Convert the following CFG's to CNF.

9. $S \rightarrow SS \mid a$

10. $S \rightarrow aSa \mid SSa \mid a$

11. $S \rightarrow aXX$
    $X \rightarrow aS \mid bS \mid a$

12. $E \rightarrow E + E$
    $E \rightarrow E * E$
    $E \rightarrow (E)$
    $E \rightarrow 7$
    The terminals here are $+ * ( ) 7$.

13. $S \rightarrow ABABAB$
    $A \rightarrow a \mid \Lambda$
    $B \rightarrow b \mid \Lambda$
    Note that Λ is a word in this language but when converted into CNF the grammar will no longer generate it.

14. $S \rightarrow SaS \mid SaSbS \mid SbSaS \mid \Lambda$

15. $S \rightarrow AS \mid SB$
    $A \rightarrow BS \mid SA$
    $B \rightarrow SS$

16. $S \rightarrow X$
     $X \rightarrow Y$
     $Y \rightarrow Z$
     $Z \rightarrow aa$

17. $S \rightarrow SS \mid A$
     $A \rightarrow SS \mid AS \mid a$

18. (i)   Find the leftmost derivation for the word *abba* in the grammar:
           $S \rightarrow AA$
           $A \rightarrow aB$
           $B \rightarrow bB \mid \Lambda$

     (ii) Find the leftmost derivation for the word *abbabaabbbabbab* in the
           CFG:
           $S \rightarrow SSS \mid aXb$
           $X \rightarrow ba \mid bba \mid abb$

19. Prove that any word that can be generated by a CFG has a right-most
     derivation.

20. Show that if L is any language that does not contain the word Λ, then
     there is a context-free grammar that generates L and that has the property
     that the right-hand side of every production is a string that starts with
     a terminal.
     In other words all productions are of the form:

     $$\text{Nonterminal} \rightarrow \text{terminal (arbitrary)}$$

CHAPTER 17

PUSHDOWN
AUTOMATA

In Chapter 15 we saw that the class of languages generated by CFG's is properly larger than the class of languages defined by regular expressions. This means that all regular languages can be generated by CFG's, and so can some nonregular languages (for example, $\{a^n b^n\}$ and PALINDROME).

After introducing the regular languages defined by regular expressions we found a class of abstract machines (FA's) with the following dual property: For each regular language there is at least one machine that runs successfully only on the input strings from that language and for each machine in the class the set of words it accepts is a regular language. This correspondence was crucial to our deeper understanding of this collection of languages. The Pumping Lemma, complements, intersection, decidability . . . were all learned from the machine aspect, not from the regular expression. We are now considering a different class of languages but we want to answer the same questions; so we would again like to find a machine formulation. We are looking for a mathematical model of some class of machines that correspond analogously to CFL's; that is, there should be at least one machine that accepts each CFL and the language accepted by each machine is context-free. We want CFL-recognizers or CFL-acceptors just as FA's are regular language recognizers and acceptors. We are hopeful that an analysis of the machines will help us understand the languages in a deeper, more profound sense, just as an analysis of FA's led to theorems about regular languages. In this chapter we develop such a new class of machines. In the next chapter we prove that these new machines do indeed correspond to CFL's in the way we desire. In subsequent chapters we shall learn that the grammars have as much to teach us about the machines as the machines do about the grammars.

To build these new machines, we start with our old FA's and throw in some new gadgets that will augment them and make them more powerful. Such an approach does not necessarily always work—a completely different design may be required—but this time it will (it's a stacked deck).

What we shall do first is develop a slightly different pictorial representation for FA's, one that will be easy to augment with the new gizmos.

We have, so far, not given a name to the part of the FA where the input string lives while it is being run. Let us call this the **INPUT TAPE.** The INPUT TAPE must be long enough for any possible input, and since any word in **a*** is a possible input, the TAPE must be infinitely long (such a tape is very expensive). The TAPE has a first location for the first letter of the input, then a second location, and so on. Therefore, we say that the TAPE is infinite in one direction only. Some people use the silly term "half-infinite" for this condition (which is like being half sober).

We draw the TAPE as shown here:

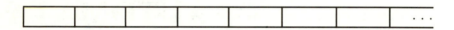

The locations into which we put the input letters are called **cells.** We name the cells with lowercase Roman numerals.

cell *i*   cell *ii*   cell *iii*

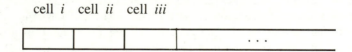

Below we show an example of an input TAPE already loaded with the input string *aaba*. The character "Δ" is used to indicate a blank in a TAPE cell.

| a | a | b | a | Δ | Δ | . . . |

The vast majority (all but four) of the cells on the input TAPE are empty, that is, they are loaded with blanks, ΔΔΔ . . . .

As we process this TAPE on the machine we read one letter at a time and eliminate each as it is used. When we reach the first blank cell we stop. We always presume that once the first blank is encountered the rest of the TAPE is also blank. We read from left to right and never go back to a cell that was read before.

As part of our new pictorial representations for FA's, let us introduce the symbols

to streamline the design of the machine. The arrows (directed edges) into or out of these states can be drawn at any angle. The START state is like a − state connected to another state in a TG by a Λ edge. We begin the process there, but we read no input letter. We just proceed immediately to the next state. A start state has no arrows coming into it.

An ACCEPT state is a shorthand notation for a dead-end final state—once entered, it cannot be left, such as:

all
letters

A REJECT state is a dead-end state that is not final.

all
letters

Since we have used the adjective "final" to apply only to accepting states in FA's, we call the new ACCEPT and REJECT states "**halt states.**" Previously we could pass through a final state if we were not finished reading the input data; halt states cannot be traversed. We can enter an ACCEPT or REJECT state but we cannot exit.

We are changing our diagrams of FA's so that every function a state performs is done by a separate box in the picture. The most important job performed by a state in an FA is to read an input letter and branch to other states depending on what letter has been read. To do this job from now on we introduce the READ states. These are depicted as diamond shaped boxes as shown below:

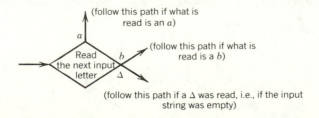

(follow this path if what is read is an a)

(follow this path if what is read is a b)

(follow this path if a Δ was read, i.e., if the input string was empty)

Here again the directions of the edges in the picture above show only one of the many possibilities. When the character Δ is read from the TAPE, it means that we are out of input letters. We are then finished processing the input string. The Δ-edge will lead to ACCEPT if the state we have stopped in is a final state and to REJECT if the processing stops in a state that is not a final state. In our old pictures for FA's we never explained how we knew we were out of input letters. In these new pictures we can recognize this fact by reading a blank from the TAPE.

These suggestions have not altered the power of our machines. We have merely introduced a new pictorial representation that will not alter their language-accepting abilities.

The FA that used to be drawn like this:

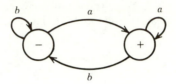

(the FA that accepts all words ending in the letter *a*) becomes, in the new symbolism, the machine below:

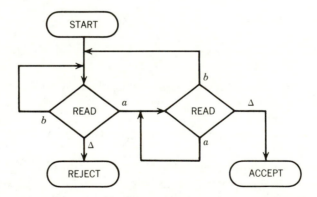

Notice that the edge from START needs no label because START reads no letter. All the other edges do require labels. We have drawn the edges as straight-line segments, not curves and loops as before. We have also used the electronic diagram notation for wires flowing into each other. For example,

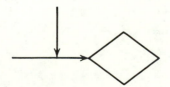

means

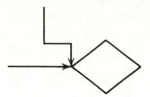

(they go the same place together).

Our machine is still an FA. The edges labeled Δ are not to be confused with Λ-labeled edges. These Δ-edges lead only from READ boxes to halt states. We have just moved the + and − signs out of the circles that used to indicate states and into adjoining ovals. The "states" are now only READ-boxes and have no final/nonfinal status.

In the FA above, if we run out of input letters in the left READ state, we will find a Δ on the INPUT TAPE and so take the Δ-edge to REJECT. Reading a Δ in a READ state that corresponds to an FA final state sends us to ACCEPT.

Let us give another example of the new pictorial notation:

EXAMPLE

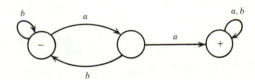

becomes

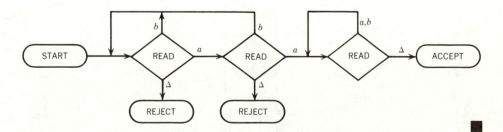

These pictures look more like the "flowcharts" we are familiar with than the old pictures for FA's did. The general study of the flowchart as a mathematical structure is part of Computer Theory but beyond our intended scope.

The reason we bothered to construct new pictures for FA's (which had perfectly good pictures already) is that it is now easier to make an addition to our machine called the **PUSHDOWN STACK** or **PUSHDOWN STORE.** This is a concept we may have already met in a course on Data Structures.

A PUSHDOWN STACK is a place where input letters (or other information) can be stored until we want to refer to them again. It holds the letters it has been fed in a long line (as many letters as we want). The operaton **PUSH** adds a new letter to the line. The new letter is placed on top of the STACK, and all the other letters are pushed back (or down) accordingly. Before the machine begins to process an input string the STACK is presumed to be empty, which means that every storage location in it initially contains a blank. If the STACK is then fed the letters a, b, c, d by this sequence of instructions:

$$\text{PUSH } a$$
$$\text{PUSH } b$$
$$\text{PUSH } c$$
$$\text{PUSH } d$$

then the top letter in the STACK is d, the second is c, the third is b, and the fourth is a. If we now execute the instruction:

$$\text{PUSH } b$$

the letter b will be added to the STACK on the top. The d will be pushed down to position 2, the c to position 3, the other b to position 4, and the bottom a to position 5.

One pictorial representation of a STACK with these letters in it is shown below. Beneath the bottom a we presume that the rest of the STACK, which, like the INPUT TAPE, has infinitely many storage locations, holds only blanks.

STACK

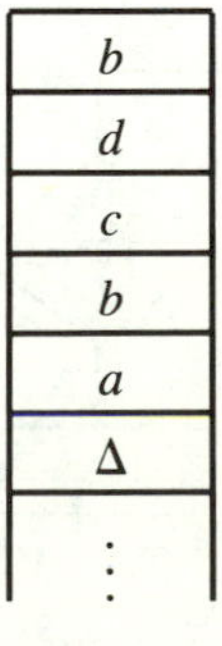

b
d
c
b
a
Δ
⋮

The instruction to take a letter out of the STACK is called **POP.** This causes the letter on the top of the STACK to be brought out of the STACK (popped). The rest of the letters are moved up one location each. A PUSH-DOWN STACK is called a **LIFO** file standing for "the LAST IN is the FIRST OUT," like a narrow crowded elevator. It is not like the normal storage area of a computer, which allows random access (we can retrieve stuff from anywhere regardless of the order in which it was fed in). A PUSHDOWN STACK lets us read only the top letter. If we want to read the third letter in the STACK we must go POP, POP, POP, but then we have additionally popped out the first two letters and they are no longer in the STACK. We also have no simple instruction for determining the bottom letter in the STACK, or for telling how many b's are in the STACK, and so forth. The only STACK operations allowed to us are PUSH and POP.

Popping an empty STACK, like reading an empty TAPE, gives us the blank character Δ.

We can add a PUSHDOWN STACK and the operations PUSH and POP to our new drawings of FA's by including as many as we want of the states:

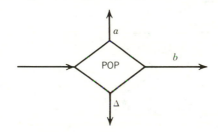

and the states:

The edges coming out of a POP state are labeled in the same way as the edges from a READ state, one (for the moment) for each character that might appear in the STACK including the blank. Note that branching can occur at POP states but not at PUSH states. We can leave PUSH states only by the one indicated route, although we can enter a PUSH state from any direction.

When FA's have been souped up with a STACK and POP and PUSH states, we call them **pushdown automata,** abbreviated **PDA**'s. These PDA's were introduced by Anthony G. Oettinger in 1961 and Marcel P. Schützenberger in 1963 and were further studied by Robert J. Evey, also in 1963.

The notion of a PUSHDOWN STACK as a data structure had been around for a while, but these mathematicians independently realized that when this structure is incorporated into an FA, its language-recognizing capabilities are increased considerably. Schützenberger developed a mathematical theory of languages encompassing both FA's and PDA's. We shall discuss this more in Chapter 18.

The precise definition will follow soon, after a few examples.

EXAMPLE

Consider the following PDA:

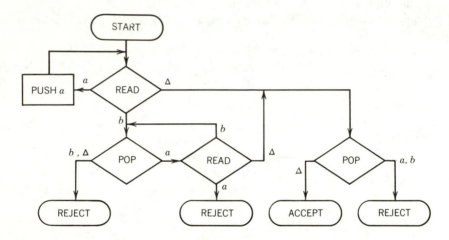

Before we begin to analyze this machine in general, let us see it in operation on the input string *aaabbb*. We begin by assuming that this string has been put on the TAPE. We always start the operation of the PDA with the STACK empty as shown:

TAPE	*a*	*a*	*a*	*b*	*b*	*b*	Δ		· · ·

STACK

Δ
⋮

We must begin at START. From there we proceed directly into the upper left READ, a state that reads the first letter of input. This is an *a*, so we cross it off the TAPE (it has been read) and we proceed along the *a* edge from the READ state. This edge brings us to the PUSH *a* state that tells us to push an *a* onto the STACK. Now the TAPE and STACK look like this:

TAPE	¢	a	a	b	b	b	Δ	· · ·

STACK

a
Δ
⋮

The edge from the PUSH *a* box takes us back to the line feeding into the same READ box, so we return to this state. We now read another *a* and proceed as before along the *a* edge to push it into the STACK. Again we are returned to the READ box. Again we read an *a* (our third), and again this *a* is pushed onto the STACK. The TAPE and STACK now look like this:

TAPE	¢	¢	¢	b	b	b	Δ	· · ·

STACK

a
a
a
Δ
⋮

After the third PUSH *a*, we are routed back to the same READ state again. This time, however, we read the letter *b*. This means that we take the *b* edge out of this state down to the lower left POP. Reading the *b* leaves the TAPE like this:

TAPE	¢	¢	¢	b̶	b	b	Δ	· · ·

The state POP takes the top element off the STACK. It is an *a*. It must be an *a* or a Δ since the only letters pushed onto the STACK in the whole program are *a*'s. If it were a Δ or the impossible choice, *b*, we would have to go to the REJECT state. However, this time, when we pop the STACK we get the letter *a* out, leaving the STACK like this:

STACK

Following the *a* road from POP takes us to the other READ. The next letter on the TAPE to be read is a *b*. This leaves the TAPE like this:

TAPE | ȼ | ȼ | ȼ | ɓ | ɓ | b | Δ | · · ·

The *b* road from the second READ state now takes us back to the edge feeding into the POP state. So we pop the STACK again and get another *a*. The STACK is now down to only one *a*.

STACK

The *a* line from POP takes us again to this same READ. There is only one letter left on the input TAPE, a *b*. We read it and leave the TAPE empty, that is, all blanks. However, the machine does not yet *know* that the TAPE is empty. It will discover this only when it next tries to read the TAPE and finds a Δ.

TAPE | ȼ | ȼ | ȼ | ɓ | ɓ | ɓ | Δ | · · ·

The *b* that we just read loops us back into the POP state. We then take the last *a* from the STACK, leaving it also empty—all blanks.

STACK

The *a* takes us from POP to the right side READ again. This time the only thing we can read from the TAPE is a blank, Δ. The Δ-edge takes us to the other POP on the right side. This POP now asks us to take a letter from the STACK, but the STACK is empty. Therefore, we say that we pop a Δ.

This means that we must follow the Δ-edge, which leads straight to the halt state ACCEPT. Therefore, the word *aaabbb* is accepted by this machine.

More than this can be observed. The language of words accepted by this machine is exactly:

$$\{a^n b^n, \quad n = 0 \quad 1 \quad 2 \quad \ldots\}$$

Let us see why.

The first part of the machine

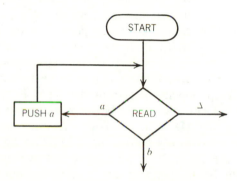

is a circuit of states that reads from the TAPE some number of a's in a row and pushes them into the STACK. This is the only place in the machine where anything is pushed into the STACK. Once we leave this circuit, we cannot return, and the STACK contains everything it will ever contain.

After we have loaded the STACK with all the a's from the front end of the input string, we read yet another letter from the input TAPE. If this character is a Δ, it means that the input word was of the form a^n, where n might have been 0 (i.e., some word in **a***).

If this is the input, we take the Δ-line all the way to the right-side POP state. This tests the STACK to see if it has anything in it. If it has, we go to REJECT. If the STACK is empty at this point, the input string must have been the null word, Λ, which we accept.

Let us now consider the other logical possibility, that after loading the front a's from the input (whether there are many or none) onto the STACK we read a b. This must be the first b in the input string. It takes us to a new section of the machine into another small circuit.

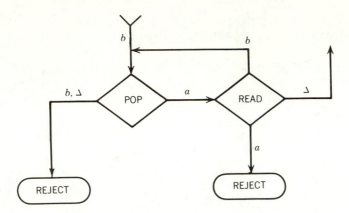

On reading this first b we immediately pop the STACK. The STACK can contain some a's or only Δ's. If the input string started with a b, we would be popping the STACK without ever having pushed anything onto it. We would then pop a Δ and go to REJECT. If we pop a b, something impossible has happened. So we go to REJECT and call the repairperson. If we pop an a we go to the lower right READ state that asks us to read a new letter.

As long as we keep popping a's from the STACK to match the b's we are reading from the TAPE, we circle between these two states happily: POP a, READ b, POP a, READ b. If we pop a Δ from the STACK, it means that we ran out of STACK a's before the TAPE ran out of input b's. This Δ-edge brings us to REJECT. Since we entered this two-state circuit by reading a b from the TAPE before popping any a's, if the input is a word of the form $a^n b^n$, then the b's will run out first.

If while looping around this circuit we hit an a on the TAPE, the READ state sends us to REJECT because this means the input is of the form

$$(\text{some } a\text{'s}) \ (\text{some } b\text{'s}) \ (\text{another } a) \ . \ . \ .$$

We cannot accept any word in which we come to an a after having read the first b. To get to ACCEPT the second READ state must read a blank and send us to the second POP state. Reading this blank means that the word ends after its clump of b's. All the words accepted by this machine must therefore be of the form **a*b*** but, as we shall now see, only some of these words successfully reach the halt state ACCEPT.

Eventually the TAPE will run out of letters and the READ state will turn up a blank. An input word of the form $a^n b^n$ puts n a's into the STACK. The first b read then takes us to the second circuit. After n trips around this circuit, we have popped the last a from the STACK and have read the other $(n-1)$ b's and a blank from the TAPE. We then exit this section to go to the last test.

We have exhausted the TAPE's supply of b's, so we should check to see

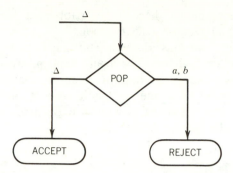

that the STACK is empty. We want to be sure we pop a Δ, otherwise we reject the word because there must have been more a's in the front than b's in the back. For us to get to ACCEPT, both TAPE and STACK must empty together. Therefore, the set of words this PDA accepts is exactly the language

$$\{a^n b^n, \quad n = 0 \quad 1 \quad 2 \quad 3 \ldots \}$$

We have already shown that the language accepted by the PDA above could not be accepted by any FA, so pushdown automata *are* more powerful than finite automata. We can say *more* powerful because all regular languages can be accepted by some PDA since they can be accepted by some FA and an FA (in the new notation) is exactly like a PDA that never uses its STACK. Propriety dictates that we not present the formal proof of this fact until after we give the formal definition of the terms involved. We present the definition of PDA's in a few pages.

We shall prove in the next chapter that PDA's are exactly the machines we need for recognizing CFL's. Every CFL can be defined as the language accepted by some PDA and the language accepted by any PDA can be defined by some CFG—a situation exactly analogous to the relationship between regular expressions and FA's—a context-free Kleene's Theorem.

Let us take a moment to consider what makes these machines more powerful than FA's. The reason is that even though they too have only finitely many states to roam among, they do have an unlimited capacity for memory. They can know where they have been, and how often. The reason no FA could accept the language $\{a^n b^n\}$ was that for large enough n the a^n part had to run around in a circuit and the machine could not keep track of how many times it had looped around. It could therefore not distinguish between $a^n b^n$ and some $a^m b^n$. However, the PDA has a primitive memory unit. It can keep track of how many a's are read in at the beginning. It can know how many times a circuit is traversed in general by putting a count cell, PUSH a, inside the loop.

Is this mathematical model then as powerful as a whole computer? Not quite yet; but that goal will be reached soon.

There are two points we must discuss. The first is that we need not restrict ourselves to using the same alphabet for input strings as we use for the STACK. In the example above, we could have read an *a* from the TAPE and then pushed an *X* into the STACK and let the *X*'s count the number of *a*'s. In this case, when we test the STACK with a POP state, we branch on *X* or Δ. The machine would then look like this:

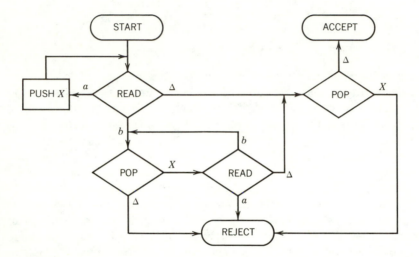

We have drawn this version of the PDA with some minor variations of display but no substantive change in function.

The READ states must provide branches for *a, b,* or Δ. The POP states must provide branches for *X* or Δ. We eliminated two REJECT states, by having all rejecting edges go into the same state.

When we do define PDA's, we shall require the specification of the TAPE alphabet Σ and the STACK alphabet Γ, which may be different. Although in Chapter 9 we used Γ to denote an output alphabet, we should not make the mistake of thinking that the STACK is an output device. It is an internal part of the PDA.

The second point that we should discuss is the possibility of nondeterminism. In our search for the machine equivalent to CFG's we saw that a memory device of some kind is required to accept the language $\{a^n b^n\}$. Is the addition of the STACK enough of a change to allow these new machines to accept all CFL's? Consideration of the language PALINDROME will soon convince us that the new machines (PDA's) will have to be nondeterministic if they are to correspond to CFG's.

This is not like biology where we are discovering what is or is not part of a kangaroo; we are inventing these machines and we can put into them whatever characteristics we need. In our new notation nondeterminism can be expressed by allowing more than one edge with the same label to leave a given branching state, READ or POP.

A **deterministic PDA** is one (like the pictures we drew above) for which every input string has a unique path through the machine. A **nondeterministic PDA** is one for which at certain times we may have to choose among possible paths through the machine. We say that an input string is accepted by such a machine if *some* set of choices leads us to an ACCEPT state. If for *all possible* paths that a certain input string can follow it always ends at a REJECT state, then the string must be rejected. This is analogous to the definition of acceptance for TG's, which are also nondeterministic. As with TG's, non-determinism here will also allow the possibility of too few as well as too many edges leading from a branch state. We shall have complete freedom not to put a *b*-edge leading out of a particular READ state. If a *b* is, by chance, read from the INPUT TAPE by that state, processing cannot continue. As with TG's, we say the machine **crashes** and the input is rejected. To have no *b*-edge leading out of a branch state (READ or POP) is the same as having exactly one *b*-edge that leads straight to REJECT.

The PDA's that are equivalent to CFG's is the class of nondeterministic ones. For FA's we found that nondeterminism (which gave us TG's and NFA's) did not increase the power of the machine to accept new languages. For PDA's, this is different. The following Venn diagram shows the relative power of these three types of machines:

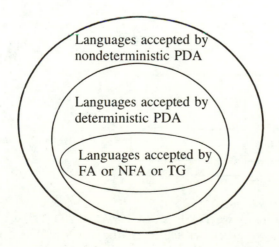

Before we give a concrete example of a language accepted by a nondeterministic PDA that cannot be accepted by a deterministic PDA, let us consider a new language.

EXAMPLE

Let us introduce the PALINDROMEX, language of all words of the form

$$s \; X \; \text{reverse}(s)$$

where s is any string in $(\mathbf{a} + \mathbf{b})$*.
The words in this language are

$$\{ X \; aXa \; bXb \; aaXaa \; abXba \; baXab \; bbXbb \; aaaXaaa \; aabXbaa \; \ldots \}$$

All these words are palindromes in that they read the same forward and backward. They all contain exactly one X, and this X marks the middle of the word. We can build a deterministic PDA that accepts the language PALINDROMEX. Surprisingly, it has the same basic structure as the PDA we had for the language $\{a^n b^n\}$.

In the first part of the machine the STACK is loaded with the letters from the input string just as the initial a's from $a^n b^n$ were pushed onto the STACK. Conveniently for us, the letters go into the STACK first letter on the bottom, second letter on top of it, and so on till the last letter pushed in ends up on top. When we read the X we know we have reached the middle of the input. We can then begin to compare the front half of the word (which is reversed in the STACK) with the back half (still on the TAPE) to see that they match.

We begin by storing the front half of the input string in the STACK with this part of the machine.

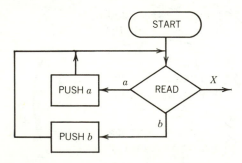

If we READ an a, we PUSH an a. If we READ a b, we PUSH a b, and on and on until we encounter the X on the TAPE.

After we take the first half of the word and stick it into the STACK, we have reversed the order of the letters and it looks exactly like the second half of the word. For example, if we begin with the input string

abbXbba

then at the moment we are just about to read the X we have:

TAPE

ȼ	ɓ	ɓ	X	b	b	a	Δ	· · ·

STACK

b
b
a
Δ

Isn't it amazing how palindromes seem perfect for PUSHDOWN STACK's?

When we read the X we do not put it into the STACK. It is used up in the process of transferring us to phase two. This is where we compare what is left on the TAPE with what is in the STACK. In order to reach ACCEPT, these two should be the same letter for letter, down to the blanks.

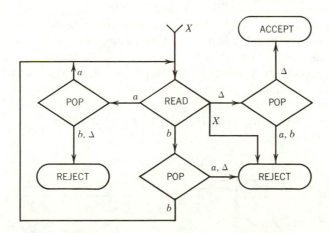

If we read an a, we had better pop an a (pop anything else and we REJECT), if we read a b, we had better pop a b (anything else and we REJECT), if we read a blank, we had better pop a blank; when we do, we accept. If we ever read a second X, we also go to REJECT.

The machine we have drawn is deterministic. The input alphabet here is $\Sigma = \{a, b, X\}$, so each READ state has four edges coming out of it.

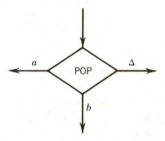

The STACK alphabet has two letters $\Gamma = \{a, b\}$, so each POP has three edges coming out of it:

At each READ and each POP there is only one direction the input can take. Each string on the TAPE generates a unique path through this PDA.

We can draw a less complicated picture for this PDA without the REJECT states if we do not mind having an input string *crash* when it has no path to follow. This means that when we are in a READ or a POP state and find there is no edge with a label corresponding to the character we have just encountered, we terminate processing, reject the input string, and say that the execution crashed. (We allowed a similar rejection process in TG's.)

The whole PDA (without REJECT's) is pictured below:

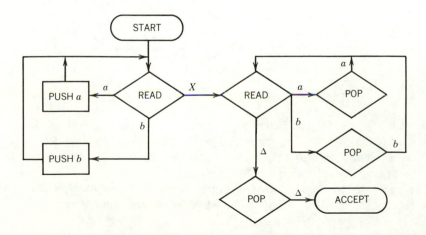

EXAMPLE

Let us now consider what kind of PDA could accept the language ODD-PALINDROME. This is the language of all strings of a's and b's that are palindromes and have an odd number of letters. The words in this language are just like the words in PALINDROMEX except that the middle letter X has been changed into an a or a b.

$$\text{ODDPALINDROME} = \{a \quad b \quad aaa \quad aba \quad bab \quad bbb \dots\}$$

The problem here is that the middle letter does not stand out, so it is harder to recognize where the first half ends and the second half begins. In fact, it's not only harder; it's impossible. A PDA, just like an FA, reads the input string sequentially from left to right and has no idea at any stage how many letters remain to be read. In PALINDROMEX we knew that X marked the spot; now we have lost our treasure map. If we accidentally push into the STACK even one letter too many, the STACK will be larger than what is left on the TAPE and the front and back will not match. The algorithm we used to accept PALINDROMEX cannot be used without modification to accept ODDPALINDROME. We are not completely lost, though. The algorithm can be altered to fit our needs by introducing one nondeterministic jump. That we choose this approach does not mean that there is not a completely different method that might work deterministically, but the introduction of nondeterminism here seems quite naturally suited to our purpose.
    Consider:

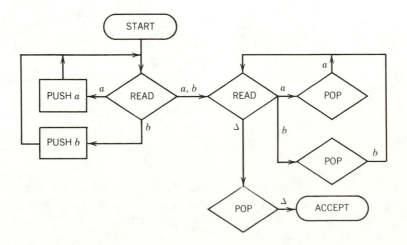

    This machine is the same as the previous machine except that we have changed the X into the choice: a or b.

The machine is now nondeterministic since the left READ state has two choices for exit edges labeled *a* and two choices for *b*:

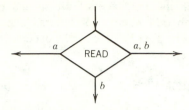

If we branch at the right time (exactly at the middle letter) along the former *X*-edge, we can accept all words in ODDPALINDROME. If we do not choose the right edge at the right time, the input string will be rejected even if it is in ODDPALINDROME. Let us recall, however, that for a word to be accepted by a nondeterministic machine (NFA or TG or PDA) all that is necessary is that *some* choice of edges does lead to ACCEPT.

For every word in ODDPALINDROME, if we make the right choices the path does lead to acceptance.

The word *aba* can be accepted by this machine if it follows the dotted path.

It will be rejected if it tries to push two, three, or no letters into the STACK before taking the right-hand branch to the second READ state.

We present a better method of tracking the action of a word on a PDA in the next example. ∎

Let us now consider a slightly different language.

EXAMPLE

Recall the language:

EVENPALINDROME $= \{s \text{ reverse}(s), \text{ where } s \text{ is in } (\mathbf{a} + \mathbf{b})^*\}$

$\qquad\qquad\qquad = \{\ \Lambda \quad aa \quad bb \quad aaaa \quad abba \quad baab \quad bbbbaaaaaa \ldots\}$

This is the language of all palindromes with an even number of letters.
    One machine to accept this language is pictured below:

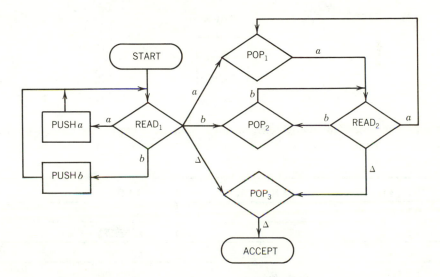

We have labeled the READ states 1 and 2 and the POP states 1, 2 and 3 so that we can identify them in discussion. These numbers do not indicate that we are to READ or POP more than one letter. They are only labels. Soda-POP, grand-POP and POP-corn would do as well. The names will help us trace the path of an input string through the machine.

This machine is nondeterministic. At READ$_1$ when we read an a from the TAPE we have the option of following an a-edge to PUSH a or an a-edge of POP$_1$. If we read a b in READ$_1$, we also have two alternatives: to go to PUSH b or to go to POP$_2$. If we read a Δ in READ$_1$, we have only one choice: to go to POP$_3$.

Let us take notice of what we have done here. In the PDA for PALINDROMEX, the X-edge took us into a second circuit, one that had the form: Read from TAPE→compare with STACK→read from TAPE→compare with STACK . . . . In this machine, we begin the process of "read from

TAPE→compare with STACK" in READ$_1$. The first letter of the second half of the word is read in READ$_1$, then we immediately go to the POP that compares the character read with what is on top of the STACK. After this we cycle READ$_2$→POP→READ$_2$→POP→ . . . .

It will be easier to understand this machine once we see it in action. Let us run the string *babbab*. Initially we have:

TAPE	*b*	*a*	*b*	*b*	*a*	*b*	Δ		· · ·

STACK

Δ
⋮

We can trace the path by which this input can be accepted by the successive rows in the table below:

STATE	STACK	TAPE
START	Δ · · ·	*babbab*Δ · · ·
READ$_1$	Δ · · ·	b̸*abbab*Δ · · ·
PUSH *b*	*b*Δ · · ·	b̸*abbab*Δ · · ·
READ$_1$	*b*Δ · · ·	b̸a̸*bbab*Δ · · ·
PUSH *a*	*ab*Δ · · ·	b̸a̸*bbab*Δ · · ·
READ$_1$	*ab*Δ · · ·	b̸a̸b̸*bab*Δ · · ·
PUSH *b*	*bab*Δ · · ·	b̸a̸b̸*bab*Δ · · ·
READ$_1$	*bab*Δ · · ·	b̸a̸b̸b̸*ab*Δ · · ·

If we are going to accept this input string this is where we must make the jump out of the left circuit into the right circuit. The trace continues:

POP$_2$	*ab*Δ · · ·	b̸a̸b̸b̸*ab*Δ · · ·
READ$_2$	*ab*Δ · · ·	b̸a̸b̸b̸a̸*b*Δ · · ·
POP$_1$	*b*Δ · · ·	b̸a̸b̸b̸a̸*b*Δ · · ·
READ$_2$	*b*Δ · · ·	b̸a̸b̸b̸a̸b̸Δ · · ·
POP$_2$	Δ · · ·	b̸a̸b̸b̸a̸b̸Δ · · ·
READ$_2$	Δ · · ·	b̸a̸b̸b̸a̸b̸Δ · · ·

(We have just read the first of the infinitely many blanks on the TAPE.)

POP₃	Δ · · · (Popping a blank from an empty stack still leaves blanks)	b̸ab̸b̸ab̸ΔΔ · · · (Reading a blank from an empty tape still leaves blanks)
ACCEPT	Δ · · ·	b̸ab̸b̸ab̸Δ · · ·

Notice that to facilitate the drawing of this table we have rotated the STACK so that it reads left to right instead of top to bottom.

Since this is a nondeterministic machine, there are other paths this input could have taken. However, none of them leads to acceptance.

Below we trace an unsuccessful path.

STATE	STACK	TAPE
START	Δ	babbab
READ₁ (We had no choice but to go here)	Δ	b̸abbab
PUSH b (We could have chosen to go to POP₂ instead)	b (We know there are infinitely many blanks underneath this b)	b̸abbab (Notice that the TAPE remains unchanged except by READ statements)
READ₁ (We had no choice but to go here from PUSH b	b	b̸ab̸bab
POP₁ (Here we exercised bad judgment and made a poor choice, PUSH a would have been better)	Δ (When we pop the b, what is left is all Δ's)	b̸ab̸bab
CRASH (This means that when we were in POP₁ and found a b on top of the STACK we tried to take the b-edge out of POP₁. However, there is no b-edge out of POP₁.)		

Another unsuccessful approach to accepting the input *babbab* is to loop around the circuit $READ_1 \rightarrow PUSH$ six times until the whole string has been pushed onto the STACK. After this, a Δ will be read from the TAPE and we have to go to POP_3. This POP will ask if the STACK is empty. It won't be, so the path will CRASH right here.

The word Λ is accepted by this machine through the sequence:

$$START \rightarrow READ_1 \rightarrow POP_3 \rightarrow ACCEPT \qquad \blacksquare$$

As above, we shall not put all the ellipses (. . .) into the tables representing traces. We understand that the TAPE has infinitely many blanks on it without having to write:

$$\not b \not a \not b bab\Delta \ . \ . \ .$$

As we shall see in Theorem 39, deterministic PDA's do not accept all context-free languages. The machine we need for our purpose is the nondeterministic pushdown automaton. We shall call this machine the PDA and only use DPDA (deterministic pushdown automaton) on special occasions (Chapter 21). There is no need for the abbreviation NPDA, any more than there is for NTG (nondeterministic transition graph).

In constructing our new machines we had to make several architectural decisions. Should we include a memory device?—yes. Should it be a stack, a queue or random access?—a stack. One stack or more?—one. Deterministic?—no. Finitely many states?—yes. Can we write on the INPUT TAPE?—no. Can we reread the input?—no. Remember we are not trying to discover the structure of a naturally occurring creature; we are concocters trying to invent a CFL-recognizing machine. The test of whether our decisions are correct will come in the next chapter.

We can now give the full definition of PDA's.

DEFINITION

A **pushdown automaton, PDA,** is a collection of eight things:

1. An alphabet Σ of input letters.
2. An input TAPE (infinite in one direction). Initially the string of input letters is placed on the TAPE starting in cell i. The rest of the TAPE is blank.
3. An alphabet Γ of STACK characters.
4. A pushdown STACK (infinite in one direction). Initially the STACK is empty (contains all blanks).
5. One START state that has only out-edges, no in-edges.

6. Halt states of two kinds: some ACCEPT and some REJECT. They have in-edges and no out-edges

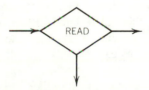

7. Finitely many nonbranching PUSH states that introduce characters onto the top of the STACK. They are of the form

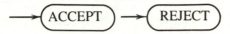

where X is any letter in Γ.

8. Finitely many branching states of two kinds:
   (i) States that read the next unused letter from the TAPE

which may have out-edges labeled with letters from Σ and the blank character Δ, with no restrictions on duplication of labels and no insistance that there be a label for each letter of Σ, or Δ.
And
   (ii) States that read the top character of the STACK

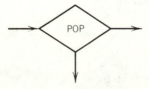

which may have out-edges labeled with the letters of Γ and the blank character Δ, again with no restrictions.

We further require that the states be connected so as to become a connected directed graph.

To run a string of input letters on a PDA means to begin from the START state and follow the unlabeled edges and those labeled edges that apply (making choices of edges when necessary) to produce a path through the graph. This path will end either at a halt state or will crash in a branching state when there is no edge corresponding to the letter/character read/popped. When letters are read from the TAPE or characters are popped from the STACK they are used up and vanish.

An input string with a path that ends in ACCEPT is said to be **accepted.** An input string that can follow a selection of paths is said to be accepted if at least one of these paths leads to ACCEPT. The set of all input strings accepted by a PDA is called the **language accepted** by the PDA, or the **language recognized** by the PDA. ∎

We should make a careful note of the fact that we have allowed more than one exit edge from the START state. Since the edges are unlabeled this branching has to be nondeterministic. We could have restricted the START state to only one exit edge. This edge could immediately lead into a PUSH state in which we would add some arbitrary symbol to the STACK, say a *Weasel*. The PUSH *Weasel* would then lead into a POP state having several edges coming out of it all labeled *Weasel*. POP goes the *Weasel*, and we make our nondeterministic branching. Instead of this we allow the START state itself to have several out-edges.

Even though these are nondeterministic like TG's, unlike TG's we do not allow edges to be labeled with words, only with single characters. Nor do we allow Λ-edges. Edges labeled with Δ are completely different.

PDA's as we have defined them are only language acceptors. Later we shall consider adding output capabilities.

We have not, as some authors do, specified that the STACK has to be empty at the time of accepting a word. Some go so far as to define acceptance by empty STACK as opposed to halt states. We shall address this point with a theorem later in this chapter.

EXAMPLE

Consider the language generated by the CFG:

$$S \rightarrow S + S \,|\, S * S \,|\, 4$$

The terminals are $+$, $*$, and 4 and the only nonterminal is S.

The following PDA accepts this language:

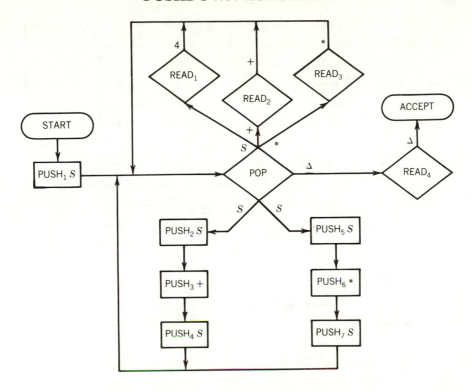

This is a funny looking PDA with one POP, four READ's and seven PUSH's.

Instead of proving that this machine accepts exactly the language generated by this CFG, we only trace the acceptance of the string

$$4 \ + \ 4 \ * \ 4$$

This machine offers plenty of opportunity for making nondeterministic choices. The path we illustrate is one to acceptance; there are many that fail.

STATE	STACK	TAPE
START	Δ	4 + 4 * 4
PUSH₁ S	S	4 + 4 * 4
POP	Δ	4 + 4 * 4
PUSH₂ S	S	4 + 4 * 4
PUSH₃ +	+ S	4 + 4 * 4
PUSH₄ S	S + S	4 + 4 * 4

STATE	STACK	TAPE
POP	$+ S$	$4 + 4 * 4$
READ$_1$	$+ S$	$+ 4 * 4$
POP	S	$+ 4 * 4$
READ$_2$	S	$4 * 4$
POP	Δ	$4 * 4$
PUSH$_5$ S	S	$4 * 4$
PUSH$_6$ $*$	$* S$	$4 * 4$
PUSH$_7$ S	$S * S$	$4 * 4$
POP	$* S$	$4 * 4$
READ$_1$	$* S$	$* 4$
POP	S	$* 4$
READ$_3$	S	4
POP	Δ	4
READ$_1$	Δ	Δ
POP	Δ	Δ
READ$_4$	Δ	Δ
ACCEPT	Δ	Δ

Note that this time we have erased the TAPE letters read instead of striking them. ■

THEOREM 26

For every regular language L there is some PDA that accepts it.

PROOF

We have actually discussed this matter already, but we could not formally prove anything until we had settled on the definition of a PDA.

Since L is regular, it is accepted by some FA. The constructive algorithm for converting an FA into an equivalent PDA was presented at the beginning of this chapter. ■

One important difference between a PDA and an FA is the length of the path formed by a given input. If a string of seven letters is fed into an FA, it follows a path exactly seven edges long. In a PDA, the path could be longer or shorter. The PDA below accepts the regular language of all words beginning with an *a*. But no matter how long the input string, the path is only one or two edges long.

Since we can continue to process the blanks on the TAPE even after all input letters have been read, we can have arbitrarily long or even infinite paths caused by very short input words. For example, the following PDA accepts only the word *b*, but it must follow a seven-edge path to acceptance:

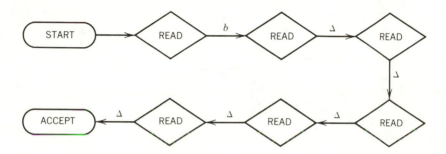

The following machine accepts all words that start with an *a* in a path of two edges and loops forever on any input starting with a *b*. (We can consider this an infinite path if we so desire.)

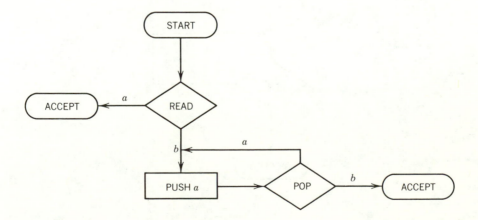

We shall be more curious about the consequences of infinite paths later. The following result will be helpful to us in the next chapter.

THEOREM 27

Given any PDA, there is another PDA that accepts exactly the same language with the additional property that whenever a path leads to ACCEPT the STACK and the TAPE contain only blanks.

PROOF

We present a constructive algorithm that will convert any PDA into a PDA with the property mentioned.

Whenever we have the machine part:

we replace it with the diagram below:

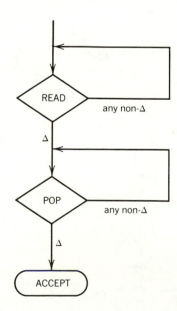

Technically speaking, we should have labeled the top loop "any letter in Σ" and the bottom loop "any character in Γ."

The new PDA formed accepts exactly the same language and finishes all successful runs with empty TAPE and empty STACK. ∎

PROBLEMS

Convert the following FA's into equivalent PDA's:

1.

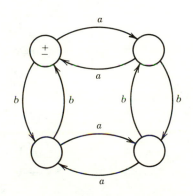

2.

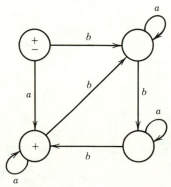

Consider the following deterministic PDA:

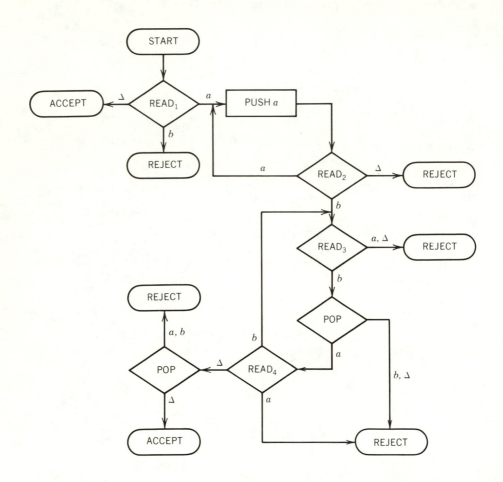

Using a trace table like those in this chapter, show what happens to the INPUT TAPE and STACK as each of the following words proceeds through the machine.

3.　(i)　*abb*

　　(ii)　*abab*

　　(iii)　*aabb*

　　(iv)　*aabbbb*

4. (i)   What is the language accepted by this PDA?

    (ii)   Find a CFG that generates this language.

    (iii) Is this language regular?

5. Consider the following PDA.

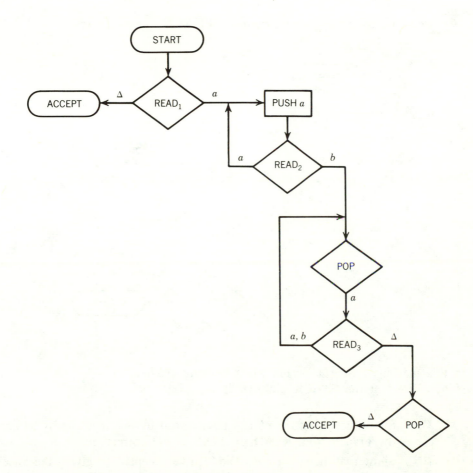

Trace the following words on this PDA:

(i)   *aaabbb*

(ii)   *aaabab*

(iii)   *aaabaa*

(iv)   *aaaabb*

6. Prove that the language accepted by the machine in Problem 5 is

    $L = \{a^n S,$ where S starts with b and length$(S) = n\}$.

7. Find a CFG that defines the language in Problem 6.

8. Prove that the language of the machine in Problem 5 is not regular.

Consider the following nondeterministic PDA

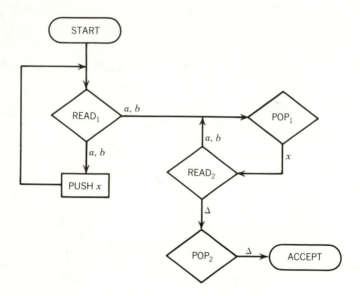

In this machine REJECT occurs when a string crashes.
Notice here that the STACK alphabet is $\Gamma = \{x\}$.

9. (i)   Show that the string ab can be accepted by this machine by taking
         the branch from READ$_1$ to POP$_1$ at the correct time.
    (ii) Show that the string $bbba$ can also be accepted by giving the trace
         that shows when to take the branch.

10. Show that this PDA accepts the language of all words with an even
    number of letters (excluding Λ). Remember, it is also necessary to show
    that all words with odd length can never lead to ACCEPT.

11. Here we have a nondeterministic PDA for a language that could have
    been accepted by an FA. Find such an FA. Find a CFG that generates
    this language.

Consider the following nondeterministic PDA:

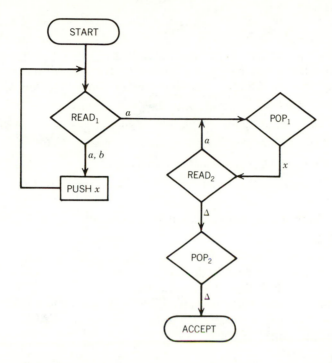

Here the STACK alphabet is again

$$\Gamma = \{x\}$$

12. (i) Show that the word *aa* can be accepted by this PDA by demonstrating a trace of its path to ACCEPT.

(ii) Show that the word *babaaa* can be accepted by this PDA by demonstrating a trace of its path indicating exactly where we must take the branch from $READ_1$ to $READ_2$

(iii) Show that the string *babaaab* cannot be accepted.

(iv) Show that the string *babaaaa* cannot be accepted.

13. (i) Show that the language of this machine is

$$\text{TRAILINGCOUNT} = \{s \ a^{\text{length}(s)}\}$$
= {any string *s* followed by as many *a*'s as *s* has letters}

(ii) We know that this language is not regular; show that there is a CFG that generates it.

14.   Build a deterministic PDA to accept the language $\{a^n b^{n+1}\}$.
      (As always, when unspecified the condition on n is assumed to be $n = 1\ 2\ 3\ \ldots$)

15.   Let the input alphabet be $\Sigma = \{a,\ b,\ c\}$ and let L be the language of all words in which all the a's come before the b's and there are the same number of a's as b's and arbitrarily many c's that can be in front, behind, or among the a's and b's. Some words in L are abc, $caabcb$, $ccacaabcccbccbc$.

      (i)   Write out all the words in this language with six or fewer letters.

      (ii)   Show that the language L is not regular.

      (iii) Find a PDA (*deterministic*) that accepts L.

      (iv)   Find a CFG that generates L.

16.   Find a PDA (nondeterministic) that accepts all PALINDROMES where the alphabet is $\Sigma = \{a,b\}$.

17.   We have seen that an FA with N states can be converted into an equivalent PDA with N READ states (and no POP states). Show that for any FA with N states there is some PDA with only one READ state (and several POP states) but which uses N different STACK symbols and accepts the same language.

18.   Let L be some regular language in which all the words happen to have an even length. Let us define the new language Twist (L) to be the set of all the words of L twisted, where by twisted we mean the first and second letters have been interchanged, the third and fourth letters have been interchanged, etc.
      For example, if

$$L = \{ba\ abba\ babb\ldots\}$$

$$\text{Twist } (L) = \{ab\ baab\ abbb\ldots\}$$

      Build a PDA that accepts Twist (L).

19.   Given any language L that does not include Λ let us define its cousin language $|L|$ as follows: for any string of a's and b's, if the word formed by concatenating the second, fourth, sixth,... letters of this string is a word in L then the whole string is a word in $|L|$. For instance, if bbb is a word in L then $ababbbb$ and $bbababa$ are both words in $|L|$.

(i)   Show that if there is some PDA that accepts L then there is some PDA that accepts |L|.

(ii)   If L is regular, is |L| necessarily regular too?

20.   Let L be the language of all words that have the same number of a's and b's and that, as we read them from left to right, never have more b's than a's. For example,

$$abaaabbabb$$

is good but

$$abaabbba$$

is no good since at a certain point we had four b's but only three a's. All the words in L with six letters are:

aaabbb   aababb   aabbab
abaabb   ababab

(i)   Write out all the words in L with eight letters (there are 14).

(ii)   Find a PDA that accepts L.

(iii) Prove that L is not regular.

(iv)   Find a CFG that defines L.

(v)   If we think of an a as an open parenthesis "(" and a b as a close parenthesis ")" then L is the language of the sequences of parentheses that might occur in arithmetic expressions. Explain.

CHAPTER 18

CFG = PDA

We are now ready to prove that the set of all languages accepted by PDA's is the same as the set of all languages generated by CFG's.

We prove this in two steps.

THEOREM 28

Given a language L generated by a particular CFG, there is a PDA that accepts exactly L.

THEOREM 29

Given a language L that is accepted by a certain PDA, there exists a CFG that generates exactly L.

These two important theorems were both discovered independently by Schützenberger, Chomsky, and Evey.

PROOF OF THEOREM 28

The proof will be by constructive algorithm. From Theorem 24 in Chapter 16, we can assume that the CFG is in CNF. (The problem of Λ will be handled later.)

Before we describe the algorithm that associates a PDA with a given CFG in its most general form, we shall illustrate it on one particular example. Let us consider the folowing CFG in CNF

$$S \rightarrow SB$$
$$S \rightarrow AB$$
$$A \rightarrow CC$$
$$B \rightarrow b$$
$$C \rightarrow a$$

We now propose the nondeterministic PDA pictured below.

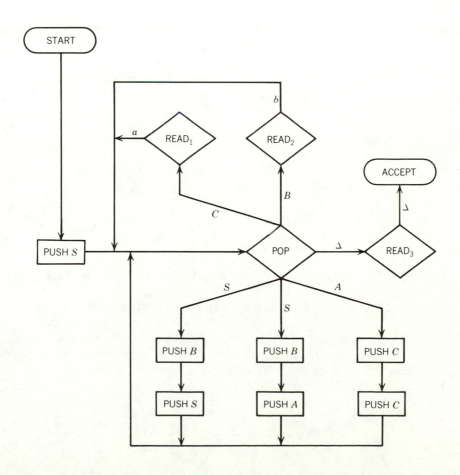

In this machine the STACK alphabet is

$$\Gamma = \{S, A, B, C\}$$

while the TAPE alphabet is only

$$\Sigma = \{a, b\}$$

We begin by pushing the symbol S onto the top of the STACK. We then enter the busiest state of this PDA, the central POP. In this state we read the top character of the STACK.

The STACK will always contain nonterminals exclusively. Two things are possible when we pop the top of the STACK. Either we replace the removed nonterminal with two other nonterminals, thereby simulating a production (these are the edges pointing downward) or else we do not replace the nonterminal at all but instead we go to a READ state, which insists we read a specific terminal from the TAPE or else it crashes (these edges point upward). To get to ACCEPT we must have encountered READ states that wanted to read exactly those letters that were originally on the INPUT TAPE in their exact order. We now show that to do this means we have simulated a left-most derivation of the input string in this CFG.

Let us consider a specific example. The word *aab* can be generated by left-most derivation in this grammar as follows:

Working-String Generation	Production Used	
$S \Rightarrow AB$	$S \rightarrow AB$	Step 1
$\Rightarrow CCB$	$A \rightarrow CC$	Step 2
$\Rightarrow aCB$	$C \rightarrow a$	Step 3
$\Rightarrow aaB$	$C \rightarrow a$	Step 4
$\Rightarrow aab$	$B \rightarrow b$	Step 5

In CNF all working strings in left-most derivations have the form:

(string of terminals) (string of Nonterminals)

To run this word on this PDA we must follow the same sequence of productions, keeping the STACK contents at all times the same as the string of nonterminals in the working string of the derivation.

We begin at START with

STACK	TAPE
Δ	*aab*

Immediately we push the symbol S onto the STACK.

STACK	TAPE
S	aab

We then head into the central POP. The first production we must simulate is $S \rightarrow AB$. We pop the S and then we PUSH B, PUSH A arriving at this:

STACK	TAPE
AB	aab

Note that the contents of the STACK is the same as the string of nonterminals in the working string of the derivation after Step 1.

We again feed back into the central POP. The production we must now simulate is a $A \rightarrow CC$. This is done by popping the A and following the path PUSH C, PUSH C.

The situation is now:

STACK	TAPE
CCB	aab

Notice that here again the contents of the STACK is the same as the string of nonterminals in the working string of the derivation after Step 2.

Again we feed back into the central POP. This time we must simulate the production $C \rightarrow a$. We do this by popping the C and then reading the a from the TAPE. This leaves:

STACK	TAPE
CB	¢ab

We do not keep any terminals in the STACK, only the nonterminal part of the working string. Again the STACK contains the string of nonterminals in Step 3 of the derivation. However, the terminal that would have appeared in front of these in the working string has been cancelled from the front of the TAPE. Instead of keeping the terminals in the STACK, we erase them from the INPUT TAPE to ensure a perfect match.

The next production we must simulate is another $C \rightarrow a$. Again we POP C and READ a. This leaves:

STACK	TAPE
B	¢¢b

Here again we can see that the contents of the STACK is the string of nonterminals in the working string in Step 4 of the derivation. The whole working string is *aaB,* the terminal part *aa* corresponds to what has been struck from the TAPE.

This time when we enter the central POP we simulate the last production in the derivation, $B \to b$. We pop the B and read the b. This leaves:

STACK	TAPE
Δ	a̸a̸b̸

This Δ represents the fact that there are no nonterminals left in the working string after Step 5. This, of course, means that the generation of the word is complete.

We now reenter the POP, and we must make sure that both STACK and TAPE are empty.

$$\text{POP } \Delta \to \text{READ}_3 \to \text{ACCEPT}$$

The general principle is clear. To accept a word we must follow its left-most derivation from the CFG. If the word is

$$a\,b\,a\,b\,b\,b\,a\,a\,b$$

and at some point in its left-most Chomsky derivation we have the working string

$$a\,b\,a\,b\,b\,Z\,W\,V$$

then at this point in the corresponding PDA-processing the status of the STACK and TAPE should be

STACK	TAPE
ZWV	a̸b̸a̸b̸b̸baab

the used-up part of the TAPE being the string of terminals and the contents of the STACK being the string of nonterminals of the working string. This process continues until we have derived the entire word. We then have

STACK	TAPE
Δ	a̸b̸a̸b̸b̸b̸a̸a̸b̸

At this point we POP Δ, go to READ$_3$, and ACCEPT.

There is noticeable nondeterminism in this machine at the POP state. This parallels, reflects, and simulates the nondeterminism present in the process of generating a word. In a left-most derivation if we are to replace the nonterminal N we have one possibility for each production that has N as the left side. Similarly in this PDA we have one path leaving POP for each of these possible productions. Just as the one set of productions must generate any word in the language, the one machine must have a path to accept any legal word once it sits on the INPUT TAPE. The point is that the choices of which lines to take out of the central POP tell us how to generate the word through left-most derivation, since each branch represents a production.

It should also be clear that any input string that reaches ACCEPT has got there by having each of its letters read by simulating Chomsky productions of the form:

$$\text{Nonterminal} \rightarrow \text{terminal}$$

This means that we have necessarily formed a complete left-most derivation of this word through CFG productions with no terminals left over in the STACK. Therefore, every word accepted by this PDA is in the language of the CFG.

One more example may be helpful. Consider the randomly chosen CFG (in CNF) below:

$$
\begin{array}{lll}
S \rightarrow AB & B \rightarrow AB & B \rightarrow a \\
A \rightarrow BB & A \rightarrow a & B \rightarrow b
\end{array}
$$

By the same technique as used before, we produce the following PDA:

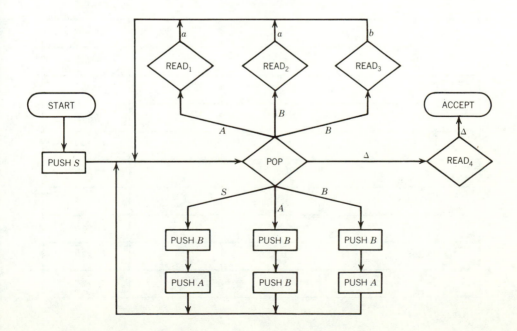

We shall trace simultaneously how the word *baaab* can be generated by this CFG and how it can be accepted by this PDA.

Left-most derivation	State	STACK	TAPE
	START	Δ	baaab
S	PUSH S	S	baaab
	POP	Δ	baaab
	PUSH B	B	baaab
⇒ AB	PUSH A	AB	baaab
	POP	B	baaab
	PUSH B	BB	baaab
⇒ BBB	PUSH B	BBB	baaab
	POP	BB	baaab
⇒ bBB	READ₃	BB	b̸aaab
	POP	B	b̸aaab
	PUSH B	BB	b̸aaab
⇒ bABB	PUSH A	ABB	b̸aaab
	POP	BB	b̸aaab
⇒ baBB	READ₁	BB	b̸a̸aab
	POP	B	b̸a̸aab
⇒ baaB	READ₂	B	b̸a̸a̸ab
	POP	Δ	b̸a̸a̸ab
	PUSH B	B	b̸a̸a̸ab
⇒ baaAB	PUSH A	AB	b̸a̸a̸ab
	POP	B	b̸a̸a̸ab
⇒ baaaB	READ₁	B	b̸a̸a̸a̸b
	POP	Δ	b̸a̸a̸a̸b

Left-most derivation	State	STACK	TAPE
$\Rightarrow baaab$	READ$_3$	Δ	¢¢¢¢¢
	POP	Δ	¢¢¢¢¢
	READ$_4$	Δ	¢¢¢¢¢
	ACCEPT	Δ	¢¢¢¢¢

At every stage we have the following equivalence:

working string
= (letters cancelled from TAPE) (string of nonterminals from STACK)

At the beginning this means:

$$\text{working string} = S$$
$$\text{letters cancelled} = \text{none}$$
$$\text{string of nonterminals in STACK} = S$$

At the end this means:

$$\text{working string} = \text{the whole word}$$
$$\text{letters cancelled} = \text{all}$$
$$\text{STACK} = \Delta$$

Now that we understand this example, we can give the rules for the general case.

If we are given a CFG in CNF as follows:

$$X_1 \rightarrow X_2 X_3$$

$$X_1 \rightarrow X_3 X_4$$

$$X_2 \rightarrow X_2 X_2$$

$$\cdots$$

$$X_3 \rightarrow a$$

$$X_4 \rightarrow a$$

$$X_5 \rightarrow b$$

$$\cdots$$

where the start symbol $S = X_1$, and the other nonterminals are X_2, X_3, . . . we build the following machine:

Begin with

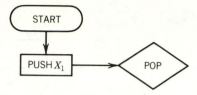

For each production of the form:

$$X_i \rightarrow X_j X_k$$

we include this circuit from the POP back to itself:

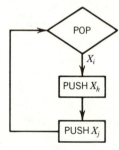

For all productions of the form

$$X_i \rightarrow b$$

we include this circuit:

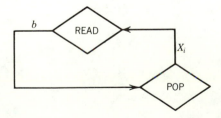

When the stack is finally empty, which means we have converted our last nonterminal to a terminal and the terminals have matched the INPUT TAPE, we follow this path:

From the reasons and examples given above, we know that all words generated by the CFG will be accepted by this machine and all words accepted will have left-most derivations in the CFG.

This does not quite finish the proof. We began by assuming that the CFG was in CNF, but there are some context-free languages that cannot be put into CNF. They are the languages that include the word Λ. In this case, we can convert all productions into one of the two forms acceptable to CNF while the word Λ must still be included.

To include this word, we need to add another circuit to the PDA, a simple loop at the POP

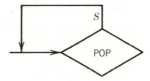

This kills the nonterminal S without replacing it with anything and the next time we enter the POP we get a blank and proceed to accept the word. ■

EXAMPLE

The language PALINDROME (including Λ) can be generated by the following CFG in CNF (plus one Λ-production)

$$S \rightarrow AR_1 \qquad S \rightarrow a$$

$$R_1 \rightarrow SA \qquad S \rightarrow b$$

$$S \rightarrow BR_2 \qquad A \rightarrow a$$

$$R_2 \rightarrow SB \qquad B \rightarrow b$$

$$S \rightarrow AA \qquad S \rightarrow \Lambda$$

$$S \rightarrow BB$$

The PDA that the algorithm in the proof of Theorem 28 instructs us to build is:

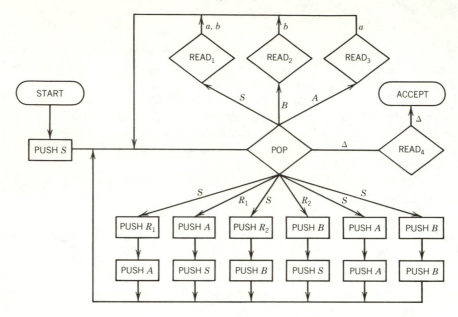

Let us examine how the input string abaaba is accepted by this PDA.

Leftmost Derivation	State	Tape	Stack
	START	abaaba	Δ
	PUSH S	abaaba	S
	POP	abaaba	Δ
	PUSH R_1	abaaba	R_1
$S \Rightarrow AR_1$	PUSH A	abaaba	AR_1
	POP	abaaba	R_1
$\Rightarrow aR_1$	READ$_3$	$\cancel{a}baaba$	R_1
	POP	$\cancel{a}baaba$	Δ
	PUSH A	$\cancel{a}baaba$	A
$\Rightarrow aSA$	PUSH S	$\cancel{a}baaba$	SA
	POP	$\cancel{a}baaba$	A
	PUSH R_2	$\cancel{a}baaba$	R_2A
$\Rightarrow aBR_2A$	PUSH B	$\cancel{a}baaba$	BR_2A
	POP	$\cancel{a}baaba$	R_2A
$\Rightarrow abR_2A$	READ$_2$	$\cancel{a}\cancel{b}aaba$	R_2A
	POP	$\cancel{a}\cancel{b}aaba$	A
	PUSH B	$\cancel{a}\cancel{b}aaba$	BA

Leftmost Derivation	State	Tape	Stack
$\Rightarrow abSBA$	PUSH S	ɇbaaba	SBA
	POP	ɇbaaba	BA
	PUSH A	ɇbaaba	ABA
$\Rightarrow abAABA$	PUSH A	ɇbaaba	$AABA$
	POP	ɇbaaba	ABA
$\Rightarrow abaABA$	READ$_3$	ɇɇaaba	ABA
	POP	ɇɇaaba	BA
$\Rightarrow abaaBA$	READ$_3$	ɇɇɇaba	BA
	POP	ɇɇɇaba	A
$\Rightarrow abaabA$	READ$_2$	ɇɇɇɇba	A
	POP	ɇɇɇɇba	Δ
$\Rightarrow abaaba$	READ$_3$	ɇɇɇɇɇΔ	Δ
	POP	ɇɇɇɇɇΔ	Δ
	READ$_4$	ɇɇɇɇɇΔ	Δ
	ACCEPT	ɇɇɇɇɇΔ	Δ

Notice how different this is from the PDA's we developed in Chapter 17 for the languages EVENPALINDROME and ODDPALINDROME. ■

We have actually proven a stronger theorem than Theorem 28. We have proven that every CFL can be accepted by a PDA that has only one POP state. After we have proven Theorem 29, we shall know that every language accepted by a PDA is a CFL and therefore every PDA is equivalent to a PDA with exactly one POP state.

Now we have to prove the other half of the equivalence theorem, that every language accepted by a PDA is context-free.

PROOF OF THEOREM 29

This is a long proof by constructive algorithm. In fact, it is unquestionably the most tortuous proof in this book; parental consent is required. We shall illustrate each step with a particular example. It is important, though, to realize that the algorithm we describe operates successfully on all PDA's and we are not merely proving this theorem for one example alone.

The requirements for a proof are that it convince and explain. The following arguments should do both if we are sufficiently perseverant.

Before we can convert a PDA into a CFG we have to convert it into a standard form, which we call **conversion form.** To achieve this conversion form, it is necessary for us to introduce a new "marker state" called a **HERE** state. We can put the word HERE into a box shaped like a READ state in the middle of any edge and we say that we are passing through that state any time we travel on the edge that it marks. Like the READ and the POP states, the HERE states can be numbered with subscripts.

One use of a HERE state is so that

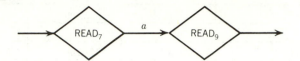

can become

Notice that a HERE state does not read the TAPE nor pop the STACK. It just allows us to describe being on the edge as being in a state. A HERE state is a legal fiction—a state with no status, but we do permit branching to occur at such points. Because the edges leading out of HERE states have no labels, this branching is necessarily nondeterministic.

DEFINITION (inside the Proof of Theorem 29)

A PDA is in **conversion form** if it meets all of the following conditions:

1. There is only one ACCEPT state.
2. There are no REJECT states.
3. Every READ or HERE is followed immediately by a POP; that is, every edge leading out of any READ or HERE state goes directly into a POP state.
4. No two POP's exist in a row on the same path without a READ or HERE between them whether or not there are any intervening PUSH states. (POP's must be separated by READ's or HERE's.)
5. All branching, deterministic or nondeterministic, occurs at READ or HERE states, none at POP states, and every edge has only one label (no multiple labels).
6. Even before we get to START, a "bottom of STACK" symbol $ is placed on the STACK. If this symbol is ever popped in the processing, it must be replaced immediately. The STACK is never popped beneath this symbol. Right before entering ACCEPT this symbol is popped out and left out.

7. The PDA must begin with the sequence:

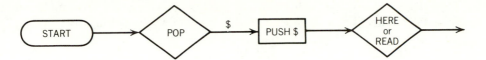

8. The entire input string must be read before the machine can accept the word. ∎

It is now our job to show that all the PDA's as we defined them before can be made over into conversion form without affecting the languages they accept.

Condition 1 is easy to accommodate. If we have a PDA with several ACCEPT states, let us simply erase all but one of them and have all the edges that formerly went into the others feed into the one remaining:

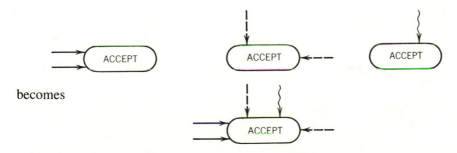

becomes

Condition 2 is also easy. Since we are dealing with nondeterministic machines, if we are at a state with no edge labeled with the character we have just read or popped we simply crash. For an input string to be accepted, there must be a safe path to ACCEPT; the absence of such a path is tantamount to REJECT. Therefore, we can erase all REJECT states and the edges leading to them without affecting the language accepted by the PDA:

becomes simply

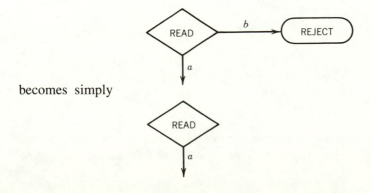

If a *b* is read in this READ state, there is no path to follow and CRASH = REJECT must occur.

Now let us consider Condition 3. A READ in a certain PDA might not have a POP immediately following it; we might find something like this:

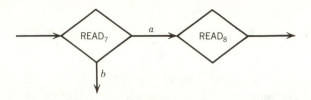

What we do is insert a POP and immediately put back on the STACK whatever might have been removed by this additional POP.

We need to have a PUSH for every letter of Γ every time we do this.

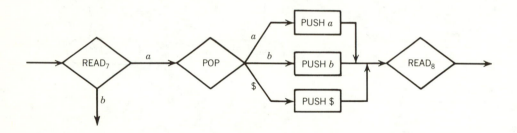

This looks like a silly waste of states, but it does mean that we can satisfy condition 3 without changing the language accepted.

We may need to insert some HERE states to satisfy Condition 4:

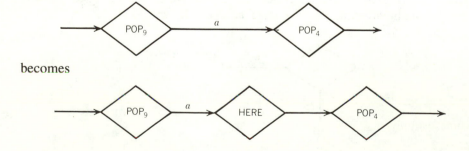

becomes

To satisfy Condition 5, we must convert all branching at POP states into branching at READ or HERE states. This is done as follows.

This:

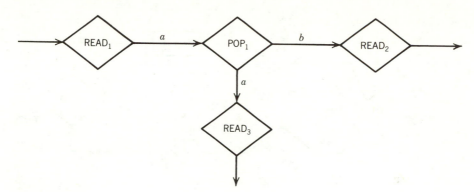

becomes this:

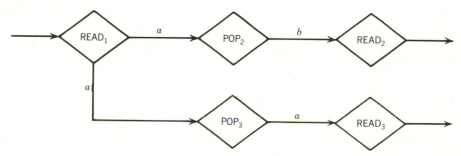

If the POP_1 state in the original picture was going to pop a b and branch to $READ_2$, then in the modified version below, its path through the machine must be the one that at $READ_1$ takes the a-edge to POP_2, not the a-edge to POP_3. If an a was going to be popped by POP_1, the path to POP_3 has to be taken to avoid crashing. All paths through these two segments of PDA's are the same, but in the second picture the deterministic branching at POP_1 has been replaced by nondeterministic branching at $READ_1$.

We must also modify the funny extra POP x — PUSH x situations that we introduced for Condition 3. Instead of using:

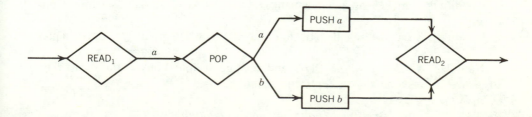

which entailed branching at the POP state, we must use the equivalent:

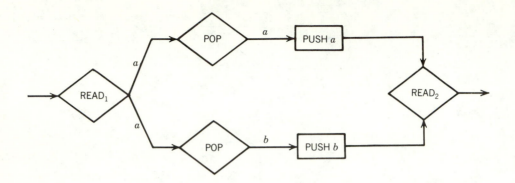

Instead of a deterministic branch at a POP state, we have made a non-deterministic branch at a READ state or a HERE state.

Condition 6 is another easy one. We simply presume that the STACK initially looks like:

STACK

$
Δ

When we change a PDA into conversion form, we must also remember that instead of popping a Δ from an empty STACK we shall find the symbol $. If we wanted (for some reason) to POP several Δ's off of an empty STACK, we shall have to be satisfied with several POP $ — PUSH $ combinations. They work just as well.

If we ever have a PDA that wants to accept an input string without emptying the whole STACK (including $), we could just insert some states that empty the STACK harmlessly right before the ACCEPT, exactly as we did in the proof of Theorem 27.

Condition 7 makes no new demands if the STACK already satisfies Condition 6.

Condition 8 can be satisfied by the algorithm of Theorem 27 from Chapter 17.

Now let us take a whole PDA and change it into conversion form. The PDA we use is one that accepts the language

$$\{a^{2n}b^n\} = \{aab \quad aaaabb \quad aaaaaabbb \ldots\}$$

The PDA is:

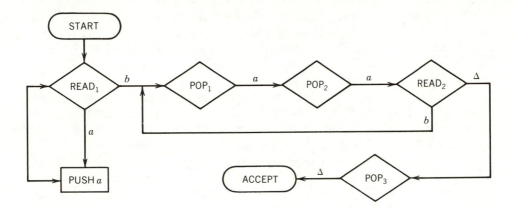

Every a from the beginning of the input tape is pushed onto the STACK. Then for every b that follows, two a's are popped. Acceptance comes if both TAPE and STACK empty at the same time. The words accepted must therefore be of the form $a^{2n}b^n$ for $n = 1, 2, 3 \ldots$.

Here we have already deleted the REJECT state and useless READ and POP alternative edges. To make this PDA satisfy all the conditions for conversion form, we must remake it into:

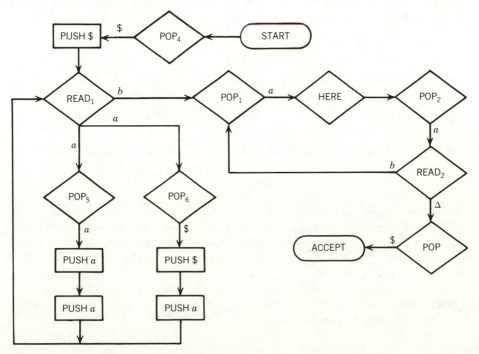

To begin with, we must start with the sequence demanded by Condition 7. This makes us insert a new POP state called POP$_4$. Now in the original machine we began a circuit "READ$_1$—PUSH a—READ$_1$—PUSH a . . .". Because of Condition 3, every READ must be followed by a POP so the pair "READ$_1$—PUSH a" must become "READ$_1$—POP$_5$—PUSH a—PUSH a." The first PUSH is to return the a that was popped out. The second PUSH *adds* the a to the STACK. The first time through this loop, the top of the STACK does not contain an a yet and what is popped is the $, which must immediately be returned to the STACK. This is the purpose of the nondeterministic branch "POP$_6$—PUSH $—PUSH a." This branch also *adds* an a to the STACK. This branch will be taken the first time out of READ$_1$ but if ever again it will cause a CRASH and lead to the acceptance of no new words.

The next violation of conversion form in the original picture was that POP$_1$ was immediately followed by POP$_2$ without a READ in between. This is fixed by inserting a HERE. (There is only one HERE state in this whole machine, so there is no reason to number it.)

The last change is that instead of POP$_3$ finding a blank, it should find the stack-end symbol $.

The new form of this PDA obviously accepts exactly the same language as before, $\{a^{2n}b^n\}$. (By our convention, when the range of n is unspecified, it is presumed to be $n = 1,2,3. . . .$)

Now that we have put this PDA into conversion form, we can explain why we ever wanted to impose these eight conditions on a poor helpless machine. Any PDA in conversion form can be considered as a collection of primitive parts—**path segments**—each of the form:

From	To	Reading	Popping	Pushing
START or READ HERE	READ or HERE ACCEPT	One or no input letters	Exactly one STACK character	Any string onto the STACK

The states START, READ, HERE, and ACCEPT are called the **joints** of the machine. Between two consecutive joints on a path exactly one character is popped and any arbitrary number can be pushed. Because no edge has a multiple label, between any two joints the machine can read no letters at all from the INPUT TAPE or else exactly one specified letter. This was the purpose of imposing all the conversion conditions.

The PDA above can be drawn as a set of joints with "arcs" (path segments) between them much like a TG.

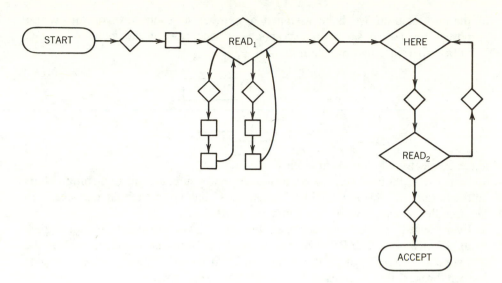

Once a PDA is in conversion form, we can describe the entire machine as a list of all the primitive joint-to-joint path segments (the "arcs" mentioned above). Such a list is called a **summary table.** A summary table for a PDA satisfies the same purpose as a transition table for an FA. It explains the total action on the inputs without recourse to pictorial representation. This may seem like a step backwards, since the pictures make more sense than the tables—which is why we do not commonly use tables for FA's. However, for the purpose of completing the proof of Theorem 29 (which is what we are still in the midst of doing), the summary table will be very useful.

The PDA we have just converted corresponds to the summary table below.

From where	To where	READ what	POP what	PUSH what	Row Number
START	READ$_1$	Λ	$	$	1
READ$_1$	READ$_1$	a	$	$a$$	2
READ$_1$	READ$_1$	a	a	aa	3
READ$_1$	HERE	b	a	—	4
HERE	READ$_2$	Λ	a	—	5
READ$_2$	HERE	b	a	—	6
READ$_2$	ACCEPT	Δ	$	—	7

In the last column we have assigned a number to each row for our future purposes. Each path segment corresponds to one row of the table.

Notice that in Row$_2$ we summarized

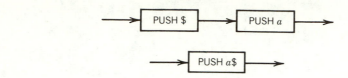

as

since it means add the $ first, then the *a*.

In our definition of conversion form, we made sure that all branching occurs at the joints READ and HERE. This means that no branching can occur in the middle of any row of the summary table.

Every word that can be accepted by the PDA corresponds to some path from START to ACCEPT. We can view these paths as made up not of the components "edges" but of the components "rows of summary table." A path is then broken into a sequence of these path segments.

For example, in the PDA above the word *aaaabb* can be accepted by the machine through the path

START — POP$_4$ — PUSH $ — READ$_1$ — POP$_6$ — PUSH $ — PUSH *a* — READ$_1$ — POP$_5$ — PUSH *a* — PUSH *a* — READ$_1$ — POP$_5$ — PUSH *a* — PUSH *a* — READ$_1$ — POP$_5$ — PUSH *a* — PUSH *a* — READ$_1$ — POP$_1$ — HERE — POP$_2$ — READ$_2$ — POP$_1$ — HERE — POP$_2$ — READ$_2$ — POP$_3$ — ACCEPT

This is a nondeterministic machine, and there are other paths that this input could take, but they all crash somewhere; only this path leads to acceptance. Instead of this long list of states, we could describe the path of this word through the machine as a sequence of rows from the summary table. The path above can be described as

Row$_1$—Row$_2$—Row$_3$—Row$_3$—Row$_4$—Row$_5$—Row$_6$—Row$_5$—Row$_7$

Let us repeat that acceptance by a PDA is determined by the existence of a path from START to ACCEPT. In FA's, paths correspond in a natural fashion to strings of letters. In a PDA paths correspond in a natural way to strings of Row's from the summary table.

The approach that we have taken for PDA's is to define them originally by a pictorial representation and imagine a correspondence between input strings and paths through the machine-graph. To abstract the grammar (CFG) of the language that the PDA accepts, we have had to begin by changing our PDA's first into conversion form and then into summary tables. This is to make an algebraic nonpictorial representation of our PDA's that we can then convert into a grammar. Most authors define PDA's originally as summary tables of some kind and the pictorial representations as directed graphs are rarely given. The proof of Theorem 29 in such a treatment is much shorter, since the proof can begin at the point we have just reached. Something is lost, though, in not seeing a PDA as a picture. This is best illustrated by comparing the summary table above with the first pictorial representation of the PDA. It is much easier to understand the looping and the language from the picture.

As definitions, both the pictures and the tables describe the same type of language-accepting device. The question of which is superior cannot be answered without knowing the specific application. Our application is education and the most understandable formulation is the best.

Notice that the HERE state reads nothing from the TAPE, so we have put Λ in the "READ-what" column. We could put a dash or a ϕ there just as well. A blank (Δ) would be wrong, since it means something else; to say that we read a Δ means the TAPE must be empty. A Λ on the other hand means, by convention, that we do not read the TAPE.

The order in which we put the rows in the summary table does not matter as long as every path segment of the PDA between two consecutive joints is represented as some row.

The summary table carries in it all the information that is found in the pictorial representation of the PDA. Every path through the PDA is a sequence of rows of the summary table. However, not every sequence of rows from the summary table represents a viable path. Right now it is very important for us to determine which sequences of rows *do* correspond to possible paths through the PDA, since the *paths* are directly related to the language accepted.

Some sequences of rows are impossible; for example, we cannot immediately follow Row_4 with Row_6 because Row_4 leaves us in HERE while Row_6 begins in $READ_2$. We must always be careful that the end joints connect up logically.

This requirement is necessary but not sufficient to guarantee that a sequence of rows can be a path. Row_1 leaves us in $READ_1$ and Row 3 starts in $READ_1$, yet Row_1-Row_3 cannot be the beginning of a path. This is because Row_1 pushes a $, whereas Row_3, which pops an a obviously presumes that the top of the STACK is an a. We must have some information about the STACK before we can string rows together.

Even if we arranged the rows so that the pushes and pops match up, we still might get into trouble. A path formed by a sequence of rows with four Row_3's and six Row_5's is impossible. This is true for a subtle reason. Six Row_5's will pop six a's from the STACK, however, since Row_2 can only be used once to obtain one a in the STACK and four Row_3's can contribute only four more a's to the STACK, we are short one a.

The question of which sequences of rows make up a path is very tricky. To represent a path, a sequence of rows must be **joint consistent** (the rows meet up end to end) and **STACK consistent** (when a row pops a character, it should be there, at the top of the STACK).

Let now us define the **row-language** of a particular PDA represented by a summary table. It is the language whose alphabet letters are the names of the rows in the summary table

$$\Sigma = \{\text{Row}_1 \quad \text{Row}_2 \quad \ldots \quad \text{Row}_7\}$$

and having as legal words all those sequences of alphabet letters that correspond to paths from START to ACCEPT that might possibly be followed by some input strings, that is, all sequences from START to ACCEPT that are joint consistent and STACK consistent.

Clearly, all valid words in this language begin with Row_1 and end with Row_7, but as we saw above, there are more requirements than just those.

Consider, for example,

$$\text{Row}_5\text{Row}_5\text{Row}_3\text{Row}_6$$

This is a string of length four, but this string is not a word in the row-language for three reasons: (1) It does not represent a path that begins with START or ends with ACCEPT; (2) it is not joint consistent; (3) it is not STACK consistent.

Not only are we going to look for rules to tell us which strings of rows are words, but we shall produce a CFG for the row-language. From this CFG we can produce another CFG, a grammar for the language of strings of a's and b's accepted by the original PDA.

Let us pause here to outline the global strategy of this proof.

1. We start with any PDA drawn as defined in Chapter 17.
2. We redraw the PDA to meet the requirements of conversion form.
3. From the machine in conversion form, we build a summary table and number the rows.
4. Every word accepted by the PDA corresponds to at least one path from START to ACCEPT and, as we shall soon see, every stack-consistent path from START to ACCEPT corresponds to some word. Therefore we define the row-language to be the set of all sequences of rows that correspond to paths.
5. We determine a CFG that generates all the words in the row-language.
6. We convert this CFG for the row-language into a CFG that generates all the words in the original language of a's and b's that are accepted by the PDA, thus proving Theorem 29.

We are now up to Step 5.

We had to build half this house before we could take our first look at the blueprints.

One thing we have to do is to keep track of the contents of the STACK. Since we are going to want to produce a CFG that generates the row-language, we need to introduce nonterminals that contain the information we need to ensure joint and STACK consistency. We have to know about the beginning and end positions of the path segments to which certain row strings correspond and about the contents of the STACK. It is not necessary to maintain any information about what characters are read from the TAPE. If what is on the TAPE is what the rows want to read then the input string will be accepted. Once we know what the rows are we can find an input word that gives them what they want to read. We shall see the implications of this observation later, but every joint- and STACK-consistent path actually is the path through the PDA taken by some input string.

The nonterminals in the row-language grammar have the following form:

$$Net(X,Y,Z)$$

where the X and Y can be any joint; START, HERE, or ACCEPT, and Z is any character from the stack alphabet Γ. This whole expression is *one* nonterminal even though it is at least 10 printer's symbols long. These odd nonterminals stand for the following sentence:

There is some path going from joint X to joint Y, perhaps passing through some other joints (READ or HERE states), which has the net effect on the STACK of removing the symbol Z, where by "net effect" we mean that while there might be extra things put onto the STACK during the path, they are eventually removed and the STACK is never popped below the initial Z that is on the top of the STACK to begin with and that is popped out somewhere along the way.

We have never seen a nonterminal be such a complicated looking item as $Net(X,Y,Z)$, but we have had nonterminals before with meanings that could be expressed in a sentence (as in the CFG for EQUAL).

This complicated description of the "net effect" on the STACK means, for instance, that the sequence of the STACK operations:

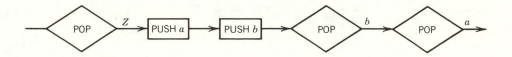

has the net effect of popping one Z since it represents the stack states:

z
?

?

a
?

b
a
?

a
?

?

The net STACK effect is the same as the simple POP Z, and no character was presumed to be in the STACK below the top Z. The symbol "?" here represents the unknown and unexamined part of the STACK. The picture

by itself is also an acceptable sequence for a STACK operation governed by a nonterminal $Net(X,Y,Z)$.
However

is not, because it presupposes knowledge about what is in the STACK under the top Z. If there were a b under the Z initially, this sequence would fail (crash). We never presume knowledge of what is available in the STACK in the statement $Net(X,Y,Z)$ beyond knowing that Z is on top.

For a given PDA some set of all the possible sentences $Net(X,Y,Z)$ are true and some are false. Our job, given a PDA, is to determine which Net statements are true and how they fit together. To do this, we must first examine every row of the table to see which ones have the net effect of popping exactly one letter. There are other paths that are composed of several rows that can also be described by a single Net statement, but we shall discover these by a separate procedure later.

Let us recall the summary table that we have developed for the PDA for the language $\{a^{2n}b^n\}$. Row$_4$ of this table says essentially:

$$Net(\text{READ}_1,\text{HERE},a)$$

which means, "we can go from READ$_1$ to HERE at the total cost of popping an a from the top of the stack."

In other words, Row$_4$ is a single Net row. However, let us suppose that we have a row in the summary table for some arbitrary PDA that looks like this:

FROM	TO	READ	POP	PUSH	ROW
READ$_9$	READ$_3$	b	b	abb	11

As it stands, Row$_{11}$ is not a Net-style sentence because the trip from READ$_9$ to READ$_3$ does not subtract one letter from the STACK; the net effect is rather that it adds two. However, there is a particular way that Row$_{11}$ can interact with some other Net-style sentences. For instance, if we knew that the following three nonterminals could be realized as path segments for this machine

$$Net(\text{READ}_3,\text{READ}_7,a)$$

$$Net(\text{READ}_7,\text{READ}_1,b)$$

$$Net(\text{READ}_1,\text{READ}_8,b)$$

then, using Row$_{11}$, we could conclude that the nonterminal:

$$Net(\text{READ}_9,\text{READ}_8,b)$$

could also be realized as a path segment. This is because we can go first from $READ_9$ to $READ_3$ using Row_{11} which eats the b at the top of the STACK but leaves the letters abb in its place, with the net effect of adding ab. The first a takes us from $READ_3$ to $READ_7$ by the path implied by $Net(READ_3,READ_7,a)$. The next b takes us from $READ_7$ along some path to $READ_1$, as guaranteed by $Net(READ_7,READ_1,b)$. Then the last b takes us from $READ_1$ to $READ_8$ by some path guaranteed by the last Net. The total cost of the trip has been the top b. Thanks to the abb we added, during this whole trip we have never popped the STACK beneath the top b.

Let us write this as:

$Net(READ_9,READ_8,b)$

$\rightarrow Row_{11}Net(READ_3,READ_7,a)Net(READ_7,READ_1,b)Net(READ_1,READ_8,b)$

In other words, the sentence that says that we can go from $READ_9$ to $READ_8$ at the cost of b can be replaced by the concatenation of the sentences Row_{11}, $Net \ldots Net \ldots Net \ldots$.

This will be a production in our row-language. We begin with the non-terminal $Net(READ_9,READ_8,b)$, and we produce a string that has one terminal, Row_{11}, and some nonterminals, $Net \ldots Net \ldots Net \ldots$. Notice that Row_{11} takes us from $READ_9$ to $READ_3$, the first Net from $READ_3$ to $READ_7$, the second from $READ_7$, to $READ_1$, and the last from $READ_1$ to $READ_8$, giving us the trip promised on the left side of the production at the appropriate cost.

This hypothetical Row_{11} that we are presuming exists for some PDA could also be used in other productions, for example,

$Net(READ_9,READ_{10},a)$

$\rightarrow Row_{11}Net(READ_3,READ_2,a)Net(READ_2,READ_2,b)Net(READ_2,READ_{10},b)$

assuming, of course, that these additional Net's are available, by which we mean realizable by actual paths.

The general formulation for creating productions from rows of the summary table is as follows:

If the summary table includes the row

FROM	TO	READ	POP	PUSH	ROW
$READ_x$	$READ_y$	u	w	$m_1m_2 \ldots m_n$	i

then for any sequence of joint states, $S_1, S_2 \ldots S_n$, we include the row-language CFG production

$$Net(\text{READ}_x,\ S_n, w)\ \rightarrow\ Row_i\ Net(\text{READ}_y, S_1, m_1)\ \ldots\ Net(S_{n-1}, S_n, m_n)$$

This is a great number of productions and a large dose of generality all at once. Let us illustrate the point on an outrageous, ludicrous example.

Suppose that someone offered us a ride from Philadelphia to L.A. if we would trade him our old socks for his sunglasses and false teeth. We would say "terrific" because we could then go from Philadelphia to Denver for the price of the old socks. How? First we get a ride to L.A. by trading the socks to him for the sunglasses and false teeth. Then we find someone who will drive us from L.A. to Chicago for a pair of sunglasses and another nice guy who will drive us from Chicago to Denver for a pair of false teeth.

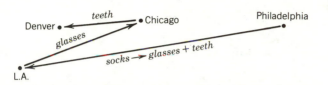

FROM	TO	READ	POP	PUSH	ROW
Phila	L.A.	anything	socks	sunglasses, false teeth	77

$Net(\text{Phila,Denver,socks})$
$\rightarrow Row_{77}\ Net(\text{L.A.,Chi,shades})Net(\text{Chi,Denver,teeth})$

The fact that we have written this production does not mean that it can ever be part of the derivation of an actual word in the row-language. The idea might look good on paper, but where do we find the clown who will drive us from Chicago to Denver for the used choppers?

So too with the other productions formed by this general rule.

We can replace $Net(\text{this and that})$ with $Net(\text{such and such})$, but can we ever boil it all down to a string of rows? We have seen in working with CFG's in general, that replacing one nonterminal with a string of others does not always lead to a word in the language.

In the example of the PDA for which we built the summary table, Row_3 says that we can go from READ_1 back to READ_1 and replace an a with aa. This allows the formation of many productions of the form:

$$Net(\text{READ}_1, X, a)\ \rightarrow\ Row_3\ Net(\text{READ}_1, Y, a)Net(Y, X, a)$$

where X and Y could be READ_1, READ_2, or READ_3—or even HERE. Also X could be ACCEPT, as in this possibility:

$Net(\text{READ}_1,\text{ACCEPT},a) \rightarrow \text{Row}_3 \ Net(\text{READ}_1,\text{READ}_2,a)Net(\text{READ}_2,\text{ACCEPT},a)$

There are three rules for creating productions in what we shall prove is a CFG for the row-language of a PDA presented to us in a summary table.

Rule 1 We have the nonterminal S, which starts the whole show, and the production

$$S \rightarrow Net(\text{START},\text{ACCEPT},\$)$$

which means that we can consider any total path through the machine as a trip from START to ACCEPT at the cost of popping one symbol, $\$$, and never referring to the STACK below $\$$.

This rule is the same for all PDA's.

Rule 2 For every row of the summary table that has no PUSH entry, such as:

FROM	TO	READ	POP	PUSH	ROW
X	Y	anything	Z	—	i

we include the production:

$$Net(X,Y,Z) \rightarrow \text{Row}_i$$

This means that $Net(X,Y,Z)$, which stands for the hypothetical trip from X to Y at the net cost Z, is really possible by using Row_i alone. It is actualizable in this PDA.

Let us remember that since this is the row-language we are generating, this production is in the form:

$$\text{Nonterminal} \rightarrow \text{terminal}$$

In general, we have no guarantee that there are any such rows that push nothing, but if no row decreases the size of the STACK, it can never become empty and the machine will never accept any words.

For completeness we restate the expansion rule above.

Rule 3 For each row in the summary table that has some PUSH we introduce a whole family of productions. For every row that pushes n characters onto the STACK, such as:

FROM	TO	READ	POP	PUSH	ROW
X	Y	anything	Z	$m_1 \ldots m_n$	i

for *all sets* of n READ, HERE, or ACCEPT states $S_1, S_2 \ldots S_n$, we create the productions:

$$Net(X, S_n, Z) \rightarrow Row_i \, Net(Y, S_1, m_1) \ldots Net(S_{n-1}, S_n, M_n)$$

Remember the fact that we are creating productions does not mean that they are all useful in the generation of words. We merely want to guarantee that we get *all* the useful productions, and the useless ones will not hurt us.

No other productions are necessary.

We shall prove in a moment that these are all the productions in the CFG defining the row-language. That is, the language of all sequences of rows representing every word accepted by the machine can be generated by these productions from the start symbol S.

Many productions come from these rules. As we have observed, not all of them are used in the derivation of words because some of these *Net*-variables can never be realized as actual paths, just as we could include the nonterminal $Net(NY, LA, 5¢)$ in the optimistic hope that some airline will run a great sale. Only those nonterminals that can be eventually replaced by strings of solid terminals will ever be used in producing words in the row-language.

This is like the case with this CFG:

$$S \rightarrow X \mid Y$$

$$X \rightarrow aXX$$

$$Y \rightarrow ab$$

The production $X \rightarrow aXX$ is totally useless in producing words.

We shall now prove that this CFG with all the *Net*'s is exactly the CFG for the row-language. To do that, we need to show two things: first, that every string generated by the CFG is a string of rows representing an actual path through the PDA from START to ACCEPT, and second, that all the paths corresponding to accepted input strings are equivalent to row-words generated by this CFG.

Before we consider this problem in the abstract, let us return to the concrete illustration of the summary table for the PDA that accepts

$$\{a^{2n}b^n\}$$

We shall make a complete list of all the productions that can be formed from the rows of the summary table using the three rules above.

Rule 1, always, gives us only the production:

PROD 1 $S \rightarrow Net(\text{START},\text{ACCEPT},\$)$

Rule 2 applies to Rows 4, 5, 6, and 7, creating the productions:

PROD 2 $Net(\text{READ}_1,\text{HERE},a) \rightarrow \text{Row}_4$
PROD 3 $Net(\text{HERE},\text{READ}_2,a) \rightarrow \text{Row}_5$
PROD 4 $Net(\text{READ}_2,\text{HERE},a) \rightarrow \text{Row}_6$
PROD 5 $Net(\text{READ}_2,\text{ACCEPT},\$) \rightarrow \text{Row}_7$

Lastly, Rule 3 applies to Rows 1, 2, and 3. When applied to Row$_1$ it generates:

$$Net(\text{START},X,\$) \rightarrow \text{Row}_1 \; Net(\text{READ}_1,X,\$)$$

where X can take on the different values READ$_1$, READ$_2$, HERE, or ACCEPT. This gives us these four new productions:

PROD 6 $Net(\text{START},\text{READ}_1,\$)$ $\rightarrow$ Row$_1$ $Net(\text{READ}_1,\text{READ}_1,\$)$
PROD 7 $Net(\text{START},\text{READ}_2,\$)$ $\rightarrow$ Row$_1$ $Net(\text{READ}_1,\text{READ}_2,\$)$
PROD 8 $Net(\text{START},\text{HERE},\$)$ $\rightarrow$ Row$_1$ $Net(\text{READ}_1,\text{HERE},\$)$
PROD 9 $Net(\text{START},\text{ACCEPT},\$)$ $\rightarrow$ Row$_1$ $Net(\text{READ}_1,\text{ACCEPT},\$)$

When applied to Row$_2$, Rule 3 generates:

$$Net(\text{READ}_1,X,\$) \rightarrow \text{Row}_2 \; Net(\text{READ}_1,Y,a) \; Net(Y,X,\$)$$

where X can be any joint state but START, and Y can be any joint state but START or ACCEPT (since we cannot return to START or leave ACCEPT).

The new productions derived from Row$_2$ are of the form above with all possible values for X and Y:

PROD 10 $Net(\text{READ}_1,\text{READ}_1,\$)$
                $\rightarrow \text{Row}_2 Net(\text{READ}_1,\text{READ}_1,a)Net(\text{READ}_1,\text{READ}_1,\$)$
PROD 11 $Net(\text{READ}_1,\text{READ}_1,\$)$
                $\rightarrow \text{Row}_2 Net(\text{READ}_1\text{READ}_2,a)Net(\text{READ}_2,\text{READ}_1,\$)$
PROD 12 $Net(\text{READ}_1,\text{READ}_1,\$)$
                $\rightarrow \text{Row}_2 Net(\text{READ}_1,\text{HERE},a)Net(\text{HERE},\text{READ}_1,\$)$

Prod 13 $Net(READ_1,READ_2,\$)$
  $\rightarrow Row_2Net(READ_1,READ_1,a)Net(READ_1,READ_2,\$)$

Prod 14 $Net(READ_1,READ_2,\$)$
  $\rightarrow Row_2Net(READ_1,READ_2,a)Net(READ_2,READ_2,\$)$

Prod 15 $Net(READ_1READ_2,\$)$
  $\rightarrow Row_2Net(READ_1,HERE,a)Net(HERE,READ_2,\$)$

Prod 16 $Net(READ_1,HERE,\$)$
  $\rightarrow Row_2Net(READ_1,READ_1,a)Net(READ_1,HERE,\$)$

Prod 17 $Net(READ_1,HERE,\$)$
  $\rightarrow Row_2Net(READ_1,READ_2,a)Net(READ_2,HERE,\$)$

Prod 18 $Net(READ_1,HERE,\$)$
  $\rightarrow Row_2Net(READ_1,HERE,a)Net(HERE,HERE,\$)$

Prod 19 $Net(READ_1,ACCEPT,\$)$
  $\rightarrow Row_2Net(READ_1,READ_1,a)Net(READ_1,ACCEPT,\$)$

Prod 20 $Net(READ_1,ACCEPT,\$)$
  $\rightarrow Row_2Net(READ_1,READ_2,a)Net(READ_2,ACCEPT,\$)$

Prod 21 $Net(READ_1,ACCEPT,\$)$
  $\rightarrow Row_2Net(READ_1,HERE,a)Net(HERE,ACCEPT,\$)$

When Rule 3 is applied to Row_3, it generates productions of the form:

$$Net(READ_1,X,a) \rightarrow Row_3 \ Net(READ_1,Y,a) \ Net(Y,X,a)$$

where X can be $READ_1$, $READ_2$, HERE, or ACCEPT and Y can only be $READ_1$, $READ_2$, or HERE.
This gives 12 new productions:

Prod 22 $Net(READ_1,READ_1,a)$
  $\rightarrow Row_3Net(READ_1,READ_1,a)Net(READ_1,READ_1a)$

Prod 23 $Net(READ_1,READ_1,a)$
  $\rightarrow Row_3Net(READ_1,READ_2,a)Net(READ_2,READ_1,a)$

Prod 24 $Net(READ_1,READ_1,a)$
  $\rightarrow Row_3Net(READ_1,HERE,a)Net(HERE,READ_1,a)$

Prod 25 $Net(READ_1,READ_2,a)$
  $\rightarrow Row_3Net(READ_1,READ_1,a)Net(READ_1,READ_2,a)$

Prod 26 $Net(READ_1,READ_2,a)$
  $\rightarrow Row_3Net(READ_1,READ_2,a)Net(READ_2,READ_2,a)$

Prod 27 $Net(READ_1,READ_2,a)$
  $\rightarrow Row_3Net(READ_1,HERE,a)Net(HERE,READ_2,a)$

PROD 28 $Net(READ_1, HERE, a)$
       $\rightarrow Row_3Net(READ_1, READ_1, a)Net(READ_1, HERE, a)$

PROD 29 $Net(READ_1, HERE, a)$
       $\rightarrow Row_3Net(READ_1, READ_2, a)Net(READ_2, HERE, a)$

PROD 30 $Net(READ_1, HERE, a)$
       $\rightarrow Row_3Net(READ_1, HERE, a)Net(HERE, HERE, a)$

PROD 31 $Net(READ_1, ACCEPT, a)$
       $\rightarrow Row_3Net(READ_1, READ_1, a)Net(READ_1, ACCEPT, a)$

PROD 32 $Net(READ_1, ACCEPT, a)$
       $\rightarrow Row_3Net(READ_1, READ_2, a)Net(READ_2, ACCEPT, a)$

PROD 33 $Net(READ_1, ACCEPT, a)$
       $\rightarrow Row_3Net(READ_1, HERE, a)Net(HERE, ACCEPT, a)$

This is the largest CFG we have ever tried to handle. We have:

         7 terminals: $Row_1 \ Row_2, \ldots \ Row_7$

    29 nonterminals: S, 16 of the form $Net(, , \$)$

                         12 of the form $Net(, , a)$

    33 productions: PROD 1 . . . PROD 33

We know that not all of these will occur in an actual derivation starting at S. For example, $Net(READ_2, ACCEPT, a)$ cannot happen, since to go from $READ_2$ to ACCEPT we must pop a $\$$, not an a.

To see which productions can lead toward words, let us begin to draw the left-most total language tree of the row-language. By "left-most" we mean that from every working string node we make one branch for each production that applies to the left-most nonterminal. Branching only on the left-most nonterminal avoids considerable duplication without losing any words of the language, because all words that can be derived have left-most derivations (Theorem 25).

In this case the tree starts simply as:

$$S$$
$$\downarrow$$
$$Net(START, ACCEPT, \$) \qquad\qquad (1)$$
$$\downarrow$$
$$Row_1Net(READ_1, ACCEPT, \$) \qquad\qquad (1,9)$$

This is because the only production that has S as its left-hand side is PROD 1. The only production that applies after that is PROD 9. The numbers in parentheses at the right show which sequence of productions was used to arrive

at each node in the tree. The left-most (and only) nonterminal now is
$Net(\text{READ}_1,\text{ACCEPT},\$)$. There are exactly three productions that can apply
here:

$$\text{PROD } 19 \qquad \text{PROD } 20 \qquad \text{PROD } 21$$

So the tree now branches as follows:

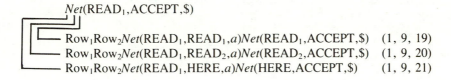

$Net(\text{READ}_1,\text{ACCEPT},\$)$

$\text{Row}_1\text{Row}_2Net(\text{READ}_1,\text{READ}_1,a)Net(\text{READ}_1,\text{ACCEPT},\$) \qquad (1,\,9,\,19)$
$\text{Row}_1\text{Row}_2Net(\text{READ}_1,\text{READ}_2,a)Net(\text{READ}_2,\text{ACCEPT},\$) \qquad (1,\,9,\,20)$
$\text{Row}_1\text{Row}_2Net(\text{READ}_1,\text{HERE},a)Net(\text{HERE},\text{ACCEPT},\$) \qquad (1,\,9,\,21)$

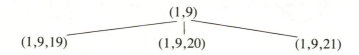

(1,9)

(1,9,19) (1,9,20) (1,9,21)

Let us consider the branch $(1,9,19)$. Here the left-most nonterminal is
$Net(\text{READ}_1,\text{READ}_1,a)$. The productions that apply to this nonterminal are PROD
22, PROD 23, and PROD 24. Application of PROD 23 gives us an expression
that includes $Net(\text{READ}_2,\text{READ}_1,a)$, but there is no production for which this
Net is the left-hand side. (This corresponds to the fact that there are no paths
from READ_2 to READ_1 in this PDA.) Therefore, PROD 23 can never be used
in the formation of a word in this row-language.

This is also true of PROD 24, which creates the expression $Net(\text{HERE},$
$\text{READ}_1,a)$. No matter how many times we apply PROD 22, we still have a
factor of $Net(\text{READ}_1,\text{READ}_1,a)$. There is no way to remove this nonterminal
from a working string. Therefore, any branch incorporating this nonterminal
can never lead to a string of only terminals. The situation is similar to this
CFG:

$$S \rightarrow b \mid X$$

$$X \rightarrow aX$$

We can never get rid of the X. So we get no words from starting with $S \rightarrow X$.
Therefore, we might as well drop this nonterminal from consideration.

We could produce just as many words in the row-language if we dropped
PROD 22, PROD 23, and PROD 24. Therefore, we might as well eliminate PROD
19, since this created the situation that led to these productions, and it can
give us no possible lines, only hopeless ones. We now see that we might as
well drop the whole branch $(1,9,19)$.

Now let us examine the branch (1,9,20). The left-most nonterminal here is $Net(\text{READ}_1,\text{READ}_2,a)$. The productions that apply to this nonterminal are

PROD 25   PROD 26   PROD 27.

Of these, PROD 25 generates a string that involves $Net(\text{READ}_1,\text{READ}_1,a)$, which we saw before led to the death of the branch (1,9,19). So PROD 25 is also poison.

We have no reason at the moment not to apply PROD 26 or PROD 27. The tree, therefore, continues:

```
┌─(1, 9, 20)
│  └─Row₁Row₂Row₃Net(READ₁,READ₂,a)Net(READ₂READ₂a)Net(READ₂,ACCEPT,$)  (1, 9, 20, 26)
└──Row₁Row₂Row₃Net(READ₁,HERE,a)Net(HERE,READ₂,a)Net(READ₂,ACCEPT,$)  (1, 9, 20, 27)
```

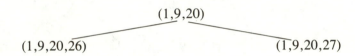

$$(1,9,20)$$

$$(1,9,20,26) \qquad\qquad (1,9,20,27)$$

Let us continue the process along one branch of the tree.

$$(1,9,20,27)$$
$$\downarrow$$
$$\text{Row}_1\text{Row}_2\text{Row}_3\text{Row}_4Net(\text{HERE},\text{READ}_2,a)Net(\text{READ}_2,\text{ACCEPT},\$) \qquad (1,9,20,27,2)$$
$$\downarrow$$
$$\text{Row}_1\text{Row}_2\text{Row}_3\text{Row}_4\text{Row}_5Net(\text{HERE},\text{ACCEPT},\$) \qquad (1,9,20,27,2,3)$$
$$\downarrow$$
$$\text{Row}_1\text{Row}_2\text{Row}_3\text{Row}_4\text{Row}_5\text{Row}_7 \qquad (1,9,20,27,2,3,5)$$

This is the shortest word in the entire row-language. The total language tree is infinite.

In this particular case, the proof that this is the CFG for the row-language is easy, and it reflects the ideas in the general proof that the CFG formed by the three rules we stated is the desired CFG.

For one thing, it is clear that every derivation from these rules is a realizable path of rows. This is because each production says:

We can make this trip at this cost

if

We can make these trips at these costs

If it all boils down to a set of Rows, then the subtrips can be made along the deterministic edges of the PDA corresponding to the rows of the summary table: When we put them together, the longer trip based on these path segments becomes realizable.

How do we know that every path through the PDA is derivable from the productions that the rules create? Every trip through the PDA can be broken up into the segments of net cost. The STACK is set initially at $ and row by row some things are popped and some are pushed. Some rows push more than one letter and some push none. The ones that push more than one letter are the ones that enable us to execute the rows that pop but do not push. This is STACK economics. We can write down directly,

"The profit from Row$_i$ is such and such."

"The cost of Row$_j$ is so and so."

For the machine to operate properly, the total cost must be equal to the profit plus the initial $, and the profit must come first. We can never be in debt more than one $. (That is why we chose the symbol "$.")

For example, let us examine the word Row$_1$Row$_2$Row$_3$Row$_4$Row$_5$Row$_7$:

Row$_1$	Row$_2$	Row$_3$	Row$_4$	Row$_5$	Row$_7$
Net change	Net change	Net change	Net change	Net change	Net change
0	$+a$	$+a$	$-a$	$-a$	$-\$$

The table shows that as soon as we have a row with a profit we must decide where to spend it. If Row$_3$ has a profit of $+a$, then we can say we will spend it on Row$_5$. Row$_3$ enables Row$_5$ to follow it.

From	To	READ	POP	PUSH	Row
READ$_1$	READ$_1$		a	aa	3
HERE	READ$_2$		a	—	5

This matching is summarized by the production:

$Net(\text{READ}_1,\text{READ}_2,a) \rightarrow \text{Row}_3 Net(\text{READ}_1,\text{HERE},a)Net(\text{HERE},\text{READ}_2,a)$

which is our PROD 27.

Any allocation we can make of the STACK profit from the push rows to the STACK losses of the nonpush rows must correspond to a production in the grammar we have created since the rules we gave for CFG production formation included all possible ways of spending the profit.

Let us look at a typical abstract case of the application of Rule 3. Let us start with some hypothetical Row$_H$ below

From	To	READ	POP	PUSH	Row
A	B	C	D	EFG	H

and generate all productions of the form:

$$Net(A,Z,D) \rightarrow Row_H Net(B,X,E)Net(X,Y,F)Net(Y,Z,G)$$

This tells us to distribute the profit of Row$_H$, which is EFG, in all possible ways to pass through any sequence of joints X,Y,Z. We start at A and do Row$_H$. We are now in B and have to spend EFG. We travel from B, but by the time we get to X we have spent the top E. We may have passed through many other states and popped and pushed plenty, but when we reach X the E is gone and the F and G are on the top of the STACK. Similarly, by the time we get to Y the F is gone and by Z the G is gone.

Any trip from A to Z that nets D and starts with Row$_H$ must be of this form. After Row$_H$ an E is on top of the STACK. At some point that E must be popped. Let us call the joint that we get to when the E is popped X. Call the joint we get to when the F is first popped Y. The joint we get to when the G is popped must be Z, since that fulfills $Net(A,Z,D)$.

All trips of the right-side form are trips that go from A to Z at net cost D, and all $Net(A,Z,D)$ must be of the right-side form.

This argument shows that this CFG generates the row-language corresponding to all trips through the PDA.

Where are we now in the proof of Theorem 29? Let us recapitulate.

I. Starting with any PDA as defined in the previous section, we can convert it into conversion form without changing its language.

II. From conversion form we can build a summary table that has all the information about the PDA broken into rows, each of which describes a simple path between joint states (READ, HERE, START, and AC-CEPT). The rows are of the form:

From	To	READ	POP	PUSH	Row Number

III. There is a set of rules describing how to create a CFG for the language whose words are all the row sequences corresponding to all the paths through the PDA that can be taken by input strings on their way to acceptance.

The rules create productions of the three forms:

Rule 1 $S \rightarrow Net(\text{START},\text{ACCEPT},\$)$

Rule 2 $Net(X,Y,Q) \rightarrow \text{Row}_i$

Rule 3 $Net(A,B,C) \rightarrow \text{Row}_i\ Net(A,X,Y)\ \ldots\ Net(Q,B,W)$

What we need now to complete the proof of Theorem 29 (to which we are dedicating our natural-born lives) is to create the CFG that generates the *language* accepted by the PDA—not just its row-language, but the language of strings of a's and b's. The grammar for the row-language is a good start but it is not the grammar we are looking for which is the CFG for the language of strings accepted by the PDA.

We can finish this off in one simple step. In the summary table every row had an entry that we have ignored until now, that is, the READ column.

Every row reads a, b, Λ, or Δ from the INPUT TAPE. There is no ambiguity because an edge from a READ state cannot have two labels. So every row sequence corresponds to a sequence of letters read from the INPUT TAPE. In order for this path to be successfully followed through the PDA the TAPE must first be loaded with the word that is the concatenation of the READ demands of the rows. We can convert the row-language into the language of the PDA by adding to the CFG for the row-language the set of productions created by a new rule, Rule 4.

Rule 4 For every row

From	To	READ	POP	Push	Row
A	B	C	D	EFGH	I

create the production:

$$\text{Row}_I \rightarrow C$$

For example, in the summary table for the PDA that accepts that language $\{a^{2n}b^n\}$ we have seven rows. Therefore we create the seven new productions:

PROD 34 $\text{Row}_1 \rightarrow \Lambda$

PROD 35 $\text{Row}_2 \rightarrow a$

PROD 36 $\text{Row}_3 \rightarrow a$

PROD 37 $\text{Row}_4 \rightarrow b$

PROD 38 $\text{Row}_5 \rightarrow \Lambda$

PROD 39 $\text{Row}_6 \rightarrow b$

PROD 40 $\text{Row}_7 \rightarrow \Delta$

The symbols, Row_1, Row_2 . . . that used to be terminals in the row-language are now nonterminals. From every row sequence we can produce a word. For example,

$$Row_1 Row_2 Row_3 Row_4 Row_5 Row_7$$

becomes:

$$\Lambda \; a \; a \; b \; \Lambda \; \Delta$$

Treating Δ like a Λ (to be painfully technical, by the production $\Delta \rightarrow \Lambda$) we have the word:

$$a \; a \; b$$

Clearly this word can be accepted by this PDA by following the path

$$Row_1 - Row_2 - Row_3 - Row_4 - Row_5 - Row_7$$

The derivations of the words from the productions of this CFG not only tell us which words are accepted by this PDA but also indicate a *path* by which the words may be accepted, which may be useful information.

Remember that since this is a nondeterministic machine, there may be several paths that accept the same word. But for every legitimate word there will be at least one complete path to ACCEPT.

The language generated by this CFG is exactly the language accepted by the PDA originally. Therefore, we may say that, for any PDA there is a CFG that generates the same language the machine accepts. ∎

EXAMPLE

We shall now illustrate the complete process of equivalence, as given by the two theorems in this chapter, on one simple example. We shall start with a CFG and convert it into a PDA (using the algorithm of Theorem 28), and we then convert this very PDA back into a CFG (using the algorithm of Theorem 29).

The language of this illustration is the collection of all strings of an even number of a's:

$$EVENA = (aa)^+ = a^{2n} = \{aa \quad aaaa \quad aaaaaa \ldots\}$$

One obvious grammar for this language is

$$S \rightarrow SS \mid aa$$

The left-most total language tree begins:

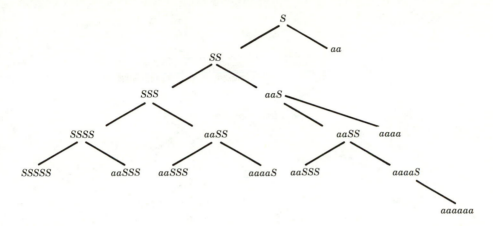

Before we can use the algorithm of Theorem 28 to build a PDA that accepts this language, we must put it into CNF. We therefore first employ the algorithm of Theorem 24:

$$S \rightarrow SS \mid AA$$

$$A \rightarrow a$$

The PDA we produce by the algorithm of Theorem 28 is:

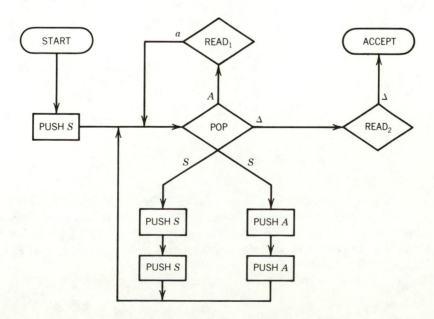

We shall now use the algorithm of Theorem 29 to turn this machine back into a CFG. First we must put this PDA into conversion form:

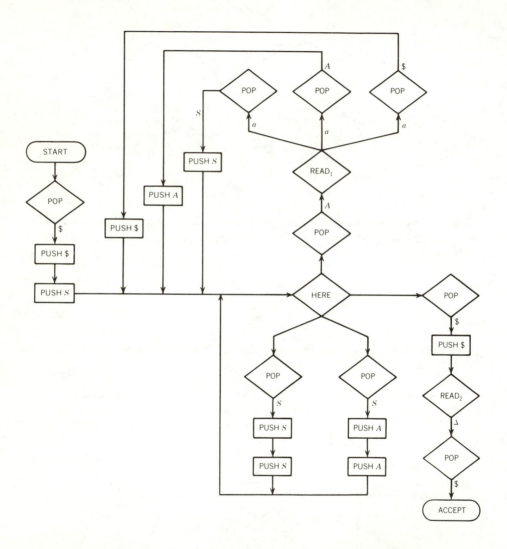

Notice that the branching that used to take place at the grand central POP must now take place at the grand central HERE. Notice also that since we insist there be a POP after every READ, we must have three POP's following READ$_1$. Who among us is so brazen as to claim to be able to glance at this machine and identify the language it accepts?

The next step is to put this PDA into a summary table:

From	TO	READ	POP	PUSH	ROW
START	HERE	—	$	S$	1
HERE	HERE	—	S	SS	2
HERE	HERE	—	S	AA	3
HERE	READ$_1$	—	A	—	4
READ$_1$	HERE	a	S	S	5
READ$_1$	HERE	a	$	$	6
READ$_1$	HERE	a	A	A	7
HERE	READ$_2$	—	$	$	8
READ$_2$	ACCEPT	Δ	$	—	9

We are now ready to write out all the productions in the row-language. We always begin with the production from Rule 1:

$$S \rightarrow Net(\text{START,ACCEPT},\$)$$

There are two rows with no PUSH parts and they give us, by Rule 2:

$$Net(\text{HERE,READ}_1,A) \rightarrow \text{Row}_4$$

$$Net(\text{READ}_2,\text{ACCEPT},\$) \rightarrow \text{Row}_9$$

From Row$_1$ we get 12 productions of the form:

$$Net(\text{START},X,\$) \rightarrow \text{Row}_1 Net(\text{HERE},Y,\$)Net(Y,X,\$)$$

where X = HERE, READ$_1$, READ$_2$, or ACCEPT and Y = HERE, READ$_1$ or READ$_2$.

From Row$_2$ we get eight productions of the form:

$$Net(\text{HERE},X,S) \rightarrow \text{Row}_2 \; Net(\text{HERE},Y,S) \; Net(Y,X,S)$$

where X = HERE, READ$_1$, READ$_2$, or ACCEPT and Y = HERE or READ$_1$.

From Row$_3$ we get eight productions of the form:

$$Net(\text{HERE},X,S) \rightarrow \text{Row}_3 \; Net(\text{HERE},Y,A)Net(Y,X,A)$$

where X = HERE, READ$_1$, READ$_2$, or ACCEPT and Y = HERE or READ$_1$.

From Row_5 we get the four productions:

$$Net(READ_1, X, S) \rightarrow Row_5 \ Net(HERE, X, S)$$

where X = HERE, $READ_1$, $READ_2$, or ACCEPT.
From Row_6 we get the four productions:

$$Net(READ_1, X, \$) \rightarrow Row_6 \ Net(HERE, X, \$)$$

where X = HERE, $READ_1$, $READ_2$, or ACCEPT.
From Row_7 we get the four productions:

$$Net(READ_1, X, A) \rightarrow Row_7 \ Net(HERE, X, A)$$

where X = HERE, $READ_1$, $READ_2$, or ACCEPT.
From Row_8 we get the one production:

$$Net(HERE, ACCEPT, \$) \rightarrow Row_8 \ Net(READ_2, ACCEPT, \$).$$

All together, this makes a grammar of 44 productions for the row-language.
We shall now do something we have not discussed before. We can trim from the row-language grammar all the productions that are never used in the derivation of words. For example, in the simple grammar

$$S \rightarrow a \mid X \mid Ya$$

$$X \rightarrow XX$$

it is clear that only the production $S \rightarrow a$ is ever used in the derivation of words in the language. The productions $S \rightarrow X$, $S \rightarrow Ya$ and $X \rightarrow XX$, as well as the nonterminals X and Y, are all useless.

We have not previously demonstrated an algorithm for pruning grammars, but we can develop one now, from the principles of common sense (tenets heretofore eschewed).

At all times we shall look only at the formal grammar, never at the original PDA, since the insight we can find in this simple PDA will not always be so easy to come by in more complicated cases. We must try to follow rules that can apply in all cases.

Our question is: In a derivation from S to a string of the terminals, Row_1, Row_2, . . . , Row_8, which productions can obviously never be used?

If we are ever to turn a working string into a string of solid terminals, we need to use some productions at the end of the derivation that do not introduce nonterminals into the string. In this grammar only two productions are of the form:

$$Nonterminal \rightarrow string \ of \ terminals$$

They are:

$$Net(HERE,READ_1,A) \rightarrow Row_4$$

and

$$Net(READ_2,ACCEPT,\$) \rightarrow Row_9$$

If any words are generated by this row-language grammar at all, then one of these productions must be employed as the last step in the derivation.

In the step before the last, we should have a working string that contains all terminals except for one of the possible nonterminals $Net(HERE,READ_1,A)$ or $Net(READ_2,ACCEPT,\$)$.

Still counting backward from the final string, we ask: What production could have been used before these two productions to give us such a working string? It must be a production in which the right side contains all terminals and one or both of the nonterminals above.

Of the 44 productions, there are only two that fit this description:

$$Net(HERE,ACCEPT,\$) \rightarrow Row_8 \; Net(READ_2, ACCEPT,\$)$$

$$Net(READ_1,READ_1,A) \rightarrow Row_7 \; Net(HERE,READ_1,A)$$

This gives us two more useful nonterminals, $Net(HERE,ACCEPT,\$)$ and $Net(READ_1,READ_1,A)$.

We have now established that any working string containing terminals and some of the four nonterminals:

$$Net(HERE,READ_1, A)$$

$$Net(READ_2,ACCEPT,\$)$$

$$Net(HERE,ACCEPT,\$)$$

$$Net(READ_1,READ_1,A)$$

can be turned by these productions into a string of all terminals.

Again we ask the question: What could have introduced these nonterminals into the working string?

There are only two productions with right sides that have only terminals and these four nonterminals. They are:

$$Net(HERE,READ_1,S) \rightarrow Row_3Net(HERE,READ_1,A)Net(READ_1,READ_1,A)$$

and

$$Net(READ_1,ACCEPT,\$) \rightarrow Row_6 \; Net(HERE,ACCEPT,\$)$$

We shall call these two nonterminals "useful" as we did before. We can now safely say that any working string that contains terminals and these six nonterminals can be turned into a word.

Again we ask the question: How can these new useful nonterminals show up in a word? The answer is that there are only two productions with right sides that involve only nonterminals known to be useful. They are:

$$Net(READ_1, READ_1, S) \rightarrow Row_5 \ Net(HERE, READ_1, S)$$

and

$$Net(START, ACCEPT, \$) \rightarrow Row_1 \ Net(HERE, READ_1, S) Net(READ_1, ACCEPT, \$)$$

So now we can include $Net(READ_1, READ_1, S)$ and $Net(START, ACCEPT, \$)$ on our list of useful symbols because we know that any working string that contains them and the other useful symbols can be turned by the productions into a word of all terminals. This technique should be familiar by now. From here we can almost smell the blue paint.

Again we ask which of the remaining productions have useful right sides, that is, which produce strings of only useful symbols? Searching through the list we find two more. They are:

$$Net(HERE, READ_1, S) \rightarrow Row_2 Net(HERE, READ_1, S) Net(READ_1, READ_1, S)$$

and

$$S \rightarrow Net(START, ACCEPT, \$)$$

This makes both $Net(HERE, READ_1, S)$ and S useful. This is valuable information since we know that any working string working composed only of useful symbols can be turned into a string of all terminals. When applied to the working string of just the letter S, we can conclude that there is some language that can be generated from the start symbol. The row-language therefore contains some words.

When we now go back through the list of 44 productions looking for any others that have right sides composed exclusively of useful symbols we find no new productions. In other words, each of the other remaining productions introduces onto its right-side some nonterminal that cannot lead to a word.

Therefore, the only useful part of this grammar lies within the 10 productions we have just considered above. Let us recapitulate them:

PROD 1 $S \rightarrow Net(START, ACCEPT, \$)$

PROD 2 $Net(START, ACCEPT, \$) \rightarrow Row_1 Net(HERE, READ_1, S) Net(READ_1, ACCEPT, \$)$

PROD 3 $Net(HERE,READ_1,S) \rightarrow Row_2Net(HERE,READ_1,S)Net(READ_1,READ_1,S)$

PROD 4 $Net(HERE,READ_1,S) \rightarrow Row_3Net(HERE,READ_1,A)Net(READ_1,READ_1,A)$

PROD 5 $Net(HERE,READ_1,A) \rightarrow Row_4$

PROD 6 $Net(READ_1,READ_1,S) \rightarrow Row_5Net(HERE,READ_1,S)$

PROD 7 $Net(READ_1,ACCEPT,\$) \rightarrow Row_6Net(HERE,ACCEPT,\$)$

PROD 8 $Net(READ_1,READ_1,A) \rightarrow Row_7Net(HERE,READ_1,A)$

PROD 9 $Net(HERE,ACCEPT,\$) \rightarrow Row_8Net(READ_2,ACCEPT,\$)$

PROD 10 $Net(READ_2,ACCEPT,\$) \rightarrow Row_9$

We can now make an observation from looking at the grammar that could have been made by looking at the PDA alone. For this particular machine and grammar, each row appears in only one production.

The CFG above is the grammar for the row-language. To obtain the grammar for the actual language of the PDA, we must also include the following productions:

PROD 11 $Row_1 \rightarrow \Lambda$

PROD 12 $Row_2 \rightarrow \Lambda$

PROD 13 $Row_3 \rightarrow \Lambda$

PROD 14 $Row_4 \rightarrow \Lambda$

PROD 15 $Row_5 \rightarrow a$

PROD 16 $Row_6 \rightarrow a$

PROD 17 $Row_7 \rightarrow a$

PROD 18 $Row_8 \rightarrow \Lambda$

PROD 19 $Row_9 \rightarrow \Lambda$

This grammar is too long and has too many nonterminals for us simply to look at it and tell immediately what language it generates. So we must perform a few obvious operations to simplify it. We have been very careful never to claim that we have rules that will enable us to understand the language of a CFG. However, there are a few tricks we can employ to help us a little.

First, let us observe that if N is a nonterminal that appears on the left side of productions all of which are of the form:

$$N \rightarrow \text{string of terminals}$$

then we can eliminate N from the CFG entirely by substituting these right-side strings for N wherever N occurs in the productions (and of course dropping the productions from N). This is similar to the way in which we eliminated unit productions in Chapter 16. This simplification will not change the language generated by the CFG.

This trick applies to the CFG before us in many places. For example, the production

$$\text{Row}_6 \rightarrow a$$

is of this form and this is the only production from this nonterminal. We can therefore replace the nonterminal Row$_6$ throughout the grammar with the letter a.

Not only that, but the production

$$\text{Row}_2 \rightarrow \Lambda$$

is also of the form specified in the trick. Therefore, we can use it to eliminate the nonterminal Row$_2$ from the grammar. In fact, all the nonterminals of the form Row$_i$ can be so eliminated.

PROD 1 is a unit production, so we can use the algorithm for eliminating unit productions (given in Theorem 22) to combine it with PROD 2. The result is:

$$S \rightarrow Net(\text{HERE},\text{READ}_1,S)Net(\text{READ}_1,\text{ACCEPT},\$)$$

As we said before any nonterminal N that has only one production:

$$N \rightarrow \text{some string}$$

can be eliminated from the grammar by substituting the right-side string for N everywhere it appears.

As we shall presently show this rule can be used to eliminate all the nonterminals in the present CFG except for the symbol S and $Net(\text{HERE},\text{READ}_1,S)$, which is the left side of two different productions.

We shall illustrate this process in separate stages. First, we obtain:

PROD 1 and 2 $S \rightarrow Net(\text{HERE},\text{READ}_1,S)Net(\text{READ}_1,\text{ACCEPT},\$)$

PROD 3 $Net(\text{HERE},\text{READ}_1,S) \rightarrow Net(\text{HERE},\text{READ}_1,S)$
$Net(\text{READ}_1,\text{READ}_1,S)$

PROD 4 and 5 $Net(\text{HERE},\text{READ}_1,S) \rightarrow Net(\text{READ}_1,\text{READ}_1,A)$

PROD 6 $Net(\text{READ}_1,\text{READ}_1,S) \rightarrow aNet(\text{HERE},\text{READ}_1,S)$

PROD 7 $Net(\text{READ}_1,\text{ACCEPT},\$) \rightarrow aNet(\text{HERE},\text{ACCEPT},\$)$

PROD 8 and 5 $Net(\text{READ}_1,\text{READ}_1,A) \rightarrow a$

PROD 9 and 10 $Net(\text{HERE},\text{ACCEPT},\$) \rightarrow \Lambda$

Notice that the READ$_2$'s completely disappear.

We can now combine PROD 9 and 10 with PROD 7. PROD 8 and 5 can be combined with PROD 4 and 5. Also PROD 6 can be combined with PROD 1 and 2 to give:

$$S \rightarrow Net(\text{HERE},\text{READ}_1,S)a$$

Now let us rename the nonterminal $Net(\text{HERE},\text{READ}_1,S)$ calling it X. The entire grammar has been reduced to

$$S \rightarrow Xa$$

$$X \rightarrow XaX$$

$$X \rightarrow a$$

This CFG generates the same language as the PDA. However, it is not identical to the CFG with which we started. To see that this CFG does generate EVENA, we draw the beginning of its left-most total language tree.

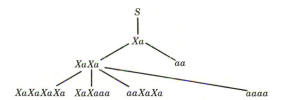

It is clear what is happening. All words in the language have only a's as letters. All working strings have an even number of symbols (terminals plus nonterminals). The production $S \rightarrow Xa$ can be used only once in any derivation, from then on the working string has an even length. The substitution $X \rightarrow XaX$ would keep an even-length string even just as $X \rightarrow a$ would.

So the final word must have an even number of letters in it, all a's. We must also show that all even-length strings of a's can be derived. To do this, we can say, that to produce a^{2n} we use $S \rightarrow Xa$ once, then $X \rightarrow XaX$ left-most $n-1$ times, and then $X \rightarrow a$ exactly n times.

For example, to produce a^8:

$$S \Rightarrow \underline{X}a \Rightarrow \underline{X}aXa \Rightarrow \underline{X}aXaXa \Rightarrow \underline{X}aXaXaXa \Rightarrow aa\underline{X}aXaXa$$
$$\Rightarrow aaaa\underline{X}aXa \Rightarrow aaaaaa\underline{X}a \Rightarrow a^8 \qquad \blacksquare$$

Before finishing our discussion of Theorem 29 we should say a word about condition 8 in the definition of conversion form. On the surface it seems that we never made use of this property of the PDA in our construction of the CFG. We didn't. However, it is an important factor in showing that the CFG generates the language accepted by the machine. According to our definition of PDA it is possible for a machine to accept an input string without reading the whole string. One example is a machine that accepts all strings beginning with an *a*. From START we go to a READ state which checks the first letter. If it is an *a* we accept. The path through the machine that the word *abb* takes is identical to the path for the word *aaa*. If we converted this machine into a CFG the row-language version of a successful path would correspond only to the word *a*. However, if we insist on condition 8 then each row-language word will correspond to a different unique word in the language of the PDA.

PROBLEMS

For each of the CFG's below, construct a PDA that accepts the same language they generate, using the algorithm of Theorem 28.

1. (i) $S \rightarrow aSbb \mid abb$

    (ii) $S \rightarrow SS \mid a \mid b$

2. $S \rightarrow XaaX$
    $X \rightarrow aX \mid bX \mid \Lambda$

3. $S \rightarrow aS \mid aSbS \mid a$

4. $S \rightarrow XY$
    $X \rightarrow aX \mid bX \mid a$
    $Y \rightarrow Ya \mid Yb \mid a$

5. $S \rightarrow Xa \mid Yb$
    $X \rightarrow Sb \mid b$
    $Y \rightarrow Sa \mid a$

6. (i) $S \rightarrow Saa \mid aSa \mid aaS$

    (ii)   How many words of length 12 are there in this language?

7. (i) $S \rightarrow (S)(S) \mid a$
           Parentheses are terminals here.

    (ii)   How many words are there in this language with exactly four *a*'s?

8. (i) $S \rightarrow XaY \mid YbX$
$X \rightarrow YY \mid aY \mid b$
$Y \rightarrow b \mid bb$

(ii) Draw the total language tree.

9. Explain briefly why it is not actually necessary to convert a CFG into CNF to use the algorithm of Theorem 28 to build a PDA that accepts the same language.

10. Let us consider the set of all regular expressions to be a language over the alphabet

$$\Sigma = \{\mathbf{a} \ \mathbf{b} \ (\ ) \ + \ * \ \Lambda\}$$

Let us call this language REGEX.

(i) Prove that REGEX is nonregular.

(ii) Prove that REGEX is context-free by producing a grammar for it.

(iii) Draw a PDA that accepts REGEX.

(iv) Draw a deterministic PDA that accepts REGEX.

11. (i) Draw a PDA in conversion form that has twice as many READ states as POP states.

(ii) Draw a PDA in conversion form that has twice as many POP states as READ states.

12. (i) In a summary table for a PDA, can there be more rows with PUSH than rows with no PUSH?

(ii) In a summary table for PDA, can there be more rows that PUSH more than one letter than there are rows that PUSH no letter?

(iii) On a path through a PDA generated by a word in the language of the PDA, can there be more rows that PUSH more than one letter than rows that PUSH no letters?

13. Consider the PDA used as an example in the proof of Theorem 29, the PDA for the language $\{a^{2n}b^n\}$. Of the 33 productions listed in this chapter as being in the CFG for the row-language, it was shown that some (for example, PROD 22, PROD 23, PROD 24, and PROD 19) can be dropped from the grammar since they can never be used in the derivation of any word in the row-language. Which of the remaining 23 nonterminals can be used in any productions? Why?

14. Write out the reduced CFG for the row-language formed by deleting the useless nonterminals in Problem 13 above. Draw the total language tree to demonstrate that the language accepted by the PDA is in fact $\{a^{2n}b^n\}$.

15.   Consider this PDA:

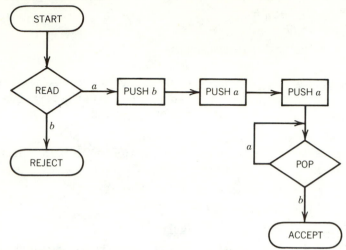

   (i)   What is the language of words it accepts?
   (ii)   Put it into conversion form.
   (iii)   Build a summary table for this PDA.

16.   (i)   Write out the CFG for the row-language. Do not list useless *Nets*.
      (ii)   Write out the CFG for the language accepted by this machine.

17.   (i)   Simplify the CFG of Problem 16 by deleting unused productions.
      (ii)   Prove this CFG generates the language of the machine above.

18.   Starting with the CFG

$$S \rightarrow aSb \mid ab$$

   for $\{a^n b^n\}$
   (i)   Put this CFG into CNF.
   (ii)   Take this CNF and make a PDA that accepts this language.
   (iii)   Take this PDA and put it into conversion form. (Feel free to eliminate useless paths and states.)
   (iv)   Now take this PDA and build a summary table for it.

19.   (i)   From the summary table produced in Problem 18, write out the productions of the CFG that generate the row-language of the PDA.
      (ii)   Convert this to the CFG that generates the actual language of the PDA (not the row-language).

20.   Prove that every context-free language over the alphabet $\{a,b\}$ can be accepted by a PDA with three READ states.

CHAPTER 19

CONTEXT-FREE LANGUAGES

In Part I after finding machines that act as acceptors or recognizers for regular languages, we discussed some properties of the whole class of regular languages. We showed that the union, the product, the Kleene closure, the complement, and the intersection of regular languages are all regular. We are now at the same point in our discussion of context-free languages. In this section we prove that the union, the product, and the Kleene closure of context-free languages are context-free. What we shall not do is show that the complement and intersection of context-free languages are context-free. Rather, we show in the next two chapters that this is not true in general.

THEOREM 30

If L_1 and L_2 are context-free languages, then their union, $L_1 + L_2$, is also a context-free language. In other words, the context-free languages are closed under union.

421

PROOF 1 (by Grammars)

This will be a proof by constructive algorithm, which means that we shall show how to create the grammar for $L_1 + L_2$ out of the grammars for L_1 and L_2.

Since L_1 and L_2 are context-free languages, there must be some CFG's that generate them.

Let the CFG for L_1 have the start symbol S and the nonterminals A, B, C . . . Let us change this notation a little by renaming the start symbol S_1 and the nonterminals A_1, B_1, C_1 . . . All we do is add the subscript 1 onto each character. For example, if the grammar were originally

$$S \rightarrow aS \mid SS \mid AS \mid \Lambda$$
$$A \rightarrow AA \mid b$$

it would become

$$S_1 \rightarrow aS_1 \mid S_1S_1 \mid A_1S_1 \mid \Lambda$$
$$A_1 \rightarrow A_1A_1 \mid b$$

where the new nonterminals are S_1 and A_1.

Notice that we leave the terminals alone. Clearly, the language generated by this CFG is the same as before, since the added 1's do not affect the strings of terminals derived.

Let us do something comparable to a CFG that generates L_2. We add a subscript 2 to each symbol. For example,

$$S \rightarrow AS \mid SB \mid \Lambda$$
$$A \rightarrow aA \mid a$$
$$B \rightarrow bB \mid b$$

becomes

$$S_2 \rightarrow A_2S_2 \mid S_2B_2 \mid \Lambda$$
$$A_2 \rightarrow aA_2 \mid a$$
$$B_2 \rightarrow bB_2 \mid b$$

Again we should note that this change in the names of the nonterminals has no effect on the language generated.

Now we build a new CFG with productions and nonterminals that are those of the rewritten CFG for L_1 and the rewritten CFG for L_2 plus the new start symbol S and the additional production:

$$S \rightarrow S_1 \mid S_2$$

Because we have been careful to see that there is no overlap in the use of nonterminals, once we begin $S \rightarrow S_1$ we cannot then apply any productions from the grammar for L_2. All words with derivations that start $S \rightarrow S_1$ belong to L_1, and all words with derivations that begin $S \rightarrow S_2$ belong to L_2.

All words from both languages can obviously be generated from S. Since we have created a CFG that generates the language $L_1 + L_2$, we conclude it is a context-free language.   ∎

EXAMPLE

Let L_1 be PALINDROME. One CFG for L_1 is

$$S \rightarrow aSa \mid bSb \mid a \mid b \mid \Lambda$$

Let L_2 be $\{a^n b^n \text{ where } n \geq 0\}$. One CFG for L_2 is

$$S \rightarrow aSb \mid \Lambda$$

Theorem 30 recommends the following CFG for $L_1 + L_2$:

$$S \rightarrow S_1 \mid S_2$$
$$S_1 \rightarrow aS_1a \mid bS_1b \mid a \mid b \mid \Lambda$$
$$S_2 \rightarrow aS_2b \mid \Lambda$$

∎

No guarantee was made in this proof that the grammar proposed for $L_1 + L_2$ was the simplest or most intelligent CFG for the union language, as we can see from the following.

EXAMPLE

One CFG for the language EVENPALINDROME is

$$S \rightarrow aSa \mid bSb \mid \Lambda$$

One CFG for the language ODDPALINDROME is

$$S \rightarrow aSa \mid bSb \mid a \mid b$$

Using the algorithm of the proof above we produce the following CFG for PALINDROME:

$$\text{PALINDROME} = \text{EVENPALINDROME} + \text{ODDPALINDROME}$$

$$S \rightarrow S_1 \mid S_2$$
$$S_1 \rightarrow aS_1a \mid bS_1b \mid \Lambda$$
$$S_2 \rightarrow aS_2a \mid bS_2b \mid a \mid b$$

We have seen more economical grammars for this language before. ■

No stipulation was made in this theorem that the set of terminals for the two languages had to be the same.

EXAMPLE

Let L_1 be PALINDROME over the alphabet $\Sigma_1 = \{a,b\}$, while L_2 is $\{c^n d^n$ where $n \geq 0\}$ over the alphabet $\Sigma_2 = \{c,d\}$. Then one CFG that generates $L_1 + L_2$ is:

$$S \rightarrow S_1 \mid S_2$$
$$S_1 \rightarrow aS_1a \mid bS_1b \mid a \mid b \mid \Lambda$$
$$S_2 \rightarrow cS_2d \mid \Lambda$$

This is a language over the alphabet $\{a,b,c,d\}$. ■

In the proof of this theorem we made use of the fact that context-free languages are generated by context-free grammars. However, we could also have proven this result using the alternative fact that context-free languages are those accepted by PDA's.

PROOF 2 (by Machines)

Since L_1 and L_2 are context-free languages, we know (from the previous chapter) that there is a PDA_1 that accepts L_1 and a PDA_2 that accepts L_2.

We can construct a PDA_3 that accepts the language of $L_1 + L_2$ by amalgamating the START states of these two machines. This means that we draw only one START state and from it come all the edges that used to come from either prior START state.

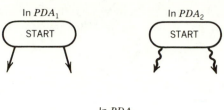

becomes

In PDA_3

Once an input string starts on a path on this combined machine, it follows the path either entirely within PDA_1 or entirely within PDA_2 since there are no cross-over edges.

Any input reaching an ACCEPT state has been accepted by one machine or the other and so is in L_1 or in L_2. Also any word in $L_1 + L_2$ can find its old path to acceptance on the subpart of PDA_3 that resembles PDA_1 or PDA_2. ∎

Notice how the nondeterminism of the START state is important in the proof above. We could also do this amalgamation of machines using a single-edge START state by weaseling our way out, as we saw in Chapter 17.

EXAMPLE

Consider these two machines:

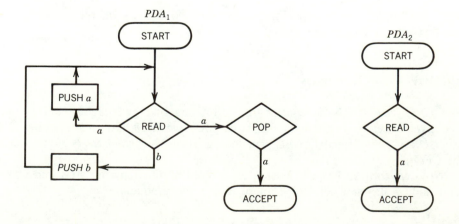

PDA_1 accepts the language of all words that contain a double a. PDA_2 accepts all words that begin with an a. The machine for $L_1 + L_2$ is:

PDA_3

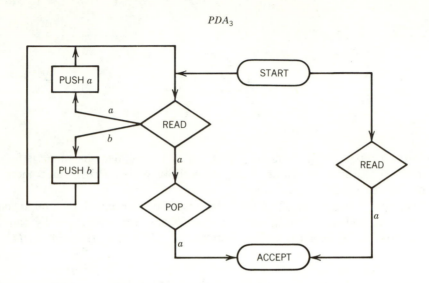

Notice that we have drawn PDA_3 with only one ACCEPT state by combining the ACCEPT states from PDA_1 and PDA_2.

This was not mentioned in the algorithm in the proof, but it only simplifies the picture without changing the substance of the machine. ■

THEOREM 31

If L_1 and L_2 are context-free languages, then so is L_1L_2. In other words, the context-free languages are closed under product.

PROOF 1 (by Grammars)

Let CFG_1 and CFG_2 be context-free grammars that generate L_1 and L_2, respectively. Let us begin with the same trick we used last time: putting a 1 after every nonterminal in CFG_1 (including S) and a 2 after every nonterminal in CFG_2.

Now we form a new CFG using all the old productions in CFG_1 and CFG_2 and adding the new START symbol S and the production

$$S \rightarrow S_1 S_2$$

Any word generated by this CFG has a front part derived from S_1 and a rear derived from S_2. The two sets of productions cannot cross over and interact with each other because the two sets of nonterminals are completely disjoint. It is therefore in the language L_1L_2.

The fact that any word in L_1L_2 can be derived in this grammar should be no surprise. ∎

(We have taken a little liberty with mathematical etiquette in our use of the phrase ". . . should be no surprise." It is more accepted to use the cliches "obviously . . ." or "clearly . . ." or "trivially . . .". But it is only a matter of style. A proof only needs to explain enough to be convincing. Other virtues a proof might have are that it be interesting lead to new results or be constructive. The proof above is at least the latter.)

EXAMPLE

Let L_1 be PALINDROME and CFG_1 be

$$S \rightarrow aSa \mid bSb \mid a \mid b \mid \Lambda$$

Let L_2 be $\{a^n b^n$ where $n \geq 0\}$ and CFG_2 be

$$S \rightarrow aSb \mid \Lambda$$

The algorithm in the proof recommends the CFG:

$$S \rightarrow S_1 S_2$$
$$S_1 \rightarrow aS_1a \mid bS_1b \mid a \mid b \mid \Lambda$$
$$S_2 \rightarrow aS_2b \mid \Lambda$$

for the language L_1L_2. ∎

(?)PROOF 2 (by Machines)

For the previous theorem we gave two proofs: one grammatical and one mechanical. There is an obvious way to proceed to give a machine proof for this theorem too. The front end of the word should be processed by one PDA and the rear end of the word processed on the second PDA. Let us see how this idea works out.

If we have PDA_1 that accepts L_1 and PDA_2 that accepts L_2, we can try to build the machine PDA_3 that accepts L_1L_2 as follows.

Draw a black dot. Now take all the edges of PDA_1 that feed into any ACCEPT state and redirect them into the dot. Also take all the edges that come from the START state of PDA_2 and draw them coming out of the dot. Erase the old PDA_1 ACCEPT and the old PDA_2 START states.

becomes

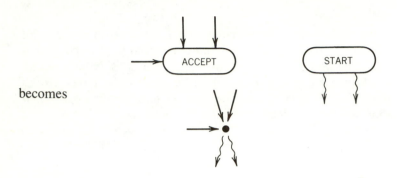

This kind of picture is not legal in a pushdown automaton drawing because we did not list "a black dot" as one of the pieces in our definition of PDA. The black dot is not necessary. We wish to connect every state that leads to ACCEPT-PDA_1 to every state in PDA_2 that comes from START-PDA_2. We can do this by edges drawn directly pointing from one machine to another. Alternately the edges from PDA_1 can lead into a new artificial state: PUSH *OVER*, that is followed immediately by POP *OVER* whose nondeterministic edges all labeled *OVER* continue to PDA_2. Let us call this the black dot.

For an input string to be accepted by the new PDA its path must first reach the black dot and then proceed from the dot to the ACCEPT states of PDA_2. There is no path from the START (of PDA_1) to ACCEPT (of PDA_2) without going through the dot. The front substring with a path that leads up to the dot would be accepted by PDA_1, and the remaining substring with a path that leads from the dot to ACCEPT would be accepted by PDA_2. Therefore, all words accepted by this new machine are in the language L_1L_2.

It is also obvious that any word in L_1L_2 is accepted by this new machine. Not so fast.

We did not put an end-of-proof mark, ■, after the last sentence because the proof actually is not valid. It certainly sounds valid. But it has a subtle flaw, which we shall illustrate.

When an input string is being run on PDA_1 and it reaches ACCEPT, we may not have finished reading the entire INPUT TAPE. The two PDA's that were given in the example above (which we have redrawn below) illustrate this point perfectly. In the first we reach the ACCEPT state right after reading a double *a* from the INPUT TAPE. The word *baabbb* will reach ACCEPT on this machine while it still has three *b*'s unread.

The second machine presumes that it is reading the first letter of the L_2 part of the string and checks to be sure that the very first letter it reads is an a.

If we follow the algorithm as stated above, we produce the following. From

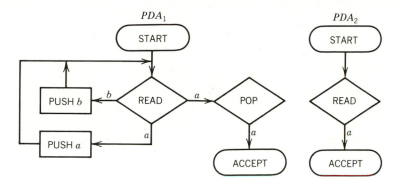

we get

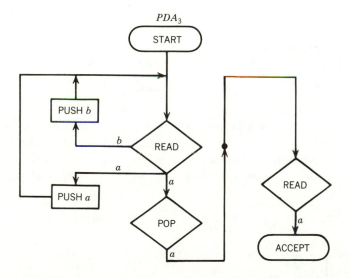

The resultant machine will reject the input string $(baabbb)(aa)$ even though it is in the language L_1L_2 because the black dot is reached after the third letter and the next letter it reads is a b, not the desired a, and the machine will crash. Only words containing aaa are accepted by this machine.

For this technique to work, we must insist that PDA_1, which accepts L_1, have the property that it reads the whole input string before accepting. In other words, when the ACCEPT state is encountered, there must be no unread input left. What happens if we try to modify PDA_1 to meet this requirement? Suppose we use PDA_1 version 2 as below, which employs a technique from the proof of Theorem 27:

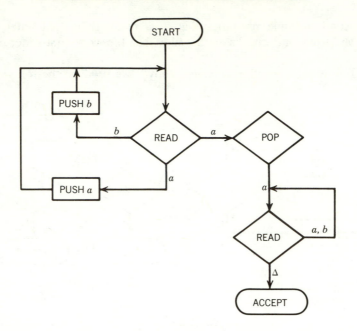

This machine does have the property that when we get to ACCEPT there is nothing left on the TAPE. This is guaranteed by the READ loop right before ACCEPT. However, when we process the input (*baabbb*)(*aa*), we shall read all eight letters before reaching ACCEPT and there will be nothing left to process on PDA_2 because we have *insisted* that the TAPE be exhausted by the first machine. Perhaps it is better to leave the number of letters read before the first ACCEPT up to the machine to decide nondeterministically.

If we try to construct PDA_3 using PDA_1 version 3 as shown below, with a nondeterministic feed into the black dot, we have another problem.

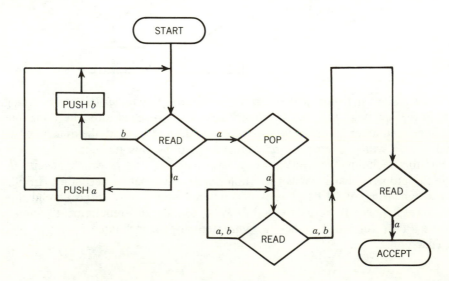

This conglomerate will accept the input $(baabbb)(bba)$ by reading the first two b's of the second factor in the PDA_1 part and then branching through the black dot to read the last letter on the second machine. However, this input string actually is in the language L_1L_2, since it is also of the form $(babbbbb)(a)$.

So this PDA_3 version works in this particular instance, but does it work in *all cases?* Are we convinced that even though we have incorporated some nondeterminism there are no undesirable strings accepted?

As it stands, the discussion above is no proof. Luckily this problem does not affect the first proof, which remains valid. This explains why we put the "?" in front of the word "proof" above. No matter how rigorous a proof appears, or how loaded with mathematical symbolism, it is always possible for systematic oversights to creep in undetected. The reason we have proofs at all is to try to stop this. But we never really know. We can never be sure that human error has not made us blind to substantial faults. The best we can do, even in purely symbolic abstract mathematics, is to try to be very very clear and complete in our arguments, to try to understand what is going on, and to try many examples.

THEOREM 32

If L is a context-free language, then L^* is one too. In other words, the context-free languages are closed under Kleene star.

PROOF

Let us start with a CFG for the language L. As always, the start symbol for this language is the symbol S. Let us as before change *this symbol* (but no other nonterminals) to S_1 throughout the grammar. Let us then add to the list of productions the new production:

$$S \to S_1 S \mid \Lambda$$

Now we can, by repeated use of this production, start with S and derive:

$$S \Rightarrow S_1 S \Rightarrow S_1 S_1 S \Rightarrow S_1 S_1 S_1 S \Rightarrow S_1 S_1 S_1 S_1 S$$
$$\Rightarrow S_1 S_1 S_1 S_1 S_1 S \Rightarrow S_1 S_1 S_1 S_1 S_1$$

Following each of these S_1's independently through the productions of the original CFG, we can form any word in L^* made up of five concatenated words from L. To convince ourselves that the productions applied to the various separate word factors do not interfere in undesired ways we need only think of the derivation tree. Each of these S_1's is the root of a distinct branch. The productions along one branch of the tree do not effect those on another. Similarly, any word in L^* can be generated by starting with enough copies of S_1. ∎

EXAMPLE

If the CFG is

$$S \rightarrow aSa \mid bSb \mid a \mid b \mid \Lambda$$

(which generates PALINDROME), then one possible CFG for PALINDROME* is

$$S \rightarrow XS \mid \Lambda$$
$$X \rightarrow aXa \mid bXb \mid a \mid b \mid \Lambda$$

Notice that we have used the symbol X instead of the nonterminal S_1, which was indicated in the algorithm in the proof. Of course, this makes no difference.   ■

PROBLEMS

In Problems 1 through 14, find CFG's for the indicated languages over $\Sigma = \{a, b\}$. When n appears as an exponent, it means $n = 1, 2, 3, \ldots$

1.   All words that start with an a or are of the form $a^n b^n$.

2.   All words that start with a b or are of the form $a^n b^n$.

3.   All words that have an equal number of a's and b's or are of the form $a^n b^n$.

4.   All words of the form $a^m b^n$, where $m > n$ or the form $a^n b^n$.

5.   All words in EVEN-EVEN*.

6.   All words of the form

$a^n b^n a^m b^m$, where $n, m = 1$ 2 3 $\ldots$ but m need not $= n$
$= \{abab \quad aabbab \quad abaabb \ldots .aaaabbbbab \; aaabbbaaaabbb \ldots \}$

7. All words of the form

$$a^x b^y a^z, \text{ where } x, y, z = 1\ 2\ 3 \ldots \text{ and } x + z = y$$
$$= \{abba \quad aabba \quad abbbaa \quad aabbbbaa \ldots\}$$

Hint: The concatenation of a word of the form $a^n b^n$ with a word of the form $b^m a^m$ gives a word of the form $a^x b^y a^z$, where $y = x + z$.

8. All words of the form

$$a^n b^{2n} a^m b^{2m}, \text{ where } n, m = 1\quad 2\quad 3\quad \ldots \text{ but } m \text{ need not } = n$$
$$= \{abbabb \quad abbaabbbb \quad aabbbbabb \ldots\}$$

9. All words of the form

$$a^x b^y a^z, \text{ where } x, y, z = 1\quad 2\quad 3\quad \ldots \text{ and } y = 2x + 2z$$
$$= \{abbbba \quad abbbbbbaa \quad aabbbbbbba \ldots\}$$

10. All words of the form

$$a^x b^y a^z, \text{ where } x, y, z = 1\quad 2\quad 3\quad \ldots \text{ and } y = 2x + z$$
$$= \{abbba \quad abbbbaa \quad aabbbbba \ldots\}$$

11. (i) All words of the form

$$a^x b^y a^z, \text{ where } x, y, z = 1\quad 2\quad 3\quad \ldots$$
$$\text{and}$$
$$y = 5x + 7z$$

   (ii) For any two positive integers p and q the language of all words of the form

$$a^x b^y a^z, \text{ where } x, y, z = 1\quad 2\quad 3\quad \ldots$$
$$\text{and}$$
$$y = px + qz$$

12.   (i)   All words of the form

$$a^x b^y a^z b^w, \text{ where } x, y, z, w = 1 \quad 2 \quad 3 \quad \ldots$$
$$\text{and}$$
$$y > x \qquad \text{and} \qquad z > w$$
$$\text{and}$$
$$x + z = y + w$$

Hint: Think of these words as:

$$(a^p \, b^p) \, (b^q \, a^q) \, (a^r \, b^r)$$

(ii)   What happens if we throw away the restrictions $y > x$ and $z > w$?

13.   (i)   Find a CFG for the language of all words of the form

$$a^n b^n \text{ or } b^n a^n, \text{ where } n = 1 \quad 2 \quad 3 \quad \ldots$$

(ii)   Is the Kleene closure of the language in part (i) the language of all words with an equal number of a's and b's that we have called EQUAL?

(iii)   Using the algorithm from Theorem 32, find the CFG that generates the closure of the language in part (i).

(iv)   Compare this to the CFG for the language EQUAL given before.

(v)   Write out all the words in

(Language of part (i))*

that have eight or fewer letters.

14.   Use the results of Theorems 30, 31, and 32 and a little ingenuity and the recursive definition of regular languages to provide a new proof that all regular languages are context-free.

15.   (i) Find a CFG for the language:

$$L_1 = \mathbf{a(bb)}^*$$

(ii)   Find a CFG for the language L_1^*.

Using the appropriate algorithm from this chapter,

(iii)   Find a CFG for the language $L_2 = \mathbf{(bb)}^*\mathbf{a.}$

(iv)   Find a CFG for L_2^*.

(v)   Find a CFG for

$$L_3 = \mathbf{bba}^*\mathbf{bb} + \mathbf{bb}$$

(vi)   Find a CFG for L_3*

(vii) Find a CFG for

$$L_1* + L_2* + L_3*$$

(viii) Compare the CFG in (vii) to

$$S \rightarrow aS \mid bbS \mid \Lambda$$

Show that they generate the same language.

16. A *substitution* is the action of taking a language L and two strings of terminals called s_a and s_b and changing every word of L by substituting the string s_a for each a and the string s_b for each b in the word. This turns L into a completely new language. Let us say for example that L was the language defined by the regular expression:

$$\mathbf{a*(bab* + aa)*}$$

and say that:

$$s_a = bb \qquad s_b = a$$

then L would become the language defined by the regular expression

$$\mathbf{(bb)*(abba* + bbbb)*}$$

(i)   Prove that after any substitution any regular language is still regular.
(ii)   Prove that after any substitution a CFL is still context-free.

17. Find PDA's that accept
(i) $\{a^n b^m$, where $n, m = 1 \quad 2 \quad 3 \ldots$ and $n \neq m\}$
(ii) $\{a^x b^y a^z$, where $x, y, z = 1 \quad 2 \quad 3 \ldots$ and $x + z = y.\}$
(iii) $L_1 L_2$, where
       $L_1 = $ all words with a double a
       $L_2 = $ all words that end in a

18. If L is any language, then we can define L^+ as the collection of all words that are formed by concatenating at least one word from L. This is related to the definition of $L*$ in the same way just as the regular expression $\mathbf{a^+}$ is related to the regular expression $\mathbf{a*}$.
(i)   If Λ is a word in L, show that $L^+ = L*$
(ii)   Show that L^+ is always the product of the languages L and $L*$:

$$L^+ = LL*$$

(iii)   If L is a CFL, we have shown how to find a CFG that generates $L*$. Show how to find a CFG that generates L^+.

(iv)   If L is a CFL, show how to build a PDA for $L*$. Show how to build a PDA for L^+ from the PDA for L.

19.   Let L_1 be any finite language and let L_2 be accepted by PDA_2. Show how to build a PDA that accepts L_1L_2.

20.   (i)   Some may think that the machine argument that tried to prove Theorem 31 could be made into a real proof by using the algorithms of Theorem 27 to convert the first machine into one that empties its STACK and TAPE before accepting. If while emptying the TAPE a nondeterministic leap is made to the START state of the second machine, it appears that we can accept exactly the language L_1L_2. Demonstrate the folly of this belief.

(ii)   Show that Theorem 31 can have a machine proof if the machines are those developed in Theorem 28.

(iii)   Provide a machine proof for Theorem 32.

CHAPTER 20

NON-CONTEXT-FREE
LANGUAGES

We are now going to answer the most important question about context-free languages: Are all languages context-free? No.

To prove this we have to make a very careful study of the mechanics of word production from grammars. Let us consider a CFG that is in Chomsky normal form. All of its productions are of the form:

$$\text{Nonterminal} \rightarrow \text{Nonterminal Nonterminal}$$

or else

$$\text{Nonterminal} \rightarrow \text{terminal}$$

Let us, for the moment, abandon the disjunctive BNF notation:

$$N \rightarrow \ldots \,|\, \ldots \,|\, \ldots \,|\, \ldots$$

and instead write each production as a separate line and number them:

PROD 1 $N \rightarrow \ldots$
PROD 2 $N \rightarrow \ldots$
PROD 3 $N \rightarrow \ldots$

. . .   . . .

In the process of a particular left-most derivation for a particular word in a context-free language, we have two possibilities:

1.   No production has been used more than once.
2.   At least one production has been repeated.

Every word with a derivation that satisfies the first possibility can be defined by a string of production numbers that has no repetitions. Since there are only finitely many productions to begin with, there can be only finitely many words of this nature.

For example, if there are 106 productions,

PROD 1

PROD 2

PROD 3

. . .

PROD 106

then there are exactly 106! possible permutations of them. Some of these sequences of productions when applied to the start symbol S will lead to the generation of a word by left-most derivation and some (many) will not.

Suppose we start with S and after some partial sequence of applications of productions we arrive at a string of all terminals. Since there is no left-most nonterminal, let us say that the remaining productions that we may try to apply leave this word unchanged.

We are considering only left-most derivations. If we try to apply a production with a left-side nonterminal that is not the same as the left-most nonterminal in the working string, the system crashes—the sequence of productions does not lead to a word.

For example, consider the CFG for EVENPALINDROME:

PROD 1 $S \rightarrow aSa$
PROD 2 $S \rightarrow bSb$
PROD 3 $S \rightarrow \Lambda$

All possible permutations of the three productions are:

PROD 1	$S \Rightarrow aSa$		PROD 1	$S \Rightarrow aSa$
PROD 2	$\Rightarrow abSba$		PROD 3	$\Rightarrow aa$
PROD 3	$\Rightarrow abba$		PROD 2	$\Rightarrow aa$
PROD 2	$S \Rightarrow bSb$		PROD 2	$S \Rightarrow bSb$
PROD 1	$\Rightarrow baSab$		PROD 3	$\Rightarrow bb$
PROD 3	$\Rightarrow baab$		PROD 1	$\Rightarrow bb$
PROD 3	$S \Rightarrow \Lambda$		PROD 3	$S \Rightarrow \Lambda$
PROD 1	$\Rightarrow \Lambda$		PROD 2	$\Rightarrow \Lambda$
PROD 2	$\Rightarrow \Lambda$		PROD 1	$\Rightarrow \Lambda$

The only words in EVENPALINDROME that can be generated without repetition of production are Λ, aa, bb, $abba$, and $baab$. Notice that $aaaa$, which is just as short as $abba$, cannot be produced without repeating PROD 1.

In general, not all sequences of productions lead to left-most derivations. For example, consider the following CFG for the language ab^*:

$$
\begin{array}{ll}
\text{PROD 1} & S \rightarrow XY \\
\text{PROD 2} & X \rightarrow a \\
\text{PROD 3} & Y \rightarrow bY \\
\text{PROD 4} & Y \rightarrow \Lambda
\end{array}
$$

Only productions with a left side that is S can be used first. The only possible first production in a left-most derivation here is PROD 1. After this, the left-most nonterminal is X, not Y, so that PROD 3 does not apply yet. The only sequences of productions (with no production used twice) that lead to words in this case are:

PROD 1	$S \Rightarrow XY$		PROD 1	$S \Rightarrow XY$
PROD 2	$\Rightarrow aY$		PROD 2	$\Rightarrow aY$
PROD 3	$\Rightarrow abY$	and	PROD 4	$\Rightarrow a$
PROD 4	$\Rightarrow ab$		PROD 3	$\Rightarrow a$

So the only words in this language that can be derived without repeated productions are a and ab.

THEOREM 33

Let G be a CFG in Chomsky normal form. Let us call the productions of the form:

$$\text{Nonterminal} \to \text{Nonterminal Nonterminal}$$

live and the productions of the form:

$$\text{Nonterminal} \to \text{terminal}$$

dead.

There are only finitely many words in the language generated by G with a left-most derivation that does not use any of the live productions at least twice. In other words, if we are restricted to using the live productions at most once each, we can generate only finitely many words by left-most derivations.

PROOF

The question we shall consider is: How many nonterminals are there in the working strings at different stages in the production of a word?

Suppose we start (in some abstract CFG in CNF that we need not specify) with:

$$S \Rightarrow AB$$

The right side, the working string, has exactly two nonterminals. If we apply the live production:

$$A \to XY$$

we get:

$$\Rightarrow XYB$$

which has three nonterminals. Now applying the dead production:

$$X \to b$$

we get:

$$\Rightarrow bYB$$

with two nonterminals. But now applying the live production:

$$Y \to SX$$

we get:

$$\Rightarrow bSXB$$

with three nonterminals again.

Every time we apply a live production we increase the number of nonterminals by one. Every time we apply a dead production we decrease the number of nonterminals by one. Since the net result of a derivation is to start with one nonterminal, S, and end up with none (a word of solid terminals), the net effect is to lose a nonterminal. Therefore, in all cases, to arrive at a string of only terminals, we must apply one more dead production than live production.

For example (again these derivations are in some arbitrary, uninteresting CFG's in CNF),

$S \Rightarrow b$		$S \Rightarrow XY$		$S \Rightarrow AB$
		$\Rightarrow aY$		$\Rightarrow XYB$
		$\Rightarrow aa$		$\Rightarrow bXB$
	or		or	$\Rightarrow bSXB$
				$\Rightarrow baXB$
				$\Rightarrow baaB$
				$\Rightarrow baab$
0 live		1 live		3 live
1 dead		2 dead		4 dead

Let us suppose that the grammar G has exactly

$$p \text{ live productions}$$

and

$$q \text{ dead productions}$$

Since any derivation that does not reuse a live production can have at most p live productions, it must have at most $(p + 1)$ dead productions. Each letter in the final word comes from the application of some dead production. Therefore, all words generated from G without repeating any live productions have at most $(p + 1)$ letters in them.

Therefore, we have shown that the words of the type described in this theorem cannot be more than $(p + 1)$ letters long. Therefore, there can be at most finitely many of them. ∎

Notice that this proof applies to any derivation, not just left-most derivations. However, we are interested only in the left-most situation.

Suppose that a left-most Chomsky derivation used the same live production twice. What would be the consequences?

Let us start with a CFG for the language NONNULLPALINDROME:

$$S \rightarrow aSa \mid bSb \mid a \mid b \mid aa \mid bb$$

We can easily see that all palindromes except Λ can be generated from this grammar. We "Chomsky-ize" it as follows:

Original Form	Form of Theorem 23	CNF
$S \rightarrow aSa$	$S \rightarrow ASA$	$S \rightarrow AX$
$S \rightarrow bSb$	$S \rightarrow BSB$	$X \rightarrow SA$
$S \rightarrow a$	$S \rightarrow a$	$S \rightarrow BY$
$S \rightarrow b$	$S \rightarrow b$	$Y \rightarrow SB$
$S \rightarrow aa$	$S \rightarrow AA$	$S \rightarrow AA$
$S \rightarrow bb$	$S \rightarrow BB$	$S \rightarrow BB$
$A \rightarrow a$		$S \rightarrow a$
$B \rightarrow b$		$S \rightarrow b$
		$A \rightarrow a$
		$B \rightarrow b$

The left-most derivation of the word *abaaba* in this grammar is:

$$
\begin{aligned}
S &\Rightarrow AX \\
&\Rightarrow a\ X \\
&\Rightarrow a\ SA \\
&\Rightarrow a\ BYA \\
&\Rightarrow ab\ YA \\
&\Rightarrow ab\ SBA \\
&\Rightarrow ab\ AABA \\
&\Rightarrow aba\ ABA \\
&\Rightarrow abaa\ BA \\
&\Rightarrow abaab\ A \\
&\Rightarrow abaaba
\end{aligned}
$$

When we start with a CFG in CNF, in *all* left-most derivations, each intermediate step is a working string of the form:

$\Rightarrow$ (string of solid terminals) (string of solid Nonterminals)

This is a special property of *left-most Chomsky working strings*. To emphasize this separation of the terminals and the nonterminals in the derivation above, we have inserted a meaningless space between the two substrings.

Let us consider some arbitrary, unspecified CFG in CNF.

Suppose that we employ some live production, say,

$$Z \rightarrow XY$$

twice in the derivation of some word w in this language. That means that at one point in the derivation, just before the duplicated production was used the first time, the left-most Chomsky working string had the form

$$\Rightarrow (s_1)\ Z\ (s_2)$$

where s_1 is a string of terminals and s_2 is a string of nonterminals. At this point the left-most nonterminal is Z. We now replace this Z with XY according to the production and continue the derivation. Since we are going to apply this production again at some later point, the left-most Chomsky working string will sometime have the form:

$$\Rightarrow (s_1)\ (s_3)\ Z\ (s_4)$$

where s_1 is the same string of terminals unchanged from before (once the terminals have been derived in the front they stay put, nothing can dislodge them) s_3 is a newly formed string of terminals, and s_4 is the string of non-terminals remaining. We are now about to apply the production $Z \rightarrow XY$ for the second time.

Where did this second Z come from? Either the second Z is a **tree descendant** of the first Z or else it comes from something in the old s_2. By the phrase "tree descendant" we mean that in the derivation tree there is an ever-downward path from one Z to the other.

Let us look at an example of each possibility.

Case 1. Let us consider an arbitrary grammar:

$$S \rightarrow AZ$$
$$Z \rightarrow BB$$
$$B \rightarrow ZA$$
$$A \rightarrow a$$
$$B \rightarrow b$$

as we proceed with the derivation of some word we find:

$$S \Rightarrow AZ$$
$$\Rightarrow aZ$$
$$\Rightarrow aBB$$
$$\Rightarrow abB$$
$$\Rightarrow abZA$$

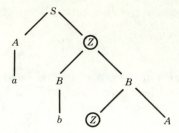

As we see from the derivation tree, the second Z was derived (descended) from the first. We can see this from the diagram because there is a downward path from the first Z to the second.

On the other hand we could have something like this.

Case 2. In the arbitrary grammar:

$$S \rightarrow AA$$
$$A \rightarrow BC$$
$$C \rightarrow BB$$
$$A \rightarrow a$$
$$B \rightarrow b$$

as we proceed with the derivation of some word we find:

$$S \Rightarrow AA$$
$$\Rightarrow BCA$$
$$\Rightarrow bCA$$
$$\Rightarrow bBBA$$

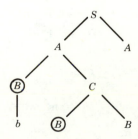

Two times the left-most nonterminal is B, but the second B is not descended from the first B in the tree. There is no downward path from the first B to the second B.

We shall now show that in an infinite language we can always find an example of Case 1.

THEOREM 34

If G is a CFG in CNF that has

$$p \text{ live productions}$$

and

$$q \text{ dead productions}$$

and if w is a word generated by G that has more than 2^p letters in it, then somewhere in every derivation tree for w there is an example of some non-terminal (call it Z) being used twice as the left-most nonterminal where the second Z is descended from the first Z.

PROOF

Why did we include the arithmetical condition that:

$$\text{length}(w) > 2^p?$$

This condition ensures that the production tree for w has more than p rows (generations). This is because at each row in the derivation tree the number of symbols in the working string can at most double.

For example, in some abstract CFG in CNF we may have a derivation tree that looks like this:

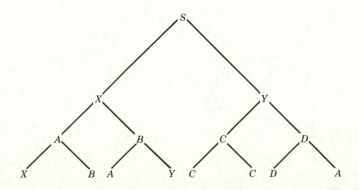

(In this figure the nonterminals are chosen completely arbitrarily.) If the bottom row has more than 2^p letters, the tree must have more than $p + 1$ rows.

Let us consider the last terminal that was one of the letters formed on the bottom row of the derivation tree for w by a dead production, say,

$$X \rightarrow b$$

The letter b is not necessarily the right-most letter in w, but it is a letter formed after more than p generations of the tree. That means it has more than p direct ancestors up the tree.

From the letter b we trace our way back up through the tree to the top, which is the start symbol S. In this backward trace we encounter one nonterminal after another in the inverse order in which they occurred in the derivation. Each of these nonterminals represents a production. If there are more than p rows to retrace, then there have been more than p productions in the ancestor path from b to S.

But there are only p different live productions possible in the grammar G; so if more than p have been used in this ancestor-path, then some live productions have been used more than once.

The nonterminal on the left side of this repeated live production has the property that it occurs twice (or more) on the descent line from S to b. This then is a nonterminal that proves our theorem.

Before stamping the end-of-proof box, let us draw an illustration, a totally arbitrary tree for a word w in a grammar we have not even written out:

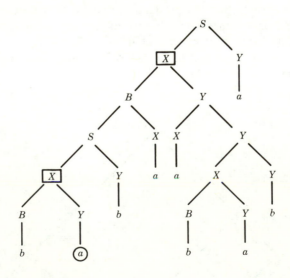

The word w is *babaababa*. Let us trace the ancestor-path of the circled terminal a from the bottom row up.

a came from Y by the production $Y \rightarrow a$
Y came from X by the production $X \rightarrow BY$
X came from S by the production $S \rightarrow XY$
S came from B by the production $B \rightarrow SX$
B came from X by the production $X \rightarrow BY$
X came from S by the production $S \rightarrow XY$

If the ancestor chain is long enough, one production must be used twice. In this example, $X \rightarrow BY$ is used twice and $S \rightarrow XY$ is used twice. The two X's that have boxes drawn around them satisfy the conditions of the theorem. One of them is descended from the other in the derivation tree of w. ∎

DEFINITION

In a given derivation of a word in a given CFG a nonterminal is said to be **self-embedded** if it ever occurs as a tree descendant of itself. ◙

Theorem 34 says that in any CFG all sufficiently long words have left-most derivations that include a self-embedded nonterminal.

EXAMPLE

Consider the CFG for NONNULLPALINDROME

$$S \rightarrow AX \qquad S \rightarrow b$$
$$X \rightarrow SA \qquad S \rightarrow AA$$
$$S \rightarrow BY \qquad S \rightarrow BB$$
$$Y \rightarrow SB \qquad A \rightarrow a$$
$$S \rightarrow a \qquad B \rightarrow b$$

There are six live productions, so, according to Theorem 34, it would require a word of more than $2^6 = 64$ letters to guarantee that each derivation has a self-embedded nonterminal in it.

If we are only looking for one example of a self-embedded nonterminal we can find such a tree much more easily than that. Consider this derivation tree for the word *aabaa*.

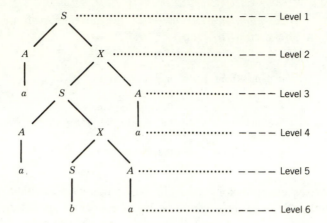

This tree has six levels, so it cannot quite *guarantee* a self-embedded non-terminal, but it has one anyway. Let us begin with the *b* on level 6 and trace its path back up to the top:

"The *b* came from *S* which came from *X*, which came from *S*, which came from *X*, which came from *S*".

In this way we find that the production $X \rightarrow SA$ was used twice in this tree segment:

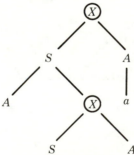

The self-embedded nonterminal that we find in the example above, using the algorithm given in the proof of Theorem 34, is not just a nonterminal that is descended from itself. It is more. It is a nonterminal, say *Z*, that was replaced by a certain production that later gave birth to another *Z* that was also replaced by the *same production* in the derivation of the word. Specifically, the first *X* was replaced by the production $X \rightarrow SA$ and so was its descendant. We can use this fact, with the self-embedded *X*'s in this example to make some new words.

The tree above proceeds from *S* down to the first *X*. Then from the *second* *X* the tree proceeds to the final word. But once we have reached the second

X, instead of proceeding with the generation of the word as we have it here, we could instead have repeated the same sequence of productions that the first X initiated, thereby arriving at a third X. The second can cause the third exactly as the first caused the second. From this third X we could proceed to a final string of all terminals in a manner exactly as the second X did.

Let us review this logic once more slowly. The first X can start a subtree that produces the second X, and the second X can start a subtree that produces all terminals, but it does not have to. *Instead the second can begin a subtree exactly like the first's*. This will then produce a *third X*. From this third X we can produce a string of all terminals as the second X used to. Instead of having this list of productions applied

Down	$S \rightarrow \cdots$
to the	$\cdots$
first X	$\cdots$
	$X \rightarrow \cdots$
Down	$\cdots$
to the	$\cdots$
second X	$X \rightarrow \cdots$
Down	$\cdots$
to the	$\cdots$
end of the	
word	

the middle section of productions could have been repeated:

Down to the	$S \rightarrow \cdots$
first X	$\cdots$
	$\cdots$
	$X \rightarrow \cdots$
Down to the	$\cdots$
second X	$\cdots$
	$X \rightarrow \cdots$
Repeat the	$\cdots$
last section of	$\cdots$
productions	$X \rightarrow \cdots$
Now down to	$\cdots$
the end of	$\cdots$
the word	

Everyone should feel the creeping sensation of familiarity. Is this not like finding a circuit and looping around it an extra time?

Let us illustrate this process with a completely arbitrary concrete example.

Suppose we have these productions in a nonsense CFG to illustrate the point.

$$S \rightarrow AB$$
$$S \rightarrow BC$$
$$A \rightarrow BA$$
$$C \rightarrow BB$$
$$B \rightarrow AB$$
$$A \rightarrow a$$
$$B \rightarrow b$$
$$C \rightarrow b$$

One word that has a self-embedded nonterminal is *aabab*.

Step Number	Derivation	Productions Used
1	$S \Rightarrow AB$	$S \rightarrow AB$
2	$\Rightarrow BAB$	$A \rightarrow BA$
3	$\Rightarrow ABAB$	$B \rightarrow AB$
4	$\Rightarrow aBAB$	$A \rightarrow a$
5	$\Rightarrow aABAB$	$B \rightarrow AB$
6	$\Rightarrow aaBAB$	$A \rightarrow a$
7	$\Rightarrow aabAB$	$B \rightarrow b$
8	$\Rightarrow aabaB$	$A \rightarrow a$
9	$\Rightarrow aabab$	$B \rightarrow b$

From line 2 to line 3 we employed the production $B \rightarrow AB$. This same production is employed from line 4 to line 5. Not only that, but the second left-most B is a descendant of the first.

Therefore, we can make new words in this language by repeating the sequence of productions used in lines 3, 4, and 5 as if the production for line 5 was the beginning of the same sequence again:

Derivation	Productions Used	
$S \Rightarrow AB$	$S \rightarrow AB$	
$\Rightarrow BAB$	$A \rightarrow BA$	
$\Rightarrow ABAB$	$B \rightarrow AB$	
$\Rightarrow aBAB$	$A \rightarrow a$	Identical
$\Rightarrow aABAB$	$B \rightarrow AB$	sequence
$\Rightarrow aaBAB$	$A \rightarrow a$	of
$\Rightarrow aaABAB$	$B \rightarrow AB$	productions
$\Rightarrow aaaBAB$	$A \rightarrow a$	

⇒ *aaabAB*	$B \rightarrow b$
⇒ *aaabaB*	$A \rightarrow a$
⇒ *aaabab*	$B \rightarrow b$

The sequence can be repeated as often as we wish.

Derivation	Productions Used
S ⇒ *AB*	$S \rightarrow AB$
⇒ *BAB*	$A \rightarrow BA$
⇒ *ABAB*	$B \rightarrow AB$
⇒ *aBAB*	$A \rightarrow a$
⇒ *aABAB*	$B \rightarrow AB$
⇒ *aaBAB*	$A \rightarrow a$
⇒ *aaABAB*	$B \rightarrow AB$
⇒ *aaaBAB*	$A \rightarrow a$
⇒ *aaaABAB*	$B \rightarrow AB$
⇒ *aaaaBAB*	$A \rightarrow a$
⇒ *aaaaABAB*	$B \rightarrow AB$
⇒ *aaaaaBAB*	$A \rightarrow a$
⇒ *aaaaabAB*	$B \rightarrow b$
⇒ *aaaaabaB*	$A \rightarrow a$
⇒ *aaaaabab*	$B \rightarrow b$

Identical repeated sequences of productions

This repetition can be explained in tree diagrams as follows. What is at first

Derivation tree for *aabab*

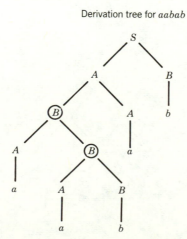

can become

Derivation tree for *aaaaabab*

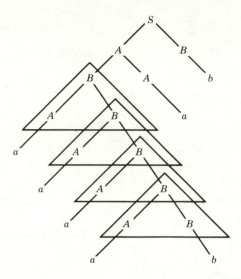

Even though the self-embedded nonterminals must be along the same descent line in the tree, they do not have to be consecutive nodes (as in the example above) but may be more distant relatives.

For the arbitrary CFG

$$S \rightarrow AB$$
$$A \rightarrow BC$$
$$C \rightarrow AB$$
$$A \rightarrow a$$
$$B \rightarrow b$$

One possible derivation tree is

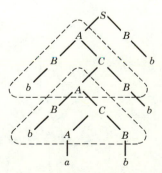

In this case we find the self-embedded nonterminal *A* in the dotted triangle. Not only is *A* self-embedded, but it has already been used twice the same way (two identical dotted triangles).

Again we have the option of repeating the sequence of productions in the triangle as many times as we want.

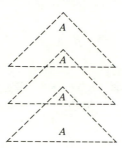

This is why in the last theorem it was important that the repeated nonterminals be along the same line of descent.

This entire situation is analogous to the Pumping Lemma of Chapter 11, so it should be no surprise that this technique was discovered by the same people: Bar-Hillel, Perles, and Shamir. The following theorem, called "the Pumping Lemma for context-free languages," states the consequences of reiterating a sequence of productions from a self-embedded nonterminal.

THEOREM 35

If *G* is any CFG in CNF with *p* live productions and *w* is any word generated by *G* with length greater than 2^p, then we can break *w* up into five substrings:

$$w = u\ v\ x\ y\ z$$

such that *x* is not Λ and *v* and *y* are not both Λ and such that all the words

$$\left.\begin{array}{l} uvxyz \\ uvvxyyz \\ uvvvxyyyz \\ uvvvvxyyyyz \\ \quad .\ .\ . \end{array}\right\} = uv^nxy^nz \quad \text{for } n = 1,\ 2,\ 3,\ .\ .\ .$$

can also be generated by *G*.

PROOF

From our previous theorem, we know that if the length of w is greater than 2^p, then there are repeated nonterminals along the same descent line in each tree diagram for w; that is, there are always self-embedded nonterminals.

Let us now fix in our minds one specific derivation of w in G. Let us call one self-embedded nonterminal P and let the production it uses to regenerate itself be

$$P \to QR$$

(These names are all arbitrary.)

Let us suppose that the tree for w looks like this:

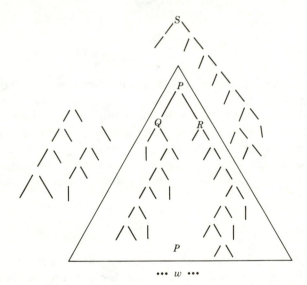

The triangle indicated encloses the whole part of the tree generated from the first P down to where the second P is produced. It is not clear whether the second P comes from the Q-branch or the R-branch of the tree, nor does it matter.

Let us divide w into these five parts:

u = the substring of all the letters of w generated to the left of the triangle above. (This may be Λ.)

v = the substring of all the letters w generated by the derivation inside the triangle to the left of the lower nonterminal P.

(This may be Λ.)

x = the substring of w descended from the lower P.

(This may not be Λ since this nonterminal must turn into some terminals.)

$y =$ the substring of w of the terminals generated by the derivation inside the triangle to the right of the lower P.

(This may be Λ, but, as we shall see, not if $v = \Lambda$.)

$z =$ the substring of all the letters of w generated to the right of the triangle. (This may be Λ.)

Pictorially:

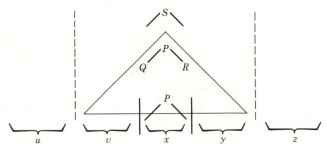

For example, the following is a complete tree in an unspecified grammar.

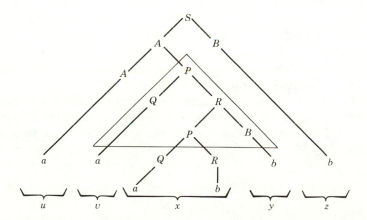

Now it is possible that either u or z or both might be Λ, as in the following example where S is the self-embedded nonterminal and all the letters of w are generated inside the triangle:

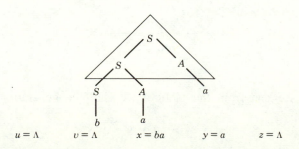

However, either v is not Λ or y is not Λ or both are not Λ. This is because in the picture

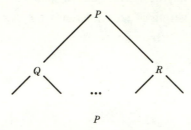

even though the lower P can come from the upper Q or from the upper R, there must still be some other letters in w that come from the other branch, the branch that does not produce this P.

This is important, since if it were ever possible that

$$v = y = \Lambda$$

then

$$u\ v^n\ x\ y^n\ z$$

would not be an interesting collection of words.

Now let us ask ourselves, what happens to the end word if we change the derivation tree by repeating the productions inside the triangle? In particular, what is the word generated by this doubled tree (which we know to be a valid derivation tree in G)?

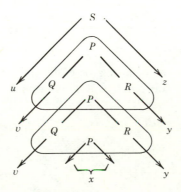

As we see can from the picture, we shall be generating the word

$$u\ v\ v\ x\ y\ y\ z$$

Remember that u, v, x, y, z are all strings of a's and b's, and this is another word generated by the same grammar. The u part comes from S to the left of the whole triangle. The first v is what comes from inside the first triangle to the left of the second P. The second v comes from the stuff in the second triangle to the left of the third P. The x part comes from the third P. The first y part comes from the stuff in the second triangle to the right of the third P. The second y comes from the stuff in the first triangle to the right of the second P. The z, as before, comes from S from the stuff to the right of the first triangle.

It may be helpful for a minute to forget grammars and concentrate on tree surgery. We start with two identical derivations of w drawn as trees. From the first tree we clip off the branch growing from the first P. On the second tree we clip off the branch growing from the second P. Then we graft the branch from the first tree onto the second tree at the cut node. The resultant tree is necessarily a possible derivation tree in this grammar. What word does it produce? The grafted branch from the first tree produces the string vxy. The pruned branch the second tree lost produced only the string x. Replacing x by vxy turns $uvxyz$ into $uvvxyyz$.

If we tripled the triangle we would get

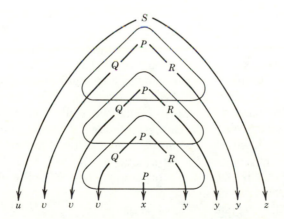

which is a derivation tree for the word

$$u \; v \; v \; v \; x \; y \; y \; y \; z$$

which must therefore also be in the language generated by G.

In general, if we repeat the triangle n times we get a derivation tree for the word

$$u \; v^n \; x \; y^n \; z$$

which must therefore also be in the language generated by G. ∎

EXAMPLE

We shall analyze a specific case in detail and then consider the situation in its full generality. Let us consider the following CFG in CNF:

$$S \rightarrow PQ$$
$$Q \rightarrow QS \mid b$$
$$P \rightarrow a$$

The word *abab* can be derived from these productions by the following derivation tree.

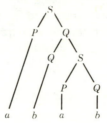

Here we see three instances of self-embedded nonterminals. The top S has another S as a descendant. The Q on the second level has two Q's as descendants, one on the third level and one of the fourth level. Notice, however, that the two P's are not descended one from the other, so neither is self-embedded. For the purposes of our example, we shall focus on the self-embedded Q's of the second and third levels, although it would be just as good to look at the self-embedded S's. The first Q is replaced by the production $Q \rightarrow QS$, while the second is replaced by the production $Q \rightarrow b$. Even though the two Q's are not replaced by the same productions, they are self-embedded and we can apply the technique of this theorem.

If we draw this diagram:

$$S \Rightarrow PQ$$
$$\Rightarrow aQ$$
$$\Rightarrow aQS$$
$$\Rightarrow abS$$
$$\Rightarrow abPQ$$
$$\Rightarrow abaQ$$
$$\Rightarrow abab$$

we can see that the word w can be broken into the five parts *uvxyz* as follows.

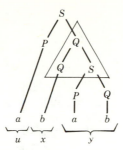

We have located a self-embedded nonterminal Q and we have drawn a triangle enclosing the descent from Q to Q. The u-part is the part generated by the tree to the left of the triangle. This is only the letter a. The v-part is the substring of w generated inside the triangle to the left of the repeated nonterminal. Here, however, the repeated nonterminal Q, *is* the left-most character on the bottom of the triangle. Therefore, $v = \Lambda$. The x-part is the substring of w descended directly from the second occurrence of the repeated nonterminal (the second Q). Here that is clearly the single letter b. The y-part is the rest of w generated inside the triangle, that is, whatever comes from the triangle to the right of the repeated nonterminal. In this example this refers to everything that descends from the second S, which is the only thing at the bottom of the triangle to the right of the Q. What is descended from this S is the substring ab. The z-part is all that is left of w, that is, the substring of w that is generated to the right of the triangle. In this case, that is nothing, $z = \Lambda$.

$$u = a \qquad v = \Lambda \qquad x = b \qquad y = ab \qquad z = \Lambda$$

The following diagram shows what would happen if we repeated the triangle from the second Q just as it descends from the first Q.

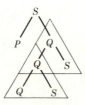

If we now fill in the picture by adding the terminals that descend from the P, the Q, and the S's, as we did in the original tree, we complete the new derivation tree as follows.

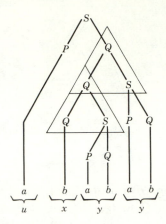

Here we can see that the repetition of the triangle does not effect the *u*-part. There was one *u*-part and there still is only one *u*-part. If there were a *z*-part, that too would be left alone, since these are defined outside the triangle. There is no *v*-part in this example, but we can see that the *y*-part (its right-side counterpart) has become doubled. Each of the two triangles generates exactly the same *y*-part. In the middle of all this the *x*-part has been left alone. There is still only one bottom repeated nonterminal from which the *x*-part descends. The word with this derivation tree can be written as *uvvxyyz*.

$$u\ v\ v\ x\ y\ y\ z\ =\ a\ \Lambda\ \Lambda\ b\ ab\ ab\ \Lambda$$
$$=\ ababab$$

If we had tripled the triangle instead of only doubling it, we would obtain

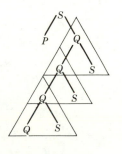

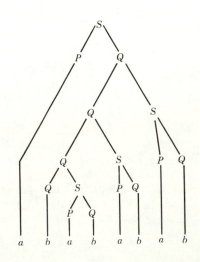

This word we can easily recognize as

$$u \; v \; v \; v \; x \; y \; y \; y \; z = a \; \Lambda \; \Lambda \; \Lambda \; b \; ab \; ab \; ab \; \Lambda$$

In general, after n occurrences of the triangle we obtain a derivation of the word

$$u \; v^n \; x \; y^n \; z$$

■

Now that we understand this specific example in excruciating detail, we can speed up our analysis of the general case.

In general, a derivation tree with a self-embedded nonterminal N looks like this.

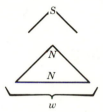

Let us decompose w into the five substrings u,v,x,y,z as defined above.

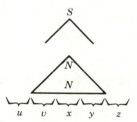

Let us reiterate the production sequence from N to N as it occurs in the triangle.

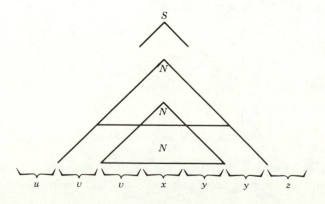

And again

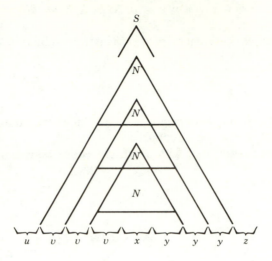

After n triangles we have

$$u \underbrace{v \ldots v}_{n \text{ of them}} x \underbrace{y \ldots y}_{n \text{ of them}} z$$

$$= u \quad v^n \quad x \quad y^n z$$

All the trees we have described are valid derivation trees in our initial grammar, so all the words they generate must be in the language generated by that grammar. ∎

As before, the reason this is called the Pumping Lemma and not the Pumping Theorem is that it is to be used for some presumedly greater purpose. In particular, it is used to prove that certain languages are not context-free or as we shall say, they are **non-context-free.**

EXAMPLE

Let us consider the language:

$$\{a^n b^n a^n \quad \text{for } n = 1\ 2\ 3 \ldots\}$$
$$= \{aba \quad aabbaa \quad aaabbbaaa \ldots\}$$

Let us think about how this language could be accepted by a PDA. As we read the first a's, we must accurately store the information about exactly how many a's there were, since $a^{100}b^{99}a^{99}$ must be rejected but $a^{99}b^{99}a^{99}$ must be accepted. We can put this count into the STACK. One obvious way is to put the a's themselves directly into the STACK, but there may be other ways of doing this. Next we read the b's and we have to ask the STACK if the number of b's is the same as the number of a's. The problem is that asking the STACK this question makes the STACK forget the answer afterward, since we pop stuff out and cannot put it back until we see that the STACK is empty. There is no temporary storage possible for the information that we have popped out. The method we used to recognize the language $\{a^n b^n\}$ was to store the a's in the STACK and then destroy them one-for-one with the b's. After we have checked that we have the correct number of b's, the STACK is empty. No record remains of how many a's there were originally. Therefore, we can no longer check whether the last clump of a's in $a^n b^n a^n$ is the correct size. In answering the first question, the information was lost. This STACK is like a student who forgets the entire course after the final exam.

All we have said so far is, "We don't see how this language can be context-free since we cannot think of a PDA to accept it." This is, of course, no proof. Maybe someone smarter can figure out the right PDA.

Suppose we try this scheme. For every a we read from the initial cluster we push two a's into the STACK. Then when we read b's we match them against the first half of the a's in the STACK. When we get to the last clump of a's we have exactly enough left in the STACK to match them also. The proposed PDA is this.

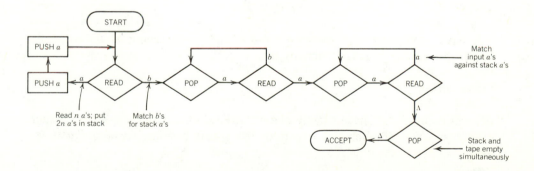

The problem with this idea is that we have no way of checking to be sure that the b's use up exactly *half* of the a's in the STACK. Unfortunately, the word $a^{10}b^8a^{12}$ is also accepted by this PDA. The first 10 a's are read and 20 are put into the STACK. Next 8 of these are matched against b's. Lastly, the 12 final a's match the a's remaining in the STACK and the word is accepted even though we do not want it in our language.

The truth is that nobody is ever going to build a PDA that accepts this language. This can be proven using the Pumping Lemma. In other words, we can prove that the language $\{a^n b^n a^n\}$ is non-context-free.

To do this, let us assume that this language could be generated by some CFG in CNF. No matter how many live productions this grammar has, some word in this language is bigger than 2^p. Let us assume that the word

$$w = a^{200}b^{200}a^{200}$$

is big enough (if it's not, we've got a bag full of much bigger ones).

Now we show that *any* method of breaking w into five parts

$$w = u \, v \, x \, y \, z$$

will mean that

$$u \, v^2 \, x \, y^2 \, z$$

cannot be in $\{a^n b^n a^n\}$.

There are many ways of demonstrating this, but let us take the quickest.

Observation

All words in $\{a^n b^n a^n\}$ have exactly one occurrence of the substring ab no matter what n is. Now if either the v-part or the y-part has the substring ab in it, then

$$u \, v^2 \, x \, y^2 \, z$$

will have more than one substring of ab, and so it cannot be in $\{a^n b^n a^n\}$. Therefore, neither v nor y contains ab.

Observation

All words in $\{a^n b^n a^n\}$ have exactly one occurrence of the substring ba no matter what n is. Now if either the v part or the y part has the substring ba in it, then

$$u \, v^2 \, x \, y^2 \, z$$

has more than one such substring, which no word in $\{a^n b^n a^n\}$ does. Therefore, neither v nor y contains ba.

The only possibility left is that v and y must be all a's, all b's, or Λ otherwise they would contain either ab or ba. But if v and y are blocks of one letter, then

$$u \, v^2 \, x \, y^2 \, z$$

has increased one or two clumps of solid letters (more a's if v is a's, etc.).

However, there are three clumps of solid letters in the words in $\{a^n b^n a^n\}$, and not all three of those clumps have been increased equally. This would destroy the form of the word.

For example, if

$$a^{200} b^{200} a^{200}$$

$$= \underset{u}{a^{200} b^{70}} \ \underset{v}{b^{40}} \ \underset{x}{b^{90} a^{82}} \ \underset{y}{a^3} \ \underset{z}{a^{115}}$$

then

$$u \, v^2 \, x \, y^2 \, z$$

$$= (a^{200} b^{70}) \, (b^{40})^2 \, (b^{90} a^{82}) \, (a^3)^2 \, (a^{115})$$

$$= a^{200} b^{240} a^{203}$$

$$\neq a^n b^n a^n \text{ for any } n$$

The b's and the second clump of a's were increased, but not the first a's. The exponents are no longer the same.

We must emphasize that there is *no possible* decomposition of this w into $uvxyz$. It is not good enough to show that *one* partition into five parts does not work. It should be understood that we have shown that *any* attempted partition into $uvxyz$ must fail to have $uvvxyyz$ in the language.

Therefore, the Pumping Lemma cannot successfully be applied to the language $\{a^n b^n a^n\}$ at all. But the Pumping Lemma does apply to all context-free languages.

Therefore, $\{a^n b^n a^n\}$ is not a context-free language. ∎

EXAMPLE

Let us take, just for the duration of this example, a language over the alphabet $\Sigma = \{a,b,c\}$. Consider the language:

$$\{a^n b^n c^n \text{ for } n = 1 \, 2 \, 3 \dots \}$$

$$= \{ \, abc \qquad aabbcc \qquad aaabbbccc \dots \}$$

We shall now prove that this language is non-context-free.
Suppose it were context-free and suppose that the word

$$w = a^{200} b^{200} c^{200}$$

is large enough so that the Pumping Lemma applies to it. That means larger than 2^p, where p is the number of live productions. We shall now show that no matter what choices are made for the five parts u, v, x, y, z:

$$u \ v^2 \ x \ y^2 \ z$$

cannot be in the language.

Again we begin with some observations.

Observation

All words in $a^n b^n c^n$ have:

> Only one substring ab
>
> Only one substring bc
>
> No substring ac
>
> No substring ba
>
> No substring ca
>
> No substring cb

no matter what n is.

If v or y is not a solid block of one letter (or Λ), then

$$u \ v^2 \ x \ y^2 \ z$$

would have more of some of the two-letter substrings ab, ac, ba, bc, ca, cb than it is supposed to have. On the other hand, if v and y are solid blocks of one letter (or Λ), then one or two of the letters a, b, c would be increased in the word $uvvxyyz$ while the other letter (or letters) would not increase in quantity. But all the words in $a^n b^n c^n$ have equal numbers of a's, b's, and c's. Therefore, the Pumping Lemma cannot apply to the language $\{a^n b^n c^n\}$, which means that this language is non-context-free. ■

Theorem 13 and Theorem 35 have certain things in common. They are both called "Pumping Lemma," and they were both proven by Bar-Hillel, Perles, and Shamir. What else?

THEOREM 13

If w is a word in a regular language L and w is *long enough*, then w can be decomposed into three parts:

$$w = x \ y \ z$$

such that all the words

$$x \ y^n \ z$$

must also be in L. ■

THEOREM 35

If w is a word in a context-free language L and w is *long enough,* then w can be decomposed into five parts:

$$w = u \, v \, x \, y \, z$$

such that all the words

$$u \, v^n \, x \, y^n \, x$$

must also be in L. ∎

The proof of Theorem 13 is that the path for w must be so long that it contains a sequence of edges that we can repeat indefinitely. The proof of Theorem 35 is that the derivation for w must be so long that it contains a sequence of productions that we can repeat indefinitely.

We use Theorem 13 to show that $\{a^n b^n\}$ is not regular because it cannot contain both xyz and $xyyz$.

We use Theorem 35 to show that $\{a^n b^n a^n\}$ is not context-free because it cannot contain both $uvxyz$ and $uvvxyyz$.

One major difference is that the Pumping Lemma for regular languages acts on the machines while the Pumping Lemma for context-free languages acts on the algebraic representation, the grammar. Is it possible to pump a PDA? Is it possible to pump a regular expression? The symbol "$\Rightarrow$" we have been using means "after one substitution turns into" as in $S \Rightarrow XS$ or $AbXSB \Rightarrow AbXSb$.

There is another useful symbol that is employed in this subject. It is "$\overset{*}{\Rightarrow}$" and it means "after some number of substitutions turns into." For example, for the CFG:

$$S \rightarrow SSS \mid b$$

we could write:

$$S \overset{*}{\Rightarrow} bbb$$

instead of:

$$S \Rightarrow SSS \Rightarrow SSb \Rightarrow Sbb \Rightarrow bbb$$

In the CFG:

$$S \rightarrow SA \mid BS \mid BB \qquad X \rightarrow \Lambda$$
$$A \rightarrow X \mid a \qquad B \rightarrow b$$

we called A nullable because $A \rightarrow X$ and $X \rightarrow \Lambda$. In the new notation we could write:

$$A \overset{*}{\Rightarrow} \Lambda$$

In fact, we can give a neater definition for the word nullable based on the symbol $\overset{*}{\Rightarrow}$. It is:

$$N \text{ is } \textbf{nullable} \text{ if } N \overset{*}{\Rightarrow} \Lambda$$

This would have been of only marginal advantage in the proof of Theorem 21, since the meaning of the word nullable is clear enough anyway. It is usually our practice to introduce only that terminology and notation necessary to prove our theorems.

The use of the $*$ in the combination symbol $\overset{*}{\Rightarrow}$ is analogous to the Kleene use of $*$. It still means some undetermined number of repetitions.

In this chapter we made use of the human ability to understand pictures and to reason from them abstractly. Language and mathematical symbolism are also abstractions; the ability to reason from them is also difficult to explain. But it may be helpful to reformulate the argument in algebraic notation using $\overset{*}{\Rightarrow}$.

Our definition of a self-embedded nonterminal was one that appeared among its own descendants in a derivation tree. This can be formulated symbolically as follows:

DEFINITION

In a particular CFG, a nonterminal N is called **self-embedded** if there are strings of terminals v and y not both null, such that

$$N \overset{*}{\Rightarrow} vNy \qquad\qquad \blacksquare$$

This definition does not involve any tree diagrams, any geometric intuition, or any possibility of imprecision.

The Pumping Lemma can now be stated as follows.

Algebraic Form of the Pumping Lemma

If w is a word in a CFL and if w is long enough, [length(w) $> 2^p$], then there exists a nonterminal N and strings of terminals u, v, x, y, and z (where v and y are not both Λ) such that:

$$w = uvxyz$$

$$S \overset{*}{\Rightarrow} uNz$$

$$N \overset{*}{\Rightarrow} vNy$$

$$N \overset{*}{\Rightarrow} x$$

and therefore

$$u \ v^n \ x \ y^n \ z$$

must all be words in this language for any n.

The idea in the Algebraic Proof is

$$S \overset{*}{\Rightarrow} uNz$$

$$\overset{*}{\Rightarrow} u \ (vNy) \ z$$

$$= (uv) \ N \ (yz)$$

$$\overset{*}{\Rightarrow} (uv) \ (vNy) \ (yz)$$

$$= (uv^2) \ N \ (y^2z)$$

$$\overset{*}{\Rightarrow} (uv^2) \ (vNy) \ (y^2z)$$

$$= uv^3 \ N \ y^3z$$

$$\overset{*}{\Rightarrow} uv^n \ N \ y^nz$$

$$\overset{*}{\Rightarrow} uv^n \ x \ y^nz. \qquad \blacksquare$$

Some people are more comfortable with the algebraic argument and some are more comfortable reasoning from the diagrams. Both techniques can be mathematically rigorous and informative. There is no need for a blood feud between the two camps.

There is one more similarity between the Pumping Lemma for contex-free languages and the Pumping Lemma for regular languages. Just as Theorem 13 required Theorem 14 to finish the story, so Theorem 35 requires Theorem 36 to achieve its full power.

Let us look in detail at the proof of the Pumping Lemma. We start with a word w of more than 2^p letters. The path from some bottom letter back up to S contains more nonterminals than there are live productions. Therefore, some nonterminal is repeated along the path. Here is the new point: If we look for the first repeated nonterminal backing up from the letter, the second occurrence will be within p steps up from the terminal row (the bottom). Just because we said that length(w) $> 2^p$ does not mean it is only a little bigger. Perhaps length(w) $= 10^p$. Even so, the upper of the first self-embedded non-terminal pair scanning from the bottom encountered is within p steps of the bottom row in the derivation tree.

What significance does this have? It means that the total output of the upper of the two self-embedded nonterminals produces a string not longer than 2^p letters in total. The string it produces is vxy. Therefore, we can say that

$$\text{length } (vxy) < 2^p$$

This observation turns out to be very useful, so we call it a theorem: the Pumping Lemma with Length.

THEOREM 36

Let L be a CFL in CNF with p live productions.

Then any word w, in L with length $> 2^p$ can be broken into five parts:

$$w = uvxyz$$

such that

$$\text{length } (vxy) \leq 2^p$$
$$\text{length } (x) > 0$$
$$\text{length } (v) + \text{length } (y) > 0$$

and such that all the words

$$\left. \begin{array}{c} uvvxyyz \\ uvvvxyyyz \\ uvvvvxyyyyz \\ \cdot\ \ \cdot\ \ \cdot \end{array} \right\} uv^n\, xy^n\, z$$

are all in the language L.   ■

The discussion above has already proven this result.

We now demonstrate one application of a language that cannot be shown to be non-context-free by Theorem 35 but can be by Theorem 36.

EXAMPLE

Let us consider the language:

$$L = \{a^n b^m a^n b^m\}$$

where n and m are integers 1, 2, 3 . . . and n does not necessarily equal m.

$$L = \{abab \quad aabaab \quad abbabb \quad aabbaabb \quad aaabaaab \ldots \}$$

If we tried to prove that this language was non-context-free using Theorem 35 we could have

$$u = \Lambda$$
$$v = \text{first } a\text{'s} = a^x$$
$$x = \text{middle } b\text{'s} = b^y$$
$$y = \text{second } a\text{'s} = a^x$$
$$z = \text{last } b\text{'s} = b^y$$
$$uv^n\, xy^n\, z$$
$$= \Lambda\,(a^x)^n\, b^y\, (a^x)^n\, b^y$$

all of which *are* in L. Therefore we have no contradiction and the Pumping Lemma does apply to L.

Now let us try a Theorem 36-type approach. If L did have a CFG that generates it, let that CFG in CNF have p live productions. Let us look at the word

$$a^{2^p}\, b^{2^p}\, a^{2^p}\, b^{2^p}$$

This word has length long enough for us to apply Theorem 36 to it. But from Theorem 36 we know:

$$\text{length}(vxy) < 2^p$$

so v and y cannot be solid blocks of one letter separated by a clump of the other letter, since the separator letter clump is longer than the length of the whole substring vxy.

By the usual argument (counting substrings of "ab" and "ba"), we see that v and y must be one solid letter. But because of the length condition the letters must all come from the same clump. Any of the four clumps will do:

$$a^{2^p}\, b^{2^p}\, a^{2^p}\, b^{2^p}$$

However, this now means that some words not of the form

$$a^n b^m a^n b^m$$

must also be in L. Therefore, L is non-context-free. ∎

The thought that unifies the two Pumping Lemmas is that if we have a finite procedure to recognize a language, then some word in the language is so long that the procedure must begin to repeat some of its steps and at that point we can pump it further to produce a family of words. But what happens if the finite procedure can have infinitely many different steps? We shall consider this possibility in Chapter 24.

PROBLEMS

1.   Study this CFG for EVENPALINDROME:

$$S \rightarrow aSa$$
$$S \rightarrow bSb$$
$$S \rightarrow \Lambda$$

     List all the derivation trees in this language that do not have two equal nonterminals on the same line of descent, that is, that do not have a self-embedded nonterminal.

2.   Consider the CNF for NONNULLEVENPALINDROME given below:

$$S \rightarrow AX$$
$$X \rightarrow SA$$
$$S \rightarrow BY$$
$$Y \rightarrow SB$$
$$S \rightarrow AA$$
$$S \rightarrow BB$$
$$A \rightarrow a$$
$$B \rightarrow b$$

     (i)   Show that this CFG defines the language it claims to define.
     (ii)   Find all the derivation trees in this grammar that do not have a self-embedded nonterminal.
     (iii) Compare this result with Problem 1.

3.   The grammar defined in Problem 2 has six live productions. This means that the second theorem of this section implies that all words of more than $2^6 = 64$ letters must have a self-embedded nonterminal. Find a

better result. What is the smallest number of letters that guarantees that a word in this grammar has a self-embedded nonterminal in each of its derivations. Why does the theorem give the wrong number?

4. Consider the grammar given below for the language defined by **a*ba***.

$$S \rightarrow AbA$$
$$A \rightarrow Aa \mid \Lambda$$

(i) Convert this grammar to one without Λ-productions.
(ii) Chomsky-ize this grammar.
(iii) Find all words that have derivation trees that have no self-embedded nonterminals.

5. Consider the grammar for $\{a^n b^n\}$:

$$S \rightarrow aSb \mid ab$$

(i) Chomsky-ize this grammar.
(ii) Find all derivation trees that do not have self-embedded nonterminals.

6. Instead of the concept of *live productions* in CNF, let us define a *live nonterminal* to be one appearing as the left side of a live production. A *dead nonterminal*, N, is one with only productions of the single form:

$$N \rightarrow \text{terminal}$$

If m is the number of live nonterminals in a CFG in CNF, prove that any word w of length more than 2^m will have self-embedded nonterminals.

7. Illustrate the theorem in Problem 6 on the CFG in Problem 2.

8. Apply the theorem of Problem 6 to the following CFG for NONNULLPALINDROME:

$$
\begin{array}{ll}
S \rightarrow AX & S \rightarrow a \\
X \rightarrow SA & S \rightarrow b \\
S \rightarrow BY & A \rightarrow a \\
Y \rightarrow SB & B \rightarrow b \\
S \rightarrow AA & \\
S \rightarrow BB &
\end{array}
$$

9. Why must the repeated nonterminals be along the same line of descent for the trick of reiteration in Theorem 34 to work?

10. Prove that the language

$$\{a^n b^n a^n b^n \quad \text{for } n = 1\ 2\ 3\ 4 \ldots\}$$
$$= \{abab \quad aabbaabb \ldots\}$$

is non-context-free.

11. Prove that the language

$$\{a^n b^n a^n b^n a^n \quad \text{for } n = 1\ 2\ 3\ 4 \ldots\}$$
$$= \{ababa \quad aabbaabbaa \ldots\}$$

is non-context-free.

12. Let L be the language of all words of any of the following forms:

$$\{a^n, \quad a^n b^n, \quad a^n b^n a^n, \quad a^n b^n a^n b^n, \quad a^n b^n a^n b^n a^n \ldots \text{for } n = 1\ 2\ 3 \ldots\}$$
$$= \{a\ aa\ ab\ aaa\ aba\ aaaa\ aabb\ aaaaa\ ababa\ aaaaaa\ aaabbb\ aabbaa \ldots\}$$

    (i)   How many words does this language have with 105 letters?
    (ii) Prove that this language is non-context-free.

13. Is the language

$$\{a^n b^{2n} a^n \quad \text{for } n = 1\ \ 2\ \ 3 \quad \ldots\}$$
$$= \{abbba \quad aabbbbbbaa \ldots\}$$

context-free? If so, find a CFG for it. If not, prove so.

14. Consider the language:

$$\{a^n b^n c^m \quad \text{for } n, m = 1\ \ 2\ \ 3 \ldots, n \text{ not necessarily} = m\}$$
$$= \{abc \quad abcc \quad abbc \quad aabbcc \ldots\}$$

Is it context-free? Prove that your answer is correct.

15. Show that the language

$$\{a^n b^n c^n d^n \quad \text{for } n = 1\ \ 2\ \ 3 \ldots\}$$
$$= \{abcd \quad aabbccdd \ldots\}$$

is non-context free.

16. Let us recall the definition of *substitution* given in Chapter 19, Problem 16. Given a language L and two strings s_a and s_b, a substitution is the replacement of every a in the words in L by the string s_a and the replacement of every b by the string s_b. In Chapter 19 we proved that if L is any CFL and s_a and s_b are any strings, then the replacement language is also a CFL. Use this theorem to provide an alternative proof of the fact that $\{a^n b^n c^n\}$ is a non-context-free language.

17. Using the result about replacements from Problem 16, provide two other proofs of the fact that the language in Problem 15 is non-context-free.

18. Why does the Pumping Lemma argument not show that the language PALINDROME is not context-free? Show how v and y can be found such that $uv^n xy^n z$ are all also in PALINDROME no matter what the word w is.

19. Let VERYEQUAL be the language of all words over $\Sigma = \{a,b,c\}$ that have the same number of a's and b's and c's.

    VERYEQUAL
        $= \{abc \quad acb \quad bac \quad bca \quad cab \quad cba \quad aabbcc \quad aabcbc \dots \}$

    Notice that the order of these letters does not matter.
    Prove that VERYEQUAL is non-context-free.

20. The language EVENPALINDROME can be defined as all words of the form

$$s \ \text{reverse}(s)$$

    where s is any string of letters from $\{a,b\}^*$. Let us define the language UPDOWNUP as:
    $L = \{$all words of the form $s(\text{reverse}(s))s$ where s is in $(a + b)^*\}$
        $= \{aaa \quad bbb \quad aaaaaa \quad abbaab \quad baabba \ bbbbbb$
            $\dots aaabbaaaaaab\}$

    Prove that L is non-context-free.

CHAPTER 21

INTERSECTION
AND
COMPLEMENT

In Chapter 19 we proved that the union, product, and Kleene star closure of context-free languages are also context-free. This left open the question of intersection and complement. We now close this question.

THEOREM 37

The intersection of two context-free languages may or may not be context-free.

PROOF

We shall break this proof into two parts: may and may not.

May

All regular languages are context-free (Theorem 19). The intersection of two regular languages is regular (Theorem 12). Therefore, if L_1 and L_2 are regular and context-free then

$$L_1 \cap L_2$$

is both regular and context-free.

May Not

Let

$$L_1 = \{a^n b^n a^m, \quad \text{where } n,m = 1\ 2\ 3\ \dots$$
$$\text{but } n \text{ is not necessarily the same as } m\}$$
$$= \{aba \quad abaa \quad aabba \dots\}$$

To prove that this language is context-free, we present a CFG that generates it.

$$S \to XA$$
$$X \to aXb \mid ab$$
$$A \to aA \mid a$$

We could alternately have concluded that this language is context-free by observing that it is the product of the CFL $\{a^n b^n\}$ and the regular language **aa***
Let

$$L_2 = \{a^n b^m a^m, \quad \text{where } n,m = 1\ 2\ 3\ \dots$$
$$\text{but } n \text{ is not necessarily the same as } m\}$$
$$= \{aba \ aaba \ abbaa \dots\}$$

Be careful to notice that these two languages are different.

To prove that this language is context-free, we present a CFG that generates it:

$$S \to AX$$
$$X \to aXb \mid ab$$
$$A \to aA \mid a$$

Alternately we could observe that L_z is the product of the regular language **aa*** and the CFL $\{b^n a^n\}$.

Both languages are context-free, but their intersection is the language

$$L_3 = L_1 \cap L_2 = \{a^n b^n a^n \quad \text{for } n = 1\ 2\ 3\ \dots\}$$

since any word in both languages has as many starting a's as middle b's (to be in L_1) and as many middle b's as final a's (to be in L_2).

But in Chapter 20 we proved that this language L_3 is non-context-free. Therefore, the intersection of two context-free languages can be non-context-free. ∎

EXAMPLE (May)

If L_1 and L_2 are two CFL's and if L_1 is contained in L_2, then the intersection is L_1 again, which is still context-free, for example,

$$L_1 = \{a^n \quad \text{for } n = 1\ 2\ 3\ \ldots\}$$
$$L_2 = \text{PALINDROME}$$

L_1 is contained in L_2; therefore,

$$L_1 \cap L_2 = L_1$$

which is context-free.

Notice that in this example we do not have the intersection of two regular languages since PALINDROME is nonregular. ■

EXAMPLE (May)

Let:

$$L_1 = \text{PALINDROME}$$
$$L_2 = \text{language of } \mathbf{a^+b^+a^+} = \text{language of } \mathbf{aa^*bb^*aa^*}$$

In this case,

$$L_1 \cap L_2$$

is the language of all words with as many final a's as initial a's with only b's in between.

$$L_1 \cap L_2 = \{a^n b^m a^n \quad n,m = 1\ 2\ 3\ \ldots$$

$$\text{where } n \text{ is not necessarily equal to } m\}$$
$$= \{aba \quad abba \quad aabaa \quad aabbaa \ldots\}$$

This language is still context-free since it can be generated by this grammar:

$$S \rightarrow aSa \mid aBa$$
$$B \rightarrow bB \mid b$$

or accepted by this PDA:

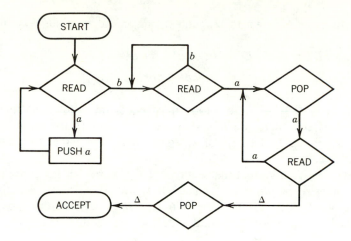

First, all the front a's are put into the STACK. Then the b's are ignored. Then we alternately READ and POP a's till both the INPUT TAPE and STACK run out simultaneously.

Again note that these languages are not both regular (one is, one is not). ∎

We mention that these two examples are not purely regular languages because the proof of the theorem as given might have conveyed the wrongful impression that the intersection of CFL's is a CFL only when the CFL's are regular.

EXAMPLE (May Not)

Let L_1 be the language

      EQUAL = all words with the same number of a's and b's

We know this language is context-free because we have seen a grammar that generates it:

$$S \rightarrow bA \mid aB$$
$$A \rightarrow bAA \mid aS \mid a$$
$$B \rightarrow aBB \mid bS \mid b$$

Let L_2 be the language

$$L_2 = \{a^n b^m a^n \quad n,m = 1\ 2\ 3\ldots\ n = m \text{ or } n \neq m\}$$

The language L_2 was shown to be context-free in the previous example. Now:

$$L_3 = L_1 \cap L_2 = \{a^n b^{2n} a^n \quad \text{for } n = 1\,2\,3\,\ldots\}$$
$$= \{abba \quad aabbbbaa \ldots\}$$

To be in $L_1 = $ EQUAL, the b-total must equal the a-total, so there are $2n$ b's in the middle if there are n a's in the front and in the back.

We use the Pumping Lemma of Chapter 20 to prove that this language is non-context-free.

As always, we observe that the sections of the word that get repeated cannot contain the substrings ab or ba, since all words in L_3 have exactly one of each substring. This means that the two repeated sections (the v-part and y-part) are each a clump of one solid letter. If we write some word w of L_3 as

$$w = u\,v\,x\,y\,z$$

then we can say of v and y that they are either all a's or all b's or one is Λ. However, if one is solid a's, that means that to remain a word of the form $a^n b^m a^n$ the other must also be solid a's since the front and back a's must remain equal. But then we would be increasing both clumps of a's without increasing the b's, and the word would then not be in EQUAL. If neither v nor y have a's, then they increase the b's without the a's and again the word fails to be in EQUAL.

Therefore, the Pumping Lemma cannot apply to L_3, so L_3 is non-context-free. ■

The question of when the intersection of two CFL's is a CFL is apparently very interesting. If an algorithm were known to answer this question it would be printed right here. Instead we shall move on to the question of complements. The story of complements is similarly indecisive.

THEOREM 38

The complement of a context-free language may or may not be context-free.

PROOF

The proof is in two parts:

May

If L is regular, then L' is also regular and both are context-free.

May Not

This is one of our few proofs by indirect argument.

Suppose the complement of *every* context-free language were context-free. Then if we started with two such languages, L_1 and L_2, we would know that L_1' and L_2' are also context-free. Furthermore,

$$L_1' + L_2'$$

would have to be context free by Theorem 30.

Not only that but,

$$(L_1' + L_2')'$$

would also have to be context-free, as the complement of a context-free language. But,

$$(L_1' + L_2')' = L_1 \cap L_2$$

and so the intersection of L_1 and L_2 must be context-free. But L_1 and L_2 are any arbitrary CFL's, and therefore *all* intersections of context-free languages would have to be context-free. But by the previous theorem we know that this is not the case.

Therefore, not all context-free languages have context-free complements. ∎

EXAMPLE (May)

All regular languages have been covered in the proof above. There are also some nonregular but context-free languages that have context-free complements. One example is the language of palindromes with an X in the center, PALINDROMEX. This is a language over the alphabet $\{a, b, X\}$.

$$= \{w \ X \ \text{reverse}(w), \text{ where } w \text{ is any string in } (\mathbf{a}+\mathbf{b})^*\}$$
$$= \{X \ aXa \ bXb \ aaXaa \ abXba \ baXab \ bbXbb \ \ldots \}$$

This language can be accepted (as we have seen in Chapter 17) by a deterministic PDA such as the one below:

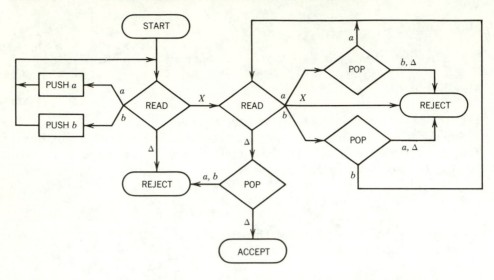

Since this is a deterministic machine, every input string determines some path from START to a halt state, either ACCEPT or REJECT. We have drawn in all possible branching edges so that no input crashes. The strings not accepted all go to REJECT. In every loop there is a READ statement that requires a fresh letter of input so that no input string can loop forever. (This is an important observation, although there are other ways to guarantee no infinite looping.)

To construct a machine that accepts exactly those input strings that this machine rejects, all we need to do is reverse the status of the halt states from ACCEPT to REJECT and vice versa. This is the same trick we pulled on FA's to find machines for the complement language.

In this case, the language L' of all input strings over the alphabet $\Sigma = \{a, b, X\}$ that are not in L is simply the language accepted by:

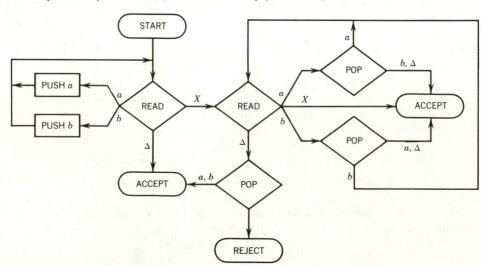

We may wonder why this trick cannot be used to prove that the complement of any context-free language is context-free, since they all can be defined by PDA's. The answer is *nondeterminism*.

If we have a nondeterministic PDA then the technique of reversing the status of the halt states fails.

Let us explain why. Remember that when we work with nondeterministic machines we say that any word that has *some* path to ACCEPT is in the language of that machine. In a nondeterministic PDA a word may have two possible paths, the first of which leads to ACCEPT and the second of which leads to REJECT. We accept this word since there is at least one way it can be accepted. Now if we reverse the status of each halt state we still have two paths for this word: the first now leads to REJECT and the second now leads to ACCEPT. Again we have to accept this word since at least one path leads to ACCEPT. The same word cannot be in both a language and its complement, so the halt-status-reversed PDA does not define the complement language.

Let us be more concrete about this point. The following (nondeterministic) PDA accepts the language NONNULLEVENPALINDROME:

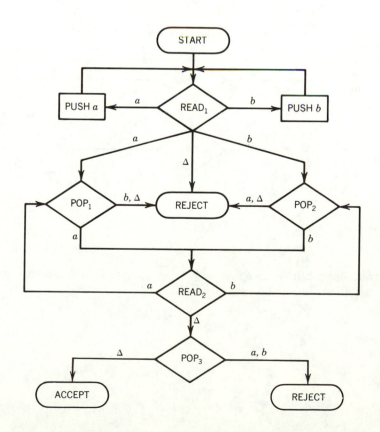

We have drawn this machine so that, except for the nondeterminism at the first READ, the machine offers no choice of path, and every alternative is labeled. All input strings lead to ACCEPT or REJECT, none crash or loop forever.

Let us reverse the status of the halt states to create this PDA

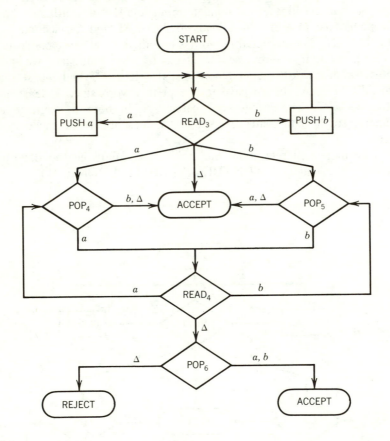

The word *abba* can be accepted by both machines. To see how it is accepted by the first PDA, we trace its path.

STATE	STACK	TAPE
START	Δ	abba
READ 1	Δ	ⱥbba
PUSH a	a	ⱥbba
READ 1	a	ⱥƀba
PUSH b	ba	ⱥƀba
READ 1	ba	ⱥƀƀa
(Choice) POP 2	a	ⱥƀƀa
READ 2	a	ⱥƀƀⱥ
POP 1	Δ	ⱥƀƀⱥ
READ 2	Δ	ⱥƀƀⱥΔ
POP 3	Δ	ⱥƀƀⱥΔ
ACCEPT		

To see how it can be accepted by the second PDA we trace this path:

STATE	STACK	TAPE
START	Δ	abba
READ 3	Δ	ⱥbba
PUSH a	a	ⱥbba
READ 3	a	ⱥƀba
(Choice) POP 5	Δ	ⱥƀba
ACCEPT		

There are many more paths this word can take in the second PDA that also lead to acceptance. Therefore halt-state reversal does not always change a PDA for L into a PDA for L'. ∎

We still owe an example of a context-free language with a complement that is non-context-free.

EXAMPLE (May Not)

Whenever we are asked for an example of a non-context-free language $\{a^n b^n a^n\}$ springs to mind. We seem to use it for everything. Surprisingly enough, its complement is context-free, as we shall now show.

This example takes several steps. First let us define the language M_{pq} as follows:

$$M_{pq} = \{a^p b^q a^r, \quad \text{where } p, q, r = 1\ 2\ 3 \dots$$
$$\text{but } p > q \text{ while } r \text{ is arbitrary}\}$$
$$= \{aaba \quad aaaba \quad aabaa \quad aaabaa \quad aaabba \dots\}$$

We know this language is context-free because it is accepted by the following CFG:

$$S \rightarrow AXA$$
$$X \rightarrow aXb \mid ab$$
$$A \rightarrow aA \mid a$$

The X part is always of the form $a^n b^n$, and when we attach the A-parts we get a string defined by the expression:

$$(\mathbf{aa}^*)\ (a^n b^n)\ (\mathbf{aa}^*)$$
$$= a^p b^q a^r, \text{ where } p > q$$

(*Note:* We are mixing regular expressions with things that are not regular expressions, but the meaning is clear anyway.)

This language can be shown to be context-free in two other ways. We could observe that M_{pq} is the product of the three languages $\mathbf{a}^+$ and $\{a^n b^n\}$ and $\mathbf{a}^+$

$$M_{pq} = \{\mathbf{a}^+\}\ \{a^n b^n\}\ \{\mathbf{a}^+\}$$

Since the product of two context-free languages is context-free, so is the product of three context-free languages.

We could also build a PDA to accept it. The machine would have three READ statements. The first would read the initial clump of a's and push them into the STACK. The second would read b's and correspondingly pop a's. When the second READ hits the first a of the third clump it knows the b's are over, so it pops another a to be sure the initial clump of a's (in the STACK) was larger than the clump of b's. Even when the input passes this test the machine is not ready to accept. We must be sure that there is nothing else on the INPUT TAPE but unread a's. If there is a b hiding behind these a's the input must be rejected. We therefore move into the third READ state which loops as long as a's are read, crashes if a b is read, and accepts as soon as a blank is encountered.

Let us also define another language:

$$M_{qp} = \{a^p b^q a^r, \quad \text{where } p, q, r = 1\ 2\ 3\ \ldots$$
$$\text{but } q > p \text{ whiie } r \text{ is arbitrary}\}$$
$$= \{abba \quad abbaa \quad abbba \quad abbaaa \quad aabbba \ldots\}$$

This language too is context-free since it can be generated by

$$S \rightarrow XBA$$
$$X \rightarrow aXb \mid ab$$
$$B \rightarrow bB \mid b$$
$$A \rightarrow aA \mid a$$

which we can interpret as

$$X \overset{*}{\Rightarrow} a^n b^n$$
$$B \overset{*}{\Rightarrow} \mathbf{b}^+$$
$$A \overset{*}{\Rightarrow} \mathbf{a}^+$$

Together this gives:

$$(a^n b^n)(\mathbf{bb^*})(\mathbf{aa^*})$$
$$= a^p b^q a^r, \quad \text{where } q > p$$

We can also write M_{qp} as the product of three context-free languages:

$$M_{qp} = \{a^n b^n\} \ \{\mathbf{b^+}\} \ \{\mathbf{a^+}\}$$

Of course, there is also a PDA that accepts this language (see Problem 2 below).

Let us also define the language

$$M_{pr} = \{a^p b^q a^r, \quad \text{where } p, q, r = 1\ 2\ 3\ \ldots$$
$$\text{but } p > r \text{ while } q \text{ is arbitrary}\}$$
$$= \{aaba \quad aaaba \quad aabba \quad aaabaa \ldots\}$$

This language is also context-free, since it can be generated by the CFG

$$S \rightarrow AX$$
$$X \rightarrow aXa \mid aBa$$
$$B \rightarrow bB \mid b$$
$$A \rightarrow aA \mid a$$

First we observe:

$$A \overset{*}{\Rightarrow} \mathbf{a}^+ \quad \text{and} \quad B \overset{*}{\Rightarrow} \mathbf{b}^+$$

Therefore, the X-part is of the form

$$a^n \mathbf{bb}^* a^n$$

So the words generated are of the form

$$(\mathbf{aa}^*)(a^n \mathbf{bb}^* a^n)$$
$$= a^p b^q a^r, \quad \text{where } p > r$$

We can see that this language is the product of context-free languages after we show that $\{a^n \mathbf{b}^+ a^n\}$ is context-free (see Problem 3 below).

Let us also define the language

$$M_{rp} = \{a^p b^q a^r, \quad \text{where } p, q, r = 1\ 2\ 3 \ldots$$
$$\text{but } r > p \text{ while } q \text{ is arbitrary}\}$$
$$= \{abaa \quad abaaa \quad aabaaa \quad abbaaa \ldots\}$$

One CFG for this language is

$$S \rightarrow XA$$
$$X \rightarrow aXa \mid aBa$$
$$B \rightarrow bB \mid b$$
$$A \rightarrow aA \mid a$$

which gives

$$A \overset{*}{\Rightarrow} \mathbf{a}^+$$
$$B \overset{*}{\Rightarrow} \mathbf{b}^+$$

$$X \overset{*}{\Rightarrow} a^n \mathbf{b}^+ a^n$$

$$S \overset{*}{\Rightarrow} (a^n \mathbf{bb}^* a^n)(\mathbf{aa}^*)$$

$$= a^p b^q a^r, \text{ where } r > p$$

We can see that this language too is the product of context-free languages when we show that $\{a^n \mathbf{b}^+ a^n\}$ is context-free.

Let us also define the language

$$M_{qr} = \{a^p b^q a^r, \quad \text{where } p, q, r = 1\, 2\, 3 \ldots$$

$$\text{but } q > r \text{ while } p \text{ is arbitrary}\}$$

$$= \{abba \quad aabba \quad abbba \quad abbbaa \ldots\}$$

One CFG for this language is

$$S \rightarrow ABX$$
$$X \rightarrow bXa \mid ba$$
$$B \rightarrow bB \mid b$$
$$A \rightarrow aA \mid a$$

which gives:

$$(\mathbf{aa}^*)(\mathbf{bb}^*)(b^n a^n)$$
$$= a^p b^q a^r, \text{ where } q > r$$

$$M_{qr} = \{\mathbf{a}^+\}\, \{\mathbf{b}^+\}\, \{b^n a^n\}$$

This language could also be defined by PDA (Problem 4 below).

Let us also define:

$$M_{rq} = \{a^p b^q a^r, \quad \text{where } p, q, r = 1\quad 2\quad 3\quad \ldots$$

$$\text{but } r > q \text{ while } p \text{ is arbitrary}\}$$

$$= \{abaa \quad aabaa \quad abaaa \quad abbaaa \ldots\}$$

One CFG that generates this language is

$$S \rightarrow AXA$$
$$X \rightarrow bXa \mid ba$$
$$A \rightarrow aA \mid a$$

which gives

$$(\mathbf{aa}*)(b^n a^n)(\mathbf{aa}*)$$
$$= a^p b^q a^r, \text{ where } r > q$$
$$M_{rq} =$$
$$\{\mathbf{a}^+\} \, \{b^n a^n\} \, \{\mathbf{a}^+\}$$

This can also be accepted by a PDA (Problem 5 below).

We need to define one last language.

$M = \{$the complement of the language defined by $\mathbf{aa}*\mathbf{bb}*\mathbf{aa}*\}$
$= \{$all words not of the form $a^p b^q a^r$ for $p, q, r = 1\ 2\ 3\ \ldots\}$
$= \{a \quad b \quad aa \quad ab \quad ba \quad bb \quad aaa \quad aab \quad abb \quad baa \quad bab \ldots\}$

M is context-free since it is regular (the complement of a regular language is regular by Theorem 11 and all regular languages are context-free by Theorem 26).

We could build a PDA for this language too (Problem 6 below).

Let us finally assemble the language L, the union of these seven languages.

$$L = M_{pq} + M_{qp} + M_{pr} + M_{rp} + M_{qr} + M_{rq} + M$$

L is context-free since it is the union of context-free languages (Theorem 30).

What is the complement of L? All words that are *not* of the form

$$a^p b^q a^r$$

are in M, which is in L, so they are not in L'. This means that L' contains only words of the form

$$a^p b^q a^r$$

But what are the possible values of p, q, and r? If $p > q$, then the word is in M_{pq}, so it is in L and not in L'. Also, if $q > p$, then the word is in M_{qp}, so it is in L and not in L'. Therefore, $p = q$ for all words in L'.

If $q > r$, then the word is in M_{qr} and hence in L and not in L'. If $r > q$, the word is in M_{rq} and so in L and not L'. Therefore, $q = r$ for all words in L'.

Since $p = q$ and $q = r$, we know that $p = r$. Therefore, the words

$$a^n b^n a^n$$

are the only possible words in L'. All words of this form are in L' since none of them is any of the M's. Therefore,

$$L' = \{a^n b^n a^n \quad \text{for} \quad n = 1 \quad 2 \quad 3 \quad \ldots\}$$

But we know that this language is non-context-free from Chapter 20. Therefore, we have constructed a CFL, L, that has a non-context-free complement. ■

We might observe that we did not need M_{pr} and M_{rp} in the formation of L. The union of the other five alone completely defines L. We included them only for the purposes of symmetry.

THEOREM 39

A deterministic PDA (DPDA) is a PDA for which every possible input string corresponds to a unique path through the machine. If we further require that no input loops forever, we say that we have a DPDA that always stops. Not all languages that can be accepted by PDA's can be accepted by a DPDA that always stops.

PROOF

The language L defined in the previous example is one such language. It can be generated by CFG's, so it can be accepted by some PDA. Yet if it were acceptable by any deterministic PDA that always stops, then its complement would have to be context-free, since we could build a PDA for the complement by reversing ACCEPT and REJECT states. However, the complement of this language is not a context-free language. Therefore, no such deterministic machine for L exists. L can be accepted by some PDA but not by any DPDA that always stops. ■

It is also true that the language PALINDROME cannot be accepted by a deterministic PDA that always stops, but this is harder to prove. It can be proven that any language accepted by a DPDA can also be accepted by a DPDA that always stops. This means that the better version of Theorem 39 is "Not all CFL's can be accepted by DPDA's," or to put it another way

$$\text{PDA} \neq \text{DPDA}$$

We shall defer further discussion of this point to Problem 20 below.

Although we cannot tell what happens when we intersect two general CFL's, we can say something useful about a special case.

THEOREM 40

The intersection of a context-free language with a regular language is always context-free.

PROOF

We prove this by a constructive algorithm of the sort we developed for Kleene's Theorem is Chapter 7.

Let C be a context-free language that is accepted by the PDA, P. Let R be a regular language that is accepted by the FA, F. We now show how to take P and F and construct a PDA from them called A that will have the property that the language that A accepts is exactly $C \cap R$.

The method will be very similar to the method we used to build the FA to accept the union of two regular languages. Before we start, let us assume P is in the form of Theorem 27 so that it reads the whole input string before accepting.

If the states of F are called x_1, x_2, . . . and the READ and POP states of P are called y_1, y_2, . . . then the new machine we want to build will have states labeled "x_i and y_j," meaning that the input string would now be in state x_i if running on F and in state y_j if running on P. We do not have to worry about the PUSH states of P since no branching takes place there. At a point in the processing when the PDA A wants to accept the input string, it must first consult the status of the current simulated x-state. If this x-state is a final state, the input can be accepted because it is accepted on both machines.

This is a general theoretical discussion. Let us now look at an example.

Let C be the language EQUAL of words with the same total number of a's and b's. Let the PDA to accept this language be:

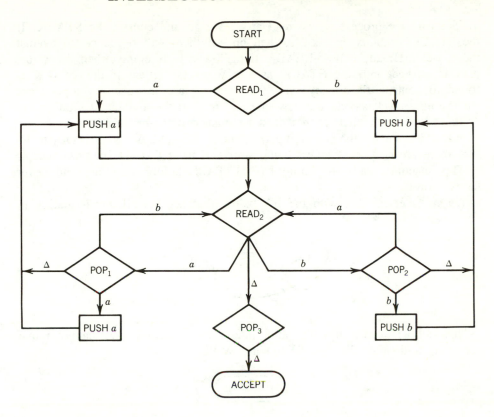

This is a new machine to us, so we should take a moment to dissect it. At every point in the processing the STACK will contain whichever letter has been read more, a or b, and will contain as many of that letter as the number of extra times it has been read. If we have read from the TAPE six more b's than a's, then we shall find six b's in the STACK. If the STACK is empty at any time, it means an equal number of a's and b's have been read.

The process begins in START and then goes to $READ_1$. Whatever we read in $READ_1$ is our first excess letter and is pushed onto the STACK. The rest of the input string is read in $READ_2$.

If during the processing we read an *a*, we go and consult the STACK. If the STACK contains excess *b*'s, then one of them will be cancelled against the *a* we just read, POP$_1$—READ$_2$. If the STACK is empty, then the *a* just read is pushed onto the STACK as a new excess letter. If the STACK is found to contain *a*'s already, then we must replace the one we popped out for testing as well as add the new one just read to the amount of total excess in the STACK. In all, two *a*'s must be pushed onto the STACK.

When we are finally out of input letters in READ$_2$, we go to POP$_3$ to be sure there are no excess letters being stored in the STACK. Then we accept.

This machine reads the entire INPUT TAPE before accepting and never loops forever.

Let us intersect this with the FA below that accepts all words ending in the letter *a*

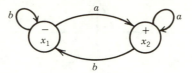

Now let us manufacture the joint intersection machine. We cannot move out of x_1 until after the first READ in the PDA.

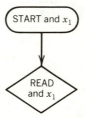

At this point in the PDA we branch to separate PUSH states each of which takes us to READ$_2$. However, depending on what is read in READ$_1$, we will either want to be in "READ$_2$ and x_1" or "READ$_2$ and x_2," so these must be two different states:

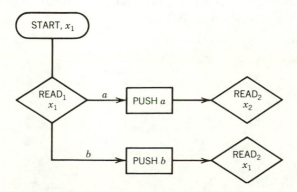

From "READ$_2$ and x_2" if we read an a we shall have to be in "POP$_1$ and x_2," whereas if we read a b we shall be in "POP$_2$ and x_1." In this particular machine, there is no need for "POP$_1$ and x_1" since POP$_1$ can only be entered by reading an a and x_1 can only be entered by reading a b. For analogous reasons, we do not need a state called "POP$_2$ and x_2" either.

We shall eventually need both "POP$_3$ and x_1" and "POP$_3$ and x_2" because we have to keep track of the last input letter.

Even if "POP$_3$ and x_1" should happen to pop a Δ, it cannot accept since x_1 is not a final state and so the word ending there is rejected by the FA.

The whole machine looks like this.

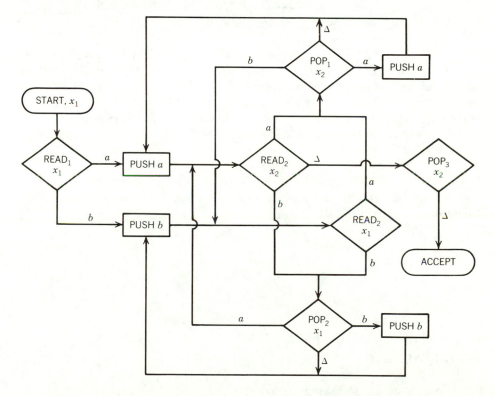

We did not even bother drawing "POP$_3$ x_1." If a blank is read in "READ$_2$, x_1" the machine peacefully crashes.

This illustrates the technique for intersecting a PDA with an FA. The process is straightforward. Mathematicians with our current level of sophistication can extract the general principles of this constructive algorithm and should consider this proof complete. ■

EXAMPLE

Let us consider the language DOUBLEWORD:

DOUBLEWORD = {ww where w is an string of a's and b's}

= {Λ aa bb $aaaa$ $abab$ $baba$ $bbbb$ $aaaaaa$ . . . }

Let us assume for a moment that DOUBLEWORD were a CFL. Then when we intersect it with any regular language, we must get a context-free language. Let us intersect DOUBLEWORD with the regular language defined by

aa*bb*aa*bb*

A word in the intersection must have both forms, this means it must be

ww where $w = a^n b^m$ for some n and m = 1 2 3 . . .

This observation may be obvious, but we shall prove it anyway. If w contained the substring ba, then ww would have two of them, but all words in **aa*bb*aa*bb*** have exactly one such substring. Therefore, the substring ba must be the crack in between the two w's in the form ww. This means w begins with a and ends with b. Since it has no ba, it must be $a^n b^m$.

The intersection language is therefore:

$$\{a^n b^m a^n b^m\}$$

But we showed in the last chapter that this language was non-context-free. Therefore, DOUBLEWORD cannot be context-free either.   ■

PROBLEMS

1.   Which of the following are context-free?

(i)   **(a)(a + b)*** ∩ ODDPALINDROME

(ii)   EQUAL ∩ {$a^n b^n a^n$}

(iii)   {$a^n b^n$} ∩ PALINDROME′

(iv)   EVEN-EVEN′ ∩ PALINDROME

(v)   {$a^n b^n$}′ ∩ PALINDROME

(vi)   PALINDROME ∩ {$a^n b^{n+m} a^m$ where n,m = 1,   2,   3 . . .
$n = m$ or $n \neq m$}

(vii)   PALINDROME′ ∩ EQUAL

2. Build a PDA for M_{qp} as defined above.

3. Show that $\{a^n\mathbf{b}^+a^n\}$ is a CFL.

4. Build a PDA for M_{qr} as defined above.

5. Build a PDA for M_{rq} as defined above.

6. Build a PDA for M as defined above.

7. (i)　Show that

$$L_1 = \{a^pb^qa^rb^p, \quad \text{where } p,q,r \text{ are arbitrary whole numbers}\}$$

is context-free.

(ii)　Show that

$$L_2 = \{a^pb^qa^pb^s\}$$

is context-free.

(iii)　Show that

$$L_3 = \{a^pb^pa^rb^s\}$$

is context-free.

(iv)　Show that

$$L_1 \cap L_2 \cap L_3$$

is non-context-free.

8. Recall the language VERYEQUAL over the alphabet $\Sigma = \{a,b,c\}$

VERYEQUAL = {all strings of a's, b's, and c's that have the same total number of a's as b's as c's}

Prove that VERYEQUAL is non-context-free by using a theorem in this chapter. (Compare with Chapter 20, Problem 19.)

9. (i)　Prove that the complement of the language L

$$L = \{a^nb^m, \quad \text{where } n \neq m\}$$

is context-free but that neither L nor L' is regular.

(ii) Show that:

$$L_1 = \{a^n b^m, \quad \text{where } n \geq m\}$$

and

$$L_2 = \{a^n b^m, \quad \text{where } m \geq n\}$$

are both context-free and not regular.

(iii) Show that their intersection is context-free and nonregular.

(iv) Show that their union is regular.

10. (i) Prove that the language

$$L_1 = \{a^n b^m a^{n+m}\}$$

is context-free.

(ii) Prove that the language

$$L_2 = \{a^n b^n a^m, \text{ where either } n = m \text{ or } n \neq m\}$$

is context-free.

(iii) Is their intersection context-free?

11. In this chapter we proved that the complement of $\{a^n b^n a^n\}$ is context-free. Prove this again by exhibiting one CFG that generates it.

12. Consider all the strings in $(a+b+c)^*$.
    We have shown that $\{a^n b^n c^n\}$ is non-context-free. Is its complement context-free?

13. (i) Let L be a CFL. Let $S = \{w_1, w_2, w_3, w_4\}$ be a set of four words from L. Let M be the language of all the words of L except for those in S (we might write $M = L - S$). Show that M is context-free.

    (ii) Let R be a regular language contained in L. Let "$L - R$" represent the language of all words of L that are not words of R. Prove that $L - R$ is a CFL.

14. (i) Show that:

$$L = \{ab^n ab^n a\}$$

is nonregular but context-free.

(ii) Show that:

$$L = \{ab^n ab^m a, \quad \text{where } n \neq m \quad \text{or} \quad n = m\}$$

is regular.

(iii) Find a regular language that when intersected with a context-free language becomes nonregular but context-free.

15. (i) Show that the language

$$L = \{a^n b^m, \text{ where } m = n \text{ or } m = 2n\}$$

cannot be accepted by a deterministic PDA

(ii) Show that L is the union of two languages that can be accepted by deterministic PDA's.

(iii) Show that the union of languages accepted by DPDA's is not necessarily a language accepted by a DPDA.

(iv) Show that the intersection of languages accepted by DPDA's is not necessarily a language accepted by a DPDA.

16. The algorithm given in the proof of Theorem 40 looks mighty inviting. We are tempted to use the same technique to build the intersection machine of two PDA's. However we know that the intersection of two CFL's is not always a CFL.

(i) Explain why the algorithm fails when it attempts to intersect two PDA's.

(ii) Can we adapt it to intersect two DPDA's?

17. (i) Take a PDA for PALINDROMEX and intersect it with an FA for **a*Xa***. (This means actually build the intersection machine.)

(ii) Analyze the resultant machine and show that the language it accepts is $\{a^n X a^n\}$.

18. (i) Intersect a PDA for $\{a^n b^n\}$ with an FA for **a(a+b)***. What language is accepted by the resultant machine?

(ii) Intersect a PDA for $\{a^n b^n\}$ with an FA for **b(a+b)*** What language is accepted by the resultant machine?

(iii) Intersect a PDA for $\{a^n b^n\}$ with an FA for **(a+b)* aa(a+b)***

(iv) Intersect a PDA for $\{a^n b^n\}$ with an FA for EVEN-EVEN.

19. Intersect a PDA for PALINDROME with an FA that accepts the language of all words of odd length. Show, by examining the machine, that it accepts exactly the language ODDPALINDROME.

20. Show that any language that can be accepted by a DPDA can be accepted by a DPDA that always stops. To do this, show how to modify an existing DPDA to eliminate the possibility of infinite looping. Infinite looping can occur in two ways:

    1. The machine enters a circuit of edges that it cannot leave and that never reads the TAPE.

    2. The machine enters a circuit of edges that it cannot leave and that reads infinitely many blanks from the TAPE.

    Show how to spot these two situations and eliminate them by converting them to REJECT's.

CHAPTER 22

PARSING

We have spent a considerable amount of time discussing context-free languages, even though we have proven that this class of languages is not all encompassing. Why should we study in so much detail, grammars so primitive that they cannot even define the set $\{a^n b^n a^n\}$?

We are not merely playing an interesting intellectual game. There is a more practical reason: Computer programming languages are context-free. (We must be careful here to say that the languages in which the words are computer language *instructions* are context-free. The languages in which the words are computer language *programs* are mostly not.) This makes CFG's of fundamental importance in the design of compilers.

Let us begin with the definition of what constitutes a valid storage location **identifier** in a higher-level language such as ADA, BASIC, COBOL,. . . . These user-defined names are often called **variables.** In some languages their length is limited to a maximum of six characters, where the first must be a letter and each character thereafter is either a letter or a digit. We can summarize this by the CFG:

$$identifier \rightarrow letter \ (letter \ + \ digit \ + \ \Lambda)^5$$
$$letter \rightarrow A \mid B \mid C \mid \ldots \mid Z$$
$$digit \rightarrow 0 \mid 1 \mid 2 \mid 3 \ldots \mid 9$$

Notice that we have used a regular expression for the right side of the first production instead of writing out all the possibilities:

$$identifier \rightarrow letter \mid letter\ letter \mid$$
$$letter\ digit \mid letter\ letter\ letter \mid$$
$$letter\ letter\ digit \mid letter\ digit\ digit \mid \ldots$$

There are 63 different strings of nonterminals represented by

$$letter\ (letter\ +\ digit\ +\ \Lambda)^5$$

and the use of this shorthand notation is more understandable than writing out the whole list.

The first part of the process of compilation is the **scanner.** This program reads through the original source program and replaces all the user-defined identifier names which have personal significance to the programmer, such as DATE, SALARY, RATE, NAME, MOTHER, . . . , with more manageable computer names that will help the machine move this information in and out of the registers as it is being processed. The scanner is also called a lexical analyzer because its job is to build a lexicon (which is from Greek what "dictionary" is from Latin).

A scanner must be able to make some sophisticated decisions such as recognizing that DO33I is an identifier in the assignment statement

$$DO33I = 1100$$

while DO33I is part of a loop instruction in the statement

$$DO33I = 1,100$$

(or in some languages DO33I = 1TO100).

Other character strings, such as IF, ELSE, END, . . . , have to be recognized as reserved words even though they also fit the definition of identifier.

All this aside, most of what a scanner does can be performed by an FA, and scanners are usually written with this model in mind.

Another task a compiler must perform is to "understand" what is meant by arithmetic expressions such as

$$A3J * S + (7 * (BIL + 4))$$

After the scanner replaces all numbers and variables with the identifier labels $i_1, i_2, \ldots$, this becomes:

$$i_1 * i_2 + (i_3 * (i_4 + i_5))$$

The grammars we presented earlier for AE (arithmetic expression) were ambiguous. This is not acceptable for programming since we want the computer to know and execute exactly what we mean by this formula.

Two possible solutions were mentioned earlier.

1. Require the programmer to insert parentheses to avoid ambiguity. For example, instead of the ambiguous $3 + 4 * 5$ insist on

$$(3 + 4) * 5$$

or

$$3 + (4 * 5)$$

2. Find a new grammar for the same language that is unambiguous because the interpretation of "operator hierarchy" (that is $*$ before $+$) is built into the system.

Programmers find the first solution too cumbersome and unnatural. Fortunately, there are grammars (CFG's) that satisfy the second requirement.

We present one such for the operations $+$ and $*$ alone, called PLUS-TIMES. The rules of production are:

$$S \rightarrow E$$
$$E \rightarrow T + E \mid T$$
$$T \rightarrow F * T \mid F$$
$$F \rightarrow (E) \mid i$$

Loosely speaking, E stands for an expression, T for a term in a sum, F for a factor in a product, and i for any identifier. The terminals clearly are

$$+ \quad * \quad (\quad) \quad i$$

since these symbols occur on the right side of productions but never on the left side.

To generate the word $i + i * i$ by left-most derivation we must proceed:

$$S \Rightarrow E$$
$$\Rightarrow T + E$$
$$\Rightarrow F + E$$
$$\Rightarrow i + E$$
$$\Rightarrow i + T$$
$$\Rightarrow i + F * T$$

$$\Rightarrow i + i * T$$
$$\Rightarrow i + i * F$$
$$\Rightarrow i + i * i$$

The syntax tree for this is

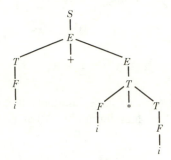

It is clear from this tree that the word represents the addition of an identifier with the product of two identifiers. In other words, the multiplication will be performed before the addition, just as we intended it to be in accordance with conventional operator hierarchy. Once the computer can discover a derivation for the formula, it can generate a machine-language program to accomplish the same task.

Given a word generated by a particular grammar, the task of finding its derivation is called **parsing.**

Until now we have been interested only in whether a string of symbols was a word in a certain language. We were worried only about the possibility of generation by grammar or acceptance by machine. Now we find that we want to know more. We want to know not just whether a string *can* be generated by a CFG but also *how*. We contend that if we know the (or one of the) derivation tree(s) of a given word in a particular language, then we know something about the *meaning* of the word. This chapter is different from the other chapters in this part because here we are seeking to understand what a word says by determining how it can be generated.

There are many different approaches to the problem of CFG parsing. We shall consider three of them. The first two are general algorithms based on our study of derivation trees for CFG's. The third is specific to arithmetical expressions and makes use of the correspondence between CFG's and PDA's.

The first algorithm is called **top-down parsing.** We begin with a CFG and a **target word.** Starting with the symbol S, we try to find some sequence of productions that generates the target word. We do this by checking all possibilities for left-most derivations. To organize this search we build a tree of all possibilities, which is like the whole language tree of Chapter 14. We grow each branch until it becomes clear that the branch can no longer present a viable possibility; that is, we discontinue growing a branch of the whole language tree as soon as it becomes clear that the target word will never appear on that branch, even generations later. This could happen, for example, if the branch includes in its working string a terminal that does not appear anywhere in the target word or does not appear in the target word in a corresponding position. It is time to see an illustration.

Let us consider the target word

$$i + i * i$$

in the language generated by the grammar PLUS-TIMES.

We begin with the start symbol S. At this point there is only one production we can possibly apply, $S \rightarrow E$. From E there are two possible productions:

$$E \rightarrow T + E \qquad E \rightarrow T$$

In each case, the left-most nonterminal is T and there are two productions possible for replacing this T.

The top-down left-most parsing tree begins as shown below:

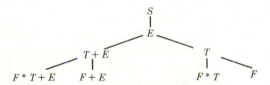

In each of the bottom four cases the left-most nonterminal is F, which is the left side of two possible productions.

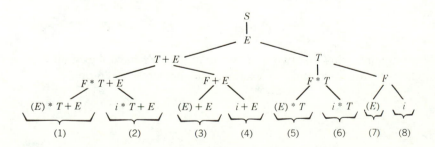

Of these, we can drop branches number 1, 3, 5, and 7 from further consideration because they have introduced the terminal character "(", which is not the first (or any) letter of our word. Once a terminal character appears in a working string, it never leaves. Productions change the nonterminals into other things, but the terminals stay forever. All four of those branches can produce only words with parentheses in them, not $i + i * i$. Branch 8 has ended its development naturally in a string of all terminals but it is not our target word, so we can discontinue the investigation of this branch too. Our pruned tree looks like this:

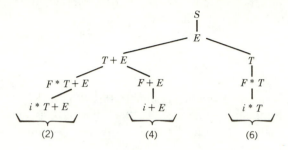

Since branches 7 and 8 both vanished, we dropped the line that produced them:

$$T \Rightarrow F$$

All three branches have actually derived the first two terminal letters of the words that they can produce. Each of the three branches left starts with two terminals that can never change. Branch 4 says the word starts with "$i + $", which is correct, but branches 2 and 6 can now produce only words that start "$i * $", which is not in agreement with our desired target word. The second letter of all words derived on branches 2 and 6 is $*$; the second letter of the target word is $+$. We must kill these branches before they multiply.

Deleting branch 6 prunes the tree up to the derivation $E \Rightarrow T$, which has proved fruitless as none of its offshoots can produce our target word. Deleting branch 2 tells us that we can eliminate the left branch out of $T + E$. With all of the pruning we have now done, we can conclude that any branch leading to $i + i * i$ must begin

$$S \Rightarrow E \Rightarrow T + E \Rightarrow F + E \Rightarrow i + E$$

Let us continue this tree two more generations. We have drawn all derivation possibilities. Now it is time to examine the branches for pruning.

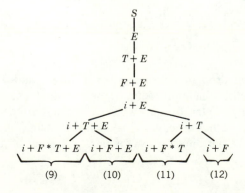

At this point we are now going to pull a new rule out of our hat. Since no production in any CFG can decrease the length of the working string of terminals and nonterminals on which it operates (each production replaces one symbol by one or more), once the length of a working string has passed five it can never produce a final word of length only five. We can therefore delete branch 9 on this basis alone. No words that it generates can have as few as five letters.

Another observation we can make is that even though branch 10 is not too long and even though it begins with a correct string of terminals, it can still be eliminated because it has produced another + in the working string. This is a terminal that all descendants on the branch will have to include. However, there is no second + in the word we are trying to derive. Therefore, we can eliminate branch 10, too.

This leaves us with only branches 11 and 12 which continue to grow.

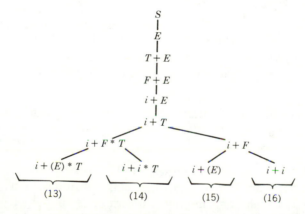

Now branches 13 and 15 have introduced the forbidden terminal "(", while branch 16 has terminated its growth at the wrong word. Only branch 14 deserves to live.

(At this point we draw the top half of the tree horizontally.)

$$S \Rightarrow E \Rightarrow T + E \Rightarrow F + E \Rightarrow i + E \Rightarrow i + T \Rightarrow i + F * T$$

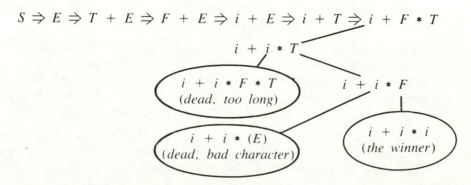

In this way we have discovered that the word $i + i * i$ can be generated by this CFG and we have found the one left-most derivation which generates it.

To recapitulate the algorithm: From every live node we branch for all productions applicable to the left-most nonterminal. We kill a branch for having the wrong initial string of terminals, having a bad terminal anywhere in the string, simply growing too long, or turning into the wrong string of terminals.

Using the method of tree search known as **backtracking** it is not necessary to grow all the live branches at once. Instead we can pursue one branch downward until either we reach the desired word or else we terminate it because of a bad character or excessive length. At this point we back up to a previous node to travel down the next road until we find the target word or another dead end, and so on. Backtracking algorithms are more properly the subject of a different course. As usual, we are more interested in showing what can be done, not in determining which method is best.

We have only given a beginner's list of reasons for terminating the development of a node in the tree. A more complete set of rules is:

1. *Bad Substring:* If a substring of solid terminals (one or more) has been introduced into a working string in a branch of the total-language tree, all words derived from it must also include that substring unaltered. Therefore, any substring that does not appear in the target word is cause for eliminating the branch.

2. *Good Substrings But Too Many:* The working string has more occurrences of the particular substring than the target word does. In a sense Rule 1 is a special case of this.

3. *Good Substrings But Wrong Order:* If the working string is *YabXYbaXX* but the target word is *bbbbaab,* then both substrings of terminals developed so far, *ab* and *ba,* are valid substrings of the target word but they do not occur in the same order in the working string as in the word. So the working string cannot develop into the target word.

4. *Improper Outer-terminal Substring:* Substrings of terminals developed at the beginning or end of the working string will always stay at the ends at which they first appear. They must be in perfect agreement with the target word or the branch must be eliminated.

5. *Excess Projected Length:* If the working string is *aXbbYYXa* and if all the productions with a left side of *X* have right sides of six characters, then the shortest length of the ultimate words derived from this working string must have length at least $1 + 6 + 1 + 1 + 1 + 1 + 6 + 1 = 18$. If the target word has fewer than 18 letters, kill this branch.

6. *Wrong Target Word:* If we have only terminals left but the string is not the target word, forget it. This is a special case of Rule 4, where the substring is the entire word.

There may be even more rules depending on the exact nature of the grammar.

EXAMPLE

Let us recall the CFG for the language EQUAL:

$$S \rightarrow aB \mid bA$$
$$A \rightarrow a \mid aS \mid bAA$$
$$B \rightarrow b \mid bS \mid aBB$$

The word *bbabaa* is in EQUAL. Let us determine a left-most derivation for this word by top-down parsing.

From the start symbol S the derivation tree can take one of two tracks.

All words derived from branch 1 must begin with the letter a, but our target word does not. Therefore, by Rule 4, only branch 2 need be considered. The left-most nonterminal is A. There are three branches possible at this point.

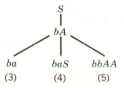

Branch 3 is a completed word but not our target word. Branch 4 will generate only words with an initial string of terminals *ba*, which is not the case with *bbabaa*. Only branch 5 remains a possibility. The left-most nonterminal in the working string of branch 5 is the first A. Three productions apply to it:

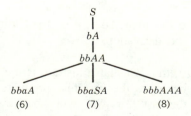

Branches 6 and 7 seem perfectly possible. Branch 8, however, has generated the terminal substring *bbb*, which all of its descendants must bear. This substring does not appear in our target word, so we can eliminate this branch from further consideration.

In branch 6 the left-most nonterminal is the A, in branch 7 it is the S.

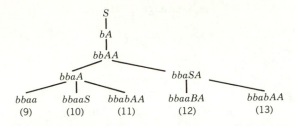

Branch 9 is a string of all terminals, but not the target word. Branch 10 has the initial substring *bbaa*; the target word does not. This detail also kills branch 12. Branch 11 and branch 13 are identical. If we wanted *all* the left-most derivations of this target word, we would keep both branches growing. Since we need only one derivation, we may just as well keep branch 13 and drop branch 11 (or vice versa); whatever words can be produced on one branch can be produced on the other.

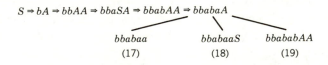

Only the working string in branch 14 is not longer than the target word. Branches 15 and 16 can never generate a six-letter word.

$$S \Rightarrow bA \Rightarrow bbAA \Rightarrow bbaSA \Rightarrow bbabAA \Rightarrow bbabaA$$

bbabaa	*bbabaaS*	*bbababAA*
(17)	(18)	(19)

Branches 18 and 19 are too long, so it is a good thing that branch 17 is our word. This completes the derivation. ∎

The next parsing algorithm we shall illustrate is the **bottom-up parser.** This time we do not ask what were the first few productions used in deriving the word, but what were the last few. We work backward from the end to the front, the way sneaky people do when they try to solve a maze.

Let us again consider as our example the word $i + i * i$ generated by the CFG PLUS-TIMES

If we are trying to reconstruct a left-most derivation, we might think that the last terminal to be derived was the last letter of the word. However, this is not always the case. For example, in the grammar

$$S \rightarrow Abb$$
$$A \rightarrow a$$

the word *abb* is formed in two steps, but the final two *b*'s were introduced in the first step of the derivation, not the last. So instead of trying to reconstruct specifically a left-most derivation, we have to search for any derivation of our target word. This makes the tree much larger. We begin at the bottom of the derivation tree, that is, with the target word itself, and step by step work our way back up the tree seeking to find when the working string was the one single *S*.

Let us reconsider the CFG PLUS-TIMES:

$$S \rightarrow E$$
$$E \rightarrow T + E \mid T$$
$$T \rightarrow F * T \mid F$$
$$F \rightarrow (E) \mid i$$

To perform a bottom-up search, we shall be reiterating the following step: Find all substrings of the present working string of terminals and nonterminals that are right halves of productions and substitute back to the nonterminal that could have produced them.

Three substrings of $i + i * i$ are right halves of productions; namely, the three *i*'s, anyone of which could have been produced by an *F*. The tree of possibilities begins as follows:

$$
\begin{array}{ccc}
 & i + i * i & \\
F + i * i & i + F * i & i + i * F
\end{array}
$$

Even though we are going from the bottom of the derivation tree to the top *S*, we will still draw the tree of possibilities, as all our trees, from the top of the page downward.

We can save ourselves some work in this particular example by realizing that all of the *i*'s come from the production $F \rightarrow i$ and the working string we should be trying to derive is $F + F * F$. Strictly speaking, this insight should not be allowed since it requires an idea that we did not include in the algorithm to begin with. But since it saves us a considerable amount of work, we succumb to the temptation and write in one step

$$
\begin{array}{c}
i + i * i \\
\mid \\
F + F * F
\end{array}
$$

Not all the F's had to come from $T \rightarrow F$. Some could have come from $T \rightarrow F * T$, so we cannot use the same trick again.

$$i + i * i$$
$$F + F * F$$
$$T + F * F \qquad F + T * F \qquad F + F * T$$

The first two branches contain substrings that could be the right halves of $E \rightarrow T$ and $T \rightarrow F$. The third branch has the additional possibility of $T \rightarrow F * T$. The tree continues

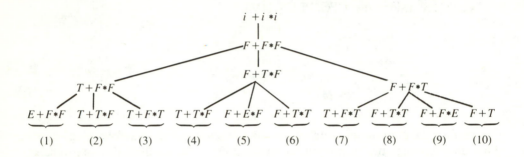

We never have to worry about the length of the intermediate strings in bottom-up parsing since they can never exceed the length of the target word. At each stage they stay the same length or get shorter. Also, no bad terminals are ever introduced since no new terminals are ever introduced at all, only nonterminals. These are efficiencies that partially compensate for the inefficiency of not restricting ourselves to left-most derivations.

There is the possibility that a nonterminal is bad in certain contexts. For example, branch 1 now has an E as its left-most character. The only production that will ever absorb that E is $S \rightarrow E$. This would give us the nonterminal S, but S is not in the right half of any production. It is true that we want to end up with the S; that is the whole goal of the tree. However, we shall want the entire working string to be that single S, not a longer working string with S as its first letter. The rest of the expression in branch 1, " $+ F * F$ ", is not just going to disappear. So branch 1 gets the ax. The E's in branch 5 and branch 9 are none too promising either, as we shall see in a moment.

When we go backward, we no longer have the guarantee that the "inverse" grammar is unambiguous even though the CFG itself might be. In fact, this backward tracing is probably not unique, since we are not restricting ourselves to finding a left-most derivation (even though we could with a little more thought; see Problem 10 below). We should also find the trails of right-most derivations and whatnot. This is reflected in the occurrence of repeated expressions in the branches. In our example, branch 2 is now the same as branch 4, branch 3 is the same as branch 7, and branch 6 is the same as branch 8. Since we are interested here in finding any *one* derivation, not *all* derivations, we can safely kill branches 2, 3, and 6 and still find a derivation—if one exists.

The tree grows ferociously, like a bush, very wide but not very tall. It would grow too unwieldy unless we made the following observation.

Observation

No intermediate working string of terminals and nonterminals can have the substring "$E * $". This is because the only production that introduces the $*$ is

$$T \rightarrow F * T$$

so the symbol to the immediate left of a $*$ is originally F. From this F we can only get the terminals ")" or "i" next to the star. Therefore, in a top-down derivation we could never create the substring "$E * $" in this CFG, so in bottom-up this can never occur in an intermediate working string leading back to S. Similarly, "$E + $" and "$ * E$" are also forbidden in the sense that they cannot occur in any derivation. The idea of forbidden substrings is one that we played with in Chapter 3. We can now see the importance of the techniques we introduced there for showing certain substrings never occur (and everybody thought Theorems 2, 3, and 4 were completely frivolous). With the aid of this observation we can eliminate branches 5 and 9.

The tree now grows as follows (pruning away anything with a forbidden substring):

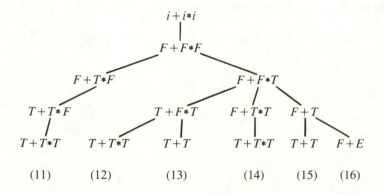

Branches 11, 12, and 13 are repeated in 14 and 15, so we drop the former. Branch 14 has nowhere to go, since none of the T's can become E's without creating forbidden substrings. So branch 14 must be dropped. From branches 15 and 16 the only next destination is "$T + E$", so we can drop branch 15 since 16 gets us there just as well by itself. The tree ends as follows:

$$i+i*i \Leftarrow F+F*F \Leftarrow F+F*T \Leftarrow F+T \Leftarrow F+E \Leftarrow T+E \Leftarrow E \Leftarrow S$$

which is the same as

$$S \Rightarrow E \Rightarrow T+E \Rightarrow F+E \Rightarrow F+T \Rightarrow F+F * T \Rightarrow F+F * F \Rightarrow i+i * i$$

(The symbol $\Leftarrow$ used above should be self-explanatory.)

EXAMPLE

Let us again consider the grammar:

$$S \rightarrow aB \mid bA$$
$$A \rightarrow a \mid aS \mid bAA$$
$$B \rightarrow b \mid bS \mid aBB$$

and again let us search for a derivation of a target word, this time through bottom-up parsing. Let us analyze the grammar before parsing anything.

If we ever encounter the working string

$$bAAaB$$

in a bottom-up parse in this grammar, we shall have to determine the working strings from which it might have been derived. We scan the string looking for any substrings of it that are the right sides of productions. In this case there are five of them:

$$b \quad bA \quad bAA \quad a \quad aB$$

Notice how they may overlap. This working string could have been derived in five ways:

$$BAAaB \Rightarrow bAAaB \quad (B \rightarrow b)$$
$$SAaB \;\; \Rightarrow bAAaB \quad (S \rightarrow bA)$$

$$AaB \quad \Rightarrow bAAaB \quad (A \to bAA)$$
$$bAAAB \Rightarrow bAAaB \quad (A \to a)$$
$$bAAS \quad \Rightarrow bAAaB \quad (S \to aB)$$

Let us make some observations peculiar to this grammar.

1. All derivations in this grammar begin with either $S \to aB$ or $S \to bA$, so the only working string that can ever begin with a nonterminal is the working string is S. For example the pseudo-working string $AbbA$ cannot occur in a derivation.

2. Since the application of each rule of production creates one new terminal in the working string, in any derivation of a word of length 6 (or n), there are exactly 6 (or n) steps.

3. Since every rule of production is in the form

   Nonterminal $\to$ (*one terminal*) (*string of 0, 1, or 2 Nonterminals*)

   in a left-most derivation we take the first nonterminal from the string of nonterminals and replace it with terminals followed by nonterminals. Therefore, all working strings will be of the form

   terminal terminal . . . terminal Nonterminal Nonterminal . . . Nonterminal
   $$= terminal^* \; Nonterminal^*$$
   $$= (string \; of \; terminals) \; (string \; of \; Nonterminals)$$

If we are searching backward and have a working string before us, then the working strings it could have come from have all but one of the same terminals in front and a small change in nonterminals where the terminals and the nonterminals meet. For example,

$$baabbababaBBABABBBAAAA$$

could have been left-most produced only from these three working strings.

$$baabbabab\underline{A}BBABABBBAAAA,$$
$$baabbabab\underline{S}BABABBBAAAA,$$
$$baabbabab\underline{B}ABABBBAAAA$$

We now use the bottom-up algorithm to find a left-most derivation for the target word *bbabaa*.

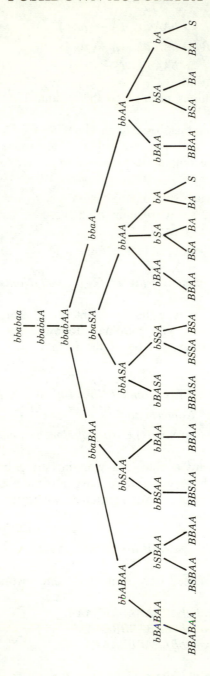

On the bottom row there are two S's. Therefore, there are two left-most derivations of this word in this grammar:

$$S \Rightarrow bA \Rightarrow bbAA \Rightarrow bbaSA \Rightarrow bbabAA \Rightarrow bbabaA \Rightarrow bbabaa$$
$$S \Rightarrow bA \Rightarrow bbAA \Rightarrow bbaA \Rightarrow bbabAA \Rightarrow bbabaA \Rightarrow bbabaa$$

Notice that all the other branches in this tree die simultaneously, since they now contain no terminals. ■

There are, naturally, dozens of programming modifications possible for both parsing algorithms. This includes using them in combination, which is a good idea since both start out very effectively before their trees start to spread.

Both of these algorithms apply to all CFG's. For example, these methods can apply to the following CFG definition of a small programming language:

$S \rightarrow$ ASSIGNMENT\$ | GOTO\$ | IF\$ | IO\$

ASSIGNMENT\$ $\rightarrow i = ALEX$

GOTO\$ $\rightarrow GOTO\ NUMBER$

IF\$ $\rightarrow IF$ CONDITION *THEN* S | *IF* CONDITION *THEN* S *ELSE* S

CONDITION $\rightarrow ALEX = ALEX$ | $ALEX \neq ALEX$ | $ALEX > ALEX$

CONDITION $\rightarrow$ CONDITION *AND* CONDITION

          | CONDITION *OR* CONDITION | *NOT* CONDITION

IO\$ $\rightarrow READ\ i$ | $PRINT\ i$

(where *ALEX* stands for algebraic expression). Notice that the names of the types of statements all end in \$ to distinguish them as a class.

The terminals are

$$\{ = GOTO\ IF\ THEN\ ELSE \neq > AND\ OR\ NOT\ READ\ PRINT \}$$

plus whatever terminals are introduced in the definitions of i, *ALEX*, and *NUMBER*.

In this grammar we might wish to parse the expression:

$$IF\ i > i\ THEN\ i = i + i * i$$

so that the instruction can be converted into machine language. This can be done by finding its derivation from the start symbol. The problem of code generation from a derivation tree is the easiest part of compiling and too language dependent for us to worry about in this course.

Our last algorithm for "understanding" words in order to evaluate expressions is one based on the prefix notation mentioned in Chapter 14. This applies not only to arithmetic expressions but also to many other programming language instructions as well.

We shall assume that we are now using *postfix* notation, where the two operands immediately precede the operator:

$A + B$	becomes	$A\ B\ +$
$(A + B) * C$	becomes	$A\ B\ +\ C\ *$
$A * (B + C * D)$	becomes	$A\ B\ C\ D\ *\ +\ *$

An algorithm for converting standard infix notation into postfix notation was given in Chapter 14. Once an expression is in postfix, we can evaluate it without finding its derivation from a CFG, although we originally made use of its parsing tree to convert the infix into postfix in the first place. We are assuming here that our expressions involve only numerical values for the identifiers (i's) and only the operations $+$ and $*$, as in the language PLUS-TIMES.

We can evaluate these postfix expressions by a new machine similar to a PDA. Such a machine requires three new states.

1. $\boxed{\text{ADD}}$: This state pops the top two entries off the STACK, adds them, and pushes the result onto the top of the STACK.
2. $\boxed{\text{MPY}}$: This state pops the top two entries off the STACK, multiplies them, and pushes the result onto the top of the STACK.
3. $\overline{/\text{PRINT}/}$: This prints the entry that is on top of the stack and accepts the input string. It is an output and a halt state.

The machine to evaluate postfix expressions can now be built as below, where the expression to be evaluated has been put on the INPUT TAPE in the usual fashion—one character per cell starting in the first cell.

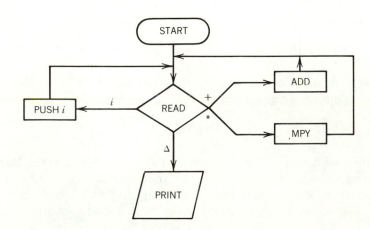

Let us trace the action of this machine on the input string:

$$7\ 5\ +\ 2\ 4\ +\ *\ 6\ +$$

which is postfix for

$$(7\ +\ 5)\ *\ (2\ +\ 4)\ +\ 6\ =\ 78$$

STATE	STACK	TAPE
START	Δ	7 5 + 2 4 + * 6 +
READ	Δ	5 + 2 4 + * 6 +
PUSH *i*	7	5 + 2 4 + * 6 +
READ	7	+ 2 4 + * 6 +
PUSH *i*	5 7	+ 2 4 + * 6 +
READ	5 7	2 4 + * 6 +
ADD	12	2 4 + * 6 +
READ	12	4 + * 6 +
PUSH *i*	2 12	4 + * 6 +
READ	2 12	+ * 6 +
PUSH *i*	4 2 12	+ * 6 +
READ	4 2 12	* 6 +
ADD	6 12	* 6 +
READ	6 12	6 +
MPY	72	6 +
READ	72	+
PUSH *i*	6 72	+
READ	6 72	Δ
ADD	78	Δ
READ	78	Δ
PRINT	78	Δ

Notice that when we arrive at PRINT the stack has only one element in it.

What we have been using here is a PDA with arithmetic and output capabilities. Just as we expanded FA's to Mealy and Moore machines, we can expand PDA's to what are called **pushdown transducers.** These are very important but belong to the study of the Theory of Compilers.

The task of converting infix arithmetic expressions (normal ones) into postfix can also be accomplished by a pushdown transducer as an alternative to depending on a dotted line circling a parsing tree. This time all we require is a PDA with an additional PRINT instruction. The input string will be read off of the TAPE character by character. If the character is a number (or, in our example, the letters *a*, *b*, *c*), it is immediately printed out, since the operands in postfix occur in the same order as in the infix equivalent. The operators, however, + and * in our example, must wait to be printed until after the second operand they govern has been printed. The place where the operators wait is, of course, the STACK. If we read $a + b$, we print a, push $+$, print b, pop $+$, print $+$. The output states we need are

and

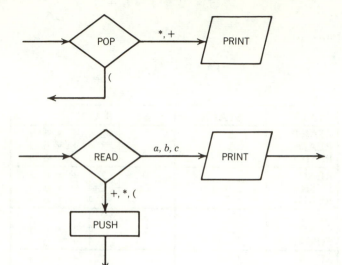

"POP-PRINT" prints whatever it has just popped, and the READ-PRINT prints the character just read. The READ-PUSH pushes whatever character "$+$" or "$*$" or "(" labels the edge leading into it. These are all the machine parts we need.

One more comment should be made about when an operator is ready to be popped. The second operand is recognized by encountering (1) a right parenthesis, (2) another operator having equal or lower precedence, or (3) the end of the input string.

When a right parenthesis is encountered, it means that the infix expression is complete back up to the last left parenthesis.

For example, consider the expression

$$a * (b + c) + b + c$$

The pushdown transducer will do the following:

1. Read a, print a
2. Read $*$, push $*$

3.   Read (, push (

4.   Read *b,* print *b*

5.   Read +, push +

6.   Read *c,* print *c*

7.   Read), pop +, print +

8.   Pop (

9.   Read +, we cannot push + on top of * because of operator precedence, so pop *, print *, push +

10.   Read *b,* print *b*

11.   Read +, we cannot push + on top of +, so print +

12.   Read *c,* print *c*

13.   Read Δ, pop +, print +.

The resulting output sequence is

$$abc + * b + c +$$

which indeed is the correct postfix equivalent of the input. Notice that operator precedence is "built into" this machine. Generalizations of this machine can handle any arithmetic expressions including $-$, $/$, and $**$.

The diagram of the pushdown transducer to convert infix to postfix is given on page 522.

The table on page 523 traces the processing of the input string:

$$(a + b) * (b + c * a)$$

Notice that the printing takes place on the right end of the output sequence.

One trivial observation is that this machine will never print any parentheses. No parentheses are needed to understand postfix or prefix notation. Another is that every operator and operand in the original expression will be printed out. The major observation is that if the output of this transducer is then fed into the previous transducer, the original infix arithmetic expression will be evaluated correctly. In this way we can give a PDA an expression in normal arithmetic notation, and the PDA will evaluate it.

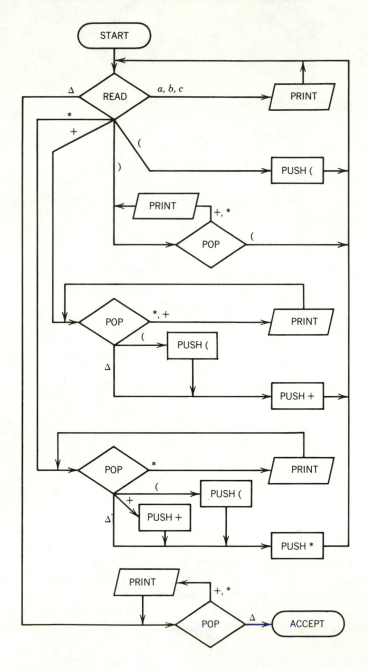

STATE	STACK	TAPE	OUTPUT
START	Δ	$(a + b) * (b + c * a)$	
READ	Δ	$a + b) * (b + c * a)$	
PUSH (	(	$a + b) * (b + c * a)$	
READ	(	$+ b) * (b + c * a)$	
PRINT	(	$+ b) * (b + c * a)$	a
READ	(	$b) * (b + c * a)$	a
POP	Δ	$b) * (b + c * a)$	a
PUSH (	(	$b) * (b + c * a)$	a
PUSH +	+ (	$b) * (b + c * a)$	a
READ	+ (	$) * (b + c * a)$	a
PRINT	+ (	$) * (b + c * a)$	ab
READ	+ (	$* (b + c * a)$	ab
POP	(	$* (b + c * a)$	ab
PRINT	(	$* (b + c * a)$	$ab +$
POP	Δ	$* (b + c * a)$	$ab +$
READ	Δ	$(b + c * a)$	$ab +$
POP	Δ	$(b + c * a)$	$ab +$
PUSH *	*	$(b + c * a)$	$ab +$
READ	*	$b + c * a)$	$ab +$
PUSH (	(*	$b + c * a)$	$ab +$
READ	(*	$+ c * a)$	$ab +$
PRINT	(*	$+ c * a)$	$ab + b$
READ	(*	$c * a)$	$ab + b$
POP	*	$c * a)$	$ab + b$
PUSH (	(*	$c * a)$	$ab + b$
PUSH +	+ (*	$c * a)$	$ab + b$
READ	+ (*	$* a)$	$ab + b$
PRINT	+ (*	$* a)$	$ab + bc$
READ	+ (*	$a)$	$ab + bc$
POP	(*	$a)$	$ab + bc$
PUSH +	+ (*	$a)$	$ab + bc$
PUSH *	* + (*	$a)$	$ab + bc$
READ	* + (*	$)$	$ab + bc$
PRINT	* + (*	$)$	$ab + bca$

STATE	STACK	TAPE	OUTPUT
READ	* + (*	Δ	ab + bca
POP	+ (*	Δ	ab + bca
PRINT	+ (*	Δ	ab + bca *
POP	(*	Δ	ab + bca *
PRINT	(*	Δ	ab + bca * +
POP	*	Δ	ab + bca * +
READ	*	Δ	ab + bca * +
POP	Δ	Δ	ab + bca * +
PRINT	Δ	Δ	ab + bca * + *
POP	Δ	Δ	ab + bca * + *
ACCEPT	Δ	Δ	ab + bca * + *

PROBLEMS

Using top-down parsing, find the left-most derivation in the grammar PLUS-TIMES for the following expressions.

1. $i + i + i$
2. $i * i + i * i$
3. $i * (i + i) * i$
4. $((i) * (i + i)) + i$
5. $(((i)) + ((i)))$

Using bottom-up parsing, find any derivation in the grammar PLUS-TIMES for the following expressions.

6. $i * (i)$
7. $((i) + ((i)))$
8. $(i * i + i)$
9. $i * (i + i)$
10. $(i * i) * i$

The following is a version of an unambiguous grammar for arithmetic expressions employing $-$ and $/$ as well as $+$ and $*$.

$$S \rightarrow E$$
$$E \rightarrow T \mid E + T \mid E - T \mid - T$$
$$T \rightarrow F \mid T * F \mid T / F$$
$$F \rightarrow (E) \mid i$$

Find a left-most derivation in this grammar for the following expressions using the parsing algorithms specified.

11. $((i + i) - i * i) / i - i$

     (Do this by inspection, that means guesswork. Do we divide by zero here?)

12. $i / i + i$ (Top-down)

13. $i * i / i - i$ (Top-down)

14. $i / i / i$ (Top-down)

     Note that this is not ambiguous in this particular grammar. Do we evaluate right to left or left to right?

15. $i - i - i$ (Bottom-up)

16. Using the second pushdown transducer, convert the following arithmetic expressions to postfix notation and then evaluate them on the first pushdown transducer.

     (i) $2 * (7 + 2)$

     (ii) $3 * 4 + 7$

     (iii) $(3 + 5) + 7 * 3$

     (iv) $(3 * 4 + 5) * (2 + 3 * 4)$ *Hint:* The answer is 238.

17. Design a pushdown transducer to convert infix to prefix.

18. Design a pushdown transducer to evaluate prefix.

19. Create an algorithm to convert prefix to postfix.

20. The transducers we designed in this chapter to evaluate postfix notation and to convert infix to postfix have a funny quirk: they can accept some bad input strings and process them as if they were proper.

     (i)   For each machine, find an example of an accepted bad input.

     (ii)   Correct these machines so that they accept only proper inputs.

CHAPTER 23

DECIDABILITY

In Part II we have been laying the foundations of the Theory of Formal Languages. Among the many avenues of investigation we have left open are some questions that seem very natural to ask, such as the following.

1. How can we tell whether or not two different CFG's define the same language?

2. Given a particular CFG, how can we tell whether or not it is ambiguous?

3. Given a CFG, how can we tell whether or not it has an equivalent PDA that is deterministic?

4. Given a CFG that is ambiguous, how can we tell whether or not there is a different CFG that generates the same language but is not ambiguous?

5. How can we tell whether or not the complement of a given context-free language is also context-free?

6. How can we tell whether or not the intersection of two context-free languages is also context-free?

7. Given two context-free grammars, how can we tell whether or not they have a word in common?

8. Given a CFG, how can we tell whether or not there are any words that it *does not* generate? (Is its language all $(\mathbf{a} + \mathbf{b})^*$ or not?)

These are very fine questions, yet, alas, they are unanswerable. There are no algorithms to resolve any of these questions. This is not because computer theorists have been too lazy to find them. No algorithms have been found because no such algorithms exist—anywhere—ever.

We are using the word "exist" in a special philosophical sense. Things that have not yet been discovered but that can someday be discovered we still call existent, as in the sentence, "The planet Jupiter existed long before it was discovered by man." On the other hand, certain concepts lead to mathematical contradictions, so they cannot ever be encountered, as in, "The planet on which $2 + 2 = 5$," or "The smallest planet on which $2 + 2 = 5$," or "The tallest married bachelor." In Part III we shall show how to prove that some computer algorithms are just like married bachelors in that their very existence would lead to unacceptable contradictions. Suppose we have a question that requires a decision procedure. If we prove that no algorithm can exist to answer it, we say that the question is undecidable. Questions 1 through 8 are undecidable.

This is not a totally new concept to us; we have seen it before, but not with this terminology. In geometry, we have learned how to bisect an angle given a straightedge and compass. We cannot do this with a straightedge alone. No algorithm exists to bisect an angle using just a straightedge. We have also been told (although the actual proof is quite advanced) that even with a straightedge and compass we cannot trisect an angle. Not only is it true that no one has ever found a method for trisecting an angle, nobody ever will. And that is a theorem that has been proven.

We shall not present the proof that questions 1 through 8 are undecidable, but toward the end of the book we will prove something very similar.

What Exists	What Does Not Exist
1. What is known	1. Married bachelors
2. What will be known	2. Algorithms for questions 1 through 8 above
3. What might have been known but nobody will ever care enough to figure it out	3. A good 5¢ cigar
. . .	. . .

There are, however, some other fundamental questions about CFG's that we can answer.

1. Given a CFG, can we tell whether or not it generates any words at all? This is the question of **emptiness.**

2. Given a CFG, can we tell whether or not the language it generates is finite or infinite? This is the question of **finiteness.**

3.   Given a CFG and a particular string of letters w, can we tell whether or not w can be generated by the CFG? This is the question of **membership.**

Now we have a completely different story. The answer to each of these three easier questions is "yes." Not only do algorithms to make these three decisions exist, but they are right here on these very pages. The best way to prove that an algorithm exists is to spell it out.

THEOREM 41

Given any CFG, there is an algorithm to determine whether or not it can generate any words.

PROOF

The proof will be by constructive example. We show there exists such an algorithm by presenting one.

In Theorem 21 of Chapter 16 we showed that every CFG that does not generate Λ can be written without Λ-productions.

In that proof we showed how to decide which nonterminals are nullable. The word Λ is a word generated by the CFG if and only if S is nullable. We already know how to decide whether the start symbol S is nullable:

$$S \overset{*}{\Rightarrow} \Lambda?$$

Therefore, the problem of determining whether Λ is a word in the language of any CFG has already been solved.

Let us assume now that Λ is not a word generated by the CFG. In that case, we can convert the CFG to CNF preserving the entire language.

If there is a production of the form

$$S \rightarrow t$$

where t is a terminal, then t is a word in the language.

If there are no such productions we then propose the following algorithm.

Step 1   For each nonterminal N that has some productions of the form

$$N \rightarrow t$$

where t is a terminal or string of terminals, we choose one of these productions and throw out all other productions for which N is on the left side. We then replace N by t in all the productions in which N is on the right side, thus eliminating the nonterminal N altogether. We may have changed the grammar so that it no longer accepts the same language. It may no longer be in CNF. That is fine with us. Every word that can be generated from the new grammar could have been generated by the old CFG. If the old CFG generated any words, then the new one does also.

Step 2   Repeat Step 1 until either it eliminates S or it eliminates no new nonterminals. If S has been eliminated, then the CFG produces some words, if not then it does not. (This we need to prove.)

The algorithm is clearly finite, since it cannot run Step 1 more times than there are nonterminals in the original CNF version. The string of nonterminals that will eventually replace S is a word that could have been derived from S if we retraced in reverse the exact sequence of steps that lead from the terminals to S.

If Step 2 makes us stop while we still have not replaced S, then we can show that no words are generated by this CFG. If there were any words in the language we could retrace the tree from any word and follow the path back to S.

For example, if we have the derivation tree:

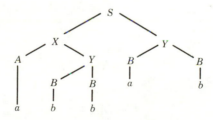

then we can trace backward as follows (the relevant productions can be read from the tree):

$$B \rightarrow b$$

must be a production, so replace all B's with b's:

$$Y \rightarrow BB$$

is a production, so replace Y with bb:

$$A \rightarrow a$$

is a production, so replace A with a:

$$X \rightarrow AY$$

is a production, so replace X with abb.

$$S \rightarrow XY$$

is a production, so replace S with $abbbb$.

Even if the grammar included some other production; for example

$$B \rightarrow d \qquad \text{(where } d \text{ is some other terminal)}$$

we could still retrace the derivation from $abbbb$ to S, but we could just as well end up replacing S by $adddd$—if we chose to begin the backup by replacing all B's by d instead of by b.

The important fact is that some sequence of backward replacements will reach back to S if there is any word in the language.

The proposed algorithm is therefore a decision procedure. ∎

EXAMPLE

Consider this CFG:

$$S \rightarrow XY$$
$$X \rightarrow AX$$
$$X \rightarrow AA$$
$$A \rightarrow a$$
$$Y \rightarrow BY$$
$$Y \rightarrow BB$$
$$B \rightarrow b$$

Step 1 Replace all A's by a and all B's by b. This gives:

$$S \rightarrow XY$$
$$X \rightarrow aX$$
$$X \rightarrow aa$$
$$Y \rightarrow bY$$
$$Y \rightarrow bb$$

Step 1   Replace all X's by aa and all Y's by bb

$$S \rightarrow aabb$$

Step 1   Replace all S's by $aabb$.

Step 2   Terminate Step 1 and discover that S has been eliminated. Therefore, the CFG produces at least one word.   ■

EXAMPLE

Consider this CFG:

$$S \rightarrow XY$$
$$X \rightarrow AX$$
$$A \rightarrow a$$
$$Y \rightarrow BY$$
$$Y \rightarrow BB$$
$$B \rightarrow b$$

Step 1   Replace all A's by a and all B's by b. This gives:

$$S \rightarrow XY$$
$$X \rightarrow aX$$
$$Y \rightarrow bY$$
$$Y \rightarrow bb$$

Step 1   Replace all Y's by bb. This gives:

$$S \rightarrow Xbb$$
$$X \rightarrow aX$$

Step 2   Terminate Step 1 and discover that S is still there. This CFG generates no words.   ■

EXAMPLE

Consider this CFG:

$$S \rightarrow XY$$
$$X \rightarrow ZX$$
$$Z \rightarrow a$$
$$X \rightarrow AX$$

$$X \rightarrow ZZ$$
$$Y \rightarrow BB$$
$$B \rightarrow b$$
$$A \rightarrow XA$$

Step 1   Replace all Z's by a and all B's by b. This gives:

$$S \rightarrow XY$$
$$X \rightarrow aX$$
$$X \rightarrow AX$$
$$X \rightarrow aa$$
$$Y \rightarrow bb$$
$$A \rightarrow XA$$

Step 1   Replace all X's by aa and all Y's by bb. This gives:

$$S \rightarrow aabb$$
$$A \rightarrow aaA$$

Step 1   Replace all S's with $aabb$. This gives:

$$A \rightarrow aaA$$

Step 2   Terminate Step 1 and discover that S has been eliminated. This CFG generates at least one word, even though when we terminated Step 1 there were still some productions left. We notice that the nonterminal A can never be used in the derivation of a word.   ■

As a final word on this topic, we should note that this algorithm does not depend on the CFG's being in CNF, as we shall see in the problems below.

We have not yet gotten all the mileage out of the algorithm in the previous theorem. We can use it again to prove:

THEOREM 42

There is an algorithm to decide whether or not a given nonterminal X in a given CFG is ever used in the generation of words.

PROOF

Following the algorithm of the previous theorem until no new nonterminals can be eliminated will tell us which nonterminals can produce strings of terminals. Clearly, all nonterminals left cannot produce strings of terminals and all those replaced can.

However, it is not enough to know that a particular nonterminal (call it X) can produce a string of terminals. We must also determine whether it can be reached from S in the middle of a derivation.

In other words, there are two things that could be wrong with X.

1. X produces strings of terminals but cannot be reached from S. For example in

$$S \rightarrow Ya \mid Yb$$
$$Y \rightarrow ab$$
$$X \rightarrow aY \mid b$$

2. X can be reached from S but only in working strings that involve useless nonterminals that prevent word derivations. For example in

$$S \rightarrow Ya \mid Yb \mid a$$
$$Y \rightarrow XZ$$
$$X \rightarrow ab$$
$$Z \rightarrow Y$$

Here Z is useless in the production of words, so Y is useless in the production of words, so X is useless in the production of words.

The algorithm that will resolve these issues is of the blue paint variety.

Step 1   Use the algorithm of Theorem 41 to find out which nonterminals cannot produce strings of terminals. Call these **useless.**

Step 2   Purify the grammar by eliminating all productions involving the useless nonterminals. If X has been eliminated, we are done. If not, proceed.

Step 3   Paint all X's blue.

Step 4   If any nonterminal is the left side of a production with anything blue on the right, paint it blue, and paint all occurrences of it throughout the grammar blue, too.

Step 5   The key to this approach is that all the remaining productions are guaranteed to terminate. This means that *any* blue on the right gives us blue on the left (not just *all* blue on the right, the way we pared down the row grammar in Chapter 18). Repeat Step 4 until nothing new is painted blue.

Step 6   If S is blue, X is a useful member of the CFG, since there are words with derivations that involve X-productions. If not, X is not useful.

Obviously, this algorithm is finite, since the only repeated part is Step 4 and that can be repeated only as many times as there are nonterminals in the grammar.

It is also clear that if X is used in the production of some word, then S will be painted blue, since if we have

$$S \Rightarrow \ldots \Rightarrow (\text{blah}) \; X \; (\text{blah}) \Rightarrow \ldots \Rightarrow \text{word}$$

then the nonterminal that put X into the derivation in the first place will be blue, and the nonterminal that put that one in will be blue, and the nonterminal from which that came will be blue . . . up to S.

Now let us say that S is blue. Let us say that it caught the blue through this sequence: X made A blue and A made B blue and B made C blue . . . up to S. The production in which X made A blue looked like this:

$$A \rightarrow (\text{blah}) \; X \; (\text{blah})$$

Now the two (blah)'s might not be strings of terminals, but it must be true that any nonterminals in the (blah)'s can be turned into strings of terminals because they survived Step 2. So we know that there is a derivation from A to a string made up of X with terminals

$$A \overset{*}{\Rightarrow} (\text{string of terminals}) \; X \; (\text{string of terminals})$$

We also know that there is a production of the form

$$B \Rightarrow (\text{blah}) \; A \; (\text{blah})$$

that can likewise be turned into

$$B \overset{*}{\Rightarrow} (\text{string of terminals}) \; A \; (\text{string of terminals})$$
$$\overset{*}{\Rightarrow} (\text{string of terminals}) \; X \; (\text{string of terminals})$$

We now back all the way up to S and realize that there is a derivation

$$S \overset{*}{\Rightarrow} (\text{string of terminals}) \; X \; (\text{string of terminals})$$
$$\overset{*}{\Rightarrow} (\text{word})$$

Therefore, this algorithm is exactly the decision procedure we need to decide if X is actually ever used in the production of a word in this CFG.   ■

EXAMPLE

Consider the CFG

$$S \rightarrow ABa \mid bAZ \mid b$$
$$A \rightarrow Xb \mid bZa$$
$$B \rightarrow bAA$$
$$X \rightarrow aZa \mid aaa$$
$$Z \rightarrow ZAbA$$

We quickly see that X terminates (goes to all terminals, whether or not it can be reached from S). Z is useless (because it appears in all of its productions). A is blue. B is blue. S is blue. So X must be involved in the production of words. To see one such word we can write:

$$A \rightarrow Xb$$
$$B \rightarrow bAA$$

Now since A is useful, it must produce some string of terminals. In fact,

$$A \overset{*}{\Rightarrow} aaab$$

So,

$$B \overset{*}{\Rightarrow} bAaaab$$
$$\Rightarrow bXbaaab$$

Now

$$S \rightarrow ABa$$
$$\overset{*}{\Rightarrow} aaabBa$$
$$\overset{*}{\Rightarrow} aaabbXbaaaba$$

We know that X is useful, so this is a working string in the derivation of an actual word in the language of this grammar. ∎

The last two theorems have been part of a project, designed by Bar-Hillel, Perles, and Shamir to settle a more important question.

THEOREM 43

There is an algorithm to decide whether a given CFG generates an infinite language or a finite language.

PROOF

The proof will be by constructive algorithm. We shall show that there exists such a procedure by presenting one. If any word in the language is long enough to apply the Pumping Lemma (Theorem 35) to, we can produce an infinite sequence of new words in the language.

If the language is infinite, then there must be some words long enough so that the Pumping Lemma applies to them. Therefore, the language of a CFG is infinite if and only if the Pumping Lemma can be applied.

The essence of the Pumping Lemma was to find a self-embedded nonterminal X, that is, one such that some derivation tree starting at X leads to another X.

We shall show in a moment how to tell if a particular nonterminal is self-embedded, but first we should also note that the Pumping Lemma will work only if the nonterminal that we pump is involved in the derivation of any words in the language. Without the algorithm of Theorem 42, we could be building larger and larger trees, none of which are truly derivation trees. For example, in the CFG:

$$S \rightarrow aX \mid b$$
$$X \rightarrow XXb$$

the nonterminal X is certainly self-embedded, but the language is finite nonetheless.

So the first step is:

Step 1   Use the algorithm of Theorem 42 to determine which nonterminals are not used to produce any words. Eliminate all productions involving them.

Step 2   Use the following algorithm to test each of the remaining nonterminals in turn to see if it is self-embedded. When a self-embedded one is discovered stop.
To test X:
   (i)   Change all X's on the left side of productions into the Russian letter Ж, but leave all the X's on the right side of productions alone.
   (ii)   Paint all X's blue.

(iii)   If Y is any nonterminal that is the left side of any production with some blue on the right side, then paint all Y's blue.

(iv)   Repeat Step 2 (iii) until nothing new is painted blue.

(v)   If Ж is blue, the X is self-embedded; if not, not.

Step 3   If any nonterminal left in the grammar after Step 1 is self-embedded, the language generated is infinite. If not, then the language is finite.

   The explanation of why this procedure is finite and works is identical to the explanation in the proof of Theorem 42.   ■

EXAMPLE

Consider the grammar:

$$S \rightarrow ABa \mid bAZ \mid b$$
$$A \rightarrow Xb \mid bZa$$
$$B \rightarrow bAA$$
$$X \rightarrow aZa \mid bA \mid aaa$$
$$Z \rightarrow ZAbA$$

This is the grammar of the previous example with the additional production $X \rightarrow bA$. As before, Z is useless while all other nonterminals are used in the production of words. We now test to see if X is self-embedded.

   First we trim away Z:

$$S \rightarrow ABa \mid b$$
$$A \rightarrow Xb$$
$$B \rightarrow bAA$$
$$X \rightarrow bA \mid aaa$$

Now we introduce:

$$S \rightarrow ABa \mid b$$
$$A \rightarrow Xb$$
$$B \rightarrow bAA$$
$$Ж \rightarrow bA \mid aaa$$

Now the paint:

$$X \text{ is blue}$$
$$A \rightarrow Xb, \text{ so } A \text{ is blue}$$
$$Ж \rightarrow bA, \text{ so } Ж \text{ is blue}$$

$$B \rightarrow A, \text{ so } B \text{ is blue}$$
$$S \rightarrow ABa, \text{ so } S \text{ is blue}$$

Conclusion:

Ж is blue, so the language generated by this CFG is infinite.   ■

We now turn our attention to the last decision problem we can handle for CFG's.

THEOREM 44

Given a CFG and a word w in the same alphabet, we can decide whether or not w can be generated by the CFG.

PROOF

This theorem should have a one-word proof: "Parsing." When we try to parse w in the CFG we arrive at a derivation or a dead-end. Let us carefully explain why this is a decision procedure.

If we were using top-down parsing, we would start with S and produce the total language tree until we either found the word w or terminated all branches for the reasons given in Chapter 21: forbidden substring, working string too long, and so on.

Let us now give a careful argument to show that this is a finite process. Assume that the grammar is in CNF.

First let us show that starting with S we need exactly $(\text{length}(w) - 1)$ applications of live productions $N \rightarrow XY$, to generate w, and exactly $\text{length}(w)$ applications of dead productions, $N \rightarrow t$. This is clear since live productions increase the number of symbols in the working string by one, and dead productions do not increase the total number of symbols at all but increase the number of terminals by one. We start with one symbol and end with $\text{length}(w)$ symbols. Therefore we have applied $(\text{length}(w) - 1)$ live productions. Starting with no terminals in the working string (S alone), we have finished up with $\text{length}(w)$ terminals. Therefore, we have applied exactly $\text{length}(w)$ dead productions. If we count as a step one use of any production rule, then the total number of steps in the derivation of w must be:

$$\text{number of live productions} + \text{number of dead productions}$$
$$= 2 \text{ length}(w) - 1$$

Therefore, once we have developed the total language tree this number of levels down, either we have produced w or else we never will.

Therefore, the process is finite and takes at most

$$p^{2 \text{length}(w) \, - \, 1}$$

steps where p is the number of productions in the grammar. ∎

There is one tricky point here. We have said that this algorithm is a decision procedure since it is finite. However, the number

$$p^{2 \text{length}(w) \, - \, 1}$$

can be phenomenally large. We must be careful to note that the algorithm is called *finite* because once we are given the grammar (in CNF) and the word w, we can predict ahead of time (before running the algorithm) that the procedure must end within a known number of steps. This is what it means for an algorithm to be a finite decision procedure. It is conceivable that for some grammar we could not specify an upper bound on the number of steps the derivation of w might have. We might then have to consider suggestions such as, "Keep trying all possible sequences of productions no matter how long." However, this would not be a decision procedure since if w is not generatable by the grammar our search would be infinite, but at no time would we know that we could not finally succeed. We shall see some non-context-free grammars later that have this unhappy property.

The decision procedure presented in the proof above is adequate to prove that the problem has an algorithmic solution, but in practice the number of steps is often much too large even to think of ever doing the problem this way. Although this is a book on *theory* and such mundane considerations as *economy* and *efficiency* should not, in general, influence us, the number of steps in the algorithm above is too gross to let stand unimproved.

We now present a much better algorithm discovered by John Cocke and subsequently published by Tadao Kasami (1965) and Daniel H. Younger (1967), called the **CYK algorithm.**

Let us again assume that the grammar is in CNF.

First let us make a list of all the nonterminals in the grammar, including S.

$$S \quad N_1 \quad N_2 \quad N_3 \ldots$$

These will be the column headings of a large table. Under each symbol let us list all the single-letter terminals that they can generate. These we read off from the dead productions, $N \rightarrow t$.

It is possible that some nonterminals generate no single terminals, in which case we leave the space under them blank.

On the next row below this we list for each nonterminal all the words of length 2 that it generates. For N_1 to generate a word of length 2 it must have a production of the form $N_1 \rightarrow N_2 N_3$, where N_2 generates a word of length

1 and N_3 also generates a word of length 1. We do not rely on human insight to construct this row, but follow a mechanical procedure: For each production of the form $N_1 \to N_2N_3$, we multiply the set of words of length 1 that N_2 generates (already in the table) by the set of words of length 1 that N_3 generates (this set is also already in the table). This product set we write down on the table in row 2 under the column N_1.

Now we construct the next row of the table: all the words of length 3. A nonterminal N_1 generates a word of length 3 if it has a live production $N_1 \to N_2N_3$ and N_2 generates a word of length 1 and N_3 generates a word of length 2 or else N_2 generates a word of length 2 and N_3 generates a word of length 1. To produce the list of words in row 3 under N_1 mechanically, we go to row 1 under N_2 and multiply that set of words by the set of words found in row 2 under N_3. To this we add (also in row 3) the product of row 2 under N_1 times row 1 under N_3. We must do this for every live production to complete row 3.

We continue constructing this table. The next row has all the words of length 4. Those derived from N_1 by the production $N_1 \to N_2 N_3$ are the union of the products:

$$\text{(all words of length 1 from } N_2) \text{ (all words of length 3 from } N_3)$$
$$+ \ \text{(all words of length 2 from } N_2) \text{ (all words of length 2 from } N_3)$$
$$+ \ \text{(all words of length 3 from } N_2) \text{ (all words of length 1 from } N_3)$$

All the constituent sets of words mentioned here have already been calculated in this table.

We continue this table until we have all words of lengths up to length(w) generated by each nonterminal. We then check to see if w is among those generated from S. This will definitively decide the question.

We can streamline this procedure slightly by eliminating from the table all small words generated that cannot be substrings of w since these could not be part of the forming of w. Also at the next-to-the-last row of words (of (length(w) $-$ 1)) we need only generate the entries in those columns X and Y for which there is a production of the form

$$S \to XY$$

and then the only entry we need calculate in the last row (the row of words of length w) is the one under S.

EXAMPLE

Consider the CFG:

$$S \to XY$$

$$X \rightarrow XA$$
$$Y \rightarrow AY$$
$$A \rightarrow a$$
$$X \rightarrow a \mid b$$
$$Y \rightarrow a$$

Let us test to see if the word *babaa* is generated by this grammar. First we write out the nonterminals as column heads.

S	X	Y	A

The first row is the list of all the single terminals each generates.

S	X	Y	A
	a b	a	a

Notice that S generates no single terminal. Now to construct the next row of the table we must find all words of length 2 generated by each nonterminal.

	S	X	Y	A
Length 1		a b	a	a
Length 2	aa ba	aa ba	aa	

The entries in row 2 in the S column come from the live production $S \rightarrow XY$, so we multiply the set of words generated by X in row 1 times the words generated by Y in row 1. Also $X \rightarrow XA$ and $Y \rightarrow AY$ give multiplications that generate the words in row 2 in the X and Y columns. Notice that A is the left side of no live production, so its column has stopped growing. A produces no words longer than one letter.

The third row is

	S	X	Y	A
Length 1		a b	a	a
Length 2	aa ba	aa ba	aa	
Length 3	aaa baa	aaa baa	aaa	

The entry for column S comes from $S \to XY$:

> (all words of length 1 from X) (all words of length 2 from Y)
> + (all words of length 2 from X) (all words of length 1 from Y)
> $= \{a + b\} \{aa\} + \{aa + ba\} \{a\}$
> $= aaa + baa + aaa + baa$
> $= aaa + baa$

Notice that we have eliminated duplications. However we should eliminate more. Our target word w does not have the substring aaa, so retaining that possibility cannot help us form w. We eliminate this string from the table under column S, under column X, and under column Y. We can no longer claim that our table is a complete list of all words of lengths 1, 2, or 3 generated by the grammar, but it is a table of all strings generated by the grammar that may help derive w. We continue with row 4.

	S	X	Y	A
Length 1		$a\ b$	a	a
Length 2	$aa\ bb$	$aa\ ba$	aa	
Length 3	baa	baa		
Length 4	$aaaa$ $baaa$	$baaa$		

In column S we have

> (all words of length 1 from X) (all words of length 3 from Y)
> + (all words of length 2 from X) (all words of length 2 from Y)
> + (all words of length 3 from X) (all words of length 1 from Y)
> $= \{a + b\} \{\text{nothing}\} + \{aa + ba\} \{aa\} + \{baa\} \{a\}$
> $= aaaa + baaa + baaa$
> $= aaaa + baaa$

To calculate row 4 in column X, we use the production $X \to XA$

> (all words of length 1 from X) (all words of length 3 from A)
> + (all words of length 2 from X) (all words of length 2 from A)
> + (all words of length 3 from X) (all words of length 1 from A)
> $= \{a + b\} \{\text{nothing}\} + \{aa + ba\} \{\text{nothing}\} + \{baa\} \{a\}$
> $= baaa$

Row 4 in column Y is done similarly:

(all words of length 1 from A) (all words of length 3 from Y)
+ (all words of length 2 from A) (all words of length 2 from Y)
+ (all words of length 3 from A) (all words of length 1 from Y)
$$= \{a\} \{\text{nothing}\} + \{\text{nothing}\} \{aa\} + \{\text{nothing}\} \{a\}$$
$$= \text{nothing}$$

Again we see that we have generated some words that are not possible substrings of w. Both $aaaa$ and $baaa$ are unacceptable and will be dropped. This makes the whole row empty. No four-letter words generated by this grammar are substrings of w.

The next row is as far as we have to go, since we have to know only all the five-letter words that are generated by S to decide the fate of our target word $w = babaa$. These are:

(all words of length 1 from X) (all words of length 4 from Y)
+ (all words of length 2 from X) (all words of length 3 from Y)
+ (all words of length 3 from X) (all words of length 2 from Y)
+ (all words of length 4 from X) (all words of length 1 from Y)
$$= \{a + b\} \{\text{nothing}\} + \{aa + ba\} \{\text{nothing}\} + \{baa\} \{aa\}$$
$$+ \{\text{nothing}\} \{a\}$$
$$= baaaa$$

The only five-letter word in this table is $baaaa$, but unfortunately $baaaa$ is not w, so we know conclusively that w is not generated by this grammar. This was not so much work, especially when compared with the

$$p^{2 \ \text{length}(w) \ - \ 1} = 6^9 = 10,077,696$$

strings of productions the algorithm proposed in the proof of Theorem 44 would have made us check. ∎

Let's run through this process quickly on one more example.

EXAMPLE

Consider the grammar:

$$S \rightarrow AX \mid BY$$
$$X \rightarrow SA$$

$$Y \rightarrow SB$$
$$A \rightarrow a$$
$$B \rightarrow b$$
$$S \rightarrow a \mid b$$

This is a CNF grammar for ODDPALINDROME. Let w be the word *ababa*. This word does not contain a double a or a double b, so we should eliminate all generated words that have either substring. However, for the sake of making the table a complete collection of odd palindromes of length 5 or less, we shall not make use of this efficient shortcut.

S has two live productions, so the words generated by S of length 5 are:

(all words of length 1 from A) (all words of length 4 from X)

+ (all words of length 2 from A) (all words of length 3 from X)

+ (all words of length 3 from A) (all words of length 2 from X)

+ (all words of length 4 from A) (all words of length 1 from X)

+

(all words of length 1 from B) (all words of length 4 from Y)

+ (all words of length 2 from B) (all words of length 3 from Y)

+ (all words of length 3 from B) (all words of length 2 from Y)

+ (all words of length 4 from B) (all words of length 1 from Y)

The CYK table is:

	S	X	Y	A	B
Length 1	*a b*			*a*	*b*
Length 2		*aa ba*	*ab bb*		
Length 3	*aaa aba* *bab bbb*				
Length 4		*aaaa abaa* *baba bbba*	*aaab abab* *babb bbbb*		
Length 5	*aaaaa aabaa* *ababa abbba* *baaab babab* *bbabb bbbbb*				

We do find w among the words of length 5 generated from S.

If we had eliminated all words with double letters, we would have had an even quicker search; but since we know what this language looks like, we write out the whole table to get an understanding of the meaning of the nonterminals X and Y. ■

PROBLEMS

Decide whether or not the following grammars generate any words using the algorithm of Theorem 40.

1. $S \rightarrow aSa \mid bSb$

2. $S \rightarrow XY$
   $X \rightarrow SY$
   $Y \rightarrow SX$
   $X \rightarrow a$
   $Y \rightarrow b$

3. $S \rightarrow AB$
   $A \rightarrow BC$
   $C \rightarrow DA$
   $B \rightarrow CD$
   $D \rightarrow a$
   $A \rightarrow b$

4. $S \rightarrow XS$
   $X \rightarrow YX$
   $Y \rightarrow YY$
   $Y \rightarrow XX$
   $X \rightarrow a$

5. $S \rightarrow AB$
   $A \rightarrow BSB$
   $B \rightarrow AAS$
   $A \rightarrow CC$
   $B \rightarrow CC$
   $C \rightarrow SS$
   $A \rightarrow a \mid b$
   $C \rightarrow b \mid bb$

6. Modify the proof of Theorem 40 so that it can be applied to any CFG, not just those in CNF.

For each of the following grammars decide whether the language they generate is finite or infinite using the algorithm in Theorem 43.

7. $S \rightarrow XS \mid b$
   $X \rightarrow YZ$
   $Z \rightarrow XY$
   $Y \rightarrow ab$

8. $S \rightarrow XS \mid b$
      $X \rightarrow YZ$
      $Z \rightarrow XY$
      $X \rightarrow ab$

9. $S \rightarrow XY \mid bb$
      $X \rightarrow YX$
      $Y \rightarrow XY \mid SS$

10. $S \rightarrow XY \mid bb$
      $X \rightarrow YY$
      $Y \rightarrow XY \mid SS$

11. $S \rightarrow XY$
      $X \rightarrow AA \mid YY \mid b$
      $A \rightarrow BC$
      $B \rightarrow AC$
      $C \rightarrow BA$
      $Y \rightarrow a$

12. $S \rightarrow XY$
      $X \rightarrow AA \mid XY \mid b$
      $A \rightarrow BC$
      $B \rightarrow AC$
      $C \rightarrow BA$
      $Y \rightarrow a$

13.   (i) $S \rightarrow SS \mid b$
            $X \rightarrow SS \mid SX \mid a$
      (ii) $S \rightarrow XX$
            $X \rightarrow SS \mid a$

14.   Modify Theorem 43 so that the decision procedure works on all CFG's, not just those in CNF.

15.   Prove that all CFG's with only the one nonterminal S and one or more live productions and one or more dead productions generate an infinite language.

For the following grammars and words decide whether or not the word is generated by the grammar using the CYK algorithm.

16. $S \rightarrow SS$ $w = abba$
      $S \rightarrow a$
      $S \rightarrow bb$

17. $S \rightarrow XS$ $w = baab$
    $X \rightarrow XX$
    $X \rightarrow a$
    $S \rightarrow b$

18. (i) $S \rightarrow XY$ $w = abbaa$
           $X \rightarrow SY$
           $Y \rightarrow SS$
           $X \rightarrow a \mid bb$
           $Y \rightarrow aa$

    (ii) $S \rightarrow AB \mid CD \mid a \mid b$ $w = bababab$
           $A \rightarrow a$
           $B \rightarrow SA$
           $C \rightarrow DS$
           $D \rightarrow b$

19. Modify the CYK-algorithm so that it applies to any CFG, not just those in CNF.

20. We stated at the beginning of this chapter that the problem of determining whether a given PDA accepts all possible inputs is undecidable. This is not true for deterministic PDA's. Show how to decide whether the language accepted by a DPDA is all of $(a + b)^*$ or not.

PART III

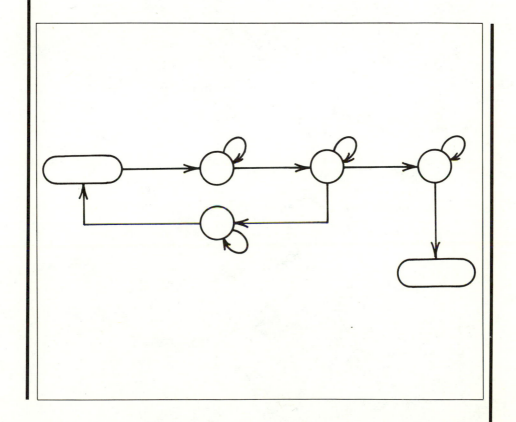

TURING
THEORY

CHAPTER 24

TURING
MACHINES

At this point it will help us to recapitulate the major themes of the previous two parts and outline all the material we have yet to present in the rest of the book all in one large table.

Language Defined by	Corresponding Acceptor	Nondeterminism = determinism?	Language Closed Under	What Can be Decided	Example of Application
Regular expression	Finite automaton Transition graph	Yes	Union, product, Kleene star, intersection, complement	Equivalence, emptiness, finiteness, membership	Text editors, sequential circuits
Context-free grammar	Pushdown automaton	No	Union, product, Kleene star	Emptiness finiteness membership	Programming language statements, compilers
Type 0 grammar	Turing machine, Post machine, 2PDA, nPDA	Yes	Union, product, Kleene star	Not much	Computers

We see from the lower right entry in the table that we are about to fulfill the promise made in the introduction. We shall soon provide a mathematical model for the entire family of modern-day computers. This model will enable us not only to study some theoretical limitations on the tasks that computers can perform, it will also be a model that we can use to show that certain operations *can* be done by computer. This new model will turn out to be surprisingly like the models we have been studying so far.

Another interesting observation we can make about the bottom row of the table is that we take a very pessimistic view of our ability to decide the important questions about this mathematical model (which as we see is called a Turing machine).

We shall prove that we cannot even decide if a given word is accepted by a given Turing machine. This situation is unthinkable for FA's or PDA's, but now it is one of the unanticipated facts of life—a fact with grave repercussions.

There is a definite progression in the rows of this table. All regular languages are context-free languages, and we shall see that all context-free languages are Turing machine languages. Historically, the order of invention of these ideas is:

1. Regular languages and FA's were developed by Kleene, Mealy, Moore, Rabin, and Scott in the 1950s.

2. CFG's and PDA's were developed later, by Chomsky, Oettinger, Schützenberger, and Evey, mostly in the 1960s.

3. Turing machines and their theory were developed by Alan Mathison Turing and Emil Post in the 1930s and 1940s.

It is less surprising that these dates are out of order than that Turing's work predated the invention of the computer itself. Turing was not analyzing a specimen that sat on the table in front of him; he was engaged in inventing the beast. It was directly from the ideas in his work on mathematical models that the first computers were built. This is another demonstration that there is nothing more practical than a good abstract theory.

Since Turing machines will be our ultimate model for computers, they will necessarily have output capabilities. Output is very important, so important that a program with no output statements might seem totally useless because it would never convey to humans the result of its calculations. We may have heard it said that the one statement every program must have is an output statement. This is not exactly true. Consider the following program (written in no particular language):

1. READ X

2. IF $X = 1$ THEN END

3. IF $X = 2$ THEN DIVIDE X BY 0

4. IF $X > 2$ THEN GOTO STATEMENT 4

Let us assume that the input is a positive integer. If the program terminates naturally, then we know X was 1. If it terminates by creating overflow or was interrupted by some error message warning of illegal calculation (crashes), then we know that X was 2. If we find that our program was terminated because it exceeded our alloted time on the computer, then we know X was greater than 2. We shall see in a moment that the same trichotomy applies to Turing machines.

DEFINITION

A **Turing machine,** denoted TM, is a collection of six things:

1. An alphabet Σ of input letters, which for clarity's sake does not contain the blank symbol Δ.

2. A TAPE divided into a sequence of numbered cells each containing one character or a blank. The input word is presented to the machine one letter per cell beginning in the left-most cell, called cell i. The rest of the TAPE is initially filled with blanks, Δ's.

cell i	cell ii	cell iii	cell iv	cell v	
					. . .

3. A TAPE HEAD that can in one step read the contents of a cell on the TAPE, replace it with some other character, and reposition itself to the next cell to the right or to the left of the one it has just read. At the start of the processing, the TAPE HEAD always begins by reading the input in cell i. The TAPE HEAD can never move left from cell i. If it is given orders to do so, the machine crashes.

4. An alphabet, Γ, of characters that can be printed on the TAPE by the TAPE HEAD. This can include Σ. Even though we allow the TAPE HEAD to print a Δ we call this erasing and do not include the blank as a letter in the alphabet Γ.

5. A finite set of states including exactly one START state from which we begin execution (and which we may reenter during execution) and some (maybe none) HALT states that cause execution to terminate when we enter them. The other states have no functions, only names:

$$q_1, q_2, q_3, \ldots \quad \text{or} \quad 1, 2, 3, \ldots$$

6.   A **program,** which is a set of rules that tell us, on the basis of the letter the TAPE HEAD has just read, how to change states, what to print and where to move the TAPE HEAD. We depict the program as a collection of directed edges connecting the states. Each edge is labeled with a triplet of information:

(letter, letter, direction)

The first letter (either Δ or from Σ or Γ) is the character the TAPE HEAD reads from the cell to which it is pointing. The second letter (also Δ or from Γ) is what the TAPE HEAD prints in the cell before it leaves. The third component, the direction, tells the TAPE HEAD whether to move one cell to the right, *R,* or one cell to the left, *L.*

No stipulation is made as to whether every state has an edge leading from it for every possible letter on the TAPE. If we are in a state and read a letter that offers no choice of path to another state, we *crash;* that means we terminate execution unsuccessfully. To terminate execution of a certain input successfully we must be led to a HALT state. The word on the input TAPE is then said to be *accepted* by the TM.

A crash also occurs when we are in the first cell on the TAPE and try to move the TAPE HEAD left.

By definition, all Turing machines are **deterministic.** This means that there is no state q that has two or more edges leaving it labeled with the same first letter.

For example,

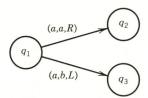

is not allowed.   ∎

EXAMPLE

The following is the TAPE from a Turing machine about to run on the input *aba*

i	ii	iii	iv	v	vi	
a	b	a	Δ	Δ	Δ	. . .

TAPE HEAD

The program for this TM is given as a directed graph with labeled edges as shown below

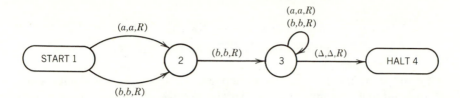

Notice that the loop at state 3 has two labels. The edges from state 1 to state 2 could have been drawn as one edge with two labels.

We start, as always, with the TAPE HEAD reading cell i and the program in the start state, which is here labeled state 1. We depict this as

1

a̲ba

The number on top is the number of the state we are in. Below that is the current meaningful contents of the string on the TAPE up to the beginning of the infinite run of blanks. It is possible that there may be a Δ inside this string. We underline the character in the cell that is *about to be read*.

At this point in our example, the TAPE HEAD reads the letter *a* and we follow the edge (*a,a,R*) to state 2. The instructions of this edge to the TAPE HEAD are "read an *a*, print an *a*, move right."

The TAPE now looks like this:

i	ii	iii	iv	
a	b	a	Δ	. . .

Notice that we have stopped writing the words "TAPE HEAD" under the indicator under the TAPE. It is still the TAPE HEAD nonetheless.

We can record the execution process by writing:

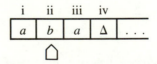

At this point we are in state 2. Since we are reading the *b* in cell ii, we must take the ride to state 3 on the edge labeled (*b,b,R*). The TAPE HEAD replaces the *b* with a *b* and moves right one cell. The idea of replacing a letter with itself may seem silly, but it unifies the structure of Turing machines.

We could instead have constructed a machine that uses two different types of instructions: either print or move, not both at once. Our system allows us to formulate two possible meanings in a single type of instruction.

(a, a, R) means move, but do not change the TAPE cell

(a, b, R) means move and change the TAPE cell

This system does not give us a one-step way of changing the contents of the TAPE cell without moving the TAPE HEAD, but we shall see that this too can be done by our TM's.

Back to our machine. We are now up to

$$\begin{matrix} 1 \\ a\underline{b}a \end{matrix} \rightarrow \begin{matrix} 2 \\ ab\underline{a} \end{matrix} \rightarrow \begin{matrix} 3 \\ aba\underline{\ } \end{matrix}$$

The TAPE now looks like this.

i	ii	iii	iv	
a	b	a	Δ	. . .

We are in state 3 reading an *a*, so we loop. That means we stay in state 3 but we move the TAPE HEAD to cell iv.

$$\begin{matrix} 3 \\ ab\underline{a} \end{matrix} \rightarrow \begin{matrix} 3 \\ aba\underline{\Delta} \end{matrix}$$

This is one of those times when we must indicate a Δ as part of the meaningful contents of the TAPE.

We are now in state 3 reading a Δ, so we move to state 4.

$$\begin{matrix} 3 \\ aba\underline{\Delta} \end{matrix} \rightarrow \begin{matrix} 4 \\ aba\Delta\underline{\Delta} \end{matrix}$$

The input string *aba* has been accepted by this TM. This particular machine did not change any of the letters on the TAPE, so at the end of the run the TAPE still reads *aba*Δ . . . . This is not a requirement for the acceptance of a string, just a phenomenon that happened this time.

In summary, the whole execution can be depicted by the following **execution chain,** also called a **process chain,** or a **trace of execution,** or simply a **trace:**

$$\underset{aba}{1} \to \underset{aba}{2} \to \underset{aba}{3} \to \underset{aba\Delta}{3} \to \text{HALT}$$

This is a new use for the arrow. It is neither a production nor a derivation.

Let us consider which input strings are accepted by this TM. Any first letter, a or b, will lead us to state 2. From state 2 to state 3 we require that we read the letter b. Once in state 3 we stay there as the TAPE HEAD moves right and right again, moving perhaps many cells until it encounters a Δ. Then we get to the HALT state and accept the word. Any word that reaches state 3 will eventually be accepted. If the second letter is an a, then we crash at state 2. This is because there is no edge coming from state 2 with directions for what happens when the TAPE HEAD reads an a.

The language of words accepted by this machine is: All words over the alphabet $\{a,b\}$ in which the second letter is a b.

This is a regular language because it can also be defined by the regular expression:

$$(a+b)b(a+b)*$$

This TM is also reminiscent of FA's, making only one pass over the input string, moving its TAPE HEAD always to the right, and never changing a letter it has read. TM's can do more tricks, as we shall soon see. ∎

EXAMPLE

Consider the following TM.

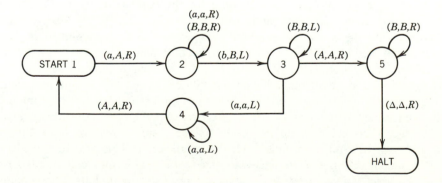

We have only drawn the program part of the TM, since initial appearance of the TAPE depends on the input word. This is a more complicated example of a TM. We analyze it by first explaining what it does and then recognizing how it does it.

The language this TM accepts is $\{a^n b^n\}$.

By examining the program we can see that the TAPE HEAD may print any of the letters a, A or B, or a Δ, and it may read any of the letters a, b, A or B or a blank. Technically, the input alphabet is $\Sigma = \{a, b\}$ and the output alphabet is $\Gamma = \{a, \quad A, \quad B\}$, since Δ is the symbol for a blank or empty cell and is not a legal character in an alphabet. Let us describe the algorithm, informally in English, before looking at the directed graph that is the program.

Let us assume that we start with a word of the language $\{a^n b^n\}$ on the TAPE. We begin by taking the a in the first cell and changing it to the character A. (If the first cell does not contain an a, the program should crash. We can arrange this by having only one edge leading from START and labeling it to read an a.) The conversion from a to A means that this a has been counted. We now want to find the b in the word that pairs off with this a. So we keep moving the TAPE HEAD to the right, without changing anything it passes over, until it reaches the first b. When we reach this b, we change it into the character B, which again means that it too has been counted. Now we move the TAPE HEAD back down to the left until it reaches the first uncounted a. The first time we make our descent down the TAPE this will be the a in cell ii.

How do we know when we get to the first uncounted a? We cannot tell the TAPE HEAD to "find cell ii." This instruction is not in its repertoire. We can, however, tell the TAPE HEAD to keep moving to the left until it gets to the character A. When it hits the A we bounce one cell to the right and there we are. In doing this the TAPE HEAD passed through cell ii on its way down the TAPE. However, when we were first there we did not recognize it as our destination. Only when we bounce off of our marker, the first A encountered, do we realize where we are. Half the trick in programming TM's is to know where the TAPE HEAD is by bouncing off of landmarks.

When we have located this left-most uncounted a we convert it into an A and begin marching up the TAPE looking for the corresponding b. This means that we skip over some a's and over the symbol B, which we previously wrote, leaving them unchanged, until we get to the first uncounted b. Once we have located it, we have found our second pair of a and b. We count this second b by converting it into a B, and we march back down the TAPE looking for our next uncounted a. This will be in cell iii. Again, we cannot tell the TAPE HEAD, "find cell iii." We must program it to find the intended cell. The same instructions as given last time work again. Back down to the first A we meet and then up one cell. As we march down we walk through a B and some a's until we first reach the character A. This will be the second A, the one in cell ii. We bounce off this to the right, into cell iii, and find an a. This we convert to A and move up the TAPE to find its corresponding b.

This time marching up the TAPE we again skip over a's and B's until we find the first b. We convert this to B and march back down looking for the first unconverted a. We repeat the pairing process over and over.

What happens when we have paired off all the a's and b's? After we have converted our last *b* into a *B* and we move left looking for the next *a* we find that after marching left back through the last of the *B*'s we encounter an *A*. We recognize that this means we are out of little *a*'s in the initial field of *a*'s at the beginning of the word.

We are about ready to accept the word, but we want to make sure that there are no more *b*'s that have not been paired off with *a*'s, or any extraneous *a*'s at the end. Therefore we move back up through the field of *B*'s to be sure that they are followed by a blank, otherwise the word initially may have been *aaabbbb* or *aaabbba*.

When we know that we have only *A*'s and *B*'s on the TAPE, in equal number, we can accept the input string.

The following is a picture of the contents of the TAPE at each step in the processing of the string *aaabbb*. Remember, in a trace the TAPE HEAD is indicated by the underlining of the letter it is about to read.

$$\underline{a}\ a\ a\ b\ b\ b$$

$$A\ \underline{a}\ a\ b\ b\ b$$

$$A\ a\ \underline{a}\ b\ b\ b$$

$$A\ a\ a\ \underline{b}\ b\ b$$

$$A\ a\ \underline{a}\ B\ b\ b$$

$$A\ \underline{a}\ a\ B\ b\ b$$

$$\underline{A}\ a\ a\ B\ b\ b$$

$$A\ \underline{a}\ a\ B\ b\ b$$

$$A\ A\ \underline{a}\ B\ b\ b$$

$$A\ A\ a\ \underline{B}\ b\ b$$

$$A\ A\ a\ B\ \underline{b}\ b$$

$$A\ A\ a\ \underline{B}\ B\ b$$

$$A\ A\ \underline{a}\ B\ B\ b$$

$$A\ \underline{A}\ a\ B\ B\ b$$

$$A\ A\ \underline{a}\ B\ B\ b$$

$$A\ A\ A\ \underline{B}\ B\ b$$

$$A \ A \ A \ B \ \underline{B} \ b$$

$$A \ A \ A \ B \ B \ \underline{b}$$

$$A \ A \ A \ B \ \underline{B} \ B$$

$$A \ A \ A \ \underline{B} \ B \ B$$

$$A \ A \ \underline{A} \ B \ B \ B$$

$$A \ A \ A \ \underline{B} \ B \ B$$

$$A \ A \ A \ B \ \underline{B} \ B$$

$$A \ A \ A \ B \ B \ \underline{B}$$

$$A \ A \ A \ B \ B \ B \ \underline{\Delta}$$

HALT

Based on this algorithm we can define a set of states that have the following meanings:

State 1   This is the start state, but it is also the state we are in whenever we are about to read the lowest unpaired a. In a PDA we can never return to the START state, but in a TM we can. The edges leaving from here must convert this a to the character A and move the TAPE HEAD right and enter state 2.

State 2   This is the state we are in when we have just converted an a to an A and we are looking for the matching b. We begin moving up the TAPE. If we read another a, we leave it alone and continue to march up the TAPE, moving the TAPE HEAD always to the right. If we read a B, we also leave it alone and continue to move the TAPE HEAD right. We cannot read an A while in this state. In this algorithm all the A's remain to the left of the TAPE HEAD once they are printed. If we read Δ while we are searching for the b we are in trouble because we have not paired off our a. So we crash. The first b we read, if we are lucky enough to find one, is the end of the search in this state. We convert it to B, move the TAPE HEAD left and enter state 3.

State 3   This is the state we are in when we have just converted a b to B. We should now march left down the TAPE looking for the field of unpaired a's. If we read a B, we leave it alone and keep moving left. If and when we read an *a,* we have done our job. We must then go to state 4, which will try to find the left-most unpaired *a.* If we encounter the character *b* while moving to the left, something has gone very wrong and we should crash. If, however, we encounter the character *A* before we hit an *a,* we know that used up the pool of unpaired *a*'s at the beginning of the input string and we may be ready to terminate execution. Therefore, we leave the *A* alone and reverse directions to the right and move into state 5.

State 4   We get here when state 3 has located the right-most end of the field of unpaired *a*'s. The TAPE and TAPE HEAD situation looks like this:

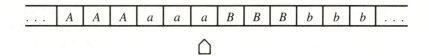

In this state we must move left through a block of solid *a*'s (we crash if we encounter a *b,* a *B,* or a Δ) until we find an *A.* When we do, we bounce off it to the right, which lands us at the left-most uncounted *a.* This means that we should next be in state 1 again.

State 5   When we get here it must be because state 3 found that there were no unpaired *a*'s left and it bounced us off the right-most *A.* We are now reading the left-most *B* as in the picture below:

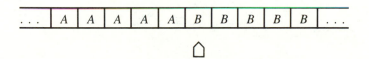

It is now our job to be sure that there are no more *a*'s or *b*'s left in this word. We want to scan through solid *B*'s until we hit the first blank. Since the program never printed any blanks, this will indicate the end of the input string. If there are no more surprises before the Δ, we then accept the word by going to the state HALT. Otherwise we crash. For example, *aabba* would become *AABBa* and then crash because while searching for the Δ we find an *a.*

This explains the TM program that we began with. It corresponds to the description above state for state and edge for edge.

Let us trace the processing of the input string *aabb* by looking at its execution chain:

This explains the TM program that we began with. It corresponds to the description above state for state and edge for edge.

Let us trace the processing of the input string *aabb* by looking at its execution chain:

$$\begin{matrix} 1 & & 2 & & 2 & & 3 & & 4 & & 1 \\ a\underline{a}bb & \to & A\underline{a}bb & \to & Aa\underline{b}b & \to & Aa\underline{B}b & \to & \underline{A}aBb & \to & A\underline{a}Bb \end{matrix}$$

$$\begin{matrix} 2 & & 2 & & 3 & & 3 & & 5 & & 5 \\ \to & AA\underline{B}b & \to & AAB\underline{b} & \to & AA\underline{B}B & \to & A\underline{A}BB & \to & AA\underline{B}B & \to & AABB\underline{} \end{matrix}$$

$$\begin{matrix} 5 \\ \to AABB\underline{\Delta} \to HALT \end{matrix}$$

It is clear that any string of the form $a^n b^n$ will reach the HALT state. To show that any string that reaches the HALT state must be of the form $a^n b^n$ we trace backward. To reach HALT we must get to state 5 and read a Δ. To be in state 5 we must have come from state 3 from which we read an A and some number of B's while moving to the right. So at the point we are in state 3 ready to terminate, the TAPE and TAPE HEAD situation is as shown below:

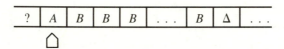

To be in state 3 means we have begun at START and circled around the loop some number of times.

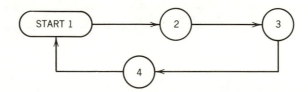

Every time we go from START to state 3 we have converted an a to an A and a b to a B. No other edge in the program of this TM changes the contents of any cell on the TAPE. However many B's there are, there are just as many A's. Examination of the movement of the TAPE HEAD shows that all the A's stretch in one connected sequence of cells starting at cell i. To go from state 3 to HALT shows that the whole TAPE has been converted to A's then B's followed by blanks. Putting this all together, to get to HALT the input word must be $a^n b^n$ for some $n > 0$. ∎

EXAMPLE

Consider the following TM

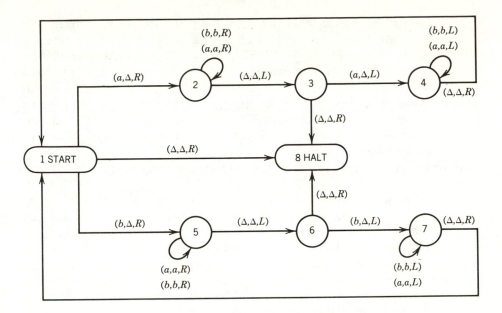

This looks like another monster, yet it accepts the familiar language PALINDROME and does so by a very simple deterministic algorithm.

We read the first letter of the input string and erase it, but we remember whether it was an *a* or a *b*. We go to the last letter and check to be sure it is the same as what used to be the first letter. If not, we crash, but if so, we erase it too. We then return to the front of what is left of the input string and repeat the process. If we do not crash while there are any letters left, then when we get to the condition where the whole TAPE is blank we accept the input string. This means that we reach the HALT state. Notice that the input string itself is no longer on the TAPE.

The process, briefly, works like this:

a b b a b b a

b b a b b a

b b a b b

b a b b

b a b

a b

a

Δ

We mentioned above that when we erase the first letter we remember what it was as we march up to the last letter. Turing machines have no auxiliary memory device, like a PUSHDOWN STACK, where we could store this information, but there are ways around this. One possible method is to use some of the blank space further down the TAPE for making notes. Or, as in this case, the memory comes in by determining what path through the program the input takes. If the first letter is an *a*, we are off on the state 2—state 3—state 4 loop. If the first letter is a *b*, we are off on the state 5—state 6—state 7 loop.

All of this is clear from the descriptions of the meanings of the states below:

State 1   When we are in this state, we read the first letter of what is left of the input string. This could be because we are just starting and reading cell i or because we have been returned here from state 4 or state 7. If we read an *a*, we change it to a Δ (erase it), move the TAPE HEAD to the right, and progress to state 2. If we read a *b*, we erase it and move the TAPE HEAD to the right and progress to state 5. If we read a Δ where we expect the string to begin, it is because we have erased everything, or perhaps we started with the input word Λ. In either case, we accept the word and we shall see that it is in EVENPALINDROME.

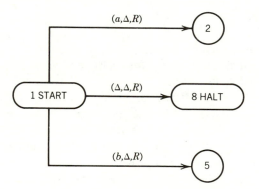

State 2   We get here because we have just erased an *a* from the front of the input string and we want to get to the last letter of the remaining input string to see if it too is an *a*. So we move to the right through all the *a*'s and *b*'s left in the input until we get to the end of the string at the first Δ. When that happens we back up one cell (to the left) and move into state 3.

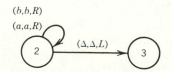

State 3   We get here only from state 2, which means that the letter we erased at the start of the string was an *a* and state 2 has requested us now to read the last letter of the string. We found the end of the string by moving to the right until we hit the first Δ. Then we bounced one cell back to the left. If this cell is also blank, then there are only blanks left on the TAPE. The letters have all been successfully erased and we can accept the word. So we go to HALT. If there is something left of the input string, but the last letter is a *b*, the input string was not a palindrome. Therefore we crash by having no labeled edge to go on. If the last non-Δ letter is an *a*, then we erase it, completing the pair, and begin moving the TAPE HEAD left, down to the beginning of the string again to pair off another set of letters. We should note that if the word is accepted by going from state 3 to HALT then the *a* that is erased in moving from state 1 to state 2 is not balanced by another erasure but was the last letter left in the erasure process. This means that it was the middle of a word in ODDPALINDROME:

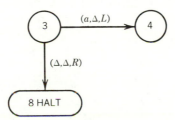

Notice that when we read the Δ and move to HALT we still need to include in the edge's label instructions to write something and move the TAPE HEAD somewhere. The label (Δ, *a*, R) would work just as well, or (Δ, *B*, R). However, (Δ, *a*, L) might be a disaster. We might have started with a one-letter word, say *a*. State 1 erases this *a*. Then state 2 reads the Δ in cell ii and returns us to cell i where we read the blank. If we try to move left from cell i we crash on the very verge of accepting the input string.

State 4   Like state 2, this is a travel state searching for the beginning of what is left of the input string. We keep heading left fearlessly because we know that cell i contains a Δ, so we shall not fall off the edge of the earth and crash by going left from cell i. When we hit the first Δ, we back up one position to the right, setting ourselves up in state 1 ready to read the first letter of what is left of the string:

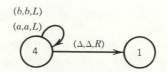

State 5   We get to state 5 only from state 1 when the letter it has just erased was a *b*. In other words, state 5 corresponds exactly to state 2 but for strings beginning with a *b*. It too searches for the end of the string:

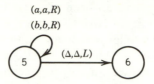

(a,a,R)
(b,b,R)

(Δ,Δ,L)

5   6

State 6   We get here when we have erased a *b* in state 1 and found the end of the string in state 5. We examine the letter at hand. If it is an *a*, then the string began with *b* and ended with *a*, so we crash since it is not in PALINDROME. If it is a *b*, we erase it and hunt for the beginning again. If it is a Δ, we know that the string was an ODDPALINDROME with middle letter *b*. This is the twin of state 3.

State 7   This state is exactly the same as state 4. We try to find the beginning of the string.

Putting all these states together, we get the picture we started with.

Let us trace the running of this TM on the input string *ababa:*

$$
\begin{array}{ccccccccc}
1 & & 2 & & 2 & & 2 & & 2 \\
a\underline{b}aba & \rightarrow & \Delta\underline{b}aba & \rightarrow & \Delta b\underline{a}ba & \rightarrow & \Delta ba\underline{b}a & \rightarrow & \Delta bab\underline{a}
\end{array}
$$

$$
\begin{array}{ccccccccc}
& & 2 & & 3 & & 4 & & 4 & & 4 \\
\rightarrow & & \Delta baba\underline{\Delta} & \rightarrow & \Delta bab\underline{a} & \rightarrow & \Delta ba\underline{b}\Delta & \rightarrow & \Delta b\underline{a}b\Delta & \rightarrow & \Delta\underline{b}ab\Delta
\end{array}
$$

$$
\begin{array}{ccccccccc}
& & 4 & & 5 & & 5 & & 5 & & 5 \\
\rightarrow & & \underline{\Delta}bab\Delta & \rightarrow & \Delta\underline{b}ab\Delta & \rightarrow & \Delta\Delta\underline{a}b\Delta & \rightarrow & \Delta\Delta a\underline{b}\Delta & \rightarrow & \Delta\Delta ab\underline{\Delta}
\end{array}
$$

$$
\begin{array}{ccccccccc}
& & 6 & & 7 & & 7 & & 1 & & 2 \\
\rightarrow & & \Delta\Delta a\underline{b}\Delta & \rightarrow & \Delta\Delta\underline{a}\Delta\Delta & \rightarrow & \Delta\Delta\underline{a}\Delta\Delta & \rightarrow & \Delta\Delta\underline{a}\Delta\Delta & \rightarrow & \Delta\Delta\Delta\Delta\underline{\Delta}
\end{array}
$$

$$
\begin{array}{ccccc}
& & 3 & & 8 \\
\rightarrow & & \Delta\Delta\Delta\underline{\Delta}\Delta & \rightarrow & \text{HALT}
\end{array}
$$

(See Problem 7 below for comments on this machine.) ■

Our first example was no more than a converted FA, and the language it accepted was regular. The second example accepted a language that was context-free and nonregular and the TM given employed separate alphabets for writing and reading. The third machine accepted a language that was also context-free but that could be accepted only by a nondeterministic PDA, whereas the TM that accepts it is deterministic.

We have seen that we can use the TAPE for more than a PUSHDOWN STACK. In the last two examples we ran up and down the TAPE to make observations and changes in the string at both ends and in the middle. We shall see later that the TAPE can be used for even more tasks: It can be used as work space for calculation and output.

In these three examples the TM was already assembled. In this next example we shall design the Turing machine for a specific purpose.

EXAMPLE

Let us build a TM to accept the language EVEN-EVEN—the collection of all strings with an even number of a's and an even number of b's.

Let this be our algorithm:

Starting with the first letter let us scan up the string replacing all the a's by A's. During this phase we shall skip over all b's. Let us make our first replacement of A for a in state 1, then our second in state 2, then our third in state 1 again, and so on alternately until we reach the first blank. If the first blank is read in state 2, we know that we have replaced an odd number of a's and we must reject the input string. We do this by having no edge leaving state 2 which wants to read the TAPE entry Δ. This will cause a crash. If we read the first blank in state 1, then we have replaced an even number of a's and must process b's. This could be done by the program segment below:

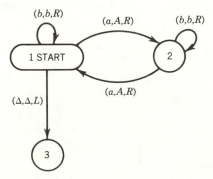

Now suppose that from state 3 we go back to the beginning of the string replacing b's by B's in two states: the first B for b in state 3, the next in state 4, then in state 3 again, and so on alternately, all the time ignoring

the A's. If we do this we run into a subtle problem. Since the word starts
in cell i, we do not have a blank space to bounce off when we are reading
back down the string. When we read what is in cell i we do not know
we are in cell i and we try to move the TAPE HEAD left, thereby crashing.
Even the input strings we want to accept will crash.

There are several ways to avoid this. The solution we choose for now
is to change the a's and b's at the same time as we first read up the string.
This will allow us to recognize input strings of the form EVEN-EVEN
without having to read back down the TAPE.

Let us define the four states:

State 1   We have read an even number of a's and an even number of b's.
State 2   We have read an even number of a's and an odd number of b's.
State 3   We have read an odd number of a's and an even number of b's.
State 4   We have read an odd number of a's and an odd number of b's.

If we are in state 1 and we read an a we go to state 3. There is no need
to change the letters we read into anything else since one scan over the input
string settles the question of acceptance. If we read a b from state 1, we leave
it alone and go to state 2 and so on. This is the TM:

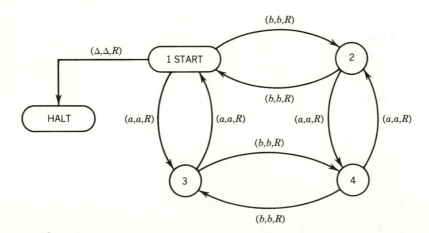

If we run out of input in state 1, we accept the string by going to HALT
along the edge labeled (Δ,Δ,R).

This machine should look very familiar. It is the FA that accepts the language EVEN-EVEN dressed up to look like a TM.   ∎

This leads us to the following observation.

THEOREM 45

Every regular language has a TM that accepts exactly it.

PROOF

Consider any regular language L. Take an FA that accepts L. Change the edge labels a and b to (a,a,R) and (b,b,R), respectively. Change the $-$ state to the word START. Erase the plus sign out of each final state and instead add to each of these an edge labeled (Δ,Δ,R) leading to a HALT state. Voilà, a TM.

We read the input string moving from state to state in the TM exactly as we would on the FA. When we come to the end of the input string, if we are not in a TM state corresponding to a final state in the FA, we crash when the TAPE HEAD reads the Δ in the next cell. If the TM state corresponds to an FA final state, we take the edge labeled (Δ,Δ,R) to HALT. The acceptable strings are the same for the TM and the FA.   ■

The connection between TM's and PDA's will be shown in Chapter 26. Let us consider some more examples of TM's.

EXAMPLE

We shall now design a TM that accepts the language EQUAL, that is, the language of all strings with the same number of a's and b's. EQUAL is a nonregular language, so the trick of Theorem 45 cannot be employed.

Since we want to scan up and down the input string, we need a method of guaranteeing that on our way down we can find the beginning of the string without crashing through the left wall of cell i. One way of being safe is to insert a new symbol, #, at the beginning of the input TAPE in cell i to the left of the input string. This means we have to shift the input string one cell to the right without changing it in any way except for its location on the TAPE. This problem arises so often that we shall write a program segment to achieve this that will be used in the future as a standard preprocessor or subroutine called **INSERT #.**

Over the alphabet $\Sigma = \{a,b\}$ we need only 5 states.

State 1   START
State 2   We have just read an a.
State 3   We have just read a b.
State 4   We have just read a Δ.
State 5   Return to the beginning. This means leave the TAPE HEAD reading cell ii.

The first part of the TM is this:

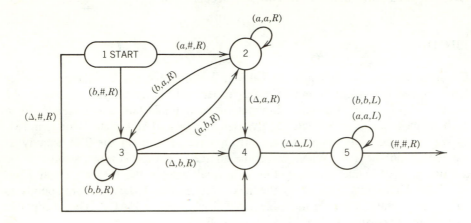

We start out in state 1. If we read an *a*, we go to state 2 and replace the *a* in cell i with the beginning-of-TAPE symbol #. Once we are in state 2, we know we owe the TAPE an *a*, so whatever we read next we print the *a* and go to a state that remembers whatever symbol was just read. There are two possibilities. If we read another *a*, we print the prior *a* and still owe an *a*, so we stay in state 2. If we read a *b*, we print the *a* we owed and move to state 3, owing the TAPE a *b*.

Whenever we are in state 3 we read the next letter, and as we go to a new state we print the old *b* we already read but do not yet print the new letter. The state we go to now must remember what the new letter was and print it only after reading yet another letter. We are always paying last month's bill. We are never up to date until we read a blank. This lets us print the last *a* or *b* and takes us to state 4.

Eventually, we get to state 5. In state 5 we rewind the TAPE HEAD moving backward to the #, and then we leave ourselves in cell ii. There we are reading the first letter of the input string and ready to connect the edge from state 5 into the START state of some second process.

The idea for this algorithm is exactly like the Mealy machine of Chapter 9, which added 1 to a binary input string.

The problem we have encountered and solved is analogous to the problem of shifting a field of data one storage location up the TAPE. Writing-over causes erasing, so a temporary storage location is required. In this case, the information is stored in the program by the identity of the state we are in. Being in state 2, 3, or 4 tells us what we have just read.

Some authors define a TM so that the input string is placed on the TAPE beginning in cell ii with a complimentary # already placed in cell i. Some people like to begin running a TM with the input string surrounded on the

TAPE with #'s in front and at the end. For example, before we processed the input *babb* we would make the TAPE look like this:

#	b	a	b	b	#	Δ	. . .

Such requirements would obviate the need for using INSERT #, but it is still a very useful subroutine and we shall want it later.

Variations of this subroutine can be written to

1. Insert any other character into cell i while moving the data to the right.

2. Insert any character into any specified cell leaving everything to the left as it is and moving the entire TAPE contents on the right one cell down the TAPE.

3. Insert any character into any cell, on a TAPE with input strings from any alphabet.

Let us illustrate the operation of INSERT # on the input string *abba:*

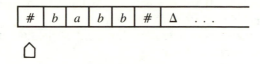

$$\begin{array}{ccccccc} 1 & \rightarrow & 2 & \rightarrow & 3 & \rightarrow & 3 \\ a\underline{b}ba & & \#\underline{b}ba & & \#a\underline{b}a & & \#ab\underline{a} \end{array}$$

The last state is "unknown" because we are in whatever state we got to on our departure from state 5. We cannot specify it in general because INSERT # will be used in many different programs. Here "unknown" will be called state 6.

Thus far, we have been doing bookkeeping. We have not addressed the question of the language EQUAL. We can now begin the algorithm of pairing off *a*'s and *b*'s. The method we use is to X out an *a* and then X out a *b* and repeat this until nothing at all is left. There are many good ways to accept EQUAL; the one we shall use is not the most efficient, but Turing machines run on imagination, which is cheaper than petroleum.

In state 6 we start at the left of the input string and scan upward for the first *a*. When we find it, we change it to an X and move to state 7. This state returns the TAPE HEAD to cell ii by backing up until it bumps off the symbol #. Now we scan upward looking for the first unchanged *b*. If we hit the end of the word before we find the matching *b*, we read a Δ and crash because the input string has more *a*'s than *b*'s. If we do find an unused *b*, then in state 8 we change it to an X. In state 9 we return the TAPE HEAD to cell ii and state 6 to repeat the whole process. If, in state 6, while searching for the first unused *a* we find there are no more left (by encountering a Δ), we go to state 10. State 10 begins at the end of the string and rewinds us to cell ii reading only *X*'s. If it encounters any unused *b*'s, it crashes. In that case we have cancelled all the *a*'s but not all the *b*'s, so the input must have had more *b*'s than *a*'s. If the TAPE HEAD can get all the way back to # reading only *X*'s, then every letter in the input string has been converted to *X* and the machine accepts the string.

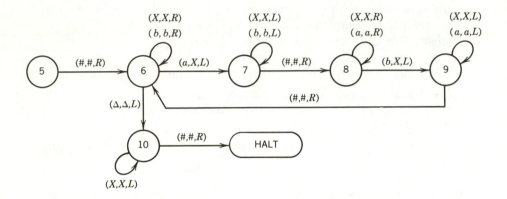

Let us follow the operation on *baab* starting in state 6. Starting in state 6 means that we have already inserted a # to the left of the input on the TAPE in states 1 through 5.

$$
\begin{array}{ccccc}
6 & 6 & 7 & 7 & 8 \\
\#\underline{b}aab & \#b\underline{a}ab & \#b\underline{X}ab & \#\underline{b}Xab & \#\underline{b}Xab
\end{array}
$$

$$
\rightarrow
\begin{array}{ccccc}
9 & 6 & 6 & 6 & 7 \\
\#\underline{X}Xab & \#X\underline{X}ab & \#XX\underline{a}b & \#XX\underline{a}b & \#X\underline{X}Xb
\end{array}
$$

$$
\rightarrow
\begin{array}{ccccc}
7 & 7 & 8 & 8 & 8 \\
\#\underline{X}XXb & \#\underline{X}XXb & \#\underline{X}XXb & \#X\underline{X}Xb & \#XX\underline{X}b
\end{array}
$$

$$
\rightarrow
\begin{array}{ccccc}
8 & 9 & 9 & 9 & 9 \\
\#XXX\underline{b} & \#XXX\underline{X} & \#XX\underline{X}X & \#X\underline{X}XX & \#\underline{X}XXX
\end{array}
$$

$$
\rightarrow
\begin{array}{ccccc}
6 & 6 & 6 & 6 & 6 \\
\#\underline{X}XXX & \#X\underline{X}XX & \#XX\underline{X}X & \#XXX\underline{X} & \#XXXX\underline{\Delta}
\end{array}
$$

$$
\rightarrow
\begin{array}{ccccc}
10 & 10 & 10 & 10 & \underline{10} \\
\#XXX\underline{X}\Delta & \#XX\underline{X}X & \#X\underline{X}XX & \#\underline{X}XXX & \underline{\#}XXXX
\end{array}
\rightarrow \text{HALT}
$$

Notice that even after we have turned all a's and b's to X's, we still have many steps left to check that there are no more non-X characters left. ■

EXAMPLE

Now we shall consider a valid but problematic machine to accept the language of all strings that have a double a in them somewhere:

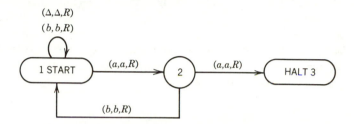

The problem is that we have labeled the loop at the start state with the extra option (Δ,Δ,R). This is still a perfectly valid TM because it fits all the clauses in the definition. Any string without a double a that ends in the letter a will get to state 2, where the TAPE HEAD will read a Δ and crash. What happens to strings without a double a that end in b? When the last letter of the input string has been read, we are in state 1. We read the first Δ and return to state 1, moving the TAPE HEAD further up the TAPE full of Δ's. In fact, we loop forever in state 1 on the edge labeled (Δ,Δ,R).

All the strings in $\{a,b\}^*$ can be divided into three sets:

1. Those with a double a. They are accepted by the TM.
2. Those without aa that end in a. They crash.
3. Those without aa that end in b. They loop forever. ■

Unlike on an FA, on a TM an input string cannot just run out of gas in some middle state. Since the input string is just the first part of an infinite TAPE, there are always infinitely many Δ's to read after the meaningful input has been exhausted.

These three possibilities exist for every TM, although for the examples we met previously the third set is empty. This last example is our first TM that can loop forever.

We have seen that certain PDA's also loop forever on some inputs. In Part II this was a mild curiosity; in Part III it will be a major headache.

DEFINITION

Every Turing machine T over the alphabet Σ divides the set of strings Σ^* into three classes:

1. ACCEPT(T) is the set of all strings leading to a HALT state. This is also called the *language accepted* by T.
2. REJECT(T) is the set of all strings that crash during execution by moving left from cell i or by being in a state that has no exit edge that wants to read the character the TAPE HEAD is reading.
3. LOOP(T) is the set of all other strings, that is, strings that loop forever while running on T. ∎

We shall consider this issue in more detail later. For now we should simply bear in mind the resemblance of this definition to the output-less computer program at the beginning of this chapter.

EXAMPLE

Let us consider the non-context-free language $\{a^n b^n a^n\}$. This language can be accepted by the following interesting procedure:

Step 1   We presume that we are reading the first letter of what remains on the input. Initially this means we are reading the first letter of the input string, but as the algorithm progresses we may find ourselves back in this step reading the first letter of a smaller remainder. If no letters are found (a blank is read), we go to HALT. If what we read is an a, we change it to a * and move the TAPE HEAD right. If we read anything else, we crash. This is all done in state 1.

Step 2   In state 2 we skip over the rest of the a's in the initial clump of a's looking for the first b. This will put us in state 3. Here we search for the *last b* in the clump of b's: We read b's continually until we encounter the first a (which takes us to state 4) and then bounce off that a to the left. If after the b's we find a Δ instead of an a, we crash. Now that we have located the last b in the clump we do something clever: We change it into an a, and we move on to state 5. The reason it took so many TM states to do this simple job is that if we allowed, say, state 2 to skip over b's as well as a's, it would merrily skip its way to the end of the input. We need a separate TM state to keep track of where we are in the data.

Step 3   The first thing we want to do here is find the end of the clump of a's (this is the second clump of a's in the input). We do this in state 5 by reading right until we get to a Δ. If we read a b after this second clump of a's, we crash. If we get to the Δ we know that the input is in fact of the form **a*b*a***. When we have located the end of this clump we turn the last *two* a's into Δ's. Because we changed the last b into an a this is tantamount to killing off a b and an a. If we had turned that b into a Δ, it would have meant Δ's in the middle of the input string and we would have had trouble telling where the real ends of the string were. Instead, we turned a b into an a and then erased two a's off the end.

Step 4 We are now in state 8 and we want to return to state 1 and do this whole thing again. Nothing could be easier. We skip over a's and b's, moving the Tape Head left until we encounter one of the *'s that fill the front end of the Tape. Then we move one cell to the right and begin again in state 1.

The TM looks like this:

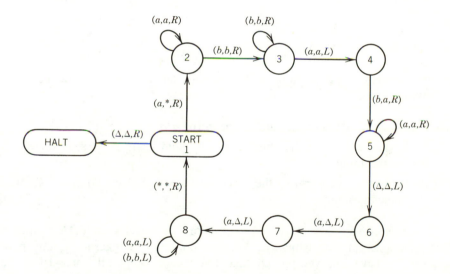

Let us trace the action of this machine on the input string *aaabbbaaa*:

$$
\begin{array}{ccccc}
\text{START} & 2 & 2 & 2 & 3 \\
\underline{a}aabbbaaa & *\underline{a}abbbaaa & *a\underline{a}bbbaaa & *aa\underline{b}bbaaa & *aab\underline{b}baaa
\end{array}
$$

$$
\begin{array}{ccccc}
3 & 3 & 4 & 5 & 5 \\
*aabb\underline{b}aaa & *aabbb\underline{a}aa & *aabb\underline{b}aaa & *aabba\underline{a}aa & *aabbaa\underline{a}a
\end{array}
$$

$$
\begin{array}{ccccc}
5 & 5 & 6 & 7 & 8 \\
*aabbaaa\underline{a} & *aabbaaaa\underline{\Delta} & *aabbaaa\underline{a} & *aabbaa\underline{a} & *aabba\underline{a}
\end{array}
$$

$$
\begin{aligned}
&\rightarrow \frac{8}{*aabb\underline{a}a}
\rightarrow \frac{8}{*aabb\underline{a}a}
\rightarrow \frac{8}{*aab\underline{b}aa}
\rightarrow \frac{8}{*aa\underline{b}baa}
\rightarrow \frac{8}{*a\underline{a}bbaa}\\[2mm]
&\rightarrow \frac{8}{*\underline{a}abbaa}
\rightarrow \frac{1}{*a\underline{a}bbaa}
\rightarrow \frac{2}{**\underline{a}bbaa}
\rightarrow \frac{2}{**a\underline{b}baa}
\rightarrow \frac{3}{**ab\underline{b}aa}\\[2mm]
&\rightarrow \frac{3}{**abb\underline{a}a}
\rightarrow \frac{4}{**abb\underline{a}a}
\rightarrow \frac{5}{**aba\underline{a}a}
\rightarrow \frac{5}{**aba\underline{a}a}
\rightarrow \frac{5}{**abaaa\underline{\Delta}}\\[2mm]
&\rightarrow \frac{6}{**abaa\underline{a}}
\rightarrow \frac{7}{**aba\underline{a}}
\rightarrow \frac{8}{**ab\underline{a}}
\rightarrow \frac{8}{**a\underline{b}a}
\rightarrow \frac{8}{**\underline{a}ba}\\[2mm]
&\rightarrow \frac{8}{**\underline{a}ba}
\rightarrow \frac{1}{**\underline{a}ba}
\rightarrow \frac{2}{***\underline{b}a}
\rightarrow \frac{3}{***b\underline{a}}
\rightarrow \frac{4}{***b\underline{a}}\\[2mm]
&\rightarrow \frac{5}{***\underline{a}a}
\rightarrow \frac{5}{***aa\underline{\Delta}}
\rightarrow \frac{6}{***a\underline{a}}
\rightarrow \frac{7}{***\underline{a}}
\rightarrow \frac{8}{***\underline{\ }}\\[2mm]
&\rightarrow \frac{1}{***\underline{\Delta}}
\rightarrow \frac{\text{HALT}}{***\Delta\underline{\Delta}}
\end{aligned}
$$

After designing the machine and following the trace several things should be obvious to us:

1. The only words accepted are of the form $a^n b^n a^n$ (here $n = 0,1,2,3 \ldots$)
2. When the machine halts, the TAPE will hold as many *'s as there were b's in the input.
3. If the input was $a^m b^m a^m$, the TAPE HEAD will be in cell $(m + 2)$ when the machine halts. ■

This example suggests that TM's are more powerful than PDA's since no PDA could accept this language. We can only say "suggests" at this point, because we have not yet proven that TM's can accept all context-free languages. The possibility remains that there might be some language that a PDA accepts that a TM cannot. We have to wait until a later chapter to prove that TM's can accept all context-free languages.

Let us do two last examples, both of TM subroutines.

EXAMPLE

In building the TM for EQUAL, we developed a TM subroutine that can insert a character in front of an input string on a TM TAPE. We mentioned that a slight modification allows us to use this routine to insert any new character at any point in a TM TAPE and shift the rest of the input one cell to the right.

Let us consider how to do this. We start with some arbitrary string on the TAPE. Let us just say for the purpose of example that what is on the TAPE is a string of *a*'s, *b*'s, and *X*'s with Δ's after it. Suppose further that the TAPE HEAD is pointing to the very cell in the middle of the string where we want to insert a new character, let us say a *b*. We want everything to the right of this spot moved one cell up the TAPE.

What we need is a symbol unlike any that is on the TAPE now, say *Q*. The following TM subroutine will accomplish this job:

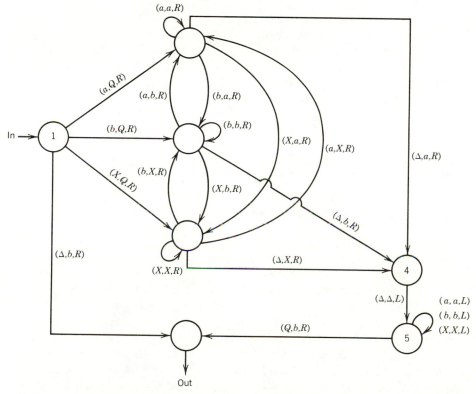

Notice that we leave the TAPE HEAD reading the next cell after the cell where the insertion occurred.

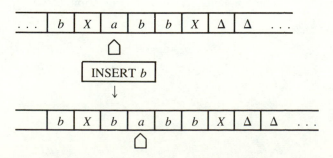

Note that the exact program of the subroutine INSERT depends on the exact alphabet that it is required to act on. If there could be any of 15 different symbols on the TAPE we need 15 different loops in the insertion routine, one separate loop to shift each character. To be very very precise, we should say that there is a whole family of subroutines called INSERT—one for each alphabet and each character to be inserted.   ■

EXAMPLE

For our last example we shall build a TM subprogram that deletes, that is, it erases the contents of the cell the TAPE HEAD is initially pointing to, moving the contents of each of the nonempty cells to its right down one cell to the left to close up the gap and leaving the TAPE HEAD positioned one cell past where it was at the start. For example:

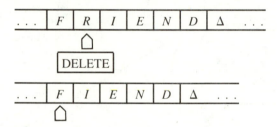

Just as with INSERT, the exact program of DELETE depends on the alphabet of letters found on the TAPE.

Let us suppose the characters on the TAPE are from the alphabet {a,b,c}

One subroutine to do this job is shown on the next page.

What we have done here is (1) erased the target cell, (2) moved to the right end of the non-Δ data, (3) worked our way back down the TAPE running the inverse of INSERT. We could just as easily have done the job on one pass up the TAPE, but then the TAPE HEAD would have been left at the end of the data and we would have lost our place; there would be no memory of where the deleted character used to be. The way we have written it, the TAPE HEAD is left in the cell immediately after the deletion cell.

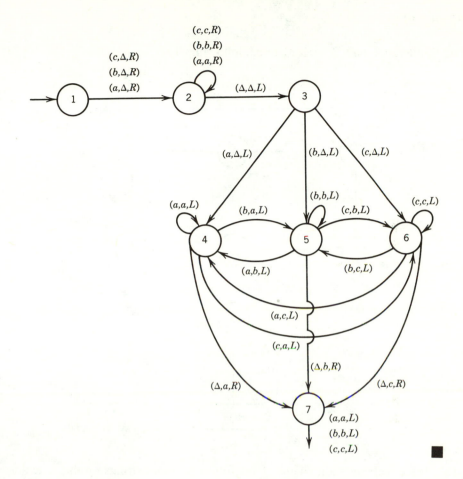

PROBLEMS

For Problems 1 and 2, consider the following TM:

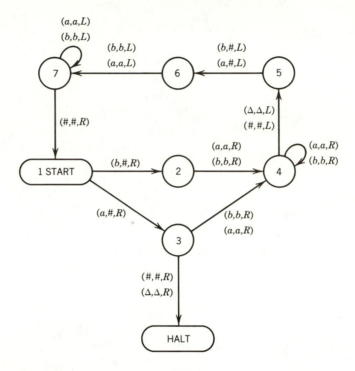

1. Trace the execution chains of the following input strings on this machine.
    (i)   *aaa*
    (ii)   *aba*
    (iii) *baaba*
    (iv)   *ababb*

2. The language accepted by this TM is all words with an odd number of letters that have *a* as the middle letter. Show that this is true by explaining the algorithm the machine uses and the meaning of each state. Pay attention to the two necessary parts that must always be demonstrated:
    (i)   Anything that has an *a* in the middle will get to HALT
    and
    (ii)   Anything that gets to HALT has an *a* in the middle.

3. (i)   Build a TM that accepts the language of all words that contain the substring *bbb*.

    (ii)   Build a TM that accepts the language of all words that do not contain the substring *bbb*.

4. Build a TM that accepts the language ODDPALINDROME.

5. Build a TM that accepts all strings with more a's than b's.

6. (i) Build a TM that accepts the language $\{a^n b^{n+1}\}$.

   (ii) Build a TM that accepts the language $\{a^n b^{2n}\}$.

7. (i) Show that the TM given in this chapter for the language PALINDROME has more states than it needs by coalescing states 4 and 7.

   (ii) Show that the TM given above for the language $\{a^n b^n\}$ can be drawn with one fewer state.

Problems 8, 9, and 10 refer to the following TM. We assume that the input string is put on the TAPE with the symbol # inserted in front of it in cell i. For example, the input ba will be run with the TAPE initially in the form $\#ba\Delta$ .... In this chapter we saw how to do this using TM states. Here, consider it already done. The TM is then:

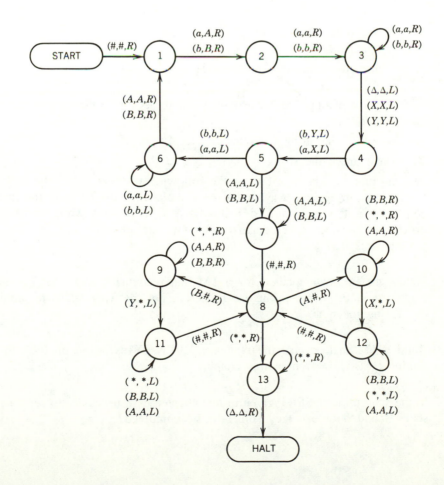

8. Trace the execution chains of the following input strings on this machine.

   (i)   *aa*

   (ii)   *aaa*

   (iii) *aaaa*

   (iv)   *aabaab*

   (v)   *abab*

9. The language this TM accepts is DOUBLEWORD, the set of all words of the form *ww* where *w* is a nonnull string in {*a,b*}*.

   DOUBLEWORD = {*aa*   *bb*   *aaaa*   *abab*   *baba*   *bbbb*
                  aaaaaa   *aabaab* . . . }

   (i)   Explain the meaning of each state and prove that all words in DOUBLEWORD are accepted by this TM.

   (ii)   Show that all words not in DOUBLEWORD are rejected by this machine.

10. (i)   Show that states 11 and 12 can be combined without changing the language.

    (ii) What other changes can be made?

11. Return to the example in the text of a TM to accept EVEN-EVEN based on the algorithm

    1. Move up the string changing *a*'s to *A*'s

    2. Move down the string changing *b*'s to *B*'s

    We can modify this algorithm in the following way: To avoid the problem of crashing on the way down the TAPE change the letter in the first cell to *X* if it is an *a* and to *Y* if it is a *b*. This way, while charging down the TAPE we can recognize when we are in cell i.
       Draw this TM.

12. Follow the up-down method for a TM that recognizes EVEN-EVEN as explained in Problem 11 but use INSERT, not the *X, Y* trick, to build the Turing machine.

13. Build a TM that accepts the language EVEN-EVEN based on the subroutine DELETE given in this chapter.

14. In the subroutine INSERT given in this chapter, is it necessary to separate states 4 and 5 or can they somehow be combined?

15. On the TM given in this chapter for the language $\{a^n b^n a^n\}$, trace the following words:

 (i)   *aabbaa*

 (ii)   *aabbaaa*

 (iii)   *aabaa*

 (iv)   *aabbaabb*

 (v)   Characterize the nature of the different input strings that crash in each of the eight states.

16. Build a TM to accept the language $\{a^n b^n a^n\}$ based on the following algorithm:

 (i)   Check that the input is in the form **a*b*a***.

 (ii)   Use DELETE in an intelligent way.

17. Trace the subroutine DELETE in the following situations:

 (i)

 (ii)

 (iii)

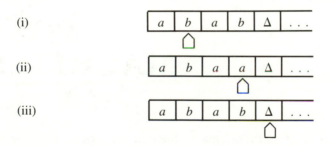

18. Draw a TM that does the same job as DELETE but leaves the TAPE HEAD pointing to the first blank cell. One way to do this is by reading a letter, putting it into the cell behind it and moving two cells up the TAPE.

19. (i)   Draw a TM that loops forever on all words ending in *a* and crashes on all others.

 (ii)   Draw a TM that loops forever on the input string *bab* leaving the TAPE different each time through the loop.

20. Draw a TM that accepts the language PALINDROME', the complement of PALINDROME. This is, although we did not prove so, a non-context-free language.

CHAPTER 25

POST MACHINES

We have used the word "algorithm" many times in this book. We have tried to explain what an algorithm is by saying that it is a procedure with instructions so carefully detailed that no further information is necessary. The person/machine executing the algorithm should know how to handle any situation that may possibly arise. Without the need for applying any extra intelligence it should be possible to complete the project. Not only that, but before even begining we should be able, just by looking at the algorithm and the data, to predict an upper limit on the number of steps the entire process will take. This is the guarantee that the procedure is finite.

All of this sounds fine, but it still does not really specify what an algorithm is. This is an unsatisfactory definition, since we have no precise idea of what a "procedure" is. Essentially, we have merely hidden one unknown word behind another. Intuitively, we know that arithmetic operations are perfectly acceptable steps in an algorithm, but what else is? In several algorithms we have allowed ourselves the operation of painting things blue without specifying what shade or how many coats. An algorithm, it seems, can be made of almost anything.

The question of determining appropriate components for mathematical algorithms was of great interest earlier in this century. People were discovering

584

that surprisingly few basic operations were sufficient to perform many sophisticated tasks, just as shifting and adding are basic operations that can be used to replace hard-wired multiplication in a computer. The hope was to find a small set of basic operations and a machine that could perform them all, a kind of "universal algorithm machine," since it could run any algorithm. The mathematical model itself would provide a precise definition of the concept of algorithm. We could use it to discuss in a meaningful way the possibility of finding algorithms for all mathematical problems. There may even be some way to make it program itself to find its own algorithms so that we need never work on mathematics again.

In 1936, the same fruitful year Turing introduced the Turing machine, Emil Leon Post (1897–1954) created the Post machine, which he hoped would prove to be the "universal algorithm machine" sought after. One condition that must be satisifed by such a "universal algorithm machine" (we have kept this phrase in quotes because we cannot understand it in a deeper sense until later) is that *any language* that can be precisely defined by humans (using English or pictures or hand signals) should be accepted (or recognized) by some version of this machine. This would make it more powerful than an FA or a PDA. There are nonregular languages and non-context-free languages, but there should not be any non-Turing or non-Post languages. In this part of the book we shall see to what extent Post and Turing succeeded in achieving their goal.

DEFINITION

A **Post machine,** denoted **PM,** is a collection of five things:

1. The alphabet Σ of input letters plus the special symbol $\#$. We generally use $\Sigma = \{a,b\}$

2. A linear storage location (a place where a string of symbols is kept) called the **STORE,** or **QUEUE,** which initially contains the input string. This location can be read, by which we mean the *left-most* character can be removed for inspection. The STORE can also be added to, which means a new character can be concatenated onto the *right* of whatever is there already. We allow for the possibility that characters not in Σ can be used in the STORE, characters from an alphabet Γ called the **store alphabet.**

3. READ states, for example,

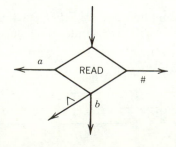

which remove the left-most character from the STORE and branch accordingly. The only branching in the machine takes place at the READ states. There *may be* a branch for every character in Σ or Γ. Note the Λ branch that means that an empty STORE was read. PM's are deterministic, so no two edges from the READ have the same label.

4.   ADD states:

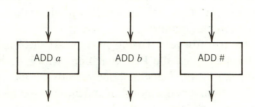

which concatenate a character onto the *right* end of the string in STORE. This is different from PDA PUSH states, which concatenate characters onto the *left*. Post machines have no PUSH states. No branching can take place at an ADD state. It is possible to have an ADD state for every letter in Σ and Γ.

5.   A START state and some halt states called ACCEPT and REJECT:

If we are in a READ state and there is no labeled edge for the character we have read then we crash, which is equivalent to taking a labeled edge into a REJECT state. We can draw our PM's with or without REJECT states.   ■

The STORE is a first-in first-out or FIFO stack in contradistinction to a PUSHDOWN or LIFO STACK. The contents of an originally empty STORE after the operations

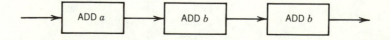

is the string

$$abb$$

If we then read the STORE, we take the a branch and the STORE will be reduced to bb.

A Post machine does not have a separate INPUT TAPE unit. In processing a string, we assume that the string was initially loaded into the STORE and we begin executing the program from the START state on. If we wind up in an ACCEPT state, we accept the input string. If not, not. At the moment we accept the input string the STORE could contain anything. It does not have to be empty nor need it contain the original input string.

As usual, we shall say that the language defined (or accepted) by a Post machine is the set of strings that it accepts. A Post machine is yet another language recognizer or acceptor.

As we have defined them, Post machines are deterministic, that is, for every input string there is only one path through the machine; we have no alternative at any stage. We could also define a nondeterministic Post machine, NPM. This would allow for more than one edge with the same label to come from a READ state. It is a theorem that, in their strength as language acceptors, NPM = PM. This we shall discuss in Chapter 27.

Let us study an example of a PM.

EXAMPLE

Consider the PM below:

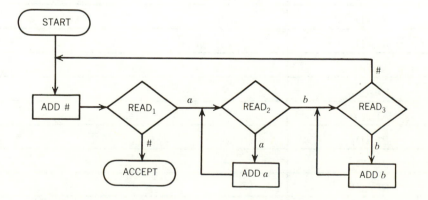

As required by our definition, this machine is deterministic. We have not drawn the edges that lead to REJECT states but instead we allow the path to crash in the READ state if there is no place for it to go.

Let us trace the processing of the input *aaabbb* on this PM.

STATE	STORE	
START	*aaabbb*	
ADD #	*aaabbb#*	(Note this point)
READ$_1$	*aabbb#*	
READ$_2$	*abbb#*	
ADD *a*	*abbb#a*	
READ$_2$	*bbb#a*	
ADD *a*	*bbb#aa*	
READ$_2$	*bb#aa*	
READ$_3$	*b#aa*	
ADD *b*	*b#aab*	
READ$_3$	*#aab*	
ADD *b*	*#aabb*	
READ$_3$	*aabb*	
ADD #	*aabb#*	(Note this point)
READ$_1$	*abb#*	
READ$_2$	*bb#*	
ADD *a*	*bb#a*	
READ$_2$	*b#a*	
READ$_3$	*#a*	
ADD *b*	*#ab*	
READ$_3$	*ab*	
ADD #	*ab#*	(Note this point)
READ$_1$	*b#*	
READ$_2$	*#*	
READ$_3$	Λ	
ADD #	*#*	(Note this point)
READ$_1$	Λ	
ACCEPT		

The trace makes clear to us what happens. The **#** is used as an end-of-input string signal (or flag). In READ$_1$ we check to see if we are out of input; that is, are we reading the end-of-input signal **#**? If so, we accept the string. If we read a b, the string crashes. So nothing starting with a b is accepted. If the string starts with an a, this letter is consumed by READ$_1$; that is the trip from READ$_1$ to READ$_2$ costs one a that is not replaced. The loop at READ$_2$ puts the rest of the a's from the front cluster of a's behind the **#**. The first b read is consumed in the trip from READ$_2$ to READ$_3$. At READ$_3$ the rest of the first cluster of b's is stripped off the front and appended onto the back, behind the a's that are behind the **#**.

After the b's have been transported we expect to read the character **#**. If we read an a, we crash. To survive the trip back from READ$_3$ to ADD **#** the input string must have been originally of the form **a*b***.

In each pass through the large circuit READ$_1$–READ$_2$–READ$_3$–READ$_1$, the string loses an a and a b. Note the markers we have indicated along the side. To be accepted, both a's and b's must run out at the same time, since if there were more a's than b's the input string would crash at READ$_2$ by reading a **#** instead of a b, and if the input string had more b's than a's, it would crash in state READ$_1$ by reading a b.

Therefore the language accepted by this PM is $\{a^n b^n\}$ (in this case including Λ). ∎

Post machines look considerably like PDA's, and, in fact, PDA's can accept the language $\{a^n b^n\}$ as the PM above does. However, we have seen that $\{a^n b^n a^n\}$ is non-context-free and cannot be accepted by a PDA. So to show that PM's have some extra power beyond PDA's we demonstrate one that accepts this language.

EXAMPLE

Consider the PM below:

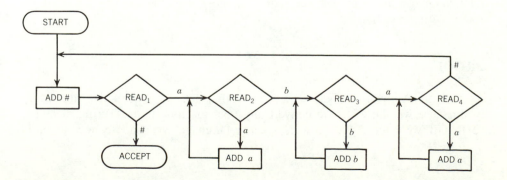

This machine is very much like the PM in the previous example. We start with a string in the STORE. We add a # to the back of it. We accept it in state READ$_1$ if the string was initially empty. If it starts with a *b*, we crash. If it starts with an *a*, we use up this letter getting to READ$_2$. Here we put the entire initial clump of *a*'s (all the way up to the first *b*) behind the #. We read the first *b* and use it up getting to READ$_3$. Here we put the rest of the clump of *b*'s behind the *a*'s behind the #. We had then better read another *a* to get to READ$_4$. In READ$_4$ a bunch of *a*'s (minus the one it costs to get there) are placed in the store on the right, behind the *b*'s that are behind the *a*'s that are behind the #. After we exhaust these *a*'s, we had better find a # or we crash. After reading the # off the front of the STORE we replace it at the back of the STORE in the state ADD #. To make this return to ADD #, the input string must originally have been of the form **a*b*a***. Every time through this loop we use up one *a* from the first clump, one *b* from the *b* clump, and one *a* from the last clump.

The only way we ever get to ACCEPT is to finish some number of loops and find the STORE empty, since after ADD # we want to read # in state READ$_1$. This means that the three clumps are all depleted at the same time, which means that they must have had the same number of letters in them initially. This means that the only words accepted by this PM are those of the form $\{a^n b^n a^n\}$. ∎

We should not think that we have *proven* that PM's accept a *larger* class of languages than do PDA's. We have only demonstrated that PM's accept *some* context-free languages and *some* non-context-free languages. In Chapter 27 we shall show that PM's do in fact accept *all* CFL's. We shall then have to face the question, "Do they accept *all* non-CFL's?" This will be answered in Chapter 29.

Before we relate PM's to PDA's, we shall compare them to TM's, as Post himself did with the following two theorems.

THEOREM 46

Any language that can be accepted by a Post machine can be accepted by some Turing machine.

PROOF

As with many theorems before, we prove this one by constructive algorithm. In this case we show how to convert any Post machine into a Turing machine, so that if we have a PM to accept some language we can see how to build a TM that will process all input strings exactly the same way as the PM, leading to HALT only when the PM would lead to ACCEPT.

We know that PM's are made up of certain components, and we shall show how to convert each of these components into corrresponding TM components that function the same way. We could call this process *simulating* a PM on a TM.

The easiest conversion is for the START state, because we do not change it at all. TM's also begin all execution at the START state.

The second easiest conversion is for the ACCEPT state. We shall rename it HALT because that is what the accepting state is called for TM's.

The next easiest conversion is for the REJECT states. TM's have no reject states, they just crash if no path can be found for the letter read by the TAPE HEAD. So we simply delete the REJECT states. (We often do this for PM's too.)

Now before we proceed any further, we should address the question of converting the PM's STORE into the TM's TAPE. The STORE contains a string of letters with the possibility of some occurrences of the symbol #.

Most often there will be only one occurrence of the symbol # somewhere in the middle of the string, but even though this is usual in practice, it is not demanded by the definition. We have seen the # used as a marker of the end of the original input, but the definition of PM's allows us to put any number of them in the STORE.

We now describe how we can use the TM TAPE to keep track of the STORE. Suppose the contents of the STORE look like

$$x_1 x_2 x_3 x_4 x_5$$

where the x's are from the PM input alphabet Σ or the symbol # and none of them is Δ. We want the corresponding contents of the TM TAPE to be

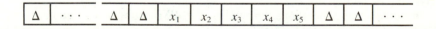

with the TAPE HEAD pointing to one of the x's. Notice that we keep some Δ's on the left of the STORE information, not just on the right, although there will only be finitely many Δ's on the left, since the TAPE ends in that direction.

We have drawn the TM TAPE picture broken because we do not know exactly where the x's will end up on the TAPE. The reason for this is that the PM eats up stuff from the left of the STORE and adds on stuff to the right. If at some point the STORE contains *abb* and we execute the instructions

READ – ADD a – READ – ADD a – ADD b – READ,

the TM TAPE will change like this:

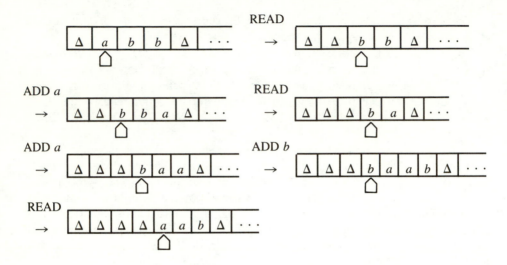

The non-Δ information wanders up to the right while Δ's accumulate on the left.

Immediately after the START state on the TM we shall employ the pre-processor INSERT (from Chapter 24) to insert a Δ in cell i and to move the whole non-Δ initial input string one cell to the right up the TAPE.

We do this so that the first PM operation simulated is like all the others in that the non-Δ information on the TM TAPE has at least one Δ on each side of it, enabling us to locate the right-most and left-most ends of the input string by bouncing off Δ's.

There are two operations by which the PM changes the contents of the STORE: ADD and READ. Let us now consider how a TM can duplicate the corresponding actions on its TAPE.

If the PM at some point executes the state

the TM must change its TAPE from something like

$$\cdots \;\Delta\; \Delta\; x_1\; x_2\; x_3\; x_4\; \Delta\; \Delta\; \cdots$$

to

$$\cdots \;\Delta\; \Delta\; x_1\; x_2\; x_3\; x_4\; y\; \Delta\; \Delta\; \cdots$$

To do this, the TAPE HEAD must move to the right end of the non-Δ characters, locate the first Δ and change it to y. This can be done as follows:

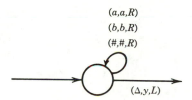

We have illustrated this in the case where $\Sigma = \{a,b\}$, but if Σ had more letters it would only mean more labels on the loop. Notice also that we have left the TAPE HEAD again pointing to some non-Δ character. This is important. We do not want the TAPE HEAD wandering off into the infinitely many blanks on the right.

There is only one other PM state we have to simulate; that is the READ state. The READ state does two things. It removes the first character from the STORE and it branches in accordance with what it has removed. The other states we have simulated did not involve branching.

For a TM to remove the left-most non-Δ character, the TAPE HEAD must move leftward until the first blank it encounters. It should then back up one cell to the right and read the non-Δ character in that cell. This it must turn into a Δ and move itself right, never moving beyond the string of non-Δ's. This process will require two states in the TM:

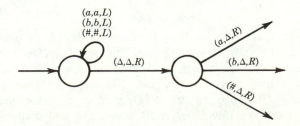

Notice that we leave the second state along different edges, depending on which character is being erased. This is equivalent to the PM instruction:

We should also note that because we were careful to insert a Δ in cell i in front of the input string we do not have to worry about moving the TAPE HEAD left from cell i and crashing while searching for the Δ on the left side.

If while processing a given input the STORE ever becomes empty, then the TM TAPE will become all Δ's. It is possible that the PM may wish to READ an empty STORE and branch accordingly. If this alternative is listed in the PM, it should also be in the TM.

becomes

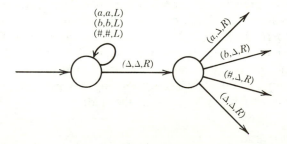

If the TAPE is all Δ's, the TAPE HEAD reads the cell it is pointing to, which contains a Δ, and moves to the right, "thinking" that it is now in the non-Δ section of the TAPE. It then reads this cell and finds another Δ, which it leaves as a Δ and moves right again. The program branches along the appropriate edge. Just because the STORE is empty does not mean that the program is over. We might yet ADD something and continue. The TM simulation can do the same.

Thus we can convert every PM state to a TM state or sequence of states that have the same function. The TM so constructed will HALT on all words that the PM sends to ACCEPT. It will crash on all words that the PM sends to REJECT (or on which the PM crashes), and it will loop forever on those same inputs on which the PM loops forever. ■

EXAMPLE

Recall that our first PM of this chapter was

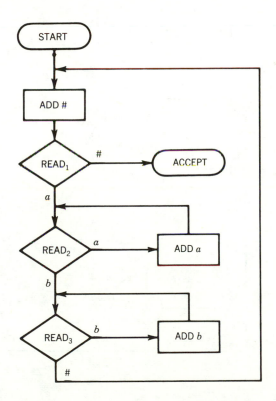

This PM accepts the language $\{a^n b^n\}$.

This time we have drawn the machine vertically to facilitate its conversion into a TM. Following the algorithm in the proof, we produce the next machine, where, for the sake of simplicity, we have omitted the Δ-inserting preprocessor and assume that the input string is placed on the TM TAPE starting in cell ii with a Δ in cell i.

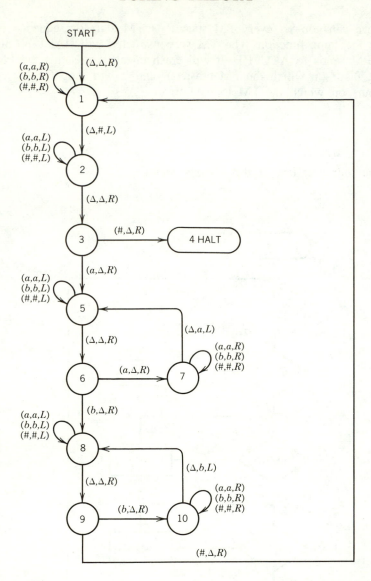

Notice that

TM State	Corresponds to	PM State
START		START
1		ADD #
2 and 3		READ 1
4		ACCEPT
5 and 6		READ 2
7		ADD a
8 and 9		READ 3
10		ADD b

We really should not have put the end-of-proof box on our discussion of Theorem 46 as we did, because the proof is not over until we fully understand exactly how the separately simulated components fit together to form a coherent TM. In the example above, we see that edges between the independently simulated states always have TM labels determined from the PM. We can now claim to understand the algorithm of Theorem 46.

In the TM we just constructed we have encountered a situation that plagues many Turing machines: piles of tedious multiple-edge labels that all say about the same thing:

$$(a,a,L)$$
$$(b,b,L)$$
$$(\Delta,\Delta,L)$$
$$(\#,\#,L)$$
$$(*,*,L)$$

This is proper Turing machine format for the instruction "If we read an a, a b, a Δ, a $\#$, or a $*$, leave it unchanged and move the TAPE HEAD left." Let us now introduce a shortened form of this sentence: $(a,b,\Delta,\#,*;=,L)$

DEFINITION (Inside of an Example)

If a, b, c, d, e are TM TAPE characters, then $(a,b,c,d,e;=,L)$ stands for the instructions

$$(a,a,L) \ (b,b,L) \ . \ . \ . \ (e,e,L)$$

Similarly we will employ $(a,b,c,d,e; =,R)$ for the set of labels

$$(a,a,R) \ (b,b,R) \ \ldots \ (e,e,R) \qquad \blacksquare$$

Let us trace the processing of the input string *aabb*:

$$
\begin{array}{cccc}
\text{START} & 1 & 1 & 1 \\
\Delta a\underline{a}bb & \Delta a\underline{a}bb & \Delta aa\underline{b}b & \Delta aab\underline{b} \\
\to & \to & \to &
\end{array}
$$

$$
\begin{array}{cccc}
1 & 1 & 2 & 2 \\
\Delta aab\underline{b} & \Delta aabb\underline{\Delta} & \Delta aab\underline{b}\# & \Delta aa\underline{b}b\# \\
\to & \to & \to &
\end{array}
$$

$$
\begin{array}{cccc}
2 & 2 & 2 & 3 \\
\Delta a\underline{a}bb\# & \Delta \underline{a}abb\# & \underline{\Delta}aabb\# & \Delta a\underline{a}bb\# \\
\to & \to & \to &
\end{array}
$$

$$
\begin{array}{cccc}
5 & 5 & 6 & 7 \\
\Delta\Delta\underline{a}bb\# & \Delta\Delta a\underline{b}b\# & \Delta\Delta a\underline{b}b\# & \Delta\Delta\Delta\underline{b}b\# \\
\to & \to & \to &
\end{array}
$$

$$
\begin{array}{cccc}
7 & 7 & 7 & 5 \\
\Delta\Delta\Delta b\underline{b}\# & \Delta\Delta\Delta bb\underline{\#} & \Delta\Delta\Delta bb\#\underline{\Delta} & \Delta\Delta\Delta bb\#\underline{a} \\
\to & \to & \to &
\end{array}
$$

$$
\begin{array}{cccc}
5 & 5 & 5 & 6 \\
\Delta\Delta\Delta b\underline{b}\#a & \Delta\Delta\Delta\underline{b}b\#a & \Delta\Delta\underline{\Delta}bb\#a & \Delta\Delta\Delta\underline{b}b\#a \\
\to & \to & \to &
\end{array}
$$

$$
\begin{array}{cccc}
8 & 8 & 9 & 10 \\
\Delta\Delta\Delta\Delta\underline{b}\#a & \Delta\Delta\Delta\Delta b\underline{\#}a & \Delta\Delta\Delta\Delta b\underline{\#}a & \Delta\Delta\Delta\Delta\Delta\underline{\#}a \\
\to & \to & \to &
\end{array}
$$

$$
\begin{array}{cccc}
10 & 10 & 8 & 8 \\
\Delta\Delta\Delta\Delta\Delta\#\underline{a} & \Delta\Delta\Delta\Delta\Delta\#a\underline{\Delta} & \Delta\Delta\Delta\Delta\Delta\#a\underline{b} & \Delta\Delta\Delta\Delta\Delta\#\underline{a}b \\
\to & \to & \to &
\end{array}
$$

$$
\begin{array}{cccc}
8 & 9 & 1 & 1 \\
\Delta\Delta\Delta\Delta\Delta\underline{\#}ab & \Delta\Delta\Delta\Delta\Delta\underline{\#}ab & \Delta\Delta\Delta\Delta\Delta\Delta\underline{a}b & \Delta\Delta\Delta\Delta\Delta\Delta a\underline{b} \\
\to & \to & \to &
\end{array}
$$

$$
\begin{array}{cccc}
1 & 2 & 2 & 2 \\
\Delta\Delta\Delta\Delta\Delta\Delta ab\underline{\Delta} & \Delta\Delta\Delta\Delta\Delta\Delta a\underline{b}\# & \Delta\Delta\Delta\Delta\Delta\Delta\underline{a}b\# & \Delta\Delta\Delta\Delta\Delta\underline{\Delta}ab\# \\
\to & \to & \to &
\end{array}
$$

$$
\begin{array}{cccc}
3 & 5 & 5 & 6 \\
\Delta\Delta\Delta\Delta\Delta\Delta\underline{a}b\# & \Delta\Delta\Delta\Delta\Delta\Delta\Delta\underline{b}\# & \Delta\Delta\Delta\Delta\Delta\Delta\underline{\Delta}b\# & \Delta\Delta\Delta\Delta\Delta\Delta\Delta\underline{b}\# \\
\to & \to & \to &
\end{array}
$$

$$
\begin{array}{cccc}
8 & 8 & 9 & 1 \\
\Delta\Delta\Delta\Delta\Delta\Delta\Delta\underline{\#} & \Delta\Delta\Delta\Delta\Delta\Delta\Delta\Delta\underline{\#} & \Delta\Delta\Delta\Delta\Delta\Delta\Delta\underline{\#} & \Delta\Delta\Delta\Delta\Delta\Delta\Delta\Delta\Delta\underline{\Delta} \\
\to & \to & \to &
\end{array}
$$

$$
\begin{array}{ccc}
2 & 3 & \\
\Delta\Delta\Delta\Delta\Delta\Delta\Delta\Delta\underline{\Delta}\# & \Delta\Delta\Delta\Delta\Delta\Delta\Delta\Delta\underline{\Delta}\# & \Delta\Delta\Delta\Delta\Delta\Delta\Delta\Delta\Delta\underline{\Delta} \qquad \text{HALT} \\
\to & \to & \to
\end{array}
$$

Here we have decided that the initial Δ's from cell i up to the data are significant and have included them in the trace.

We can see from this execution chain that this is a TM that accepts $\{a^nb^n\}$. We already know that there are other (smaller) TM's that do the same job. The algorithm never guaranteed to find the best TM that accepts the same language, only to prove the existence of one such by constructive algorithm. ■

We should note that the alphabet that appears on the TM TAPE produced by this algorithm is the same as the STORE alphabet of the PM.

We have now shown that any language that can be accepted by a Post machine can also be accepted by some Turing machine; however, that is only half the story.

THEOREM 47

Any language that can be accepted by a Turing machine can be accepted by some Post machine.

PROOF

This proof will again be by constructive algorithm. We start by assuming that we have an appropriate Turing machine for a certain language and from the TM we shall build a PM that operates on input strings in exactly the same way, step by step. Again we shall be doing a simulation.

Before continuing with this proof, we should note that we intend to use a STORE alphabet that is larger than usual. Normally we expect the STORE to contain the letters of the alphabet from the input-string language plus the symbol #. Here we are going to put any character from the TM TAPE alphabet (which can be much larger, with many special symbols) into the STORE. In particular, the character Δ may have to be placed in the STORE as well as A, B, C, . . . If there are any who have philosophical qualms about adding Δ to the store as a character let them not think of it as a blank but as the first letter of Dionysius. The simulation will work just as well. The language ultimately accepted by the PM will have only the letters of the input string language of the TM, but other characters may be employed in the processing, just as with TM's.

We already have some feel for the correspondence between these two machines from our last theorem. Still, one great problem stands out. In TM's we can read and change a character in the middle of the string, whereas with PM's we can only read the left-most character and add to the right end. How can PM's simulate the action of TM's? A clever trick is needed here that makes use of the extra symbol # that PM's have, which we shall assume is not in either of the TM's alphabets, Γ or Σ. (If the TM did use this symbol in its TAPE alphabet Γ, then change it to boldface or italics or blue paint without changing the operation of the TM and freeing # as a symbol special to the PM.)

We shall make a correspondence between # and the position of the TAPE HEAD. Characters to the left of the TAPE HEAD on the TM TAPE will be placed to the right of the symbol # on the PM STORE and characters to the right (or at) the TAPE HEAD will be placed to the left of #.

By these confusing words we mean to describe the correspondence of

	i	ii	iii	iv	v	vi	vii	viii		
TAPE:	X_1	X_2	X_3	X_4	X_5	X_6	X_7	X_8	Δ ·	· · ·

in the TM with

$$\text{STORE:} \quad X_4 \ X_5 \ X_6 \ X_7 \ X_8 \ \# \ X_1 \ X_2 \ X_3$$

in the PM.

Why do we do this? Because when the TAPE HEAD is reading cell iv as it is in the TM above it reads the character X_4. Therefore we must be set to read X_4 in the PM, which means it had better be the left-most character in the STORE.

Here comes the beauty of this method of representation.

Suppose while the TAPE HEAD is reading cell iv, as above, we execute the instruction (X_4, Y, R). This gives us the TM situation:

	i	ii	iii	iv	v	vi	vii	viii	ix	
TAPE:	X_1	X_2	X_3	Y	X_5	X_6	X_7	X_8	Δ	$\cdots$

To maintain the correspondence we must be able to convert the STORE in the PM to:

$$\text{STORE:} \quad X_5 \ X_6 \ X_7 \ X_8 \ \# \ X_1 \ X_2 \ X_3 \ Y$$

This conversion can be accomplished by the PM instructions (states):

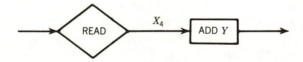

The X_4 is stripped off the front and a Y is stuck on the back, a very easy PM operation. Notice that both TM and PM are now set to read X_5.

Let us pause for a moment to see exactly how this conversion works. On the next page on the left is a Turing machine that converts the input word cat into the word dog and crashes on all other inputs. This TM uses only right TAPE HEAD moves, so we can convert it easily to the PM on the left using the correspondence shown above:

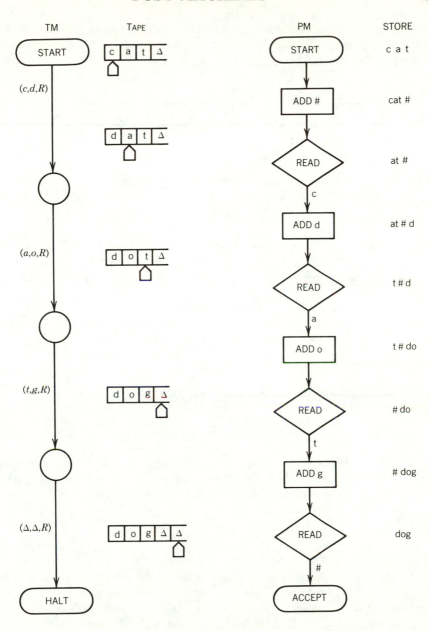

Notice how the correspondence between TAPE and STORE is preserved with every instruction. Let us return to the simulation.

Suppose instead that we started with the original TAPE as above with TAPE HEAD reading cell iv and we were asked to execute the instruction (X_4, Y, L). This would leave the TAPE as:

	i	ii	iii	iv	v	vi	vii	viii	ix	
TAPE:	X_1	X_2	X_3	Y	X_5	X_6	X_7	X_8	Δ	$\cdots$

This TAPE-status corresponds to the STORE contents:

$$X_3 \ Y \ X_5 \ X_6 \ X_7 \ X_8 \ \# \ X_1 \ X_2$$

It is not so immediately obvious how a PM can change the STORE contents $X_4 \ X_5 \ X_6 \ X_7 \ X_8 \ \# \ X_1 \ X_2 \ X_3$ into this string, but it can be done.

To execute the instruction (X_4,Y,L) properly, we begin by executing (X_4,Y,R) as before:

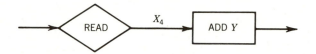

which will convert the contents of the STORE into

$$X_5 \ X_6 \ X_7 \ X_8 \ \# \ X_1 \ X_2 \ X_3 \ Y$$

and now we need to find a PM subroutine (part of a PM) that can take a character from the back end of the STORE and put it on the front end. Running this subroutine *twice* produces the correct TAPE simulation:

$$X_3 \ Y \ X_5 \ X_6 \ X_7 \ X_8 \ \# \ X_1 \ X_2$$

The following is such a subroutine. Our task is to use the operations "take from the left" and "add to the right" to simulate the operation "take one from the right and add it to the left." Can this be done? Surprisingly, it can. Roughly as follows: Stick a marker on the back, read two characters at a time, if neither is the marker stick them back onto the right in their correct order; if the second is the marker we put them back on the right in reverse order; this leaves the marker in front of the end symbol. Then we make one more pass through all the data, cycling from left to right and stopping when the marker is encountered. A more precise description is given below:

In general, let us suppose that the initial contents of an STORE are:

$$Z_1 \ Z_2 \ Z_3 \ . \ . \ . \ Z_{10}$$

where the Z's are all from some finite alphabet called Π. For the purposes of illustration, let us say:

$$\Pi = \{a,b,c\}$$

Let us also choose some distinguished symbol that is not in the alphabet Π. Let us say "$\$$" is such a symbol.

The algorithm we use is this:

Step 1   Add $\$$ on to the right of the STORE.

Step 2   Read two characters from the left of the STORE. This will take many READ statements since we wish to preserve distinct paths for any combination of symbols that may have been read. For ourselves let us refer to these as symbol ONE and symbol TWO.

Step 3   If TWO is $\$$, then we know ONE was originally the last character in the STORE. We ADD the character $\$$ to the STORE and *then* the character ONE and go to Step 5.

Step 4   If TWO is not $\$$, then ONE was not the original last character in the STORE so we

(i)   ADD the character called ONE to the right side of the STORE.

(ii)   Rename for ourselves the character called TWO as ONE, that is, the first symbol of the next pair of symbols.

(iii)   Read a new character from the left of the STORE and call it TWO.

(iv)   Go back to Step 3.

Step 5   When we get here from Step 3 the contents of the STORE look like this:

$$Z_1\, Z_2\, Z_3 \ldots Z_8\, Z_9\, \$\, Z_{10}$$

This means that we know that the $\$$ has now been moved *in front* of the character that was originally the last (right-most) symbol in the STORE.

(i)   We now read a character and call it ONE.

(ii)   If ONE is not $\$$, we add it to the right of the STORE and go back to step 5(i).

(iii)   If ONE is $\$$, we stop.

This is a much tougher algorithm to understand from the abstract description than it is to understand from illustration.

Before writing the PM program that performs this algorithm, let us see it work on a specific example. Let the STORE begin with the contents *abbc*.

We proceed as follows:

Step	STORE	ONE	TWO
1	abbc$		
2	bc$	a	b
Skip 3 since TWO is not $			
4(i)	bc$a		b
4(ii)	bc$a	b	
4(iii)	c$a	b	b
Skip 3, since TWO is not $			
4(i)	c$ab		b
4(ii)	c$ab	b	
4(iii)	$ab	b	c
Skip 3 since TWO is not $			
4(i)	$abb		c
4(ii)	$abb	c	
4(iii)	abb	c	$
3	abb$c		
5(i)	bb$c	a	
5(ii)	bb$ca		
5(i)	b$ca	b	
5(ii)	b$cab		
5(i)	$cab	b	
5(ii)	$cabb		
5(i)	cabb	$	
5(iii)	cabb		
	STOP		

The last letter became the first letter just as was desired.
    One last example, very quickly, on the string 1 2 3 4:

$$1\ 2\ 3\ 4$$
$$1\ 2\ 3\ 4\ \$$$
$$2\ 3\ 4\ \$\ 1$$
$$3\ 4\ \$\ 1\ 2$$
$$4\ \$\ 1\ 2\ 3$$

But now that $ is the second symbol, the two symbols 4 and $ go on the back end reversed. Now once more through the whole queue:

$$1\ 2\ 3\ \$\ 4$$
$$2\ 3\ \$\ 4\ 1$$
$$3\ \$\ 4\ 1\ 2$$
$$\$\ 4\ 1\ 2\ 3$$

Just kill the $

$$4\ \ 1\ \ 2\ \ 3$$

as desired. The last shall be first.

In PM's we do not have extra storage locations called ONE and TWO to use as we did in the columns in the previous table. We have to keep track of which letters have been read by knowing what state we are in. The Post machinery for this job is:

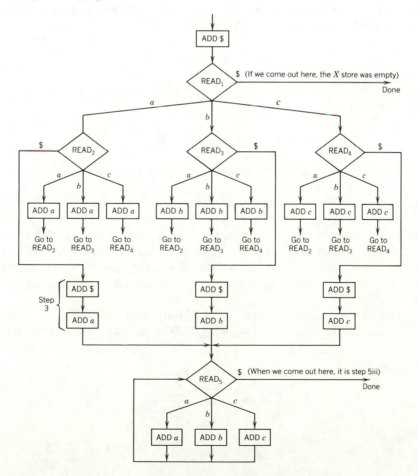

To keep the picture understandable, we have labeled some edges "Go to READ" and not drawn the connection. If we drew all the necessary lines the PM would look like spaghetti.

In $READ_1$ we read a character, say a. We do not know yet whether we want to add this character directly on the back of the STORE or whether it was the original right-most character, in which case we would want to mark it as such. Therefore, before adding anything, we read another character, say c. We now know that the a was not the fellow we are looking for (the former last character in the STORE, Z_{10}), so we add it to the back of the STORE without further discussion. However, the possibility arises that this c is our sought after last character. We go to state $READ_4$. Being in $READ_4$ means that we have just read a c, and we look at the next character in the STORE. If it is a \$, then this c is our Z_{10} and we prepare the final stages by adding \$ then c to the back of the STORE. If the next character after c is not \$ but, say, b, then we add c to the STORE and continue from state $READ_3$. Being in $READ_3$ means we have just read a b and we want to read another character. Eventually we know we must encounter the \$ (since we put it there ourselves) and when we do, we execute step 3, of adding the last two characters back onto the store in reverse order. The STORE contents will have been successfully converted to:

$$Z_1 \ Z_2 \ldots Z_8 \ Z_9 \ \$ \ Z_{10}$$

Now the three lines join to enter the $READ_5$ loop, which clearly leaves the STORE containing:

$$Z_{10} \ Z_1 \ Z_2 \ldots Z_9$$

as desired. We have successfully taken the original STORE and moved the right-most character to the left end.

Notice that if we tried to run this subroutine on an empty STORE, $READ_1$ would have sent us to "done" without changing anything.

Notice also the similarity between the READ states here and the states in the TM subroutine INSERT. The states keep track of what has just been read. If we had to be anthropomorphic we could say they are short-term memory devices or visceral learning, but fortunately no one is forcing us to be anthropomorphic.

Let us call this whole segment of a PM by a new name SUB. We can now feel free to design a machine with SUB as a state, drawn like this:

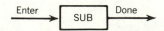

This machine will still be a PM since we can replace SUB with the actual PM program shown above, provided, of course, that we know the alphabet of characters in the STORE.

Let us recall that SUB was created to help us simulate TM instructions on a PM. We can execute almost all instructions of the form (X_4, Y, L) in the PM with this sequence:

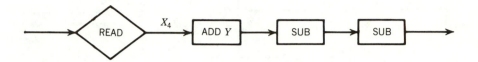

We say "almost" because we have the problem of what to do when the TM is instructed to move left when the TAPE HEAD is at cell i: Consider the TAPE situation below:

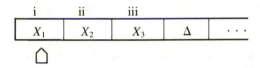

Here (X_1, Y, L) causes a crash. Let us see what this instruction means when performed by the PM simulation.

In our PM version, we would start with the STORE contents:

$$X_1 \ X_2 \ X_3 \ \#$$

We would then execute the sequence READ – ADD – SUB – SUB. The contents of the STORE changes as shown below:

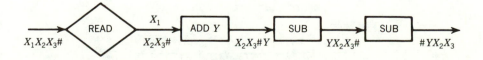

Since we have agreed in our simulation to keep the character that is in the TM cell being read by the TAPE HEAD to the left of the # in the PM store, the final STORE contents makes no sense. It does somewhat "represent" a crash in that it shows that the TAPE HEAD is not reading anything, but it does not crash the PM. The PM could conceivably still continue processing the input and eventually reach ACCEPT. To be sure the PM stops processing, we must include in every PM simulation of a leftward TM move a test to see whether the first symbol in the STORE has become #.

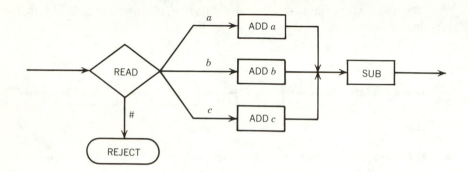

After we read a non-# character, we stick it onto the back of the STORE with ADD and move it back up to the front with SUB. If the left-most character in the STORE was not #, no harm is done by this routine; if it was, then the PM stops.

Now we have a completely accurate treatment for (X,Y,L), but we have not fully covered the (X,Y,R) case yet. Another difficulty, similar to the problem we have just treated, arises when we want to move the TAPE HEAD right beyond the non-Δ's on the TAPE. If the TAPE status is like this:

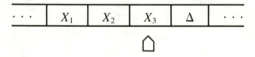

and the TM wants to execute the move

$$(X_3,Y,R)$$

we end up with:

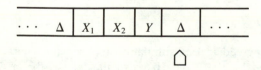

In the PM simulation of this, the STORE begins by containing

$$X_3 \# X_1 X_2$$

and after READ-ADD it contains:

$$\#X_1X_2Y$$

which is again a meaningless formulation in our correspondence. When a move right causes the # to be the first character of the STORE we should insert a Δ in front of # in the STORE to achieve

$$\Delta\#X_1X_2Y$$

which does correspond to the TM's TAPE status. The problem arose here because the actual contents of a TM TAPE includes an infinite number of Δ's that we may read, but these cannot all be kept in the PM's STORE waiting for us. The best we can do is to recognize when we need to insert a new Δ into the STORE.

We can do this as before with a test after READ-ADD. The proper simulation of (X,Y,R) is therefore this:

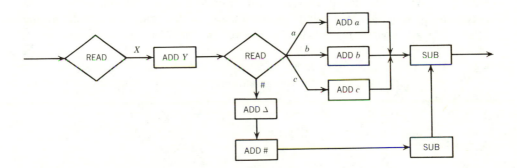

This then is the completely accurate PM routine corresponding to the TM instruction (X,Y,R).

Remember that SUB is itself composed of many PM states. So we see that even a small TM will be converted into a huge PM by this method. The simulation is almost complete. All branching and TAPE modification that the TM requires can be performed by the PM we have designed. In any case where the TM accepts the input string by landing in HALT the PM will accept the string by landing in ACCEPT and vice versa.

To start the PM, we must make it initially resemble the TM. The TM begins its procesing by having the input string already on its TAPE:

i	ii	iii	iv	v		
X_1	X_2	X_3	X_4	X_5	Δ	$\cdots$

while a PM running on the same input according to the rules of PM's must start with the STORE containing exactly the same input string:

$$X_1 \ X_2 \ X_3 \ X_4 \ X_5$$

However, the STORE contents corresponding to the TM status would be

$$X_1 \ X_2 \ X_3 \ X_4 \ X_5 \ \#$$

To begin the correspondence, we have to add a $\#$ to the right. Therefore, our initial sequence in the PM must always be

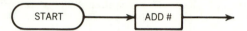

Now the correspondence is complete; all words accepted by the TM will be accepted by the PM. All input strings that crash on one will crash on the other, and all input strings that loop forever on the TM will do the same on the PM. ∎

This is a very inefficient conversion algorithm, so we shall illustrate it on a very small TM.

EXAMPLE

Consider this TM:

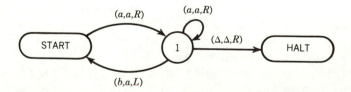

This machine accepts all words starting with an a and in so doing it turns the input into a string of solid a's. When converted into a PM by the algorithm above, the resultant machine is:

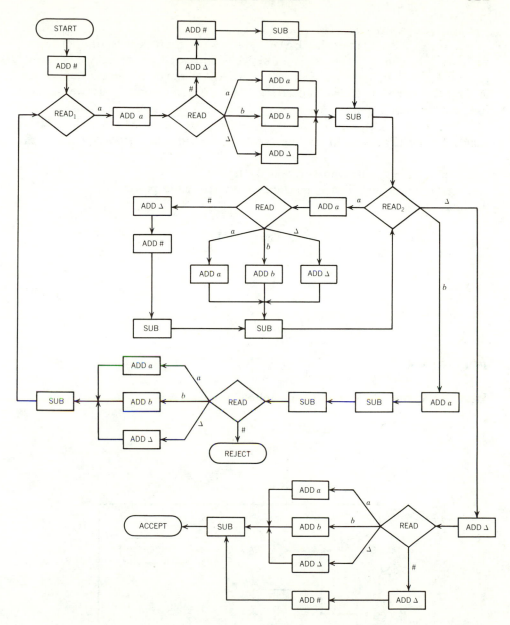

Here READ₁ represents the START state of the TM not in its capacity to initiate the process (START-ADD # does that) but in its capacity as a state to loop back to and out of.

READ$_2$ represents the TM state 1.

We get to READ$_2$ through READ$_1$ by a process equivalent to (a,a,R). Here we read either an a, b, or Δ. If an a, we loop back by a process equivalent to (a,a,R); if a b, then we go back to READ$_1$ through a process equivalent to (b,a,L); and if a Δ, we proceed to ACCEPT, not directly as we should like but through a process equivalent to (Δ,Δ,R) (not really efficient at all.) This is not even a picture of the whole PM because each of the eight SUB's stands for the 24-state PM routine constructed in the last proof.   ■

Taken together, Theorems 46 and 47 tell us:

Post machines and Turing machines have the same power.

We may write:

$$PM = TM$$

PROBLEMS

Problems 1 through 4 refer to the following PM:

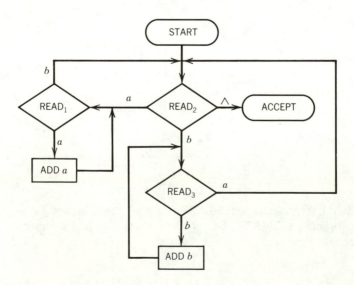

1. Trace the paths of the following input strings on this PM. At every step name the current state and the contents of the STORE.

    (i)   *abab*

    (ii)   *baabba*

    (iii) *aaabbb*

    (iv)   *aabbbb*

    (v)   *bbabaaa*

2. (i)   Show that if an input has exactly one more *a* than *b* it will crash on this PM in state $READ_1$.

   (ii)   Show that if an input string has exactly one more *b* than *a* it will crash on this PM in state $READ_3$.

   (iii) Show that if an input string has more than one more *a* than *b* or more than one more *b* than *a* then it will loop forever on this PM.

3. Show that the language accepted by this PM is EQUAL, all words with the same number of *a*'s and *b*'s.

4. Draw a PM that accepts the language UNEQUAL, the complement of EQUAL.

5. Draw a PM that accepts the language $\{a^n b^{3n}\}$.

6. Draw a PM that accepts the language EVENPALINDROME. (*Hint:* Use the subroutine SUB.)

7. (i)   Draw a PM that accepts the language ODDPALINDROME.

   (ii)   Draw a PM that accepts the language PALINDROME.

8. Draw a PM that accepts the language EVENPALINDROME' (the complement of EVENPALINDROME).

9. (i)   Explain why, even though a PM is deterministic, the complement of a language accepted by a PM might not be accepted by any PM.

   (ii)   Find an example of a PM that does not accept the complementary language by reversing ACCEPT and REJECT states.

   (iii) Find a PM which accepts exactly the same language if its ACCEPT and REJECT states are reversed.

10. Prove that all regular languages can be accepted by some PM. (This is not hard. Simply follow the line of argument in the proof of Theorem 26.)

11. (i) Convert the following TM into a PM using the algorithm of Theorem 47 (make use of the subroutine SUB).

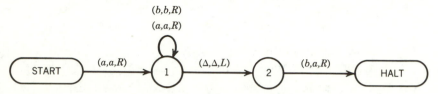

   Run the following input strings on both the TM and the PM.
   (ii) *a*
   (iii) *ab*
   (iv) *abb*
   (v) What is the language accepted by the two machines?
   (vi) Build a smaller PM that accepts the same language.

12. (i) Build a PM that takes in any string of *a*'s and *b*'s and leaves in its STORE the complement string that has the *a*'s and *b*'s switched.

   (ii) Build a PM that takes in any string of *a*'s and *b*'s and exchanges the first and last letters and then accepts.

13. (i) Build a PM that accepts the language of all words that have an *a* as the middle letter. (These words obviously must have odd length).

   (ii) Prove that this language is nonregular.

   (iii) Prove that this language is context-free.

14. Convert the PM built in Problem 13 into a TM by the algorithm in this chapter.

15. Build a PM that accepts the language of all words with more *a*'s than *b*'s by using the following algorithm:

   Step 1 On one pass through the data, look for a pair of consecutive letters that are unequal and cancel them both.

   Step 2 Repeat the operation above until there are no letters to cancel.

   Step 3 If there is an *a* left, accept the word.

   Run this machine on the following input strings:

(i)   *aabb*

(ii)   *aaabb*

(iii) *ababa*

(iv)   *ababab*

16.   Build a PM that takes any input from the language defined by $(a + b)^*$ and deletes all substrings of the form *aaa*, leaving all else in the word intact.

17.   Build a PM that sorts the letters of a string. That is, if *aba* is fed in, the machine leaves *aab* in its STORE and accepts. Also, *bbbaba* becomes *aabbbb*.

18.   Build a PM that starts with any string *s* from $(a + b)^*$ and leaves

$$s \; b^{\text{length } (s)}$$

This is the language TRAILINGCOUNT we have seen before in the Problems to Chapter 11.

19.   (i)   Outline a TM that takes any input string of *a*'s and *b*'s and runs to HALT leaving on its TAPE the same string reversed.

      (ii)   Outline a PM that does the same thing.

20.   Let *L* be a language accepted by the Post machine *P*. Let the transpose of *L*, L^T, be the language of all the words in *L* spelled backward.
      The word *X* is in L^T if reverse(*X*) is in *L*. Prove that there is some *PM*, *G*, that accepts L^T.

CHAPTER 26

MINSKY'S THEOREM

We shall soon see that Turing machines are fascinating and worthy of extensive study, but they do not seem at first glance like a natural development from the machines that we had been studying before. There was a natural extension from FA's to PDA's that made it easy to prove that all regular languages could also be accepted by PDA's. There is no such natural connection between PDA's and TM's; that is, a TM is not a souped-up PDA with extra gizmos. The TM, like the Mealy machine, performs its operations along its edges. The Mealy machine, we presumed, prints its output somewhere, while the TM writes on its own input TAPE. It leaves little notes to itself that can later be read and changed. This is unlike a PDA. Perhaps we can add a note-pad to a PDA.

We found that the addition of a PUSHDOWN STACK made a considerable improvement in the power of an FA. What would happen if we added two PUSHDOWN STACK's, or three, or seventy?

DEFINITION

A **two-pushdown stack machine,** a **2PDA,** is ike a PDA except that it has two PUSHDOWN STACK's, STACK$_1$ and STACK$_2$. When we wish to push

616

a character x into a STACK, we have to specify which stack, either "PUSH$_1$ x" or "PUSH$_2$ x." When we pop a STACK for purposes of branching, we must specify which STACK, either "POP$_1$" or "POP$_2$." The function of the START, READ, ACCEPT, and REJECT states remains the same. The input string is placed on the same read-only INPUT TAPE. One important difference is that we shall insist that a 2PDA be deterministic, that is, branching will only occur at the READ and POP states and there will be at most one edge from any state for any given character. ■

Since we have made 2PDA's deterministic, we cannot be certain whether they are even as powerful as PDA's; that is, we cannot be certain that they can accept every CFL since the deterministic PDA's cannot.

We shall soon see that 2PDA's are actually stronger than PDA's. They can accept all CFL's and some languages that are non-context-free.

EXAMPLE

Consider the 2PDA below:

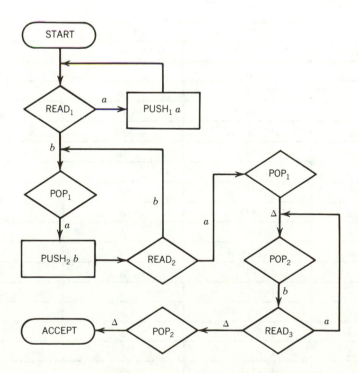

There are many REJECT states that we have not drawn in. As far as we are concerned, it is fine for the machine to crash when it reads or pops a character for which there is no path. This does not make the machine non-deterministic.

We have numbered the READ states but not the POP's because they already have numeric labels designating which STACK is to be popped and extra numbers would be confusing.

The first thing that happens to an input string is that the initial clump of a's is stripped away and put into $STACK_1$ in a circuit involving $READ_1$. Then a b takes us into a circuit involving $READ_2$ where we pop an a from $STACK_1$ for every b we read from the INPUT TAPE. Every time we pass through this circuit we push a b into $STACK_2$. When we are done with the b's from the TAPE we read an a, which takes us to a POP_1 where we check to make sure that $STACK_1$ is now empty. If we pass this test we know that there were as many b's in the b-clump as a's in the a-clump. We now enter a circuit involving $READ_3$ that reads through another clump of a's from the input and matches them against the number of b's we have put into $STACK_2$ in the previous circuit. If the INPUT TAPE and $STACK_2$ both become empty at the same time, then there were as many a's at the end of the TAPE as b's in $STACK_2$. This would mean that the whole initial input string was of the form $a^n b^n a^n$.

We can check this by processing *aabbaa* as follows.

TAPE	STATE	STACK$_1$	STACK$_2$
aabbaa	START	Δ	Δ
abbaa	READ$_1$	Δ	Δ
abbaa	PUSH$_1$ a	a	Δ
bbaa	READ$_1$	a	Δ
bbaa	PUSH$_1$ a	aa	Δ
baa	READ$_1$	aa	Δ
baa	POP$_1$	a	Δ
baa	PUSH$_2$ b	a	b
aa	READ$_2$	a	b
aa	POP$_1$	Δ	b
aa	PUSH$_2$ b	Δ	bb
a	READ$_2$	Δ	bb
a	POP$_1$	Δ	bb
a	POP$_2$	Δ	b
Δ	READ$_3$	Δ	b
Δ	POP$_2$	Δ	Δ
Δ	READ$_3$	Δ	Δ
Δ	POP$_2$	Δ	Δ
Δ	ACCEPT	Δ	Δ

So we see that a 2PDA can accept one language that a PDA cannot. Are there languages that a 2PDA cannot accept? Is a 3PDA stronger? Is a non-deterministic 2PDA stronger? Which is stronger, a 2PDA or a PM? The subject could, at this point, become very confusing. However, many of these questions are settled by a theorem of Marvin Minsky (1961).

THEOREM 48

$$2PDA = TM$$

In other words, any language accepted by a 2PDA can be accepted by some TM and any language accepted by a TM can be accepted by some 2PDA.

PROOF

In the first part of this proof we shall show that if the language L can be accepted by some 2PDA, then we can construct a TM that will also accept it. There may be several 2PDA's that accept L, so we fix our attention on one of them, call it P.

This demonstration will, of course, be by constructive algorithm. We shall show how to construct a TM that parallels the actions of the 2PDA. (We have also used the word "corresponds" instead of "parallels" or "stimulates" or "duplicates" or "emulates" or "processes exactly the same way." These are not technical words, but they help to make the idea clear.)

The 2PDA has three locations where it stores information; the INPUT TAPE, STACK₁, and STACK₂. The TM we build has only one information storage location, the TAPE. Therefore, we must put on the TAPE the information found in all three 2PDA locations. There is other information that is carried in the knowledge of what state we are in, but that will correspond easily between the 2PDA and the TM.

Suppose at some stage in the process the 2PDA has this status:

TAPE	$X_1 X_2 X_3 X_4$
STACK₁	$Y_1 Y_2 Y_3 Y_4 Y_5$
STACK₂	$Z_1 Z_2$

where the X's, Y's, and Z's are letters from the input and stack alphabets of the 2PDA. Our definition of 2PDA's was sketchy and did not mention whether each STACK had its own alphabet or whether there was some other rule. Since a STACK does not *have* to use all of the characters in its STACK alphabet, there is no real difference, so let us assume that the X's are from Σ and the Y's and Z's from Γ.

In our setup we encode these three strings on the TM TAPE as follows:

Step 1.

Assume the character # is not used by the 2PDA (if it is, find another special symbol).

Step 2.

In the first section of the TM TAPE we store the input string. Initially we inserted a Δ in cell i moving the data unchanged up the TAPE and later, as the letters of input are read by the 2PDA, we change them one-by-one into Δ's on the TM TAPE. The status of the TM TAPE corresponding to the current status of the 2PDA TAPE as described above may be:

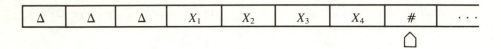

In what we have pictured above, two letters from the input string, those that were in cell ii and cell iii, have been read by the 2PDA and thus converted into Δ's on the TM. Since the number of letters in the input string cannot be increased (a 2PDA can read its TAPE but not write on it), we can put a permanent marker "#" on the TM TAPE at the end of the input string before we begin running. Throughout our processing the marker will stay exactly where it is. This # will be the home base for the TAPE HEAD. After simulating any action of the 2PDA, the TM TAPE HEAD will return to the # before beginning its next operation.

In our model the TM instructions that simulate the operation of the 2PDA state below:

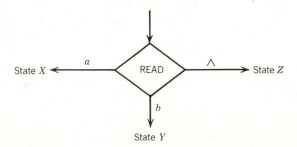

must accomplish the following chores:

(i)   Move the TAPE HEAD to the left to find the rightmost of the front Δ's.

(ii)   Bounce back to the right to find the next input letter to be read, in other words, scan right for the first non-Δ.

(iii)   If this character is #, the input has been exhausted; otherwise

(iv)   Change this letter into a Δ and back up one space to the left (so that we do not accidentally step on the # without knowing it).

(v)   Branch according to what was read and changed to a Δ; if it was an *a*, take an edge to the simulation of state *X*, if a *b*, take an edge to state *Y*, if a #, take an edge to state *Z*.

(vi)   Before continuing the processing, return the TAPE HEAD to # by moving right until it is encountered.

In TM notation this looks like this:

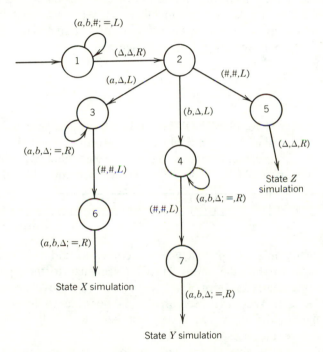

Notice that we are making use of the multiple instruction notation defined in the previous chapter:

$$(p,q,r,s; = ,R) \text{ stands for } (p,p,R), (q,q,R), (r,r,R), (s,s,R)$$

In state 1 we are looking for the Δ's at the beginning of the TAPE. We get to state 2 when we have found one and bounced off to the right either onto the first letter of the remainder of the string or else back onto #. If the string was empty when we go to read it, we follow the edge from state 2 to state 5. The edge from state 5 bounces us off the Δ that is to the left of # and leaves the TAPE HEAD reading the # as we want.

If the first letter of the remainder of the input string when we began was an a, we follow the edge from state 2 to state 3. On this edge we changed the a to a Δ and bounced left. We did this so as not to cross the # accidentally (which could be the next symbol on the TAPE). In state 3 we move right, hunting for the #. We find it and bounce left into state 6. Here we move *one* letter to the right and we know the TAPE HEAD is about to read #. If the first letter of the remaining input were a b rather than an a, we would proceed to states 4 and 7 similarly. This takes care of the complete simulation of the read statement.

The reason we make such a fuss about knowing where we leave the TAPE HEAD is not that it matters in the simulation of any particular step but because it helps us glue the simulated steps together. This is somewhat like building a house and returning the hammer to the tool shed after driving in each nail. It is not efficient, but we never lose the hammer.

Step 3.

The contents of the two PUSHDOWN STACKS will appear to the right of the # on the TM TAPE. We could place this information on the TAPE in the obvious fashion: first the contents of $STACK_1$, then another # marker, and then the contents of $STACK_2$. The TAPE would then look like this:

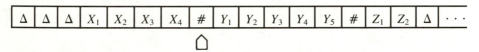

This is perfectly fine except that when it comes to adding a character onto $STACK_1$ we have to shift the entire $STACK_2$ sequence to the right and when we delete (pop) a character from $STACK_1$ we have to move everything down one cell to the left. We have seen that it is possible to insert or delete a character in the middle of a TM TAPE, but here we shall do it a different way for illustrative purposes.

The following trick makes all the work of the extra subroutines unnecessary. Let us store the stack contents on the TM TAPE backward, that is, Y_5 to the left of Y_4 to the left of Y_3 . . . up to the first letter Y_1. The same for Z_2, then Z_1. Since these are PUSHDOWN STACKS we shall be adding and deleting on the right. This means that we do not have to disturb the rest of the contents of $STACK_2$ when a character is added or popped.

We can make this apply to $STACK_1$ as well by this trick: Place the $STACK_1$ and $STACK_2$ character strings in *alternate cells* starting to the right of #. The TAPE which corresponds to the status of the 2PDA P shown above, is this:

| Δ | Δ | Δ | X_1 | X_2 | X_3 | X_4 | # | Y_5 | Z_2 | Y_4 | Z_1 | Y_3 | Δ | Y_2 | Δ | Y_1 | Δ | $\cdots$ |

In this way the active ends of both STACK's point outward into fields of Δ's. Notice that since STACK$_2$ has fewer characters than STACK$_1$ the further-out STACK$_1$ characters are separated by Δ's. This is the potential growing room where STACK$_2$ can be increased without making STACK$_1$ move at all. Similarly, STACK$_1$ can grow or shrink without making us move any of STACK$_2$.

The TAPE HEAD always starts by reading the #. If we wish to scan over STACK$_1$, we move it one cell, then two more, then two more, then two more, and so on. If the TAPE HEAD wants to read STACK$_2$, it must, from #, move two cells, then two more, then two more, and so on.

Let us assume that the stack characters in the 2PDA are a, b, and c. Our overall plan is this. The 2PDA moves from state to state to state changing its TAPE and STACK's. What we shall do is build a TM that stores on its TAPE (as shown above) the current status of the 2PDA TAPE and STACK's. As the 2PDA moves through its program from READ to PUSH$_1$ to POP$_2$ and so on, the TM will simulate the same action. The TAPE HEAD starts at # and after simulating a READ, POP, or PUSH it returns to # having changed the TM TAPE to reflect the new status of the 2PDA. When the 2PDA transfers into its ACCEPT state, the TM will move into its HALT state.

We have already seen the simulation of a READ statement. We have yet to show how to duplicate the action of the POP's and PUSH's. We can simulate the 2PDA command:

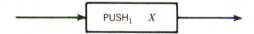

by this corresponding TM program segment:

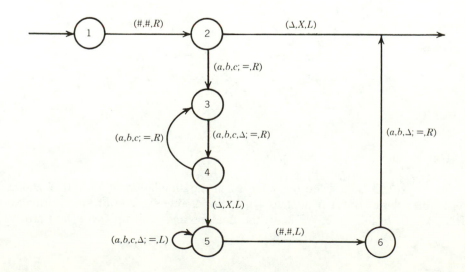

We start at state 1 reading the # and moving one cell to the right. This puts us in the midst of the character string from $STACK_1$ (spelled backward). If in state 2 we read a Δ, it means that $STACK_1$ was empty. We convert this Δ into an X and move the TAPE HEAD back to # with the one instruction (Δ,X,L).

If while reading this cell we find a non-Δ (an a, b, or c), we are reading the last (right-most) character in $STACK_1$. We leave this alone, taking the edge $(a,b,c;=,R)$, and go to state 3.

In state 3 we realize we are reading a character (or Δ) from $STACK_2$, so we ignore it and read on to state 4.

In state 4 we are again reading a cell belonging to $STACK_1$. If this contains Δ, we have just gone past the end of the contents of $STACK_1$.

We change the Δ to an X and begin marching home to #. All this is done with the instruction (Δ,X,L). We are then in state 5. However, if we read a non-Δ in state 4 we have not found the end of the character string for $STACK_1$. We then go back to state 3 because the next cell to the right contains information about $STACK_2$. From 3 we ignore what we read and go to state 4 again, where we examine another cell with $STACK_1$ information to see whether it is blank, that is, to see whether we have found the top of $STACK_1$. In state 3 we read those TAPE cells that store $STACK_2$ and in state 4 we read the cells in between them, which are those that store $STACK_1$.

We keep looping back and forth between states 4 and 3 until we get to the Δ in front of the $STACK_1$ string. When there, we replace it with X and begin our search for the home base, #. State 5 locates the # and state 6 leaves the TAPE HEAD there.

We have joined the edges from state 2 and 6 because they will both lead into whatever state comes after the "$PUSH_1\ X$" instruction.

Before demonstrating the TM equivalent of "$PUSH_2\ X$," let us give the TM formulation for the 2PDA state POP_1:

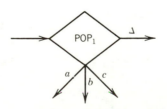

This is shown on the next page.

States 1, 2, 3, and 4 are the same as in the simulation of $PUSH_1\ X$ above. As before, if we read a Δ in state 4 it is the Δ after the end of the information in $STACK_1$. In this case, we leave the Δ alone and back up two cells (through

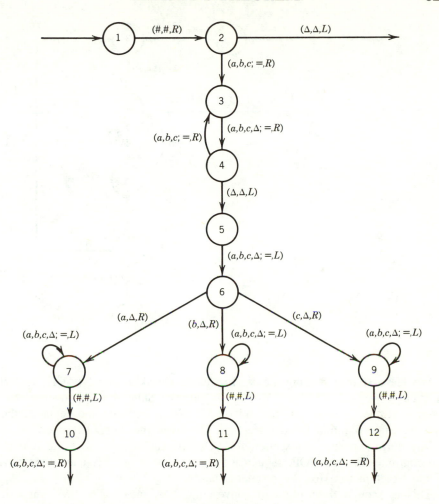

state 5) and in state 6 we read the top character in $STACK_1$. We branch while setting this equal to Δ. Along each branch we first hunt for # (states 7, 8, or 9) and we leave the TAPE HEAD on it (states 10, 11, or 12). We have not only removed a character from the top of $STACK_1$ as POP_1 does, but we have also branched in one of four different directions depending on what that character was.

To complete the description of the 2PDA stack operations we have to describe how to execute "$PUSH_2$ X" and "POP_2."

To execute a "$PUSH_2$ X" we have to move the TAPE HEAD two cells to the right initially, not just one as with $PUSH_1$ X.

The following TM sequence accomplishes this task:

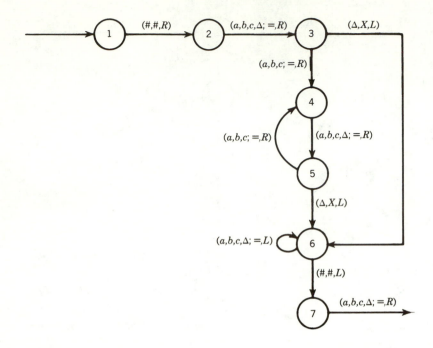

We leave state 1 reading the #. In state 2 we skip over STACK$_1$ material. In state 3 we see whether STACK$_2$ is empty. State 4 skips over STACK$_1$ material. State 5 hunts for the end of STACK$_2$, finds it, and replaces the Δ with X. State 6 hunts for the #. State 7 leaves the TAPE HEAD on #.

The corresponding TM section for POP$_2$ begins with these same five steps and continues like the POP$_1$ sequence from its state 4 on. We leave the drawing of the exact picture for the problems below.

This is enough description to convert a 2PDA into a TM. We know how to begin by corresponding the START of the 2PDA to the START state of the TM. Then, before looking at any more of the 2PDA, we insert a Δ in cell i in front of the input string on the TM TAPE and place a # after the string and leave the TAPE HEAD there. To the right of the # are all Δ's corresponding to the fact that STACK$_1$ and STACK$_2$ start out empty. In the 2PDA as we find POP's, PUSH's, and READ's, we convert them as shown above. We crash instead of having REJECT states and we put a HALT state in place of all ACCEPT's. Thus we are done.

So far we have proven only half of Minsky's theorem. We have shown that TM's can do everything 2PDA's can do. We still have to show that any language accepted by a TM can be accepted by some 2PDA.

To make the proof of this section easier, we shall prove that any language accepted by a PM can be accepted by some 2PDA. By Theorem 47, this implies that 2PDA's can do anything TM's can do and so it is enough to prove our result.

These two machines are already considerably closer to each other than TM's and 2PDA's, since both 2PDA's and PM's operate on the ends of storage locations with instructions inside states. In TM's the instructions are on the edges; and a TAPE is much easier to access, since we can read and write in its middle. We shall show how STACK$_1$ (on the 2PDA) can act in as versatile a manner as the STORE (on the PM) with the help of her brother STACK$_2$.

The PM starts with the input string already in the STORE, so we must transfer the input string from the TAPE of the 2PDA into STACK$_1$. We do this as follows:

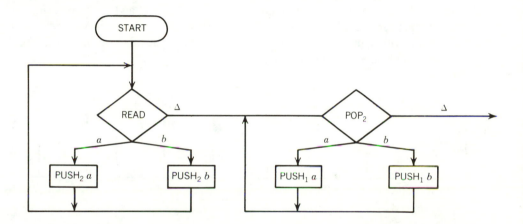

We took the letters from the TAPE and put them first in STACK$_2$. But because of the nature of a PUSHDOWN STACK, the string was reversed. If the input was initially *aabb*, what can be read from STACK$_2$ is *bbaa*. When it is transferred again to STACK$_1$, the input string is reversed again to become *aabb* as it was on the TAPE so that POP$_1$ now has an *a* as the first letter.

The two states with which a PM operates on its STORE are READ and ADD. The READ is a branch instruction and completely corresponds to the 2PDA instruction POP$_1$ by eliminating the left-most character and branching accordingly.

The ADD instruction is not so directly correspondent to any 2PDA instruction, since PUSH$_1$ introduces a new character on the left of the string in STACK$_1$ while ADD introduces a new character on the right of the string in the PM's STORE.

We can, however, simulate the action of "ADD X" with the following set of 2PDA instructions.

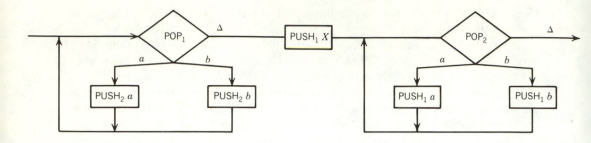

Here we first empty STACK$_1$ into STACK$_2$ (in STACK$_2$ the contents appear backward), then we insert the character X in STACK$_1$, and then we read back the string from STACK$_2$ into STACK$_1$ (it is back in correct order now). The net result is that we have an additional X on the right of the string in STACK$_1$ which means at the bottom of the stack.

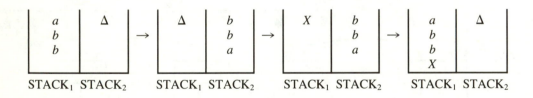

We shall keep STACK$_2$ empty at all times, except when it is being used to help arrange the data in STACK$_1$. STACK$_2$ is used only to initialize STACK$_1$ and to simulate the ADD instruction and for no other purpose.

The only other states a Post machine has are REJECT and ACCEPT, and those stay completely the same in the 2PDA. Therefore, we have finished describing this conversion process. We can completely simulate a PM on a 2PDA. Since we can simulate a TM on a PM we can conclude that we can simulate a TM on a 2PDA.

This completes the proof of Minsky's theorem. ∎

To illustrate the action of the algorithms in the proof we shall now present the mandatory examples of a 2PDA converted into a TM and a PM coverted into a 2PDA. In both cases, the conversion does not change the language accepted by the machine.

EXAMPLE

No higher purpose would be served by constucting a 3,000-state TM corresponding to a complicated 2PDA, so we choose a very simple 2PDA and claim that it is pedagogically sufficient.

One of the simplest 2PDA's is shown below:

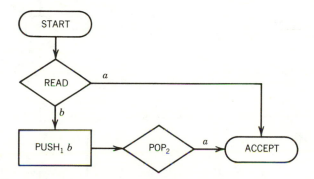

This machine accepts all words beginning with a and crashes on all words beginning with b since POP_2 cannot produce an a.

Many simple TM's can accept this language, but to know this we must *understand* the language. If we automatically follow the algorithm described in the proof of Theorem 48 we then produce a TM that must accept the same language as this 2PDA whether we know how to characterize the. language by some simple English sentence or not. That is the whole point of "proof by constructive algorithm."

The TM we must build is shown on the next page.

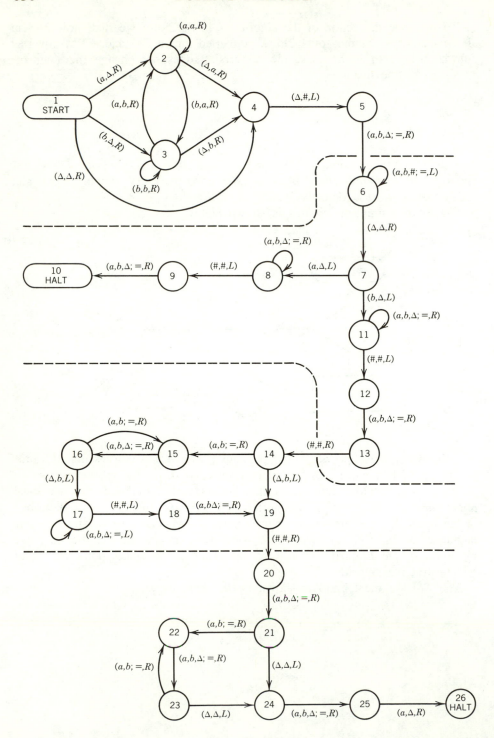

This is one of the largest machines in this book, yet the language it accepts is one of the most simplistic.

States 1 through 4 put a Δ in cell i and move the input string, without alteration, one cell to the right. From 4 to 5 the first Δ after the input is turned into the #. From 5 to 6 we position the TAPE HEAD under the #. This procedure is standard and all conversions of 2PDA's into TM's by this algorithm begin with these same five states. This process is identical to inserting a Δ in cell i as we did for PM simulation. The next part of the TM, from states 6 to 14, simulates the action of the 2PDA instruction READ. In state 6 we hunt for the beginning of the input string. In state 7 we branch to state 8 if the first letter is an a, to state 11 if it is a b. We crash in state 7 if the input is Λ. States 8, 9, and 10 reposition the TAPE HEAD under # and then state 10 accepts the input string corresponding to the a-branch from READ. Getting to state 13 repositions the TAPE HEAD under the #.

The next part of the TM, states 14 through 19, simulate the PUSH$_1$ b instruction exactly as described in the proof of Theorem 48.

States 20 through 25 simulate the POP$_2$, while state 26 corresponds to the ACCEPT state as reached by the impossible POP$_2$ a. We could have connected this up with state 10 to follow the algorithm, but the picture would be even messier.

The pleasure of running strings on this machine is reserved for Problem 16. ∎

EXAMPLE

Consider the following PM:

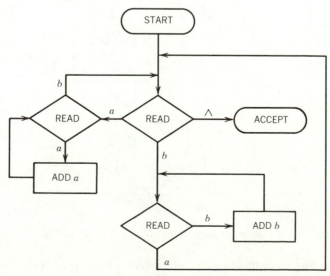

In the problem section of the last chapter this was seen to accept the language EQUAL, of all strings with the same total number of a's and b's.

When we convert this into a 2PDA by the algorithm described in the proof
of Minsky's theorem we obtain the following:

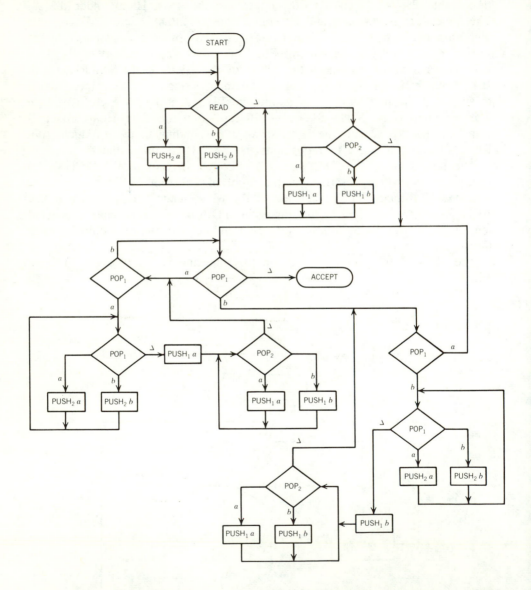

Tracing the words through this machine is left to the Problems. ■

If a pushdown automaton with two STACK's is already as powerful as a
Turing machine, it stands to reason that a PDA with three PUSHDOWN

STACK's will be even more powerful than a TM and a PDA with four STACK's even more powerful yet, and so on. This chain of reasoning is certainly true for ocean liners, but it runs aground for PDA's. None of these is any more powerful than a Turing machine.

THEOREM 49

Any language accepted by a PDA with n STACK's (where n is 2 or more), called an **nPDA,** can also be accepted by some TM. In power we have

$$n\text{PDA} = \text{TM} \quad \text{if } n \geqslant 2$$

PROOF

We shall sketch very quickly how the action of a 3PDA can be simulated by a TM as an illustration of the general idea.

Suppose that we have a 3PDA that is running on a certain input string. In the middle of the process we have some information on the INPUT TAPE and in the STACK's. Suppose the status is:

TAPE	$w_1\ w_2\ w_3\ w_4$
STACK$_1$	$x_1\ x_2$
STACK$_2$	$y_1\ y_2\ y_3\ y_4\ y_5$
STACK$_3$	$z_1\ z_2\ z_3\ z_4$

We want to represent all of this on the TAPE of the Turing machine as:

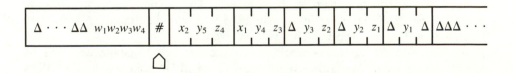

Note that we have *reversed* and *interlaced* the contents of the STACK's to the right of the # in a fashion directly analogous to the way we simulated a 2PDA on a TM in the proof of Theorem 48.

If we want to execute a 3PDA READ statement we must move to the left of # until we find the first Δ. The character to the right of this (if it is not #) is the next letter to be read. To execute a POP$_1$ or a PUSH$_1$ X, we start at # and move right one cell. If this is not empty, we skip two cells and read again. We repeat this skip-two-cells process looking for the first Δ that is in a cell representing STACK$_1$.

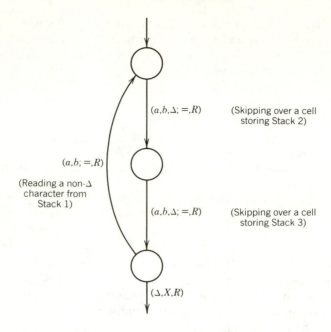

After we have found the Δ if we want to PUSH$_1$ X we change the first Δ to X by (Δ,X,R), as shown above. If we want to POP$_1$ instead, once we have found the first Δ in STACK$_1$, we back up three cells and read the non-Δ there and branch accordingly.

The same action is possible for POP$_2$, POP$_3$, PUSH$_2$ X, and PUSH$_3$ X. The method for converting a 2PDA to a TM that we gave before can also be modified to work for 3PDA's, for 4PDA's, and so on. In general, we can make a TM to duplicate the action of any nPDA.

This proves the first part of the theorem. The second thing we have to prove to establish equivalence is that an nPDA can be found to accept all languages a TM can accept. This part is even easier.

By Theorem 48 we know a 2PDA can accept any language accepted by a TM. If we leave $(n-2)$ STACKS empty, an nPDA can act like a 2PDA and accept all languages that a TM can.

Therefore, in power

$$nPDA = TM \text{ for } n \geqslant 2 \qquad \blacksquare$$

Once we reach the level of a TM, it is hard to go further. There is good reason to believe that it is impossible to go further, but that is a discussion for Chapter 31.

Symbolically we can represent the power comparison of our various mathematical models of machines as follows:

$$FA = TG = NFA < DPDA < PDA < 2PDA = nPDA = PM = TM$$

The organization of this book is finally revealed:

PART I	FA	0 PDA
PART II	PDA	1 PDA
PART II	TM	2 PDA

The machines in our highest class are all deterministic. Perhaps a nondeterministic nPDA (NnPDA), or a nondeterministic Post machine (NPM), or a nondeterministic Turing machine (NTM) would be even stronger. In the next chapter we shall see that this is not the case. All these nondeterministic machines are only equivalent in power to the TM, not stronger. Once we invent the TM we've gone about as far as we can go.

PROBLEMS

Consider the following 2PDA:

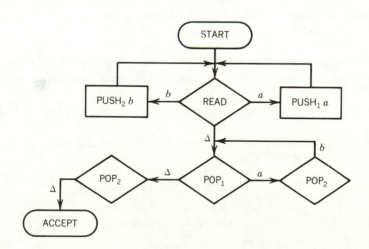

1. Trace the execution of these input strings on this machine.
   (i)   *aabb*
   (ii) *babab*

2. Prove that the language accepted by this 2PDA is the language EQUAL.

3.   Draw a 3PDA that accepts the language $\{a^n b^n a^n b^n\}$.

4.   Draw a PM that accepts the language $\{a^n b^n a^n b^n\}$.

5.   Draw a 2PDA that accepts the language $\{a^n b^n a^n b^n\}$.

6.   Let us use the alphabet $\Sigma = \{a,b,c,d\}$.
     Build a 3PDA that accepts the language $\{a^n b^n c^n d^n\}$.

7.   Outline a 2PDA that accepts the language defined in the previous problem.

Let us define the language 3EQUAL over the alphabet $\Sigma = \{a,b,c\}$ as all strings that have as many total a's as total b's as total c's.

$$3EQUAL = \{abc \quad acb \quad bac \quad bca \quad cab \quad cba \quad aabbcc$$
$$aabcbc \dots \}$$

8.   Draw a TM that accepts 3EQUAL.

9.   Draw a PM that accepts 3EQUAL.

10. (i)   Draw a 3PDA that accepts 3EQUAL.
     (ii)   Draw a 2PDA that accepts 3EQUAL.

11. Finish the proof of Theorem 48 by drawing the whole TM sequence that simulates the 2PDA state POP_2.

12. The language DOUBLEWORD is the set of all words over the alphabet $\Sigma = \{a,b\}$ that are of the form ww, where w is any string from Σ^*.

     $$DOUBLEWORD = \{aa \quad bb \quad aaaa \quad abab \quad baba \quad bbbb \quad aaaaaa \dots \}$$

     We have already seen a PM that accepts DOUBLEWORD. Draw a 2PDA that accepts DOUBLEWORD.

13. Let
     $$L = \{a^n b a^n b \text{ for } n = 1, 2, 3, \dots\}$$
     $$= \{abab \quad aabaab \quad aaabaaab \dots\}$$

     Draw a TM that accepts L.

14. Draw a PM that accepts L as defined in Problem 13.

15. Draw a 2PDA that accepts L as defined in Problem 13.

16. On the TM that was formed from the 2PDA in the example on page 630, trace the execution of the following input strings:

    (i)   *abb*

    (ii)   *baa*

17. On the 2PDA that was formed from the PM in the example on page 632, trace the execution of the following input strings:

    (i)   *abba*

    (ii)   *babab*

18. (i) Draw a 3PDA to accept the language $\{a^n b^{2n} c^n\}$ over the alphabet $\Sigma = \{a,b,c\}$.

    (ii) Draw a 2PDA to accept this language.

19. Outline a 2PDA that starts with any input string over $\Sigma = \{a,b\}$ and leaves the reverse of the same string in its STORE when it accepts.

20. Given a language L over $\Sigma = \{a,b\}$. Define the transpose of L to be the language of all words in L spelled backward.

    If L is a language accepted by a 2PDA, prove that the transpose of L, written L^T, is also a language accepted by a 2PDA.

CHAPTER 27

VARIATIONS ON THE TM

Turing machines can be drawn using different pictorial representations. Let us consider the diagram below, which looks like a cross between a Mealy and a Moore machine:

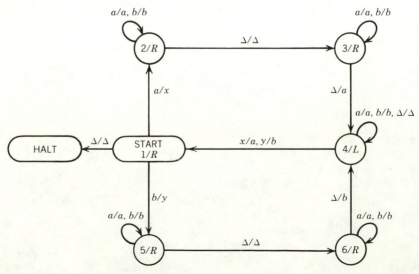

This is a new way of writing the program part of a TM; we still use the same old TAPE and TAPE HEAD. In this picture the edges are labeled as in a Mealy machine with input-slash-output instructions. An edge labeled p/q says "If the TAPE HEAD is reading a p, change it to a q and follow this arrow to the next state." The edge itself does not indicate in which direction the TAPE HEAD is to be moved. The instructions for moving the TAPE HEAD are found once we enter the next state. Inside the circles denoting states we have labels that are name-slash-move indicators. For example, $4/L$ says "You have entered state 4; please move the TAPE HEAD one cell to the left." When we commence running the machine in the START state, we do not execute its move instruction. If we reenter the start state, then we follow its move instruction.

Let us call machines drawn in this fashion **Move-in-State machines.** After analyzing the machine above, we shall prove that Move-in-State machines have the same power as TM's as we originally defined them.

The action of the Move-in-State machine drawn above is to start with any word on its TAPE, leave a space, and make an exact copy of the word on the TAPE. If we start with the word w, we end up with the string $w\Delta w$:

$baab$	becomes	$baab\Delta baab$
a	becomes	$a\Delta a$
Δ . . .	becomes	Δ . . .

The algorithm is as follows: We start in state 1. If we read an a, we take the high road: state 2 - state 3 - state 4 - state 1. If we read a b, we take the low road: state 5 - state 6 - state 4 - state 1. Suppose that we read an a. This is changed into an x as we travel along the edge labeled a/x to state 2 where the TAPE HEAD is moved right. In state 2 we now skip over all the a's and b's remaining in w, each time returning to state 2 and moving the TAPE HEAD right. When we reach the first Δ after the end of w, we take the edge labeled Δ/Δ to state 3. This edge leaves the Δ undisturbed. The TAPE HEAD is moved by state 3 to the right again. In state 3 we read through all the letters we have already copied into the second version of w until we read the first Δ. We then take the Δ/a edge to state 4. Along the edge we change the Δ into an a (this is the letter we read in state 1). State 4 moves the TAPE HEAD left, reading through all the a's and b's of the second copy of w, then through the Δ and then through the a's and b's of the part of the original w that has not already been copied.

Finally, we reach the x with which we marked the letter a that we were copying. This we change back to an a on the edge labeled x/a, y/b going to state 1. State 1 tells us to move the Tape Head to the right, so we are ready to copy the next letter of w. If this letter is an a, we take the high road again. If it is a b, we change it to a y and take the route state 5 - state 6 to find the blank that we must change to a b in the second copy. Then in state 4 we move the Tape Head back down to the y and change it back to a b and return to state 1. When we have finished copying all of w, state 1 reads a Δ and we halt.

The following is the trace of the operation of this machine on the input string *baa:*

$$
\underset{b\underline{a}a}{1} \rightarrow \underset{y\underline{a}a}{5} \rightarrow \underset{ya\underline{a}}{5} \rightarrow \underset{yaa\underline{\Delta}}{5} \rightarrow \underset{yaa\Delta\underline{\Delta}}{6}
$$

$$
\rightarrow \underset{yaa\underline{\Delta}b}{4} \rightarrow \underset{ya\underline{a}\Delta b}{4} \rightarrow \underset{y\underline{a}a\Delta b}{4} \rightarrow \underset{\underline{y}aa\Delta b}{4}
$$

$$
\rightarrow \underset{b\underline{a}a\Delta b}{1} \rightarrow \underset{bx\underline{a}\Delta b}{2} \rightarrow \underset{bxa\underline{\Delta} b}{2} \rightarrow \underset{bxa\Delta \underline{b}}{3}
$$

$$
\rightarrow \underset{bxa\Delta b\underline{\Delta}}{3} \rightarrow \underset{bxa\Delta \underline{b}a}{4} \rightarrow \underset{bxa\underline{\Delta}ba}{4} \rightarrow \underset{bx\underline{a}\Delta ba}{4}
$$

$$
\rightarrow \underset{b\underline{x}a\Delta ba}{4} \rightarrow \underset{ba\underline{a}\Delta ba}{1} \rightarrow \underset{bax\underline{\Delta}ba}{2} \rightarrow \underset{bax\Delta \underline{b}a}{3}
$$

$$
\rightarrow \underset{bax\Delta b\underline{a}}{3} \rightarrow \underset{bax\Delta ba\underline{\Delta}}{3} \rightarrow \underset{bax\Delta b\underline{a}a}{4} \rightarrow \underset{bax\Delta \underline{b}aa}{4}
$$

$$
\rightarrow \underset{bax\underline{\Delta}baa}{4} \rightarrow \underset{ba\underline{x}\Delta baa}{4} \rightarrow \underset{ba\underline{a}\Delta baa}{1} \rightarrow \text{HALT}
$$

It is not obvious that Move-in-State machines have the same power as Turing machines. Why is that? because Move-in-State machines are limited to always making the same TAPE HEAD move every time we enter a particular state, whereas with TM's we can enter a certain state having moved the TAPE HEAD left or right. For example, the TM situation shown below

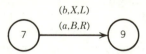

and this one also

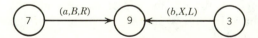

cannot simply be converted into Move-in-State TM's by adding TAPE HEAD moving instructions into state 9. However, we can get around this difficulty in a way analogous to the method we used for converting Mealy into Moore machines. The next two theorems prove

$$\text{Move-in-State} = \text{TM}$$

THEOREM 50

For every Move-in-State machine M, there is a TM, T, which accepts the same language. That is if M crashes on the input w, T crashes on the input w. If M loops on the input w, T loops on the input w. If M accepts the input w then T does too. We require even more. After halting the two machines leave exactly the same scattered symbols on the TAPE.

PROOF

The proof will be by constructive algorithm.

This conversion algorithm is simple. One-by-one, in any order, let us take every edge in M and change its labels. If the edge leads to a state that tells the TAPE HEAD to move right, change its labels from X/Y to (X,Y,R). If the edge leads to a state that tells the TAPE HEAD to move left, change its labels from X/Y to (X,Y,L). To make this description complete, we should say that any edge going into the HALT state should be given the TAPE HEAD move instruction, R.

When all edge labels have been changed, erase the move instructions from inside the states. For example,

becomes

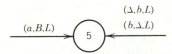

The resulting diagram is a TM in normal form that operates exactly as the Move-in-State machine did. The trace of a given input on the Move-in-State machine is the same as the trace of the same input on the converted TM. ∎

EXAMPLE

The Move-in-State machine above that copies input words will be converted by the algorithm given in this proof into the following TM.

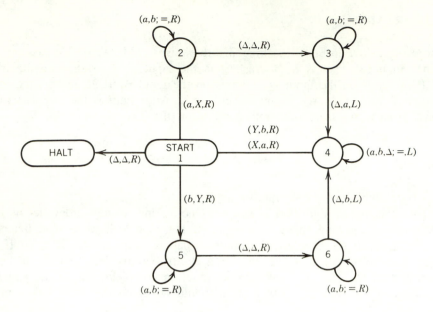

THEOREM 51

For every Turing machine T there is a Move-in-State machine M that operates in exactly the same way on all inputs—crashing, looping, or accepting. Furthermore the Move-in-State machine will always leave the same remnants on the TAPE that the TM does.

PROOF

The proof will be by constructive algorithm.

We cannot simply "do the reverse" of the algorithm in the last proof. If we try to move the TAPE HEAD instructions from the edges into the states themselves, we sometimes succeed, as with:

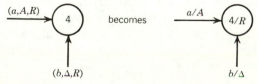

and sometimes fail, as with

depending on whether all the edges entering a given state have the same TAPE HEAD direction or not. This is a case of déjà vu. We faced the same difficulty when converting Mealy machines into Moore machines—and the solution is the same. If edges with different TAPE HEAD movement directions feed into the same state, we must make two copies of that state, one labeled move R and one labeled move L, each with a complete set of the same exit edges the original state had. The incoming edges will then be directed into whichever state contains the appropriate move instruction.

For example,

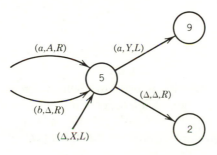

becomes

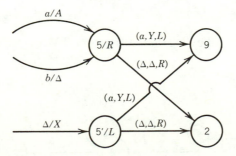

Some states become twins, some remain single. State by state we make this conversion until the TM is changed into a Move-in-State machine that acts on inputs identically to the way the old TM used to.

If the start state has to split, only one of its clones can still be called START—it does not matter which, since the edges coming out of both are the same.

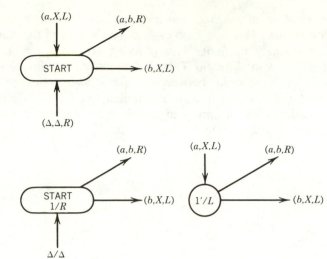

becomes

If a state that gets split loops back to itself, we must be careful to which of its personae the loops go. It all depends on what was printed on the loop edge. A loop labeled with an R will become a loop on the R twin and an edge from the L twin. The symmetric thing happens to a TM edge with an L move instruction.

This process will always convert a TM into an equivalent Move-in-State machine; equivalent both in the sense of language acceptor and in the sense of TAPE manipulator.   ■

EXAMPLE

Let us consider the following purely random TM.

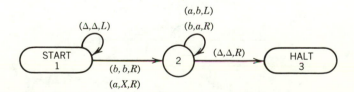

When the algorithm of the theorem above is applied to the states of this TM in order, we obtain the following conversion sequence:

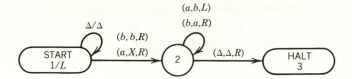

then

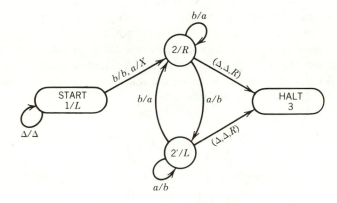

and finally:

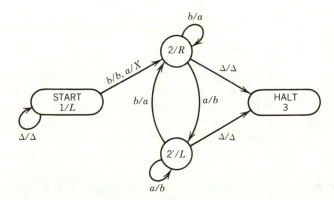

Notice that HALT 3 is the same as writing HALT 3/R, but if the edge entering HALT moved left, we would need a different state since input might crash while going into the HALT state.   ∎

We have been careful to note that when we combine the last two theorems into one statement:

$$TM = \text{Move-in-State machine}$$

we are not merely talking about their power as language recognizers but as transducers as well. Not only do the same words run to HALT on the corresponding machines, but they leave identical outputs on the input TAPE. The importance of this point will be made clear later.

Another variation on the definition of Turing machine that is sometimes encountered is the "stay-option" machine. This is a machine exactly like a TM except that along any edge we have the option of not moving the TAPE HEAD at all—the stay option. Instead of writing L or R as directions to the TAPE HEAD, we can also write S for "stay put".

On the surface this seems like a ridiculous thing to do, since it causes us to read next the character that we have just this instant printed. However, the correct use of the stay-option is to let us change states without disturbing the TAPE or TAPE HEAD, as in the example below:

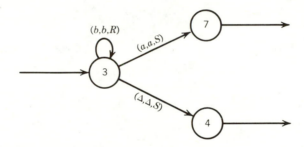

We stay in state 3 skipping over b's until we reach an a or a Δ. If we reach an a, we jump to state 7 and there decide what to do. If we reach a Δ, we go to state 4 where more processing will continue.

The question arises: Does this stay-option give us any extra real power or is it merely a method of alternate notation? Naturally we shall once again prove that the stay-option adds nothing to the power of the already omnipotent TM.

We have had some awkward moments in programming TM's, especially when we wanted to leave the TAPE HEAD pointing to a special symbol such as a * in cell i or a # in between words. We used to have to write something like:

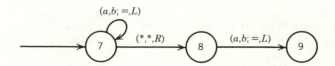

State 7 backs down the TAPE looking for the *. State 8 finds it, but the TAPE HEAD bounces off to the right. We then have to proceed to state 9 to leave the TAPE HEAD pointing to the *.

With the stay-option this becomes easier:

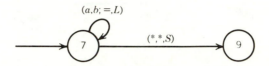

EXAMPLE

Below is a run-of-the-mill TM that crashes on Λ and otherwise changes the first letter of any input string (from a to b or b to a), leaves the TAPE HEAD in cell i, and accepts.

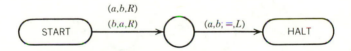

With the stay-option we can eliminate the middleman.

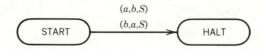

DEFINITION

Let us call a TM with a stay-option a **stay-option machine**.

We now show that the stay-option, although it may be useful in shortening programs, adds no new power to the TM.

THEOREM 52

$$\text{stay-option machine} = \text{TM}$$

In other words, for any stay-option machine there is some TM that acts the same way on all inputs, looping, crashing, or accepting while leaving the same data on the TAPE, and vice versa.

PROOF

Since a TM is only a stay-option machine in which we have not bothered to use the stay-option, it is clear that for any TM there is a stay-option machine that does the same thing—the TM itself. What remains for us to show is that if the stay-option is ever used we can replace it with other TM programming and so convert a stay-option machine into an equivalent TM.

To do this, we simply follow this replacement rule. Change any edge

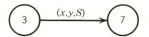

into

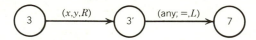

introducing a new state 3'. It is patently obvious that this does not change the processing of any input string at any stage.

In the diagrams above we have made use of a generalization of the multiple instruction symbol. We wrote (any; $=$,L) to mean the set of all instructions (x,x,L) for any x that might be read.

When all stay-option edges have been eliminated (even loops) what remains is the desired regular TM.   ■

Now that we have shown that the stay option is harmless we shall feel free to use it in the future when it is convenient.

EXAMPLE

Here we shall build a simple machine to do some subtraction. It will start with a string of the form #(0 + 1)* on its TAPE. This is a # in cell i followed by some binary number. The job of this stay-option machine is to subtract 1 from this number and leave the answer on the TAPE. This is a *binary decrementer*.

The basic algorithm is to change all the right-most 0's to 1's and the right-most 1 to 0. The only problem with this is that if the input is zero, that is of the form #0*, then the algorithm gives the wrong answer since we have no representation for negative numbers.

The machine below illustrates one way of handling this situation:

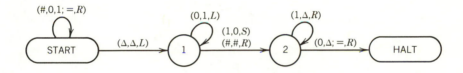

What happens with this machine is:

$$\text{START} \quad \#101001\underline{0}00$$

$$\text{becomes State 1} \quad \#101001000\underline{\Delta}$$

$$\text{becomes State 1} \quad \#101001\underline{1}11$$

$$\text{becomes State 2} \quad \#101000\underline{1}11$$

If we are in State 2 and we are reading a 0, we must have arrived there by the edge (1,0,S), so in these cases we proceed directly on to (0,0,R) HALT.

If, on the other hand we arrive in State 2 from the edge (#,#,R), it means we started with zero, #0*, on the Tape.

$$\text{START} \quad \#0\underline{0}00$$

$$\text{becomes State 1} \quad \#0000\underline{\Delta}$$

$$\text{becomes State 1} \quad \#\underline{1}111$$

$$\text{becomes State 2} \quad \#1\underline{1}11$$

Now in state 2 we must erase all these mistaken 1's. The result is that we loop with $(1,\Delta,R)$ until we HALT with (Δ,Δ,R). If the input was zero, this machine leaves an error message in the form of the single character #.

In this machine there is only one stay-option edge. Employing the algorithm from the above theorem, we leave the state 1 – state 2 edge $(\#,\#,R)$ alone but change the state 1 – state 2 edge $(1,0,S)$ as follows:

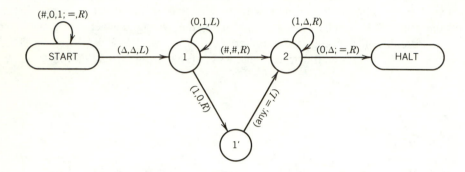

There are some other minor variations of TM's that we could investigate. One is to allow the TAPE HEAD to move more than one cell at a time such as:

$$(X,Y,3R) = (\text{read } X, \text{write } Y, \text{move 3 cells to the right})$$

This is equivalent to:

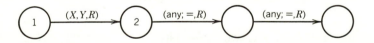

Some other instructions of this ilk are

$$(X,Y,2L) \text{ or } (X,Y,33R).$$

It is clear that these variations do not change the power of a TM as acceptor or transducer; that is, the same input strings are accepted and the stuff they leave on the TAPE is the same.

This is in fact so obvious that we shall not waste a theorem on it (however, see the problems below).

In addition to variations involving the move instructions, it is also possible to have variations on the TAPE structure. The first of these we shall consider is the possibility of having more than one TAPE.

The picture below shows the possibility of having four TAPE's stacked one on top of the other and one TAPE HEAD reading them all at once:

TAPE 1	a	b	b	a	a	· · ·
TAPE 2	Δ	Δ	Δ	Δ	Δ	· · ·
TAPE 3	b	Δ	Δ	a	Δ	· · ·
TAPE 4	b	b	a	b	b	· · ·

In this illustration the TAPE HEAD is reading cell iii of TAPE 1, cell iii of TAPE 2, cell iii of TAPE 3, and cell iii of TAPE 4 at once. The TAPE HEAD can write something new in each of these cells and then move to the left to read the four cell ii's or to the right to read the four cell iv's.

DEFINITION

A **k-track Turing machine, kTM,** has k normal TM TAPES and one TAPE HEAD that reads corresponding cells on all TAPES simultaneously and can write on all TAPES at once. There is also an alphabet of input letters Σ and an alphabet of TAPE characters Γ. The input strings are taken from Σ, while the TAPE HEAD can write any character from Γ.

There is a program of instructions for the TAPE HEAD consisting of a START state, ACCEPT states, other states, and edges between states labeled:

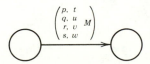

where p, q, r, s, t, u, v, w, . . . are all in Γ and M is R or L, meaning that if what is read from TAPE 1 is p, from TAPE 2 is q, from TAPE 3 is r, from TAPE 4 is s, and so on, then what will be written on TAPE 1 is t, on TAPE 2 is u, on TAPE 3 is v, and on TAPE 4 is w, and so on. The TAPE HEAD will be moved in the direction indicated by M.

To operate a kTM we start with an input string from Σ^* on TAPE 1 starting in cell i, and if we reach ACCEPT we say that the string is in the language

of the *k*TM. We also say that the contents of *all* the TAPES is the output
produced by this input string.   ■

This is a very useful modification of a TM. In many applications it allows
a natural correspondence between the machine algorithm and traditional hand
calculation, as we can see from the examples below. Notice that we use the
words track and TAPE interchangeably for a *k*TM.

EXAMPLE

When a human adds a pair of numbers in base 10, the algorithm followed
is usually to line them up in two rows, find the right-hand column, perform
the addition column by column moving left, remembering whether there are
carries and stopping when the last column has been added.
   The following 3TM performs this algorithm exactly as we were taught in
Third Grade except that it uses a column of $'s to mark the left edge.

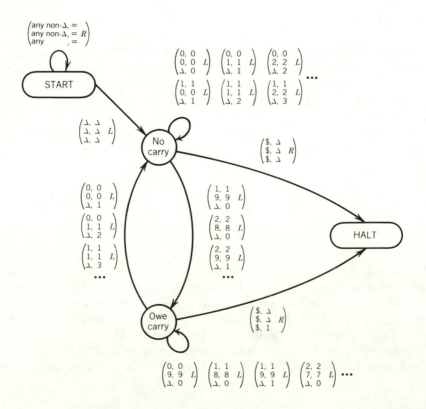

The loop from no-carry back to itself takes care of all combinations:

$$\begin{pmatrix} u, & u \\ v, & v & L \\ \Delta, & u+v \end{pmatrix}$$

where $u + v$ is less than 10.

The edges from no-carry to owe-carry are labeled:

$$\begin{pmatrix} u, & u \\ v, & v & L \\ \Delta, & u+v-10 \end{pmatrix}$$

where $u + v \geq 10$.

The loop from owe-carry back to itself is:

$$\begin{pmatrix} u, & u \\ v, & v & L \\ \Delta, & u+v-9 \end{pmatrix}$$

where $u + v \geq 9$.

The edge from owe-carry to no-carry is:

$$\begin{pmatrix} u, & u \\ v, & v & L \\ \Delta, & u+v+1 \end{pmatrix}$$

where $u + v \leq 8$.

The phrase "any non-Δ" in the instruction for the loop at START is self-explanatory.

We have not exactly followed the rules about the input being found on TAPE 1 only but have assumed that it has been loaded into the TAPES as in this picture:

$	4	2	9	Δ	$\cdots$
$	9	3	3	Δ	$\cdots$
$	Δ	Δ	Δ	Δ	$\cdots$

$\Box$

with \$'s in all three cell i's. We have also assumed that the two numbers to be added are in cells ii, iii, . . . on TAPE 1 and TAPE 2, and TAPE 3 is blank from cell ii on.

We trace this input on this 3TM:

START
$ 4 2 9
→ $ 9 3 3
$ Δ Δ Δ

START
$ 4 2 9
→ $ 9 3 3
$ Δ Δ Δ

START
$ 4 2 9
→ $ 9 3 3
$ Δ Δ Δ

START
$ 4 2 9
→ $ 9 3 3
$ Δ Δ Δ

START
$ 4 2 9 Δ
→ $ 9 3 3 Δ
$ Δ Δ Δ Δ

No-carry
$ 4 2 9
→ $ 9 3 3
$ Δ Δ Δ

Owe-carry
$ 4 2 9
→ $ 9 3 3
$ Δ Δ 2

No-carry
$ 4 2 9
→ $ 9 3 3
$ Δ 6 2

Owe-carry
$ 4 2 9
→ $ 9 3 3
$ 3 6 2

HALT
Δ 4 2 9
→ Δ 9 3 3
1 3 6 2

The correct total, 1362, is found on TAPE 3 only. The stuff left on the other TAPES is not part of the answer. We could have been erasing TAPE 1 and TAPE 2 along the way, but this way is closer to what humans do.

We should have started with both input numbers on TAPE 1 and let the machine transfer the second number to TAPE 2 and put the \$'s in the cell i's, but these chores are not difficult.

Moving the last non-Δ character from TAPE 1 to cell ii of TAPE 2 can be accomplished by this subroutine.

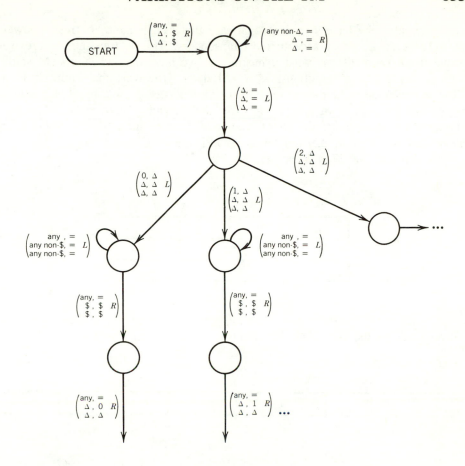

The rest of the copying and erasing can be done similarly with one subtle difficulty that we defer till the problems below. ∎

Considering TM's as tranducers has not seemed very important to us before. In a PDA we never considered the possibility that what was left in the STACK when the input was accepted had any deep significance. Usually it was nothing. In our early TM examples the TAPE often ended up containing random garbage. But, as the example above shows, the importance of the machine might not be simply that the input was accepted but what **output** was generated in the process. This is a theme that will become increasingly important to us as we approach the back cover.

We should now have a theorem that says that kTM's have no greater power than TM's do as either acceptors or transducers. This is true, but before we prove it we must discuss what it means. As we have defined it, a kTM starts with a single line of input just as a TM does. However, the output from a kTM is presumed to be the entire status of all k TAPES. How can a TM possibly hope to have output of this form? We shall adapt a convention of correspondence that employs the interlacing-cells interpretation of the TM output TAPE that we used in the simulation of nPDA's in Chapter 26.

We say that the 3TM TAPE status

a	d	g	$\cdots$
b	e	h	$\cdots$
c	f	i	$\cdots$

corresponds to the one-TAPE TM status

a	b	c	d	e	f	g	h	i	$\cdots$

This is an illustration for three tracks, but the principle of correspondence we are using applies equally well to k-tracks.

We can now prove our equality theorem.

THEOREM 53

(i) Given any TM and any k, there is a kTM that acts on all inputs exactly as the TM does (that means either loops, crashes, or leaves a corresponding output).

(ii) Given any kTM for any k, there is a TM that acts on all inputs exactly as the kTM does (that means loops, crashes, or leaves a corresponding output).

In other words, as acceptor or transducer:

$$\text{TM} = k\text{TM}$$

PROOF

(i) One might think that part (i) of this proof is trivial. All we have to do is leave TAPE 2, TAPE 3, . . . , TAPE k always all blank and change every TM edge label from (X,Y,Z) into

$$\begin{pmatrix} X, Y \\ \Delta, \Delta \ Z \\ \Delta, \Delta \end{pmatrix}$$

The end result on TAPE 1 will be exactly the same as on the original TM. This would be fine except that under our definition of correspondence

a	b	c	d	· · ·
Δ	Δ	Δ	Δ	· · ·
Δ	Δ	Δ	Δ	· · ·

does not correspond to the TM TAPE status

a	b	c	d	· · ·

but rather to the TM TAPE status

a	Δ	Δ	b	Δ	Δ	c	Δ	Δ	d	Δ	Δ	· · ·

To have a kTM correspond to a TM once we have adopted our definition of correspondence, we must convert the answer TAPE on the kTM from

a	b	c	d	· · ·
Δ	Δ	Δ	Δ	· · ·
Δ	Δ	Δ	Δ	· · ·

into this form:

a	d · · ·
b	· · ·
c	· · ·

The subroutine to do this begins as follows:

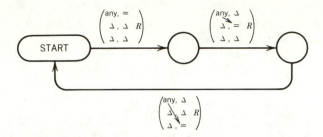

This notation should be transparent. The arrow from "any" to "=" means that into the location of the "=" we shall put whatever symbol occupied the location of the "any."

We now arrive at

a	Δ	Δ	d	· · ·
Δ	b	Δ	Δ	· · ·
Δ	Δ	c	Δ	· · ·

We need to write a variation of the DELETE subroutine that will delete a character from one row without changing the other two rows.

To do this we start with the subprogram DELETE exactly as we already constructed it and we make k (in this case 3) offshoots of it. In the first we replace every edge label as follows:

$$(X, \ Y, \ Z)$$

becomes

$$\begin{pmatrix} X, Y \\ \text{any}, = \ Z \\ \text{any}, = \end{pmatrix}$$

This, then, will be the subroutine that deletes a character from the first row leaving the other two rows the same; call it DELETE-FROM-ROW-1. If on the TAPE

1	4	7	10	· · ·
2	5	8	11	· · ·
3	6	9	12	· · ·

we run DELETE-FROM-ROW-1 while the TAPE HEAD is pointing to column 3, the result is

1	4	10	Δ	· · ·
2	5	8	11	· · ·
3	6	9	12	· · ·

We build DELETE-FROM-ROW-2 and DELETE-FROM-ROW-3 similarly. Now we rewind the TAPE HEAD to column one and do as follows:

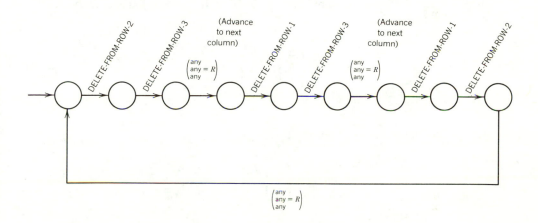

Thus we convert the TAPE

a	Δ	Δ	d	· · ·
Δ	b	Δ	Δ	· · ·
Δ	Δ	c	Δ	· · ·

into

a	d	· · ·
b	Δ	· · ·
c	Δ	· · ·

To get out of this endless loop, all we need is an end-of-data marker and a test to tell us when we have finished converting the answer on track 1 into the k-track form of the answer. We already know how to insert these things, so we call this the conclusion of the proof of part (i).

(ii) We shall now show that the work of a kTM can be performed by a simple TM. Surprisingly, this is not so hard to prove.

Let us assume that the kTM we have in mind has $k = 3$ and uses the TAPE alphabet $\Gamma = \{a,b,\$\}$. (Remember, Δ appears on the TAPE but is not an alphabet letter.) There are only $4 \times 4 \times 4 = 64$ different possibilities for columns of TAPE cells. They are:

$$\begin{pmatrix}\Delta\\\Delta\\\Delta\end{pmatrix}\begin{pmatrix}\Delta\\\Delta\\a\end{pmatrix}\begin{pmatrix}\Delta\\\Delta\\b\end{pmatrix}\begin{pmatrix}\Delta\\\Delta\\\$\end{pmatrix}\cdots\begin{pmatrix}a\\\$\\b\end{pmatrix}\cdots\begin{pmatrix}\$\\\$\\\$\end{pmatrix}$$

The TM we shall use to simulate this 3TM will have a TAPE alphabet of $64 + 3$ characters:

$$\Gamma = \left\{a,\, b,\, \$,\, \begin{pmatrix}\Delta\\\Delta\\\Delta\end{pmatrix},\, \begin{pmatrix}\Delta\\\Delta\\a\end{pmatrix},\, \ldots,\, \begin{pmatrix}\$\\\$\\\$\end{pmatrix}\right\}$$

We are calling such symbols as

$$\begin{pmatrix}a\\a\\\Delta\end{pmatrix}$$

a *single* TAPE character, meaning that it can fit into *one* cell of the TM and can be used in the labels of the edges in the program. For example,

will be a legal simple instruction on our simple TM.

These letters are admittedly very strange but so are some others soon to appear.

We are now ready to simulate the 3TM in three steps.

Step 1   The input string $X_1X_2X_3 \ldots$ will be fed to the 3TM on TAPE 1 looking like this:

X_1	X_2	X_3	$\cdots$
Δ	Δ	Δ	$\cdots$
Δ	Δ	Δ	$\cdots$

Since our TM is to operate on the same input string, it will begin like this:

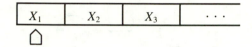

To begin the simulation we must convert the whole string to triple-decker characters corresponding to the 3TM. We could use something like these instructions:

$$\left(a, \begin{pmatrix} a \\ \Delta \\ \Delta \end{pmatrix}, R\right) \quad \left(\$, \begin{pmatrix} \$ \\ \Delta \\ \Delta \end{pmatrix}, R\right) \quad \left(b, \begin{pmatrix} b \\ \Delta \\ \Delta \end{pmatrix}, R\right) \quad \left(\Delta, \begin{pmatrix} \Delta \\ \Delta \\ \Delta \end{pmatrix}, R\right)$$

We must have some way of telling when the string of X's is done. Let us say that if the X's are a simple input word, they contain no Δ's and therefore we are done when we reach the first blank. The program should be:

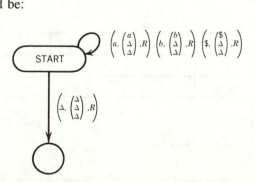

We shall now want to rewind the TAPE HEAD to cell i so we should, as usual, have marked cell i when we left it so that we could back up without crashing. (This is left as a problem below.) If the 3TM ever needs to read cells beyond the initial ones used for the input string, the simulating TM will have to remember to treat the new Δ's encountered as though they were:

$$\begin{pmatrix} \Delta \\ \Delta \\ \Delta \end{pmatrix}$$

Step 2   Copy the 3TM program exactly for use by the simulating TM. Every 3TM instruction

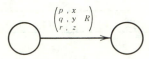

becomes

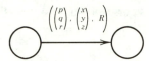

which is a simple TM instruction.

Step 3   If the 3TM crashes on a given input, so will the TM. If the 3TM loops forever on a given input, so will the simple TM. If the 3TM reaches a HALT state, we need to decode the answer on the TM. This is because the 3TM final result:

d	*g*	*j*	*m*	Δ	· · ·
e	*h*	*k*	Δ	Δ	· · ·
f	*i*	*l*	Δ	Δ	· · ·

will sit on the TM as this:

$\begin{pmatrix} d \\ e \\ f \end{pmatrix}$	$\begin{pmatrix} g \\ h \\ i \end{pmatrix}$	$\begin{pmatrix} j \\ k \\ l \end{pmatrix}$	$\begin{pmatrix} m \\ \Delta \\ \Delta \end{pmatrix}$	Δ	· · ·

but the TM TAPE status corresponding to the 3TM answer is actually

d	e	f	g	h	i	j	k	l	m	Δ	Δ	$\cdots$

we must therefore convert the TM TAPE from triple-decker characters to simple single-letter strings.

This requires a state with 64 loops like the one below:

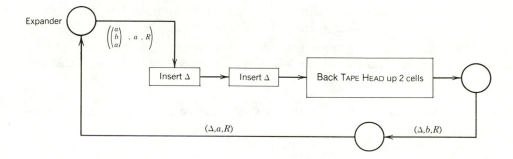

Once the answer has been converted into a simple string, we can halt. To know when to halt is not always easy because we may not always recognize when the 3TM has no more non-Δ data. Reading 10 of these:

$$\begin{pmatrix} \Delta \\ \Delta \\ \Delta \end{pmatrix}$$

does not necessarily mean that we have transcribed all the useful information from the 3TM. However, we can tell when the simple TM is finished expanding triples. When the expander state reads a single Δ, it knows that it has hit that part of the original TM TAPE not needed in the simulation of the 3TM. So we add the branch

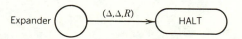

This completes the conversion of the 3TM to a TM. The algorithm for k other than 3 is entirely analogous. ■

We shall save the task of providing concrete illustrations of the algorithms in this theorem for the Problem section.

The next variation of a TM we shall consider is actually Turing's own original model. He did not use the concept of a "half-infinite" TAPE. His TAPE was infinite in both directions, which we call **doubly infinite** or *two-way infinite*. (The TAPES as we defined them originally are called *one-way infinite* TAPES.)

The input string is placed on the TAPE in consecutive cells somewhere and the rest of the TAPE is filled with blanks. There are infinitely many blanks to the left of the input string as well as to the right of it. This seems to give us two advantages:

1. We do not have to worry about crashing by moving left from cell i, because we can always move left into some ready cell.

2. We have two work areas not just one in which to do calculation, since we can use the cells to the left of the input as well as those further out to the right.

By convention, the TAPE HEAD starts off pointing to the left-most cell containing nonblank data.

The input string *abba* would be depicted as:

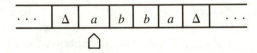

We shall number the cells once an input string has been placed on the TAPE by calling the cell the TAPE HEAD points to cell i. The cells to the right are numbered as usual with increasing lowercase Roman numerals. The cells to the left are numbered with zero and negative lowercase Roman numerals. (Let us not quibble about whether the ancient Romans knew of zero and negative numbers.)

	−v	−iv	−iii	−ii	−i	0	i	iii	iii	iv	v	vi	
⋯	Δ	Δ	Δ	Δ	Δ	Δ	a	b	b	a	Δ	Δ	⋯

THEOREM 54

TM's with two-way TAPES are exactly as powerful as TM's with one-way TAPES both as language acceptors and transducers.

PROOF

The proof will be by constructive algorithm.

First we must show that every one-way TM can be simulated by a two-way TM. We cannot get away with saying "Run the same program on the two-way TM and it will give the same answer" because in the original TM if the TAPE HEAD is moved left from cell i the input crashes, whereas on the two-way TM it will not crash. To be sure that the two-way TM does crash every time its TAPE HEAD enters cell 0 we must proceed in a special way.

Let ☺ be a symbol not used in the alphabet Γ for the one-way TM. Insert ☺ in cell 0 on the two-way TM and return the TAPE HEAD to cell i.

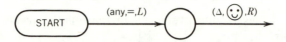

From here let the two-way TM follow the exact same program as the one-way TM.

Now if, by accident, while simulating the one-way TM the two-way TM ever moves left from cell i it will not crash immediately as the one-way TM would, *but* when it tries to carry out the *next* instruction it will read the ☺ in cell 0 and find that there is no edge for that character in the program of the one-way machine. This will cause a crash, and the input word will be rejected.

One further refinement is enough to finish the proof. (This is one of the subtlest of subtleties in anything we have yet seen.) The one-way TM may end on the instruction:

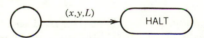

where this left move could conceivably cause a crash preventing successful termination at HALT. To be sure that the one-way TM also crashes in its simulation it must read the last cell it moves to. We must change the one-way TM program to:

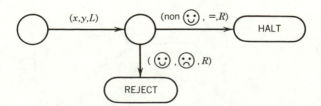

We have yet to prove that anything a two-way TM can do can also be done by a one-way TM. And we won't. What we shall prove is that anything that can be done by a two-way TM can be done by some 3TM. Then by the previous theorem a two-way TM must also be equivalent to a one-way TM.

Let us start with some particular two-way TM. Let us wrap the doubly infinite TAPE around to make the figure below:

cell i	cell ii	cell iii	cell iv	cell v	. . .
cell 0	cell −i	cell −ii	cell −iii	cell −iv	. . .

Furthermore, let us require every cell in the middle row to contain one of the five symbols: Δ, $\uparrow$, $\downarrow$, $\uparrow\uparrow$, $\downarrow\downarrow$.

The arrow will tell us which of the two cells in the column we are actually reading. The double arrows, for the tricky case of going around the bend, will appear only in the first column.

If we are in a positively numbered cell and we wish to simulate on the 3TM the two-way TM instruction:

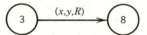

we can simply write this as:

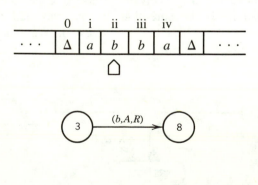

where S is the stay-option for the TAPE HEAD. The second step is necessary to put the correct arrow on track 2. We do not actually need S. We could always move one more left and then back.

For example,

	0	i	ii	iii	iv		
. . .	Δ	a	b	b	a	Δ	. . .

⌂

causes

	i	ii	iii	iv	
. . .	a	A	b	a	. . .

⌂

Analogously,

a	b	b	a	Δ	· · ·
↑↑	↑	Δ	Δ	Δ	· · ·
Δ	Δ	Δ	Δ	Δ	· · ·

$$
\begin{array}{ccc}
\boxed{3} & \xrightarrow{\left(\begin{smallmatrix} b\,,\,A \\ \uparrow\,,\,\Delta\;\;R \\ any,\,= \end{smallmatrix}\right)} & \boxed{3'} & \xrightarrow{\left(\begin{smallmatrix} any,\,= \\ \Delta\,,\,\uparrow\;\;S \\ any,\,= \end{smallmatrix}\right)} & \boxed{8}
\end{array}
$$

causes

a	A	b	a	Δ	· · ·
↑↑	Δ	↑	Δ	Δ	· · ·
Δ	Δ	Δ	Δ	Δ	· · ·

If we were in a negatively numbered cell and asked to move R, we would need to move left in the 3TM.

$$
\boxed{3} \xrightarrow{(b,A,R)} \boxed{8}
$$

could become

$$
\begin{array}{ccc}
\boxed{3} & \xrightarrow{\left(\begin{smallmatrix} any,\,= \\ \downarrow\,,\,\Delta\;\;L \\ b\,,\,A \end{smallmatrix}\right)} & \boxed{3''} & \xrightarrow{\left(\begin{smallmatrix} any,\,= \\ \Delta\,,\,\downarrow\;\;S \\ any,\,= \end{smallmatrix}\right)} & \boxed{8}
\end{array}
$$

This is because in the two-way TM moving right from cell -iii takes us to cell -ii, which in the 3TM is to the left of cell -iii.

In the two-way TM the TAPE status

		−iii	−ii	−i	0	i	ii	
· · ·	Δ	b	a	a	b	Δ	Δ	· · ·

and the instruction

$$
\boxed{3} \xrightarrow{(b,A,R)} \boxed{8}
$$

causes

	−iii	−ii	−i	0	i	ii	
· · ·	Δ	A	a	a	b	Δ	Δ	· · ·

(pointer below cell −i)

as desired.

Analogously, in the 3TM the TAPE status

i	ii	iii	iv	v	
Δ	Δ	Δ	Δ	Δ	· · ·
↓ ↓	Δ	Δ	↓	Δ	· · ·
b	a	a	b	Δ	· · ·
0	−i	−ii	(pointer)	−iv	

and the instructions

$$3 \xrightarrow{\left(\begin{array}{c} \text{any, =} \\ \downarrow, \Delta\ L \\ b, A \end{array}\right)} 3'' \xrightarrow{\left(\begin{array}{c} \text{any, =} \\ \Delta, \downarrow\ S \\ \text{any, =} \end{array}\right)} 8$$

will cause the result

i	ii	iii	iv	v	
Δ	Δ	Δ	Δ	Δ	· · ·
↓ ↓	Δ	↓	Δ	Δ	· · ·
b	a	a	A	Δ	· · ·
0	−i	(pointer)	−iii	−iv	

as desired.

The tricky part comes when we want to move right from cell 0. That we are in cell 0 can be recognized by the double down arrow on the middle TAPE.

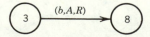

$$3 \xrightarrow{(b,A,R)} 8$$

can also be

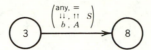

This means that we are now reading cell i having left an *A* in cell 0.

There is one case yet to mention. When we move from cell -i to the right to cell 0, we do not want to lose the double arrow there. So instead of just

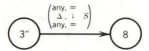

we also need

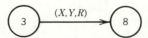

The full 3TM equivalent to the two-way TM instruction

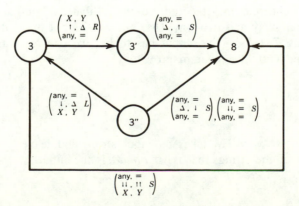

is therefore

By analogous reasoning, the equivalent of the left move

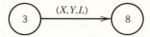

is therefore

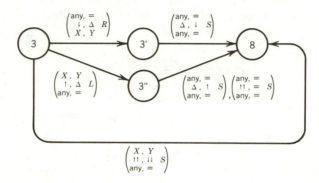

where 3′ is used when moving left from a negative cell, 3″ for moving left from a positive cell, the second label on 3″ to 8 for moving left from cell ii into cell i, and the bottom edge for moving left from cell i into cell 0.

We can now change the program of the two-way TM instruction by instruction (edge by edge) until it becomes the analogous program for the 3TM.

Any input that loops/crashes on the two-way TM will loop/crash on the 3TM. If an input halts, the output found on the two-way TM corresponds to the output found on the 3TM as we have defined correspondence. This means it is the same string, wrapped around. With a little more effort, we could show that any string found on track 1 and track 3 of a 3TM can be put together on a regular half-infinite TAPE TM.

Since we went into this theorem to prove that the output would be the same for the one-way and two-way TM, but we did not make it explicit where on the one-way TM TAPE the output has to be, we can leave the matter right where it is and call this theorem proven. ∎

EXAMPLE

The following two-way TM takes an input string and leaves as output the *a*-*b* complement of the string; that is, if *abaaa* is the input, we want the output to be *babbb*.

The algorithm we follow is this:

1. In cell 0 place a *.
2. Find the last nonblank letter on the right and erase it. If it is a *, halt; if it is an *a*, go to step (3); if it is a *b*, go to step (4).
3. Find the first blank on the left, change it to a *b*, go to step (2).
4. Find the first blank on the left, change it to an *a*, go to step (2).

The action of this algorithm on *abaaa* is:

$$abaaa \rightarrow *abaaa \rightarrow *abaa \rightarrow b*abaa$$
$$\rightarrow b*aba \rightarrow bb*aba \rightarrow bb*ab \rightarrow bbb*ab$$
$$\rightarrow bbb*a \rightarrow abbb*a \rightarrow abbb* \rightarrow babbb*$$
$$\rightarrow babbb$$

If we follow this method, the output is always going to be left in the negatively numbered cells. However, on a two-way TAPE this does not have to be shifted over to start in cell i since there is no way to distinguish cell i. The output is

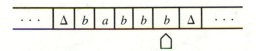

which can be considered as centered on the TAPE (infinitely many Δ's to the right, infinitely may Δ's to the left).

The program for this algorithm is:

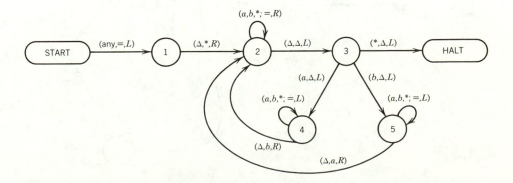

Let us trace the working of this two-way TM on the input *ab*:

$$
\begin{array}{c}
\textbf{START} \\
\begin{array}{c|c} i & ii \\ \hline \underline{a} & b \end{array}
\end{array}
\rightarrow
\begin{array}{c}
1 \\
\begin{array}{c|c|c} 0 & i & ii \\ \hline \underline{\Delta} & a & b \end{array}
\end{array}
\rightarrow
\begin{array}{c}
2 \\
\begin{array}{c|c|c} 0 & i & ii \\ \hline * & \underline{a} & b \end{array}
\end{array}
\rightarrow
\begin{array}{c}
2 \\
\begin{array}{c|c|c} 0 & i & ii \\ \hline * & a & \underline{b} \end{array}
\end{array}
$$

$$
\rightarrow
\begin{array}{c}
2 \\
\begin{array}{c|c|c|c} 0 & i & ii & iii \\ \hline * & a & b & \underline{\Delta} \end{array}
\end{array}
\rightarrow
\begin{array}{c}
3 \\
\begin{array}{c|c|c} 0 & i & ii \\ \hline * & a & \underline{b} \end{array}
\end{array}
\rightarrow
\begin{array}{c}
5 \\
\begin{array}{c|c|c} 0 & i & ii \\ \hline * & \underline{a} & \Delta \end{array}
\end{array}
\rightarrow
\begin{array}{c}
5 \\
\begin{array}{c|c} 0 & i \\ \hline \underline{*} & a \end{array}
\end{array}
$$

$$
\rightarrow
\begin{array}{c}
5 \\
\begin{array}{c|c|c} -i & 0 & i \\ \hline \underline{\Delta} & * & a \end{array}
\end{array}
\rightarrow
\begin{array}{c}
5 \\
\begin{array}{c|c|c} -i & 0 & i \\ \hline a & \underline{*} & a \end{array}
\end{array}
\rightarrow
\begin{array}{c}
2 \\
\begin{array}{c|c|c} -i & 0 & i \\ \hline a & * & \underline{a} \end{array}
\end{array}
\rightarrow
\begin{array}{c}
2 \\
\begin{array}{c|c|c|c} -i & 0 & i & ii \\ \hline a & * & a & \underline{\Delta} \end{array}
\end{array}
$$

$$
\rightarrow
\begin{array}{c}
3 \\
\begin{array}{c|c|c} -i & 0 & i \\ \hline a & * & \underline{a} \end{array}
\end{array}
\rightarrow
\begin{array}{c}
4 \\
\begin{array}{c|c|c} -i & 0 & i \\ \hline a & * & \underline{\Delta} \end{array}
\end{array}
\rightarrow
\begin{array}{c}
4 \\
\begin{array}{c|c} -i & 0 \\ \hline \underline{a} & * \end{array}
\end{array}
\rightarrow
\begin{array}{c}
4 \\
\begin{array}{c|c|c} -ii & i & 0 \\ \hline \underline{\Delta} & a & * \end{array}
\end{array}
\rightarrow
\begin{array}{c}
2 \\
\begin{array}{c|c|c} -ii & -i & 0 \\ \hline b & \underline{a} & * \end{array}
\end{array}
$$

$$
\rightarrow
\begin{array}{c}
2 \\
\begin{array}{c|c|c} -ii & -i & 0 \\ \hline b & a & \underline{*} \end{array}
\end{array}
\rightarrow
\begin{array}{c}
2 \\
\begin{array}{c|c|c|c} -ii & -i & 0 & i \\ \hline b & a & * & \underline{\Delta} \end{array}
\end{array}
\rightarrow
\begin{array}{c}
3 \\
\begin{array}{c|c|c} -ii & -i & 0 \\ \hline b & a & \underline{*} \end{array}
\end{array}
\rightarrow
\begin{array}{c}
\textbf{HALT} \\
\begin{array}{c|c} -ii & -i \\ \hline b & \underline{a} \end{array}
\end{array}
$$

When converted to a 3TM, this program begins as follows:

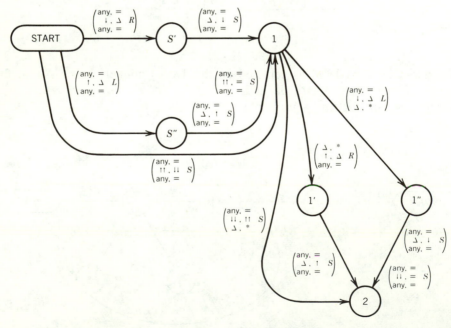

The task of completing this picture is left for the Problem section. ∎

There are other variations possible for Turing machines. We recapitulate the old ones and list some new ones below:

Variation 1:   Move-in-state machines
Variation 2:   Stay-option machines
Variation 3:   Multiple-track machines
Variation 4:   Two-way infinite TAPE machines
Variation 5:   One TAPE, but multiple TAPE HEADS
Variation 6:   Many TAPES with independently moving TAPE HEADS
Variation 7:   Two-dimensional TAPE (a whole plane of cells, like infinitely many tracks)
Variation 8:   Two-dimensional TAPE with many independent TAPE HEADS
Variation 9:   Make any of the above nondeterministic

At this point we are ready to address the most important variation: nondeterminism.

DEFINITION

A **nondeterministic Turing machine, NTM,** is defined like a TM but allows more than one edge leaving any state with the same first entry (the character to be read) in the label; that is, in state Q if we read a Y, we may have several choices of paths to pursue:

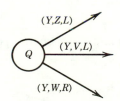

An input string is accepted by an NTM if there is *some* path through the program that leads to HALT even if there are some choices of path that loop or crash. ■

We do not consider an NTM as a transducer because a given input may leave many possible outputs. There is even the possibility of infinitely many different outputs for one particular input as below:

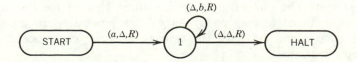

This NTM accepts only the input word a, but it may leave on its Tape any of the infinitely many choices in the language defined by the regular expression **b***, depending on how many times it chooses to loop in state 1 before proceeding to HALT.

For a nondeterminitic TM, T, we do not bother to separate the two types of nonacceptance states reject (T) and loop (T). A word can possibly take many paths through T. If some loop, some crash and some accept we say that the word is accepted. What should we do about a word that has some paths that loop and some that crash but none that accept? Rather than distinguish crash from loop we put them into one set equal to

$$\{a,b\}^* \ - \ \text{Accept(T)}$$

Two NTM's are considered equivalent as language acceptors if

$$\text{Accept}(T_1) = \text{Accept}(T_2)$$

no matter what happens to the other input strings.

THEOREM 55

Any language accepted by an NTM can be accepted by a (deterministic) TM.

PROOF

An NTM can have a finite number of choice positions, such as:

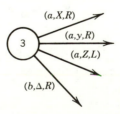

where by the phrase "choice position" we mean a state with nondeterministic branching, that is with several edges leaving it with labels that have the same first component. The picture above offers three choices for the situation of being in state 3 and reading an a. As we are processing an input string if we are in state 3 and the TAPE HEAD reads an a we can proceed along any of the paths indicated.

Let us now number each edge in the entire machine by adding a number label next to each edge instruction. These extra labels do not influence the running of the machine, they simply make description of paths through the machine easier. For example, the NTM below:

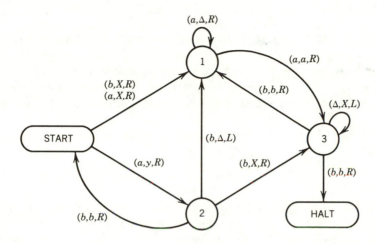

(which does nothing interesting in particular) can be instruction numbered to look like this:

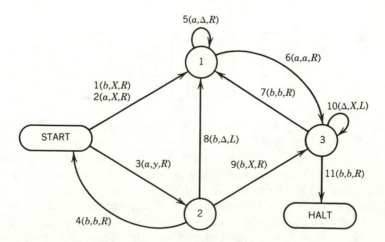

There is no special order for numbering the edge instructions. The only requirement is that each instruction receive a different number.

In the deterministic TM it is the input sequence that uniquely determines a path through the machine (a path that may or may not crash). In an NTM every string of numbers determines at most one path through the machine (which also may or may not crash). The string of numbers:

$$1 - 5 - 6 - 10 - 10 - 11$$

represents the path:

START – state 1 – state 1 – state 3 – state 3 – state 3 – HALT

This path may or may not correspond to a possible processing of an input string—but it is a path through the graph of the program nonetheless.

Some possible sequences of numbers are obviously not paths, for example,

$$9 - 9 - 9 - 2 - 11$$
$$2 - 5 - 6$$
$$1 - 4 - 7 - 4 - 11$$

The first does not begin at START, the second does not end in HALT, the third asks edge 7 to come after edge 4 but these do not connect.

To have a path traceable by an input string, we have to be careful about the TAPE contents as well as the edge sequence. To do this, we propose a three-track Turing machine on which the first track has material we shall discuss later, the second track has a finite sequence of numbers (one per cell) in the range of 1 to 11, and the bottom track has an input sequence. For example,

						$\cdots$
11	4	6	6	Δ	Δ	$\cdots$
a	b	a	Δ	Δ	Δ	$\cdots$

What we are doing is proving NTM = TM by proving NTM = 3TM. Remember, the 3TM is deterministic.

In trying to run an NTM we shall sometimes be able to proceed in a deterministic way (only one possibility at a state), but sometimes we may be at a state from which there are several choices. At this point we would like to call up our Mother on the telephone and ask her advice about which path to take. Mother might say to take edge number 11 at this juncture and she might be right, branch number 11 does move the processing along a path that will lead to HALT. On the other hand, she might be way off base. Branch 11? Why, branch 11 isn't even a choice at our current crossroads. (Some days mothers give better advice than other days.)

One thing is true. If a particular input can be accepted by a particular NTM, then there is some finite sequence of numbers (each less than the total number of instructions, 11 in the NTM above) that label a path through the machine for that word. If Mother gives us all possible sequences of advice, one at a time, eventually one sequence of numbers will constitute the guidance that will help us follow a path to HALT. If the input string cannot be accepted, nothing Mother can tell us will help. For simplicity we presume that we ask Mother's advice even at deterministic states.

So, our 3TM will work as follows:

On this track we run the input using Mother's advice
On this track we generate Mother's advice
On this track we keep a copy of the original input string

If we are lucky and the string of numbers on track 2 is good advice, then track 1 will lead us to HALT.

If the numbers on track 2 are not perfect advice for nondeterministic branching, then track 1 will lead us to a crash. Track 1 cannot loop forever, since it has to ask Mother's advice at every state and Mother's advice is always a finite string of numbers.

If Mother's advice does not lead to HALT, it will cause a crash or simply run out and we shall be left with no guidance. If we are to crash or be without Mother's advice, what we do instead of crashing is start all over again with a new sequence of numbers for track 2. We

1.   Erase track 1.

2.   Generate the *next sequence* of Mother's advice.

3.   Recopy the input from where it is stored on track 3 to track 1.

4.   Begin again to process track 1 making the branching shown on track 2.

What does this mean: generate the *next sequence* of Mother's advice? If the NTM we are going to simulate has 11 states, then Mother's advice is a *word* in the regular language defined by

$$(1 + 2 + 3 + \ldots + 11)^*$$

We have a natural ordering for these words (the words are written with hyphens between the letters):

```
  1   2   3  ...9  10  11
  1-1  1-2 ... 1-11  2-1  2-2  2-3 . . .. . . 11-11
  1-1-1  1-1-2  1-1-3 . . . 11-11-10  11-11-11
  1-1-1-1. . . .
```

If a given input can be accepted by the NTM, then at least one of these words is good advice.

Our 3TM works as follows:

1. Start with Δ's on track 1 and track 2 and the input string in storage on track 3.

2. Generate the next sequence of Mother's advice and put it on track 2. (When we start up, the "next sequence" is just the number 1 in cell i.)

3. Copy track 3 onto track 1.

4. Run track 1, always referring to Mother's advice at each state.

5. If we get to HALT, then halt.

6. If Mother's advice is imperfect and we almost crash, then erase track 1 and go to step 2.

Mother's advice could be imperfect in the following ways:

i. The edge she advises is unavailable at the state we are in.

ii. The edge she advises is available but its label requires that a different letter be read by the TAPE HEAD than the letter our TAPE HEAD is now reading from track 1.

iii. Mother is fresh out of advice; for example, Mother's advice on this round was a sequence of five numbers, but we are taking our sixth edge.

Let us give a few more details of how this system works in practice. We are at a certain state reading the three tracks. Let us say they read:

The bottom track does not matter when it comes to the operation of a run, only when it comes time to start over with new advice.

We are in some state reading a and 6. If Mother's advice is good, there is an edge from the state we are in that branches on the input a. But let us not be misled, Mother's advice is not necessarily to take edge 6 at this juncture.

To find the current piece of Mother's advice we need to move the TAPE HEAD to the first unused number in the middle track. *That* is the correct piece of Mother's advice. After thirty edges we are ready to read the thirty-first piece of Mother's advice. The TAPE HEAD will probably be off reading some different column of data for track 1, but when we need Mother's advice we have to look for it.

We find the current piece of Mother's advice and turn it into another symbol that shows that it has been used. We do not erase it because we may need to know what it was later to calculate the next sequence of Mother's advice if this sequence does not take us to HALT. We go back to the column where we started (shown above) and try to follow the advice we just looked up. Suppose the next Mother's advice number is 9. We move the TAPE HEAD back to this column (which we must have marked when we left it to seek Mother's advice) and we return in one of the 11 states that remembers what Mother's advice was. State 1 wants to take edge 1 always. State 2 wants to take edge 2. And so on. So when we get back to our column we have a state that knows what it wants to do and now we must check that the TAPE HEAD is reading the right letter for the edge we wish to take. We can either proceed (if Mother has been good to us) or restart (if something went wrong).

Notice that if the input string *can* be accepted by the NTM, eventually track 2 will give advice that causes this; but if the input *cannot* be accepted, the 3TM will run forever, testing infinitely many unsuccessful paths.

There are still a number of petty details to be worked out to complete this proof, such as:

1. How do we generate the next sequence of Mother's advice from the last? (We can call this incrementation.)

2. How do we recopy track 3 onto track 1?

3. How do we mark and return to the correct column?

4. Where do we store the information of what state in the NTM we are supposed to be simulating?

Unfortunately, these four questions are all problems at the end of the chapter; to answer them here would compromise their integrity. So we cannot do that. Instead, we are forced to write an end-of-proof mark right here. ∎

We have shown a TM can do what an NTM can do. Obviously an NTM can do anything that a TM can do, simply by not using the option of non-determinism. Therefore:

THEOREM 56

$$\text{TM} = \text{NTM}$$ ∎

The next theorem may come as a surprise, not that the result is so amazing but that it is strange that we have not been able to prove this before.

THEOREM 57

Every CFL can be accepted by some TM.

PROOF

We know that every CFL can be accepted by some PDA (Theorem 28) and
that every PDA PUSH can be written as a sequence of PM instructions ADD
and SUB. What we were not able to conclude before is that a PM could do
everything a PDA could do because PDA's could be nondeterministic while
PM's could not. If we convert a nondeterministic PDA into PM form we get
a nondeterministic PM.

If we further apply the conversion algorithm of Theorem 46 to this nondeterministic PM, we convert the nondeterministic PM into a nondeterministic
TM.

Using our last theorem, we know that every NTM has an equivalent TM.

Putting all of this together, we conclude that any language accepted by a
PDA can be accepted by some TM.   ■

PROBLEMS

1. Convert these TM's to Move-in-State machines:

    (i)

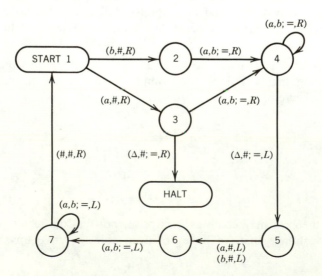

(ii)

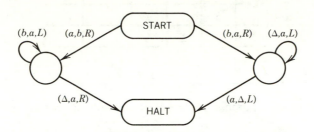

2. (i) Draw a Move-in-State machine for the language ODDPALINDROME.

    (ii) Draw a Move-in-State machine for the language $\{a^n b^n\}$

3. Draw a Move-in-State machine for the language EQUAL.

4. Draw a Move-in-State machine for the language: All words of odd length with a as the middle letter.

5. (i)   Show that an NTM can be converted, using the algorithm in this chapter, into a nondeterministic Move-in-State machine.
    (ii) Show that nondeterminism does not increase the power of a Move-in-State machine.

6. Discuss briefly how to prove that multiple-cell-move instructions such as $(x, y, 5R)$ and $(x, y, 17L)$ do not increase the power of a TM.

7. In the description of the algorithm for the 3TM that does decimal addition "the way humans do," we skimmed too quickly over the conversion of data section.
    The input is presumed to be placed on track 1 as two numbers separated by delimiters. For example,

$	8	9	$	2	6	$	Δ	
$	Δ							
$	Δ							

The question of putting the second number onto the second track has a problem that we ignored in the discussion in the chapter.
If we first put the last digit from track 1 into the first empty cell of track 2 and repeat, we arrive at

$	8	9	$	Δ	· · ·
$	6	2	Δ	· · ·	
$	Δ	Δ	Δ	· · ·	

with the second number reversed. Show how to correct this.

8. Problem 7 still leaves one question unanswered. What happens to input numbers of unequal length? For example, how does $345$1 convert to 345 + 1 instead of 345 + 100? Once this is answered, is the decimal adder finished?

9. Outline a decimal adder that adds more than two numbers at a time.

10. In the proof that 3TM = TM (Theorem 53), solve the problem posed in the chapter above: How can we mark cell i so that we do not back up through it moving left?

11. (i) Write a 3TM to do binary addition on two n-bit numbers.
    (ii) Describe a TM that multiplies two 2-bit binary numbers, called an MTM.

12. Using the algorithm in Theorem 53 (loosely), convert the 3TM in Problem 11 into a simple TM.

13. (i)   Complete the conversion of the a-b complementer from 2-way TM to 3TM that was begun in the chapter above.
    (ii) Show how this task could be done by virtually the same algorithm on a TM as on a 2-way TM.

14. (i)   Outline an argument that shows how a 2-way TM could be simulated on a 4PDA and therefore on a TM.
    (ii) Show the same method works on a 3PDA.

15. Outline an argument that shows that a 2-way TM could be simulated on a TM using interlaced sequences of TAPE cells.

16. On a TM, outline a program that inputs a word in $(1 + 2 + \ldots + 11)^*$ and leaves on the TAPE the next word in the language (the next sequence of Mother's advice).

17. Write a 2TM program to copy the contents of track 2 onto track 1 where track 2 has a finite string of a's and b's ending in Δ's. (For the proof of Theorem 55 in the chapter we needed to copy track 3 onto track 1 on a 3TM. However, this should be enough of an exercise.)

18. (i) Write a 3TM program that finds Mother's advice (locates the next unused symbol on the second track) and returns to the column it was processing. Make up the required marking devices.

    (ii) Do the same as in (i) above but arrange to be in a state numbered 1 through 11 that corresponds to the number read from the Mother's advice sequence.

19. If this chapter had come immediately after Chapter 24, we would now be able to prove Post's Theorem and Minsky's Theorem using our new results. Might this shorten the proof of Post's or Minsky's Theorem? That is, can nondeterminism or multitracks be of any help?

20. Show that a nondeterministic nPDA has the same power as a deterministic 2PDA.

$$N n\text{PDA} = \text{D2PDA}$$

CHAPTER 28

RECURSIVELY ENUMERABLE LANGUAGES

We have an independent name and an independent description for the languages accepted by FA's: the languages are called **regular,** and they can be defined by regular expressions. We have an independent name and an independent description for the languages accepted by PDA's: the languages are called **context-free,** and they can be generated by context-free-grammars. In this chapter and Chapter 30 we discuss the characteristics of the languages accepted by TM's. They will be given an independent name and an independent description. The name will be type 0 languages and the description will be by a new style of generating grammar. But before we investigate this other formulation we have a problem still to face on the old front. Is it clear what we mean by "the class of languages accepted by TM's?" A Turing machine is a little different from the previous machines in that there are some words that are neither accepted nor crash, namely, those that cause the machine to loop around a circuit forever. These forever-looping words create a new kind of problem.

For every TM, T, which runs on strings from the alphabet Σ, we saw that we can break the set of all finite strings over Σ into three disjoint sets:

$$\Sigma^* = \text{accept}(T) + \text{loop}(T) + \text{reject}(T)$$

We are led to two possible definitions for the concept of what languages are recognized by Turing machines. Rather than debate which is the "real" definition for the set of languages accepted by TM's we give both possibilities a name and then explore their differences.

DEFINITION

A language L over the alphabet Σ is called **recursively enumerable** if there is a Turing machine T that accepts every word in L and either rejects or loops for every word in the language L', the complement of L (every word in Σ^* not in L).

$$\text{accept}(T) = L$$
$$\text{reject}(T) + \text{loop}(T) = L'$$

■

EXAMPLE

The TM on page 575 accepts the language $L = \{a^n b^n a^n\}$ and loops or rejects all words not in L. Therefore $\{a^n b^n a^n\}$ is recursively enumerable. ■

A more stringent requirement for a TM to recognize a language is given by the following.

DEFINITION

A language L over the alphabet Σ is called **recursive** if there is a Turing machine T that accepts every word in L and rejects every word in L', that is,

$$\text{accept}(T) = L$$
$$\text{reject}(T) = L'$$
$$\text{loop}(T) = \phi$$

EXAMPLE

The following TM accepts the language of all words over $\{a,b\}$ that start with
a and crashes on (rejects) all words that do not.

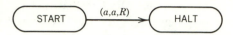

Therefore, this language is recursive. ■

This term "recursively enumerable" is often abbreviated "r.e.," which is
why we never gave an abbreviation for the term "regular expression." The
term "recursive" is not usually abbreviated. It is obvious that every recursive
language is also recursively enumerable, because the TM for the recursive
language can be used to satisfy both definitions. However, we shall see in
Chapter 29 that there are some languages that are r.e. but not recursive. This
means that *every* TM that accepts these languages must have some words on
which it loops forever.

We should also note that we could have defined r.e. and recursive in terms
of PM's or 2PDA's as well as in terms of TM's, since the languages that
they accept are the same. It is a point that we did not dwell on previously,
but because our conversion algorithms make the operations of the machines
identical section by section any word that loops on one will also loop on the
corresponding others. If a TM, T, is converted by our methods into a PM,
P, and a 2PDA, A, then not only does

$$\text{accept}(T) \ = \ \text{accept}(P) \ = \ \text{accept}(A)$$

but also

$$\text{loop}(T) \ = \ \text{loop}(P) \ = \ \text{loop}(A)$$

and

$$\text{reject}(T) \ = \ \text{reject}(P) \ = \ \text{reject}(A)$$

Therefore, languages that are recursive on TM's are recursive on PM's and
2PDA's as well. Also, languages that are r.e. on TM's are r.e. on PM's and
2PDA's, too.

Turing used the term "recursive" because he believed, for reasons we discuss
in Chapter 31, that any set defined by a recursive definition could be defined

by a TM. We shall also see that he believed that any calculation that could be defined recursively by algorithm could be performed by TM's. That was the basis for his belief that TM's are a universal algorithm device (see Chapter 31). The term "enumerable" comes from the association between accepting a language and listing or generating the language by machine. To enumerate a set (say the squares) is to generate the elements in that set one at a time (1,4,9,16 . . .). We take up this concept again later.

There is a profound difference between the meanings of recursive and recursively enumerable. If a language is regular and we have an FA that accepts it, then if we are presented a string w and we want to know whether w is in this language, we can simply run it on the machine. Since every state transition eats up a letter from w, in exactly length(w) steps we have our answer: yes (if the last state is a final state) or no (if it is not). This we have called an effective decision procedure. However, if a language is r.e. and we have a TM that accepts it, then if we are presented a string w and we would like to know whether w is in the language, we have a harder time. If we run w on the machine, it may lead to a HALT right away. On the other hand, we may have to wait. We may have to extend the execution chain seven billion steps. Even then, if w has not been accepted or rejected, it still eventually might be. Worse yet, w might be in the loop set for this machine, and we shall never get an answer. A recursive language has the advantage that we shall at least someday get the answer, even though we may not know how long it will take.

We have seen some examples of TM's that do their jobs in very efficient ways. There are some TM's, on the other hand, that take much longer to do simple tasks. We have seen a TM with a few states that can accept the language PALINDROME. It compares the first and last letter on the input TAPE, and, if they match, it erases them both. It repeats this process until the TAPE is empty and then accepts the word.

Now let us outline a worse machine for the same language:

1. Replace all a's on the TAPE with the substring *bab*.
2. Translate the non-Δ data up the TAPE so that it starts in what was formerly the cell of the last letter.
3. Repeat step 2 one time for every letter in the input string.
4. Replace all b's on the TAPE with the substring *aabaa*.
5. Run the usual algorithm to determine whether or not what is left on the TAPE is in PALINDROME.

The TM that follows this algorithm also accepts the language PALINDROME. It has more states than the first machine, but it is not fantastically large. However, it takes many, many steps for this TM to determine whether *aba* is or is not a palindrome. While we are waiting for the answer, we may mistakenly think that the machine is going to loop forever. If we knew that the language was recursive and the TM had no loop set, then we would have the faith to wait for the answer.

Not all TM's that accept a recursive language have no loop set. A language is recursive if *at least one* TM accepts it and rejects its complement. Some TM's that accept the same language might loop on some inputs.

Let us make some observations about the connection between recursive languages and r.e. languages.

THEOREM 58:

If the language L is recursive, then its complement L' is also recursive. In other words, the recursive languages are closed under complementation.

PROOF

It is easier to prove this theorem using Post machines than TM's. Let us take a language L that is recursive. There is then some PM, call it P, for which all the words in L lead to ACCEPT and all the words in L' crash or lead to REJECT. No word in Σ^* loops forever on this machine.

Let us draw in all the REJECT states so that no word crashes but instead is rejected by landing in a REJECT. To do this for each READ we must specify an edge for each possible character read. If any new edges are needed we draw:

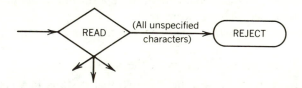

Now if we reverse the REJECT and ACCEPT states we have a new machine that takes all the words of L' to ACCEPT and all the words of L to REJECT and still never loops.

Therefore L' is shown to be recursive on this new PM. We used the same trick to show that the complement of a regular language is regular (Theorem 11), but it did not work for CFL's since PDA's are nondeterministic (Theorem 38). ■

We cannot use the same argument to show that the complement of a recursively enumerable set is recursively enumerable, since some input string might make the Post machine loop forever. Interchanging the status of the

ACCEPT and REJECT states of a Post machine P to make P' keeps the same set of input strings in loop (P).

We might imagine that since:

$$\text{accept}(P) \text{ becomes reject}(P')$$
$$\text{loop}(P) \text{ stays loop}(P')$$
$$\text{reject}(P) \text{ becomes accept}(P')$$

We have some theorem that if accept(P) is r.e., then so is reject(P), since it is the same as accept(P'). However, just by looking at a language L that is r.e. we have no way of determining what the language reject(P) might look like. It might very well be no language at all. In fact, for every r.e. language L we can find a PM such that:

$$\text{accept}(P) = L$$
$$\text{loop}(P) = L'$$
$$\text{reject}(P) = \phi$$

We do this by changing all the REJECT states into infinite loops. Start with a PM for L and replace each

with

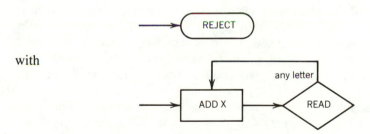

One interesting observation we can make is the following.

THEOREM 59

If L is r.e. and L' is r.e., then L is recursive.

PROOF

From the hypotheses we know that there is some TM, say T_1, that accepts L and some TM, say T_2, that accepts L'. From these two machines we want, by constructive algorithm, to build a machine T_3 that accepts L and rejects L' (and therefore does not loop forever on any input string).

We would like to do something like this. First, interchange accept and reject on T_2 so that the modified machine (call it T_2') now rejects L' but loops or accepts all the words in L. Now, build a machine, T_3, that starts with an input string and alternately simulates one step of T_1 and then one step of T_2' on this same input. If an input string is in L, it must eventually be accepted by T_1 (or even by T_2'). If an input is in L', it will definitely be rejected by T_2' (maybe even by T_1). Therefore, this combination machine proves that L is recursive. What we want is this:

$$\text{accept}(T_1) = L$$
$$\text{accept}(T_2) = L'$$
$$\text{so reject}(T_2') = L'$$
$$T_3 = T_1 \text{ and } T_2',$$
$$\text{so accept}(T_3) = L$$
$$\text{reject}(T_3) = L'$$

This is like playing two games of chess at once and moving alternately on one board and then the other. We win on the first board if the input is in L, and we lose on the second if the input is in L'. When either game ends, we stop playing both.

The reason we ask for alternation instead of first running on T_1 and then, if necessary (to reject some words from L'), running on T_2' is that T_1 might never end its processing. If we knew it would not loop forever, we would not need T_2' at all. We cannot tell when a TM is going to run forever (this will be discussed later); otherwise, we could choose to run on T_1 or T_2', whichever terminates.

This strategy has a long way to go before it becomes a proof. What does it mean to say "Take a step on T_1 and then one on T_2'"? By "a step" we mean "travel one edge of a path." But one machine might be erasing the input string before the other has had a chance to read it.

One solution is to use the results of Chapter 27 and to construct a two-TAPE machine. However, we use a different solution. We make two copies of the input on the TAPE before we begin processing. Employing the same method as in the proof of Theorem 49, we devote the odd-numbered cells on the TAPE to T_1 and the even cells to T_2'. That way, each has a work space as well as input string storage space.

It would be no problem for us to write a program that doubles every input string in this manner. If the input string is originally:

i	ii	iii		
a	b	a	Δ	$\cdots$

It can very easily be made into:

i	ii	iii	iv	v	vi		
a	a	b	b	a	a	Δ	⋯

with one copy on the evens and one on the odds. But before we begin to write such a "preprocessor" to use at the beginning of T_3, we should make note of at least one problem with this idea.

We must remember that Turing machine programs are very sensitive to the placement of the TAPE HEAD. This must be taken into account when we alternate a step on T_1 with a step on T_2'. When we finish a T_1 move we must be able to return the TAPE HEAD to the correct even-numbered cell—the one it is supposed to be about to read in simulating the action of T_2'.

Suppose, for instance, that we have a T_1 move that leaves the TAPE HEAD in cell vii. When we resume on T_1 we want the simulation to pick up there. In between we do a T_2' step that leaves the TAPE HEAD in some new cell, say xii. To be sure of picking up our T_1 simulation properly, we have to know that we must return to cell vii. Also, we have to find cell xii again for the next T_2' step. We accomplish this by leaving a marker showing where to resume on the TAPE.

We have to store these markers on the T_3 TAPE. We already have T_1 information and T_2' information in alternating cells. We propose to use every other even-numbered cell as a space for a T_1 marker, and every other odd-numbered cell as a space for a T_2' marker.

For the time being, let us use the symbol * in the T_3 cell two places before the one at which we want to resume processing. The T_3 TAPE is now composed of four interlaced sequences, as shown:

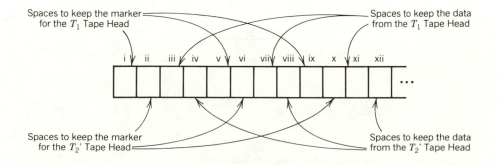

If the word *aba* is the input string to both machines, we do not just want to start with

i	ii	iii	iv	v	vi	
a	a	b	b	a	a	Δ

$\cdots$

but with

i	ii	iii	iv	v	vi	vii	viii	ix	x	xi	xii	
*	*	a	a	Δ	Δ	b	b	Δ	Δ	a	a	Δ

$\cdots$

The * in cell i indicates that the TAPE HEAD on T_1 is about to read the character in cell iii. The * in cell ii indicates that the TAPE HEAD on T_2' is about to read the character in cell iv. The a in cell iii is the character in the first cell on the TAPE for T_1. The a in cell iv is the character in the first cell on the TAPE for T_2. The Δ in cell v indicates that the TAPE HEAD on T_1 is *not* about to read the b in cell vii (which is in the second cell on the TAPE of T_1). If the TAPE HEAD were about to read this cell, a * would be in cell v.

Cells iii, vii, xi, xv, . . . (it is a little hard to recognize an arithmetic progression in Roman numerals) always contain the contents of the TAPE on T_1.

Cells iv, viii, xii, xvi, . . . always contain the contents of the TAPE on T_2'.

In the cells i, v, ix, xiii, . . . we have all blanks except for one * that indicates where the TAPE HEAD on T_1 is about to read.

In the cells ii, vi, x, xiv, . . . we also have all blanks except for the * that indicates where the TAPE HEAD on T_2' is about to read. For example,

TAPE T_3 =

i	ii	iii	iv	v	vi	vii	viii	ix	x	xi	xii	xiii	xiv	xv	xvi	
Δ	Δ	a	b	Δ	Δ	b	a	*	Δ	b	a	Δ	*	a	b	

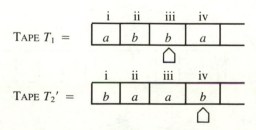

TAPE T_1 =

i	ii	iii	iv	
a	b	b	a	

TAPE T_2' =

i	ii	iii	iv	
b	a	a	b	

Even now we do not have enough information.

When we turn our attention back to T_1 after taking a step on T_2', we have forgotten which state in the program of T_1 we were at last time. We do remember what the contents of the T_1 TAPE were and where the T_1 TAPE HEAD was when we left, but we do not remember which state we were in on T_1.

The information in the program of T_1 can be kept in the program of T_3. But unless we remember which state we were last in we cannot resume the processing.

This information about last states can be stored on the T_3 TAPE. One method for doing this is to use the series of cells in which we have placed the TAPE HEAD markers *. Instead of the uninformative symbol * we may use a character from this alphabet:

$$\{ q_1 \quad q_2 \quad q_3 \quad q_4 \quad \ldots \}$$

where the q's are the names of the states in the Turing machine T_1. We can also use them to indicate the current state of processing in T_2' if we use the same names for the states in the T_2' program.

What we suggest is that if the T_3 TAPE has the contents below:

Δ	Δ	a	b	q_4	Δ	b	b	Δ	q_2	a	b	Δ	Δ	Δ	Δ	$\cdots$

it means that the current state of the T_1 TAPE is:

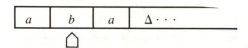

and the processing is in program state q_4 on T_1, while the current state of the T_2' TAPE is

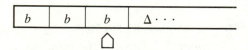

and the process is in program state q_2 on T_2'.

Notice that *where* the q's occur on the T_3 TAPE tells us where the TAPE HEADS are reading on T_1 and T_2' and *which* q's they are tells us which states the component machines are in.

One point that should be made clear is that although

$$\{ q_1 \quad q_2 \quad q_3 \quad \ldots \}$$

is an infinite alphabet, we never use the whole alphabet to build any particular T_3.

If T_1 has 12 states and T_2' has 22 states, then we rename the states of T_1 to be

$$q_1 \quad q_2 \quad \cdots \quad q_{12}$$

and the states of T_2' to be

$$q_1 \quad q_2 \quad \cdots \quad q_{22}$$

We shall assume that the states have been numbered so that q_1 is the START state on both machines.

The T_3 we build will have the following TAPE alphabet:

$\Gamma \;=\;$ {all the characters that can appear on the TAPE of T_1 or on the TAPE of T_2' plus the 22 characters $q_1 \ q_2 \ \ldots \ q_{22}$ plus two new characters different from any of these, which we shall call #1 and #2.}

As we see, Γ is finite.

These new characters #1 and #2 will be our left-end bumpers to keep us from crashing while backing up to the left on our way back from taking a step on either machine T_1 or T_2'.

Our basic strategy for the program of T_3 is as follows.

Step 1   Set up the T_3 TAPE. By this we mean that we take the initial input string, say,

b	a	a	$\Delta \cdots$

and turn it into:

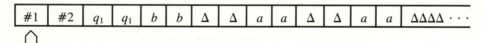

which represents the starting situation for both machines.

Step 2   Simulate a move on T_1. Move to the right two cells at a time to find the first q indicating which state we are in on T_1. At this point we must branch, depending on which q we have read. This branching will be indicated in the T_3 program. Now proceed two more cells (on the T_3 TAPE) to get to the letter read in this state on the simulated T_1. Do now what T_1 wants us to do (leave it alone or change it). Now erase the q we read two cells to the left (on the T_3 TAPE) and, depending on whether T_1 wants to move its TAPE HEAD to the right or left, insert a new q on the T_3 TAPE. Now return to home (move left until we encounter #1 and bounce from it into #2 in cell ii).

Step 3   Simulate a move on T_2'. Move to the right two cells at a time to find the first q indicating which state we are in on the simulated T_2'. Follow the instructions as we did in step 2; however, leave the TAPE HEAD reading #1 in cell i.

Step 4   Execute step 2 and step 3 alternately until one of the machines (T_1 or T_2') halts. When that happens (and it must), if T_1 halted the input is accepted, if T_2' halted, let T_3 crash so as to reject the input.

These may be understandable verbal descriptions, but how do we implement them on a Turing machine?

First, let us describe how to implement step 1. Here we make use of the subroutine developed in Chapter 24 that inserts a character in a cell on a TM TAPE and moves all succeeding information one cell to the right. This subroutine we called INSERT.

To do the job required in step 1, we must follow the program below:

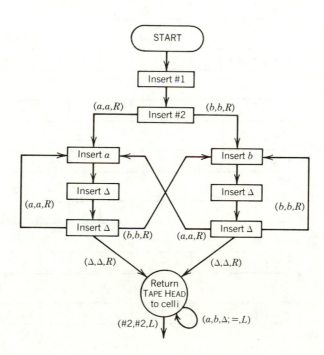

Let us follow the workings of this on the simple input string *ba:*

	b	*a*	Δ · · ·						

Insert #1: ⌂

#1	*b*	*a*	Δ · · ·						

Insert #2: ⌂

#1	#2	*b*	*a*	Δ · · ·					

Read the *b*,
leave it alone: ⌂

#1	#2	*b*	*a*	Δ · · ·					

But insert
another *b*: ⌂

#1	#2	*b*	*b*	*a*	Δ · · ·				

and insert a Δ: ⌂

#1	#2	*b*	*b*	Δ	*a*	Δ · · ·			

and insert
another Δ: ⌂

#1	#2	*b*	*b*	Δ	Δ	*a*	Δ · · ·		

Read the *a*,
leave it alone: ⌂

#1	#2	*b*	*b*	Δ	Δ	*a*	Δ · · ·		

But insert
another *a*: ⌂

#1	#2	*b*	*b*	Δ	Δ	*a*	*a*	Δ · · ·	

and insert a Δ: ⌂

#1	#2	*b*	*b*	Δ	Δ	*a*	*a*	Δ	Δ · · ·

and insert
another Δ: ⌂

#1	#2	*b*	*b*	Δ	Δ	*a*	*a*	Δ	Δ	Δ · · ·

Read the Δ and
return the
TAPE HEAD to
cell i: ⌂

#1	#2	*b*	*b*	Δ	Δ	*a*	*a*	Δ · · ·	

So we see that Step 1 can be executed by a Turing machine leaving us ready for Step 2.

To implement Step 2, we move up the TAPE reading every other cell:

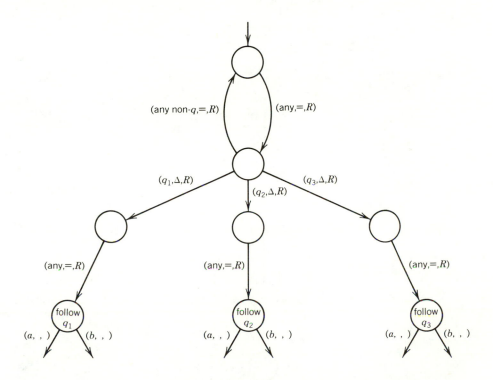

The top two states in this picture are searching for the q in the appropriate track (odd-numbered cells). Here we skip over the even cells. When we find a q, we erase it and move right two cells. (We have drawn the picture for 3 possible q-states, but the idea works for any number of states. How many are required depends on the size of the machine.) Then we branch depending on the letter. On this level, the bottom level in the diagram above, we encode all the information of T_1. The states that are labeled "follow q_1," "follow q_2," and so on refer to the fact that q_1 is a state in T_1, which acts a certain way when an a is read or a b is read. It changes the contents of the cell and moves the TAPE HEAD. We must do the same. Let us take the example that in q_6 the machine T_1 tells us to change b to a and move the TAPE HEAD to the right and enter state q_{11} on T_1:

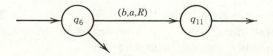

In the program for T_3 we must write:

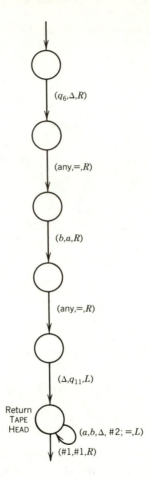

First we erase the TAPE-HEAD-and-state marker q_6. Then we skip a cell to the right. Then we read a b and change it to an a. Then we skip another cell. Then, in a formerly blank cell, we place the new T_1 TAPE-HEAD-and-state marker q_{11}. Then we return to the left end of the TAPE having executed one step of the processing of the input on the machine T_1.

The simulation of any other T_1 instruction is just as simple. In this manner the whole program of T_1 can be encoded in the program of T_3 and executed one step at a time using only some of the TAPE of T_3 (the odd-numbered cells).

Step 3 is implemented the same way, except that we return the TAPE HEAD to cell i, not cell ii.

Step 4 really has nothing extra for us to do. Since Step 2 leaves us in the correct cell to start Step 3 and Step 3 leaves us in the correct cell to execute Step 2, we need only connect them like this:

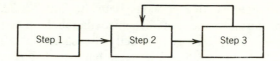

and the steps will automatically alternate.

The language this machine accepts is L, since all words in L will lead to HALT's while processing on T_1. All words in L' will lead to crashes while processing on T_2'.

Therefore, T_3 proves that L is a recursive language.   ■

Again, the machines produced by the algorithm in this proof are very large (many, many states) and it is hard to illustrate this method in any but the simplest examples.

EXAMPLE

Consider the language:

$$L = \{\text{all words starting with } b\}$$

which is regular since it can be defined by the regular expression $\mathbf{b(a+b)}^*$.
L can be accepted by the following TM, T_1:

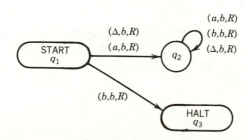

$$\text{accept}(T_1) = L$$
$$\text{loop}(T_1) \;\; = L'$$
$$\text{reject}(T_1) \;\; = \phi$$

This silly machine tries to turn the whole TAPE into b's if the input string is in L'. This process does not terminate. On this machine we loop forever in state q_2 for each word in L'. When we do, the Tape is different after each loop, so we have an example where the process loops forever even though the TAPE never returns to a previous status. (Unlike a TM, a computer has only finite memory, so we can recognize that a loop has occurred because the memory eventually returns to exactly the same status.)

The machine T_1 proves that L is r.e., but not that L is recursive.

The TM below, T_2,

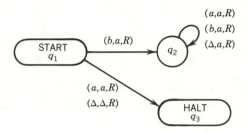

accepts the language L' and loops on L.

From these two machines together, we can make a T_3 that accepts L and rejects L'.

We shall not repeat the complicated implementation involved in Step 1 of the algorithm (setting up the TAPE), since that was explained above and is always exactly the same no matter which T_1 and T_2' are to be combined. So let us assume that the TAPE has been properly prepared. We now examine Steps 2 and 3.

First we modify T_2 to become T_2' so that it accepts what it used to reject and rejects what it used to accept, leaving

$$\text{loop}(T_2) = \text{loop}(T_2')$$

The resultant T_2' we build is:

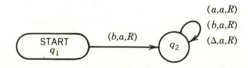

which now crashes on all the words it used to accept, that is, T_2' crashes for all input strings from L', and only those.

We could have turned q_3 into a reject state, but it is simpler just to eliminate it altogether.

Once Step 1 is out of the way and the TAPE HEAD is reading #1 in cell i, the program for Step 2 is:

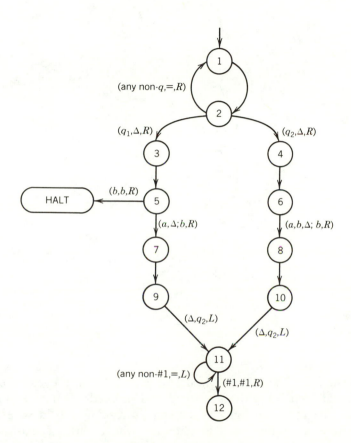

Note: All unlabeled edges should have the label "(any, = ,R)."

State 11 is a transition state between state 2 and state 3 since it locates the #2.

Step 3 is programmed as follows. [Again all unlabeled edges should have the label "(any, = ,R)."]

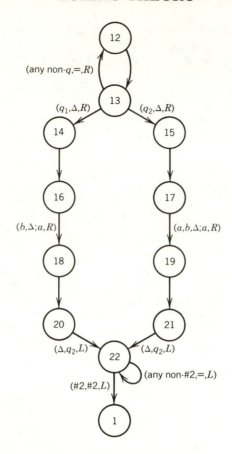

Notice how Step 2 and Step 3 lead into each other in a cycle. Step 2 ends at state 12 and Step 3 begins at state 12 and proceeds to state 1, and so on. In this case, the cycle can only be broken by reading a *b* in state 5, which leads to HALT or reading an *a* in state 16, which causes a crash.

This T_3 accepts L and rejects L', so it proves that L is recursive.

The pleasure of running inputs on this machine is deferred until the problem section.   ■

The first question that comes to most minds now is, "So what? Is the result of Theorem 59 so wonderful that it was worth a multipage proof?" The answer to this is not so much to defend Theorem 59 itself but to examine the proof.

We have taken two different Turing machines (they could have been completely unrelated) and combined them into one TM that processes an input as though it were running simultaneously on both machines. This is such an important possibility that it deserves its own theorem.

THEOREM 60

If T_1 and T_2 are TM's, then there exists a TM, T_3, such that

$$\text{accept}(T_3) \ = \ \text{accept}(T_1) \ + \ \text{accept}(T_2).$$

In other words, the union of two recursively enumerable languages is recursively enumerable; the set of recursively enumerable languages is closed under union.

PROOF

The algorithm in the proof of Theorem 59 is all that is required. First we must alter T_1 and T_2 so that they both loop instead of crash on those words that they do not accept. This is easy to do. Instead of letting an input string crash at q_{43}:

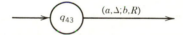

because there is no edge for reading a b, remake this into:

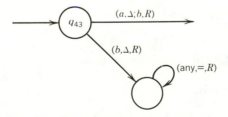

Now nothing stops the two machines from running in alternation, accepting any words and only those words accepted by either. The algorithm for producing T_3 can be followed just as given in the proof of Theorem 59.

On the new machine

$$\begin{aligned}
\text{accept } (T_3) &= \text{accept } (T_1) \ + \ \text{accept } (T_2) \\
\text{loop } (T_3) &= \text{loop } (T_1) \cap \text{loop } (T_2) \\
\text{reject } (T_3) &= \text{reject } (T_1) \cap \text{reject } (T_2) \\
&\quad + \ \text{reject } (T_1) \cap \text{loop } (T_2) \\
&\quad + \ \text{loop } (T_1) \cap \text{reject } (T_2)
\end{aligned}$$

(See Problem 15 below.)

There is a small hole in the proof of Theorem 60. It is important to turn all rejected words into words that loop forever so that one machine does not crash while the other is on its way to accepting the word. However, the example of how to repair this problem given in the proof above does not cover all cases. It is also possible, remember, for a machine to crash by moving the TAPE HEAD left from cell i. To complete the proof we should also show how this can be changed into looping. This is left to Problem 12 below. ■

The fact that the union or intersection of two recursive languages is also recursive follows from this theorem (see Problem 20 below).

PROBLEMS

Show that the following languages over $\{a,b\}$ are recursive by finding a TM that accepts them and crashes for every input string in their respective complements.

1. The language of all words that do not have the substring ab.

2. EVEN-EVEN

3. (i) EQUAL
   (ii) All words with one more a than b's.

4. ODDPALINDROME

5. (i) All words with a triple letter (either aaa or bbb).
   (ii) All words with either the substring ab or the substring ba.

6. DOUBLEWORD

7. TRAILINGCOUNT

8. All words with the form $b^n a^n b^n$ for $n = 1,2,3, \ldots$.

9. All words of the form $a^x b^y$, where $x < y$ and x and y are $1,2,3, \ldots$.

10. Prove algorithmically that all regular languages are recursive.

11. Are all CFL's recursive?

12. Finish the proof of Theorem 60 as per the comment that follows it, that is, take care of the possibility of crashing on a move left from cell i.

Assume that a Step 1 subroutine is working and that the input string $x_1x_2x_3$ is automatically put on the TM TAPE as:

#1	#2	q_1	q_1	x_1	x_1	Δ	Δ	x_2	x_2	Δ	Δ	x_3	x_3	Δ	· · ·

The following are some choices for input strings $x_1x_2x_3$ to run on the T_3 designed in the example on pages 701 and 702. Trace the execution of each.

13. (i)   *ab*

   (ii)   *bbb*

14. (i)   Λ

   (ii)   What is the story with Λ in general as a Step 1 possibility?

15. Explain the formulas for accept, loop and reject of T_3 in the proof of Theorem 60.

Consider the following TM's:

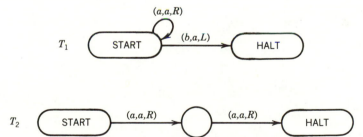

16. What are accept(T_1), loop(T_1), and reject(T_1)? Be careful about the word *b*.

17. What are accept(T_2), loop(T_2), and reject(T_2)?

18. Assume that there is a Step 1 subroutine already known, so that we can simply write:

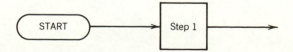

Using the method of the proof of Theorem 46, draw the rest of the TM that accepts the language:

$$\text{accept}(T_1) \; + \; \text{accept}(T_2).$$

19. Trace the execution of these input strings on the machine of Problem 18.
  (i) Λ
  (ii) b
  (iii) aab
  (iv) ab

20. (i)   Prove that the intersection of two recursive languages is recursive.
  (ii)   Prove that the union of two recursive languages is recursive.

  Hint: There is no need to produce any new complicated algorithms. Proper manipulation of the algorithms in this chapter will suffice.

CHAPTER 29

THE ENCODING OF TURING MACHINES

Turing machines do seem to have immense power as language acceptors or language recognizers, yet there are some languages that are not accepted by any TM, as we shall soon prove.

Before we can describe one such language, we need to develop the idea of encoding Turing machines.

Just as with FA's and PDA's, we do not have to rely on pictorial representations for TM's. We can make a TM into a summary table and run words on the table as we did with PDA's in Chapter 18. The algorithm to do this is not difficult. First we number the states 1, 2, 3, . . . and so on. By convention we always number the START state 1 and the HALT state 2. Then we convert every instruction in the TM into a row of the table as shown below

From	To	Read	Write	Move
1	3	a	a	L
3	1	Δ	b	R
8	2	b	a	R

. . .

where the column labeled "move" indicates which direction the TAPE HEAD is to move.

EXAMPLE

The Turing machine shown below

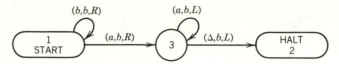

can be summarized by the following table:

From	To	Read	Write	Move
1	1	b	b	R
1	3	a	b	R
3	3	a	b	L
3	2	Δ	b	L

Since we know that state 1 is START and state 2 is HALT, we have all the information in the table necessary to operate the TM.   ■

We now introduce a coding whereby we can turn any row of the TM into a string of a's and b's.
Consider the general row

From	To	Read	Write	Move
X_1	X_2	X_3	X_4	X_5

where X_1 and X_2 are numbers, X_3 and X_4 are characters from $\{a,b,\#\}$ or Δ, and X_5 is a direction (either L or R).
We start by encoding the information X_1 and X_2 as:

$$a^{X_1}ba^{X_2}b$$

which means a string of a's of length X_1 concatenated to a b concatenated to a string of a's X_2 long concatenated to a b. This is a word in the language defined by $\mathbf{a^+ba^+b}$.
Next X_3 and X_4 are encoded by this table.

X_3,X_4	Code
a	aa
b	ab
Δ	ba
$\#$	bb

Next we encode X_5 as follows.

X_5	Code
L	a
R	b

Finally, we assemble the pieces by concatenating them into one string. For example, the row

From	To	Read	Write	Move
6	2	b	a	L

becomes

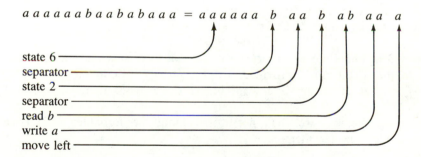

$$a\,a\,a\,a\,a\,a\,b\,a\,a\,b\,a\,b\,a\,a\,a = a\,a\,a\,a\,a\,a \quad b \quad a\,a \quad b \quad a\,b \quad a\,a \quad a$$

state 6
separator
state 2
separator
read b
write a
move left

Every string of a's and b's that is a row is of the form definable by the regular expression:

$$\mathbf{a^{+}ba^{+}b(a+b)^{5}}$$
$$= \text{(at least one } a\text{) } b \text{ (at least one } a\text{) } b \text{ (five letters)}$$

It is also true that every word defined by this regular expression can be interpreted as a row of a TM summary table with one exception: We cannot leave a HALT state. This means that $\mathbf{aaba^{+}b(a + b)^{5}}$ defines a forbidden sublanguage.

Not only can we make any row of the table into a string, but we can also make the whole summary table into one long string by concatenating the strings that represent the rows.

EXAMPLE

The summary table shown above can be made into a string of a's and b's as follows:

From	To	Read	Write	Move	Code for Each Row
1	1	b	b	R	$a\,b\,a\,b\,a\,b\,a\,b\,b$
1	3	a	b	R	$a\,b\,a\,a\,a\,b\,a\,a\,a\,b\,b$
3	3	a	b	L	$a\,a\,a\,b\,a\,a\,a\,b\,a\,a\,a\,b\,a$
3	2	Δ	b	L	$a\,a\,a\,b\,a\,a\,b\,b\,a\,a\,b\,a$

One one-word code for the whole machine is:

$$abababababbabaaabaaabbaaabaaabaaabaaaabaabbaaba$$

This is not the only one-word code for this machine since the order of the rows in the table is not rigid. Let us also not forget that there are many other methods for encoding TM's, but ours is good enough. ∎

It is also important to observe that we can look at such a long string and decode the TM from it provided that the string is in the proper form, that is, as long as the string is a word in the Code Word Language (CWL).

(For the moment we shall not worry about the forbidden HALT-leaving strings. We consider them later.)

$$\text{CWL} = \text{the language defined by } (\mathbf{a^+ba^+b(a + b)^5})^*$$

The way we decode a string in CWL is this:

Step 1 Count the initial clump of a's and fill in that number in the first entry of the first empty row of the table.

Step 2 Forget the next letter; it must be a b.

Step 3 Count the next clump of a's and fill in that number in the second column of this row.

Step 4 Skip the next letter; it is a b.

Step 5 Read the next two letters. If they are aa, write an a in the Read box of the table. If they are ab, write a b in the table. If they are ba, write a Δ in the table. If they are bb, write a # in the table.

Step 6 Repeat Step 5 for the table Write entry.

Step 7 If the next letter is an *a*, write an *L* in the fifth column of the table; otherwise, write an *R*. This fills in the Move box and completes the row.

Step 8 Starting with a new line of the table, go back to Step 1 operating on what remains of the string. If the string has been exhausted, stop. The summary table is complete.

EXAMPLE

Consider the string:

$$a\,b\,a\,a\,a\,b\,a\,a\,a\,a\,b\,a\,a\,a\,b\,a\,a\,a\,b\,a\,a\,a\,a\,b\,a\,a\,a\,b\,a\,a\,b\,a\,b\,a\,b\,a$$

The first clump of *a*'s is one *a*. Write 1 in the first line of the table. Drop the *b*. The next part of the string is a clump of three *a*'s. Write 3 in row 1 column 2. Drop the *b*. Now "*aa*" stands for *a*. Write *a* in column 3. Again "*aa*" stands for *a*. Write *a* in column 4. Then "*b*" stands for *R*. Write this in column 5, ending row 1. Starting again, we have a clump of three *a*'s so start row 2 by writing a 3 in column 1. Drop the *b*. Three more *a*'s, write a 3. Drop the *b*. Now "*aa*" stands for *a*; write it. Again "*aa*" stands for *a*; write it. Then "*b*" stands for *R*. Finish row 2 with this *R*. What is left is three *a*'s, drop the *b*, two *a*'s, drop the *b*, then "*ab*" and "*ab*" and "*a*" meaning *b* and *b* and *L*. This becomes row 3 of the table. We have now exhausted the CWL word and have therefore finished a table.

The table and machine are:

From	To	Read	Write	Move
1	3	*a*	*a*	*R*
3	3	*a*	*a*	*R*
3	2	*b*	*b*	*L*

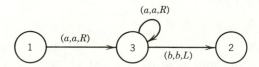

The result of this encoding process is that every TM corresponds to a word in CWL. However, not all words in CWL correspond to a TM. There is a little problem here since when we decode a CWL string we might get an improper TM such as one that is nondeterministic or repetitive (two rows the same) or violates the HALT state, but this should not dull our enthusiasm for the code words. These probems will take care of themselves, as we shall see.

The code word for a TM contains all the information of the TM yet it can be considered as merely a name — or worse yet, input. Since the code for every TM is a string of a's and b's, we might ask what happens if this string is run as input on the very TM it stands for? We shall feed each TM its own code word as input data. Sometimes it will crash, sometimes loop, sometimes accept.

Let us define the language ALAN as follows:

DEFINITION

ALAN = { all the words in CWL that are *not* accepted by the TM's they represent or that do not represent any TM }

∎

EXAMPLE

Consider the TM

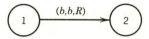

The table for this machine is simply:

From	To	Read	Write	Move
1	2	b	b	R

The code word for this TM is:

$$abaabababb$$

But if we try to run this word on the TM as input, it will crash in state 1 since there is no edge for the letter a leaving state 1.

Therefore, the word

$$abaabababb$$

is in the language ALAN.

∎

EXAMPLE

The words

$$a\ a\ b\ a\ b\ a\ a\ a\ a\ a \quad \text{and} \quad a\ a_{,}a\ b\ a\ a\ b\ a\ a\ a\ a$$

are in CWL but do not represent any TM, the first because it has an edge leaving HALT and the second because it has no START state. Both words are in ALAN.   ∎

EXAMPLE

In one example above we found the TM corresponding to the CWL word

$$a\ b\ a\ a\ a\ b\ a\ a\ a\ b\ a\ a\ a\ b\ a\ a\ a\ b\ a\ a\ a\ a\ b\ a\ a\ a\ b\ a\ a\ b\ a\ b\ a\ b\ a$$

When this word is run on the TM it represents, it is accepted. This word is *not* in ALAN.   ∎

EXAMPLE

If a TM accepts all inputs, then its code word is not in ALAN. If a TM rejects all inputs, then its code word is in ALAN. Any TM that accepts the language of all strings with a double a will have a code word with a double a and so will accept its own code word. The code words for these TM's are not in ALAN. The TM we built in Chapter 24 to accept the language PALINDROME has a code word that is not a PALINDROME (and see problem 8 below). Therefore, it does not accept its code word and its code word is in ALAN.   ∎

We shall now prove that the language ALAN is not recursively enumerable. We prove this by contradiction. Let us begin with the supposition that ALAN is r.e.. In that case there would be some TM that would accept all the words in ALAN. Let us call one such Turing Machine T. Let us denote the code word for T as code(T). Now we ask the question:

Is code(T) a word in the language ALAN or not?

There are clearly only two possibilities: Yes or No.
Let us work them out with the precision of Euclidean Geometry.

CASE 1: code(T) is in ALAN.

CLAIM	REASON
1. T accepts ALAN	1. definition of T
2. ALAN contains no code word that is accepted by the machine it represents	2. definition of ALAN
3. code(T) is in ALAN	3. hypothesis
4. T accepts the word code(T)	4. from 1 and 3
5. code(T) is not in ALAN	5. from 2 and 4
6. contradiction	6. from 3 and 5
7. code(T) is not in ALAN	7. the hypothesis (3) must be wrong because it led to a contradiction

Again, let us use complete logical rigor.

CASE 2: code(T) is not in ALAN.

CLAIM	REASON
1. T accepts ALAN	1. definition of T
2. If a word is not accepted by the machine it represents it is in ALAN	2. definition of ALAN
3. code(T) is not in ALAN	3. hypothesis
4. code(T) is not accepted by T	4. from 1 and 3
5. code(T) is in ALAN	5. from 2 and 4
6. contradiction	6. from 3 and 5
7. code(T) is in ALAN	7. the hypothesis (3) must be wrong because it led to a contradiction

Both cases are impossible; therefore the assumption that ALAN is accepted by some TM is untenable. ALAN is not recursively enumerable.

THEOREM 61

Not all languages are recursively enumerable. ■

This argument usually makes people's heads spin. It is very much like the old "liar paradox," which dates back to the Megarians (attributed sometimes to Eubulides and sometimes to the Cretan Epimenides) and runs like this. A man says, "Right now, I am telling a lie." If it is a lie, then he is telling the truth by confessing. If it is the truth, he must be lying because he claims he is. Again, both alternatives lead to contradictions.

If someone comes up to us and says "Right now, I am telling a lie." we can walk away and pretend we did not hear anything. If someone says to us, "If God can do anything can he make a stone so heavy that He cannot lift it," we can burn him as a blaspheming heretic. If someone asks us, "In a certain city the barber shaves all those who do not shave themselves and only those. Who shaves the barber?" we can answer, the barber is a woman. However, here we have used this same old riddle not to annoy Uncle Charlie, but to provide a mathematically rigorous proof that there are languages that Turing machines cannot recognize.

We can state this result in terms of computers. Let us consider the set of all preprogrammed computers—dedicated machines with a specific program chip inside. For each machine we can completely describe the circuitry in English. This English can be encoded using ASCII into a binary string. When these binary strings are run on computers they either run and cause the word "YES" to be printed or they do not. Let ALAN be the language of all bit strings that describe computers that do *not* run successfully on the computers they describe (they do not cause the word "YES" to be printed). There is no computer that has the property that all the bit strings in ALAN make it type "YES," but no other bit strings do. This is because if there were such a computer then the bit string that describes it would be in ALAN and at the same time would not be in ALAN for the reasons given above. The fact that no computer can be built that can identify when a bit string is in ALAN means that there is no computer that can analyze all circuitry descriptions and recognize when particular bit strings run on the computers described. This means that there is no computer that can do this task today and there never will be, since any computer that could perform this task could recognize the words in ALAN.

We have now fulfilled a grandiose promise that we made in Chapter 1. We have described a task that is reasonable to want a computer to do that no computer can do. Not now, not ever. We are beginning to see how our abstract theoretical discussion is actually leading to a practical consideration of computers. It is still a little too soon for us to pursue this point.

The liar paradox and other logical paradoxes are very important in Computer Theory as we can see by the example of the language ALAN (and one more surprise that we shall meet later). In fact, the whole development of the computer came from the same kind of intellectual concern as was awakened by consideration of these paradoxes.

The study of Logic began with the Greeks (in particular Aristotle and Zeno of Elea) but then lay dormant for millenia. The possibility of making Logic a branch of mathematics began in 1666 with a book by Gottfried Wilhelm von Leibniz, who was also the coinventor of Calculus and an early computer man (see Chapter 1). His ideas were continued by George Boole in the nineteenth century.

About a hundred years ago, Georg Cantor invented Set Theory and immediately a connection was found between Set Theory and Logic. This allowed the paradoxes from Logic, previously a branch of Philosophy, to creep into Mathematics. That Mathematics could contain paradoxes had formerly been an unthinkable situation. When Logic was philosophical and rhetorical, the paradoxes were tolerated as indications of depth and subtlety. In Mathematics, paradoxes are an anathema. After the invention of Set Theory, there was a flood of paradoxes coming from Cesare Burali-Forti, Cantor himself, Bertrand Russell, Jules Richard, Julius König, and many other mathematical logicians. This made it necessary to be much more precise about which sentences do and which sentences do not describe meaningful mathematical operations. This led to Hilbert's question of the decidability of mathematics and then to the development of the Theory of Algorithms and to the work of Gödel, Turing, Post, Church (whom we shall meet shortly), Kleene, and von Neumann, which in turn led to the computers we all know (and love). In the meantime, mathematical Logic, from Gottlob Frege, Russell, and Alfred North Whitehead on, has been strongly directed toward questions of decidability.

The fact that the language ALAN is not recursively enumerable is not its only unusual feature. The language ALAN is defined in terms of Turing machines. It cannot be described to people who do not know what TM's are. It is quite possible that all the languages that can be thought of by people who do not know what TM's are are recursively enumerable. (This sounds like its own small paradox.) This is an important point because, since computers are TM's (as we shall see in Chapter 31), and since our original goal was to build a universal algorithm machine, we want TM's to accept practically everything. Theorem 61 is definitely bad news. If we are hoping for an even more powerful machine to be defined in Part IV of this book that will accept all possible languages, we shall be disappointed for reasons soon to be discussed.

Since we have an encoding for TM's, we might naturally ask about the language MATHISON:

DEFINITION:

MATHISON
   = { all words in CWL that *are* accepted by their corresponding TM } ∎

MATHISON is surprising because it *is* recursively enumerable.

THEOREM 62

MATHISON is recursively enumerable.

PROOF

We prove this by constructive algorithm.

We shall design a Turing machine called *UTM* that starts with a CWL word on its TAPE and interprets the code word as a TM and then it pretends to be that TM and operates on the CWL word as if it were the input to the simulated TM (see Problem 14 below). For this purpose we shall need to have two copies of the word from MATHISON: one to keep unchanged as the instructions for operation and one to operate on; one copy as cookbook one as ingredients; one copy as program one as data. The picture below should help us understand this. Starting with the TAPE

CWL word	Δ	· · ·

we insert markers and copy the string to make the *UTM* TAPE contain this:

#	CWL word	$	2nd copy of CWL word	Δ	· · ·

$\leftarrow$ Program $\rightarrow$ $\leftarrow$ Data $\rightarrow$

Now using the information to the left of the $, *UTM* processes the input string it finds on the right of the $.

We shall not give the full details of *UTM* because it has many very lengthy components, but we shall describe it in enough detail to convince a reasonable person that this machine does exist. We may even induce an industrious fanatic to build one.

UTM should never change the information between the # and the $ because this is the set of instructions it must follow to process the string on the right of the $. However, to facilitate the processing we shall alter the form.

UTM will separate the codes for the different rows encoded in the word from MATHISON by spaces. It will use a marker, *, in front of the row that it has just executed, as shown on the next page.

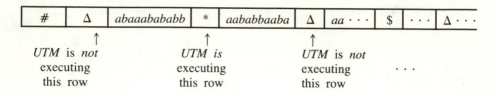

In the example above, *UTM* is just now executing the row

From	To	Read	Write	Move
2	1	Δ	b	L

We say "executing the row" because the row, being a substring of a CWL word, represents an instruction in a TM that has been encoded.

Before beginning the simulation, *UTM* must adjust the form of the data string to the right of $. It has to keep track of where the simulated TAPE HEAD operating on the input data was last reading. Remember that in operation *UTM* goes back and forth; it does something to the data section (to the right of $) and then runs back to the program section (to the left of $) for further instructions, then back to data, back to program, and so on. Just as it leaves a marker to show where it was last reading in the program section, it must leave one in the data section.

UTM accomplishes this with the same trick we used in the proof of Theorem 59. In the data section of the TAPE, where we simulate the TAPE of the encoded TM, we store its word (the one we are testing to see whether or not it is in MATHISON) in every other cell. The alternate cells are left blank. In one of these we will put the marker * to indicate the place where the simulated TAPE HEAD was left after its last simulated move.

The TAPE initially looks like this.

The * to the right of the $ is in front of the simulated TAPE HEAD. The * to the left of the $ is in front of the encoded row that we are simulating.

To figure out which encoded row we must execute next, we must first figure out what letter the TAPE HEAD of the simulated machine is reading. This we do by finding the * after the $ and reading the next cell. We return the *UTM* TAPE HEAD to # along different paths in the *UTM* program depending on whether we have just read an *a* or a *b* (or whatever characters are used in Γ on the TM being simulated).

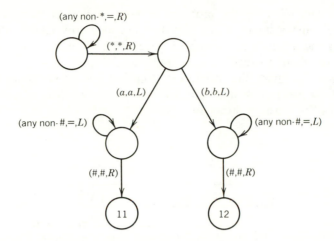

If we returned to # (on the *UTM* TAPE) via state 11 (in the *UTM* program), the letter read by the TAPE HEAD on the simulated machine was an *a*, if via state 12, the letter read by the simulated TAPE HEAD was a *b*.

We still cannot determine which row is to be executed next until we determine what state on the simulated TM we were left in by the last instruction executed. So now we must find out what row we last executed. We look for the * before the $. We consider what state the row just executed took us to on the simulated TM:

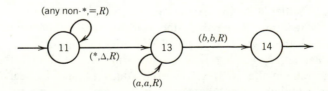

In state 14 we are about to count the number of *a*'s before the next *b*. This number will be the number of the state that the simulated TM is now in. It is also the number of *a*'s that must begin the code for the next instruction to be executed, since the state we are left in is the state we must start from.

Knowing the number of the state the simulated TM is in and the letter the simulated TM is reading in that state will uniquely determine which encoded row the *UTM* must execute next. The *UTM* must be sure that the row it executed last had its marker changed from * to Δ so that it can mark the new encoded row with a * without leaving any confusing old markers lying about.

We still have to solve the problem of how to find an encoded row that starts at the same state in which this last encoded row ended. In this code this is the same as finding a string of *a*'s after a blank as long as the string of *a*'s we are about to read in state 14.

To do this, we mark this particular string of *a*'s by changing the first to *A;* then we go back to # and, one by one, when we find a Δ we examine the length of the ensuing string of *a*'s.

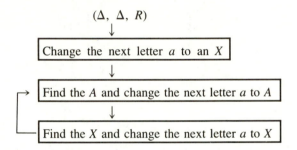

We get off the merry-go-round if an *a* is not matched by an *a* and a *b* by a *b*. If we do not find an exact matching clump of *a*'s, we change the *X*'s back to *a*'s, the *A*'s back to *a*'s (except the first), and move on to the next Δ to begin the comparison process again.

If the two clumps of *a*'s match, we have success. We have found a row that starts from the state the last row left us in.

Once we have found a row that begins with the correct state, we must check to see whether this row expects us to read the letter that the simulated TAPE HEAD is reading. Remember, the starting state number and letter read totally determine the row because our TM's are deterministic. Fortunately, we remember what letter is being read by the simulated TM because this information is inherent in the *UTM* state. Both states 11 and 12 search for a row matching the simulated state; however, if we are searching in a path from *UTM* state 11 the path keeps the memory that the next criterion for the row is that the letter read be an *a*. If the search for the next row is carried through *UTM* state 12, it knows that the next requirement for a prospective row is to read a *b*.

To check the READ portion of the encoded row, we use the *UTM* program on the next page.

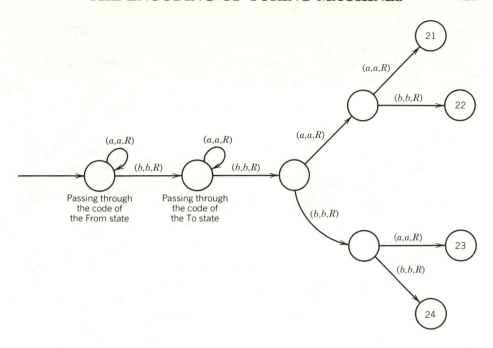

If we get to state 21, the READ letter for that row is an *a*. If we get to state 22, the READ letter for that row is a *b*. If state 23, the character is Δ. If state 24, the character is #.

If the character in the READ part of the row agrees with the character we have read after the * in the input section, we know we have found the correct row to execute. If not, we hunt for the next Δ and examine the next encoded row, to see if it is the right one and so on.

Once we have found the correct encoded row to execute next, we mark it with a * in front (so we can find it later) and determine what character it wants us to write, and in which direction it wants us to move the simulated TAPE HEAD.

We then toddle off up the TAPE, past $, to the * and make the indicated change in the contents of the cell after the *, and move the * according to the directions of the row being simulated.

The way we carry this information up the *UTM* TAPE is to follow various alternate paths in the *UTM* program: one path hunts for the * after the $ remembering that it wants to print a *b* and move the simulated TAPE HEAD marking * left; one path knows to print a Δ and move the * right.

There must be a separate possible path for each of the (finitely many) separate possibilities. Reading the row to be executed tells the *UTM* which path to follow up the TAPE.

We must always check to see whether a row puts us in state 2. If so, we halt. The test to see whether a row leads to halt is this.

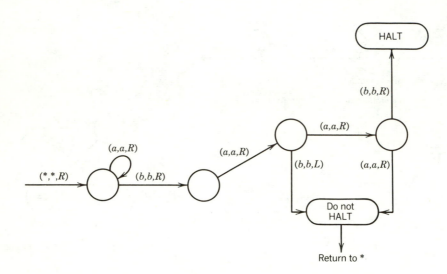

If while looking for the possible next row to execute we read the $, we crash since the machine we are trying to simulate does not have an edge leaving the state it is in labeled with the letter it is reading.

The machine we have been designing will test to see whether a code word from CWL can be accepted by the TM it encodes. This machine will accept exactly the language MATHISON.

If the input word does not represent a machine or the machine does not reach HALT on the input of its own code word, then the *UTM* will loop or crash. Therefore, this *UTM* proves that MATHISON is recursively enumerable. ∎

UTM is a very interesting machine that we shall discuss further in a moment, but first let us draw some more conclusions from Theorem 62.

Let us reason as follows:

1. CWL is regular because it is defined by a regular expression.
2. The complement of CWL in {*a,b*}*, called CWL′, is therefore also regular (Theorem 11).
3. CWL′ is r.e. (Theorem 45).

4.   CWL′ + MATHISON is r.e. (Theorem 60).

5.   The complement of (CWL′ + MATHISON) is ALAN, since ALAN is all code words not in MATHISON.

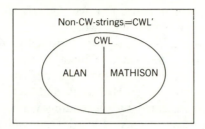

6.   But ALAN is not r.e. (Theorem 61).

Therefore, we have proven:

THEOREM 63

The complement of a recursively enumerable language may not be recursively enumerable.   ■

We know that MATHISON is a r.e. language, but is it recursive? CWL′ is regular and therefore also recursive. Even though it was not proven in the text (but see Chapter 28, Problem 20), the union of two recursive languages is also recursive. Therefore, if MATHISON is recursive so is:

$$\text{MATHISON} + \text{CWL}' = \text{ALAN}' = \text{the complement of ALAN}$$

But, by Theorem 58, this would mean that ALAN is recursive, which is not true, ALAN is not even r.e.. Therefore we have proven:

THEOREM 64

There are recursively enumerable languages that are not recursive.   ■

In other words, there are languages that are accepted by TM's but only by TM's that must loop forever on some inputs. There does not exist an algorithm that changes all loop words into reject words for all machines. The possibility that some inputs to a TM loop forever is unpleasant but unavoidable. This is at the heart of what makes some problems undecidable. The TM that makes the decision might loop forever. This prevents the TM from being considered a decision procedure.

Let us return now to consider the machine *UTM* we outlined for the proof of Theorem 62. It has a program section and a data section and when we ran it it simulated the action of the program on the data. However, at no time did we make use of the fact that the data word was the same as the program word. What would happen if we fed *UTM* a program word from CWL and a completely arbitrary data word?

If we start by placing a # on its TAPE originally, then the code word for some arbitary TM, then a $, then any input string sitting in alternate cells, *UTM* will simulate the execution of the encoded TM operating on the given input string. It will terminate at HALT if and only if the given string is accepted by the TM represented by the coding word.

To build a machine that accepts MATHISON, which is what Theorem 62 was about, we made the first action of *UTM* be to make two copies of the string fed it as input and then we began operation on that form. From now on, we skip that step and say that the input to *UTM* must be in the form

$$\# \ (a \ + \ b)^* \ \$ \ (a \ + \ b)^*$$

Here we have the beginning of a stored-program computer. The information on the left of the $ is the program (or algorithm) we feed in and the string on the right of the $ is the data. *UTM* then executes the requested operations on the given data. The program for *UTM* itself never changes. The operations it performs change based on the instructions (the encoded TM) and the data (the input string).

This *UTM*, which can simulate the action of any TM on any input, is called the **Universal Turing Machine.** Turing designed it in 1936, and it is not only the foundation of all Computer Theory, but it was also the conceptual archetype of the early computers.

The simple operations a Turing machine executes (read, move, write) can be implemented electronically. This is not by any means the simplest way to build a computer, but it did provide a theoretical proof that electronic computers could be built, that is only to say computers that do what TM's do. We have seen TM's only as acceptors, not as arithmetic calculators. In Chapter 31 we shall see them as full computers.

The design of the first stored-program computer that performed arithmetic operations and branched on logical comparisons and could modify its program, and so on, as modern computers do, was constructed by von Neumann and coworkers within a few years of Turing's work.

We mentioned earlier in this chapter that Theorem 61 proved that there could not be a computer that pretested programs to tell if they will run successfully. One word will explain why the existence of *UTM* does not contradict this: loop. If the input is accepted by the encoded TM, then *UTM* will halt; however, if the input loops on the encoded TM, then it must also loop forever on *UTM*. *UTM* is therefore *not* an effective decision procedure.

We shall discuss this further in Chapter 31 (Theorem 76).

Before we leave this chapter there is one point that deserves further attention. In the Universal Turing Machine we made use of auxiliary symbols in the TAPE alphabet Γ. We used #, $, *, A, and X, as well as a and b. However, the TM's we encoded were presumed to use only the symbols a, b, and # and Δ. This is fair since there is a theorem that we did not prove that says that any recursively enumerable language over the alphabet $\{a, b\}$ can be accepted by a TM that employs only the symbols a and b in its TAPE alphabet. Of course, it also uses blanks on the TAPE. But we do not even need this theorem.

If we should want to consider a language over a larger alphabet, say

$$\{p, \ q, \ r, \ s, \ t\}$$

then we can encode these letters and make the whole language into words over $\{a,b\}$.

This can be done as follows. Start with the correspondence

Letter		Code
p	=	*aaa*
q	=	*aab*
r	=	*aba*
s	=	*abb*
t	=	*baa*

Now every string over $\{p,q,r,s,t\}$ will become a string over $\{a,b\}$.

$$pqqstp = a\,a\,a\,a\,a\,b\,a\,a\,b\,a\,b\,b\,b\,a\,a\,a\,a\,a$$

If a certain language over $\{p,q,r,s,t\}$ is r.e., then so is the encoded language and vice versa. An instruction of the form (p, s, R) converts into instructions that say "Read three cells. If they contain *aaa*, then change them to *abb* and leave the TAPE HEAD three cells to the right of where it started."

It is for this reason that we have concentrated on languages over the alphabet $\Sigma = \{a,b\}$ for 99% of this book. We should also admit that we secretly realize that the languages we are most interested in are sets of bit strings to be fed into digital computers. In this case, $a = 0$, $b = 1$, (or vice versa).

PROBLEMS

Convert the following TM's first into summary tables and then into their code
words in CWL. What are the six languages accepted by these TM's?

1.

2.

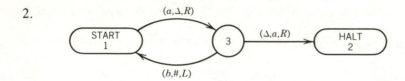

3.

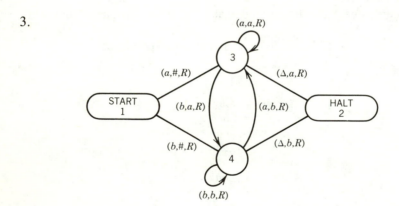

4.

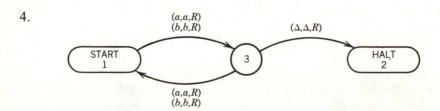

5.

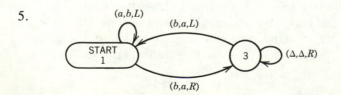

6.

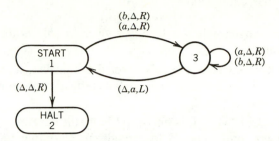

7. Run each of the six encoded words on their respective machines to see which are in the language ALAN.

8. Can the code word for any TM be a palindrome? Prove your answer.

Decode the following words from CWL into their corresponding TM's and run them on their corresponding TM's to see which are in ALAN and which are in MATHISON.

9. *a b a a b b b b a b*

10. *a b a a b a a b b a*

11. *a b a a b a a b b b*

12. *a b a a a b a a a b b a a a b a a b a b b b b*

13. *a b a a a b a a a b a a a a b a a b a b b a b*

14. *a b a b a b a b a b*

15. Let L be a language and L' its complement. Prove that one of the following three cases must be true:
    (i)   Both L and L' are recursive.
    (ii) Neither L nor L' is r.e.
    (iii) One is r.e., but not recursive while the other is not r.e.

16. In Chapter 20 we showed that the language $\{a^n b^n c^n\}$ over the alphabet $\{a, b, c\}$ is non-context-free. Encode this language into a language over the alphabet $\{a, b\}$. Is the encoded language context-free?

17. (i) Working with the alphabet $\{a, b, c\}$ there is a language defined by the regular expression

    a*b (ca + bb)*

    Encode this language into a language over $\{a, b\}$. Is the encoded language regular?

    (ii) Show that if a language is regular over one alphabet, then it is still regular when encoded in a different alphabet, by any substitution code.

18. What happens to a CFL when it is encoded? Is it still necessarily context-free? (Of course you are supposed to provide an algorithm to construct the grammar if the answer is yes and to provide an example if the answer is no.)

19. In this chapter we skipped over one interesting problem. Given a TM, there are many different ways we can write its summary table (we can arrange the rows in many different orders). Each way of writing the summary table gives a slightly different code word. In other words, the same TM can have many different code words. Show that this problem does not change any of the theorems in this chapter.

20. (Oddly enough, this problem has nothing to do with Computer Theory, yet it has everything to do with the contents of this chapter.)

    In the English language we can observe that some adjectives apply to themselves. For example the word "short" is a fairly short word. We might say: "Short" is short. Also the adjective "polysyllabic" is indeed polysyllabic. Some other possible adjectives of this type are "unfrequent", "melodious", "unhyphenated", "English", "harmless". Let us call all of these adjectives that describe themselves *homothetic*. Let us call all other adjectives (those that do not decribe themselves) *heterothetic*. For example, the words "gymnastic", "myopic", "recursive" are all heterothetic adjectives. The word "heterothetic" is an adjective and therefore like all adjectives it is either homothetic or heterothetic. Which is it?

CHAPTER 30

THE CHOMSKY HIERARCHY

We have not yet developed all the information presented in the table at the beginning of Chapter 24. For one thing, we have not discovered the language structures that define recursively enumerable sets independent of the concept of TM's. This we shall do now.

Why were context-free languages called "context-free"? The answer is that if there is a production $N \rightarrow t$, where N is a nonterminal and t is a terminal, then the replacement of t for N can be made in *any* situation in any working string. This gave us the uncomfortable problem of the itchy itchy itchy bear in Chapter 13. It could give us even worse problems.

As an example, we could say that in English the word "base" can mean cowardly, while "ball" can mean a dance. If we employ the CFG model we could introduce the productions:

$$base \rightarrow cowardly$$

$$ball \rightarrow dance$$

and we could modify some working string as follows:

$$baseball \Rightarrow cowardly \ dance$$

What is wrong here is that although "base" *can* sometimes mean cowardly it does not always have that option. In general, we have many synonyms for any English word; each is a possibility for substitution:

base → foundation | alkali | headquarters | safety-station | cowardly | mean

However, it is not true in English that base can be replaced by any one of these words in each of the sentences in which it occurs. What matters is the *context* of the phrase in which the word appears. English is therefore not an example of a CFL. This is true even though, as we saw in Chapter 13, the model for context-free languages was originally abstracted from human language grammars. Still, in English we need more information before proceeding with a substitution. This information can be in the form of the knowledge of the adjoining words:

base line → starting point

base metal → not precious metal

way off base → very mistaken | far from home

Here we are making use of some of the context in which the word sits to know which substitutions are allowed, where by "context" we mean the adjoining words in the sentence. The term "context" could mean other things, such as the general topic of the paragraph in which the phrase sits, however for us "context" means some number of the surrounding words.

Instead of replacing one character by a string of characters as in CFG's, we are now considering replacing one whole string of characters (terminals and nonterminals) by another. This is a new kind of production and it gives us a new kind of grammar. We carry over all the terminology from CFG's such as *"working string"* and *"the language generated."* The only change is in the form of the productions. We are developing a new mathematical model that more accurately describes the possible substitutions occurring in English and other human languages. There is also a useful connection to Computer Theory, as we shall see.

DEFINITION

A **phrase-structure grammar** is a collection of three things:

1 An alphabet Σ of letters called **terminals.**
2 A finite set of symbols called **nonterminals** that includes the **start symbol** S.
3 A finite list of productions of the form:

$$\text{String } 1 \to \text{String } 2$$

where String 1 can be any string of terminals and nonterminals that contains at least one nonterminal and where String 2 is any string of terminals and nonterminals whatsoever.

A **derivation** in a phrase-structure grammar is a series of working strings beginning with the start symbol S, which, by making substitutions according to the productions, arrives at a string of all terminals, at which point generation must stop.

The **language generated** by a phrase-structure grammar is the set of all strings of terminals that can be derived starting at S. ■

EXAMPLE

The following is a phrase-structure grammar over $\Sigma = \{a, b\}$ with nonterminals X and S:

$$\text{PROD 1} \quad S \rightarrow XS \mid \Lambda$$
$$\text{PROD 2} \quad X \rightarrow aX \mid a$$
$$\text{PROD 3} \quad aaaX \rightarrow ba$$

This is an odd set of rules. The first production says that we can start with S and derive any number of symbols of type X, for example,

$$S \Rightarrow XS$$
$$\Rightarrow XXS$$
$$\Rightarrow XXXS$$
$$\Rightarrow XXXXS$$
$$\Rightarrow XXXX$$

The second production shows us that each X can be any string of a's (with at least one a):

$$X \Rightarrow aX$$
$$\Rightarrow aaX$$
$$\Rightarrow aaaX$$
$$\Rightarrow aaaaX$$
$$\Rightarrow aaaaa$$

The third production says that any time we find three a's and an X we can replace these four symbols with the two-terminal string ba.

The following is a summary of one possible derivation in this grammar:

$$S \overset{*}{\Rightarrow} XXXXX$$
$$\overset{*}{\Rightarrow} aaaaaXXXX \qquad (\text{after } X \overset{*}{\Rightarrow} aaaaa)$$

$$\Rightarrow aabaXXXX \qquad \text{(by Prod 3)}$$

$$\Rightarrow aabaaaXXX \qquad \text{(after } X \overset{*}{\Rightarrow} aa\text{)}$$
$$\Rightarrow aabbaXX \qquad \text{(Prod 3)}$$

$$\Rightarrow aabbaaaX \qquad \text{(after } X \overset{*}{\Rightarrow} aa\text{)}$$
$$\Rightarrow aabbba \qquad \text{(after Prod 3)} \qquad \blacksquare$$

This is certainly a horse of a different color. The algorithms that we used for CFG's must now be thrown out the window. Chomsky Normal Form is out. Sometimes applying a production that is not a Λ-production still makes a working string get shorter. Terminals that used to be in a working string can disappear. Left-most derivations do not always exist. The CYK algorithm does not apply. We can't tell the terminals from the nonterminals without a scorecard. It is no longer possible just to read the list of nonterminals off of the left sides of productions.

All CFG's are phrase-structure grammars in which we restrict ourselves as to what we put on the left-side of productions. So all CFL's can be generated by phrase-structure grammars. Can any other languages be generated by them?

THEOREM 65

At least one language that cannot be generated by a CFG can be generated by a phrase-structure grammar.

PROOF

To prove this assertion by constructive methods we need only demonstrate one actual language with this property. A nonconstructive proof might be to show that the assumption:

$$\text{phrase-structure grammar} = \text{CFG}$$

leads to some devious contradiction, but as usual, we shall employ the preferred constructive approach here. (Theorem 61 was proved by devious contradiction and see what became of that.)

Consider the following phrase-structure grammar over the alphabet $\Sigma = \{a, b\}$.

$$\begin{array}{lll}
\text{Prod 1} & S \rightarrow aSBA \\
\text{Prod 2} & S \rightarrow abA \\
\text{Prod 3} & AB \rightarrow BA \\
\text{Prod 4} & bB \rightarrow bb \\
\text{Prod 5} & bA \rightarrow ba \\
\text{Prod 6} & aA \rightarrow aa
\end{array}$$

We shall show that the language generated by this grammar is $\{a^n b^n a^n\}$, which we have shown in Chapter 20 is non-context-free.

First let us see one example of a derivation in this grammar:

$$
\begin{array}{ll}
S \Rightarrow aSBA & \text{PROD 1} \\
\Rightarrow aaSBABA & \text{PROD 1} \\
\Rightarrow aaaSBABABA & \text{PROD 1} \\
\Rightarrow aaaabABABABA & \text{PROD 2} \\
\Rightarrow aaaabBAABABA & \text{PROD 3} \\
\Rightarrow aaaabBABAABA & \text{PROD 3} \\
\Rightarrow aaaabBBAAABA & \text{PROD 3} \\
\Rightarrow aaaabBBAABAA & \text{PROD 3} \\
\Rightarrow aaaabBBABAAA & \text{PROD 3} \\
\Rightarrow aaaabBBBAAAA & \text{PROD 3} \\
\Rightarrow aaaabbBBAAAA & \text{PROD 4} \\
\Rightarrow aaaabbbBAAAA & \text{PROD 4} \\
\Rightarrow aaaabbbbAAAA & \text{PROD 4} \\
\Rightarrow aaaabbbbaAAA & \text{PROD 5} \\
\Rightarrow aaaabbbbaaAA & \text{PROD 6} \\
\Rightarrow aaaabbbbaaaA & \text{PROD 6} \\
\Rightarrow aaaabbbbaaaa & \text{PROD 6} \\
= a^4 b^4 a^4 &
\end{array}
$$

To generate the word $a^m b^m a^m$ for some fixed number m (we have used n to mean any power in the defining symbol for this language), we could proceed as follows.

First we use PROD 1 exactly $(m - 1)$ times. This gives us the working string:

$$
\underbrace{aa \ldots a}_{m-1} \quad S \quad \underbrace{BABA \ldots BA}_{\substack{(m-1) \text{ B's alternating} \\ \text{with} \\ (m-1) \text{ A's}}}
$$

Next we apply PROD 2 once. This gives us the working string:

$$
\underbrace{aa \ldots a}_{m} \quad b \quad \underbrace{ABAB \ldots BA}_{\substack{m \text{ A's} \\ m - 1 \text{ B's}}}
$$

Now we apply PROD 3 enough times to move the B's in front of the A's. Note that we should not let our mathematical background fool us into thinking that $AB \rightarrow BA$ means that the A's and B's commute. No. We cannot replace BA with AB—only the other way around. The A's can move to the right through the B's. The B's can move to the left through the A's. We can only separate them into the arrangement B's then A's. We then obtain the working string:

$$\underbrace{aa \ldots a}_{m} \quad b \quad \underbrace{BB \ldots B}_{m-1} \quad \underbrace{AA \ldots A}_{m}$$

Now using PRODS 4, 5, and 6, we can move left through the working string converting B's to b's and then A's to a's.

We will finally obtain:

$$\underbrace{aa \ldots a}_{m} \quad \underbrace{bb \ldots b}_{m} \quad \underbrace{aa \ldots a}_{m}$$

$$= a^m b^m a^m$$

We have not yet proven that $\{a^n b^n a^n\}$ is the language generated by the original grammar, only that all such words can be derived. To finish the proof, we must show that no word not in $\{a^n b^n a^n\}$ can be generated. We must show that every word that is derived *is* of the form $a^n b^n a^n$ for some n.

Let us consider some unknown derivation in this phrase-structure grammar. We begin with the start symbol S and we *must* immediately apply either PROD 1 or PROD 2. If we start with PROD 2, the only word we can generate is *aba*, which is of the approved form.

If we begin with a PROD 1, we get the working string:

$$a\ SBA$$

which is of the form:

$$\underbrace{\rule{2cm}{0pt}}_{\text{some } a\text{'s}} \quad S \quad \underbrace{\rule{3cm}{0pt}}_{\text{equal } A\text{'s and } B\text{'s}}$$

The only productions we can apply are PRODS 1, 2, and 3, since we do not yet have any substrings of the form bB, bA, or aA. PROD 1 and PROD 3 leave the form just as above, whereas once we use PROD 2 we immediately obtain a working string of the form:

$$\underbrace{\rule{2cm}{0pt}}_{a\text{'s}} \quad abA \quad \underbrace{\rule{3cm}{0pt}}_{\text{equal } A\text{'s and } B\text{'s}}$$

If we never apply PROD 2, we never remove the character S from the working string and therefore we never obtain a word. PROD 2 can be applied only one time, since there is never more than one S in the working string.

Therefore, in every derivation before we have applied PROD 2 we have applied some (maybe none) PROD 1's and PROD 3's. Let the number of PROD 1's we have applied be m. We shall now demonstrate that the final word generated must be

$$a^{m+1}b^{m+1}a^{m+1}$$

Right after PROD 2 is applied the working string looks like this:

$$\underbrace{\qquad\qquad}_{\text{exactly } m \ a\text{'s}} \quad abA \quad \underbrace{\qquad\qquad}_{\substack{\text{exactly } m \ A\text{'s} \\ m \ B\text{'s} \\ \text{in some order}}}$$

The only productions we can apply now are PRODS 3, 4, 5, and 6. Let us look at the working string this way:

$$a^{m+1} \quad b \quad \underbrace{|\text{nonterminals}|}_{\substack{m+1 \ A\text{'s} \\ m \quad B\text{'s}}}$$

Any time we apply PROD 3 we are just scrambling the right half of the string, the sequence of nonterminals. When we apply PROD 4, 5, or 6 we are converting a nonterminal into a terminal, but it must be the nonterminal on the border between the left-side terminal string and the right-side nonterminal string. We always keep the shape:

$$\text{terminals} \qquad \text{Nonterminals}$$

(just as with leftmost Chomsky derivations), until we have all terminals. The A's eventually become a's and the B's eventually become b's. However, none of the rules PROD 4, PROD 5, or PROD 6 can create the substring ab. We can create bb, ba, or aa, but never ab. From this point on the pool of A's and B's will be converted into a's and b's without the substring ab. That means it must eventually assume the form $b*a*$.

$$a^{m+1}b \quad \underbrace{|\text{nonterminals}|}_{\substack{m+1 \ A\text{'s} \\ m \quad B\text{'s}}}$$

must become

$$a^{m+1} \quad b \quad b^m \quad a^{m+1}$$

which is what we wanted to prove. ∎

As with CFG's, it is possible to define and construct a *total language tree* for a phrase-structure grammar. To every node we apply as many productions as we can along different branches. Some branches lead to words, some may not. The total language tree for a phrase-structure language may have very short words way out on very long branches (which is not the case with CFL's). This is because productions can sometimes shorten the working string, as in the example:

$$S \rightarrow aX$$
$$X \rightarrow aX$$
$$aaaaaaX \rightarrow b$$

The derivation for the word *ab* is:

$$S \Rightarrow aX$$
$$\Rightarrow aaX$$
$$\Rightarrow aaaX$$
$$\Rightarrow aaaaX$$
$$\Rightarrow aaaaaX$$
$$\Rightarrow aaaaaaX$$
$$\Rightarrow aaaaaaaX$$
$$\Rightarrow ab$$

EXAMPLE

The total language tree for the phrase-structure grammar for $\{a^n b^n a^n\}$ above begins

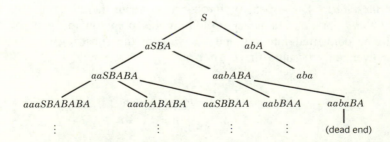

Notice the interesting thing that can happen in a phrase-structure grammar. A working string may contain nonterminals and yet no production can be applied to it. Such a working string is not a word in the language of the grammar it is a dead end. ∎

The **phrase-structure languages** (those languages generated by phrase-structure grammars) are a larger class of languages than the CFL's. This is fine with us, since CFG's are inadequate to describe all the languages accepted by Turing machines.

We found that the languages accepted by FA's are also those definable by regular expressions and that the languages accepted by PDA's are also those definable by CFG's. What we need now is some method of defining the languages accepted by Turing machines that does not make reference to the machines themselves (simply *calling* them recursively enumerable contributes nothing to our understanding). Perhaps phrase-structure languages are what we need. (Good guess.) Also, since we already know that some languages cannot be accepted by TM's, perhaps we can find a method of defining *all possible* languages, not just the r.e. languages. Although we have placed very minimal restrictions on the shape of their productions, phrase-structure grammars do not have to be totally unstructured, as we see from the following result.

THEOREM 66

If we have a phrase-structure grammar that generates the language L, then there is another grammar that also generates L that has the same alphabet of terminals and in which each production is of the form:

$$\text{string of Nonterminals} \rightarrow \text{string of terminals and Nonterminals}$$

(where the left side cannot be Λ but the right side can).

PROOF

This proof will be by constructive algorithm using the same trick as in the proof of Theorem 23.

Step 1   For each terminal $a, b, \ldots$ introduce a *new* nonterminal (one not used before): $A, B, \ldots$ and change every string of terminals and nonterminals into a string of nonterminals above by using the new symbols. For example,

$$aSbXb \rightarrow bbXYX$$

becomes

$$ASBXB \rightarrow BBXYX$$

Step 2   Add the new productions

$$A \rightarrow a$$
$$B \rightarrow b$$

These replacements and additions obviously generate the same language and fit the desired description. In fact, the new grammar fits a stronger requirement. Every production is either:

string of Nonterminals $\rightarrow$ string of Nonterminals

or

one Nonterminal $\rightarrow$ one terminal

(where the right side can be Λ but not the left side)   ■

EXAMPLE

The phrase-structure grammar over the alphabet $\{a,b\}$, which generates $\{a^n b^n a^n\}$, which we saw above:

$$S \rightarrow aSBA$$
$$S \rightarrow abA$$
$$AB \rightarrow BA$$
$$bB \rightarrow bb$$
$$bA \rightarrow ba$$
$$aA \rightarrow aa$$

turns into the following, when the algorithm of Theorem 66 is applied to it:

$$S \rightarrow XSBA$$
$$S \rightarrow XYA$$
$$AB \rightarrow BA$$
$$YB \rightarrow YY$$
$$YA \rightarrow YX$$
$$XA \rightarrow XX$$
$$X \rightarrow a$$
$$Y \rightarrow b$$

Notice that we had to choose new symbols, X and Y, because A and B were already being employed as nonterminals.

■

DEFINITION

A phrase-structure grammar is called **type 0** if each production is of the form:

non-empty string of Nonterminals $\rightarrow$ any string of terminals and Nonterminals

■

The second grammar above is type 0. Actually, what we have shown by Theorem 66 is that all phrase-structure grammars are equivalent to type 0 grammars in the sense that they generate the same languages.

Some authors *define* type 0 grammars by exactly the same definition as we gave for phrase-structure grammars. Now that we have proven Theorem 66, we may join the others and use the two terms interchangeably, forgetting our original definition of type 0 as distinct from phrase-structure. As usual, the literature on this subject contains even more terms for the same grammars, such as *unrestricted grammars* and *semi-Thue* grammars.

Beware of the sloppy definition that says that type 0 includes all productions of the form:

any string $\rightarrow$ any string

since that would allow one string of terminals (on the left) to be replaced by some other string (on the right). This goes against the philosophy of what a *terminal* is, and we do not allow it. Nor do we allow frightening productions of the form: $\Lambda \rightarrow$ *something* which could cause letters to pop into words indiscriminately (see *Gen*, I:3 for "$\Lambda \rightarrow$ light").

Names such as *nonterminal-rewriting grammars* and *context-sensitive-with-erasing grammars* also turn out to generate the same languages as type 0. These names reflect other nuances of Formal Language Theory into which we do not delve.

One last remark about the name type 0. It is not pronounced like the universal blood donor but rather as "type zero." The 0 is a number, and there are other numbered types.

Type 0 is one of the four classes of grammars that Chomsky, in 1959, catalogued in a hierarchy of grammars according to the structure of their productions.

The Chomsky Hierarchy of Grammars

Type	Name of Languages Generated	Production Restrictions $X \rightarrow Y$	Acceptor
0	Phrase-structure = recursively enumerable	X = any string with nonterminals Y = any string	TM
1	Context-sensitive	X = any string with nonterminals Y = any string as long as or longer than X	TM's with bounded (not infinite) TAPE, called linear-bounded automata LBA's‡
2	Context-free	X = one nonterminal Y = any string	PDA
3	Regular	X = one nonterminal Y = tN or $Y = t$ t terminal N nonterminal	FA

‡The size of the tape is a linear function of the length of the input.

We have not yet proven all the claims on this table, nor shall we. We have completely covered the cases of type 2 and type 3 grammars. Type 1 grammars are called context-sensitive because they use some information about the context of a nonterminal before allowing a substitution. However, they require that no production shorten the length of the working string, which enables us to use the top-down parsing techniques discussed in Chapter 22. Because they are very specialized, we skip them altogether. In this chapter we prove the theorem that type 0 grammars generate all recursively enumerable languages.

Two interesting languages are not on this chart. The set of all languages that can be accepted by deterministic PDA's is called simply the **deterministic context-free languages.** We have seen that they are closed under complementation, which makes more questions decidable. They are generated by what are called **LR(k)** grammars, which are grammars that generate words that can be parsed by being read from left to right taking k symbols at a time. This is a topic of special interest to compiler designers. This book is only an introduction and does not begin to exhaust the range of what a computer scientist needs to know about theory to be a competent practitioner.

The other interesting class of languages that is missing is the collection of recursive languages. No algorithm can, by looking only at the structure of the grammar, tell whether the language it generates is recursive—not counting the symbols, not describing the production strings, nothing.

These six classes of languages form a nested set as shown in the Venn diagram below.

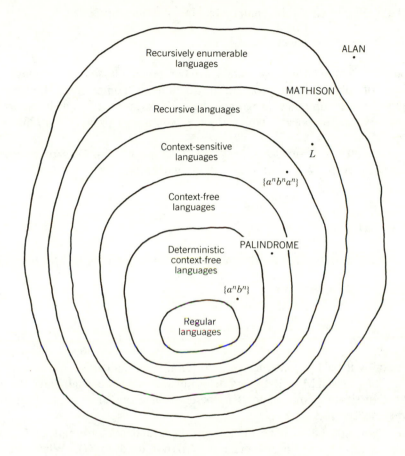

We have discussed most of the examples that show that no two of these categories are really the same. This is important, since just because a condition *looks* more restrictive does not mean it actually is in the sense that different languages fulfill it. Remember that FA = NFA.

$\{a^n b^n\}$ is deterministic context-free but not regular.

PALINDROME is context-free but not deterministic context-free. (We did not prove this. We did prove that the complement of $\{a^n b^n a^n\}$ is a CFL, but it cannot be accepted by a DPDA.)

$\{a^n b^n a^n\}$ is context-sensitive but not context-free. (The grammar we just examined above that generates this language meets the conditions for context-sensitivity.)

L stands for a language that is recursive but not context-sensitive. There are such but that proof is beyond our intended scope.

MATHISON is recursively enumerable but not recursive.

ALAN comes from outerspace.

Counting "outerspace," we actually have seven classes of languages. The language of all computer program instructions is context-free; however, the language of all computer programs themselves is r.e.. English is *probably* recursive except for poetry, which (as e.e. cummings proved in 1923) is from outerspace.

What is left for us to do is prove r.e. = type 0. This was first proven by Chomsky in 1959. We shall prove it in two parts.

THEOREM 67

If *L* is generated by a type 0 grammar *G*, then there is a TM that accepts *L*.

PROOF

The proof will be by constructive algorithm. We shall describe how to build such a TM. This TM will be nondeterministic, and we shall have to appeal to Theorem 56 to demonstrate that there is therefore also some deterministic TM that accepts *L*.

The TAPE alphabet will be all the terminals and nonterminals of *G* and the symbols $ and * (which we presume are not used in *G*). When we begin processing the TAPE contains a string of terminals. It will be accepted if it is generated by *G* but will be rejected otherwise.

Step 1   We place a $ in cell i moving the input to the right and place another $ in the cell after the input string and an *S* after that. We leave the TAPE HEAD pointing to the second $:

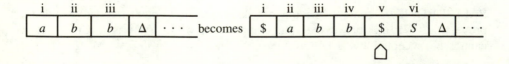

Each of these additions can be done with the subroutine INSERT.

Step 2　We create a *central state* with nondeterministic branching that simulates the replacement indicated by every possible production applied to the string of terminals and nonterminals to the right of the second $. (This state is analogous to the central POP state in the proof of Theorem 28.) There are three possible forms for the TM instructions, depending on the type of replacement we are simulating.

First, we can have a production of the form larger → smaller, such as,

$$aSbX \rightarrow Yb$$

Corresponding to this production we must have a branch coming from the central state that does the following:

1.　Scan to the right for the next occurrence on the TAPE of the substring $aSbX$.
2.　Replace it on the TAPE with $Yb**$.
3.　Delete the *'s closing up the data.
4.　Return the TAPE HEAD to the second $.
5.　Return to the central state.

We have already seen how to write TM programming to accomplish all five of these steps.
Secondly, the production could be of the form smaller → larger, such as,

$$aS \rightarrow bbXY$$

Then we:

1.　Scan to the right for the next occurrence on the TAPE of the substring aS.
2.　Insert two blanks after the S, moving the rest of the string two cells to the right.
3.　Replace the $aS\Delta\Delta$ with $bbXY$.
4.　Return TAPE HEAD to the second $, and
5.　Return to the central state.

Thirdly, both sides of the production could be the same length such as,

$$AB \rightarrow XY$$

In this case we need only

1.   Scan to the right for the next occurrence of substring *AB*.
2.   Replace *AB* with *XY*.
3.   Return the TAPE HEAD to the second $, and
4.   Return to the central state.

   Conceiveably the substring of *aSbX*, *aS* or *AB* that is replaced in the working string in the production we are trying to simulate might be the third or fourth occurrence of such a substring in the working string not the very next, as we have insisted. To account for this we must have the option while in the central state of simply advancing the TAPE HEAD to the right over the working string without causing change.

Eventually, if we have made the correct nondeterministic choices of loops around the central state, we can accomplish the simulation of any particular derivation of the input word beyond the second $. We shall have derived a twin copy of the input string.

The TAPE then looks like this:

$	input	$	twin copy	Δ $\cdots$

   Notice that we can arrive at the twin copy situation only if the input word can, in fact, be derived from the grammar *G*.

Step 3   When we have completed Step 2 we nondeterministically take a branch out of the central state that will let us compare the copy we have produced to the original input string cell by cell to be sure that they are the same. If so, we accept the input. If no sequence of simulated productions turns *S* into the input string, then the input is not in *L* and cannot be accepted by this TM.

   Since the loops out of the central state accurately parallel all possible productions in *G* at all times in the processing, the string to the right of $ will be a valid (derivable) working string in *G*. If we have nondeterministically made the wrong choices and produced a word other than the input string, or if we have jumped out of the central state too soon before the working string has been turned into a string of all terminals, we must crash during the comparison of product string and input string. No inputs not in the language of *G* can be accepted and all words derivable from *G* can be accepted by some set of nondeterministic choices. Therefore the machine accepts exactly the language *L*.   ■

EXAMPLE

Starting with the type 0 grammar:

$$S \rightarrow aSb \mid bS \mid a$$
$$bS \rightarrow aS$$

A crude outline for the corresponding TM is

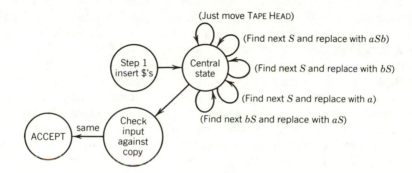

We now turn to the second half of the equivalence.

THEOREM 68

If a language is r.e., it can be generated by a type 0 grammar.

PROOF

The proof will be by constructive algorithm. We must show how to create a type 0 grammar that generates exactly the same words as are accepted by a given Turing machine. From now on we fix in our minds a particular TM.

Our general goal is to construct a set of productions that "simulate" the working of this TM. But here we run into a problem: unlike the simulations of TM's by PM's or 2PDA's, a grammar does not start with an input and run it to halt. A grammar must start with S and end up with the word. To overcome this discrepancy our grammar must first generate all possible strings of a's and b's and then test them by simulating the action of the TM upon them.

As we know, a TM can mutilate an input string pretty badly on its way to the HALT state, so our grammar must preserve a second copy of the input as a backup. We keep the backup copy intact while we act on the other as if it were running on the input TAPE of our TM. If this TM ever gets to a HALT state, we erase what is left of the mutilated copy and are left with the pristine copy as the word generated by the grammar. If the second copy does not run successfully on the TM (it crashes, is rejected, or loops forever), then we never get to the stage of erasing the working copy. Since the working copy contains nonterminals, this means that we never produce a string of all terminals. This will prevent us from ever successfully generating a word not in the language accepted by the TM. A derivation that never ends corresponds to an input that loops forever. A derivation that gets stuck at a working string with nonterminals still in it corresponds to an input that crashes. A derivation that produces a word corresponds to an input that runs successfully to HALT.

That is a rough description of the method we shall follow. The hard part is this: Where can we put the two different copies of the string so that the productions can act on only one copy, never on the other? In a derivation in a grammar, there is only one working string generated at any time. Even in phrase-structure grammars, any production can be applied to any part of the working string at any time. How do we keep the two copies separate? How do we keep the first copy intact (immune from distortion by production) while we work on the second copy?

The surprising answer to this question is that we keep the copies separate by interlacing them. We store them in alternate locations on the working string, just as we used the even and the odd numbered cells of the TM TAPE to store the contents of the two PUSHDOWN STACKS in the proof of Theorem 48.

We also use parentheses as nonterminals to keep straight which letters are in which copy. All letters following a "(" are in the first (intact) copy. All symbols before a ")" are in the second (TM TAPE simulation) copy. We say "symbol" here because we may find any symbol from the TM TAPE sitting to the left of a ")".

When we are finally ready to derive the final word because the second copy has been accepted by the TM, we must erase not only the remnants of the second copy but also the parentheses and any other nonterminals used as TM-simulation tools.

First, let us outline the procedure in even more detail, then formalize it, and then finally illustrate it.

Step 1   Eventually we need to be able to test each possible string of a's and b's to see whether it is accepted by the TM. We need enough productions to cover these cases. Since a string such as *abba* will be represented initially by the working string:

$$(aa)\ (bb)\ (bb)\ (aa)$$

the following productions will suffice:

$$S \rightarrow (aa)\ S \mid (bb)\ S \mid \Lambda$$

Later we shall see that we actually need something slightly different because of other requirements of the processing.

Remember that "(and)" are nonterminal characters in our type 0 grammar that must be erased at the final step.

Remember that the first letter in each parenthesized pair will stay immutable while we simulate TM processing on the second letter of each pair *as if* the string of second letters were the contents of TM TAPE during the course of the simulation.

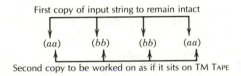

First copy of input string to remain intact

(aa)   (bb)   (bb)   (aa)

Second copy to be worked on as if it sits on TM TAPE

Step 2 Since a Turing machine can use more TAPE cells than just those that the input letters initially take up, we need to add some blank cells to the working string. We must give the TM enough TAPE to do its processing job. We do know that a TM has a TAPE with infinitely many cells available, *but* in the processing of any particular word it accepts, it employs only finitely many of those cells—a finite block of cells starting at cell i. If it tried to read infinitely many cells in one running, it would never finish and reach HALT. If the TM needs four extra cells of its TAPE to accept the word *abba*, we add four units of $(\Delta\Delta)$ to the end of the working string:

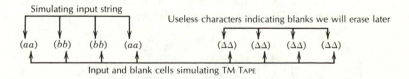

Simulating input string

Useless characters indicating blanks we will erase later

(aa) (bb) (bb) (aa)   ($\Delta\Delta$) ($\Delta\Delta$) ($\Delta\Delta$) ($\Delta\Delta$)

Input and blank cells simulating TM TAPE

Notice that we have had to make the symbol Δ a nonterminal in the grammar we are constructing.

Step 3 To simulate the action of a TM, we need to include in the working string an indication of *which* state we are in and *where* the TAPE

HEAD is reading. As with many of the TM simulations we have done before, we can handle both problems with the same device.

We shall do this as follows. Let the names of the states in the TM be q_0 (the start state) q_1 q_2. . . . We insert a q in front of the parentheses of the symbol now being read by the TAPE HEAD. To do this, we have to make all the q's nonterminals in our grammar.

Initially, the working string looks like this:

$$q_0 \ (aa) \ (bb) \ (bb) \ (aa) \ (\Delta\Delta) \ (\Delta\Delta) \ (\Delta\Delta) \ (\Delta\Delta)$$

It may sometime later look like this:

$$(aA) \ (b\Delta) \ (bX) \ q_6 \ (aA) \ (\Delta b) \ (\Delta M) \ (\Delta\Delta) \ (\Delta\Delta)$$

This will mean that the TAPE contents being simulated are $A\Delta XAbM\Delta\Delta$ and the TAPE HEAD is reading the fourth cell, while the simulated TM program is in state q_6.

To summarize, at every stage, the working string must:
1. remember the original input
2. represent the TAPE status
3. reflect the state the TM is in

Step 4   We also need to include as nonterminals in the grammar all the symbols that the TM might wish to write on its TAPE, the alphabet Γ. The use of these symbols was illustrated above.

Step 5   Now in the process of simulating the operation of the TM, the working string could look like this.

$$(aa) \ q_3 \ (bB) \ (b\Delta) \ (aA) \ (\Delta A) \ (\Delta A) \ (\Delta\Delta) \ (\Delta M)$$

The original string we are interested in is *abba,* and it is still intact in the positions just after "("'s.

The current status of the simulated TM TAPE can be read from the characters just in front of close parentheses. It is

i	ii	iii	iv	v	vi	vii	viii	
a	B	Δ	A	A	A	Δ	M	$\cdots$

The TM is in state q_3, and the TAPE HEAD is reading cell ii as we can tell from the positioning of the q_3 in the working string.

To continue this simulation, we need to be able to change

the working string to reflect the specific instructions in the particular TM, that is, we need to be able to simulate all possible changes in TAPE status that the TM program might produce.

Let us take an example of one possible TM instruction and see what productions we must include in our grammar to simulate its operation. If the TM says:

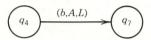

"from state q_4 while reading a b, print an A, go to state q_7, and move the TAPE HEAD left"

We need a production that causes our representation of the prior status of the TM to change into a working string that represents the outcome status of the TM. We need a production like:

$$(\text{Symbol}_1\ \text{Symbol}_2)\ q_4\ (\text{Symbol}_3\ b)$$
$$\rightarrow q_7\ (\text{Symbol}_1\ \text{Symbol}_2)\ (\text{Symbol}_3\ A)$$

where Symbol_1 and Symbol_3 are any letters in the input string (a or b) or the Δ's in the extra ($\Delta\Delta$) factors. Symbol_2 is what is in the TAPE in the cell to the left of the b being read. Symbol_2 will be read next by the simulated TAPE HEAD:

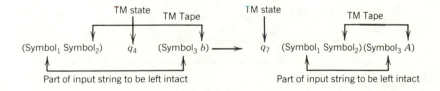

This is not just one production, but a whole family of possibilities covering all considerations of what Symbol_1, Symbol_2 and Symbol_3 are:

$$(aa)\ q_4\ (ab) \quad \rightarrow \quad q_7\ (aa)\ (aA)$$
$$(aa)\ q_4\ (bb) \quad \rightarrow \quad q_7\ (aa)\ (bA)$$
$$(aa)\ q_4\ (\Delta b) \quad \rightarrow \quad q_7\ (aa)\ (\Delta A)$$
$$(ab)\ q_4\ (ab) \quad \rightarrow \quad q_7\ (ab)\ (aA)$$
$$(ab)\ q_4\ (bb) \quad \rightarrow \quad q_7\ (ab)\ (bA)$$
$$\cdots$$
$$(bX)\ q_4\ (\Delta b) \quad \rightarrow \quad q_7\ (bX)\ (\Delta A)$$
$$\cdots$$

This is reminiscent of the technique used in the proof of Theorem 29, where one PDA-part gave rise to a whole family of productions, and for the same reasons one TM instruction can be applied to many different substring patterns.

The simulation of a TM instruction that moves the TAPE HEAD to the right can be handled the same way.

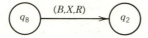

"If in a state q_8 reading a B, write an X, move the TAPE HEAD right, and go to state q_2" translates into the following family of productions:

$$q_8 \ (\text{Symbol}_1 \ B) \rightarrow (\text{Symbol}_1 \ X) \ q_2$$

where Symbol_1 is part of the immutable first copy of the input string or one of the extra Δ's on the right end. Happily, the move-right simulations do not involve as many unknown symbols of the working string.

Two consecutive cells on the TAPE that used to be

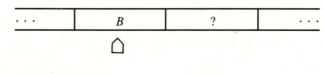

have now become

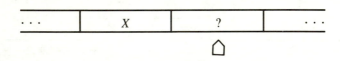

We need to include productions in our grammar for all possible values for Symbol_1.

Let us be clear here that we do not include in our grammar productions for all possible TM instructions, only for those instructions that do label edges in the specific TM we are trying to simulate.

Step 6   Finally, let us suppose that after generating the doubled form of the word and after simulating the operation of the TM on its TAPE, we eventually are led into a HALT state. This means that the input we started with is accepted by this TM. We then want to let the type 0 grammar finish the derivation of that word, in our example, the word *abba* by letting it mop up all the garbage left in the working string. The garbage is of several kinds: There are Δ's, the letters in $\Gamma = \{A,B,X,Y, \ldots\}$, the q symbol for the HALT state itself, and, let us not forget, the extra a's and b's that are lying around on what we think are TAPE-simulating locations but which just as easily could be mistaken for parts of the final word, and then, of course, the parentheses.

We also want to be very careful not to trigger this mop-up operation unless we have actually reached a HALT state.

We cannot simply add the productions:

$$\text{Unwanted symbols} \rightarrow \Lambda$$

since this would allow us to accept any input string at any time. Remember in a grammar (phrase-structure or other) we are at all times free to execute any production that can apply. To force the sequencing of productions, we must have some productions that introduce symbols that certain other productions need before they can be applied. What we need is something like:

[If there is a HALT state symbol in the working string, then every other needless Symbol and the q's] $\rightarrow \Lambda$

We can actually accomplish this conditional wipe-out in type 0 grammars in the following way: Suppose q_{11} is a HALT state. We first add productions that allow us to put a copy of q_{11} in front of each set of parentheses. This requires all possible productions of these two forms:

$$(\text{Symbol}_1 \ \text{Symbol}_2) \ q_{11} \rightarrow q_{11} (\text{Symbol}_1 \ \text{Symbol}_2) \ q_{11}$$

where Symbol_1 and Symbol_2 are any possible parenthesized pair. This allows q_{11} to propagate to the left.

We also need:

$$q_{11} (\text{Symbol}_1 \ \text{Symbol}_2) \rightarrow q_{11} (\text{Symbol}_1 \ \text{Symbol}_2) \ q_{11}$$

allowing q_{11} to propagate to the right.

This will let us spread the q_{11} to the front of each factor as soon as it makes its appearance in the working string. It is like a cold: Every factor catches it. In this example, we start with q_{11} in front of only one parenthesized pair and let it spread till it sits in front of every parenthesized pair.

(aA) (bB) q_{11} (bB) (aX) (ΔX) (ΔM)
$\Rightarrow (aA)$ q_{11} (bB) q_{11} (bB) (aX) (ΔX) (ΔM)
$\Rightarrow q_{11}$ (aA) q_{11} (bB) q_{11} (bB) (aX) (ΔX) (ΔM)
$\Rightarrow q_{11}$ (aA) q_{11} (bB) q_{11} (bB) q_{11} (aX) (ΔX) (ΔM)
$\Rightarrow q_{11}$ (aA) q_{11} (bB) q_{11} (bB) q_{11} (aX) q_{11} (ΔX) (ΔM)
$\Rightarrow q_{11}$ (aA) q_{11} (bB) q_{11} (bB) q_{11} (aX) q_{11} (ΔX) q_{11} (ΔM)

Remember, we allow this to happen only to the q's that are HALT states in the particular TM we are simulating. The q's that are not HALT states cannot be spread because we do not include such productions in our grammar to spread them.

Now we can include the garbage-removal productions:

$$q_{11} \ (a \ \text{Symbol}_1) \rightarrow a$$
$$q_{11} \ (b \ \text{Symbol}_1) \rightarrow b$$
$$q_{11} \ (\Delta \ \text{Symbol}_1) \rightarrow \Lambda$$

for any choice of Symbol_1. This will rid us of all the TAPE simulation characters, the extra Δ's, and the parentheses, leaving only the first copy of the original input string we were testing. Only the immutable copy remains; the scaffolding is completely removed.

Here are the formal rules describing the grammar we have in mind. In general, the productions for the desired type 0 grammar are the following, where we presume that S, X, Y are not letters in Σ or Γ:

PROD 1 $S \rightarrow q_0 X$
PROD 2 $X \rightarrow (aa) \ X$
PROD 3 $X \rightarrow (bb) \ X$
PROD 4 $X \rightarrow Y$
PROD 5 $Y \rightarrow (\Delta\Delta)Y$
PROD 6 $Y \rightarrow \Lambda$
PROD 7 For all TM edges of the form

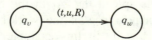

create the productions:

$$q_v \ (at) \rightarrow (au) \ q_w$$
$$q_v \ (bt) \rightarrow (bu) \ q_w$$
$$q_v \ (\Delta t) \rightarrow (\Delta u) \ q_w$$

PROD 8   For all TM edges of the form:

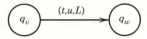

create the productions:

$$(\text{Symbol}_1 \ \text{Symbol}_2) \ q_v \ (\text{Symbol}_3 \ t) \rightarrow q_w \ (\text{Symbol}_1 \ \text{Symbol}_2) \ (\text{Symbol}_3 \ u)$$

where Symbol_1 and Symbol_3 can each be a, b, or Δ and Symbol_2 can be any character appearing on the TM TAPE, that is, any character in Γ.

This could be quite a large set of productions.

PROD 9   If q_x is a HALT state in the TM, create these productions:

$$q_x \ (\text{Symbol}_1 \ \text{Symbol}_2) \rightarrow q_x \ (\text{Symbol}_1 \ \text{Symbol}_2) \ q_x$$
$$(\text{Symbol}_1 \ \text{Symbol}_2) \ q_x \rightarrow q_x \ (\text{Symbol}_1 \ \text{Symbol}_2) \ q_x$$

$$q_x \ (a \ \text{Symbol}_2) \rightarrow a$$
$$q_x \ (b \ \text{Symbol}_2) \rightarrow b$$
$$q_x \ (\Delta \ \text{Symbol}_2) \rightarrow \Lambda$$

where $\text{Symbol}_1 = a$, b, or Δ and Symbol_2 is any character in Γ.

These are all the productions we need or want in the grammar.

Notice that productions 1 through 7 are the same for all TM's. Production sets 7, 8, and 9 depend on the particular TM being simulated.

Now come the remarks that convince us that this is the right grammar (or at least one of them). Since we must start with S, we begin with PROD 1. We can then apply any sequence of PROD 2's and PROD 3's so that for any string such as *baa* we can produce:

$$S \overset{*}{\Rightarrow} q_0 \ (bb) \ (aa) \ (aa) \ X$$

We can do this for any string whether it can be accepted by the TM or not. We have not yet formed a word, just a working string. If *baa* can be accepted by the TM, there is a certain amount of additional space it needs on the TAPE to do so, say two more cells. We can create this work space by using PROD 4, PROD 5, and PROD 6 as follows:

$$\Rightarrow q_0 \; (bb) \; (aa) \; (aa) \; Y$$

$$\Rightarrow q_0 \; (bb) \; (aa) \; (aa) \; (\Delta\Delta) \; Y$$

$$\Rightarrow q_0 \; (bb) \; (aa) \; (aa) \; (\Delta\Delta) \; (\Delta\Delta) \; Y$$

$$\Rightarrow q_0 \; (bb) \; (aa) \; (aa) \; (\Delta\Delta) \; (\Delta\Delta)$$

Other than the minor variation of leaving the Y lying around until the end and eventually erasing it, this is exactly how all derivations from this grammar must begin. The other productions cannot be applied yet since their left sides include nonterminals that have not yet been incorporated into the working string.

Now suppose that q_4 is the only HALT state in the TM. In order ever to remove the parentheses from the working string, we must eventually reach exactly this situation:

$$\overset{*}{\Rightarrow} q_4 \; (b \; ?) \; q_4 \; (a \; ?) \; q_4 \; (a \; ?) \; q_4 \; (\Delta \; ?) \; q_4 \; (\Delta \; ?)$$

where the five ?'s show some contents of the first five cells of the TM TAPE at the time it accepts the string *baa*. Notice that no rule of production can ever let us change the first entry inside a parenthesized pair. This is our intact copy of the input to our simulated TM.

We could only arrive at a working string of this form if, while simulating the processing of the TM, we entered the halt state q_4 at some stage.

$$\overset{*}{\Rightarrow} (b \; ?) \; (a \; ?) \; q_4 \; (a \; ?) \; (\Delta \; ?) \; (\Delta \; ?)$$

When this happened, we then applied PROD 9 to spread the q_4's.

Once we have q_4 in front of every open parenthesis we use PROD 9 again to reduce the whole working string to a string of all terminals:

$$\overset{*}{\Rightarrow} baa$$

All strings such as *ba* or *abba* . . . can be set up in the form:

$$q_0 \; (aa) \; (bb) \; (bb) \; (aa) \; . \; . \; . \; (\Delta\Delta) \; (\Delta\Delta) \; . \; . \; . \; (\Delta\Delta)$$

but only those that can then be TM-processed to get to the HALT state can ever be reduced to a string of all terminals by PROD 9.

In short, all words accepted by the TM can be generated by this grammar and all words generated by this grammar can be accepted by the TM. ∎

EXAMPLE

Let us consider a simple TM that accepts all words ending in a:

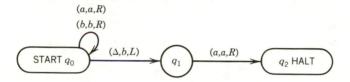

Note that the label on the edge from q_0 to q_1 could just as well have been (Δ,Δ,L), but this works too.

Any word accepted by this TM uses exactly one more cell of TAPE than the space the input is written on. Therefore, we can begin with the productions:

$$\text{PROD 1} \quad S \rightarrow q_0\ X$$
$$\text{PROD 2} \quad X \rightarrow (aa)X$$
$$\text{PROD 3} \quad X \rightarrow (bb)X$$
$$\text{PROD 4} \quad X \rightarrow (\Delta\Delta)$$

This is a minor variation omitting the need for the nonterminal Y and PROD 4, PROD 5, and PROD 6.

Now there are four labeled edges in the TM; three move the TAPE HEAD right, one left. These cause the formation of the following productions. From:

we get:

$$\text{PROD 7(i)} \quad q_0\ (aa) \rightarrow (aa)\ q_0$$
$$\text{PROD 7(ii)} \quad q_0\ (ba) \rightarrow (ba)\ q_0$$
$$\text{PROD 7(iii)} \quad q_0\ (\Delta a) \rightarrow (\Delta a)\ q_0$$

From:

(b,b,R)

q_0

we get:

$\quad$ PROD 7(iv) $\quad q_0\ (ab) \to (ab)\ q_0$
$\quad$ PROD 7(v) $\quad q_0\ (bb) \to (bb)\ q_0$
$\quad$ PROD 7(vi) $\quad q_0\ (\Delta b) \to (\Delta b)\ q_0$

From:

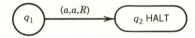

$q_1 \xrightarrow{(a,a,R)} q_2\ \text{HALT}$

we get:

$\quad$ PROD 7(vii) $\quad q_1\ (aa) \to (aa)\ q_2$
$\quad$ PROD 7(viii) $\quad q_1\ (ba) \to (ba)\ q_2$
$\quad$ PROD 7(ix) $\quad q_1\ (\Delta a) \to (\Delta a)\ q_2$

From:

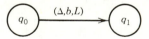

$q_0 \xrightarrow{(\Delta,b,L)} q_1$

we get:

$\quad$ PROD 8 $\quad (uv)\ q_0\ (w\Delta) \to q_1\ (uv)\ (wb)$

where u, v, and w can each be a, b, or Δ. (Since there are really 27 of these; let's pretend we have written them all out.)

Since q_2 is the HALT state, we have:

PROD 9(i)	$q_2\ (uv) \to q_2\ (uv)\ q_2$	where $u,v = a, b, \Delta$
PROD 9(ii)	$(uv)\ q_2 \to q_2\ (uv)\ q_2$	where $u,v = a, b, \Delta$
PROD 9(iii)	$q_2\ (au) \to a$	where $u = a, b, \Delta$
PROD 9(iv)	$q_2\ (bu) \to b$	where $u = a, b, \Delta$
PROD 9(v)	$q_2\ (\Delta u) \to \Lambda$	where $u = a, b, \Delta$

These are all the productions of the type 0 grammar suggested by the algorithm in the proof of Theorem 68.

Let us examine the total derivation of the word *baa:*

TM Simulation		Production No.
State **TAPE**		

$$S \Rightarrow q_0\, X \qquad\qquad 1$$
$$\Rightarrow q_0\,(bb)\,X \qquad\qquad 3$$
$$\Rightarrow q_0\,(bb)\,(aa)\,X \qquad\qquad 2$$
$$\Rightarrow q_0\,(bb)\,(aa)\,(aa)\,X \qquad\qquad 2$$

q_0 | b | a | a | Δ | $\cdots$ $\Rightarrow q_0\,(bb)\,(aa)\,(aa)\,(\Delta\Delta)$ 4

q_0 | b | a | a | Δ | $\cdots$ $\Rightarrow (bb)\,q_0\,(aa)\,(aa)\,(\Delta\Delta)$ 7v

q_0 | b | a | a | Δ | $\cdots$ $\Rightarrow (bb)\,(aa)\,q_0\,(aa)\,(\Delta\Delta)$ 7i

q_0 | b | a | a | Δ | $\cdots$ $\Rightarrow (bb)\,(aa)\,(aa)\,q_0\,(\Delta\Delta)$ 7i

q_1 | b | a | a | b | $\cdots$ $\Rightarrow (bb)\,(aa)\,q_1\,(aa)\,(\Delta b)$ $8\ u = a,$ $\;v = a,\ w = \Delta$

q_2 | b | a | a | b | $\Rightarrow (bb)\,(aa)\,(aa)\,q_2\,(\Delta b)$ 7vii

= HALT

$$\Rightarrow (bb)\,(aa)\,q_2\,(aa)\,q_2\,(\Delta b) \qquad 9\text{ii},\ u = a,\ v = a$$
$$\Rightarrow (bb)\,q_2\,(aa)\,q_2\,(aa)\,q_2\,(\Delta b) \qquad 9\text{ii},\ u = a,\ v = a$$
$$\Rightarrow q_2\,(bb)\,q_2\,(aa)\,q_2\,(aa)\,q_2\,(\Delta b) \qquad 9\text{ii},\ u = b,\ v = b$$
$$\Rightarrow b\ q_2\,(aa)\,q_2\,(aa)\,q_2\,(\Delta b) \qquad 9\text{iv}$$
$$\Rightarrow b\ a\ q_2\,(aa)\,q_2\,(\Delta b) \qquad 9\text{iii}$$
$$\Rightarrow b\ a\ a\ q_2\,(\Delta b) \qquad 9\text{iii}$$
$$\Rightarrow b\ a\ a \qquad 9\text{v}$$

Notice the the first several steps are a setting up operation and the last several steps are cleanup.

In the setting-up stages, we could have set up any string of *a*'s and *b*'s. In this respect, grammars are nondeterministic. We can apply these productions in several ways. If we set up a word that the TM would not accept, then we could never complete its derivation because cleanup can occur only once the halt state symbol has been inserted into the working string. Once we have actually begun the TM simulation, the productions are determined, reflecting the fact that TM's are deterministic.

Once we have reached the cleanup stage, we again develop choices. We could follow something like the sequence shown. Although there are other successful ways of propagating the q_2 (first to the left, then to the right, then to the left again . . .), they all lead to the same completely saturated state with a q_2 in front of everything. If they don't, the cleanup stage won't work and a terminal string won't be produced. ■

Now that we have the tool of type 0 grammars, we can approach some other results about recursively enumerable languages that were too difficult to handle in Chapter 28 when we could only use TM's for the proofs; or can we?

THEOREM 69

If L is a recursively enumerable language, then L^* is also. The recursively enumerable languages are closed under Kleene star.

PROOF?

The proof will be by the same constructive algorithm we used to prove Theorem 32. Since L is r.e. it can be generated by some type 0 grammar starting:

$$S \rightarrow \ldots$$

Let us use the same grammar but change the old symbol S to S_1 and include the new productions

$$S \rightarrow \Lambda$$
$$S \rightarrow S_1 S$$

using the new start symbol S.

This new type 0 grammar can generate any word in L^*, and only words in L^*. Therefore, L^* is r.e. Is this proof valid? See. Problem 20.

THEOREM 70

If L_1 and L_2 are recursively enumerable languages, then so is L_1L_2. The recursively enumerable languages are closed under product.

PROOF?

The proof will be by the same constructive algorithm we used to prove Theorem 31.

Let L_1 and L_2 be generated by type 0 grammars.

Add the subscript 1 to all the nonterminals in the grammar for L_1 (even the start symbol, which becomes S_1). Add the subscript 2 to all the nonterminals in the grammar for L_2 (even the start symbol, which becomes S_2).

Form a new type 0 grammar that has all the productions from the grammars for L_1 and L_2 plus the new start symbol S and the new production

$$S \rightarrow S_1 S_2$$

This grammar generates all the words in $L_1 L_2$ and only the words in $L_1 L_2$. The grammar is type 0, so the language $L_1 L_2$ is r.e. Is this proof valid? See Problem 20.

Surprisingly both of these proofs are bogus. Consider the type 0 grammar

$$S \rightarrow a$$
$$aS \rightarrow b$$

The language L generated by this grammar is the single word a, but the grammar in the "proof" of Theorem 69 generates b, which is not in L^*, and the grammar in the "proof" of Theorem 70 also generates b, which is not in LL. This illustrates the subtle pitfalls of type 0 grammars.

PROBLEMS

Consider the grammar:

$$\begin{array}{ll}
\text{PROD 1} & S \rightarrow ABS \mid \Lambda \\
\text{PROD 2} & AB \rightarrow BA \\
\text{PROD 3} & BA \rightarrow AB \\
\text{PROD 4} & A \rightarrow a \\
\text{PROD 5} & B \rightarrow b
\end{array}$$

1. Derive the following words from this grammar:
    (i)   *abba*
    (ii) *babaabbbaa*

2. Prove that every word generated by this grammar has an equal number of a's and b's.

3. Prove that all words with an equal number of a's and b's can be generated by this grammar.

4. (i)   Find a grammar that generates all words with more a's than b's.
    (ii) Find a grammar that generates all the words not in EQUAL.
    (iii) Is EQUAL recursive?

For Problems 5, 6, and 7 consider the following grammar over the alphabet $\Sigma = \{a, b, c\}$.

$$\begin{array}{ll}
\text{PROD 1} & S \rightarrow ABCS \mid \Lambda \\
\text{PROD 2} & AB \rightarrow BA \\
\text{PROD 3} & BC \rightarrow CB \\
\text{PROD 4} & AC \rightarrow CA \\
\text{PROD 5} & BA \rightarrow AB \\
\text{PROD 6} & CB \rightarrow BC \\
\text{PROD 7} & CA \rightarrow AC \\
\text{PROD 8} & A \rightarrow a \\
\text{PROD 9} & B \rightarrow b \\
\text{PROD 10} & C \rightarrow c
\end{array}$$

5. Derive the words:
    (i)   *ababcc*
    (ii) *cbaabccba*

6. Prove that all words generated by this grammar have equal numbers of a's, b's, and c's.

7. Prove that all words with an equal number of a's, b's, and c's can be generated by this grammar.

Problems 8 through 12 consider the following type 0 grammar over the alphabet $\Sigma = \{a, b\}$:

$$
\begin{array}{lll}
\text{PROD 1} & S & \to UVX \\
\text{PROD 2} & UV & \to aUY \\
\text{PROD 3} & UV & \to bUZ \\
\text{PROD 4} & YX & \to VaX \\
\text{PROD 5} & ZX & \to VbX \\
\text{PROD 6} & Ya & \to aY \\
\text{PROD 7} & Yb & \to bY \\
\text{PROD 8} & Za & \to aZ \\
\text{PROD 9} & Zb & \to bZ \\
\text{PROD 10} & UV & \to \Lambda \\
\text{PROD 11} & X & \to \Lambda \\
\text{PROD 12} & aV & \to Va \\
\text{PROD 13} & bV & \to Vb
\end{array}
$$

8. Derive the following words from this grammar.

   (i) Λ
   (ii) aa
   (iii) bb
   (iv) $abab$

9. Draw the total language tree of this grammar far enough to find all words generated of length 4 or less.

10. Show that if w is any string of a's and b's, then the word:

$$ww$$

can be generated by this grammar.

11. Suppose that in a certain generation from S we arrive at the working string

$$wUVwX$$

where w is some string of a's and b's.

(i)   Show that if we now apply PROD 10 we will end up with the word ww.

(ii)   Show that if instead we apply PROD 11 first we cannot derive any other words.

(iii)   Show that if instead we apply PROD 2 we must derive the working string

$$waUVwaX$$

(iv)   Show that if instead we apply PROD 3 we must derive the working string

$$wbUVwbX$$

12.   Use the observations in Problem 11 and the fact that UVX is of the form $wUVwX$ with $w = \Lambda$ to prove that all words generated by this grammar are in the language DOUBLEWORD $= \{ww$, where w is any string if a's and b's$\}$, which we have seen in many previous problems.

Problems 13 through 16 consider the following type 0 grammar over the alphabet $\Sigma = \{a\}$. *Note:* There is no b.

PROD 1 S $\rightarrow a$
PROD 2 S $\rightarrow CD$
PROD 3 C $\rightarrow ACB$
PROD 4 C $\rightarrow AB$
PROD 5 AB $\rightarrow aBA$
PROD 6 Aa $\rightarrow aA$
PROD 7 Ba $\rightarrow aB$
PROD 8 AD $\rightarrow Da$
PROD 9 BD $\rightarrow Ea$
PROD 10 BE $\rightarrow Ea$
PROD 11 E $\rightarrow a$

13.   Draw the total language tree of this language to find all words of five or fewer letters generated by this grammar.

14.   Generate the word $a^9 = aaaaaaaaa$.

15. (i) Show that for any $n = 1, 2 \ldots$ we can derive the working string

$$A^n B^n D$$

(ii) From $A^n B^n D$ show that we can derive the working string

$$a^{n^2} B^n A^n D$$

16. (i) Show that the working string in Problem 15(ii) generates the word

$$a^{(n+1)^2}$$

(ii) Show that the language of this grammar is
   $$\text{SQUARE} = \{a^{n^2} \quad \text{where } n = 1\ 2\ 3 \ldots \}$$
   $$= \{a \qquad aaaa \qquad a^9 \qquad a^{16} \qquad \ldots \}$$

17. Using type 0 grammars, give another proof of Theorem 60.

18. What language is generated by the grammar

   PROD 1 $S \rightarrow aXYba$
   PROD 2 $XY \rightarrow XYbZ | \Lambda$
   PROD 3 $Zb \rightarrow bZ$
   PROD 4 $Za \rightarrow aa$

Prove any claim.

19. Analyze the following type-0 grammar:

   PROD 1 $S \rightarrow A$
   PROD 2 $A \rightarrow aABC$
   PROD 3 $A \rightarrow abC$
   PROD 4 $CB \rightarrow BC$
   PROD 5 $bB \rightarrow bb$
   PROD 6 $bC \rightarrow b$

   (i) What are the four smallest words produced by this grammar?
   (ii) What is the language of this grammar?

20. Outline proofs for Theorems 69 and 70 using NkTM's.

21. In this chapter we claimed that there is a language that is recursive but not context-sensitive.

Consider

PROBLEM = {the set of words X_1, X_2, X_3 . . . where X_n represents but is not generated by the nth type 1 grammar}

Nothing we have covered so far enables us to understand this. We now explain it. This takes several steps. The first is to show that every language generated by a context-sensitive grammar is recursive. To do this note the following:

(i)   Given a context-sensitive gram*mar T in* which the terminals are a and b and a string w, show that there are only finitely many possible working strings in T with length $\leq$ length (w)

(ii)   Show that the notion of top-down parsing developed in Chapter 22 applies to context sensitive grammars as well as to CFG's. To do this explain how to draw a total language tree for a type 1 gram*mar a*nd how to prune it appropiately. Be sure to prune away any duplication of working strings. Explain why this is permissible and why it is necessary.

(iii) Using our experience from data structures courses, show how a tree of data might be encode*d an*d grown on a TM T$_{APE}$.

(iv)   Show that the facts established above should convince us that for every type 1 grammar T there is a TM that can decide whether or not w can be generated from T. There is at least one such TM for each grammar that halts on all inputs. Show that this means that all type 1 languages are recursive.

(v)   Why does this argument work for type 1 gramma*rs and y*et not carry over to show that all type 0 grammars are recursive?

The TM's we have described in part (iv) can all be encoded into strings of a's and b's (as in Chapter 29). These strings are either words in the language generated by the grammar, or they are not. To decide this, we merely have to run the string on the TM. So let us define the following language:

SELFREJECTION = {all the strings that encode the TM's of part (iv) that are rejected by their own machine}

The words in SELFREJECTION represent type 1 grammars, but they are not generated by the grammars they represent.

- (vi) Prove that the language SELFREJECTION is not type 1.

- (vii) It can be shown by a lengthy argument (that we shall not bother with here) that a TM called DAVID can be built that decides whether or not a given input string is the code word for a grammar machine as defined in part (iv). DAVID crashes if the input is not and halts if it is. Using DAVID and UTM show that SELFREJECTION is recursive.

- (viii) Notice that SELFREJECTION = PROBLEM

CHAPTER 31

COMPUTERS

The finite automata, as defined in Chapter 4, are only language acceptors. When we gave them output capabilities, as with Mealy and Moore machines in Chapter 9, we called them *transducers*. The pushdown automata of Chapter 17 similarly do not produce output but are only language acceptors. However, we recognized their potential as transducers for doing parsing in Chapter 22, by considering what is put into or left in the STACK as output.

Turing machines present a completely different situation. They always have a natural output. When the processing of any given TM terminates, whatever is left on its TAPE can be considered to be the intended, meaningful output. Sometimes the TAPE is only a scratch pad where the machine has performed some calculations needed to determine whether the input string should be accepted. In this case, what is left on the TAPE is meaningless. For example, one TM that accepts the language EVENPALINDROME works by cancelling a letter each from the front and the back of the input string until there is nothing left. When the machine reaches HALT, the TAPE is empty.

However, we may use TM's for a different purpose. We may start by loading the TAPE with some data that we want to process. Then we run the machine until it reaches the HALT state. At that time the contents of the TAPE will have been converted into the desired output, which we can interpret as the result of a calculation, the answer to a question, a manipulated file—whatever.

766

So far we have been considering only TM's that receive input from the language defined by $(a+b)^*$. To be a useful calculator for mathematics we must encode sets of numbers as words in this language. We begin with the encoding of the natural numbers as strings of a's alone:

the code for $0 = \Lambda$

the code for $1 = a$

the code for $2 = aa$

the code for $3 = aaa$

. . .

This is called **unary encoding** because it uses one digit (as opposed to binary, which uses two digits, or decimal with ten).

Every word in $(a + b)^*$ can then be interpreted as a sequence of numbers (strings of a's) separated internally by b's. For example,

$$abaa = (\text{one } a) \; b \; (\text{two } a\text{'s})$$

the decoding of $(abaa) = 1,2$

$$bbabbaa = (\text{no } a\text{'s}) \; b \; (\text{no } a\text{'s}) \; b \; (\text{one } a) \; b \; (\text{no } a\text{'s}) \; b \; (\text{two } a\text{'s})$$

the decoding of $(bbabbaa) = 0,0,1,0,2$

Notice that we are assuming that there is a group of a's at the beginning of the string and at the end even though these may be groups of no a's. For example,

$$abaab = (\text{one } a) \; b \; (\text{two } a\text{'s}) \; b \; (\text{no } a\text{'s})$$

decoded $= 1,2,0$

$$abaabb = (\text{one } a) \; b \; (\text{two } a\text{'s}) \; b \; (\text{no } a\text{'s}) \; b \; (\text{no } a\text{'s})$$

decoded $= 1,2,0,0$

When we interpret strings of a's and b's in this way, a TM that starts with an input string of a's and b's on its TAPE and leaves an output string of a's and b's on its TAPE can be considered to take in a sequence of specific input numbers and, after performing certain calculations, leave as a final result another sequence of numbers—output numbers.

We are considering here only TM's that leave a's and b's on their TAPES, no special symbols or extraneous spaces are allowed among the letters.

We have already seen TM's that fit this description that had no idea they were actually performing data processing, since the interpretation of strings of letters as strings of numbers never occurred to them. "Calculation" is one of those words that we never really had a good definition for. Perhaps we are at last in a position to correct this.

EXAMPLE

Consider the following TM called ADDER:

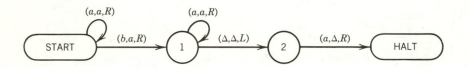

In START we skip over some initial clump of a's, leaving them unchanged. When we read a b, we change it to an a and move to state 1. In state 1 a second b would make us crash. We skip over a second clump of a's till we run out of input string and find a Δ. At this point, we go to state 2, but we move the TAPE HEAD *left*. We have now backed up into the a's. There must be at least one a here because we changed a b into an a to get to state 1. Therefore, when we first arrive at state 2 we erase an a and move the TAPE HEAD right to HALT and terminate execution.

The action of ADDER is illustrated below:

We start with:

| a | a | a | b | a | a | a | a | $\Delta \cdots$ |

which becomes in state 1:

| a | a | a | a | a | a | a | a | $\Delta \cdots$ |

which becomes by HALT:

| a | a | a | a | a | a | a | Δ | $\Delta \cdots$ |

For an input string to be accepted (lead to HALT), it has to be of the form:

$$\textbf{a*ba*}$$

If we start with the input string $a^n b a^m$, we end up with:

$$a^{n+m}$$

on the TAPE.

When we decode strings as sequences of numbers as above, we identify $a^n b a^m$ with the two numbers n and m. The output of the TM is decoded as $(n + m)$.

Under this interpretation, ADDER takes two numbers as input and leaves their sum on the TAPE as output.

This is our most primitive example of a TM intentionally working as a calculator.　■

If we used an input string not in the form **a*ba***, the machine would crash. This is analogous to our computer programs crashing if the input data is not in the correct format.

Our choice of unary notation is not essential; we could build an "adding-machine" for any other base as well.

EXAMPLE

Let us build a TM that adds two numbers presented in binary notation and leaves the answer on the TAPE in binary notation.

We shall construct this TM out of two parts. First we consider the Turing machine T_1 shown below:

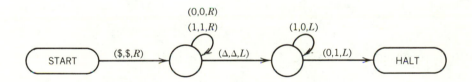

This TM presumes that the input is of the form:

$$\$(0 + 1)^*$$

It finds the last bit of the binary number and reverses it; that is, 0 becomes 1, 1 becomes 0. If the last bit was a 1, it backs up to the left and changes the whole clump of 1's to 0's and the first 0 to the left of these 1's it turns into a 1. All in all, this TM adds 1 to the binary number after the \$. If the input was of the form **\$1***, the machine finds no 0 and crashes. This adder does not work on numbers that are solid strings of 1's: 1 (1 decimal), 11 (3 decimal) 111 (7 decimal), 1111 (15 decimal), and so on. These numbers are trouble, but for all other numbers 1 can be added to their binary representations without increasing the number of bits.

In general, T_1 increments by 1.

Now let us consider the Turing machine T_2. This machine will accept a nonzero number in binary and subtract 1 from it. The input is presumed to be of the form:

$$\$(0 + 1)*\$$$

but not:

$$\$0*\$$$

The subtraction will be done in a three-step process:

Step 1   Reverse the 0's and 1's between the $'s. This is called taking the 1's complement.

Step 2   Use T_1 to add 1 to the number now between the $'s. Notice that if the original number was not 0, the 1's complement is not a forbidden input to T_1 (i.e., not all 1's).

Step 3   Reverse the 0's and 1's again.

The total result is that what was x will become $x - 1$.

The mathematical justification for this is that the 1's complement of x (if it is n-bits long) is the binary representation of the number

$$(2^n - 1) - x$$

Because when x is added to it, it becomes n solid 1's $= 2^n - 1$.

Step 1 x becomes $(2^n - 1) - x$

Step 2   Which becomes $(2^n - 1) - x + 1 = (2^n - 1) - (x - 1)$, the 1's complement of $x - 1$

Step 3   Which becomes $(2^n - 1) - [(2^n - 1) - (x - 1)] = (x - 1)$

For example,

$$\$ \ 1010 \ \$ = \text{binary for ten}$$

Step 1   Becomes $ 0101 $ = binary for five

Step 2   Becomes $ 0110 $ = binary for six

Step 3   Becomes $ 1001 $ = binary for nine

T_2 is shown on the next page.

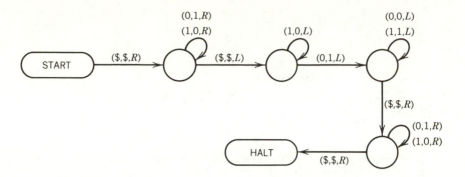

We generally say T_2 decrements by 1.

The binary adder we shall now build works as follows:
The input strings will be of the form

$$\$\ (0 + 1)^*\ \$\ (0 + 1)^*$$

which we call:

$$\$\ x\text{-part}\quad \$\ y\text{-part}$$

We shall interpret the x-part and y-part as numbers in binary that are to be added. Furthermore, we make the assumption that the total $x + y$ has no more bits than y itself. This is analogous to the addition of numbers in the arithmetic registers of a computer where we presume that there will be no overflow.

If y is the larger number and starts with the bit 0, the condition is guaranteed. If not, we can make use of the subroutine insert 0 from Chapter 24 to put enough 0's in the front of y to make the condition true.

The algorithm to calculate $x + y$ in binary will be this:

Step 1   Check the x-part to see if it is 0. If yes, halt. If no, proceed.

Step 2   Subtract 1 from the x-part using T_2 above.

Step 3   Add 1 to the y-part using T_1 above.

Step 4   Go to Step 1.

The final result will be:

$$\$\ 0^*\ \$\ (x + y \text{ in binary})$$

Let us illustrate the algorithm using decimal numbers:

$$\$\,4\,\$\,7$$

becomes	$\$\,3\,\$\,8$
becomes	$\$\,2\,\$\,9$
becomes	$\$\,1\,\$\,10$
becomes	$\$\,0\,\$\,11$

The full TM is this:

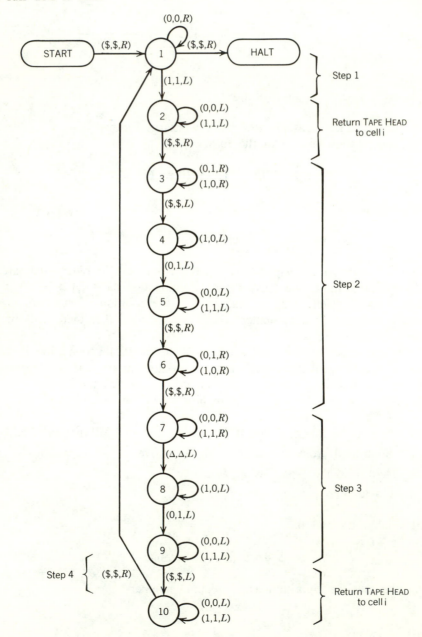

Let us run this machine on the input

$$\$ \ 10 \ \$ \ 0110$$

in an attempt to add two and six in binary.

START	1		2	3
$\underline{\$}10\$0110$	$\rightarrow \ \$1\underline{0}\$0110$	$(x \neq 0) \ \rightarrow$	$\$1\underline{0}\$0110$	$\rightarrow \ \$\underline{1}0\$0110$

3	3	4	4	5
$\rightarrow \ \$\underline{0}0\$0110$	$\rightarrow \ \$0\underline{1}\$0110$	$\rightarrow \ \$0\underline{1}\$0110$	$\rightarrow \ \$\underline{0}0\$0110$	$\rightarrow \ \$1\underline{0}\$0110$

6	6	6		7
$\rightarrow \ \$\underline{1}0\$0110$	$\rightarrow \ \$\underline{0}0\$0110$	$\rightarrow \ \$0\underline{1}\$0110$	$(x \leftarrow x - 1) \ \rightarrow$	$\$01\$\underline{0}110$

7	7	7	7	8
$\rightarrow \ \$01\$0\underline{1}10$	$\rightarrow \ \$01\$01\underline{1}0$	$\rightarrow \ \$01\$011\underline{0}$	$\rightarrow \ \$01\$0110\underline{\Delta}$	$\rightarrow \ \$01\$011\underline{0}$

9	9	9	9	
$\rightarrow \ \$01\$01\underline{1}1$	$\rightarrow \ \$01\$0\underline{1}11$	$\rightarrow \ \$01\$\underline{0}111$	$\rightarrow \ \$01\$0111$	$(y \leftarrow y + 1)$

10	10	10	1	1
$\rightarrow \ \$01\$\underline{0}111$	$\rightarrow \ \$\underline{0}1\$0111$	$\rightarrow \ \$\underline{0}1\$0111$	$\rightarrow \ \$0\underline{1}\$0111$	$\rightarrow \ \$01\$0111$

	2	2	3	3
$(x \neq 0) \ \rightarrow$	$\$\underline{0}1\$0111$	$\rightarrow \ \$\underline{0}1\$0111$	$\rightarrow \ \$\underline{0}1\$0111$	$\rightarrow \ \$1\underline{1}\$0111$

3	4	5	5	6
$\rightarrow \ \$1\underline{0}\$0111$	$\rightarrow \ \$1\underline{0}\$0111$	$\rightarrow \ \$\underline{1}1\$0111$	$\rightarrow \ \$\underline{1}1\$0111$	$\rightarrow \ \$\underline{1}1\$0111$

6	6	7	7
$\rightarrow \ \$0\underline{1}\$0111$	$\rightarrow \ \$\underline{0}0\$0111$	$(x \leftarrow x - 1) \ \rightarrow \ \$00\$\underline{0}111$	$\rightarrow \ \$00\$0\underline{1}11$

7	7	7	8	8
$\rightarrow \ \$00\$01\underline{1}1$	$\rightarrow \ \$00\$011\underline{1}$	$\rightarrow \$00\$0111\underline{\Delta}$	$\rightarrow \ \$00\$011\underline{1}$	$\rightarrow \ \$00\$01\underline{1}0$

8	8	9		10
$\rightarrow \ \$00\$0\underline{1}00$	$\rightarrow \ \$00\$\underline{0}000$	$\rightarrow \ \$00\$\underline{1}000$	$(y \leftarrow y + 1) \ \rightarrow$	$\$0\underline{0}\$1000$

10	10	1	1	1
$\rightarrow \ \$\underline{0}0\$1000$	$\rightarrow \ \$\underline{0}0\$1000$	$\rightarrow \ \$0\underline{0}\$1000$	$\rightarrow \ \$0\underline{0}\$1000$	$\rightarrow \ \$0\underline{0}\$1000$

	HALT
$(x = 0) \ \rightarrow$	$\$00\$\underline{1}000$

The correct binary total is 1000. ■

Now that we have seen how much fun binary is, let us return to unary notation for calculation.

DEFINITION

If a TM has the property that for every word it accepts, at the time it halts, it leaves one solid string of a's and b's on its TAPE starting in cell i, we call it a **computer.** The input string we call the **input** (or, **string of input numbers**), and we identify it as a sequence of nonnegative integers. The string left on the TAPE we call the **output** and identify it also as a sequence of nonnegative integers.   ∎

In the definition above, we use the semi-ambiguous word "identify" because we do not wish to restrict ourselves to unary encoding or binary encoding or any other system.

Now we finally know what a computer is. Those expensive boxes of electronics sold as computers are only approximations to the real McCoy. For one thing they almost never come with an infinite memory like a true TM. At this stage in our consideration we are dealing only with zero and the positive integers. Negative numbers and numbers with decimal points can be encoded into nonnegative integers for TM's as they are for electronic digital computers. We do not worry about this generality here.

With our primitive definition it is hard to do usual subtraction on a TM computer since we might need negative numbers. Up until we were 11 years old no one ever asked us to subtract a bigger number from a smaller one, and if we are lucky no one ever will again. This is just how a TM computer feels. Let us define the new symbol "$\dot{-}$" to use instead of the regular minus sign.

DEFINITION

If m and n are nonnegative integers, then their **simple subtraction** is defined as

$$
m \dot{-} n = \begin{cases} m - n & \text{if } m \geq n \\ \\ 0 & \text{if } m \leq n \end{cases}
$$

Essentially what $\dot{-}$ does is perform regular subtraction and then rounds all negative answers back up to 0.   ∎

Simple subtraction is often called **proper subtraction** or even **monus.**

EXAMPLE

Consider the TM below called MINUS:

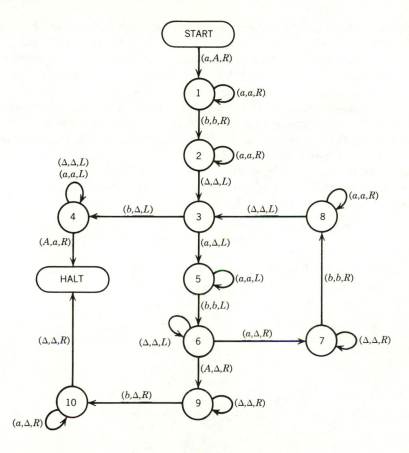

This machine works as follows. To get from START to state 3 the input on the TAPE must have been of the form:

$$a^+ \ b \ a^*$$

or else the machine would crash. This can be interpreted as starting with two numbers, the first of which is not zero.

Along the way to state 3 we have changed the first a into A—the usual expedient to guarantee that we do not accidentally move left from cell i while backing up.

For example,

<u>a</u>aabaa

becomes

$$Aaabaa$$

Notice that the TAPE HEAD is reading the last nonblank character when we enter state 3. If what is being read in state 3 is a *b*, it signifies that our task (which we have not yet explained) is done. We erase the *b* and move to state 4. This state leaves all *a*'s and *b*'s as it finds them and seeks the *A* in cell i. When this is found, it is changed back into an *a* and the process halts.

If the character read in state 3 is an *a*, a different path is followed. The *a* is erased while moving to state 5. Here we move left seeking the center *b*. When we find it, we reach state 6 and continue left in search of the last *a* of the initial group of *a*'s. We find this, erase it, and move to state 7. State 7 moves right, seeking the center *b*. We cross this going to state 8 where we seek the last *a* of the second group of *a*'s. When this is located, we return to state 3. The circuit:

$$\text{state } 3 - \text{state } 5 - \text{state } 6 - \text{state } 7 - \text{state } 8 - \text{state } 3$$

cancels the last *a* of the second group against the last *a* of the first group.

For example, what starts as

$$Aaaaabaa$$

becomes

$$Aaaa\Delta ba\Delta$$

Another time through the circuit and this becomes:

$$Aaa\Delta\Delta b\Delta\Delta$$

Now from state 3 we follow the path

$$\text{state } 3 - \text{state } 4 - \text{HALT}$$

leaving

$$aaa$$

on the TAPE alone. This is the correct result of the subtraction $5 \div 2$.

The only possible deviation from this routine is to find that the *a* that is to be cancelled from the first group is the *A* in cell i. This could happen if the two groups of *a*'s are initially the same size or if the second group is larger.

$$\underline{a}abaa \rightarrow Aabaa \rightarrow A\Delta b\underline{a} \rightarrow \underline{A}\Delta b\Delta \rightarrow \Delta\underline{\Delta}b\Delta \rightarrow \Delta. . .$$

or

$$\underline{a}abaaa \rightarrow Aabaa\underline{a} \rightarrow A\Delta ba\underline{a} \rightarrow \underline{A}\Delta ba\Delta \rightarrow \Delta\underline{\Delta}ba\Delta \rightarrow \Delta. . .$$

If this happens, states 9 and 10 erase everything on the TAPE and leave the answer zero (an all-blank TAPE). It is not recorded whether this zero is the exact answer or a rounded up answer.

If we start with $a^m ba^n$ on the TAPE, we will be left with a^{m-n} unless $m \leq n$, in which case we will be left with only blanks.

This machine then performs the operation of simple subtraction as defined by the symbol $" \div "$. ∎

Notice that although this TM starts with a string in $(\mathbf{a} + \mathbf{b})^*$ and ends with a string in $(\mathbf{a} + \mathbf{b})^*$, it does use some other symbols in its processing, (in this case, A).

DEFINITION

If a TM takes a sequence of numbers as input and leaves only one number as output, we say that the computer has acted like a mathematical **function**. Any operation that is defined on all sequences of K numbers (for some number $K \geq 1$) and that can be performed by a TM is called **Turing-computable** or just **computable.** ∎

The TM's in the last two examples, ADDER and MINUS, provide a proof of the following theorem.

THEOREM 71

Addition and simple subtraction are computable. ∎

In both of these examples, $K = 2$ (addition and subtraction are both defined on a sequence of two numbers). Both of these are functions (they leave a one-number answer).

THEOREM 72

The function MAX (x,y), which is equal to the larger of the two nonnegative integers x and $y,$ is computable.

PROOF

We shall prove this by describing a TM that does the job of MAX.

Let us use the old trick of building on previous results, in this case the machine MINUS. MINUS does make the decision as to which of the two numbers m or n is larger. If m is larger, $m \div n$ leaves an a in cell i. If n is larger than (or equal to) m, cell i will contain a Δ. However, after the program is completed it is too late to leave m or n on the TAPE, since all that remains is $m \div n$.

Instead of erasing the a's from the two groups as we do in MINUS, let us make this modification. In the first section, let us turn the a's that we want to erase into x's and let us turn the a's of the second section that we want to erase into y's. For example, what starts as

$$aaaaabaa$$

and on MINUS ends as

$$aaa$$

now should end as

$$Aaaxxbyy$$

Notice that we have left the middle b instead of erasing it, and we leave the contents of cell i A if it should have been a or, as we shall see, leave it a (if it should have been Δ).

The TM program that performs this algorithm is only a slight modification of MINUS. The picture is on the next page.

If we arrive at state 4, the first input group of a's is larger. The TAPE looks like this:

$$Aa. . . aaxx. . . xx \, byy . . . yy$$

with the TAPE HEAD reading the y to the right of the b. To finish the job of MAX we must go right to the first Δ, then sweep down leftward, erasing all the y's and the b as we go and changing x's into a's, and finally stopping after changing A into a.

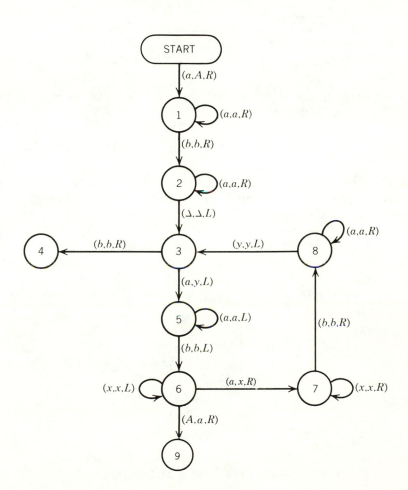

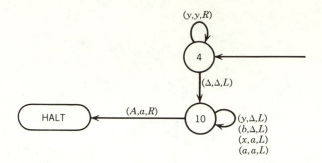

If we arrive at state 9, the second group is larger than or equal to the first. Then TAPE now looks like this:

$$a\underline{x}x. . . xxbaa. . . aayy. . . yy$$

with the TAPE HEAD reading cell ii. Here what we have to do is leave a number of a's equal to the former constitution of the second group of a's (the current a's and y's together). Now since there are as many symbols before the b as y's, all we really need to do is to erase the b and the y's, change the x's to a's, and shift the other a's one cell to the left (into the hole left by b). For example, what is now

$$axxxbaayyyy$$

becomes

$$aaaa\Delta aa\Delta\Delta\Delta$$

and then

$$aaaaaa$$

The TM program on the top of the next page does all this.

What we actually did is to change the b into an a instead of Δ. That gives us one too many a's, so in state 11 we back up and erase one.

This machine is one of many TM's that does the job of MAX.   ■

EXAMPLE

Let us trace the execution of the input $aaabaa$ on this TM.

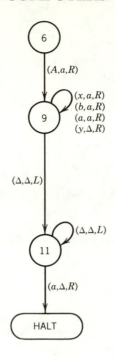

$$\text{START} \quad \underset{\text{1}}{\underline{a}aabaa} \xrightarrow{1} A\underline{a}abaa \xrightarrow{1} Aa\underline{a}baa \xrightarrow{1} Aaa\underline{b}aa$$

$$\xrightarrow{2} Aaab\underline{a}a \xrightarrow{2} Aaaba\underline{a} \xrightarrow{2} Aaabaa\underline{\Delta} \xrightarrow{3} Aaaba\underline{a} \xrightarrow{5} Aaab\underline{a}y$$

$$\xrightarrow{5} Aaa\underline{b}ay \xrightarrow{6} Aa\underline{a}bay \xrightarrow{7} Aax\underline{b}ay \xrightarrow{8} Aaxb\underline{a}y \xrightarrow{8} Aaxba\underline{y}$$

$$\xrightarrow{3} Aaxb\underline{a}y \xrightarrow{5} Aax\underline{b}yy \xrightarrow{6} Aa\underline{x}byy \xrightarrow{6} A\underline{a}xbyy \xrightarrow{7} Ax\underline{x}byy$$

$$\xrightarrow{7} Axx\underline{b}yy \xrightarrow{8} Axxb\underline{y}y \xrightarrow{3} Axx\underline{b}yy \xrightarrow{4} Axxb\underline{y}y \xrightarrow{4} Axxby\underline{y}$$

$$\xrightarrow{4} Axxbyy\underline{\Delta} \xrightarrow{10} Axxby\underline{y} \xrightarrow{10} Axxb\underline{y}\Delta \xrightarrow{10} Axx\underline{b}\Delta\Delta \xrightarrow{10} Ax\underline{x}\Delta\Delta\Delta$$

$$\xrightarrow{10} A\underline{x}a\Delta\Delta\Delta \xrightarrow{10} \underline{A}aa\Delta\Delta\Delta \rightarrow a\underline{a}a\Delta\Delta\Delta \quad \text{HALT}$$

This is the correct answer since:

$$\text{Max } (3,2) = 3$$

EXAMPLE

To give equal time to the state 9—state 11—HALT branch, we trace the execution of the input *aabaaa*:

$$
\begin{array}{cccccc}
\text{START} & 1 & 1 & 2 & 2 & 2 \\
\underline{a}abaaa & \rightarrow A\underline{a}baaa & \rightarrow Aa\underline{b}aaa & \rightarrow Aab\underline{a}aa & \rightarrow Aaba\underline{a}a & \rightarrow Aabaa\underline{a}
\end{array}
$$

$$
\begin{array}{cccccc}
 & 2 & 3 & 5 & 5 & 5 & 6 \\
\rightarrow & Aabaaa\underline{\Delta} & \rightarrow Aabaa\underline{a} & \rightarrow Aaba\underline{a}y & \rightarrow Aab\underline{a}ay & \rightarrow Aa\underline{b}aay & \rightarrow A\underline{a}baay
\end{array}
$$

$$
\begin{array}{cccccc}
 & 7 & 8 & 8 & 8 & 3 & 5 \\
\rightarrow & Ax\underline{b}aay & \rightarrow Axb\underline{a}ay & \rightarrow Axba\underline{a}y & \rightarrow Axbaa\underline{y} & \rightarrow Axba\underline{a}y & \rightarrow Axba\underline{y}y
\end{array}
$$

$$
\begin{array}{cccccc}
 & 5 & 6 & 6 & 9 & 9 & 9 \\
\rightarrow & Ax\underline{b}ayy & \rightarrow A\underline{x}bayy & \rightarrow \underline{A}xbayy & \rightarrow a\underline{x}bayy & \rightarrow aa\underline{b}ayy & \rightarrow aaa\underline{a}yy
\end{array}
$$

$$
\begin{array}{cccccc}
 & 9 & 9 & 9 & 11 & 11 & 11 \\
\rightarrow & aaaa\underline{y}y & \rightarrow aaaa\Delta\underline{y} & \rightarrow aaaa\Delta\underline{\Delta} & \rightarrow aaaa\underline{\Delta}\Delta & \rightarrow aaaa\underline{\Delta} & \rightarrow aaa\underline{a}
\end{array}
$$

$$
\begin{array}{ccc}
\rightarrow & aa\underline{a}\Delta & \text{HALT}
\end{array}
$$

■

THEOREM 73

The identity function:

$$\text{IDENTITY}(n) = n \quad \text{for all } n \geq 0$$

and the successor function:

$$\text{SUCCESSOR}(n) = n+1 \quad \text{for all } n \geq 0$$

are computable.

NOTE: These functions are defined on only one number ($K = 1$), so we expect input only of the form **a***.

PROOF

The only trick in the IDENTITY function is to crash on all input strings in bad format, that is, not of the form **a***:

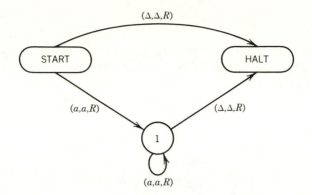

Similarly, SUCCESSOR is no problem:

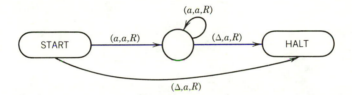

■

DEFINITION

The **"i-th of n" selector function** is the function that starts with a sequence of n nonnegative numbers and erases most of them leaving only the i-th one (whether that one is the largest or not). It is written:

$$\text{SELECT}/i/n(\ ,\ ,\ ,\ )$$

where there is space for exactly n numbers inside the parenthesis. For example,

$$\text{SELECT}/2/4\ (8,7,1,5)\ =\ 7$$
$$\text{SELECT}/4/9\ (2,0,4,1,5,9,2,2,3)\ =\ 1$$ ■

THEOREM 74

The "i-th of n" selector function is computable for every value of i and n (where we assume i is less than or equal to n).

PROOF

We shall build a TM that shows that the "third of five" selector function is computable. The other SELECTi/n functions can be constructed similarly.

The TM that operates as

$$\text{SELECT}/3/5 \ (r,s,t,u,v)$$

begins with input of the form

$$a^r ba^s ba^t ba^u ba^v$$

It marks the first cell with a *, erases the first clump of a's and the first b, the next a's and the next b, saves the next a's, and erases the next b, the next a's, the next b, and the last a's, all the time moving the TAPE HEAD to the right.

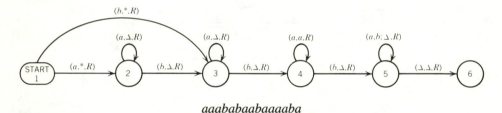

$$aaababaabaaaaba$$

becomes

$$\Delta\Delta\Delta\Delta\Delta\Delta aa\Delta\Delta\Delta\Delta\Delta\Delta\Delta$$

We must now shift the remaining a's down to the left to begin in cell i, which we marked with a *. We can use the TM subroutine DELETE Δ, which we built in Chapter 24. We keep deleting the Δ in cell i until the contents of cell i becomes an a. Then we stop. ∎

THEOREM 75

Multiplication is computable.

PROOF

Here we shall make a slight departure from previous custom. We shall assume that the two numbers of input are preceded on the TAPE by an extra letter b. This machine, called MPY, takes strings of the form $ba^m ba^n$ and leaves on the TAPE ba^{mn}. To make things easier on ourselves, we shall build a machine that rejects the input if n or m is zero; however, if we wanted to we could build the machine differently to allow multiplication by zero (see the problem section). We could also do without the initial b, but then we would have to insert a cell i symbol to prevent back-up crashes.

The algorithm this machine will follow is to place the symbol # after the input string. Then to the right of the # it will write one copy of the string a^n for each a in the string a^m, one by one erasing the a's in the first string. For example, the multiplication of 3 times 2 proceeds in these stages:

$$baaabaa\#$$
$$b\Delta aabaa\#aa$$
$$b\Delta\Delta abaa\#aaaa$$
$$b\Delta\Delta\Delta baa\#aaaaaa$$

The machine will then erase everything between and including the first b and the #. The TAPE now looks like this:

$$b\Delta\Delta\Delta\Delta\Delta\Delta\Delta aaaaaa$$

For this machine we shall spell out the process of shifting the string of a's leftward to begin in cell ii. This is a simplified version of the DELETE Δ routine of Chapter 24—"simplified" because the only data shift is a solid clump of a's and an easier method works. The reason we spell this out in detail again is that we want to make a complete trace of some runnings of the full TM and we need the entire machine drawn out for us to do it.

Let us proceed.
MPY begins like this:

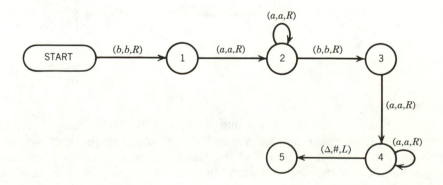

So far we have checked the form of the input (so we can crash on improper inputs) and placed the # where we want it.

Now we go back and find the first a in a^m and convert it into a Δ:

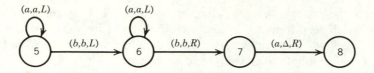

Now we find the beginning of the second factor a^n:

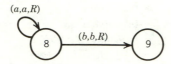

Now one by one we turn these a's in the second factor into A's and copy them on the other side of the #:

$$b\Delta aaabaa\#$$
$$\downarrow$$
$$b\Delta aaabAa\#a$$
$$\downarrow$$
$$b\Delta aaabAA\#aa$$

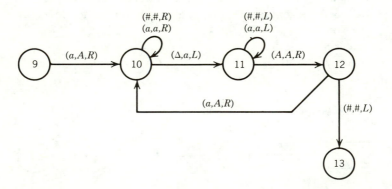

In state 9 we convert the first a into an A. In state 10 we move the TAPE HEAD to the right going through a's and the # and perhaps other a's until we find the Δ. To get to state 11 we change the first Δ to an a and start the trip back down the TAPE leftward. In state 11 we skip over a's and the # and more a's until we find the last copied A. In state 12 we look to the right of this A. If there is a #, then there are no more a's to copy and we go to state 13. If there is another a, it must be copied so we change it to A and go back to state 10.

In state 13 we must change the A's back to a's so we can repeat the process. Then we look for the next a in the first factor:

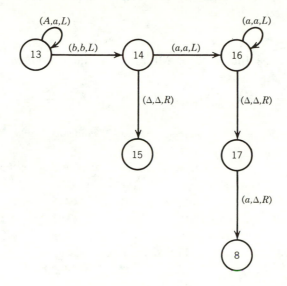

After changing the A's back to a's, we move left, through the middle b, into whatever is left of the first factor a^m. If the cell to the immediate left of b is blank, then the multiplication is finished and we move to state 15. If the cell to the left of b has an a in it, we go to state 16. Here we move leftward through the a's till we find the first Δ, then right one cell to the next a to be erased. Changing this a to a Δ, we repeat the process of copying the second factor into the Δ's after the # and a's by returning to state 8.

When we get to state 15 we have the simple job left of erasing the now useless second factor:

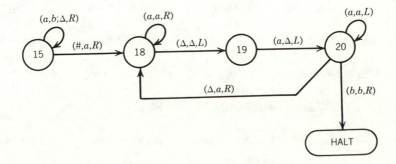

Going to state 18 we change the # into an a so we must later erase the end a. Using states 18 and 19, we find the end a and erase it. In state 20

we go back down the TAPE to the left to see if there are more Δ's in front of the answer. If so, we make one an a and go back to state 18. If not, we encounter the b in cell i and we halt. This completes the machine MPY. ■

EXAMPLE

Let us write out the full trace of MPY on the input $baabaa$:

	START		1		2		2
	b<u>a</u>abaa	→	ba<u>a</u>baa	→	baa<u>b</u>aa	→	baab<u>a</u>a
	3		4		4		5
→	baaba<u>a</u>	→	baabaa<u> </u>	→	baabaa<u>Δ</u>	→	baabaa<u>#</u>
	5		5		6		6
→	baaba<u>a</u>#	→	baab<u>a</u>a#	→	baa<u>b</u>aa#	→	ba<u>a</u>baa#
	6		7		8		8
→	b<u>a</u>abaa#	→	<u>b</u>aabaa#	→	b<u>Δ</u>abaa#	→	bΔ<u>a</u>baa#
	9		10		10		10
→	bΔa<u>b</u>aa#	→	bΔabA<u>a</u>#	→	bΔabAa<u>#</u>	→	bΔabAa#<u>Δ</u>
	11		11		11		12
→	bΔabAa<u>#</u>a	→	bΔabA<u>a</u>#a	→	bΔab<u>A</u>a#a	→	bΔabA<u>a</u>#a
	10		10		10		11
→	bΔabA<u>A</u>#a	→	bΔabAA<u>#</u>a	→	bΔabAA#a<u>Δ</u>	→	bΔabAA#<u>a</u>a
	11		11		12		13
→	bΔabA<u>A</u>#aa	→	bΔab<u>A</u>A#aa	→	bΔabA<u>A</u>#aa	→	bΔab<u>A</u>A#aa
	13		13		14		16
→	bΔab<u>A</u>a#aa	→	bΔa<u>b</u>aa#aa	→	b<u>Δ</u>abaa#aa	→	bΔ<u>a</u>baa#aa
	17		8		9		10
→	bΔ<u>a</u>baa#aa	→	bΔ<u>Δ</u>baa#aa	→	bΔΔb<u>a</u>a#aa	→	bΔΔbA<u>a</u>#aa
	10		10		10		10
→	bΔΔbA<u>a</u>#aa	→	bΔΔbAa<u>#</u>aa	→	bΔΔbAa#<u>a</u>a	→	bΔΔbAa#aa<u>Δ</u>
	11		11		11		11
→	bΔΔbA<u>a</u>#aaa	→	bΔΔbA<u>a</u>#aaa	→	bΔΔbA<u>a</u>#aaa	→	bΔΔb<u>A</u>a#aaa
	11		12		10		10
→	bΔΔ<u>A</u>a#aaa	→	bΔΔb<u>A</u>a#aaa	→	bΔΔbA<u>A</u>#aaa	→	bΔΔbAA<u>#</u>aaa
	10		10		10		11
→	bΔΔbA<u>A</u>#aaa	→	bΔΔbAA<u>#</u>aaa	→	bΔΔbAA#aaa<u>Δ</u>	→	bΔΔbAA#<u>a</u>aaa
	11		11		11		11
→	bΔΔbAA#<u>a</u>aaa	→	bΔΔbAA#<u>a</u>aaa	→	bΔΔbAA<u>#</u>aaaa	→	bΔΔbA<u>A</u>#aaaa
	12		13		13		13
→	bΔΔbAA<u>#</u>aaaa	→	bΔΔbA<u>A</u>#aaaa	→	bΔΔb<u>A</u>a#aaaa	→	bΔΔ<u>b</u>aa#aaaa
	14		15		15		15
→	bΔ<u>Δ</u>baa#aaaa	→	bΔΔ<u>b</u>aa#aaaa	→	bΔΔΔ<u>a</u>a#aaaa	→	bΔΔΔΔ<u>a</u>#aaaa
	15		18		18		18
→	bΔΔΔΔΔ<u>#</u>aaaa	→	bΔΔΔΔΔ<u>a</u>aaaa	→	bΔΔΔΔΔa<u>a</u>aaa	→	bΔΔΔΔΔaa<u>a</u>aa
	18		18		19		20
→	bΔΔΔΔΔaaaa<u>a</u>	→	bΔΔΔΔΔaaaaa<u>Δ</u>	→	bΔΔΔΔΔaaaa<u>a</u>	→	bΔΔΔΔΔaaa<u>a</u>

$$
\begin{array}{llll}
20 & 20 & 20 & 20 \\
\to b\Delta\Delta\Delta\Delta\Delta aaaa & \to b\Delta\Delta\Delta\Delta\Delta aaaa & \to b\Delta\Delta\Delta\Delta\Delta aaaa & \to b\Delta\Delta\Delta\Delta\Delta aaaa \\[4pt]
18 & 18 & 18 & 18 \\
\to b\Delta\Delta\Delta\Delta aaaaa & \to b\Delta\Delta\Delta\Delta aaaaa & \to b\Delta\Delta\Delta\Delta aaaaa & \to b\Delta\Delta\Delta\Delta aaaaa \\[4pt]
18 & 19 & 20 & 20 \\
\to b\Delta\Delta\Delta\Delta aaaaa\Delta & \to b\Delta\Delta\Delta\Delta aaaaa & \to b\Delta\Delta\Delta\Delta aaaa & \to b\Delta\Delta\Delta\Delta aaaa \\[4pt]
20 & 20 & 20 & 18 \\
\to b\Delta\Delta\Delta\Delta aaaa & \to b\Delta\Delta\Delta\Delta aaaa & \to b\Delta\Delta\Delta\Delta aaaa & \to b\Delta\Delta\Delta aaaaa \\[4pt]
18 & 18 & 18 & 18 \\
\to b\Delta\Delta\Delta aaaaa & \to b\Delta\Delta\Delta aaaaa & \to b\Delta\Delta\Delta aaaaa & \to b\Delta\Delta\Delta aaaaa\Delta \\[4pt]
19 & 20 & 20 & 20 \\
\to b\Delta\Delta\Delta aaaaa & \to b\Delta\Delta\Delta aaaa & \to b\Delta\Delta\Delta aaaa & \to b\Delta\Delta\Delta aaaa \\[4pt]
20 & 20 & 18 & 18 \\
\to b\Delta\Delta\Delta aaaa & \to b\Delta\Delta\Delta aaaa & \to b\Delta\Delta aaaaa & \to b\Delta\Delta aaaaa \\[4pt]
18 & 18 & 18 & 19 \\
\to b\Delta\Delta aaaaa & \to b\Delta\Delta aaaaa & \to b\Delta\Delta aaaaa\Delta & \to b\Delta\Delta aaaaa \\[4pt]
20 & 20 & 20 & 20 \\
\to b\Delta\Delta aaaa & \to b\Delta\Delta aaaa & \to b\Delta\Delta aaaa & \to b\Delta\Delta aaaa \\[4pt]
20 & 18 & 18 & 18 \\
\to b\Delta\Delta aaaa & \to b\Delta aaaaa & \to b\Delta aaaaa & \to b\Delta aaaaa \\[4pt]
18 & 18 & 19 & 20 \\
\to b\Delta aaaaa & \to b\Delta aaaaa\Delta & \to b\Delta aaaaa & \to b\Delta aaaa \\[4pt]
20 & 20 & 20 & 20 \\
\to b\Delta aaaa & \to b\Delta aaaa & \to b\Delta aaaa & \to b\Delta aaaa \\[4pt]
18 & 18 & 18 & 18 \\
\to baaaaa & \to baaaaa & \to baaaaa & \to baaaaa \\[4pt]
18 & 19 & 20 & 20 \\
\to baaaaa\Delta & \to baaaaa & \to baaaa & \to baaaa \\[4pt]
20 & 20 & 20 & \\
\to baaaa & \to baaaa & \to baaaa & \text{HALT} \quad \blacksquare \\
\end{array}
$$

This is how one Turing machine calculates that two times two is four. No claim was ever made that this is a *good* way to calculate that $2 \times 2 = 4$, only that the existence of MPY proves that multiplication *can* be calculated, i.e., is computable.

We are dealing here with the realm of possibility (what is and what is not possible) not optimality (how best to do it); that is why this subject is called Computer *Theory* not "A Practical Guide to Computation".

Remember that electricity flows at (nearly) the speed of light, so there is hope that an electrical Turing machine could calculate 6×7 before next April.

Turing machines are not only powerful language recognizers but they are also powerful calculators. For example, a TM can be built to calculate square roots, or at least to find the integer part of the square root.

The machine SQRT accepts an input of the form ba^n and tests all integers one at a time from one on up until it finds one whose square is bigger than n.

Very loosely, we draw this diagram:
(In the diagram we have abbreviated SUCCESSOR "SUC," which is commonly used in this field.)

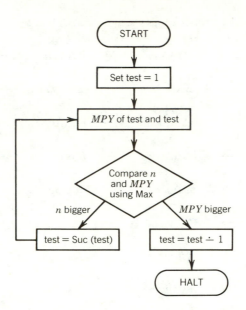

We can build SQRT out of the previous TM's we have made.

What functions cannot be computed by a Turing machine? The answer is surprising: "It is believed that there are *no* functions that can be defined by humans, whose calculation can be described by *any* well defined algorithm that people can be taught to perform, that *cannot* be computed by Turing machines. The Turing machine is believed to be the ultimate calculating mechanism."

This statement is called **Church's thesis** because Alonzo Church (1936 again) gave many sophisticated reasons for believing it. Church's original statement was a little different because his thesis was presented slightly before Turing invented his machines. Church actually said that any machine that can do a certain list of operations will be able to perform all conceivable algorithms. Turing machines can do all that Church asked, so they are one possible model of the universal algorithm machines Church described.

Unfortunately, Church's Thesis cannot be a theorem in mathematics because ideas such as "can ever be defined by humans" and "algorithm that people can be taught to perform" are not part of any branch of known mathematics. There are no axioms that deal with "people." If there were no axioms that dealt with triangles, we could not prove any theorems about triangles. There is no known definition for "algorithm" either, as used in the most general sense by practicing mathematicians, except that if we believe Church's Thesis we can define algorithms as what TM's can do. This is the way we have (up to today) resolved the old problem of, "Of what steps are all algorithms composed? What instructions are legal to put in an algorithm and what are not?"

Not all mathematicians are satisfied with this. Mathematicians like to include in their proofs such nebulous phrases as "case two can be done similarly" or "by symmetry we also know" or "the case of $n = 1$ is obvious". Many mathematicians cannot figure out what other mathematicians have written, so it is often hopeless to try to teach a TM to do so. However, our *best* definition today of what an algorithm is is that it is a TM.

Turing had the same idea in mind when he introduced his machines. He argued as follows.

If we look at what steps a human goes through in performing a calculation, what do we see? (Imagine a man doing long division, for example.) He writes some marks on a paper. Then by looking at the marks he has written he can make new marks or, perhaps, change the old marks. If the human is performing an algorithm, the rules for putting down the new marks are finite. The new marks are entirely determined by what the old marks were and where they were on the page. The rules must be obeyed automatically (without outside knowledge or original thinking of any kind). A TM can be programmed to scan the old marks and write new ones following exactly the same rules. The TAPE HEAD can scan back and forth over the whole page, row by row, and recognize the old marks and replace them with new ones. The TM can draw the same conclusions a human would as long as the human was forced to follow the rigid rules of an algorithm.

Someday someone might find a task that humans agree is an algorithm but that cannot be executed by a TM, but this has not yet happened. Nor is it likely to. People seem very happy with the Turing-Post-Church idea of what components are legal parts of algorithms.

There are faulty "algorithms" that do not work in every case that they are supposed to handle. Such an algorithm leads the human up to a certain point and then has no instruction on how to take the next step. This would foil a TM, but it would also foil many humans. Most mathematics textbooks adopt the policy of allowing questions in the problem section that cannot be completely solved by the algorithms in the chapter. Some "original thinking" is required. No algorithm for providing proofs for all the theorems in the problem section is ever given. In fact, no algorithm for providing proofs for all theorems in general is known. Better or worse than that, it can be *proved* that no such algorithm exists.

We have made this type of claim at several places throughout this book; now we can make it specific. We can say (assuming as everyone does that Church's Thesis is correct) that anything that can be done by algorithm can be done by TM. Yet we have shown in the previous chapter that there are some languages that are not recursively enumerable. That means that there is no Turing machine that acts as their acceptor, that can guarantee, for any string whatsoever, a yes answer if it is in the language. This means that the problem of deciding whether a given word is in one such particular language cannot be solved *by any algorithm*.

When we proved that the language PALINDROME is not accepted by any FA, that did not mean that there is no algorithm in the whole wide world to determine whether or not a given string is a palindrome. There are such algorithms. However, when we proved that ALAN is not r.e., we proved that there is no possible decision procedure (algorithm) to determine whether or not a given string is in the language ALAN.

Let us recall from Chapter 1 the project proposed by the great mathematician David Hilbert. When he saw the problems arising in Set Theory he asked that the following statements should be proven:

1. Mathematics is consistent. Roughly this means that we cannot prove both a statement and its opposite, nor can we prove something horrible like $1 = 2$.

2. Mathematics is complete. Roughly, this means that every true mathematical assertion can be proven. Since we might not know what "true" means, we can state this as: Every mathematical assertion can either be proven or disproven.

3. Mathematics is decidable. This, as we know, means that for every type of mathematical problem there is an algorithm that, in theory at least, can be mechanically followed to give a solution. We say "in theory" because following the algorithm might take more than a million years and still be finite.

Many thought that this was a good program for mathematical research, and most believed that all three points were true and could be proved so. One exception was the mathematician G. H. Hardy, who hoped that point 3 could never be proven, since if there were a mechanical set of rules for the solution of all mathematical problems, mathematics would come to an end as a subject for human research.

Hardy did not have to worry. In 1930 Kurt Gödel shocked the world by *proving* that points 1 and 2 are not both *true* (much less provable). Most people today hope that this means that point 2 is false, since otherwise point 1 has to be. Then in 1936, Church, Kleene, Post, and Turing showed that point 3 is false. After Gödel's theorem, all that was left of point 3 was "Is there an algorithm to decide whether a mathematical statement has a proof or a disproof, or whether it is one of the unsolvables." In other words, can one invent an algorithm that can determine if some other algorithm (possibly undiscovered) does exist which could solve the given problem. Here we are not looking for the answer but merely good advice as to whether there is even an answer. Even this cannot be done. Church showed that the first-order predicate calculus (an elementary part of mathematics) is undecidable. All hope for Hilbert's program was gone.

We have seen Post's and Turing's conception of what an algorithm is. Church's model of computation, called the **lambda calculus**, is also elegant but less directly related to Computer Theory on an elementary level, so we have not included it here. The same is true of the work of Gödel and Kleene on μ-recursive functions. Of the mathematical logicians mentioned, only Turing and von Neumann carried their theoretical ideas over to the practical construction of electronic machinery.

We have already seen Turing's work showing that no algorithm (TM) exists that can answer the question of membership in ALAN. Turing also showed that the problem of recognizing what can and cannot be done by algorithm is also undecidable, since it is related to the language ALAN.

Two other interesting models of computation can be used to define "computability by algorithm." A. A. Markov (1951) defined a system today called **Markov algorithms, MA,** which are similar to type 0 grammars, and J. C. Shepherdson and H. E. Sturgis (1963) proposed a **register machine, RM,** which is similar to a TM. Just as we suspect from Church's Thesis, these methods turned out to have exactly the same power as TM's.

Turing found the following very important example of a problem that has no possible solution, called the **Halting Problem for Turing machines.** The problem is simply this:

> Given some arbitrary TM called T and some arbitrary string w of a's and b's, is there an algorithm to decide whether T halts when given the input w?

We cannot just say, "Sure, run w on T and see what happens," because if w is in loop(T), we shall be waiting for the answer forever, and an algorithm must answer its question in a finite amount of time. This is the pull-the-plug question. Our program has been running for eleven hours and we want to know are we in an infinite loop or are we making progress. We have already discussed this matter informally with a few paragraphs following Theorem 64, but we now devote a special theorem to it.

THEOREM 76

The Halting Problem for Turing machines is *unsolvable,* which means that there does not exist any such algorithm.

PROOF

The proof will use an idea of Minsky's. Suppose there were some TM called *HPA* (halting-problem-answerer) that takes as input the code for any TM, *T*, and any word *w*, and leaves an answer on its TAPE yes or no (also in code). The code used for the Turing machines does not have to be the one we presented in Chapter 29. Any method of encoding is acceptable. We might require *HPA* to leave a blank in cell i if *w* halts on *T* and an *a* in cell i otherwise, or we could use any other possible method of writing out the answer. If one *HPA* leaves a certain kind of answer, a different *HPA* can be built to leave a different kind of answer.

Let us say *HPA* reaches HALT if *w* halts on *T* and crashes if *w* does not halt on *T*:

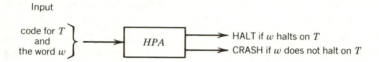

Using *HPA*, we can make a different TM called NASTY. The input into NASTY is the code of any TM. NASTY then asks whether this encoded TM can accept its own code word as input (shades of ALAN).

To do this, NASTY acts like *HPA* with the input: code-of-TM (for the machine) and also code-of-TM (for the word *w* to be tested). But we are not going to let NASTY run exactly like *HPA*. We are going to change the HALT state in *HPA* into an infinite loop:

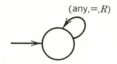

And we shall change all the crashes of *HPA* into successful HALT's. For example, if *HPA* crashes in state 7 for input *b*:

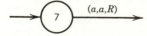

then we change it to:

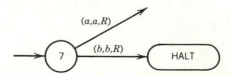

This is what NASTY does:

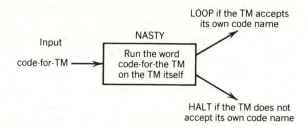

LOOP if the TM accepts
its own code name

NASTY

Input

code-for-TM ⟶ Run the word
code-for-the TM
on the TM itself

HALT if the TM does not
accept its own code name

If we pause for one moment we may sense the disaster that is about to strike.

Now what TM should we feed into this machine NASTY? Why NASTY itself, of course:

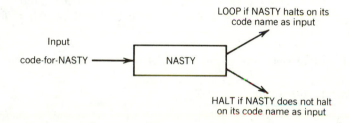

LOOP if NASTY halts on its
code name as input

Input

code-for-NASTY ⟶ NASTY

HALT if NASTY does not halt
on its code name as input

Now we see that NASTY does halt when fed its code name as input if NASTY does not halt when fed its code name as input. And NASTY loops when fed its code name if NASTY halts when fed its code name as input.

A paradox in the mold of ALAN (and the Liar paradox and Cantor's work and Gödel's theorem, and so forth). NASTY is practically the TM that would accept ALAN, except that ALAN is not r.e.

No such TM as NASTY can exist. Therefore, no such TM as *HPA* can exist (ever, not in the year 3742, not ever). Therefore, the Halting Problem for Turing machines is unsolvable. ■

This means that there are tasks that are theoretically impossible for any computer to do, be it an electronic, a nuclear, a solar, a horse-powered, or a mathematical model.

Now we see why the sections on decidability in the previous parts were so important. This is also how we found all those pessimistic ideas of what questions about CFG's were undecidable. We always prove that a question is undecidable by showing that the existence of a TM that answers it would lead to a paradox. In this way (assuming Church's Thesis), we can prove that no decision procedure can ever exist to decide whether a running TM will halt.

Let us return, for a moment, to Church's Thesis. As we mentioned before, Church's original ideas were not expressed in terms of Turing machines. Instead, Church presented a small collection of simple functions and gave logical reasons why he felt that all algorithmically computable functions could be calculated in terms of these basic functions. The functions he considered fundamental building blocks are even more primitive than the ones we already showed were TM-computable. By proving Theorems 71 through 74, we showed that TM's more than satisfy Church's idea of universal algorithm machines.

When we can show how to calculate some new function in terms of the functions we already know are Turing computable, we have shown that the new function is also Turing computable.

Proving that division is computable is saved for the Problem section. Instead, we give a related example.

EXAMPLE

A Turing machine can decide whether or not the number n is prime. This means that a TM exists called PRIME that when given the input a^n will run and halt, leaving a 1 in cell i if n is a prime and a 0 in cell i if n is not prime.

We shall outline one simple but wasteful machine that performs this task:

Step 1   Set up this string:

$$a^n baa$$

Call the a's after the b the "second field."

Step 2   Without moving the b, change some number of a's at the end of the first field into b's, the number changed being equal to the number of a's in the second field.

Step 3   Compare the two fields of a's. If the first is smaller, go to step 4. If they are of equal size, go to step 5. If the second is smaller, go to step 2.

Step 4   Restore all the a's in the first field (turn all the b's into a's except the last one). Add one more a to the second field. Compare the first and second fields. If they are the same, go to step 6. If they are different, go to step 2.

Step 5   Go to cell i. Change it to a 0. HALT

Step 6   Go to cell i. Change it to a 1. HALT.

Does this do the trick? (See Problem 19 below.)   ■

So far we have seen TM's in two of their roles as transducer and as acceptor:

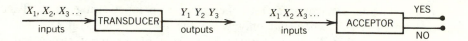

As a transducer it is a computer and as an acceptor it is a decision procedure. There is another purpose a TM can serve. It can be a generator.

GENERATOR $\xrightarrow{X_1, X_2, X_3 \dots}$

DEFINITION

A TM is said to **generate** the language

$$L = \{w_1 \ w_2 \ w_3. \ . \ . \}$$

if it starts with a blank TAPE and after some calculation prints a # followed by some word from L. Then there is some more calculation and the machine prints a # followed by another word from L. Again there is more calculation and another # and a word from L appears on the TAPE. And so on. Each word from L must eventually appear on the TAPE inside of #'s. The order in which they occur does not matter and any word may be repeated often. ∎

This definition of generating a language is also called **enumerating** it. With our last two theorems we shall show that any language that can be generated by a TM can be accepted by some TM and that any language that can be accepted by a TM can be generated by some TM. This is why the languages accepted by TM's were called **recursively enumerable.**

THEOREM 77

If the language L can be generated by the Turing machine T_g, then there is another TM, T_a, that accepts L.

PROOF

The proof will be by constructive algorithm. We shall show how to convert T_g into T_a.

To be a language acceptor T_a must begin with an input string on its TAPE and end up in HALT when and only when the input string is in L.

The first thing that T_a does is put a $ in front of the input string and a $ after it. In this way it can always recognize where the input string is no matter what else is put on the TAPE. Now T_a begins to act like T_g in the sense that T_a imitates the program of T_g and begins to generate all the words in L on the TAPE to the right of the second $. The only modification is that every time T_g finishes printing a word of L and ends with a #, T_a leaves its copy of the program of T_g for a moment to do something else. T_a instead compares the most recently generated word of L against the input string inside the $'s. If they are the same, T_a halts and accepts the input string as legitimately being in L. If they are not the same the result is inconclusive. The word may yet show up on the TAPE. T_a therefore returns to its simulation of T_g.

If the input is in L, it will eventually be accepted. If it is not, T_a will never terminate execution. It will wait forever for this word to appear on the TAPE.

$$\text{accept}(T_a) \ = \ L$$
$$\text{loop}(T_a) \ = \ L'$$
$$\text{reject}(T_a) \ = \ \phi$$

Although the description above of this machine is fairly sketchy we have already seen TM programs that do the various tasks required: inserting $, comparing strings to see if they are equal, and jumping in and out of the simulation of another TM. This then completes the proof. ∎

THEOREM 78

If the language L can be accepted by the TM T_a, then there is another TM T_g that generates it.

PROOF

The proof will be by constructive algorithm. What we would like to do is to start with a subroutine that generates all strings of a's and b's one by one in size and alphabetical order:

$$\Lambda \ a \ b \ aa \ ab \ ba \ bb \ aaa \ aab. \ . \ .$$

We have seen how to do this by TM before in the form of the binary incrementor. After each new string is generated, we run it on the machine

T_a. If T_a halts, we print out the word on the TAPE inside #'s. If T_a does not halt, we skip it and go on to the next possibility from the string generator, because this word is not in the language.

What is wrong with this idea is that if T_a does not halt it may loop forever. While we are waiting for T_a to decide, we are not printing any new words in L. The process breaks down once it reaches the first word in loop(T_a).

As a side issue, let us observe that if L is recursive then we can perform this procedure exactly as outlined above. If the testing string is in L, T_a will halt and T_g will print it out. If the test string is not in L, T_a will go to REJECT, which T_g has converted into a call for a new test string, the next word in order, from the string generator subroutine. If L is recursive, not only can we generate the words of L but we can generate them in size and alphabetical order. (An interesting theorem, which we shall leave to the Problem section, puts it the other way around: If L can be generated in size order then L is recursive.)

Getting back to the main point: How shall we handle r.e. languages that are not recursive, that do have loop–words? The answer is that while T_a begins to work on the input from the string generator, the string generator can simultaneously be making and then testing another string (the next string of a's and b's). We can do this because both machines, the string generator and the L-acceptor T_a, are part of the TM T_g. T_g can simulate some number of steps of each component machine in alternation.

Since T_g is going to do a great deal of simulating of several machines at once, we need a bookkeeping device to keep track of what is going on. Let us call this bookkeeper an **alternator**.

Let the strings in order be string 1 ($= \Lambda$), string 2 ($= a$), string 3 ($= b$), string 4 ($= aa$), and so on.

The alternator will tell T_g to do the following, where by a "step" we mean traveling one edge on a TM:

1 First simulate only one step of the operation of T_a on string 1 and set a counter equal to 1. This counter should appear on the TAPE after the last # denoting a word of L. After the last cell used by the counter should be some identifying marker, say *. The work space on which to do the calculations simulating T_a is the rest of the TAPE to the right of the *.

2 Start from scratch, which means increment the counter by one and erase everything on the TAPE to the right of the *. The counter is now 2 so we simulate two steps of the operation of T_a on string 1 and then two steps of the operation of T_a on string 2.

3 Increment the counter and start from scratch, simulate three steps of the operation of T_a on string 1 and then simulate three steps of the operation of T_a on string 2 and then simulate three steps of the operation of T_a on string 3.

4   From scratch, simulate four steps of string 1 on T_a, and four steps of string 2 on T_a, four steps of string 3 on T_a, and four steps of string 4 on T_a.

5   And so on in a loop without end.

If, in simulating k steps of the operation of string j on T_a the machine T_g should happen to accept string j, then T_g will print string j out between #'s inserted just in front of the counter.

Eventually every word of L will be examined and run on T_a long enough to be accepted and printed on T_g's TAPE.

If a particular word of L, say string 87, is accepted by T_a in 1492 steps what will happen is that once the counter reaches 87 it will start testing the string on T_a but until the counter reaches 1492 it will not simulate enough steps of the processing of string 87 on T_a to accept it. When the counter first hits 1492 T_g will simulate enough of the processing of string 87 to know it is in L and so it will print it permanently on the TAPE between #'s. From then on, in each loop when the counter is incremented it will retest string 87, reaccept it and reprint it. Any word in L will appear on the TAPE infinitely many times.

This is a complete proof once we have shown how to build the string generator, the "start from scratch adjuster", and the so-many step simulator. All of these programs can be written by anyone who has read this far in this book, and by now is an expert Turing machine programmer.   ■

As we can see, we have just begun to appreciate Turing machines; many interesting and important facts have not been covered (or even discovered). This is also true of PDA's and FA's.

For a branch of knowledge so new, this subject has already reached some profound depth. Results in Computer Theory cannot avoid being of practical importance, but at the same time we have seen how clever and elegant they may be. This is a subject with twentieth-century impact that yet retains its Old World charm.

PROBLEMS

1. Trace these inputs on ADDER and explain what happens.
   (i) *aaba*

   (ii) *aab*

   (iii) *baaa*

   (iv) *b*

2. (i) Build a TM that takes an input of three numbers in unary encoding separated by *b*'s and leaves their sum on the TAPE.
   (ii) Build a TM that takes in any number of numbers in unary encoding separated by *b*'s and leaves their sum on the TAPE.

3. Describe how to build a binary adder that takes three numbers in at once in the form

   $$\$ (0 + 1)^* \$ (0 + 1)^* \$ (0 + 1)^*$$

   and leaves their binary total on the TAPE.

4. Outline a TM that acts as a binary-to-unary converter, that is, it starts with a number in binary on the TAPE

   $$\$ (0 + 1)^* \$$$

   and leaves the equivalent number encoded in unary notation.

5. Trace these inputs on MINUS and explain what happens.
   (i) *aaabaa*

   (ii) *abaaa*

   (iii) *baa*

   (iv) *aaab*

6. Modify the TM MINUS so that it rejects all inputs not in the form

   ba*ba*

   and converts $ba^n ba^m$ into $b\ a^{n \doteq m}$

7.   MINUS does proper subtraction on unary encoded numbers. Build a TM that does proper subtraction in binary encoded inputs.

8.   Run the following input strings on the machine MAX built in the proof of Theorem 72.
     (i)   *aaaba*

     (ii)   *baaa*   (interpret this)

     (iii) *aabaa*

     (iv)   In the TM MAX above, where does the TAPE HEAD end up if the second number is larger than the first?

     (v)   Where does it end if they are equal?

     (vi)   Where does it finish if the first is larger?

9.   MAX is a unary machine, that is, it presumes its input numbers are fed into it in unary encoding. Build a machine (TM) that does the job of MAX on binary encoded input.

10. Build a TM that takes in three numbers in unary encoding and leaves only the largest of them on the TAPE.

11. Trace the following strings on IDENTITY and SUCCESSOR.
     (i)   *aa*

     (ii)   *aaaba*

12. Build machines that perform the same function as IDENTITY and SUC-CESSOR but on binary encoded input.

13. Trace the input string

                    bbaaababaaba

     on SELECT/3/5, stopping where the program given in the proof of Theorem 74 ends, that is, without the use of DELETE Δ.

14. In the text we showed that there was a different TM for SELECT/*i*/*n* for each different set of *i* and *n*. However, it is possible to design a TM that takes in a string form

                    (a*b)*

and interprets the initial clump of a's as the unary encoding of the number i. It then considers the word remaining as the encoding of the string of numbers from which we must select the ith.

(i)   Design such a TM.

(ii)   Run this machine on the input

aabaaabaabaaba

15.   On the TM MPY, from the proof of Theorem 75, trace the following inputs:

(i)   *babaa*

(ii)   *baaaba*

16.   Modify MPY so that it allows us to multiply by zero.

17.   Sketch roughly a TM that performs multiplication on binary inputs.

18.   Prove that division is computable by building a TM that accepts the input string $ba^m ba^n$ and leaves the string $ba^q ba^r$ on the TAPE where q is the quotient of m divided by n and r is the remainder.

19.   (i)   Explain why the algorithm given in this chapter for the machine PRIME works.

(ii)   Run the machine on the input 7.

(iii)   Run the machine on the input 9.

20.   Prove that if a language L can be generated in size-alphabetical order, then L is recursive.

TABLE
OF
THEOREMS

805

INDEX